KEEPERS OF THE
KEYS OF HEAVEN

A History of the Papacy

ROGER COLLINS

BASIC
BOOKS

A Member of the Perseus Books Group

New York

FOR JUDITH

AND IN MEMORY OF GILES

Books published by Basic Books are available at special discounts for bulk purchases in the
United States by corporations, institutions, and other organizations. For more information,
please contact the Special Markets Department at the Perseus Books Group, 2300 Chestnut
Street, Suite 200, Philadelphia, PA 19103, or call (800) 810-4145, ext. 5000, or e-mail
special.markets@perseusbooks.com.

Library of Congress Cataloging-in-Publication Data
    Collins, Roger, 1949–
    Keepers of the keys of heaven : a history of the papacy / Roger Collins.
        p. cm.
    Includes bibliographical references and index.
    ISBN 978-0-465-01195-7 (alk. paper)
    1. Papacy—History. I. Title.

BX955.3.C655 2009
262'.1309—dc22

                                                                                    2008039890

10 9 8 7 6 5 4 3 2 1

CONTENTS

PREFACE

Trying to describe the entire history of the papacy, an institution that has survived for nearly two thousand years, in a single volume, is probably far too ambitious an undertaking. The most substantial treatment of the subject is the thirty-volume work of Ludwig Pastor, which confined itself to the period from the late fifteenth century to the end of the eighteenth, and still failed to be comprehensive. Several lifetimes of study would be needed to master the voluminous archives of the Vatican alone. Yet even in as small a scale as that offered here, it is a worthwhile undertaking. Few if any other human institutions have survived so long and played so continuously important a role not just in the history and affairs of Europe but also of the wider world. The papacy's significance in modern times has been enormous, but it has not always had the character or exerted the influence we are familiar with today. Its story is a long and complicated one, full of incident, ideas and the interplay of personalities.

In attempting such a daunting task, I am enormously grateful for help and inspiration from many quarters. Stuart Proffitt first suggested to me the idea of a single-volume history, which was pursued with characteristic enthusiasm—and many humorous emails—by my agent, the incomparable Giles Gordon. Following Giles's untimely death I was extremely fortunate to be taken under the wing of John Saddler and now of Peter Robinson, both of whom set their seals on the project in subsequent stages, as did George Lucas in New York. Thanks are also due in many other directions, not least to Paul Harcourt and Jonathan Reilly of Maggs Brothers, who alerted me to the existence of several arcane books and manuscripts on papal history. I have been privileged to have my book pruned and greatly improved over the course of several months by the editorial skills of Norman MacAfee, while Lara Heimert at Basic Books and Ben Buchan at Weidenfeld & Nicolson have exercised benevolent oversight throughout. Walter Ficoncini and everyone at the Palazzo al Velabro made staying and working in Rome even more of a delight than it would normally be. Libraries, from those of the Vatican and the Ecole Française in Rome to New College and the National Library of Scotland in Edinburgh, have provided generous access to their collections. I am most grateful to the School of History, Classics and Archaeology in the University of Edinburgh for the Fellowship during whose tenure this book has been both researched and written. The true inspirer, guide and constant companion of both the book and its author has been my wife, Judith McClure, to whom it is dedicated.

ROGER COLLINS

The Isle of Eriska
January 2009

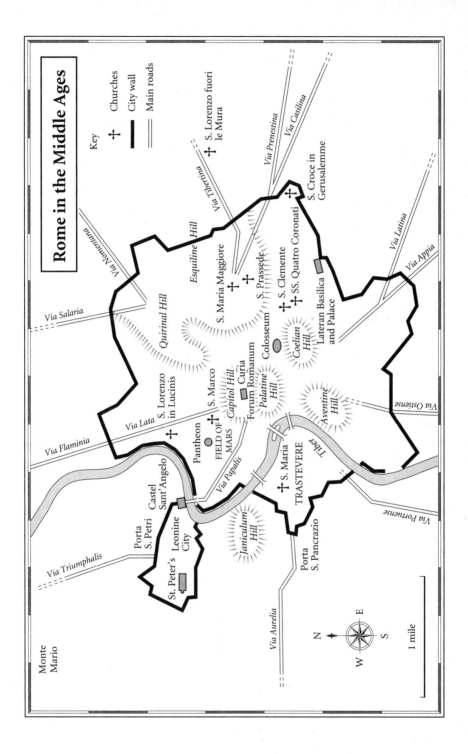

Rome in the Middle Ages

Key

✝ Churches

━━ City wall

══ Main roads

Monte Mario

Via Triumphalis

Porta S. Petri

Castel Sant'Angelo

Leonine City

St. Peter's

Via Aurelia

Porta S. Pancrazio

Janiculum Hill

Via Portuense

TRASTEVERE

✝ S. Maria in Trastevere

Tiber

Via Papalis

Pantheon

FIELD OF MARS

✝ S. Lorenzo in Lucinis

✝ S. Marco

Capitol Hill

Curia

Forum Romanum

Palatine Hill

Via Lata

Via Flaminia

Via Salaria

Quirinal Hill

Esquiline Hill

✝ S. Maria Maggiore

Via Nomentana

Via Tiburtina

✝ S. Lorenzo fuori le Mura

Via Prenestina

Via Casilina

✝ S. Croce in Gerusalemme

✝ S. Prassede

✝ S. Clemente

✝ SS. Quatro Coronati

Colosseum

Coelian Hill

Lateran Basilica and Palace

Via Latina

Via Appia

Via Ostiense

Aventine Hill

N
W E
S

1 mile

Central Italy in the Early 8th Century

Ferrara

Modena

Bologna

Ravenna

Adriatic Sea

EXARCHATE OF RAVENNA

Rimini

Fano

Arno

PENTAPOLIS

Ancona

DUCHY OF PERUGIA

Gualdo Tadino

LOMBARD TUSCANY

Perugia

DUCHY

OF

Todi

Spoleto

Terni

SPOLETO

Orte

Narni

Rieti

Mt Soracte

Nepi

Farfa

Civitavecchia

DUCHY

Tiber

SABINA

DUCHY OF

Rome

BENEVENTO

Porto

Ostia

Alatri

OF

Montecassino

ROME

Tyrrhenian Sea

Terracina

Benevento

Gaeta

Naples

```
0      20     40     60     80 miles
0        40        80      120 kms
```

Papal States in the Later Middle Ages

N
W — E
S

• Bologna
ROMAGNA

A d r i a t i c
S e a

• Rimini

Arno
Florence •

• Ancona

MARCH
OF
ANCONA

• Siena

Lake
Trasimeno

TUSCANY

Perugia • • Assisi

Orvieto •
DUCHY
OF
SPOLETO

Lake Bolsena
Sabine
Hills • Rieti

PATRIMONY
OF
ST PETER •
Viterbo

Civitavecchia

Tiber

KINGDOM
OF
SICILY

Rome
Alban
Hills
• Ostia • Anagni
CAMPAGNA
AND
MARITTIMA
• Fondi
• Terracina

T y r r h e n i a n
S e a

0   20   40   60   80 miles

0   40   80   120 kms

chapter 1

BISHOP OF ROME

(C. AD 30–180)

A Story of Bones

O ne evening in early 1942, in Rome, after the great basilica of St. Peter's had closed its doors for the night, the man in charge of the building, Monsignor Ludwig Kaas, descended into the archaeological excavations beneath it. With him was the foreman of the Vatican workforce carrying out the dig, Giovanni Segoni, who was keeping Kaas informed of everything the excavators were doing. This included their recent uncovering, just beneath St. Peter's sixteenth-century high altar, of a small wall, one side of which was covered with roughly carved inscriptions and graffiti.

The archaeologists and excavation team had gone for the day. The two men were alone. And now Segoni showed Kaas an even more recent discovery. Within the little wall, the team had found a small concealed rectangular space lined with marble. In it were bones, which the archaeologists had not yet had time to examine, let alone record. Kaas told Segoni to remove and carry them as they returned to the surface.[1] As a way of handling important archaeological evidence, few things could have been less professional, but these were most unusual excavations, carried out under conditions of utmost secrecy and rigid discipline, with a chain of command extending all the way up to the pope, Pius XII (1939–1958).[2]

The dig had begun after a discovery made in February 1939, when a tomb was being prepared for his predecessor, Pius XI (1922–1939), in the grotto underneath St. Peter's, long the site of papal burials. In the course of that work a Roman cemetery, dating to the first and second centuries AD, had been found beneath the grotto. Originally this cemetery had been on ground level and consisted of streets of tombs that looked like little houses and were owned by wealthy families. The area in which it stood had been buried when a small hill was flattened during the construction of the earliest church on the site, which was built in the mid-fourth century over what was long believed to be the burial place of St. Peter.

The presence of St. Peter in Rome, his role in the founding of the Church in the city and his martyrdom and burial there had for centuries been the subject of often heated debate between Protestants and Catholics. Excavation of a site linked to Peter's tomb, but whose results could not be predicted, could strengthen or weaken not just scholarly arguments but also the faith of hundreds of millions of believers. And so the Vatican decided that the dig should be carried out in complete secrecy, with nothing being announced until the results had been carefully reviewed. Although at first forbidden to approach the area immediately under the high altar, the excavations soon began to produce more and more intriguing results the closer they came to it, and in 1941 an extension was permitted to allow inclusion of this, the most sensitive part of the site.

As well as having the potential for theological fallout, the excavations had to be watched for any threat they might pose to the stability of the enormous church below which they were burrowing. For both reasons, while directed on a daily basis by scholars trained in archaeology and epigraphy, the study of inscriptions, overall charge resided with Monsignor Kaas. His own training and experience as a priest, a professor of canon law and a politician were very different from those of the archaeologists whose work he now had to monitor.[3] Although he never himself explained why he ordered the removal and concealment of the bones, he apparently had little sympathy with archaeologists, whom, he felt, rarely treated human remains with proper respect. In any case these bones mattered less at the time than some others that had been discovered nearby a few weeks earlier. To that other set of bones we now briefly turn.

In 1941, when digging was extended to the area below the high altar, a red painted wall was found that had probably once formed part of a small open enclosure at the back of a street of Roman house-tombs. The archaeologists hypothesised that onto this wall a narrow stone table had been built supported on two legs at the front and with a small stone roof over it. It was located immediately below what became the altar of the first Church of St. Peter's, and above which now stands the present sixteenth-century high altar. The assumption seemed irresistible that the place marked by this small stone table, which the archaeologists dated to the later second century, had been specially revered by successive generations of Christians.

Further excavation revealed that concealed below and at a slight angle to this shrine was a rectangular enclosure extending under the red wall. In other words, it pre-dated that wall and could be assumed to be the repository of whatever it was that the small table-shaped shrine was commemorating. When news of this discovery and of the presence within it of bones was mentioned to Pius XII, he himself descended into the excavations and sat on a stool beside the site while the archaeologists reverently handed out the fragments of bone into his keeping. The possibility that the relics being removed were indeed those of the first of Christ's Apostles must have been in the minds of all present. Nothing, however, could be said publicly, even when the pope's personal doctor, Riccardo Galeazzi-Lisi, to whom the bones were entrusted for examination, quickly determined that they belonged to a powerfully built man about sixty-five to seventy years old.

One consequence of the doctor's hasty verdict was that when the very small graffiti-covered wall was subsequently uncovered nearby and was found to contain more bones, they seemed of minor importance. The real significance of this wall was thought to lie in the inscriptions on it. Some of these were simple personal names like Severa or Leonta, but others were explicitly Christian prayers for the dead. One fragmentary one was interpreted as being an invocation to St. Peter. Together these inscriptions seemed to confirm the Christian significance of the site and a possible special association with the Prince of the Apostles. As it was also clear that this small wall was built after the red one that it existed to support, little attention needed to be given to bones housed in it when others had already been found below the earlier one.

Unfortunately, Pius XII's doctor had been inspired more by enthusiasm than by forensic skill, as he was not a specialist in the identification of bones. While the private discussions continued about what to do with the discoveries, it became clear that before any announcement was made, the bones should be studied more thoroughly. An expert, Professor Venerando Correnti, was called in under terms of absolute secrecy to carry out a full investigation. This caution proved wise, as he concluded that the bones came from not one man, but two, plus a woman, a chicken, a pig, a goat or sheep and possibly a mouse.[4]

While it was possible that one of the men was Peter, the discovery of the bones under the red wall could not now be included in any announcement about the excavations and their results. Finally, just before Christmas 1950, in a radio broadcast, Pius XII revealed the existence of the dig. He played down the chances of finding the physical remains of St. Peter and concentrated instead on the evidence found for early veneration of the site as the presumed burial place of the Apostle. When the official two-volume report by the archaeologists came out in 1951, it barely mentioned bones.[5] Other scholars were permitted to publish on the subject only if they agreed not to make use of any information that was not contained in the official report (and not reveal the existence of this restriction).[6] Meanwhile, the bones removed from the graffiti-covered wall remained unstudied and forgotten until 1953, the year after the death of Monsignor Kaas, when Giovanni Segoni, who had taken them from the wall, mentioned them to Professor Margherita Guarducci, an authority on inscriptions who was working on the messages on the wall. He was able to lead her to the bones themselves, in Kaas's former office, and to the wooden box in which they were said to have originally been found. She had the bones examined by Professor Correnti, who confirmed that they came from a well-built man, probably in his sixties.

The caution that had saved the Vatican from making embarrassing claims about the significance of the red-wall bones might have militated against public statements about the bones from the graffiti wall, but Guarducci was a family friend of Pope Paul VI (1963–1978). He was persuaded by her conviction that the bones were highly likely to be Peter's, because they were from a sexagenarian and located in a place long associated with the Apostle. And so, on 26 June 1968, Paul announced that the bones of St. Peter, the Prince of the Apostles, had been discovered, not mentioning the previous uncertainties and changes of opinion.[7]

If Pope Paul's statement about the discovery of Peter's bones could not be openly contested, not everyone was convinced by the claim and what lay behind it. Among the doubters was one of the two original excavators, Professor Antonio Ferrua S.J., who as an authority on epigraphy had clashed with Guarducci on other occasions.[8] While academic point scoring and personal antipathies may have added to the complexities of the various discoveries and claims made about them, it has to be admitted that the sceptics have the stronger case.

There are two crucial breaks in the chain of evidence, and the scene was contaminated twice. The first break happened as long ago as the second century. If the rectangular hollow under the red wall pre-dates the building of that wall, as indeed it must, and if the wall itself was erected in the second century, which is a less secure claim, then bones buried in that space could date from the late first century, and thus the time of Peter. However, the bones that Paul VI said were Peter's come from the graffitied wall built to buttress the red wall. A date no earlier than 200 has been suggested for its construction. So, the bones buried within it cannot have been there before that date. They may, of course, have been transferred from somewhere else, but their lack of a distinctive staining indicates that they had not previously resided in the location under the red wall in which the other set of miscellaneous human and animal bones were found. To add to all these uncertainties, it has recently been suggested that the archaeologists' reconstruction of what they regarded as a table-shaped shrine at the red wall is based more on speculation than on evidence, and that whatever its nature and purpose, it may actually date from the early fourth century rather than the end of the second. This leaves the dating of anything found under it far less secure than the excavation report implies.[9]

The second break in the chain of evidence comes with Kaas's removal of the bones from the graffitied wall in 1942. If his motive had been the reverential treatment of human remains, it has to be wondered why he did not have them reburied. More importantly, we do not know what became of them between their removal from the graffitied wall in 1942 and the handing over to Guarducci in 1953 of a set of bones said to be the same ones.

Professor Guarducci was convinced not only that they were the very same ones, but more importantly that they were indeed those of St. Peter. She dedicated her 1995 book about the discovery of the bones 'to the Church of Christ, which through providential design is founded at Rome upon the authentic and extraordinary relics of Peter.'[10] As we have seen, by more objective standards, the outcome proved at best inconclusive, but the questions that might have been answered lie at the heart of the papacy's claim to a unique authority within Christianity, and to the way that claim is so indissolubly tied to both St. Peter, considered the Prince of the Apostles, and to the city of Rome.

St. Peter and Rome

The status of the popes as successors of Peter relies upon distinct strands of argument that seem so tightly interwoven as to be inseparable. One of these relates to the role played by Peter as the first called and the leader of Jesus' twelve Apostles, and in particular on the authority given him by Christ. His standing depends upon the meaning ascribed to sayings in the Gospels of Matthew and of John, in which Jesus appears to invest him with particular responsibilities and authority. In Matt. 16. 18–19, after Peter's recognition of him as 'the Christ, the Son of the living God', Jesus says: 'And I tell you, you are Peter, and on this rock I will build my church. . . . I will give you the keys of the kingdom of heaven, and whatever you bind on earth shall be considered bound in heaven; whatever you loose on earth shall be considered loosed in heaven.'[11] At the end of John's Gospel, in the accounts of the post-Resurrection appearances, there is a prophecy about Peter's death: '"when you were young, you girded yourself and walked where you would; but when you are old, you will stretch out your hands, and another will gird you and carry you where you do not wish to go." (This he said to show by what death he was to glorify God.) And after this he said to him, "Follow me."' (John 21. 18–19)[12]

There are three widely held beliefs about what happened to Peter in the decades between the Crucifixion, traditionally dated to AD 30, and his own death around 65/70. The first is that at some point he lived in Rome. The second is that if he did not actually found the Christian community in the city, he, together with Paul, established an institutional structure for its Church, either appointing or serving as its first bishop. The third is that he was martyred in Rome during a persecution of Christians and was buried in a site near the city, whose location remained known to successive generations of his fellow believers.

That neither Peter nor Paul actually founded the Church in Rome, in the sense of establishing the first community of Christians in the city, is now generally accepted. Exactly when the first Christians appeared there is uncertain. It is clear, though, that there were a considerable number by AD 49, when the emperor Claudius (AD 41–54) expelled from Rome those Jews, generally assumed to refer to Christians, who were creating disturbances 'under the influence of *Chrestus*'.[13]

This was long before either Peter or Paul could have arrived in the city. We know from Paul's own Epistle to the Romans, written sometime around AD 56 or 58, that he had not yet visited Rome but was hoping he soon would. That he did so a year or two later under the rather different circumstances of being kept there for two years under house arrest, waiting for a trial before the emperor that probably never took place, is recorded in Acts, which ends its narrative at that point (Acts 28. 30–31). Peter's presence in Rome is much harder to document. This problem has provided intellectual ammunition over the centuries for those, not just Protestants, who have wanted to challenge papal authority by trying to undermine its historical foundations.[14]

While Peter's presence in Rome cannot be proved, it is generally accepted as highly probable on other grounds. Perhaps the most significant of these is the fact that no other Christian community claimed that it was in their city that he died and was buried. The church of Antioch, like that of Rome, came to regard Peter as its founder and first bishop, but Antioch never suggested that he remained there until his death or that he was buried there. By the early fourth century at the latest, there was a general agreement amongst Christians that Peter had been bishop in Antioch but then moved on to Rome, where he met his death.

There are two texts that might support the idea that Peter was closely associated with the Christians in Rome from an early date. One is the anonymous letter known as the First Epistle of Clement. Its author was writing on behalf of the Christian community in Rome to encourage the Corinthian Christians to settle an internal dispute, and he cites Peter and Paul: 'Peter, who because of unrighteous jealousy suffered not one or two but many trials, and having thus given his testimony went to the glorious place which was his due.'[15] This passage might imply that Peter met a violent end and so may be the earliest reference to his martyrdom.

On Paul, Clement is more eloquent: 'Through jealousy and strife Paul showed the way to the prize of endurance; seven times he was in bonds, he was exiled, he was stoned, he was a herald both in the East and the West, he gained the noble fame of his faith, he taught righteousness to all the world, and when he had reached the limits of the West he gave his testimony before rulers, and thus passed from the world and was taken up into the Holy Place, the greatest example of endurance.'[16] Again, this might substantiate the belief that Paul was martyred.

The date of this letter is not easy to establish. Often stated belief that it was written around AD 96 depends on mention in the opening section of 'sudden and repeated misfortunes and calamities', seen as a reference to persecution of Christians in the mid-90s under the emperor Domitian (81–96), but there is no certainty that such persecution actually occurred. One prominent scholar has noted that the letter could just as easily have been written twenty years later.[17]

The second piece of evidence is a mention of Peter and Paul in a letter sent to Rome's Christians by Bishop Ignatius of Antioch. At the time of writing, Ignatius was being transported to Rome to be executed as a Christian. Although he had been tried and condemned in Antioch, he was one of many sent to the imperial capital to be killed during public spectacles provided by the emperors. On his journey, Ignatius wrote a series of short letters to the Christian communities in the cities through which he passed, but he also sent one on ahead to the Christians in Rome, asking them not to appeal for clemency from the emperor. He wanted his sentence to be carried out and was worried that some well-meaning and influential fellow believers might get an imperial pardon for him, thus preventing him from following Christ's example even to death. He wrote, 'I do not order you as did Peter and Paul; they were Apostles, I am a convict; they were free, I am even now a slave.'[18] The mention of Peter and Paul and the implication that they issued commands to the Christians in Rome suggest that together they had a special relationship with the city.

The difficulties dating Ignatius' letter are even greater than with Clement's, not least as it only survives as part of a much later text. The traditional view that he wrote around the year 117 is based on nothing more than a guess made around 325, by Eusebius, bishop of Caesarea (c. 314–339/40) in his *History of the Church*. But it is now generally agreed that Ignatius' writings and execution cannot be dated more precisely than to sometime between AD 125 and 150.

If there are grounds for believing that both Peter and Paul lived in Rome and died there, does this also mean that either of them was the first bishop of the city, or that one or the other appointed someone else to that office? The claim that they did make such an appointment first appears around AD 180, in a book written in Greek by Irenaeus, bishop of Lyon in what is now southern France. This work lacks a title but has long been known as *Against the Heresies,* since its aim was to combat several variant forms of Christian belief that were then influential. Included in it is a list of all the bishops of Rome ever since the Roman church had been 'founded and set up by the two most glorious apostles Peter and Paul', who are also said to have 'delivered the ministry of the episcopate to Linus'.[19] Although neither Peter nor Paul actually created the Christian community in Rome, Irenaeus might just be implying that theirs was the formative influence on Roman Christianity in its earliest phase. If so, could his claim that they appointed the first bishop, Linus, be correct?

Irenaeus was not the only person who thought so. About twenty years after he wrote, another list appeared. Its author was a teacher and orator in Carthage in North Africa, Tertullian (died c. 212), who wrote a series of short and vigorous treatises in Latin on moral and doctrinal issues affecting the Christian community of his city. Like Irenaeus, he used the continuity of the episcopal office in Rome from the time of the Apostles as an argument against theological opponents. However, he claimed that Peter himself had been the first bishop.[20] This, together with a difference in the order of some names of the bishops, proves that Tertullian was not just copying from Irenaeus.

Cumulatively, this looks like pretty good evidence, allowing for how little of the literary output of the early Christians has been preserved, and we might be happy to accept the testimony of two independent authors writing relatively close in time to the events described. Admittedly, there is still a gap of a century to a century and a half between the presumed period in which Peter and Paul were in Rome and the time at which Irenaeus and the others were writing.[21] Ultimately, however, the testimony of these writers was in error, for the office of bishop, as Irenaeus and Tertullian understood it, simply did not exist in the time of Peter and Paul.

THE FIRST BISHOP

The early growth of the administrative organisation of the Christian movement and the emergence within it of a clerical caste remain obscure and controversial. But these were in fact separate processes. For one thing the first generations of Christians may have expected an imminent *Parousia* or Second Coming of Christ, making organisational structures unnecessary. Such a phase seems to have been short-lived, for Paul in his later letters was no longer expecting it in his own lifetime. His epistles are our best evidence for how the Christians tried to run their communities at this time. Groups of elders, similar to those found in contemporary synagogues, took the lead in each community, assisted by deacons who were responsible for the charitable care of widows, orphans and other vulnerable members. The only formal meeting was the weekly community meal. This too may be a vestige of Judaic practice, from a time when the Christians still attended synagogue services. The Pharisees as a similar rigorist group within Judaism used to meet for a meal shared only amongst themselves on the evening preceding the Sabbath, just as Christians began doing on the day following it.

Several dimly recorded processes then took place as Christianity freed itself from its Jewish roots and as expectations of an imminent Second Coming waned.[22] The communal meal, which as described by Paul was essentially a convivial occasion, divided into two separate parts. The weekly meal remained as an *agape,* or love feast, available to all, but a separate Eucharistic service for full members of the community was celebrated on a different day. Exactly when this development took place is not clear, and it probably emerged at different times in different communities. Its significance is considerable for two reasons: The Eucharistic service required a celebrant, essentially to imitate Christ's role in the Last Supper; and full membership of the community became something that had to be attained, rather than being open to all immediately after they accepted the Christian message. The transition was effected through and marked by baptism, which thus also became a sacred rite requiring the presence of an officiant. As these baptismal and Eucharistic ceremonies became formalised, the need grew for a class of ritual specialists. They were important not so much for knowing what to do, since the proceedings were relatively simple, as for possessing a special state of purity or spiritual elevation that distinguished them from fellow believers. In other words what emerged was a Christian clerical elite.

To try to decide if the ceremonies created the clergy or the clergy the ceremonies is to fail to answer the conundrum about the chicken and the egg. They probably helped each other. Clearly, neither the writings of Paul nor the Gospel narratives of the life and teaching of

Jesus indicate the presence or anticipation of a Christian priesthood or of baptism marking the transition from one level of membership of the community to another. These were developments of the late first and early second centuries.

Bishops (overseers) appeared in some Christian communities as the leaders of the groups of elders, being chosen by election and quite likely for life.[23] Probably as a second stage in this development, such existing chief elders took on the primary roles in the new sacred ceremonies that were becoming increasingly standardised. Again, it is worth stressing that there was no overall organisational structure for the Christian church in these early centuries, and thus individual groups followed different practices or gradually adopted ones that were starting to gain general agreement. This point is illustrated by the letters of Ignatius of Antioch, previously mentioned. In the messages he sent to the various Christian communities he came in contact with on his way to Rome, he almost always urged on them the importance of obedience to their bishops. This has been seen to imply that he was trying to promote acceptance of something that was still very new and controversial.[24]

One crucial consequence of the rise not just of a clergy but of a hierarchy within it was the fairly rapid marginalising and then elimination in most communities of women as office holders and leaders. As Jewish society had been very patriarchal, it may be that in some Christian groups women had never played a leading or teaching role, but there is plenty of evidence to show that they did in others. A well-documented case is that of Prisca, who shared the leadership of one of the communities in Rome with her husband, Aquila.[25] Women also served as deacons, and some groups, expecting divine guidance from the inspired utterances of individuals in some form of trance or ecstasy, allowed a special role for prophets, including women such as the four daughters of the Apostle Philip. Even after the rise of a professional clergy, there is evidence of some Christian communities having women priests as well as deacons, though the numbers decline rapidly in the course of the second and early third centuries.[26]

The decline in the role of women as leaders and teachers in the early Church seems to correlate fairly closely to the rise of a hierarchical sacramental priesthood, which needed to be set apart from lay believers, just as these latter came to be divided into the two categories of catechumens and full initiates.[27] Pressure for greater uniformity led to the disappearance of several once central features of early Christian practice and to communities that would not conform being regarded as heretical or outside the body of the true believers.

As suggested by the letters of Ignatius, from the period roughly AD 125 to 150, the emergence of a clerical hierarchy with special ritual functions and an exclusive role in the leadership of their fellow believers was well under way but no means universally welcomed by all Christian groups. His letter to the Romans is particularly important in this respect, because it helps confirm that the process had hardly begun in the city of Rome by this time. Not only were there no bishops, as we understand the word, in the time of Peter and Paul, they were actually slower to appear in Rome than in almost any other part of the Roman empire.

This is not as paradoxical as it may seem, since the sheer size of Rome would have made it hard for Christians to create a single organisational structure or congregate in one part of the city. Because the earliest Christian groups grew out of the Jewish community, their presence in Rome probably mirrored that of the Jews, with particular concentrations in certain neighborhoods, notably Trastevere. As the new faith began making converts, probably mostly amongst immigrants and across a growing range of social classes, the dispersal of Christians throughout the city intensified. Because of the persecution of Christians by Nero around AD 64, it became prudent to live and meet in small groups, and avoid congregating in public in large numbers. Because they worshiped in rooms dedicated to the purpose in private houses and kept their meetings very discreet, creating a clerical hierarchy exercising authority over the different Christian groups in the city proved a slow process.

Indications of this can be found in texts produced by Christian writers in Rome in the late first and second centuries. The author of the Epistle of Clement may have been the man of this name later described as the person responsible for drafting communications sent on behalf of the Christians of Rome to other churches.[28] But by the time of Tertullian and Irenaeus, Clement was listed as the second or third bishop of Rome.

This difference of perspective on Clement is telling. The late-second-century authors were probably reporting a tradition that had grown up in Rome in which leading figures amongst the elders of their day were retrospectively turned into bishops, to produce a continuous list of holders of the office stretching back to Peter. Why this happened can be explained, but it would be helpful to ask which of the people named by Irenaeus and Tertullian should be regarded as the first real bishop of the city. Most scholars now agree that the answer would be Anicetus, who comes in tenth on both lists, and whose episcopate likely covered the years 155 to 166.[29]

Not everyone is convinced that what has been called a monarchic bishop, with unquestioned authority over all of the Christian clergy in the city, was to be found in Rome even as early as this, and Fabian (236–250) has been proposed as the first bishop of Rome in the full sense.[30] It is probably not necessary to take so extreme a view. The idea that in principle there should be a single bishop at the head of the whole Christian community of the city existed from well before his time. On the other hand, even after 250 the authority of the bishop over all of the Christians in the city could not easily be enforced, as it was impossible to impose uniformity in so large a city, when the Christians remained legally proscribed and in danger of prosecution by the state.

Defining the Faith

If the office of bishop only appeared in Rome in the mid-second century, it might be asked why within a generation it was thought to have existed since the time of Peter and Paul, more than a century earlier. In part this was because the process was a gradual one. Although divided into many small groups centred on house-churches scattered across the city, the Christians in Rome had early on developed a sense of community, as can be seen from Paul's Epistle that addressed them as a whole. By the end of the first century, they were choosing office holders such as Clement to carry out tasks on behalf of the whole Christian body, and there were meetings of the leaders of the different house-churches, who thus formed a body of senior elders. It was then a relatively small step to choose one of these as the president of the whole community and the head of its clergy, as both the organisational structure of the local church and its forms of worship became more complex.

This may explain why Irenaeus and Tertullian's apparent rewriting of the history of Christianity in Rome provoked no evident disagreement. Why they were so keen to present the Roman church as one ruled by an unbroken succession of bishops since the time of the Apostles is another matter. What is significant is that both authors produced their lists of bishops in writings that were explicitly controversial and intended to combat theological opponents. Neither was interested in the history of the Church in Rome for its own sake. The existence of the line of bishops they described was a central plank in their arguments. Both were appealing to it as a source of authority to be preferred to that claimed by their adversaries, the Gnostics.

The various individuals and groups now known as Gnostics did not belong to a unified movement. They only came to be lumped together in a later period, when the differences in their views no longer mattered and when their beliefs had been definitively condemned and declared heretical.[31] In the first and second centuries, however, there was no absolute orthodoxy against which their interpretations of Christianity could be measured. A consensus of opinion on what constituted the authoritative books of Christian teaching, that collection of texts we call the New Testament, was only starting to form and would not be fully achieved before the fourth century.[32] There was also no individual, committee or council of leaders within the Christian movement that could pronounce on which beliefs and practices were acceptable and which were not.

This was particularly true of Rome with its numerous small groups of believers. Different Christian teachers and organisers of house-churches offered a variety of interpretations of the faith and attracted particular followings, rather in the way that modern denominations provide choice for worshipers looking for practices that particularly appeal to them on emotional, intellectual, aesthetic or other grounds. The range of opinion extended, for example, from traditional Jewish Christians, who continued to obey the ritual requirements of Judaism, to the followers of Marcion, who rejected the Old Testament and accepted only parts of just one Gospel, that of Luke.

The difference between those two extremes lay in the attitude towards the Jewish heritage of Christianity, something that became increasingly contentious as the influence of Greek ideas on the interpretation of the Christian message grew throughout the second century. One of several ways this showed itself was in the belief that the real teachings of Jesus were hidden and esoteric and could only be revealed to believers by enlightened teachers or through revelations in dreams and visions. This is the origin of the term Gnostic applied to those who came to accept such views, as it was a secret *Gnosis* or 'knowledge' that believers had to acquire through the teaching of their spiritual master.

Such a general adjective is actually inappropriate, as it implies that this was a coherent movement or body of ideas. There were almost as many different ideas of what the true but concealed message of Christianity might be as there were teachers and leaders of Gnostic groups. Most of their teachings included ideas and language borrowed from contemporary Greek philosophical and religious speculation. All that was common to them was the conviction that the literal word of the early Christian texts was deliberately misleading and was intended to conceal the real spiritual meaning within. Thus Paul was presented by several Gnostic teachers as a master of secret wisdom and even the ultimate source of authority for their particular version of the hidden knowledge.[33] This may be why their opponents increasingly emphasised Peter's authority and downplayed Paul's.

The reasons for the rise in the second century of such groups are not hard to see. With the rapid growth of conversions to Christianity amongst non-Jews, a backlash against the strict Jewish elements in Christian thought and practice was inevitable. The language and contents of the Old Testament seemed primitive or alien to those educated in the Graeco-Roman tradition, with its intellectual and cultural heritage of classical antiquity. Meanwhile the wealthier classes of the cities of the Roman empire, amongst whom Christians were now to be found, were becoming interested in new interpretations of Plato and other Greek philosophers and being drawn into membership of a growing range of esoteric mystery cults.

The widespread feeling in this period that real knowledge required teaching and initiation, and therefore the creation of different levels of membership within a religious group, also had an impact on Christianity. As we have seen, it was at this time that baptism became a rite of passage, to be approached only after long periods of instruction. Some acts of Christian worship were closed to those who had not yet attained this level of initiation, and a priestly hierarchy emerged to administer the rites and instruct the aspiring believers.

Emphasis on hidden knowledge meant that most of the writings of those later described as Gnostics are very obscure and far removed in style and contents both from the straightforward narratives of the Gospels and the open instruction of the Pauline letters. So it was long assumed that their works had little to do with Christianity. The discovery in 1945 of a cache of texts at Nag Hammadi in Egypt, likely part of the fourth-century library of a Christian monastic community, however, radically changed this view, for they were mostly previously unknown writings ranging from those that could be considered orthodox to the clearly Gnostic.[34]

The Nag Hammadi discovery has made it much easier to understand why Christian Gnostic teachers flourished in Rome in the second century. Several of them were members of the clergy, and one in particular, Valentinus, may have been a serious candidate for the office of bishop around the time it was first established.[35] Several rival and even contradictory interpretations of the Christian message could coexist in the city so long as there was no single local authority able to rule on what was and what was not acceptable belief. Resolution of such doctrinal conflicts only became imperative when one group of believers tried to impose their views on all the rest. For example, Marcion, son of a bishop from Sinope on the Black Sea, came to Rome around 139 and began teaching that Christ had never had a physical human body and so had not suffered crucifixion 'in the flesh'. He also taught that the god of the Old Testament was not the real creator God but a lesser being whose work had to be corrected by Jesus and Paul. Extreme as many of his views were, it was only when in 144 he called a meeting of the presbyters, the leaders of the various Christian communities in Rome, and tried to persuade them to accept his ideas that he was excommunicated and a large donation he had made to the charitable funds of the Roman church was returned to him.[36] Marcion soon after left the city, only to build up a much larger following in the East and found a movement that survived for another century.

While this case illustrates that contradictory beliefs could coexist within Rome's Christian community, it also shows the limits of the resources available to its leaders for imposing doctrinal unity. Excommunication came to mean far more as a sanction in later centuries, but at this time its significance was more symbolic than practical. As the importance of the Eucharistic service grew, the various Christian groups would exchange weekly gifts of their consecrated bread and wine, as a sign of fellowship. In particular, the bishop sent them to all of the various house-churches that accepted his authority. So, excommunication meant that Eucharistic elements would no longer be sent to or received from the group thus being excluded. This was not yet a spiritual sanction that threatened supernatural or other punishment; the parties concerned just had nothing more to do with each other.

After Marcion, the best-known case of excommunication in Rome in the second century occurred during the years when Victor was bishop (c. 189 to c. 198). At the time there were two methods of calculating the date of Easter, the greatest feast of the Christian year. One used the Eastern method of calculation, by which it was held on the same day as the Jewish Passover, and the other used the practice followed in Rome of celebrating it on the Sunday immediately following that festival. Victor sent letters to the leaders of all the major communities, but with limited success. Finally, he excommunicated those in Rome who refused to give up the Eastern system. For this, he was rebuked by the Christians of Lyon for being too harsh, although their bishop, Irenaeus, had only recently been emphasising the importance of the apostolic authority of the Roman bishops.

Irenaeus' interest in establishing a somewhat unhistorical continuity in the Roman episcopate from the time of the Apostles was central to his opposition to the Gnostics, which was itself a reaction to a recent persecution in Lyon in 177, in which his predecessor as bishop and many of his fellow clergy in the city had been publicly executed, often in scenes of great cruelty. His anger against the Gnostic teachers was prompted by arguments they used to justify their evading persecution, even to the extent of denying their Christian beliefs. If, in their view, the real truths of Christianity were secret and did not belong to the literal word of the Scriptures or the performance of religious rituals, then what did it matter if you denied belief in such texts or involvement in such acts of worship? The sufferings of those who confessed their faith in public may have made it seem to non-Gnostics even more important that there be greater uniformity in belief. Why should they have to face imprisonment, torture and usually very painful deaths if some who professed to be fellow believers scoffed at them for being so literal minded and unnecessarily brave?

THE APOSTOLIC SUCCESSION

The need for a recognised source of authority that could claim access to an authentic tradition of teaching going back to Jesus impelled Irenaeus and Tertullian to fix on episcopal succession as the key. Their claim was that the Apostles had founded a number of the major churches and appointed their first bishops or even been bishops themselves. In each case there had followed an unbroken succession of office holders, who passed on the authoritative teaching they had received from the founding Apostles, who themselves heard it from Jesus. This countered the claims of the Gnostic teachers to have inherited a secret teaching that traced back to Paul and others, for the Gnostics could not produce such complete and apparently well-attested lines of succession as those of the bishops of the major cities.

It was a clever argument that took on the various Gnostic teachers more or less on their own terms, and its authority survived unchallenged for centuries, even though in fact there had been no bishops before the early part of the second century. Rome was used by both

Irenaeus and Tertullian as their prime example not only because of the special significance in Christian history of both Peter and Paul but also because it was actually the only major see for which such a complete chain of episcopal succession could convincingly be constructed. We must assume that there were good records of early Christian office holders in Rome, even if they had not necessarily been bishops, from which it could be made. When around 325 Eusebius of Caesarea tried to draw up lists of holders of the office of bishop in the main Christian centres, including Alexandria, Antioch and Jerusalem, his evidence was insufficient to permit it for any case other than that of Rome, on which he drew his early information from Irenaeus.

Another problem with Irenaeus and Tertullian's argument is that it assumes a role for the Apostles in the years after the Crucifixion that may not be entirely historical. The canonical gospels tell us of the Apostles' role in Christ's ministry and preaching, but these texts are not themselves the earliest evidence for Christianity. Paul's letters, dating from the 40s to the early 60s, do not refer to the Apostles as a body exercising leadership of the movement. From his remarks, it was Peter, John and James, the brother of Jesus, who were seen as leaders of the movement. Later James, known as 'the Just' and 'the Rampart of the people', who combined an asceticism reminiscent of that of an Old Testament prophet with absolute fidelity to Jewish ritual and dietary laws, became the predominant figure.[37] During a purge of Christians in Jerusalem at the time of the Jewish Revolt in AD 66, some orthodox Jews stoned him to death. His status was inherited by other members of the family, some of whom were apparently still alive in the reign of Domitian (81–96), but by this time any leadership of the movement had long since passed from their hands.[38]

The early primacy of members of Jesus' family, together with the expectation of an imminent Second Coming, limited the need for institutional structures and authority. It is only after the destruction of the Temple in AD 70 that the first Gospel, Mark's, was written, followed by those of Matthew and Luke within another ten to twenty years. It is in their narratives that the Apostles as a group first take on a special role in the revelation and spread of Christ's teaching. This may reflect the growing sense that the End was not nigh and that Christian communities, some of which were now claiming special links with particular disciples, saw an apostolic transmission of Jesus' words as a source of direction and authority.

For example, a community of Christians is believed to have existed in western Anatolia (Asian Turkey) claiming a particular link with the Apostle John, in whose name a number of writings were produced in the late first and early second centuries. These included not just his Gospel but also the Book of Revelation and the two Epistles.[39] In the case of Peter, the First Epistle attributed to him but certainly not written by him, may well have been produced at Rome in the last decades of the first century, though this is not definitely established. If so, it is further evidence of the special relationship between the Prince of the Apostles and at least some of the Christian groups in the imperial capital. Interestingly, its theological views are essentially those of Paul.[40]

While the history of these early years may seem too vague and inconclusive, with too few three-dimensional characters or clearly delineated events, and with all too much recourse to scholarly doubt, disagreement and lack of evidence, its importance is undeniable. Why and how links were forged between the apostolic founders and a line of successors which they were supposed to have instituted and through whom their teaching was uniquely transmitted—these questions mark the first step in our enquiry. This process laid the groundwork upon which the whole edifice of papal primacy would be erected in the centuries to come.

chapter 2

PRIMACY IS GIVEN
TO PETER

(180–312)

A Persecuted Church

In AD 64, during the reign of the emperor Nero, a great fire destroyed much of the centre of Rome. According to the historian Cornelius Tacitus, writing a generation later, the populace believed the emperor had started the fire, and so, to divert attention from himself, Nero initiated a persecution of Christians—not, however, apparently, for arson.

> First, Nero had self-acknowledged Christians arrested. Then, on their information, large numbers of others were condemned—not so much for incendiarism as for their anti-social tendencies. Their deaths were made farcical. Dressed in wild animals' skins, they were torn to pieces by dogs or crucified, or made into torches to be ignited after dark as substitutes for daylight. Nero provided his Gardens for the spectacle, and exhibited displays in the Circus, at which he mingled with the crowd—or stood in a chariot, dressed as a charioteer.

But the lurid executions had an unintended consequence: 'Despite their guilt as Christians, and the ruthless punishment it deserved, the victims were pitied. For it was felt that they were being sacrificed to one man's brutality rather than for the national interest.'[1]

We do not know the names of these martyrs nor how many died. The only possible exceptions are Peter and Paul, but the early Christians in Rome never associated their deaths with Nero's persecution. The first explicit reference to their being martyred is in a letter by Bishop Dionysius of Corinth ·to his Roman counterpart, Soter (c. 166?–c. 174?), and it was only in 325 that the first Christian historian, Bishop Eusebius of Caesarea, linked the persecution under Nero with the reports of their violent deaths.[2]

The Christians in Rome suffered the earliest known persecution by the Roman state, but, compared to Christian communities elsewhere, they were slow to venerate their martyrs and record their names and dates of death. The simple explanation for this reticence must be that in Rome, as indeed other parts of the empire, Christians were embarrassed by their status as criminals condemned for their beliefs. Being liable to arrest and capital punishment was not something in which at first they gloried, and they tried to avoid provoking public anger or official retaliation by open displays of their faith. The Gospel teachings—'Render therefore to Caesar the things that are Caesar's, and to God the things that are God's' (Matt. 22.21)—and those of Paul also encouraged detachment from secular society and obedience to civil power, not confrontation.

This reticence began to disappear around the year 180. Persecution of Christians in the cities of the Rhone valley in 177 and in the small North African town of Scillium produced the earliest Western contributions to an emerging literature of martyrdom, which until the late fourth century was written anonymously. Some of the earliest texts, such as *The Passion of the Scillitan Martyrs*, took the form of trial transcripts, with vivid if invented dialogue between the martyrs and their judges.[3] Others were simpler narratives, but usually including dialogue, and most presented the fortitude of the martyrs and their sufferings as reaffirmation of their faith.[4] These 'Martyr Acts' were circulated among Christian communities across the empire to encourage and inspire. Although one such text was produced in Rome around the end of the second century, it did not result in the glorification of martyrdom then developing elsewhere in the West.[5]

Despite its earlier reluctance to record the deeds of its martyrs, Rome produced in 336 the first Western martyrology, a list of the days of the calendar year on which victims were executed and where they were buried, so these could be the dates and locations for commemoration of their deaths by the community. In a very small number of cases the actual year of death was also recorded.[6] There are twenty-one dates in this text on which one or more of forty-eight Roman martyrs were to be remembered. That for Peter and Paul is June 29, and their burials were said to have been 'in the catacombs and on the Via Ostiensis' respectively. This record also mentions the year 258, which probably refers to a reburial of Peter at that time, when Christians were facing renewed persecution. Interestingly, there is no record of his body being taken back to its presumed original place of burial, under what is now the high or papal altar of St. Peter's.

This martyrology, preserved in a collection of texts compiled in 354, contains the names of very few of the bishops of Rome of the first three centuries. For example, the only one of these from the period before c. 180 is Telesphorus (c. 130). This is significant in that it shows that very few of them were regarded as martyrs at that time. This would change, reflecting the way later generations of bishops of the city wanted to take control of all forms of religious activity within it, and veneration of martyrs became one of the most powerful forms of popular piety for both local Christians and growing numbers of pilgrims. This is why by the early sixth century almost all the bishops of the period before 312 were being commemorated as martyrs, although very few of them actually were.

If the most important developments of the role and authority of the bishops took place from the early fourth century onwards, even in the third their growing status in the community can be seen, for example, in their special burial chamber in the catacomb of San Callisto. This chamber was first used in 236 for Bishop Pontianus, who had died in exile the previous year, and his successor, Anterus, who held office for little over a month. All of the next nine bishops, up to Eutychianus (274–282), were buried in the same place. Services were held there on the anniversaries of their burials, and during one of these, on 6 August 258, Bishop Sixtus II (257–258) and four of his seven deacons were surprised and killed by imperial soldiers. The three other deacons were taken prisoner and executed soon after. One of these was Laurentius (St. Laurence), who by the early fourth century had become one of Rome's most famous and venerated martyrs. No one knows why he, but not his seven colleagues, achieved this exalted status.[7]

This was a particularly violent episode, all the more so since the victims were killed without any legal hearing. But the emperor Valerian (253–260) had issued an order that Christians found gathering in the catacombs would be subject to summary execution. While laws against Christians certainly existed, we know little of the details, as they were not copied into the legal codes compiled under the Christian emperors of the fourth century and later. It is clear, though, that until the middle of the third century there were no general persecutions, and the application of anti-Christian legislation usually resulted from denunciations of individuals and outbreaks of violence. In Rome, after Nero, punitive measures against the Christians were always related to the maintenance of public order in the city, a constant preoccupation of Roman administrators. Thus, in 235 two rival bishops of Rome, Pontianus (230–235) and Hippolytus (c. 217–235), were exiled from the city by the emperor Maximin I (235–238) because of street fighting between their followers.[8]

The origins of their dispute belong to the time of Bishop Callistus (217–222), whom Hippolytus calls a freed slave, failed banker and convicted criminal, and whom he opposed for allowing twice-married men to join the clergy and existing clerics to remarry.[9] Refusing to accept the election of Callistus, Hippolytus had then been chosen bishop by those who shared his views of the need for more vigorous punishment for moral failings.

Because of the house-church system, such rival bishops could co-exist for as long as they had the backing of some of the city's many Christian groups. But the divisions usually resulted in violent clashes between the partisans of the two claimants, and in all cases the imperial government intervened to end the bloodshed and to send one or both of the rivals into exile, as happened in 235, and would do so again in 306/7 and 308.

The first general persecution of Christians in the empire was the result of the edict of the emperor Trajan Decius (249–251) requiring all adult male citizens to perform an act of worship which involved paying for the sacrifice and ritual cooking of an animal in a temple, to be followed by publicly eating some of it and offering wine to the 'genius' or guiding spirit of the emperor. As proof a signed and dated certificate would be issued.[10]

The Christians refused to obey the edict because it contravened their prohibition on worship of idols and eating of food that had been sacrificed to them. Although they later saw this law as having been aimed exclusively at them, its real intentions were different and far more radical, as this was the first time that the Roman state had demanded a public demonstration of loyalty from all its citizens. It was a period of political instability, military defeat and economic turmoil, and so Christian opposition to the emperor's edict on religious grounds was interpreted by the government as treason.[11] As a result, the actions taken by the state against several of the bishops and clergy of Rome in the 250s were far more severe than anything since the time of Nero.

Following widespread Christian refusal to perform the sacrifices, Bishop Fabian (236–250) was arrested and died under interrogation. Cornelius (251–253) could be elected only after the emperor's death but was exiled in 252 under the equally insecure regime of Trebonianus Gallus (251–253). When a period of relative political and military tranquillity was restored by Valerian in 253, two successive bishops, Lucius I (253–254) and Stephen I (254–257), functioned freely until the situation changed again in 257 when Valerian reinstated Trajan Decius' edict. He also ordered that Christians of senatorial rank be stripped of their status and property. But after the emperor was captured by the Persians in 260, his son Gallienus (253–268) repealed these laws and restored confiscated Christian property.

PUNISHMENT OR MERCY?

Although much of the history of the Church in Rome in the third century is obscure, some events in the years 250 to 258 are unusually well illuminated, thanks to the letters of Cyprian, bishop of Carthage, the foremost city of Roman North Africa. From a wealthy and aristocratic background, Cyprian was a recent convert to Christianity when elected bishop in 248. His previous paganism mattered less than his social standing, as bishops were often chosen for their wealth and political connections, which benefited their church. He became the most prolific Christian Latin author of this period, reinforcing the intellectual reputation of the church in Africa created by Tertullian. Among Cyprian's works were collections of letters put together after his martyrdom in 258, some of which relate to his not always easy relations with Rome.

His election was followed by Decius' decree. Some Christians performed the required sacrifices, some did not but bribed officials into giving them the necessary certificates and others refused and were imprisoned or executed. Cyprian left Carthage to avoid the new law, but in Rome Bishop Fabian died under interrogation in January 250, and leadership of the Christian communities in the city was taken over by a group of priests until it was safe to hold an episcopal election fourteen months later. The leader of this priestly oligarchy was Novatian, who took a strong line against Christians who had lapsed during the persecution. He and his supporters proposed that such sinners, including those who had bought certificates of sacrifice, should only be readmitted to communion on their deathbeds and should follow a full penitential discipline until then: fasting, abstinence, continence and exclusion from the Eucharist.

The Roman clergy were uneasy about Cyprian's conduct in lying low until the emperor's edict had been revoked. He sent them a letter arguing that he had not actually gone into hiding but merely removed himself from the city, where he would have been a prime target. Having to defend himself clearly rankled, as Cyprian was quick to demand answers of his own when a dispute broke out in Rome over the election of a new bishop in March 251. Novatian had expected to be the new bishop, but another of the Roman priests, Cornelius, had been elected. He represented a majority group among the clergy who were prepared to readmit lapsed members into full communion after a limited period of exclusion. Novatian refused to accept the result of the election and was consecrated as bishop by his supporters, creating a schismatic sect within the Roman church that would survive until the fifth century. At the time, however, his hope was to gain wider recognition as the legitimate bishop of Rome, and he sent his followers to win the support of Christian leaders elsewhere. Cyprian took his time to declare for Cornelius, although their views on the reconciliation of the lapsed were similar, and he sent some African bishops to Rome to enquire about the recent election.

Acceptance by the leading bishops of the day eventually legitimised the choice of Cornelius, but there was no way that Novatian could be suppressed. He continued to be recognised by the rigorist party in Rome as the true bishop of the city, and he used his status to back those following similar policies elsewhere. Thus he orchestrated the consecration of a rigorist bishop in Carthage in opposition both to Cyprian and to another rival, recently elected by those in the city clergy who felt that the lapsed should be readmitted to communion immediately. The three bishops coexisted in mutual hostility until Cyprian was martyred in 258.

CHURCH GOVERNMENT

Cyprian's letters, together with a handful of those of other bishops preserved in Eusebius' *Ecclesiastical History,* supply vital evidence for this period. A letter of Bishop Cornelius reveals that in his day there were forty-six priests and seven deacons in the Church of Rome, along with forty-two acolytes and fifty-six readers, exorcists and doorkeepers, as well as about fifteen hundred widows and others in the care of the church. From these figures it is estimated that there were 30,000 Christians in the city.[12]

These letters also reveal the importance of synods, or regional meetings of bishops convened under the presidency of a senior or metropolitan bishop. No synod is recorded in Spain before 300 or in Gaul before 314, but they appear to have been held regularly in both Rome and Africa during much of the third century. The ideal was for two meetings to be held annually, one during Lent and the other around October. The Roman synods were attended by up to sixty bishops, but the names of the towns from which they came are not recorded.

What is striking about the synods is their central role in decision making. Excommunications of individuals or groups were discussed and announced in them, as were other current issues. The synods sent delegates to enquire into appeals or complaints from other bishoprics. In major disputes, such as the Roman election of 251, opinion was sought throughout the empire, and letters from bishops were read out publicly during the synods. Behind the scenes, such meetings may have been carefully orchestrated, not least by metropolitans such as the bishops of Rome, who always presided and proclaimed the synodal decisions. However, these meetings emphasised collegiality and consensus, as shown in the interpretation that Cyprian put on Christ's charge to Peter (Matt. 16. 18–19), which he cited as testimony to the divinely instituted authority of all bishops, not just the one who could call himself Peter's successor.

Still, in this period the bishop of Rome was pre-eminent in the respect accorded to his see by fellow bishops. As Cyprian wrote in a tract on the unity of the Church, 'Certainly the other Apostles were what Peter was, but primacy is given to Peter so that it may be shown that the church is one.'[13] It was long established that there were a small number of patriarchal sees: Antioch and Alexandria (traditionally thought to have been founded by Peter's disciple Mark) in the Eastern half of the empire, and Rome in the West. Jerusalem also had a special standing. Lacking an apostolic foundation, Carthage could not compete on these terms, though its political and economic importance gave it prominence, and its bishops regarded themselves as equal to their Roman colleagues, even receiving appeals from other Western churches against decisions made by the bishop of Rome and his synods.

CYPRIAN AND ROME

Some of Cyprian's letters contain increasingly acrimonious exchanges between himself and Bishop Stephen I of Rome (254–257). Relations began badly when some Spanish bishops lobbied Cyprian to endorse their removal from office of two colleagues, who had lapsed during the recent persecution but had secured a reversal of the sentence from Rome. In a second case some bishops in southern Gaul complained to Cyprian that Stephen had ignored their request that he curb the bishop of Arles, who was following a Novatianist line in dealing with the lapsed. In neither case do we know the outcome, but a more fundamental conflict was brewing.

Disagreements over doctrine and the treatment of the lapsed in many of the Christian communities in the Roman empire led to schisms and questioning the validity of sacraments administered by bishops seen as heretical or schismatic. This was particularly significant in the matter of baptism, a sacrament to be received only once. Cyprian and the African bishops followed the practice of colleagues in Antioch and Asia Minor in regarding sacraments administered by heretics as invalid and therefore to be repeated. Rome and the churches in Egypt took the opposite view, that the worthiness of the administrator did not affect the validity of the sacrament, which was a divine gift, and so re-baptism could not be undertaken in any circumstances. The theology behind the Roman stance would win universal acceptance in the fourth century, but in the time of Cyprian two synods of the African churches rejected baptism by heretics.[14] Stephen refused to receive, let alone read, their *acta* (acts)—the formal record of the decisions taken—and the accompanying letters from Cyprian.

Stephen also threatened to break off communion with the churches in Asia Minor if they persisted in re-baptising, and he sent letters to the leading bishops of the empire asking their support. Although only fragments of his letters have survived, they prompted heated reactions. Cyprian called the bishop of Rome 'a friend of heretics, an enemy to Christians' and described his remarks as 'arrogant or irrelevant'.[15] Bishop Firmilian of Caesarea in Cappadocia, the principal city in Asia Minor, agreed and noted that the Romans were not following the practices of the Church in Jerusalem, which he regarded as the model. He also criticised Stephen 'since he who brags so loudly of the seat of his episcopate and who insists that he holds the succession from Peter, on whom the foundations of the church were laid, is introducing many other rocks and building many new churches' and asked 'can there be "one body and one spirit" with such a man, when he himself has, perhaps, not one mind, so slippery it is, so shifting, so unstable?'[16]

Behind the vituperation lies a rejection of Stephen's claim that Rome enjoyed special authority because of its Petrine foundation and unique apostolic tradition.[17] For Firmilian the customs of Jerusalem and those recognised by Eastern councils of bishops were superior, and he held that Rome's views should be judged entirely by the degree to which they corresponded to these. Rome for him was defending heretical novelty and dividing the Church, rather than unifying it, as Stephen claimed.

Cyprian did not have such a bedrock of tradition to which to appeal, but he could call on the solidity of the views expressed by his episcopal colleagues meeting in council, whose unanimity validated the stand he was making. These conflicting opinions on the source of authority and its expression would resurface frequently in later centuries. How this particular dispute was resolved is unknown, as Stephen died in 257 and our unique light on the period is lost when Cyprian was executed in 258.

A PAPAL TRAITOR?

The remainder of the third century is almost a blank as far as the Roman church is concerned, with only the names of a succession of bishops being recorded. The savage deaths of Sixtus II and his deacons in 258 produced another episcopal hiatus, as it was impossible or unwise to elect a new bishop before the emperor Gallienus repealed his father's anti-Christian edicts in 260. Then, having recovered their property, Christians re-entered Roman society and even showed themselves willing to involve the state in their internal affairs.

When a dispute over property broke out in Antioch between two rival bishops, one of them appealed to the emperor Aurelian (270–275). The case hinged on identifying which bishop of the two was recognised by the wider Christian community in the empire. This, the emperor decided, was the one with whom the bishop of Rome and his synod would be willing to exchange letters.[18] The importance attached to the view taken by Rome in the solution of disputes amongst Christians would be extended by decisions made by emperors in the fourth century. Before then, however, came the longest and most severe period of persecution.

The emperor Diocletian (284–305) initiated in 303 what came to be called from its length and the large numbers of those believed to have perished in it the Great Persecution. It continued under his successors, but with differing degrees of enthusiasm across the empire, until formally ended by imperial decrees in 312 (West) and 313 (East). The Roman church suffered less than in the 250s, and imperial edicts prohibiting Christian worship, confiscating Christian property and requiring the surrender of copies of the Scriptures were repealed or ceased to be enforced in the city from as early as 306. Even so, some suffered for their refusal to obey. Few of their names are reliably recorded, but they would be augmented in later centuries thanks to the mistaken belief that almost any identifiable body found buried in the catacombs had to be that of a martyr.

Among the small number of names of those who actually perished at this time, preserved in the list of martyrs of the Roman church compiled around 336, is that of thirteen-year-old Agnes, later to be proclaimed patron saint of girls, and one of the most venerated saints of the city. She was denounced as a Christian after rejecting the advances of a pagan. His father, who was a magistrate, sentenced her to be stripped and sent to a brothel, but miraculously, it is said, her hair grew so long as to completely cover her nakedness. When her former suitor came to work his evil ways upon her, he was struck dead by divine intervention but was restored to life through her prayers. She was dragged once more before his father and sentenced to death. Tradition has it that her execution took place in the Stadium of Domitian, beneath what is now the Piazza Navona, a site ever since associated with her.[19] The earliest account of her martyrdom was written nearly a century later, and may reflect a particular model of sanctity more than actual events.[20]

The resumption of persecution and demands that Christians hand over their holy books produced similar reactions to those of the 250s. From fear or even a sense of duty to the emperor, some complied. This act of handing over—the Latin verb is *tradere* 'to hand over' or 'surrender'—led to their being known by their more uncompromising brethren as *traditores,* from which comes the modern English word 'traitor'. The questions of the 250s as to how to deal with Christians who faltered under persecution and who compromised or abandoned their faith reasserted themselves as tolerance returned from 306 onwards.

Among those involved was an earlier bishop of Rome, Marcellinus (295–303), who in 313 was posthumously accused of having been a *traditor* by a group of rigorist Africans. The claim that Marcellinus and two of his deacons had handed over copies of the Scriptures continued to be repeated well into the fifth century.[21] While this was just as vehemently denied in both Rome and Africa, genuine doubts exist about Marcellinus. His episcopate ended in autumn 303, though there is no record of his death, let alone that he was martyred.[22] A hiatus then ensued before the election of his successor, Marcellus, in either 305 or 306.

One plausible explanation, doubted by some, is that Marcellinus abdicated because he had compromised in some way during the short but severe opening period of the persecution.[23] Even if no longer performing his episcopal functions, he could not be replaced as bishop until after his death two or three years later. Whatever the truth about Marcellinus' conduct, his existence is not in doubt, nor the fact that he is the first bishop of Rome to be referred to as *Papa* (Father), or Pope. An abbreviated form of the word appears in a contemporary catacomb inscription erected by one of his deacons.[24] Despite its later popularity, this title was very rarely employed by the bishops of Rome themselves before the late eleventh century. It tended to be used as a term of affectionate respect when referring to them and could equally be used of other bishops, at least until the sixth century, from which time on in the West it was applied uniquely to the holder of the see of Rome. In the East the bishops of Alexandria were known as 'popes' from the third century onward.

chapter 3

THE SUCCESSOR OF
THE FISHERMAN

(312–384)

CONSTANTINE'S ROME

Beside a bridge over the Tiber just north of Rome, a battle was fought on 28 October 312 that changed the history of Christianity. The outcome would also have a dramatic impact on the bishops of Rome, turning them into functionaries of the state that had long persecuted them. The relationship with the civil power, previously one of wary neutrality or occasional hostility, would be transformed as Christianity became the religion first of an emperor and then of the whole empire.

The battle that had such far-reaching consequences was the product of rivalry between two of the four emperors then controlling the Roman world, part of a process that by 324 would see one of them, Constantine I (306–337), emerge as sole ruler of the empire. Proclaimed emperor in York in 306, controlling Britain, Gaul and Spain, he took the first step on that road by invading Italy, ruled by his brother-in-law Maxentius (306–312). Just before the battle at the Milvian Bridge, Constantine had a dream in which he was told 'to mark the heavenly sign of God on the shields of his soldiers'.[1] This was how the tutor to the emperor's son recorded the event three years later, by which time Constantine's conversion to Christianity had been publicly acknowledged. A decade later, in the East, a far more elaborate account, involving the vision of a cross in the sky that was also seen by some of his soldiers, was published by one of the emperor's theological advisors. Despite contradictions, both narratives make the battle with Maxentius into the turning point in transforming Constantine into the first Christian emperor.[2]

His British and Gallic legions overwhelmed the forces of Maxentius, who drowned in the Tiber when the bridge collapsed as he fled. The defeated emperor's head, stuck on a spear, led Constantine and his army in their triumphal entry into Rome the next day.

Although seizing power in Italy and Africa without the consent of the other rulers sharing the imperial office in 306, Maxentius had thereafter made his mark on Rome in a way unmatched since the second century, erecting massive public and private buildings, particularly around the Forum, honouring himself and his family.[3] He had also ended the persecution of Christians in his territories, the first emperor to do so. And in 310/11 he returned to Bishop Miltiades (310–314) the communal property of the Roman church that had been confiscated in 304.

For Rome's Christians, Maxentius' dispassionate tolerance was of less weight than the warm embrace of an emperor who shared their own beliefs. However, it is not known how quickly Constantine made his conversion public, and in any case he did not remain long in Rome, departing after a few months for a meeting at Milan with the Eastern emperor Licinius I (308–324), at which both agreed to end the persecution. Constantine was back in Rome briefly in 315 and again in 326 but thereafter did not return. He preferred his new imperial capital, which he named Constantinople (modern Istanbul) after himself, and on which work began after the elimination of Licinius in 324.

It has long been assumed that Constantine created magnificent new places of worship for the Christians of Rome and a residence for their bishop in a former imperial palace. The earliest history of the bishops, the *Liber Pontificalis* (Pontiff's Book), written around 540, records how, at the request of Pope Sylvester and others, the emperor constructed a series of churches, which he embellished with remarkable treasures and endowed with estates to provide a regular income for their maintenance. These churches included the Constantinian or Lateran Basilica; the original St. Peter's, 'a basilica to St. Paul', assumed to be San Paolo fuori le mura; 'a basilica in the Sessorian Palace' and others dedicated to St. Agnes, St. Laurence, and Sts. Marcellinus and Peter 'Between the Two Laurels', as well as some smaller ones in towns outside Rome.

Although compiled two centuries after Constantine's time, sometimes demonstrably inaccurate or prejudiced, the *Liber Pontificalis'* narrative of Constantine's construction projects is widely believed, thanks to detailed information about his gifts and endowments which looks as if it comes from an official source. While not exactly contemporary, these records date to the generation after Constantine, roughly in the middle of the fourth century. However, while most of the financial information is probably reliable, the setting into which it is placed in the *Liber Pontificalis* is far less so. This context matters because the story of these buildings is directly linked to that of the bishops of the city, whose social and economic standing is thought to have been transformed by Constantine's gift.

Both the chronology and the purposes of the emperor's building programme may be questioned. None of his constructions have survived intact, but traces of most survive. Where they have been studied archaeologically, none shows signs of dating from earlier than c. 330, but it is argued from the list of endowments in the *Liber Pontificalis* that work on the Constantinian Basilica could have begun in 315, when the emperor made his second short visit to Rome. By 360 this was also known as the Lateran Basilica, being on the site of what had once been the home of a noble family called the Lateranni.[4] It became the cathedral or principal church of the bishops of Rome, as it remains to the present, but exactly when that occured is not recorded.

Like the Lateran, the first basilica of St. Peter's, gradually replaced in the sixteenth century by the one we are familiar with today, has generally been regarded as Constantinian in date, as is claimed in the *Liber Pontificalis*. But as all of the properties given to provide an income for this basilica were located in the Eastern provinces of the empire, which

Constantine acquired in 324, work on St. Peter's could have begun only after that date. The mention of the burial of St. Peter himself being 'in the catacombs' in the Martyrology of 336 also suggests that a shrine in the catacomb of San Sebastiano on the Appian Way was still the centre of his cult in Rome just a year before Constantine died in 337. It is now thought that work on the basilica was not completed until the later 350s, in the reign of Constantine's son Constantius II (337–361). Suggestions have also been made that it was he or his brother Constans (337–350), with whom he partitioned the empire on their father's death, who actually commissioned the building of St. Peter's.[5]

Another of the basilicas said to have been constructed by Constantine was certainly not his. Although the *Liber Pontificalis* claims he 'built a basilica to St. Paul the apostle at the suggestion of Bishop Silvester', archaeological investigation has found no trace of a building that pre-dates the one on the presumed site of Paul's burial 'on the Ostia Road' that was built by Theodosius I (379–395), the founder of a different imperial dynasty.[6]

It seems remarkable that neither of the founding Apostles of the Church in Rome was honoured in the earliest phase of church building in the city. A basilica on the site of the presumed tomb of St. Peter was not completed until the middle of the century, and that on the burial site of St. Paul only appeared a generation later. The cult of the two Apostles that mattered so much to the bishops may not have appealed so strongly to the Christian emperors.

The Lateran apart, all the buildings that definitely date to Constantine were built outside the city walls and are called circus-shaped basilicas because their ground plan is similar to that of a typical Roman racetrack or circus, with long narrow parallel sides and one curved (apsidal) end and one square. They contained few internal structures, and archaeologists think they were used primarily as places of mass burial.[7] They include basilicas built close to the tombs of two third-century martyrs, Laurence and Gorgonius. The latter was raised over the burial ground of Maxentius' personal bodyguards, disbanded after the battle on the Milvian Bridge and whose tombstones were now deliberately smashed in its construction. Similarly, the Lateran Basilica was built on the site of the demolished barracks of the same unit, suggesting that a further aim of Constantine's building programme was obliterating the memory of his defeated predecessor.[8]

The basilica dedicated to Gorgonius also had a circular building attached to its western end, which is all that is still visible today (near the Termini railway station). Its size and design imply it was a mausoleum. If so, it could have been originally intended either for Constantine himself (who was, however, buried in his new capital of Constantinople) or for his mother, Helena, whose porphyry sarcophagus is now preserved in the Vatican Museum. Around 340 another great circus-shaped basilica was built outside the city walls, close to the burial place of St. Agnes, by Constantine's daughter Constantina. It too has a mausoleum attached to it, in which she was buried in 354.[9]

As these examples show, this phase of constructing great basilicas, several of which in their later forms still dominate the Christian topography of Rome, was entirely the product of imperial initiative. Before this period the Christians lacked any purpose-built and distinctive places of worship, gathering instead in private houses or small and discrete communally owned meeting houses. Although it has been assumed that Constantine's dramatic building programme in Rome and elsewhere was a groundbreaking attempt to remedy this lack, this is unlikely.[10] All of the basilicas other than the Lateran were associated with places of burial, which by Roman law had to be situated outside city limits. So they certainly were not built as the first churches for city congregations. Contrary to another long-held belief, which argues that the use of city-centre locations for the new buildings might have offended the majority pagan population, including the still highly influential Senate, their deliberate association with Christian burial sites meant there was never any question of their being built within the walls. In any case no thought seems to have been given to non-Christian opinion, because many of them were erected over earlier pagan civil as well as military cemeteries that were deliberately destroyed in the process.[11]

Some of Constantine's basilicas helped obliterate the memory of a previous regime, and some were intended to serve as final resting places for members of the imperial family who lived in Rome. Perhaps most of them were also built to honour particular martyr saints, but as the earliest evidence for their cults dates from after these great buildings were erected, it may be it was the existence of the basilicas that helped popularise the cults rather than vice versa. In any event, these constructions were intended more as statements of imperial piety than as a facility for the emperor's new co-religionists, who were served instead by a growing number of much smaller local churches inside the city.

St. Peter's was the largest of the Roman basilicas, thanks to the presence of a great colonnaded court in front of its main entry, but the treasures and endowments provided for it were much less in quantity and value than those given to the Lateran.[12] According to the lists in the *Liber Pontificalis*, the gifts of liturgical vessels and decorative items given by Constantine (or possibly his sons) to the Lateran weighed nearly 12,000 pounds of silver and 1,200 of gold. Estates in Italy, Sicily and Africa were also donated to produce revenue estimated at 14,384 *solidi*, the largest gold coin of the time, per annum. In comparison, the gifts and endowments for St. Peter's were much more modest, amounting to 1,720 pounds of silver and 291 of gold, with estates in Syria and Egypt generating an annual income of 3,708 gold *solidi*, together with renders of incense, papyrus and spices. Smaller still were Constantina's gifts to her basilica of St. Agnes: just 330 pounds of silver and 60 of gold, plus Italian estates producing 595 *solidi* a year.[13]

Even so, such endowments far outstripped anything that the bishops of the city could provide for the churches they founded in Rome in the fourth century, for which they often received imperial assistance. For example, when Pope Marcus (336) constructed a small basilica in a cemetery on the Via Ardeatina as his place of burial, he provided it with liturgical vessels weighing 96 pounds of silver and three farms producing annual revenue of 126 *solidi*.[14] Such comparatively modest figures underline the enormous difference in the scale of imperial and episcopal patronage at this time.

BISHOPS AND EMPEROR

It has also been thought that Constantine provided the bishops of Rome with a grand residence in a former imperial palace, but this is less than certain. The palace in question was the property of Constantine's wife and was just loaned for a meeting of bishops in 313, and in any case it was not the same building as the one attached to the Lateran Basilica, which became the main papal residence in Rome until the fifteenth century. The earliest mention of that palace dates to the pontificate of Zacharias (741–752), and there is no way of knowing when it was built.

The basilicas were imperial property, intended in some cases for dynastic burials, and there is no contemporary evidence that the emperor transferred ownership of them to the Church. The claim that he did so first appears in the account of the pontificate of Sylvester in the *Liber Pontificalis,* from the mid-sixth century. In fact, we do not know for sure when they were acquired by the bishops, but this was unlikely to have been before the end of the Constantinian dynasty in 363, and was probably later.

No pope before Celestine I (422–432) is recorded as making donations to any of these imperial basilicas, and none of the popes of the period was buried in them, choosing to be laid to rest in the catacombs or in smaller funerary basilicas of their own foundation, outside the city walls. On the other hand, a specially constructed mausoleum attached to St. Peter's served as the burial place for all members of the Western branch of the imperial dynasty of Theodosius from c. 400 to 455. It may be significant that the first pope to be buried in St. Peter's, the choice of so many of his successors, was Leo I in 461. He and his successor, Hilary (461–468), were also the first papal donors to almost all of the greater basilicas.

So it is likely that most or all of these buildings remained imperial property until the fifth century, and quite possibly the middle of it. This is not actually so surprising. The pagan temples of Rome and the endowments that supported them became the property of the state in 394, when all forms of traditional Roman religion were prohibited, and even as late as the early seventh century, when Pope

Boniface IV (608–615) wanted to turn one of them, the huge domed Pantheon, into a church, he had to ask for it as a gift from the emperor Phocas, ruling in Constantinople. In view of such tenacity, it might be wondered why the emperors gave up legal ownership of the great Constantinian basilicas. One reason may have been a 'divine fire' that seriously damaged the basilica of St. Paul's in the time of Leo I.[15] The need for repairs to this building on top of the maintenance costs of the others, now over a century old, at a time when the Western imperial government could no longer support its rapidly shrinking army and bureaucracy, may have made transfer of ownership attractive. All the more so as the Roman church was far wealthier and better endowed than it had been back in the early fourth century.

There is thus no way of knowing where the principal residence and administrative centre of the bishops was located at this time, or how they divided their time between the various churches of the city. Every pope from Sylvester (314–335) to Damasus (366–384) built basilicas in significant parts of the city, several of which developed into major churches that featured prominently in the ceremonies of the papacy's liturgical year. Particularly notable is the Basilica Liberiana, founded by Bishop Liberius (352–366) and rebuilt in the mid-fifth century as Santa Maria Maggiore, one of the great patriarchal basilicas. It seems that each pope wanted a church with which he would be particularly associated. The increasing size and magnificence of these buildings also testify to the growing wealth of the bishopric, thanks to the quantity of gifts and bequests it was now receiving from the rising number of Christian noble families in the city, as well as from imperial patronage.

Constantine's conversion did more than enhance the social standing and political influence of the leaders of the Christian communities in the empire. He also incorporated the bishops into its administrative and judicial organisation, by making them judges in cases in which Christians were involved. Initially this was confined to disputes between fellow believers but was then extended so that if one party to a case was a Christian, he could request to have it heard by a bishop rather than by a civil magistrate. While we do not know in detail how the weight of this new responsibility affected the bishops in Rome, one North African bishop around the end of the century complained that his judicial responsibilities took up far too much time, at the expense of his pastoral ones.[16]

The bishops of Rome did not enjoy easy access to the first Christian emperor, as he was scarcely ever in Rome after 312, and from 326 took up permanent residence in the East. For his part Constantine found the Roman bishops of his day less useful than he had expected. Soon after his victory over Maxentius, he had to deal with a dispute amongst his co-religionists, when some bishops in North Africa refused to accept the election of Caecilian to the see of Carthage, claiming that he had been consecrated by bishops who had been *traditores* in the Great Persecution. When in 313 the African dissidents appealed to the emperor, he referred the case to Pope Miltiades in the hope of a quick and authoritative decision.[17] As the emperor also named two Gallic bishops to sit on the tribunal alongside him, Miltiades became deliberately obstructive, turning what was intended to be a simple arbitration into a full synod of Italian bishops, and following elaborate legal procedures.[18]

The dissidents, led by a bishop Donatus, eventually stormed out, frustrated by the pope's tactics, thus allowing him to deliver a verdict in favour of Caecilian by default. Donatus and his followers, soon to be known as 'Donatists', refused to accept the result and appealed again to the emperor. They even accused the pope himself of being a *traditor*, like his predecessor Marcellinus. Constantine then handed the issue over to a synod of Gallic bishops to resolve, though with equal lack of success.

Hardly anything is known of the long pontificate of Miltiades' successor, Sylvester I (314–335), though in legends that began to take shape between the sixth and eighth centuries, he is the pope most closely associated with Constantine. In these tales Sylvester cures the emperor of leprosy, converts and baptises him, after Constantine had seen a vision of Saints Peter and Paul. As we know, Constantine's conversion actually had nothing to do with the bishops of Rome of his time, and he was baptised in Nicomedia near Constantinople just before his death. But in the Western historical tradition, all of this was forgotten, and in legend he remained, until the end of the Middle Ages, permanently associated with Pope Sylvester.

ROME AND THE ARIAN CONTROVERSY

If pope and emperor had little contact at this time, a dispute was brewing within the Church that would soon bring them into conflict. The issues involved were central in fashioning Christian doctrine, and if they are not contentious now it is because they were settled then, even at the cost of permanent divisions within the Church. Christians, only recently freed from the threat of persecution, were groping towards more complex understandings of their faith, but each question that was resolved generated new ones. In all of them the papacy had a role to play and in so doing further refined its own sense of purpose and authority.

The first of these great rifts was the debate over the Godhead known as the Arian Controversy, named for Arius, a deacon of the church of Alexandria. By 318 he was teaching that the three persons of the Trinity were neither equal nor co-eternal, that only the Father was eternal and uncreated and that the Son was, while superior to all other creatures, inferior to the Father and indeed not fully divine. The roots of his ideas go back to Origen (died 254), who had once been in charge of the Christian school in Alexandria, as well as to the widely influential contemporary Greek philosophy known as Neoplatonism. Origen remained controversial in Alexandria, and successive bishops of the see, Alexander (313–328) and Athanasius (328–373), tried to suppress Arius' views, but he could count on the support of influential Eastern bishops, some of whom had the ear of the emperor.

In 325, the first-ever large-scale council of the Church, attended by 220 or more bishops, was called by Constantine to meet under his presidency at Nicaea (now Iznik, Turkey) to resolve the dispute. Although several bishops from the Western provinces attended, Pope Sylvester did not, sending two priests and two deacons to represent him. A contemporary account reports that he was too old to make the journey, but his non-attendance helped foster the tradition that popes never attended councils that they themselves had not called.

Although the council produced a creed or statement of theological beliefs, called the Nicene, which is one of the oldest and still most authoritative of such formulations, it failed to solve the problem it was meant to address. The supporters of Arius were not won over, and other bishops found some of the theological statements of the dominant anti-Arian group disturbing. Ecclesiastical politics and clashes of personality added to the inflammatory mix, especially after Athanasius succeeded Alexander as bishop of Alexandria in 328. These theological disagreements provided another context for increasingly bitter rivalries between the two foremost patriarchal sees of the East: Alexandria and Antioch.

The sixth of the decrees issued by the Council of Nicaea had ruled that the bishop of Alexandria should exercise authority over the other episcopal dioceses of Egypt and Libya, 'as the Roman bishop did over those subject to Rome'.[19] The men who drafted this may have known what they meant, and it has long been accepted that the territorial units mentioned are civil administrative ones. But what is not clear is whether in the case of Rome this is referring to a larger or a smaller area: the 'suburbicarian' region immediately surrounding the city or Italy more generally. In the case of the bishops of Alexandria, however, in whose interests this was drafted, the wording was unambiguous. They were to exercise primatial authority over all the other bishops of Egypt and the adjacent provinces to the west.[20]

The diocese of Alexandria had previously enjoyed precedence but not disciplinary authority over other Egyptian bishoprics, so, establishing this was not easy. Athanasius tried through his patronage of the rapidly growing monastic communities of the Nile valley and occasional strong-arm tactics. But acts of violence he sanctioned, directed against the leaders of breakaway Christian communities in Egypt, gave his theological and political opponents grounds for complaining to the emperor. As Constantine was now influenced by advisors who shared some of Arius' ideas, a reversal of fortune followed. In 337 a council of bishops at Tyre condemned Athanasius, and Constantine exiled him to Gaul—an early example of how emperors would treat recalcitrant bishops.

These changes in imperial preference soon affected the bishops of Rome. Since at least the middle of the third century they had been in frequent communication with the bishops of Alexandria, thanks to the regular seaborne trade between the two cities. They exchanged views on all major theological issues, even if they were not always in agreement. Belief that the see of Alexandria had been established by Peter's disciple Mark added to the sense of a special relationship, at least on the Roman side.

In theological exchanges, Rome tended to worry about ideas that threatened belief in the unity of the Godhead. Some of the finer distinctions that the Greek Christians were trying to work into the relationship between the three persons of the Trinity perplexed the Romans, partly because of the difficulty of expressing them in Latin. In general, therefore, after 325 the bishops of Rome were interested in preserving the decisions of the Council of Nicaea as the benchmark for Christian unity and in maintaining good relations with the bishops of Alexandria.

Although Athanasius returned to Egypt on Constantine's death, his opponents were determined to get rid of him, and they had the ear of the new ruler of the Eastern half of the empire, Constantius II (337–361). Within two years Athanasius was under renewed attack. His opponents, led by Bishop Eusebius of Nicomedia, who had baptised Constantine, wrote to the new pope, Julius (337–352), to ask him to hold an Italian synod to add its condemnation to theirs. Julius responded by calling both sides to come to Rome for a general council. This was the first time that a pope had involved himself in a dispute in which the parties were outside his Western patriarchate. Julius claimed that Athanasius had been denied a fair hearing and so wanted an impartial gathering of bishops under his presidency to hear the evidence, 'so that a just conclusion might be reached'. Athanasius in the meantime had been expelled from Alexandria and was only too happy to escape to Rome, while Eusebius and his supporters refused to attend and delayed replying to the invitation until after the date suggested for the council had passed.

In Rome Julius became convinced of Athanasius' theological orthodoxy and was charmed by his charismatic personality. As the pope wrote to the Church in Egypt, when Athanasius returned triumphant to Alexandria in 346, Julius regarded it as 'a special token of divine favour that we should have had the privilege of knowing so outstanding a man'.[21]

After his vindication by the papal synod in Rome in 340, Athanasius worked his charm on the Western emperor, Constans (337–350), who persuaded his elder brother Constantius II that a council should be held on the frontier between their territories, at which the bishops from both sides could resolve their differences. So in 343 about 160 bishops converged on Sardica (modern Sofia in Bulgaria). But when Constantius' bishops discovered that Athanasius and others whom they had previously condemned and deposed were going to take part—thus implicitly reversing those verdicts—they refused to attend and instead held a council of their own at Philippopolis, in Constantius' territory. There they excommunicated Pope Julius and other Western bishops who had received Athanasius.

This breakdown in ecclesiastical harmony was mended by the threat of secular violence. After the elimination of a third brother in 340, Constans was militarily the more dominant of the two remaining emperors, and after the failure of the Council of Sardica, it was his threat of war over the issue that forced Constantius II to allow Athanasius and the other exiles to return to their sees in the East in 346. However, in 350 Constans was killed by his troops, and a general called Magnentius seized power, precipitating a civil war. It was in the final stages of this that Pope Julius I died in 352, just before Constantius II eliminated the usurper and made himself master of the whole empire.

So the new bishop of Rome, Liberius (352–366), began his pontificate in a changed political climate. Athanasius was accused of treasonable correspondence with Magnentius and went into hiding amongst the monks in upper Egypt for six years, while Constantius tried to secure consensus of support for a modified Arian theology that he and his ecclesiastical advisors favoured, involving a general condemnation of Athanasius, the standard bearer of Nicene orthodoxy. Liberius' appeals to Constantius to call a council resulted in one in 355 in which the emperor imposed his will through threats, and the pope's own representatives were coerced into signing a condemnation of Athanasius. When Liberius disowned them, he was removed from Rome in the middle of the night and brought before the emperor in Milan. When he still persisted in his support of Athanasius, Liberius was deposed and exiled to Thrace.

SCHISM AND RIOT

Back in Rome authority was taken by the archdeacon Felix, the most senior of the seven deacons, who called a meeting of the city clergy, where they refused to accept any other bishop while Liberius lived. This resolution proved short-lived, as under pressure from the emperor they subsequently met again and elected Felix himself. Athanasius later claimed Felix's ordination was carried out by imperial secret agents with three court eunuchs as the sole representatives of the populace.[22] Meanwhile, Liberius was pressured into communion with the opponents of Athanasius. In consequence some of the Roman clergy refused to recognise him, and disturbances broke out between supporters of the two popes—one in Rome and the other still in exile.

Maintaining public order in the Western imperial capital, still the largest city in the empire, was a sensitive issue, and the senator appointed to oversee its administration, the prefect of the city, kept the government regularly informed of the state of public opinion.[23] Riots in Rome were easily provoked and usually violent. For example, one broke out when a prefect requisitioned rather than bought scrap metal for work on public buildings. He had to flee the city while a mob tried to burn down his house. So when Constantius himself came to Rome in April 357, he was eager to find a solution to the division over the bishopric. An excuse for imperial clemency was provided by petitions from several leading Christian senators, said to have been egged on by their wives. Liberius was recalled from exile, but only after agreeing to share the episcopal office with Felix, an inherently unworkable compromise.

Soon after Liberius' return in August 357, Felix was expelled from the city by a mob shouting, 'One God, one Christ, one bishop!'[24] He attempted to reinstate himself the following year, when his supporters seized control of the basilica built by the late pope Julius, on the site of the present Church of Santa Maria in Trastevere, but the followers of Liberius stormed the church. Felix withdrew to an estate outside the city, still claiming to be the legitimate bishop, until his death in 365.

Liberius and Felix were not the only bishops in the city at this time. Virtually every break-away Christian community in the empire had followers in the huge imperial capital, and because these groups were not in communion with each other, they all needed the presence of bishops of their particular persuasion to carry out their baptisms, ordinations and consecrations. So, just as in the second and third centuries, several parallel clergies co-existed, refusing to recognise each other. We know most about the Donatists, the African rigorists who broke off communion with Pope Miltiades. Because of the large North African community in Rome, involved not least in grain and oil shipping, the Donatists had installed a bishop to serve the needs of their congregation in the city very soon after 313, and we have an unbroken list of names of his successors extending on into the 380s.[25] Novatianists, Melletians, Marcionites, Sabellians and others also maintained bishops and clergy of their own in Rome throughout the century.

None of this would have been possible if the state had been interested in imposing unity and in persecuting schismatic groups. However, the divisions were mainly products of disagreements over discipline, and until the early fifth century the imperial government ignored them if questions of belief were not involved. Indeed Constantine had guaranteed the Novatianists the right to own churches and cemeteries, and the state provided free transport for schismatic bishops attending councils as well as for orthodox ones.[26]

That Felix's followers occupied the Julian basilica in 358 was symbolic, as its founder, Pope Julius, had distinguished himself by his support for the Council of Nicaea and for Athanasius. This was a legacy Felix sought to claim, in contrast to Liberius, who had excommunicated Athanasius and accepted an Arian creed in order to secure his return to Rome the previous year. For some this was an inexcusable betrayal, and Liberius' reputation suffered in consequence, both in his own lifetime and after.

Traces of this decline can be found in the *Liber Pontificalis,* whose accounts of both Liberius and Felix II are in some respects misleading. Of Liberius it reports that he was exiled for three years for refusing to accept the doctrine of the Arians but subsequently agreed to be in communion with them, and that during his exile he was replaced by Felix, whom he himself consecrated. Then, on returning to Rome he remained outside the walls with the emperor's sister at her Basilica of St. Agnes, hoping, unsuccessfully, she would support him. Eventually, the emperor called a council of Arian bishops to order the pope's restoration and the expulsion of 'the catholic' Felix. Liberius' ensuing reinstatement is said to have led to 'a persecution which caused the deaths and martyrdom in church of priests and clerics'.[27]

In the *Liber Pontificalis,* this account of Liberius' pontificate is followed by a separate life of Felix, in which he is said to have called Constantius II a heretic, and as a result 'he was beheaded with many of the clerics and faithful in secret alongside the aqueduct of Trajan on 11 November'.[28] Four days later his body was recovered by Damasus (to whom we shall soon turn) and buried in the basilica Felix had founded on the Via Aurelia. It has long been recognised that this account actually repeats the equally unhistorical story of an earlier pope, Felix I (268–273), also said to have been martyred and to have built a basilica on the Via Aurelia.

What we have are confused memories of these mid-fourth-century events based on hostile propaganda put out by the rival parties of the time, which survived into the sixth century and became fixed in the authoritative record of early papal history. This was unfortunate for Liberius, at least posthumously. He may have been no hero, but he tried to make up for his lack of the martyr's spirit in the later part of his pontificate, supporting attempts in the East to restore Church unity on the basis of Nicene orthodoxy and ensuring there were no recriminations in Italy between those bishops who had accepted an Arian creed at the Council of Rimini in 359 and those who had resisted.

This revival of the pro-Nicene party was only possible because of a change of imperial regime. Constantius II died in 361, just on the eve of a civil war with his sole surviving relative, a younger cousin called Julian, who succeeded him unopposed. Although brought up a Christian, Julian had secretly converted to a philosophically inclined paganism in his youth and, once emperor, revealed his true religious persuasion. He removed all the legal privileges and responsibilities his predecessors had given to the bishops, and, since nothing suited his purposes better than having the Christians fighting among themselves, he recalled all those in exile. His reign came to an abrupt end in 363, when he was killed in a skirmish while invading the Persian empire, and after a brief interval a new imperial dynasty emerged. Its founder, Valentinian I (364–375), although a committed Christian, had no particular theological enthusiasms and was more interested in ensuring good order in the Western half of his empire, leaving the Eastern one to his brother Valens (364–378).

DAMASUS

The change in imperial priorities benefited the next pope, Damasus (366–384), one of the most significant holders of the office in its early centuries. He has not found many admirers: 'a man of much practical shrewdness and self-assertive energy . . . he quite as clearly lacked that greatness of spirit that shows so strikingly in his contemporaries, Athanasius, Basil, Gregory Nazianzen, and Ambrose. His acts, his letters, his metrical inscriptions all betray the same dry, cold temperament and are all singularly devoid of any spontaneous generosity of feeling, magnanimity of judgement or breadth of vision.'[29] There is a little too much blood on his hands and a lingering odour of scandal.

Born in Spain around 305, he had been one of Liberius' deacons, and exiled with him in 355, but changing his mind, he returned to Rome and accepted Felix as bishop. When Liberius was reinstated, he took no action against Damasus, and subsequently indicated a preference for him as his successor, perhaps to heal the rift between the two factions. But Damasus' shifting loyalties were resented by those who had never wavered in their support for Liberius. After the latter's death in September 366 a small group of clergy occupied the Julian basilica and elected Ursinus, another of the deacons, as bishop.[30] Almost simultaneously the majority of the clerical electors chose Damasus in the church in Lucinis (now San Lorenzo in Lucina), and a week later he was consecrated in the Lateran basilica—the earliest mention of it as a site of papal ceremonies.[31]

This may have been the first disputed papal election since 250, but it did not result in the same uneasy coexistence of rival claimants. Damasus' supporters—described in a hostile source as 'ruffians from the race track and gravediggers'—launched an assault on the Julian basilica, seizing control of it after three days of street fighting.[32] When the backers of Ursinus occupied the Liberian basilica, it too was stormed. In the aftermath of the fighting a neutral contemporary reported that the bodies of 137 men and women were found in the church.[33]

The controversial and violent nature of its start marked most of Damasus' pontificate. Ursinus and a group of eight priests who supported him were exiled to Gaul when renewed fighting broke out a year later.[34] They were never reconciled, and continued attempts were made to remove Damasus from office by other means. In 378 he was accused of sexual misconduct by two of his deacons, and in 380 he was charged with murder. In both cases he was cleared by synods of Italian bishops in Rome, who had to report their findings to the emperor.[35] While followers of Ursinus may have been behind these accusations, they were not Damasus' only enemies.

After his death a long petition was submitted to the emperors of the time by two priests belonging to the rigorist group founded earlier in the century by Bishop Lucifer of Cagliari. Amongst other things, they accused the former pope of forcibly breaking up one of their services and having one of their clergy so savagely beaten in the course of his arrest that he subsequently died from his injuries.[36]

Potentially more damaging were other criticisms. In a complaint to the emperor about his violent suppression of the supporters of Ursinus, he was also called 'a tickler of the ears of middle-aged women', implying that he had used his position and charm to ingratiate himself with some of the female members of his flock.[37] That personal enrichment was implied emerges from an imperial edict issued in July 370 and sent to Damasus himself, to be read out in all of the churches of Rome, forbidding all present and former members of the clergy from visiting the homes of widows and girl orphans and wards, and from receiving any gifts or legacies from them.[38] Any such property would be confiscated by the state. The law itself was much resented by both potential donors and recipients and was finally repealed in 455.[39]

Damasus was not the only subject of such gossip. Similar accusations were directed at Jerome, his advisor and secretary in his last years. It was Jerome who in a letter to Damasus in 376 had first contrasted the majesty of the bishop's office with the humble origins of its first holder: 'I am terrified by your eminence, yet your benevolence attracts me. From the priest I claim the preservation of the victim, from the shepherd the due protection of the sheep. Away with all trace of pride; let Roman majesty withdraw. It is to the successor of the fisherman that I address myself, to the disciple of the Cross.'[40] His depiction of the pope as successor to Peter the fisherman survived as a permanent feature of papal imagery.

Six years later Jerome became Damasus' secretary and was soon mired in controversy alongside him. In both their cases the rumours and innuendos reflected divisions in upper-class society in Rome. The families who made up the three orders of nobility of which the Roman Senate was composed were still by far the wealthiest and most socially prestigious in the empire. Most of them enjoyed incomes in a range of from one to four thousand pounds of gold a year, but there were a handful of the super-rich, such as the lady Melania, whose annual receipts around the year 400 totalled 120,000 pounds of gold.[41] Within this aristocracy, Christianity had gradually taken hold across the fourth century, and the majority of the senatorial families in Rome had converted by the early fifth century, becoming involved with the bishops, their policies, and their election.[42]

Even when senatorial families were divided in religious loyalties, the growth of conversion did not produce internal conflict, despite a comparable rise in imperial legislation outlawing pagan religious practices and closing temples. A brief 'pagan reaction' under the emperor Eugenius (392–394) was no more than a temporary repeal of these laws and a return to an earlier tolerance of religious diversity, as reflected in the senator Quintus Aurelius Symmachus' famous claim that 'There are many routes to so great a truth.'[43] Pope Damasus had opposed Symmachus' contention at the time it was made in 384, but his successor Siricius (384–399) and the Roman church do not seem to have suffered loss of wealth or privilege in Eugenius' short reign, not least because so many senators were by then Christians.

Where, on the other hand, a fault line can be more easily detected is within the Christian aristocracy itself over the rising appeal of the monastic movement. While large communities, inspired by the examples of outstanding ascetics and teachers such as Anthony and Pachomius, had developed in Egypt, Palestine and other Eastern provinces in the fourth century, in the West the new movement expressed itself primarily in aristocratic circles. It took the form of a life of renunciation of food and other bodily pleasures, and devotion to reading of Scripture, prayer and meditation in small closed groups, often established in noble households in town and country. Unlike the East, where rules for larger, more socially diverse communities were being written from the mid-fourth century on, the aristocratic house monasteries of the West lacked such a literature in Latin and depended much more on the personal instruction provided by popular spiritual guides and directors.[44]

One of the problems that resulted from the growing appeal of worldly renunciation and consecration to virginity was the impact on families that had prided themselves on their long histories and distinguished ancestries, real or imaginary. When heirs renounced marriage or committed themselves to chastity within it, aristocratic dynasties faced extinction and vast fortunes passing out of family control, all the more so when the monastic ideal promoted relinquishing of personal wealth. Thus, when Melania and her husband adopted a life of chastity following the deaths of their two children, they immediately began selling her family estates to fund works of charity.[45] Inevitably such situations were fraught with opportunities for conflict and for accusations against fashionable spiritual directors of self-interested manipulation of their vulnerable patrons. Jerome's rapid departure from Rome after the death of Damasus resulted from accusations of sexual impropriety between himself and his leading female disciple, a wealthy widow. An investigation ordered by Pope Siricius, who was less keen on such ascetic gurus, exonerated him, but Jerome and his aristocratic followers found the atmosphere in the city so hostile that they left to set up a community in Bethlehem.[46]

THE PETRINE THEME

Despite the various assaults on his character by his opponents, Damasus established the papacy on a stronger footing than ever before, both in the city of Rome and in the Church. He is remembered not least for a series of short poetic inscriptions he composed in honour of principal Roman martyrs and then had carved on large marble slabs.[47] Although most of these monuments have been damaged, and some entirely lost, the thirteen that survive more or less complete show how he used them to associate himself and his office with the increasingly popular cults of these martyrs.[48] Visitors to their tombs outside the city walls could not fail to notice these imposing tributes from the pope. Hitherto papal patronage had been confined to building one or two churches in each pontificate, and no pope had interfered with or patronised the constructions of his predecessors. But through his inscriptions Damasus made his presence felt in a wide range of catacomb shrines and basilicas that he himself had not built. This marks the start of a tradition of proclaiming papal links with particular buildings in Rome through monumental inscriptions, a practice much favoured by many of his successors up to the twentieth century.

The sharp decline of Arian influence in the West after the death of the emperor Constantius in 361 produced attempts to find a yardstick of theological orthodoxy against which new ideas could be measured, so as to prevent future conflicts. In 380 the Western and Eastern emperors agreed that this should be 'that religion which Peter the divine apostle gave to the Romans', which was defined as being that followed by Damasus of Rome and Patriarch Peter II of

Alexandria (373–380).[49] This imperial decree placed the same emphasis on apostolic tradition in the recognition of orthodoxy as had been demanded by late-second-century authors such as Irenaeus, but that tradition now focussed entirely upon Peter as its sole authoritative source for both East and West. What happened if the Petrine faith of Rome differed in any way from that of Alexandria was not here addressed, but this would become an important question in the fifth century. More immediately, another controversy was looming.

The replacement of the emperor Valens (364–378), who had shared the theological views of Constantius II, by a general called Theodosius (379–395), whose family came from Spain, marked the final defeat of Arianism in the Eastern half of the empire. This was ratified at a council held in Constantinople in 381. While this outcome was warmly welcomed by Damasus, who had sent representatives to the council, he strongly opposed another conciliar decision—'the bishop of Constantinople shall have pre-eminence in honour after the bishop of Rome, because Constantinople is the New Rome'—since it gave Constantinople precedence over the other Eastern metropolitan sees.[50]

While Rome's own position as sole apostolic patriarchate in the Western empire was unchallenged, it was the defiance of tradition represented by the ranking of a see that had only come into existence in 330 over the Petrine sees of the East—Antioch, of which Peter was held to be first bishop, and Alexandria, long regarded as being founded by his disciple Mark—that led Damasus to refuse to accept the decrees of this council. This was the start of a protracted resistance by Rome to what it saw as the pretensions of Constantinople.[51]

In the West the most influential ecclesiastic figure in the late fourth century was Ambrose, bishop of Milan (374–397), especially after the Western imperial court established itself in his city in 388. His physical proximity to the court enabled him to stage dramatic confrontations with the emperors when he felt their decisions were morally wrong. He was also able to put in a good word for Damasus as successive accusations reached Milan, but he himself ignored the pope's patriarchal authority.[52]

The popes of the period never left Rome and so could not make a personal impact on the secular rulers. However, the prestige of their city and of the Petrine foundation of its church gave them a unique authority. In 378 the emperor Gratian (367–383) accepted Damasus' proposal that the pope and his successors should hear judicial appeals from all churches in the Western half of the empire. This gave the pope and his advisors an equivalent role in ecclesiastical cases to that of the emperor and his consistory as the final court of appeal in all civil matters, thereby producing the kind of logical administrative structure that satisfied the Roman legal mind. What the emperor was not prepared to accept was the further suggestion that bishops of Rome by virtue of their new status as judges of appeal in ecclesiastical matters should not be answerable in court themselves for civil offences.[53] As we shall see, this question of the superiority of the papacy to all other jurisdictions would rumble on for several centuries.

PETER HIMSELF

(384–496)

GOVERNMENT OF THE CHURCH

In 416 Pope Innocent I (401–417) declared, 'in all of Italy, Gaul, Spain, Africa, Sicily and the isles that lie between them no churches have been established other than by those ordained bishop by the Venerable Apostle Peter or his successors.'[1] This was given contemporary significance when Celestine I appointed the Roman deacon Palladius as the first bishop of a Christian community in Ireland in 431. Although historically inaccurate, this claim also allowed Innocent's successor, Zosimus (417–418), to promote the myth that the Roman provinces of Gaul had been evangelised by a disciple of Peter called Trophimus, the first bishop of Arles.[2]

Zosimus' argument justified giving the bishops of Arles the new status of papal vicar (a title borrowed from the imperial administration), with authority, as the pope's deputy in the Gallic provinces, over all other metropolitans in Gaul. Unsurprisingly, the other metropolitan sees, such as Lyon and Vienne, which possessed some of the longest-established Christian communities in the West, were resentful.

Damasus had already created a similar papal vicariate in the eastern Balkans for the bishops of Thessalonica because of the transfer of the provinces of this region in 379 from the control of the Western emperor to that of his Eastern colleague. The bishoprics concerned had been under Rome's metropolitan authority, so the transfer separated their political and ecclesiastical loyalties, and the new papal vicariate was a response. Thessalonica was by far the most important city with the longest-established church in the eastern Balkans and northern Greece, so Damasus' move created no rivalries. In the case of Gaul, however, it looks as if Zosimus may have been forging a new organisational structure, mirroring that of the imperial administration, in which there were to be separate vicars for the Gallic, Spanish and African provinces. If so, the brevity of his pontificate and the degree of opposition prevented its development.

While Zosimus' attempt to elevate the status of Arles highlights the novelty of several of the claims made by the see of Rome from the late fourth century onwards, the purpose behind them was always the maintenance of tradition. As we have seen, in 378 the state had recognised the Petrine traditions of Rome and Alexandria as the touchstone of orthodoxy. The divisions within individual churches, not least in Rome itself, and in the Church as a whole across the half century that had been dominated by the Arian controversy made the definition and preservation of that unifying tradition of ever greater importance. What seemed to be the final victory over Arianism in 381 was accompanied by a determination that such division should never happen again.

So it is no surprise that the judgements and commands issued by the bishops of Rome became more authoritarian and less consensual in tone at this time and that they were largely accepted by their recipients. Much earlier correspondence between bishops, including those of Rome, had contained little more than exchanges of views amongst equals, but in the late fourth century a new type of papal letter appears, later called a 'decretal', defined as 'a letter containing a papal ruling', dealing with matters of Church discipline and sent in reply to an appeal for guidance.[3] Because these rulings were accepted as authoritative, such letters were copied and circulated, and they also began to be collected and quoted. As a result, within little more than a few decades, decretals were recognised, at least in the West, as a second source of canon or Church law, alongside the decisions taken by bishops meeting in councils.[4]

The change in tone can be seen by comparing a letter of the last years of Damasus to a synod of bishops in Gaul—who asked him for advice on nearly twenty topics, ranging from baptism to the prohibition on uncles marrying nieces—with one from the next pontificate. Damasus' reply presents the answers coming not from himself but from a Roman synod, and the reasons for several of its rulings are carefully explained.[5] This letter contrasts with one sent by Pope Siricius (384–399) early in 385 in response to some questions from Bishop Himerius of Tarragona in Spain. These queries were also formally presented to a Roman synod, but several of Siricius' rulings were far more peremptory in tone than those of Damasus, and the authority he claimed was his own, as heir to St. Peter. The recipient was also instructed to circulate the pope's reply to all of the other Spanish bishops.[6]

Orthodoxy was the ancient Petrine tradition, and what threatened it was novelty. New ideas and practices were essentially wrong by virtue of their very newness, however trivial they might seem. Thus when in 447 Pope Leo I the Great (440–461) discovered that bishops in Sicily were celebrating more baptisms in Epiphany than in Easter Week, he told them he was 'amazed that you or your predecessors could have introduced such an unreasonable innovation', adding, 'You could not have fallen into this error at all . . . if the See of the blessed Apostle Peter, which is the mother of your priestly dignity, were also your teacher in ecclesiastical procedure.'[7] But he also explained in detail why choosing the correct season for baptising was theologically significant.

This fear of the harm that could be inflicted by novelty made the holding of councils particularly sensitive. If left to themselves, groups of bishops, however large and distinguished, could endorse ideas and practices differing from those of Rome, thus threatening division within the Church. It became the fixed view of the popes from at least the time of Celestine (422–432) that councils should only confirm prior papal decisions. As Leo the Great wrote, 'For even amongst the most blessed Apostles, alike in honour, there was a certain distinction in power. Although they were all equal in being chosen, one was allowed to stand out above the others. From this arrangement there arose, also, distinctions among the bishops,' with superior authority being exercised by metropolitans and vicars, 'and through them the care of the universal church was to converge in the one see of Peter, and nothing was ever to be at odds with his leadership.'[8] This view gained little support in the East, where the lack of a single dominant metropolitanate meant that councils remained the most important source of authority, or in Africa with a strong tradition of conciliar decision making.

As the guardian of the Petrine tradition, Rome saw itself as the sole source of authoritative rulings. While there was scope in disciplinary matters for cases to be heard by the other non-apostolic metropolitans in the West, when it came to central issues of belief and practice, uncertainties could only properly be resolved in Rome, and any decisions by provincial bishops or synods should be submitted for confirmation or correction, to avoid the danger of novelty. If in principle minor matters could be determined locally, only Rome could decide what was indeed minor, and so it was wiser to consult the pope first rather than suffer the indignity of a rebuke later. Thus, Pope Siricius congratulated Himerius of Tarragona for sending his enquiries 'to the Roman church as if to the head of your body'.[9]

The precise nature of the apostolic tradition was not easily described, in that Peter had not left a body of texts or even oral instructions to guide his successors. In this sense he was more useful than Paul, fourteen of whose letters were now part of the canon of the New Testament, as defined by Innocent I in 405.[10] What was written could be debated. Peter on the other hand gave direction via his successors in the office he was held to have founded. So it is unsurprising that in the later fourth century Paul features less and less in the papal correspondence, and from the early fifth century the Prince of the Apostles clearly dominates papal ideology.[11]

As Christian theology and worship changed under new influences, the Petrine tradition needed more than a set of rules from the past. There had to be a way in which popes could make authoritative rulings on new features of Christian life, such as monasticism, that had come into existence since the apostolic age. If Peter was to be the arbiter of correct belief and practice, he had to speak to a changing world. This he could do through his successors.

While the Petrine foundation of the see had sufficed in the third and earlier fourth century as a basis for papal authority, it increasingly became the Apostle himself as a living presence in the Roman church who was presented as the direct source of rulings made by his episcopal heirs. Damasus said Peter was ever-present, showing his successors the way, and Boniface I (418–422) claimed that papal actions were in reality those of the Apostle. He also first used the image of the Apostle as the gate keeper of Heaven, controlling admission to it, as a threat to those who disregarded the orders of the Roman bishops. Leo I developed the association between the pope and St. Peter to its fullest extent in a series of sermons and letters in which he presented himself as not just Peter's successor but as, in a legal sense, Peter himself, and thus the direct inheritor of the powers that Christ had given to the first Apostle. Although such an argument may now seem far-fetched, it was firmly grounded in Roman legal thinking on the rights and duties of heirs.[12]

In some cases Rome's demand for obedience was challenged, particularly by the long-established African churches, with their annual synods that often ignored papal decisions. However, there were occasions when the Africans needed the authority of the papacy to promote a cause that mattered to them. The best-known case is that of Pelagius. Born in Britain, he was a fashionable monastic teacher in Rome for many years, patronised by members of the aristocracy, until forced to leave the city following its sack by the Goths in 410.[13] When he took refuge in Africa, Augustine, bishop of Hippo, with whom he had previously clashed over predestination and grace, persuaded the other African bishops to investigate the orthodoxy of his teaching. When condemned by a synod at Carthage, Pelagius moved on to Palestine, but Augustine and his allies were determined to achieve a universal condemnation of his ideas, and so a papal ruling was sought.

Although it was doubtless gratifying to have the Africans appealing to Rome for once, it was harder to accommodate them than might have been expected. Innocent I issued a partial condemnation of Pelagius just before his death in 417, which his successor Zosimus effectively reversed. The reason for their hesitancy was the influential support that Pelagius had enjoyed in Rome for many years and his continued aristocratic backing. Faced with papal reluctance to antagonise members of the leading senatorial families, Augustine, who had once been a professor in Milan, then the imperial capital, used his personal contacts in the government.[14] He played on imperial sensitivity to political disturbances in Rome following a riot in the city in 418 that was conveniently blamed on the supporters of Pelagius. The emperor immediately banished them, and Zosimus had to follow suit with a papal denunciation, which soon led to the general condemnation of Pelagius, his teachings and his followers in both East and West.[15]

Relations between papacy, government and local churches were complex, and the various parties could try and manipulate them to their own advantage. However, in the longer term what Rome had to offer through its system of appeals and through its role as the benchmark for apostolic doctrine and practice became increasingly attractive to individual bishops and regional churches throughout the West. Bishops threatened with deposition in local conflicts could appeal to an independent higher court, and synods uneasy at making rules that might conflict with orthodoxy could secure prior confirmation for their decisions.

In Rome itself, the bishops remained sensitive to aristocratic opinion. The greater senatorial families in the early fifth century were still wealthier and more influential than the popes, although this was about to change. The Gothic sack of 410 led to the dispersal of the aristocracy and marked the beginning of its economic decline. As an institution that continued to attract donations and bequests, the Roman church was not threatened by extinction through lack of heirs, as happened to many noble families, and it could better preserve its resources in even the most difficult times. Shared beliefs helped, as the Goths, Christians since the late fourth century, refrained from looting churches during the sack of Rome in 410, one of the event's few positive features that could later be praised by Christian apologists such as Augustine and the Spanish priest Orosius.

By this time the senatorial aristocracy was mostly Christian, but the bishops and clergy were not yet drawn from the upper classes. Only in the late fifth century was the first pope of aristocratic birth, Felix III (483–492), appointed, but the political influence of the bishops was something on which the senators came increasingly to rely. So, when in 416 the Senate wanted the emperor to help with the restoration of the city, still recovering from the Gothic sack, it asked Pope Innocent I to be one of its envoys to the imperial court.

By the middle of the fifth century the ability of the Western emperors to defend their empire was seriously in doubt. Britain had been left to fend for itself in 410, much of Spain and parts of northern and eastern Gaul were abandoned from the mid-420s and the African provinces were ceded to the Vandal kingdom in 442. Only northeastern Spain, southern Gaul and Italy were directly ruled from Ravenna, the Western imperial capital since 402. Even this reduced empire was threatened by the Huns, who had dominated the lands north of the Danube for half a century. In 452 Attila invaded Italy, and the emperor Valentinian III (425–455) could offer no resistance. Instead, a delegation of two senators and Pope Leo I met the Hun king in northern Italy and, mightily assisted by the outbreak of an epidemic in the Hun ranks, persuaded him to withdraw. Through involvement in such events the papacy acquired a prestige that enabled it to play an important role in secular affairs, especially on behalf of its city, a prominence enhanced by the rapid decline in imperial power in the West after 455.

ROME, ALEXANDRIA AND CONSTANTINOPLE

Where Rome could not carry the day was in relations with the churches in the East, especially those that saw themselves as her equal. As we have seen, friction had resulted when in 381 the Council of Constantinople awarded the see of Constantinople, only fifty years old, precedence over all the other patriarchal sees of the East. Pope Damasus had refused to accept this decision, because it violated tradition and implicitly undermined the argument that a see's authority came from its apostolic foundation. For the majority of the Eastern bishops who had voted for this decree, it was valid because it had been passed by an ecumenical council, one that represented all the Christian churches.

At the time the ambition of Constantinople had only strengthened the ties between the two Petrine sees of Rome and Alexandria. However, within a few decades this long-standing alliance was sabotaged by attempts of the bishops of Alexandria to undermine their Eastern rivals. The first of these followed the appointment of the great preacher John Chrysostom (the Golden-Mouthed) to the bishopric of Constantinople in 398. He had been trained in Antioch, whose traditions of theology and biblical interpretation differed from those of Alexandria, whose bishop, Theophilus (385–412), became doubly determined to get rid of him.

A fiery orator and a stern moralist, John did not hesitate to criticise members of the imperial family publicly from his pulpit. So, he could look for no support from that quarter when in 403 Theophilus manipulated a council packed with Egyptian bishops into declaring him deposed, on the grounds that he had given support to some fugitive monks from Egypt, known as the Four Tall Brothers, and thus, as Theophilus argued, broken the decree of the Council of Nicaea forbidding interference in the affairs of another patriarchate.[16] This was a shrewd charge, since Rome regarded the acts of Nicaea as inviolable because they had received papal confirmation.

Despite John's popular backing in Constantinople, the Eastern emperor Arcadius endorsed the council by exiling him to Armenia in 404 and persecuting his leading supporters. Some of these fled to Rome with an appeal from John to Innocent I. The pope was already uneasy about Theophilus' account of events and, learning that John had not been present when condemned by the council, tried to have him reinstated by getting the Western emperor Honorius to persuade his brother Arcadius to agree to a papal plan for a new council of bishops from East and West at Thessalonica. At the same time a synod of Italian bishops in Rome excommunicated Theophilus and his allies. In practice neither the Western emperor nor the pope could force the increasingly hostile Eastern court to reopen the case, as political relations were already tense for other reasons. Indeed their intervention led to John being sent to a harsher place of exile. His death on the way there in 407 ended the matter, leaving links between the churches of Rome and Alexandria suspended until the death of Theophilus in 412.

Relations improved in the time of Theophilus' nephew and successor, Cyril (412–444), who was keen to revive the historic alliance. He got Roman support in 430 to block creation of a new patriarchal province for the see of Jerusalem by using the good offices of the Roman deacon Leo, a leading advisor of both Celestine I and Sixtus III, who would soon become pope himself. Also with Leo's help Cyril began seeking Roman backing to condemn the theological views of a new bishop of Constantinople, Nestorius (429–431).

Unlike John Chrysostom, whose own orthodoxy had been unimpeachable, Nestorius had developed increasingly controversial interpretations of the views of the Antioch theological school, of which he had also been a product, on the relationship between the divine and human natures in Christ. He began to stress the separation of the two, not least denying to the Virgin Mary her popular title of *Theotokos* or God-bearer. This term was particularly popular in Egypt, and central to the theological tradition of the Alexandrian school, which favoured the contrary emphasis on the unity of the two natures. Strict separation of the two natures meant that the Virgin could only be the mother of the human Jesus and minimised or removed the implication that she was the Mother of God.

Cyril, who was not only the most outstanding theologian produced by the Egyptian church but also its ablest ecclesiastical politician, soon raised doubts in Rome about Nestorius' orthodoxy. He persuaded Pope Celestine I (422–432), who was briefed by Leo, that Nestorius was implicitly denying Christ's full divinity, thereby playing on Rome's long-held worry that Greek theology always tended in that direction. More astute than Theophilus, Cyril thus secured prior papal backing for a council held at Ephesus in 431 which investigated Nestorius' beliefs and deposed him from his see. He was exiled to the oasis of Kharga in Egypt until his death in 451, but his teaching was subsequently accepted by the Mesopotamian or Assyrian church that later extended its missionary activity to Central Asia and China and survives to the present.[17]

Not everything went Cyril's way in the aftermath of the Council of Ephesus. He had pushed through his agenda before either the delegates from Rome or the patriarch of Antioch arrived, and the latter objected strongly to some of the theology used by Cyril in the condemnation of Nestorius, particularly in a text called *The Twelve*

Anathemas. A formal rift between Antioch and Alexandria ensued which lasted until 433, when a formula of reconciliation was agreed, which involved a modification of some of Cyril's pronouncements on the relationship between the human and divine natures of Christ. This was greeted warmly by Pope Sixtus III (432–440) but was seen as an unacceptable defeat by some of Cyril's supporters, committed to a pure Monophysite or single-nature doctrine. So the stage was set for a new and much greater conflict than that over Nestorius.

Cyril was succeeded by Dioscorus (444–451), an uncompromising partisan of single-nature theology. At the same time this doctrine began being promoted in Constantinople by Eutyches, a fashionable monastic teacher who enjoyed the backing of Chrysaphius, the chief eunuch of the imperial court and principal advisor to the emperor Theodosius II (408–450). So flagrant did Eutyches' promotion of an extreme version of Cyril's teaching become that in 448 the patriarch of Constantinople, Flavian, had to take action against him. Eutyches wrote to Pope Leo claiming that he was being persecuted by neo-Nestorians, but although he received a guarded if approving reply, the papal attitude toward him changed completely when a full account of what was happening arrived from Flavian. Treating this in the Roman way as an appeal for papal, and thus Petrine, confirmation of true doctrine and denunciation of theological novelty, Leo wrote his most famous letter, known as his *Tomus,* or *Tome,* which contained his authoritative ruling on the dispute.

In the meantime Flavian found himself in a weak position. He faced an Eastern council to which Eutyches had appealed, which would be packed with Egyptian bishops, and again like John Chrysostom before him, he lacked imperial support, thanks to the influence of Chrysaphius. It was to this council that Leo despatched delegates bearing his *Tome,* which he regarded as fully self-sufficient.

At the Second Council of Ephesus in 449, dominated by Dioscorus, Flavian was outmanoeuvred, outvoted and deposed. He was immediately exiled by the emperor and died within a year. The bishops refused to allow Leo's *Tome* to be read out, and instead the views of Eutyches on the unity of the two natures in Christ were fully endorsed. In the intimidating atmosphere of the council, the papal representatives narrowly escaped being lynched when they spoke up in support of Flavian. Receiving their report, Leo denounced the council as a *latrocinium* or robbery, and II Ephesus has ever since been known as the 'robber council'. Leo broke off communion with Dioscorus of Alexandria and the newly appointed patriarch of Constantinople, which meant not including their names in prayers on major festivals, but he had no hope of reversing the decisions of the council while they enjoyed the backing of the Eastern court.

After the death of the emperor Theodosius II in 450, however, his sister Pulcheria, already a correspondent of the pope, married a general called Marcian, who became the new emperor, while the unpopular Chrysaphius was executed. One further consequence was that the new rulers refused to continue the annual tribute payments to the Huns instituted by Chrysaphius, leading to their invasion of Italy in 452, and Pope Leo's meeting with Attila. But long before that the pope was taking advantage of the regime change in the East to urge the emperors to order a new council, to reverse the decisions made at II Ephesus. The result was the Council of Chalcedon of 451. There the doctrines of Eutyches were condemned, and Dioscorus of Alexandria, who had refused to attend the council, was deposed and exiled, though it took imperial troops to remove him from his city.

Leo had sent another copy of his *Tome* to Chalcedon, again expecting that it would be confirmed by the bishops without discussion. This time it was read out, but only after the issues had been debated and the main decisions of the council taken. While it was publicly acclaimed by the bishops as the words of Peter, this was because they had satisfied themselves that its doctrine was in accord with what they had already agreed to be correct. Two different concepts of authority met, although without conflict on this occasion, because they were in agreement on the outcome, though not the way to it. For Leo it was for him and him alone as Peter's heir to confirm the decisions made by a council or even to tell it what conclusions to reach. For the bishops at Chalcedon, the fact that they had been called together by the emperors of both East and West, with all of the patriarchal sees represented, meant this was a truly ecumenical council, the only kind that could make authoritative decisions. If these different views did not clash in the council, they had many centuries of so doing ahead of them.

In one area Chalcedon did generate friction with Rome. Its twenty-eighth decree reinforced the one issued in 381, giving Constantinople precedence over other patriarchal sees in the East and ranking it second only to Rome: giving 'equal privileges to the most holy throne of New Rome, justly judging that the city which is honoured with the Sovereignty and the Senate, and enjoys equal privileges with the old imperial Rome, should in ecclesiastical matters also be magnified as she is, and rank next after her'.[18] Leo was furious, not least with his own delegates for failing to prevent this decree being adopted. Rome's own standing was not threatened by the elevation of Constantinople, but the decision endorsed novelty, with the newly created see being placed ahead of its more ancient counterparts, and also implicitly undermined the supremacy of the Petrine traditions of Rome and Alexandria.

Leo himself was a stickler for the preservation of properly constituted hierarchical order. In 448 in one of the more irate of his letters he rebuked a bishop of Benevento in southern Italy for 'the hasty and ill-considered' promoting of one of his more recently ordained priests over the heads of longer-established members of his clergy. The pope was if anything more annoyed with two of the passed-over priests for meekly agreeing to this and questioned if they should be allowed to keep their office if they felt so unworthy of it. Eventually, as 'an act of mercy', he decreed that the young priest should be demoted to the appropriate level and that the two who had offended by their meekness should be forced to remain perpetually subordinate to him.[19] Such a pope could never agree to Constantinople usurping the precedence of Antioch and Alexandria nor tolerate their acquiescing in it.

In practice, though, there was little Leo could do about it. Alexandria was wracked by disturbances following the exile of Dioscorus, and his successor Proterius only remained there thanks to the protection of imperial troops. He was lynched soon after the news of the emperor Marcian's death reached the city in 457, and an irreconcilable rift throughout the Eastern provinces opened between those who supported the decisions of Chalcedon and those who saw that council as a heretical betrayal of the true doctrine of the unity, or technically the hypostatic union, of Christ's natures. The latter are normally referred to by historians as Monophysites, but the term was not used at the time, and it could imply greater unity amongst the opponents of Chalcedonian theology than was the case. Out of convenience alone, it will continue to be used here.

For Marcian and Pulcheria and their successors in the East, the elevation of the status of Constantinople was a good thing, and an appropriate compliment to their imperial capital. Neither they nor the successive patriarchs of the city could sympathise with the Roman view or show much interest in accommodating it. The popes for their part were unwilling to compromise. Simplicius (468–483) rebuffed an attempt by patriarch Acacius of Constantinople to persuade him to accept the offensive twenty-eighth decree of Chalcedon, which Leo had rejected. So, the issue rumbled on for decades, only to be made worse later in the fifth century when Constantinople began calling itself 'the ecumenical patriarchate'.

The Papacy and
the End of the Empire in the West

In Leo's last years the Western Roman empire entered a final stage of disintegration, ushered in by the ending of the Theodosian dynasty with the murder of Valentinian III in 455. For the next twenty years power passed through the hands of a succession of military dictators and short-lived emperors, several of whom were not recognised by their counterparts in Constantinople. Rome was sacked in 455 by the Vandals and was the setting for the violent final stages of a civil war between an emperor and a general in 472. Direct imperial rule over any of the Western provinces other than Italy ended in the 470s, and the last de facto emperor of the West was deposed by another general in 476.

In such circumstances the close partnership ceased between the Roman church and imperial government that had been so important in the development and enforcing of papal authority since the end of the Arian controversy. As we have seen, the Western Theodosian emperors came to Rome to be buried, and they backed all papal initiatives relating to the Eastern churches. The emperors in Constantinople could never be as close geographically or in other ways, and their support was given to the patriarchs of their capital. Their main ecclesiastical concern lay in resolving the division over Monophysite theology, which produced a rival church organisation in Syria and Egypt. While the popes in Rome remained loyal political subjects of the empire for another three hundred years, from 476 they had to be increasingly self-reliant and would never be the docile court chaplains that their counterparts in the New Rome often became.

All these problems made themselves felt under Leo's immediate successors. The Suevic general Ricimer, who dominated Italy from 457 until 472, was an Arian like most of his soldiers. They came from various ethnic groups such as the Goths, Rugians, Sueves and others that had formed in the Balkans out of a mix of immigrants from north of the Danube and elements of the indigenous population at a time when Arianism was the dominant form of Christianity in the empire, and they had retained this faith even after it lost its hold more generally. Back in the 370s Bishop Ambrose of Milan had resisted attempts by the court to make him give up churches for use by the emperor's Arian troops. Nearly a century later Pope Hilary (461–468) was unable to prevent a church in Rome—later known as Santa Agata dei Goti, Saint Agatha of the Goths—being built for Ricimer's men. The next pope, Simplicius (468–483), was faced with an emperor, Anthemius (467–472), imposed from the East, who was suspected of being a pagan, and who perhaps in consequence wanted toleration for all heretical forms of Christianity. Before this could be achieved he was overthrown.

Under Simplicius the Western empire came to an end, even if in theory the emperor in Constantinople claimed authority over all the former imperial territories in the West. In practice these were now ruled by a variety of 'barbarian' kings, who had imposed themselves and their followers as military elites on the former provinces of the empire. In Italy power was taken in 476 in a coup by a general called Odoacer, but rather than setting up another puppet emperor, he recognised the formal authority of the Eastern emperor, Zeno

(474–491), and ruled the peninsula as king in his own right, appointing Roman senators to the administrative offices in Rome and in Ravenna. Through one of these, the praetorian prefect Decius Maximus Basilius, Odoacer played a direct role in securing the election of the aristocratic Pope Felix III in 483.[20]

THE ACACIAN SCHISM: ROME VERSUS CONSTANTINOPLE

Both Hilary and Simplicius had been more involved in relations with Western churches than with the East, not least in reviving the role of the bishop of Arles as papal vicar in Gaul, and then giving similar status to the bishop of Seville for the Spanish provinces. However, events were taking place in the East that led to a formal breach between the churches of Rome and Constantinople. In 475 the emperor Zeno was forced to flee Constantinople in a coup that replaced him with his brother-in-law Basiliscus. The new emperor was, however, a committed Monophysite and began working to undermine the Council of Chalcedon and secure the condemnation of its canons and the *Tome* of Pope Leo. Basiliscus' regime was quickly toppled, not least thanks to the popular resistance egged on by pro-Chalcedonian holy men such as Daniel the Stylite, who spent thirty-three years living on top of a pillar. However, for a troubled Zeno, now restored to power, this episode made it imperative that some way be found to reconcile the Monophysites, for whom the Council of Chalcedon was a symbol of all that had gone wrong in the Church.

The emperor worked with patriarch Acacius of Constantinople (472–489) to produce a formula for compromise, which he published in 482 in a document called the *Henotikon* or Edict of Reunion.[21] In it he accepted the authority of both the First Council of Ephesus, which had condemned Nestorius, and Cyril's *Twelve Anathemas*, which had later been withdrawn. Zeno gave no such status to the decrees of Chalcedon and even implied that they might contain errors. He also failed to confirm the Chalcedonian definition of faith and made no mention of Leo's *Tome*, making it impossible for Rome to even contemplate accepting the *Henotikon*. The document did not prove all that popular with the more extreme Mono-physites either, who would settle for nothing less than a complete re-versal of Chalcedon.

In the same year there was also an opportunity to heal a rift in the church of Alexandria. Here a succession of Monophysite patriarchs had been elected by the majority of the clergy, only to be exiled by the government, which tried instead to maintain a line of pro-Chalcedonian patriarchs. In 475 the regime of Basiliscus had restored the exiled Monophysite Timothy II (the Cat) as undisputed patriarch, but the Church split again following his death in 477, when his sup-porters elected Peter III Mongus (the Hoarse) and the Chalcedonian party chose the monk Timothy (called Wobbly-Hat, because of his frequent changes of theological allegiance). To make things worse, Pope Simplicius recognised a third claimant who soon fled to Rome. However, the death of Wobbly-Hat in 482 enabled Zeno and Acacius to recognise Peter Mongus (died 490) as a further step towards win-ning over the Monophysites.[22]

News of both the *Henotikon* and the recognition of Mongus by the emperor reached Rome just after the accession of Felix III in 483. He was the first pope to send legates to inform the emperor of his election, a practice that became standard until the eighth cen-tury, and so they were present in Constantinople when the name of Peter Mongus had been 'added to the diptychs', which is to say for-mally placed on a list of living and dead bishops recognised as or-thodox and who would thereafter be commemorated in the solemn liturgical celebrations of the church. Because the papal envoys did not object to a known Monophysite being thus legitimised, the pope put them on trial by a synod of bishops on their return to Rome, accusing them of taking bribes. He also refused to accept the *Henotikon* and excommunicated Patriarch Acacius, who re-sponded by striking Felix's name from the diptychs in Constantino-ple, thus initiating a schism between the two churches that would last until 519.

Such a breach in the unity of the Church as a whole was regarded as a scandal. In the political circumstances of the time the secular rulers in Italy and the empire had no particular interest in brokering a compromise, but there was pressure on the bishops to try. Constantinople made the first move, immediately after Acacius' death in 489, but Felix insisted that the names of both Acacius and Mongus had to be removed from the diptychs in the imperial capital. The new patriarch Euphemius (490–496) was a staunch supporter of Chalcedon but was unwilling to dishonour his popular predecessor, fearing such a posthumous condemnation would spark a riot. Another attempted reconciliation followed the death of Zeno, whose widow had then determined the succession by marrying a sixty-year-old financial administrator, Anastasius I (491–518), a professed Monophysite. But once again Felix III would not compromise on his demand for the removal of the offending names from the diptychs.

The election of a new pope, Gelasius I (492–496), who was of North African origin, made no difference, as he had been Felix III's archdeacon and chief advisor in his dealings with the East. Like his predecessor he rejected all overtures from Constantinople that meant compromising Rome's demand, even though there was clearly a growing unease amongst the Italian bishops over the continuance of the schism. In 495 Gelasius was persuaded by a synod to lift the excommunication on the surviving papal legate who had failed to protest at the inclusion of Mongus' name in the diptychs in 482. This was also the first occasion on which a pope was called the 'Vicar of Christ', which came in the formal acclamations at the end of the synod, a practice borrowed from the Senate, in which the assembled bishops shouted out praises of their president in unison, with the precise number of repetitions being recorded: 'Life to Gelasius (15 times), Lord Peter, you serve him (12 times), Vicar of Christ we see you (11 times), Apostle Peter we see you (6 times), Of whom the seat and also the years (37 times).'[23]

The new pope took office at a particularly difficult time, when the Gothic general Theoderic was trying to wrest control of Italy away from Odoacer and had him under siege in Ravenna. Gelasius used his own resources and food brought in from the papal estates in Italy to stave off famine in Rome, before being able to call on the now victorious Theoderic for help in 493. Although the Gothic leader had entered Italy as the result of an agreement with the former emperor

Zeno, he had no such ties to Anastasius I, and established a kingdom in Italy in his own name after murdering Odoacer. So he ignored the attempts of members of the Senate, urged on by the emperor, to persuade him to get the pope to compromise over the Acacian schism. Under Gothic rule an ecclesiastical reconciliation between Rome and Constantinople was not a priority.

Despite the brevity of his pontificate, Gelasius is amongst the most notable popes, being one of just a handful to have produced major writings, a distinction that in the first millennium he shares only with Leo the Great and Gregory the Great. The *Liber Pontificalis,* compiled about forty years later, records that he was the author of a work in five books on the doctrines of Nestorius and Eutyches, 'which are kept safe today in the archive of the church library'.[24] He also produced a treatise in two parts on Arianism and wrote hymns and liturgical prayers and prefaces. The reference to the latter led to a Mass book for the whole liturgical year put together in Rome in the mid-seventh century being wrongly identified as his work and called the 'Gelasian Sacramentary'.[25]

Unfortunately, none of Gelasius' larger-scale writings have survived. What remain are a few letters, including some short treatises that may have been briefing documents prepared for Felix III. As well as two relating to the Monophysite dispute and the Acacian schism, there is one concerned with Pelagianism, which had recently revived in Dalmatia, on the Adriatic coast of the Balkans.[26] Of special note among his letters is one he sent in 494 to the emperor Anastasius I, in which he enunciated what has come to be called the doctrine of the two swords, on the relationship between secular and ecclesiastical authority. The key idea is summed up in a single beautifully crafted sentence: 'There are two forces, august emperor, by which this world is principally governed: the sacred authority of priests and the royal power, of which the heavier is the weight of that of the bishops, as they also have to return an account to the divine enquiry for the kings of men themselves.'[27]

While this expresses a radical new view of the greater responsibilities and therefore the superior authority of the ecclesiastical over the secular ruler, it is less a manifesto for a new ordering of church-state

·relations than is sometimes claimed. It takes up a very small part of a long letter and was one of many arguments the pope was deploying to try to persuade the emperor to follow Rome's line on the Monophysite controversy. It was certainly not intended as an abstract statement of political principle. However, because this was one of forty-three letters of Gelasius to be copied into some of the earliest collections of papal decretals, it survived and was then read by reformers in both the ninth and eleventh centuries who were trying to regain for the papacy an authority they believed it had once enjoyed.[28] They frequently quoted this and other passages from early papal correspondence in support of their arguments, as we shall see in later chapters.

Gelasius' doctrine would exercise far greater influence in later times than in his own. Then, the emperor Anastasius was unmoved by this or other arguments in the letter. He showed what weight he gave to episcopal superiority when in 496 he deposed Euphemius of Constantinople on a trumped-up political charge, so he could appoint a patriarch more sympathetic to the Monophysites. Pope Gelasius was beyond the emperor's reach, but his successors were not always so fortunate, as the events of the sixth century would show.

chapter 5

THE TWO SWORDS

(496–561)

THE LAURENTIAN SCHISM

The new century opened with the longest and most bitterly contested papal election of the first millennium. Known as the Laurentian Schism, it had a part to play in the wider Acacian Schism that had divided Rome and Constantinople since 484, and re-opened questions of whether a pope could be a heretic and who could sit in judgement on him.

Gelasius I was succeeded in November 496 by Anastasius II, who sent envoys to Constantinople to announce his election and seek an end to the division between the churches. However, the pope's apparent willingness to compromise reignited the debate in Rome over the rift with Constantinople, by now the longest breach between patriarchal sees. A rigorist party in the Roman church, faithful to the memory of Felix III and Gelasius I, broke off communion with Anastasius, even before he agreed to any compromise. The rigorist view was reflected in the *Liber Pontificalis,* compiled about thirty-five years later, which claims that Anastasius fell into heresy and that his early death in November 498 was the result of being 'struck down by God's will'.[1] This account led Dante to place Anastasius in Hell.[2]

Anastasius' death turned the ensuing papal election into a contest over the resolution of the schism, but with a new secular political dimension. From the second century on, a bishop was elected by the whole Christian community of his city, but in very large centres of population such as Rome and with rising numbers of believers, this could hardly have worked in practice. Because the Senate was predominantly Christian from the later fourth century onwards, its members effectively monopolised lay involvement in papal elections.[3]

A papal election provided a forum for factional conflict. Two issues combined to make this the case in 498. An embassy from the Senate, led by its senior member, the former consul Festus, had been in Constantinople in 497 to request the emperor's recognition of the rule of the Gothic King Theoderic in Italy. This had been granted, but in return Festus promised to work to end the Acacian Schism. Whether he made headway with Anastasius II on his return is unclear, but the latter's death provided the chance to choose a pope willing to compromise with Constantinople.

At the same time there was unease amongst senators over papal control of the wealth of the Roman church. Ever since it became a property-owning corporate body in the early third century, the episcopal Church in the city had been accumulating wealth through donations and bequests. These grew in size and frequency in the fourth century, with gifts being made by emperors and senators. The expansion of papal building projects, including libraries and bath houses as well as churches and monasteries, as recorded in the *Liber Pontificalis,* from the time of Damasus onwards hints at the mounting institutional wealth that the pope controlled and administered through his deacons.[4]

The charitable activities of the Church cut across the aristocracy's traditional role as the main patrons of the city, and senators objected to donations their families had made to the Church being sold or given away. So, restricting papal control over these resources became a political objective, and in 483 the praetorian prefect Basilius issued an edict prohibiting alienation of Church property by the bishops of Rome. This law was resented by the clergy, especially because it had been issued by a lay rather than an ecclesiastical authority, and opposition to it became another policy issue in the papal election of 498.

Three days after the death of Anastasius II, the deacon Laurentius was consecrated pope in Santa Maria Maggiore, having been elected by Festus and a majority in the Senate who wanted to see relations fully restored between Rome and Constantinople in both political and ecclesiastical spheres. On the same day in the Lateran, a minority of senators led by Faustus the Black, but with most of the clergy on their side, elected another of the deacons, called Symmachus, a Sardinian convert from paganism, who represented those unwilling to compromise over the Acacian Schism.

Although the emperor Honorius had in 420 decreed that all Christians in Rome should vote in a disputed papal election, such participation was clearly regarded in 498 as impractical, and instead the issue was put before King Theoderic in Ravenna, despite his being an Arian and thus a heretic in the eyes of both parties. He decreed that the candidate chosen by the larger number of electors should win the contest, and so Symmachus was recognised as pope, with Laurentius receiving an Italian bishopric in compensation.

As in the conflict between Damasus and Ursinus in 366, this solution proved fragile because it ignored the fundamental issues behind the dispute. In 501 the supporters of Laurentius tried to reverse it by accusing Symmachus of adultery and squandering the wealth of his church. He was said to have had numerous women followers, being especially devoted to one Conditaria (Spice Woman).[5] As a retort to the charge of misuse of church property, Symmachus called a synod of sixty-five bishops in November 501, which revoked the decree of 483 forbidding papal transfer of church property.[6] By this time Symmachus and his supporters were entrenched in St. Peter's, where he built the first papal residence next to the basilica, while the other churches and districts of the city remained in the hands of his opponents.

Street fighting broke out, which the mainly pro-Symmachan sources blamed entirely on Festus and his senatorial allies, but honours may have been even. With the charges brought against the pope still unanswered and Easter of 502 approaching, Festus and others persuaded Theoderic to appoint a Visitor, a bishop from another see, to go to Rome to conduct the celebrations, along with the baptisms and ordinations normally carried out in that season. He was also to take over control of the Church's property from Symmachus.

In August the king also ordered the regular synod, meeting in the Church of Santa Croce, to hear the charges against the pope.

Symmachus demanded the removal of the Visitor as a condition for attending and then refused to continue to participate when attacked by partisans of Laurentius on his way to the synod. For nearly two months the bishops tried unsuccessfully to find a solution to the problem of how to judge someone who was their hierarchical superior and who refused to appear before them. At the same time they made persistent efforts to persuade Theoderic to try the case himself, something he claimed he was incompetent to do. In the end they proclaimed that the holder of the See of Peter could be judged by God alone and, declaring themselves in full communion with Symmachus, headed for home.

The decision that had been reached by this long synod raised a claim that would be repeated in succeeding centuries, that no man could sit in judgement on the pope and that there was no earthly jurisdiction, civil or ecclesiastical, to which he was subject. In practice this decision resulted from an argument developed out of necessity in a situation of impasse. Popes had in the past been judged. Damasus had submitted to hearings both in a Roman synod and before the emperor, and Pope Sylvester (314–335) appeared before Constantine I when faced with 'scurrilous charges'.[7] So, this claim made in 502 was not based on precedents, and those that existed argued against it. But it had a long future ahead of it.

The expedient nature of the declaration of the bishops in 502 was underlined by the criticisms it raised, and by the decision of Theoderic to allow Laurentius, who had recently taken refuge at his court, to return to Rome later that year. There, with powerful backing, he made himself master of most of the city, while Symmachus remained in St. Peter's. This unstable situation and the resulting violence in the city lasted until 506, when Theoderic made a definitive intervention on the side of Symmachus, probably because diplomatic relations with the emperor were breaking down and he no longer needed to court the approval of pro-imperial senators. Laurentius was sent into retirement on an estate owned by Festus, devoting himself to a life of asceticism, and died a year or two later. Symmachus retained the papal see unchallenged and was increasingly popular for his charitable work, until his death in 514.

Amongst the most important products of this period are texts written almost entirely by the pro-Symmachan camp justifying the view of the synod of 502. The first was a fiery rhetorical defence written in 503 by Ennodius, a deacon of Milan, who made new claims that the popes were incapable of sin and error: 'God willed the successors of the blessed Apostle Peter to owe their innocence to Heaven.'[8] This would also provide vital ammunition for later generations of papal theorists.

So too would the spurious historical texts written anonymously or ascribed to earlier authors that are known collectively as the Symmachan forgeries. This was the first occasion on which the Roman church had revisited its own history, in particular the third and fourth centuries, in search of precedents. That these were largely invented does not negate the significance of the process. Forgery is an emotive word, and it should not necessarily be assumed that the documents, including the acts of two synods, were cynically concocted to justify a particular claim. Some of the periods in question, such as the pontificates of Sylvester (314–335) and Liberius (352–366), were already being seen more through the prism of legend than that of history, and in the Middle Ages texts were often forged because their authors were convinced of the truth of what they contained. Their faked documents provided tangible evidence of what was already believed true.

The Symmachan forgeries reinterpreted some of the more embarrassing episodes in papal history, both real and imaginary. In the supposed acts of a synod held in Santa Maria Maggiore, Pope Marcellinus (295–303) admits to burning incense to idols during the Diocletianic persecution, but the bishops declare their inability to try him, because 'the first see may be judged by no man.' Similarly, in the 'Account of the Purgation of Sixtus', Pope Sixtus III (431–440) faced charges of mishandling church property and committing adultery with a nun, but a friendly senator invoked papal superiority to all earthly judgement to prevent Sixtus being brought to trial.

How convincing these forged texts seemed in the early sixth century is unknown, but when rediscovered in later centuries, they were regarded as authentic records with unequivocal legal authority. In the short term, however, their influence was limited, and their claims did not save several popes in the sixth and seventh centuries from being judged and sometimes suffering punishment at the hands of secular rulers.

It is no coincidence that the first systematic works of papal history appear at the very time the Roman church's past was being reinvented for polemical purposes. The earliest may have been a pro-Laurentian list of popes with brief accounts of their pontificates, written between 514 and 519. Only a fragment survives, but it became the model for the *Liber Pontificalis,* the collection of papal biographies, the first edition of which was compiled soon after 530. This too is lost, except for two very condensed versions, but a revised edition was prepared between 537 and the mid-540s, which extended it to the pontificate of Silverius (536–537). The collection then lapsed until sometime around 625 to 638, when a new author took it up. His task was carried on by a succession of largely anonymous writers working in the papal administration until the late ninth century.

Memories of the Laurentian Schism remained strong because many of the participants survived into subsequent decades. In 499, after his initial triumph over Laurentius, Symmachus held a synod which changed the rules of election, so that a pope could nominate his own heir. If he failed to do so, the new bishop would be chosen by the clergy of Rome, without lay involvement. Symmachus appointed his deacon Hormisdas (514–523), who had played a leading role in the synod of 501, and Hormisdas' successor, John I (523–526), was another veteran of the schism, a supporter of Laurentius until 506. The last pope with a personal link to these events was Agapitus (535–536), whose father, a priest called Gordianus, had been killed by pro-Laurentians in the street fighting.

THE POPES AND THE ARIAN KINGS

Despite initial warmth, relations between the empire and the Gothic kingdom in Italy chilled, with imperial interest in the West turning instead to the rising power of the Gallic kingdom of the Franks, created by Clovis (died c. 511). In the East in 515, the emperor Anastasius I was threatened by a pro-Chalcedonian general, who used the emperor's Monophysite sympathies, which were unpopular in Constantinople, to justify his revolt. In consequence reunion with Rome suddenly became an imperial priority, and Anastasius invited Pope Hormisdas to preside over a conference to settle the schism, only to lose interest when the rebel was defeated. Negotiations continued intermittently, but real progress required a change of dynasty.

The death of the emperor in 518 prompted a coup by the commander of the imperial guard, who was proclaimed as Justin I (518–527). A Latin speaker from the western Balkans, he was pro-Chalcedonian in his theology and determined in a way his predecessors had not been to restore ecclesiastical and other ties with Rome. In this he was encouraged by his principal advisor on these questions, his nephew and successor, Justinian. An embassy from Rome, led by the deacons Felix and Dioscorus, both of whom later became pope, secured almost everything the papacy wanted, and an agreement known as the Formula of Hormisdas was signed in 519.

Full communion was restored, and Acacius and his successors, along with Peter Mongus of Alexandria, were removed from the diptychs. However, the papal demand that the cases of all deposed bishops be submitted to Rome for trial, thus recognising the pope's supreme jurisdiction, was quietly sidestepped when the emperor reversed all depositions before the acceptance of the formula. In return Hormisdas implicitly recognised Constantinople's precedence amongst the Eastern patriarchates, something his predecessors had resisted since 381. The formula itself was frequently cited in subsequent centuries, and at the First Vatican Council of 1870 it was claimed as evidence of Eastern recognition of Rome's supremacy.

If ecclesiastical relations between Italy and the empire improved after 519, political ones took a downward turn. Imperial tolerance of Arianism in the East ended, not least because the Gothic Arian troops in imperial service had participated in a succession of failed revolts. Churches used for Arian worship were confiscated, and pressure was put on them to convert. Theoderic, who had commanded such troops in the Balkans before 490, demanded a change of policy in Constantinople, threatening reprisals against Catholic interests in Italy.

The election of John I in 523 brought a former Laurentian deacon and thus an advocate of ever closer political ties between Rome and the empire to the papal throne. He had influential friends in the Senate of like mind, including the philosopher and former government minister Boethius, to whom he was a spiritual mentor and who had dedicated three short theological treatises to him. Boethius and other leading senators had relatives in the East, as well as strong emotional attachments to the empire and to the Roman past. Other members of this circle included Symmachus, Boethius' father-in-law and author of a now lost history of Rome, his two ascetic daughters Proba and Galla and abbot Eugippius, whose *Life of St. Severinus* records the end of Roman rule in what is now eastern Austria. They also exchanged letters with some North African bishops exiled to Sardinia by the Arian Vandal kings. As a group they could be characterised as Roman patriots, ultra orthodox in their theology, and supporters of more austere forms of monasticism, resentful at being ruled by heretics and barbarians. That the Gothic regime in Ravenna regarded the new pope and his friends with suspicion is hardly surprising.

The order of the ensuing events is obscure, but Boethius was accused of treason in 524 or 525 by members of another faction in the Senate. Sentenced to death by Theoderic, he wrote his *Consolation of Philosophy* while awaiting execution. Soon afterwards a similar fate befell Symmachus. Around this time Theoderic sent John I with four leading senators and the archbishop of Ravenna to persuade the emperor Justin to reverse his anti-Arian measures. John thus became the first pope to visit Constantinople or indeed to leave Italy. He was warmly received in the imperial capital, and his status as first amongst the patriarchs was recognised in his celebrating the Easter liturgy in the presence of both the emperor and the bishop of Constantinople. Some concessions were made by Justin over the Arians, but the details are not clear.

The *Liber Pontificalis* tells us that upon his return, John personally presented the four great patriarchal basilicas of Rome with valuable gifts from the emperor. This contradicts the later claim that the pope was arrested in Ravenna immediately on arriving in Italy, but he was certainly detained soon afterwards and died in captivity on 18 May 526. His distribution of imperial largesse and connections to Boethius and Symmachus may have prompted his arrest. Lurid accounts of the fates of all three of them were soon being circulated in a propaganda war waged against the Gothic kingdom in Italy by Justin I's successor, Justinian (527–565), and helped justify its ensuing destruction.

Just as the Senate became increasingly polarised between those whose first loyalty was to the emperor in Constantinople and those who preferred to support a strong Gothic kingdom in Italy, the Roman church divided on similar lines. John I did not designate a successor, and the senators objected to the decree of Pope Symmachus that had excluded them from papal elections. So a two-month constitutional crisis after his death only ended with the appointment of the pro-Gothic Felix IV (526–530), under whom relations between papacy and monarchy became harmonious.

One consequence of entente was a royal edict confirming the papal right to hear all cases involving the clergy of the kingdom, both in civil and criminal matters. This was an important stage in a long process of securing the exemption of all clerics from secular jurisdiction. Felix also established the first Christian building in the ancient heart of Rome, when he converted a large hall, once part of the Forum of Peace of the emperor Vespasian (69–79), into a basilica dedicated to Saints Cosmas and Damian, twin doctors from Syria, martyred in the Great Persecution. The new church was entered from the Roman Forum through a former shrine to the city's legendary founder, Romulus, twin brother of Remus. The emphasis on twins and on medicine in this choice of patron saints was deliberate, as this area of the Forum had previously been associated with pagan healing cults centred on the temple of the divine twins Castor and Pollux.

The church contains one of the finest apse mosaics in Rome, although poorly restored in the seventeenth century. In it Felix himself is shown being presented to Christ by one of the two saints. This is the first time a pope was depicted in art. The new iconography—the patron saints leading the pope to Christ—was frequently reused by later pontiffs.

Divisions reasserted themselves on Felix's death, when in the Lateran a majority of the clergy and senators elected as pope the deacon Dioscorus, originally from Alexandria, while members of an opposing faction in Santa Maria Maggiore proclaimed another deacon, Boniface, pope. This was a repeat of the contested election of 498 and might have been as bitter but for Dioscorus' sudden death a month later. Constitutionally, Dioscorus was probably the rightful pope, enjoying the larger body of support, but he was never recognised as such, as the dispute was unresolved when he died. The outcome might have been the same in any case, as Boniface II (530–532) was a Goth and more acceptable to Ravenna. His now leaderless opponents submitted to him, but as the hostile compiler of the *Liber Pontificalis* writes, 'driven by jealousy and madness' Boniface required them to sign a document posthumously condemning Dioscorus, which he then placed in the papal archives.

Boniface's brief pontificate was followed by the equally short one of John II (533–535), who was the first pope to change his name on being elected. This would not become a standard papal practice until the late tenth century. John probably did so because his original name, Mercurius, was that of a pagan god, though he had used it as a priest.

John II's consecration in January 533 was delayed by ten weeks thanks to factional conflicts and a revival of the dispute over the election processes. Symmachus' attempt to exclude lay participation and allow designation of his successor by the incumbent pope had failed to take root after 514, but in 531 Boniface II tried to revive it in a Roman synod, nominating his deacon Vigilius. However, he reversed this decision at a second synod, largely because of opposition from the Senate, which continued resisting attempts to limit its participation in papal elections.

In 535 the archdeacon Agapitus was elected pope with broad support. Like several of his predecessors, he was the son of a leading member of the Roman clergy from a senatorial family. Not surprisingly he had strong views on the disputed election of 530, which the senators' candidate had lost through his premature death, and so ordered the destruction of the document that had been 'uncanonically and maliciously extorted from the priests and bishops against Dioscorus' by Boniface II.[9]

The new pope was soon engaged in planning a library and academy of Christian learning with the senator Cassiodorus, who had been a high government official under the Gothic kings Theoderic and Athalaric. It was to be located in Agapitus' family mansion, opposite the Church of Saints John and Paul on the Caelian Hill, of which the apse of the great audience hall survives. However, the scheme for the academy never got off the ground, because it depended on raising subscriptions, and war was looming. The last phase of Agapitus' brief pontificate was devoted to trying to prevent it.

The death of the young King Athalaric in 534 precipitated a crisis in the Gothic kingdom. His widowed mother, Amalasuintha, Theoderic's daughter, had been regent and was now reluctant to relinquish power. She and an elderly cousin, Theodehad, agreed that he should inherit the throne, while she retained the real authority, but this arrangement quickly proved unworkable and he had her imprisoned on an island, where in 535 she was murdered by members of the Gothic aristocracy whom she had once offended. The killing provided the excuse needed for the emperor Justinian to intervene in Italy, following the successful reconquest of Africa by his armies in 533/4. By late 535 half the army used to conquer the Vandal kingdom was in Sicily under its commander Belisarius, poised to invade Italy.

Theodehad was willing to capitulate and sent the pope to Constantinople in December 535 to negotiate with the emperor for the surrender of his kingdom in return for estates and a pension in the East. Agapitus' arrival in Constantinople in March 536 was welcomed for reasons of ecclesiastical as well as secular politics. Although both emperor and capital firmly supported the Council of Chalcedon, the Eastern provinces of the empire, especially Syria and Egypt, remained strongholds of the various Monophysite theologies that had grown in popularity and intellectual sophistication under a new generation of teachers, of whom the most outstanding was Patriarch Severus of Antioch.

While Justinian was as anxious as his predecessors to heal the breach in the Eastern church through compromise, his wife, the empress Theodora (died 548), was a committed anti-Chalcedonian, who used her influence to advance bishops of the same persuasion. A recent triumph had been the transfer in 535 of her ally Anthimus, bishop of Trebizond, to the patriarchate of Constantinople. In the same year she also secured the election of a follower of Severus of Antioch, himself now in exile in Egypt, as patriarch of Alexandria. The patriarch of Jerusalem was also known to be wavering in his support for Chalcedon. Even in Constantinople, a stronghold of pro-Chalcedonianism in the reign of Anastasius, popular opinion was volatile. When the city was spared serious damage in an earthquake in 533, some began shouting, 'Burn the document issued by the bishops of the synod of Chalcedon.'[10]

With conditions increasingly favourable, Anthimus proposed restoring church unity in the East on the basis of general acceptance of the Councils of Nicaea (325), I Constantinople (381) and I Ephesus (431) together with the *Henotikon* of Zeno, omitting and thereby implicitly condemning the Council of Chalcedon and Pope Leo's *Tome*. For this to work, the acquiescence of Agapitus was required.

The pope had been kept informed of these developments by staunchly pro-Chalcedonian correspondents in the East and so arrived in Constantinople well briefed, despite the difficulties of his journey, which had to be funded by sale of Church property. The prestige of his office remained unquestionable, and with his allies he quickly worked on the emperor to depose Patriarch Anthimus of Constantinople on the grounds that his transfer from Trebizond defied the Council of Nicaea's explicit ban on bishops changing diocese. Following this unexpected victory for the Chalcedonian party, the patriarch of Jerusalem returned to the fold, and in Alexandria a violent split amongst the Monophysites led to imperial intervention and the removal of new patriarch Theodosius to thirty years of exile. But Pope Agapitus did not long survive his triumph, dying in Constantinople in April 536. His body was returned to Rome for burial in St. Peter's. Meanwhile the empress plotted a revenge that would not be long in coming.

Her chosen instrument was the Roman deacon Vigilius, the apocrisiarius, or papal diplomatic representative, in Constantinople. This office, created at the end of the Acacian Schism, was an important one because of its holder's presence in the imperial court. Several of the apocrisiarii of the period were subsequently elected pope, as this connection was valued by emperors and electors alike.

In Italy, Agapitus' mission had failed to prevent war, and in 536 Theodehad was deposed by the Gothic army, recognising that he had no stomach for a fight, and murdered, and Wittigis, a Gothic general, took the throne. By this time Belisarius and his imperial army had crossed from Sicily and taken Naples. Here because they refused to admit him, asking just to be left in peace, 'he killed both the Goths and the Neapolitan citizens, and embarked on a sack from which he did not even spare the churches, such a sack that he killed husbands by the sword in their wives' presence and eliminated the captured sons and wives of nobles. No one was spared, not priests, not God's servants, not virgin nuns.'[11] Italy was to know much more of such conduct before the war ended two decades later.

Faced with this example, and despite swearing to King Wittigis that they would not surrender the city, the senators, strongly urged on by a new pope, opened the gates of Rome to Belisarius. The price they paid was the massacre of senatorial hostages held by the Goths in Ravenna. In Rome Agapitus had been succeeded a few months earlier by a young subdeacon, Silverius, son of the former Pope Hormisdas.

We should note that cases of bishops being the sons of clergy lack the suggestion of scandal this would arouse in later centuries. As letters of Leo the Great make clear, there was no bar to a married man being admitted to the clergy, so long as both he and his wife had not previously been married to someone else. Remarriage was entirely prohibited, and a cleric would be expected not to marry once in orders. Continence was an ideal rather than a requirement, and so children could be born to married clergy, even if some rigorists disapproved.

The *Liber Pontificalis* claims that Silverius had been imposed on the papal throne by King Theodehad and was 'ordained through force and fear' and against the opposition of the Roman clergy. They were said to have accepted him only after his ordination and merely 'to safeguard the unity of the church and religion'.[12] However, the anonymous compiler wrote this in the opening years of the next pontificate, when, as we shall see, there were strong reasons for implying that Silverius had not been legitimately elected. In the circumstances of 536, his family connections actually made him an ideal choice.

Although responsible for the welcome given to Belisarius and his army in Rome in December 536, Silverius was subsequently arrested and despatched to Constantinople, accused of treasonable correspondence with the Goths, who were now preparing to besiege the city. In so doing Belisarius acted on the orders of Theodora, transmitted by his wife Antonina, a close friend of the empress. Theodora wanted a malleable pope to reverse Agapitus' defeat of her Monophysite allies. Her choice fell on the apocrisiarius Vigilius, who was sent to Rome to be elected pope even though no case had been made against the legitimacy of Silverius' election the previous year, and his removal was achieved by secular not ecclesiastical authority. But despite the blatant irregularity of the process, Vigilius was ordained bishop on 29 March 537, soon after the Goths began to besiege Rome.

The contradictory nature of religious policy making under Justinian and Theodora was further demonstrated when Silverius, exiled to Lycia in Asia Minor by the empress, succeeded in appealing to the emperor, who ordered that he be returned to Rome for a proper investigation of the charges levelled against him. Once there, he was in the hands of his enemies and under pressure was forced to abdicate in November 537. Although Silverius then took monastic vows, he was exiled to the island of Ponza and died within weeks. The *Liber Pontificalis* claims that Pope Vigilius had him starved to death, while the contemporary imperial historian Procopius implicates an agent of Belisarius' wife in his demise.[13]

This episode caused difficulties for later generations of Catholic historians, as Vigilius had been made pope while his predecessor was still alive and in office. Silverius' subsequent forced resignation resolved the problem of the ending of his pontificate, but Vigilius' tenure of the office began eight months earlier. In the late sixteenth century, the annalist Cardinal Baronius, combating Protestant interpretations of the early history of the papacy, tried to square the circle by claiming that Vigilius had submitted himself to re-election immediately after Silverius' abdication, thus legitimising his position, but there is no evidence to support such a claim. Vigilius' installation as pope was unquestionably irregular, but this was not something about which the Church in Rome could afford to be concerned at the time.

THE THREE CHAPTERS

It may seem paradoxical that the *Liber Pontificalis* is so hostile to Silverius in its account of his election but so sympathetic in describing his deposition and death. However, the two parts of the life of this pope were written by different authors, working a century apart. The first of them, around 540, presented the official justification for the removal of Silverius, but by the time the second continued the narrative from 537 up to his own day, this pope was revered as a martyr, and it was his successor, Vigilius, who had become highly controversial.

The reason lies in something known as the Three Chapters Controversy, the result of another ill-fated attempt to settle the division in the Eastern churches over the theology of the Natures of Christ that was becoming more deeply entrenched by the decade. In the early 540s, the emperor Justinian acquired a new theological advisor, Theodore Askidas, bishop of Caesarea in Cappadocia. The bishop persuaded Justinian that reconciliation might be achieved through the condemnation of three fifth-century theologians whose ideas were particularly disliked by the Monophysites. The emperor was persuaded that the Monophysites might accept the Council of Chalcedon, to which he himself was fully committed, if the three were now proclaimed to have been supporters of Nestorius. This he did in an edict issued in 544. The nature and extent of the censure varied in each case. For one of the targets, Theodore of Mopsuestia (died 428), his person as well as his entire literary output was anathematised. With Theodoret of Cyrus (died 457/8), it was only his writings against Cyril of Alexandria that were targeted, while in the case of Ibas of Edessa (died 457), the only questionable text was an anonymous letter to a Persian called Mari, that everyone knew he had written but whose authorship was officially declared to be uncertain.

The treatment of Theodore violated the convention that individuals should not be judged in their absence or after their death, even if specific writings of theirs could be condemned. However, the greatest unease was generated by the treatment of Theodoret and Ibas, because both had been anathematised and deposed at the 'Robber Council' of Ephesus then vindicated and restored by the Council of Chalcedon. Because of their involvement in that touchstone of orthodoxy, this renewed attack on them nearly a century later was seen, particularly in the West, as yet another attempt to undermine the whole authority of Chalcedon.

There was also disquiet amongst the pro-Chalcedonian bishops in the East, and Patriarch Menas of Constantinople, who was jealous of the influence of Theodore Askidas, only agreed to accept the edict if the pope did likewise. Bishops in Western imperial territories such as the Balkans, Sicily and North Africa reacted with even greater hostility to it. Papal backing for the new policy was clearly going to be required if it was to be successful, but the advice that Vigilius was receiving from the leading African theologian of the day, the deacon Ferrandus of Carthage, was to resist it. So, in 545 the empress Theodora ordered that he be brought to Constantinople to make him fall into line. The hostile *Liber Pontificalis* claimed that imperial officials seized Vigilius in the middle of celebrating Mass in the Church of Santa Cecilia in Trastevere and put him on a ship waiting in the Tiber, while starving citizens—Rome being again under siege by the Goths—threw stones and cooking pots, shouting, 'Take your famine with you! Take your killing with you! You treated the Romans badly, may you meet evil where you are going!'[14] The last of these wishes, at least, would be granted.

Vigilius' journey was slow, as he had to remain in Sicily throughout 546 due to the current state of the war, and there he was pressured in person and through letters by Italian and African bishops opposed to the imperial edict. He also learned that Patriarch Menas had now accepted the emperor's edict, and so on arrival in Constantinople in the spring of 547 Vigilius immediately excommunicated him. This bravura display of resistance did not last long. Both emperor and empress set out to flatter the pope, and four months later he reversed his sentence on Menas. By 548 he had come round fully to Justinian's point of view and issued a private *judicatum* or judgement supporting the condemnation of the three authors. This was leaked by two of his deacons, who felt he was betraying Chalcedon, a view quickly shared in the West, where an African synod actually excommunicated him. Rumours began to circulate that back in 537 he had promised to support the empress in promoting Monophysitism in return for her making him pope and had secretly been in correspondence with the Monophysite bishops ever since.

Faced with this furious reaction, Vigilius backtracked, even though he sacked his two disloyal deacons with a vituperative letter of dismissal. He suppressed the *judicatum* and urged Justinian to suspend his edict until he could call a full council of bishops from both East and West to discuss the issue. This was agreed, but Western representatives were slow to arrive, with only two bishops turning up from the Balkans and none from Africa. When Vigilius refused to proceed until more Western delegates appeared, the exasperated emperor reissued his edict, and the pope, supported by the bishop of Milan who had been with him since Sicily, threatened to excommunicate anyone who accepted it. He then fled to one of the churches of Constantinople.

An attempt to drag him from sanctuary by his feet was thwarted by his clinging to the altar, and he was eventually persuaded to return to the palace that had been put at his disposal by the promise of more rational methods of debate. But finding himself effectively under house arrest and complaining of sinister noises in his bedroom, Vigilius and a handful of the clergy accompanying him escaped by boat to Chalcedon on the opposite side of the Bosphorus, where they took refuge in the Church of Saint Eufemia. This was too sacred and too public a place for further strong-arm methods to be employed against them, and a truce was again agreed, with the edict being suspended until a full council had assembled.

When this council met in May 553, the balance of representation remained unequal, with 165 Eastern bishops but only sixteen Western attending. Vigilius refused to come, claiming ill health, but drew up a *constitutum* or decree setting out his opposition to the condemnation of the three authors and prohibiting further discussion of the issue.[15] This was signed by the Western bishops, but Justinian prevented it being laid before the council, which completed its deliberations in June, condemning the three authors.

There still remained the matter of Vigilius' assent. Despite the stand he had taken in his *constitutum,* the pope was persuaded, not least by some of his own advisors, to accept the decisions of the council and himself condemned the three authors in letters written in December 553. The following year he was allowed to leave to return to Rome, where the Gothic war had just ended with the defeats and deaths of the last two Gothic kings. But Vigilius only got as far as Sicily, where he died in June 555.

After a ten-month gap, a new pope was ordained. Although never explained, this delay arose because the choice of pope was in the hands of the emperor. There were few senators left in Rome, many having been massacred by the Goths in 552, and the clergy were leaderless. Several of the most prominent were still in the East, including a deacon called Pelagius. Of Roman aristocratic family, he had accompanied Agapitus to Constantinople in 535 and succeeded Vigilius as papal representative there. In 551 he was back again after the calling of the council and served thereafter as Vigilius' main theological advisor. He may well have composed the *constitutum* of 553 for the pope, whom he did not follow in his change of heart later that year. Refusing to accept the Three Chapters, as the formal condemnations of Theodore, Theodoret and Ibas were known, and kept in exile in the East while Vigilius returned to Rome, Pelagius composed a substantial defence of the three authors, criticising the pope for his final capitulation and two fellow deacons for advising him to make it.

Despite this, Pelagius finally recognised the condemnation and accepted the decisions of the council when offered the papal throne by Justinian early in 556. He returned to a much damaged and depleted Rome in April and was ordained despite considerable hostility from clergy and populace. Only two bishops, rather than the required three, were willing to consecrate him. The *Liber Pontificalis,* as prejudiced against him as against Vigilius, reports an implausible tale that he had actually poisoned his predecessor and took a public oath on the Gospels that he had not done so. This story established an important precedent for how a pope could clear himself of serious charges.

It is likely, though, that Pelagius I (556–561) made a public declaration of his theological principles soon after his consecration, to try to dispel the rumours surrounding the agreement he had made with the emperor. His popularity in the city began to rise once he started using his family money to begin rebuilding Rome, severely damaged in two sieges and a three-month period of abandonment, and feed the poor. However, he also published his acceptance of the recent council, which thereafter was officially recognised as the Fifth Ecumenical Council (or the Second Council of Constantinople), and he ordered that its decrees should not be questioned or even discussed in regional synods in the West. A number of bishops in northern Italy, Sicily, the western Balkans and Africa promptly refused to accept his authority, claiming he had betrayed the faith of Chalcedon, and broke communion with him.

The result was the longest schism yet known in the Western church, lasting through the seventh century. Its initially wide geographical range shrank rapidly, however, and due to factors unrelated to the dispute itself, Rome had to make few concessions to win back its authority. In Africa, ruled by the emperor since 533, force was applied to make the bishops and leading abbots accept the imperial theology. Several were exiled to the East and others capitulated. Some who refused, including whole monastic communities, migrated, not least to Spain, where their arrival, together with libraries of books they brought with them, kick-started an intellectual renaissance in the Spanish church that lasted until the Arab conquest of 711. Their flight was further encouraged by the raiding of the settled coastal districts by the Berber tribes of the interior, which the imperial garrisons proved incapable of stopping. This persecution, warfare and migration fatally weakened the intellectual strength and independence of the African church.

In Italy the war between the imperial forces and the Goths that lasted for over twenty years inflicted lasting damage on both town and country, with massacres, looting and the destruction of farms by both sides producing famine and depopulation. The last pockets of Gothic resistance were only eliminated in 562. In these same decades, thanks to the imperial armies being overstretched in campaigns in Africa, Italy, Spain and on the eastern frontiers, the defences of the Balkans were virtually abandoned, resulting in many areas being overrun by Slavs migrating from across the Danube. Diplomatic attempts were made to regain control of the Danube through alliances with rival barbarian confederacies jostling for control. In 568 an ill-judged change of policy on the part of the new emperor Justin II (565–578) led to one of them, the *Langobardi* or Lombards, crossing the Alps and entering Italy unopposed. In less than a decade they had made themselves masters of much of the north and centre of the peninsula, with their kings ruling from Pavia, near Milan. In 579 Rome was subjected to its first siege by the new invaders. For the next two centuries the Lombards would be the greatest threat to the security of Rome and the papacy's political ties to the empire.

In the circumstances, theological differences came to seem less important while the armies of the imperial governor, the exarch, based in Ravenna, struggled militarily and diplomatically to stem the Lombard conquests. Thus in 573 Bishop Laurentius II of Milan, whose predecessor had been an uncompromising opponent of Justinian's theology, agreed to restore communion with Rome and accept the Three Chapters. Soon it was only the metropolitan province of Aquileia in northeastern Italy that continued to resist renewing ties with Rome on such terms. Pope Pelagius II (579–590) tried to persuade the exarch to force its bishops to submit, but the Lombard threat made the use of such tactics too risky. Several dioceses around the northern Adriatic remained out of communion with Rome until the time of Pope Sergius I (687–701).

Until then the rift remained an embarrassment for the papacy. In 608 the delightfully Irish abbot Columbanus (d. 615) wrote to Pope Boniface IV to tell him off for the ongoing schism, which was hampering his missionary work in the Lombard kingdom. He was less than reverential about Vigilius: 'Watch therefore, I beg you, Pope, watch and again I say watch; since perhaps Vigilius was not very vigilant.' He had also heard that Boniface was as soft on heretics as Vigilius, who had spoken up for 'those old heretics Eutyches, Nestorius and Dioscorus' at some council or another—'I do not know which.' He urged the pope to call a new council in order to resolve the matter, which he considered an emergency, not just 'a day at the races'.[16] With such a legacy, it is hardly surprising that in the mid-seventh century the compiler of the *Liber Pontificalis* looked back on the age of Vigilius and Pelagius I with a jaundiced eye and believed every story that discredited them. In their day Gelasius I's doctrine of the Two Swords had signally failed to turn itself into a reality.

~ *chapter 6* ~

SLAVE OF
THE SLAVES OF GOD

(561–687)

GREGORY THE GREAT

The enormous walls of Rome, built around AD 270 and heightened in the early fifth century, kept the Lombards out in 579, but when Pope Benedict I (575–579) died during the Lombard siege, there was no way of sending for imperial confirmation for his elected successor, Pelagius II (579–590), who was therefore consecrated without the usual long delays. Amongst his first decisions after the siege was to send to Constantinople as his new apocrisiarius a member of one of the few surviving aristocratic families in the city, Gregory, a descendent of Pope Felix III and a close relative of Pope Agapitus I.

Gregory may also have been chosen as much for his political experience as his connections, having been Rome's civil governor after the Gothic wars. Since then he had become a monk, founding a community in his own family property on the Caelian Hill, once the site of Agapitus' library.

When Gregory left for the imperial capital in 580, he took some of his monks with him and set up a monastic household in the official residence of the apocrisiarius. In Constantinople Gregory's first task was to try to persuade the emperor Tiberius II (578–582) to send reinforcements to save Rome from further threat. Here he failed, and Tiberius advised bribing the Lombards to make peace instead, using Church funds. Gregory was more successful in the ecclesiastical sphere, in 582 persuading the emperor that Eutychius, patriarch of Constantinople, had fallen into heresy when claiming that bodies would be insubstantial after the resurrection of the dead.

Gregory also made personal contacts that would be important in future years. The closest of these was with Bishop Leander of Seville (died 599), who came seeking imperial support for Hermenegild, a Gothic prince in rebellion in southern Spain against his father, Leovigild (569–586). In 587 Leander orchestrated the personal conversion from Arianism of Hermenegild's brother Reccared (586–601), and then of the Gothic kingdom as a whole at the Third Council of Toledo in 589. Because of his friendship with Leander, Gregory took close interest in Spain, where his memory and writings were thereafter especially revered.[1]

Gregory ministered to the spiritual welfare of his monastic companions by lecturing them on the historical, allegorical and moral significance of every passage in the Book of Job. This he later turned into his twenty-five-volume *Moralia in Job,* the largest literary composition by any pope of the first millennium. Gregory was the most prolific of all papal authors, composing commentaries on several works of Scripture, but his output tails off after his consecration, and some of his works derive from notes taken from his sermons and from the verbal expositions of texts delivered to his monks, that were then written up for him. His time in Constantinople and the five years that followed his return to Rome in 585, were amongst his most productive. This period ended when in 589 plague broke out and included Pelagius II amongst its victims.

The choice of Gregory (590–604) as his successor was unsurprising, as so many of the popes of this period had served as papal envoys at the imperial court and so were well known to the emperor. Gregory's own previous administrative experience was an additional incentive, and like many of his predecessors he was a deacon of the Roman church. He stands out as the first pope to be a monk, but even while living in his community prior to his election he was closely involved in the events of the day.[2]

Although someone with the habit of command, Gregory was also a believer in the classical ideal that it was wrong to pursue office. In a Christian context this meant that while taking on worldly responsibilities threatened the individual's spiritual well-being, resistance was inappropriate since service was a duty. As pope, Gregory always referred to himself in his letters as *Servus Servorum Dei* or 'Slave of the Slaves of God' (the more usual version 'Servant of the Servants of God' lacks the element of ownership inherent in the original). This became a permanent papal title, preserved by his immediate successors and thereafter appearing in formal documents. Gregory's thoughts on the proper exercise of spiritual authority were included in his *Regula Pastoralis* (Pastoral Rule), which he intended for all who have responsibility for spiritual direction.

On becoming pope, Gregory's immediate concern was the plague, which came on top of years of warfare and famine throughout the peninsula. The city of Rome had suffered sieges by both Goths and Lombards, and many of its leading families had been taken hostage when the Goths captured it in 546, briefly expelling the inhabitants. Those who survived the massacres that followed in the final phase of the war had lost much of their wealth.

As conditions changed throughout the generally disastrous middle decades of the century, the Roman church took on the responsibilities once borne by the aristocracy as patrons and benefactors to the city and its inhabitants. Its administrative organisation developed to accommodate these new roles. The seven deacons had been in charge of the financial and charitable activities of the bishopric for the fourteen districts of the city since at least the third century. Now special diaconal administrative offices and warehouses, attached to chapels, were established throughout Rome, to serve as centres for the collection and distribution of charity and food.[3] Although individual popes and clergy with family lands contributed generously from them, the principal source of the Roman church's charitable activities were its estates in Sicily and Provence. These had suffered much less than those in Italy in the recent wars.

The Roman church objected to the secular public entertainments such as chariot races and gladiatorial combats that had been paid for by the secular aristocracy up until the reign of Theoderic (493–526) and had long tried to persuade the emperors to ban the bloodier forms of Roman games.[4] Other more innocuous local festivals were also disliked because of their associations with pagan gods but were patronised by the Christian aristocracy because they were traditional and popular. Pope Gelasius I (492–496) failed to persuade the Senate to suppress the Roman festival of the Lupercalia, in which naked men in wolf masks ran through the streets, whipping women wanting children with strips of goat skin, but the horrors of the sixth century finally put an end to it.[5]

Though the penitential processions instituted by Gregory in 590 to show public remorse for the sins that had brought the plague upon the city were hardly a substitute for the Lupercalia, gradually public Church rituals became the most important annual events in the life of the city. Livelier and more popular were the growing number of annual festivals commemorating Rome's early Christian martyrs, celebrated at their places of burial and in churches dedicated to them.[6]

The need for penitential processions remained, as more flooding, plague and famine occurred under Pope Boniface IV (608–615). Another threat reasserted itself more rapidly. In 593 the Lombards renewed their attempt to take Rome, after a four-year truce. They failed thanks again to the city's walls. Gregory took a more active role than his predecessors in ensuring the military preparedness of the city and negotiating with the Lombard ruler Agilulf (590–616). Although the king was an Arian, his wife, Theodelinda, was not and so became a potential ally in the Lombard court. She may have helped Gregory negotiate a truce for Rome during a period of open war between Agilulf and the empire. The resulting treaty strained relations between the pope and the emperor Maurice (582–602), whom Gregory had known in Constantinople. But Gregory's political loyalty was never in doubt, and his actions were not aimed at emancipating Rome and its church from imperial rule.[7]

We know so much about Gregory thanks to the survival of 850 of his letters, far more than for any other pope before the twelfth century. Even in comparison with outstanding Christian authors whose letters were deliberately collected and circulated after their deaths,

Gregory's surviving output is exceptional, being, for example, roughly three times that of St. Augustine.

Even so, we possess but a fraction of the letters written in his name. A huge annual correspondence was conducted by the pope with fellow patriarchs and bishops, secular rulers, contacts at court, papal emissaries and other officials. Letters were drafted by a permanent staff of notaries working in the papal household, of whose organisation we know little. Some letters, notably those sent to the emperors or making theological pronouncements, were written by the popes themselves or close advisors. Routine ones were drawn up by the notaries following standard procedures, and a formulary, the *Liber Diurnus,* was used to provide model letters for purposes such as confirming appointments or granting requests.[8] Whether these were then approved by the pope in person we do not know. Even the grander and more personal ones may have only received a final valedictory sentence or two in the papal hand.[9] What is certain, thanks to a life of Gregory written by the Roman deacon John around 873, is that copies of letters written by the papal secretariat were entered in chronological order into huge rolls of papyrus known as registers, kept in the archives of the Roman church. This process began before Gregory's day, and papal archives certainly existed in the fourth century if not earlier.

Around 720 an Anglo-Saxon deacon called Nothelm came to Rome and copied a precious handful of letters from these correspondence rolls, not just of Gregory but of a number of his successors. Nothelm was one of very few people who ever used them, as these papyrus registers were enormous, hard to unroll, containing a lot of humdrum administrative texts of little interest to later generations, without indexing, and written in a script that would have appeared increasingly archaic and difficult to read. So, it is not surprising, though infinitely regrettable, that by the thirteenth century they had been allowed to rot away and were never copied onto the more durable medium of parchment.

That so many of Gregory's letters survive is thanks to his high reputation in subsequent centuries, particularly outside Rome. Thus, small collections of his letters were made in the eighth century from copies of the originals sent to a variety of recipients and preserved by them and their successors. But under Pope Hadrian I (772–795), a much larger edition of 684 Gregorian letters was made directly from the papyrus registers in Rome, at the request of the Frankish king Charlemagne. Luckily, there is very little overlap between the contents of this and the smaller collections, resulting in the 850 letters now known. The preservation of this correspondence is important not least for the light it sheds on one of the best-known features of Gregory's pontificate, his sending of a mission to the Anglo-Saxons. The Northumbrian monk, exegete and historian Bede (died 735; given the status of Venerable by a synod at Aachen in 836), based his narrative of these events in his *Ecclesiastical History of the People of the English* (731) on the papal letters brought back for him from Rome by Nothelm and which he included verbatim in his text. But he never saw letters relating to Gregory's diplomatic dealings with the rulers of the Franks, smoothing the way for the mission to pass through their territory in the winter of 596, as Nothelm had not copied these.[10]

One consequence of his limited information was that Bede did not know why Gregory sent the mission and put it down to 'divine inspiration'. In fact, Gregory was responding to a request from Aethelberht, king of the Cantuarii (Men of Kent). Gregory sent Augustine, prior of his monastery of St. Andrew, and forty monks on the mission and arranged for him to be consecrated as metropolitan bishop by the papal vicar in Gaul, the bishop of Arles. Augustine's seat had been intended for London, the former centre of the British provinces when under Roman rule, but instead it became fixed in Canterbury, the capital of the Kentish kingdom, because of Aethelberht's request. Gregory believed that a proper province of the Church was ready to be formed, but the refusal of the bishops of the British realms in the west to accept Augustine's authority restricted this to the Anglo-Saxon kingdoms. As these converted, new bishoprics were created for them, starting with the arrival of a second mission from Rome in 601 that brought more monks and new bishops for the sees of Rochester and London.

The presence of monks in the missions of 596/7 and 601 is a distinctively Gregorian feature. They were not there to go about preaching or serve newly founded churches, as this contradicted the ideals of community and stability that writers of rules for monks and synods of bishops always insisted on. The monks were sent to provide the kind of monastic episcopal households that Gregory himself enjoyed in Rome and which he regarded as essential for the spiritual support of the rector, the teacher-bishop.

In practice the Gregorian mission to Kent was limited in its effects, thanks to changes in the balance of power between the Anglo-Saxon kingdoms that the pope could not have foreseen. Even before the death of Aethelberht in 616, his Kentish realm was declining into a second-class status from which it would never re-emerge, while real power over lowland Britain was the subject of competition between the expanding kingdoms of Northumbria, Mercia and Wessex.

So the conversion of the Anglo-Saxons in the seventh century became a piecemeal process achieved by a mixture of influences, including those of the Church in northern Francia on Wessex and the Irish monks from Iona on Northumbria and Mercia, but in all cases the unique authority and standing of the Roman see was part of the message. The churches in the Anglo-Saxon kingdoms looked to Rome for guidance and direction to a degree unmatched in any of the other much longer-established churches of the West. They also developed a special reverence for the person of Gregory, so much so that the first ever 'Life' of him was written about a century after his death in Northumbria, in the joint male and female monastery of Whitby on the north Yorkshire coast.

THE GREGORIAN LEGACY

Gregory died in 604 after a long illness. The decades that follow have been seen as ones of reaction to some of his policies, especially his promotion of monasticism and turning of the papal household into a monastic community. Thus popes Sabinian (604–606), Deusdedit (615–618), Boniface V (619–625) and Severinus (640) are called anti-Gregorian, and Boniface III (607), Boniface IV (608–615) and Honorius (625–638), pro. Boniface IV turned his house into a monastery, while Sabinian 'filled the church with clergy'.[11]

It is hard to sustain such an argument. In the case of Sabinian's appointment of new clergy, for example, Gregory's long and debilitating illness meant that he performed far fewer ordinations than might have been expected. The only pope of these decades who expressed a clear view on Gregory was Honorius, for whom he was a model.[12] Honorius made his devotion to Gregory patent in letters he sent to the Northumbrian king Edwin (616–633), in which he urged the king to devote much time to reading the works of 'your spiritual guide and my lord of apostolic memory', in the hope that the late pope's prayers would sustain both the kingdom and its people, and bring them faultless into the presence of God.[13] His own 'Life' in the *Liber Pontificalis* was deliberately modelled on that of Gregory, and as all the papal biographies between 537 and his own were compiled at this time, Honorius probably commissioned this extension of the work, which had been left untouched for a century. Thereafter it was kept up on a more or less regular basis, pontificate by pontificate.

This period saw important advances in the transformation of Rome into a Christian city. In 609 the emperor Phocas, who had overthrown Maurice in a military revolt in 602, allowed Boniface IV to transform the Pantheon, the pagan temple of all the gods, in the Campus Martius into a church. This was the first time that a former temple was reused as a church, as hitherto such buildings were reserved for exclusively secular functions. Phocas was revered by the papacy for decreeing, at the request of Boniface III, that Rome was the head of all churches.

Even more striking was the way in which Pope Honorius was able to turn the Senate House in the Forum, built by Diocletian, into the Church of St. Hadrian, thus incidentally ensuring the long-term survival of the building. We do not know when the Senate actually ceased to exist as a functioning institution, but it must have been before this loss of its former meeting place in 630.

On the other side of the Forum from the Senate is the Palatine Hill, which had housed the imperial palaces of successive dynasties since the foundation of the Roman empire under Augustus. Little new construction took place on it after the reign of Maxentius (306–312), but recent archaeological excavation has shown continuity of occupation of some of the earlier buildings, in particular the palace of Tiberius, now hidden under the Farnese gardens. Such partial reuse of buildings, with some sections being allowed to fall into ruins, is typical of the time, with similar examples being found throughout the city. The Palatine itself remained imperial property, and those parts of the old palace still in use probably housed the much-reduced civil government. However, some time around the 620s and 630s even these limited traces of occupation came to an end.[14]

What remained was the military organisation. Rome was the centre of an administrative district known as a *ducatum* or duchy, whose forces commanded by a *dux* or duke defended the region primarily against the Lombards. Communication with the imperial governor of Italy, the exarch, whose seat was in Ravenna, depended upon a single road across the Apennines, the Via Amerina, controlled by the fortress of Perugia, the capital of an intervening duchy. This town fell to the Lombards under Agilulf in the 590s but was regained by Pope Gregory through diplomacy, in which Queen Theodelinda again played a central part. Preserving it from further threat and keeping the road open were major concerns for the papacy during most of the two centuries that followed.

While the dux and his forces answered to the exarch, their regular maintenance depended on the Roman church, which had the facilities, including store houses, necessary to replace those of the now vanished civil administration. Keeping the regional army supplied and contented became increasingly important, as conditions in Italy were extremely turbulent, and not just because of the Lombards. The overthrow of Phocas in 610 by a military expedition sent by the exarch of Africa, Heraclius, which installed his son of the same name as emperor, initiated a period of political instability throughout the empire. This was intensified when the Persians overran most of the Eastern provinces. Syria fell to them in 612, then Jerusalem in 614 and Egypt in 616. By 626 a Persian army was encamped on the opposite shore of the Bosphorus to Constantinople itself.

Little imperial interest in the West could be expected, and the exarchates in Italy and Africa had to look to their own defence. Lack of pay caused mutinies, and local army commanders were tempted to create kingdoms for themselves or bid for the empire itself. Thus, in 619 a court eunuch called Eleutherius who was sent to punish mutineers who had killed the exarch in Ravenna and to suppress a revolt by the dux of Naples, had no sooner done so than he proclaimed himself ruler of Italy, only to be killed by members of another military unit, who sent his head to the emperor in token of their loyalty.[15] In Rome in 639, during a nineteen-month wait for the imperial confirmation of Pope Severinus, the troops of the duchy tried to break into the Lateran complex because they heard that the Church was holding up distribution of their pay. The exarch then spent eight days searching the buildings before upholding the soldiers' complaint, exiling several clerical administrators and confiscating much of what he found. The *Liber Pontificalis* called this looting and claimed the impounded goods had been intended for charitable distribution. Whatever the truth, it is clear that the popes of this time had to be adept diplomats and quartermasters as well as pastors. Their political loyalties could also be questioned, as we shall see.

THE GREEK POPES

The Persian conquests in the East ended as dramatically as they had begun, when the emperor Heraclius defeated the shah in 628 and threatened his capital, Ctesiphon near Baghdad. The lost provinces were recovered, and the relic of the True Cross that had been carried off by the Persians was restored to Jerusalem in 630. Although ultimately victorious the empire had been seriously weakened by thirty years of continuous warfare on virtually all fronts, with half of its territory lost to foreign invaders for most of that time. In the circumstances, the emperor and his advisors were keen to address what they saw as the causes of the recent disasters, which they identified as theological. The continuing division of the Church over the theology of the natures of Christ and the standing of the Council of Chalcedon was held to explain the temporary loss of divine favour so obviously demonstrated by the victories of the Persians.

Patriarch Sergius had been the hero of the defence of Constantinople in 626, when the city was threatened on the European shore by

Avar nomads from across the Danube and a Persian army encamped on the other side of the Bosphorus. His public appeals to the Virgin Mary to protect the city and the procession around the walls of her most popular icon raised the morale of the defenders, while, more mundanely, the imperial fleet stopped the Persians from bringing their siege technology to support their Avar allies.

After the war Sergius tried to heal the rift in the Eastern churches, negotiating the Pact of Union with the Armenian Monophysites in 630 and starting discussions with those in Antioch and Alexandria. His principal advisor was Cyrus, a bishop and imperial favourite from Lazica in the southern Caucasus, who developed the doctrine of Monoenergism, which allowed for the separation of the divine and human natures of Christ, as demanded by the defenders of Chalcedon, while preserving a single activity. In 631 Cyrus was transferred to the patriarchate of Alexandria, where his predecessor had already indicated a willingness to accept Chalcedon if interpreted in the light of Monoenergism. The Pact of Union, which included various key statements of Cyril of Alexandria, was accepted by the Egyptian Monophysites in 633.

General reconciliation looked possible until an influential Syrian monk, Sophronius, who had spent some years in Rome during the Persian occupation, objected to the new theology. Sergius and Cyrus tried to stifle debate, attempting to convince Pope Honorius that Monoenergism was compatible with the *Tome* of Leo the Great, the Roman See's touchstone of orthodoxy. Honorius was persuaded by their argument and not only wrote to congratulate Sergius but himself developed the doctrine of the single divine energy into that of a single divine will.

Part of the problem was the linguistic divide between Greek and Latin. Western theologians were increasingly deficient in their knowledge of Greek and so could not always follow the finer points of the arguments of their Eastern colleagues, which often turned on complex ideas and a nuanced technical vocabulary. Neither Leo the Great nor Gregory mastered this level of Greek, depending instead on Latin translations and other people's interpretations when following the debates in the East. It was the same with Honorius, who heard only one side of the argument. This changed in 634 when Sophronius was elected patriarch of Jerusalem and sent out a synodical letter to fellow metropolitans explaining why Monoenergism or Monotheletism (single-will theology) contradicted the decrees of Chalcedon. Honorius then sent Sergius a second, more hesitant letter but did not revoke his earlier support.

How Sophronius would have been dealt with is unknown, as dramatic events of another sort were now taking place in the East, with the first Arab attacks on the severely weakened empires of Rome and Persia being launched in 633. The emperor Heraclius was decisively defeated at the battle of Yarmuk in 636, and Jerusalem fell to Umar, the Arab caliph or Successor to the Prophet Muhammad, later the same year. In 640 Arab armies overran Egypt and in 642 took Alexandria, and the Patriarch Cyrus and the last imperial troops left the city. None of these territories would ever be recovered, and further losses followed. Apocalyptic fears grew, causing Pope Honorius to write in 638 to the Gothic king Chintila in Spain urging him and his bishops to be 'more robust on behalf of the faith and more eager in wiping out the pernicious heresies of the unfaithful'.[16]

In the same year Sergius of Constantinople persuaded the emperor to issue a document known as the *Ekthesis,* which contained much of the Pact of Union. Honorius died before a copy reached Rome, and the emperor Heraclius made confirmation of the new pope, Severinus, conditional upon his accepting the *Ekthesis.* As the pope-elect was reluctant, twenty months passed before a face-saving formula was agreed whereby the papal envoys in Constantinople promised to try to persuade him to agree in return for receiving the imperial document of confirmation. However, the new pope died two months after his consecration in May 640. His successors all refused to sign the *Ekthesis,* and in January 641 the theology behind it was condemned at a Roman synod under John IV (640–642).

By now Christian clergy and monks from the Eastern provinces conquered by the Arabs were fleeing westwards to Italy and North Africa, producing amongst other things the election of the first Greek pope, Theodore (642–649), who had come to Rome from Jerusalem. A disciple of Sophronius, who had died in 638, he was no more disposed to accept the *Ekthesis* than his predecessors. An equally determined opponent of the imperially sponsored theology was an Eastern monk, Maximus, who arrived in Africa in 642. There he won a public debate with a former patriarch of Constantinople, Pyrrhus (638–641), who had helped draft the *Ekthesis* but had subsequently fallen from favour. Following his victory Maximus moved on to Rome in 646.

By now the imperial government in Constantinople was in a weakened state. The dying Heraclius had left power in the hands of a terminally ill son and of his second wife. With her overthrow in 641 the throne passed to a grandson who was still a minor, while the fall of Alexandria in 642 was followed by further Arab expansion into Cyrenaica and Tripolitania, and in 646 the exarch of Africa who had hosted the debate between Maximus and Pyrrhus the previous year, declared himself emperor, only to be killed in battle with an Arab raiding force in 647.

Faced with a succession of such disasters and virulent theological controversies, in 647 or 648 the young emperor Constans II (641–668) and Patriarch Paul II of Constantinople tried to impose a solution in an edict called the *Typos* (Rule), which forbade any further discussion of the question of one or two divine wills or activities. But this was seen as suppressing orthodox doctrine along with heresy. As a contemporary noted, 'the Romans won't allow the illuminating statements of the holy Fathers to be annulled simultaneously with the expressions of impure heretics, or the truth to be snuffed out simultaneously with falsehood, or the light to perish simultaneously with darkness.'[17] Anastasius, the papal apocrisiarius in Constantinople, who refused to accept the new rule, was exiled to Trebizond. Opinion in Rome remained hostile, and the 649 election of Pope Martin I, a former apocrisiarius and opponent of Monotheletism, reflected this animosity.

The new pope did not request the usual imperial confirmation and continued planning a larger than usual synod in Rome later in the year, aimed at debating the very topics on which the emperor had commanded silence. Defied, the emperor ordered his exarch, Olympius, to arrest the pope or even assassinate him, but finding opinion in the city so strongly in support of Martin, he failed to do either and instead seized power in Italy for himself. Olympius did not challenge Constans II in the East but may have intended reviving the old Western empire. The pope probably recognised his rule, as silver coins were issued in Rome in 651/2 in the name of the usurper.[18]

The synod of 105 bishops called by Martin I met in the Lateran Basilica in October 649 and condemned the *Ekthesis,* the *Typos* and all the recent patriarchs of Constantinople. In practice the bishops may have been asked to do little more than endorse a series of canons prepared in advance by the pope and Maximus, who now advised Martin, as he had Theodore. The acts of the synod include several passages from Maximus' own writings and had been written in Greek before being translated into Latin for discussion by the bishops. Even if stage-managed, the synod's decisions were an impressive Western rejection of the theology favoured in Constantinople and the emperor's attempt to stifle debate.

Copies of the synod's decrees were sent to other bishops who had not been present to secure a general condemnation of Monotheletism, though surprisingly the acts of the council did not reach England until 679 and are not recorded in Spain.[19] Art was also used to promote the decisions of the synod, with the Church of Santa Maria Antiqua in the Roman Forum being redecorated with frescoes depicting Church fathers holding scrolls on which were painted key texts that had been quoted in its acts.

However well orchestrated this papal reaction may have been, political events proved stronger. The empire began to recover militarily and economically in the early 650s. In 652 the usurper Olympius died, and an expedition was sent to restore imperial control in Italy. A new exarch, Theodore Calliopas, entered Rome without resistance in June 653 and occupied the old imperial palace on the Palatine. Two weeks later, having lulled him into a false sense of security, Calliopas arrested Pope Martin in the middle of celebrating Mass in the Lateran on a charge of treason. The pope was whisked out of the city in the middle of the night and put on a boat for Constantinople, where he arrived complaining that he had been prevented from washing for forty-seven days.[20]

The first charge against the pope was that he had conspired with Olympius, but it was further alleged that he had sent letters, money and even a theological treatise to the Arabs. In a letter to a friend, Martin denied all these accusations. He admitted that he had sent charitable donations to help monks and clergy suffering as a result of the conquests but could not see how these might have fallen into the hands of the Arabs. All in all, he felt what was happening to him was a sign of the onset of the disasters foretold as preceding the coming of the Antichrist.[21]

Although in his letters he called Olympius 'infamous', one of the usurper's officers was prepared to testify that the pope had supported his revolt. On arrival in Constantinople Martin was held in prison for three months before being tried before the Senate and sentenced to death. However, at the intervention of Patriarch Paul II of Constantinople (641–653), then on his death bed, this was commuted to a public flogging, followed by exile to the Crimea, where the pope died in 655 or 656. He had hoped that the Roman clergy would not elect a successor during his lifetime and sent a message to say that the see should be administered by the senior priest, the senior deacon and the head of the papal bureaucracy, during his absence. But Eugenius I, an elderly Roman priest, was elected pope in August 654, while Martin still lived.

Resentment in Rome over the emperor's support for Monotheletism and his treatment of the pope ran deep. Eugenius tried to restore communion with the new patriarch of Constantinople, Peter (654–666), but his room for manoeuvre was limited by popular opinion in the city. When a synodical letter containing a compromise formula that papal envoys had agreed with the patriarch was read out to the assembled clergy and laity in Santa Maria Maggiore, there was uproar, and the pope was forced to reject it. By late 656 envoys from the emperor and the patriarch were threatening the pope with the fate of his predecessor, but he died before action was taken. His successor, Vitalian (657–672), was much more conciliatory, not objecting to the patriarch's synodal letter and immediately restoring communion with Constantinople. No mention was made of the Lateran Synod of 649.

In the meantime Martin I's advisor Maximus, also removed to Constantinople after the imperial recovery of Rome, had been put on trial in 655. We have a detailed if partisan account of the hearing, written like an early martyr act, in which he was accused of betraying 'Egypt, Alexandria, Pentapolis and Africa to the Saracens'. The testimony offered in support of this extraordinary charge came from a military treasurer who said his general had asked for Maximus' blessing when planning an expedition against the Arabs, only to be told that 'God did not approve lending aid to the Roman empire during the reign of Heraclius and his kin.'[22]

Despite the seriousness of the charges, which illustrate how theology, politics and military success intertwined in these centuries, Maximus was just exiled to Thrace, from where he tried unsuccessfully to dissuade Pope Vitalian from compromising with Constantinople. His interference led to his being put on trial again in 662, along with the former papal apocrisiarius Anastasius and other disciples. This time the eighty-year-old Maximus was flogged, had his tongue and right hand cut off (symbolic punishment for speaking and writing treason), and was exiled to Lazica in the Caucasus, where he soon died. Similar penalties were imposed on Anastasius and the others.

Pope Vitalian received Constans II in Rome in 663. The emperor had aroused so much popular hostility in Constantinople through murdering his younger brother in 660 that he decided to move to the West and established himself in Sicily. In Rome, following an unsuccessful campaign against the Lombards and short of money to pay his troops, Constans ordered the gilded bronze tiles be stripped from the roof of the former Pantheon, although it was now the Church of St. Mary ad Martyres. He also removed the statue of Trajan from the top of his column, while members of his court carved his name on a number of monuments around the city, on which it can still be seen. Further offence was given to the papacy in 666 when the emperor made the metropolitan see of Ravenna autocephalous or free of the need for papal approval before a new bishop could be consecrated. Returning to his new capital of Syracuse, Constans II was murdered in his bath in 668, aged only thirty, during an abortive military coup.

Vitalian's immediate refusal to recognise the usurper in Syracuse and his support for the murdered emperor's young son Constantine IV (668–685) proved far-sighted, as the rebel was quickly eliminated and the new ruler was grateful. He reversed his father's decision on the status of the see of Ravenna, and in 682 it was made entirely subordinate to Rome. The emperor also proved much less keen than his father on enforcing the *Typos*. Since Alexandria, Antioch and Jerusalem were now firmly under Muslim rule, restoring unanimity between the two patriarchates of 'the old and the new Romes' became more important than healing the rift between the Eastern ones.

If Monoenergism or Monotheletism was no more than an ill–conceived theological fudge, solely intended to produce a probably unsustainable reconciliation between Chalcedonians and Monophysites, it is hard to understand why its supporters proved so obdurate when the emperor turned against it. But it was not intellectually untenable, and there were issues of loyalty involved. Rejection of it involved the condemnation of a line of patriarchs going back to the highly revered Sergius I. However, this is what Constantine IV now required, and he finally got his way by deposing three recalcitrant patriarchs in succession, before installing the more malleable George (679–686). A new ecumenical council was planned, to restore harmony between Rome and Constantinople and put an end to Monotheletism.

In Rome the council was supported by a new pope, Agatho (678–681), who mobilised Western metropolitans to hold synods confirming their orthodoxy. One result was a meeting of bishops of the Frankish kingdom of Neustria and Burgundy in September 679. Better documented is the Synod of Hatfield (in what is now Hertfordshire), held the same month and attended by the bishops of the Anglo-Saxon kingdoms, under the presidency of Archbishop Theodore of Canterbury. A native Greek speaker from Tarsus, living as a refugee in Rome, he had been sent to England by Pope Vitalian in 668. His Synod of Hatfield confirmed its acceptance of the decrees of the councils of Nicaea, I Constantinople, I Ephesus, Chalcedon, II Constantinople and 'the synod in the city of Rome in the time of the most blessed Pope Martin'.[23]

Pope Agatho sent seven representatives to the ecumenical council, one of whom later wrote the life of the pope in the *Liber Pontificalis* and included an eyewitness account of some of the proceedings. This Sixth General Council or Third Council of Constantinople opened in November 680 and continued intermittently until September 681. The papal legates brought a letter to the council from the pope and the acts of a synod of 125 bishops recently held in Rome.

If Agatho's letters to the emperor and council never achieved the iconic status of the *Tome* of Leo the Great, it was not for lack of trying, in that they cited a weighty array of authorities in support of the pope's definition of the faith. The pope presented St. Peter to the emperor as 'the co-worker of your most pious labours' and stressed the Petrine tradition of faith that was passed on unchanging by the Apostle's successors. Adherence to this immutable doctrine was also presented as the sine qua non of military victory: 'This is the living tradition of the Apostles of Christ . . . which keeps the Christian empire of your Clemency, which gives far-reaching victories to your most pious Fortitude from the Lord of heaven, which accompanies you in battle and defeats your foes.'[24] Constantine IV's recent defeat by the nomad Bulgars and resulting loss of much imperial territory in the eastern Balkans may have added potency to this claim.

Agatho played up the resolute orthodoxy of his predecessors, referring to Christ's promise to Peter that his faith would never fail, and how this had been handed on to 'the Apostolic pontiffs, the predecessors of my littleness'.[25] He made no reference to Pope Honorius, whose authority, along with that of Cyril of Alexandria, was claimed by the Monotheletes in their presentations to the council. As with previous ecumenical councils, the assembled bishops formulated their own view before allowing the reading of the papal letter on 15 February 681 and then acclaimed it because it concurred with what they had decided was orthodox, rather than allowing it to define orthodoxy for them. When ten days later the leading Monotheletes were condemned and physically thrown out of the council, a Roman observer noted 'at that point so many jet-black spiderwebs fell among the people that everyone was astonished at the filth of the heresies being expelled.'[26]

The outcome was satisfactory in most respects, in that the *Ekthesis* and *Typos,* and the patriarchs of Constantinople from Sergius onwards, were definitively condemned. So too were the Monothelete patriarch of Antioch and several prominent monks, who were sent to the pope to be instructed in true doctrine. As they remained obdurate they were imprisoned in monasteries in Rome. There was, however, a price for the papacy to pay for this great victory. When in the final session the bishops shouted acclamations in praise of the emperors, Senate and leading metropolitans, and anathemas against heretics, these included both 'Many years to Agatho, Pope of Rome!' and 'To Honorius the heretic, anathema!'[27] For Pope Agatho the sentiment came too late. He had died in January 681. Although the news had reached Constantinople by May, the Roman legates there were putting up a lengthy resistance to the posthumous condemnation of Honorius, which threatened the papacy's claim to be the source and defender of Apostolic tradition. To break the deadlock, the emperor refused to confirm the pope-elect, Leo II (682–683), until agreement had been secured. So, Agatho was wished a long life although dead, and Leo was not consecrated until August 682, following his acceptance of the council's judgement that one of his predecessors was a heretic. In a letter sent to Constantine IV in May 683, Leo II said of Honorius that he 'had not brightened this apostolic see with the teaching of the apostolic tradition, but dared to subvert the immaculate faith by profane treachery'.[28] But in writing to bishops in the West he was less critical of this successor of St. Peter.

chapter 7

THE KEYS OF THE KINGDOM

(687–799)

ROME AND CONSTANTINOPLE

I n 680, plague devastated Rome. According to a contemporary, 'Parents and their children, brothers and their sisters, were taken in pairs on biers to their graves.'[1] It carried off Pope Agatho in January 681 and caused the short pontificates of his successors.[2] It reappeared in Constantinople in 698 and spread all across the Mediterranean.

The Roman empire was a third the size it had been a century before. The greatest losses occurred in the East, caused by the Arab invasions from 635 onwards, but much of the western Balkans and northern Greece were colonised by the Slavs, and the Lombard conquests in Italy proved equally irreversible. Further shrinkage followed, with the Bulgars overrunning the eastern Balkans in 680 and the Arabs completing their conquest of the African provinces in 698.

In light of Pope Agatho's letter to Constantine IV in 680 describing Christ as the emperor's 'colleague in reigning' and promising Constantine military victory because of his loyalty to the apostolic tradition, these disasters needed explaining. The unchecked presence of heresy was an obvious answer, and the popes were not alone in making such a connection: The Monothelete controversy was so protracted and bitter because both sides felt that only their success would please God.

Such feelings were not confined to the clerical elite. A military coup in 711 installed an emperor of Armenian origin, Philippicus, who was so committed to Monotheletism that he began his reign by destroying an icon depicting the Sixth Ecumenical Council of 680/1. When he sent a decree to Rome containing Monothelete statements, Pope Constantine refused to receive it.

More significantly, the inhabitants of Rome also refused to recognise the new emperor, saying they would not accept his laws, use his name to date documents or employ his coins as legal tender.[3] An icon depicting all of the Ecumenical Councils, including the Sixth, was set up by pope and people in St. Peter's as a further sign of resistance. Never before had the city or its bishop so defied an emperor over an issue of theology. Philippicus did not last long, being deposed in a coup in 713, but the Roman reaction to him marks an important stage in the erosion of papal loyalty to the emperors in Constantinople.

Equally apparent was the growing political loyalty to the popes, and not just in Rome. Since the mid-sixth century, emperors had deposed popes at will. But this was increasingly resented, and Martin I, exiled by Constans II in 653, became a symbol of resistance. Pope John VII (705–707) included a painting of Martin in the Church of Santa Maria Antiqua, part of the bishop's palace he built on the Palatine Hill, depicting Martin as a martyr, although he had been condemned as a traitor to the emperor whose grandson was then ruling in Constantinople.

Emperors still expected papal obedience, but after Martin this could no longer be obtained forcibly. Justinian II (685–695 and 705–711) called a council in Constantinople in 691, attended by papal delegates who signed the acts. The pope, Sergius I (687–701), however, refused even to open the box containing a copy of its decrees sent to him to sign, because they included such 'novel errors' as more lenient treatment of clerics who married widows or took second wives, ignoring the fifth-century rulings of Pope Leo the Great. Leo's memory was particularly revered in the papal household at this time, and a new collection of his sermons was issued, highlighting his views on Rome's unique Petrine authority.

When Sergius persisted in refusing to sign, the emperor sent Zacharias, the head of the imperial bodyguard, to arrest him. However, when units of the army of the exarch of Italy and of the Roman duchy discovered what was happening, they mutinied to stop the pope being carried off to Constantinople, and the terrified Zacharias had to hide under the pope's bed and be taken under Sergius' protection, before being ejected from the city 'with injuries and insults'.[4]

In 695 Justinian II was deposed in a coup, something the author of the 'Life of Sergius' attributed to the emperor's treatment of the pope,[5] though he was restored ten years later. Rome's refusal to accept his council of 691 remained an unresolved issue. The emperor seemed conciliatory, asking John VII to confirm just those of its decrees he accepted, but the pope returned the document without comment or signature.[6] After the short-lived Sisinnius (708), who suffered so badly with arthritis that he could not feed himself, Constantine I (708–715) became pope, the first to include an ordination ceremony of crowning with a mitre.

In 710 Justinian summoned Constantine to Constantinople, and in October he set out with a substantial retinue, including the *secundicerius,* the deputy chief of the papal bureaucracy, the *sacellarius* or paymaster, the head of the papal bodyguards known as the *defensores* (defenders), and the *nomenclator*, the master of ceremonies of the papal court. Soon after the pope's departure a new exarch arrived in Rome and beheaded four other leading members of the papal entourage, including the *vicedominus,* in charge of the papal palace, the *arcarius,* keeper of the treasury, and the *ordinator,* or deputy *nomenclator*. We do not know why they were executed, but all these titles give us insight into the organisation of the papal household, which was modelled on the emperor's.

This is not the only evidence of Eastern influence in Rome at this time. The Arab conquests and the Slav settlements in the Balkans led to many refugees arriving in Italy, including communities of monks. Several of these were established in Rome by sympathetic popes, and numerous Greek-speaking monastic houses were founded, especially around the Aventine Hill. A second Greek and Syrian migration took place around 661 when Constans II began settling military units in Sicily and southern Italy, as part of his plan to move the imperial government to the West. The exarchs and other senior officials were almost always sent to Italy from the East.

Several popes of the period were sons of officers and civil officials of Eastern origin. Pope Conon (686–687) was the son of an officer from Thrace, brought up in Sicily. John V (685–686) was born in Syria. Sergius (687–701) was of Syrian origin, but born in Sicily, and the father of John VII had been the custodian of the imperial palaces in Rome. In fact, virtually every pope between 678 (Agatho) and 772 (Stephen III) was of Eastern origin or came from Sicily, where Greek was the dominant language of the social elite. Greek was used in several monasteries in Rome and appears in inscriptions and on wall paintings in the city throughout this period.

Constantinople gave Constantine a magnificent reception: He was escorted into the city by the emperor's son Tiberius.[7] Further ceremonies marked the ensuing meeting with Justinian: The emperor kissed the pope's feet, and Constantine subsequently celebrated Mass for Justinian and his court. All existing papal privileges, such as the freedom from the need for imperial confirmation before a pope could be enthroned that had been granted by Constantine IV in 681, were confirmed. As for the council of 691, the pope accepted the offer of confirming only those canons that Rome found acceptable.

Justinian II was entirely redeemed in papal eyes and was called 'the Christian and orthodox emperor'.[8] Pope Constantine returned to Rome in October 711. Soon came the news that Justinian and his son had been killed in a revolt and a Monothelete, Philippicus (711–713), had succeeded him. In 717 the Arabs began a year-long siege of Constantinople, which had it succeeded might have destroyed the empire.

HOLY IMAGES

Out of this period of political instability and military threat emerged the new imperial dynasty of the Isaurians, founded by Leo III (717–741), a general from the Syrian frontier. His success in holding the capital, largely thanks to the secret weapon known as Greek Fire, and in restoring order reopened the question of why God had permitted the Christian empire to suffer such disasters. A new theological explanation was suggested: the empire's defiance of the Second Commandment by its worship of images.

It was an issue with a long history. Bishop Epiphanius of Salamis (died 404) had insisted that depicting Christ and the saints in art was idolatrous, but, in the late fourth and early fifth centuries, a distinctive Christian iconography emerged, one we are familiar with today, including Christ with long hair and beard and St. Peter with short curly white hair and beard.[9]

The veneration of saints, not least the martyrs of the persecutions, grew in popularity, as did their role as intercessors and intermediaries between the worshiper and the court of heaven. Painted images of the saints, known as icons, became channels of communication between believers and the object of their reverence, and some particularly prominent ones served as talismans of a city's security and prosperity, as when the icon of the Virgin Hodegetria was carried round the walls of Constantinople during the Avar siege of 626.[10]

There remained a current of opposition to images in some Christian circles, especially in this period in the eastern frontier provinces, so it was not surprising that the new Syrian-born emperor, Leo III, regarded the image-venerating traditions of Constantinople and his Western territories as the explanation of the empire's recent catastrophes. Assisted by clerics who shared his view he attempted to eradicate the devotion to icons, inflaming an already combustible situation in Italy, where opposition to the empire was running high over taxes.

In 715 Constantine had been succeeded by Gregory II (715–731), one of the few native Roman popes of the period. Born in 669, he was highly experienced, having served under Pope Sergius as the first recorded holder of the offices of *sacellarius* (paymaster) and *bibliothecarius* or librarian (actually meaning head of the papal administration), and as deacon he had accompanied his predecessor to Constantinople. As pope he followed the lead of his namesake, Gregory the Great, turning his family home into a monastery. He restored several monasteries and churches in and around Rome. Like his predecessor Sisinnius, he ordered lime for repairing the city walls, a process that, alas, involved the burning of antique marble statues and fittings.[11]

The need for restoring the city's defences was acute with the empire so weak, but Gregory also relied on diplomacy to restrain the

Lombards, now ruled by Liutprand (712–744). Although usually described in imperial and papal correspondence as 'unspeakable' and barbaric, the Lombards recognised that their kingdom needed to co-exist with both empire and papacy in Italy. They had abandoned Arianism in the mid-seventh century and recognised the patriarchal authority of the pope in Italy. Even their more powerful kings, such as Liutprand, were reluctant to try and take over Rome and its lands.

For the emperor Leo III, the empire's weakened economic state in the early 720s meant that Italy should pay for its own defence, and so he increased the tax on land, including that owned by the Church. Because the see of Rome was the greatest landowner in Italy, Gregory, busy with his programmes of restoration, protested, inspiring members of the secular elite throughout imperial territories in Italy to do the same, leading to a taxpayers' strike. For the first time a pope had become a figurehead in political resistance to an emperor on an issue that was not theological.

In 724 Leo instigated a plot to murder Gregory, but it was uncovered, and the conspirators were immediately lynched by the Roman mob, further proof of the pope's popularity. In 725, the exarch Paul marched on Rome, only to be faced outside the city by the armies of the duchy of Rome and the Lombard dukes of Spoleto and Benevento, and forced to retreat. The Roman troops blinded their own duke for his involvement in the plot and invaded the neighboring duchy of Campania, killing its duke and his son because they had backed the imperial cause. All this precipitated a revolt in Ravenna and the murder of the exarch.

Although this sounds like a papally inspired nationalist revolt, Gregory remained loyal to the empire throughout his pontificate, as did his immediate successors. The crisis evaporated, and when in 729 a new exarch formed an alliance with Liutprand, enabling the king to impose his authority on the Lombard dukes of Spoleto and Benevento, Rome's recent allies, the imperial army entered Rome without resistance, the tax question having been settled.

However, the argument over image veneration was coming to a head, after Leo sent letters to Gregory in 726 to win his support. The papal replies may have been preserved in the acts of the Second

Council of Nicaea of 787, which reversed the iconoclast or image-destroying policies of the Isaurian emperors. In the first of these, Gregory insisted that Christian doctrine could not be dictated by secular rulers.[12] The contrasting view of absolute imperial authority over the Church emerges clearly from Leo's letter, in which he had stated: *Imperator sum et sacerdos* (I am emperor and priest).[13] The pope rejected this contention, adding, 'emperors who lived pious lives hardly ever objected to obeying pontiffs.'[14]

From the early fourth century, the Eastern churches had felt that Church and empire were interdependent and that imperial power was essential in directing Christian society. The patriarchs of Constantinople only refused to cooperate with the emperors when they interfered in doctrinal questions, as these could only be changed with the consent of all churches expressed through a council. So, when in January 730 Leo III tried to persuade Patriarch Germanus of Constantinople to support publicly his opposition to image veneration, the reply came back: 'If I am Jonah, cast me into the sea. For without an ecumenical council it is impossible for me, O emperor, to innovate in matters of faith.'[15]

True to the Eastern traditions of not resisting imperial authority, Germanus accepted his own immediate deposition and retired to his family estates. Because a mixed assembly of lay and clerical notables, and not a church council, had carried out the deposition, the pope held it to be invalid and regarded the emperor's new patriarch, Anastasius (730–754), as a usurper. Gregory II refused to accept Anastasius' letter announcing his appointment, and so Rome and Constantinople were out of communion when Gregory died in February 731.

His successor, an elderly priest of Syrian origin who became Gregory III (731–741), was chosen in a most unusual way: by popular acclamation during the funeral of his predecessor. Boniface III (607–608) had decreed that there should be no discussion of the succession to a pope while he was still living, and that the election of a new one should take place three days after burial of the old one. By the late 680s the army of the duchy of Rome had joined the clergy and the populace as a third constituent of the body of electors, though we still do not know how the process was carried out in practice. The late seventh century saw several disputed elections, usually with majority groups in the clergy and the army supporting rival candidates, who were normally the senior priest and the senior deacon. But in 731 Gregory III was chosen by 'the whole people from the greatest to the least' while standing by the bier of Gregory II. Spontaneous acclamation thereafter became a recognised alternative to formal election, even in later centuries when the process of selection was restricted to the College of Cardinals.[16]

Gregory III resembled his predecessor in more than name. He sent letters to the emperor announcing his election but also condemning iconoclasm and the treatment of Germanus. These were carried by a priest called George, who became so frightened by the hostile atmosphere in Constantinople that he returned them undelivered. Although Gregory thought of unfrocking him for his feebleness, the pope was persuaded to let him off with a penance: going back to Constantinople with an even more robust condemnation of the emperor. This time the unfortunate priest got no further than Sicily, where he was detained for a year by the governor.

The same fate befell the next papal messenger, carrying the acts of a large synod of ninety-three Italian bishops that had met in November 731 and decreed, 'if anyone thenceforth . . . should remove, destroy, profane and blaspheme against the sacred images of our God and Lord Jesus Christ, of his mother the ever-virgin immaculate and glorious Mary, of the blessed apostles and of all the saints, let him be driven forth from the body and blood of Our Lord Jesus Christ and from the unity and membership of the entire church.'[17] Other papal letters and appeals from Italian bishops and civic leaders were similarly intercepted on their way to Constantinople, as they had to be delivered to become legally effective.

Some papal letters were eventually smuggled into Constantinople, and in 733 the emperor Leo III decided to crush resistance in Italy. He sent a fleet with reinforcements for the exarch, only to lose it in a storm in the Adriatic. Further such losses could not be contemplated, and Leo turned to other methods, transferring ownership of all of the papal estates in Sicily, southern Italy and the western Balkans to the patriarchate of Constantinople. This vastly reduced the economic resources of the Roman see, leaving it dependent on what it owned in the duchy of Rome.

For all the bitterness of the theological conflict and the loss of properties, Gregory III remained loyal to the emperor in secular matters. In 733 he persuaded the Lombard king to hand back Ravenna, which Liutprand had just captured from the exarch. Recognising the obvious military weakness of the imperial territories in Italy and the inability of the exarch to defend them, Gregory also completed the project begun by his predecessor of restoring the walls of Rome. He then made treaties for mutual defence against Liutprand with the Lombard dukes of Spoleto and Benevento, but this led the king to invade the duchy of Rome in 739 and seize four key fortress towns to frighten the pope into breaking with the dukes, whom he regarded as rebels. Fearing that Liutprand's real aim was the capture of Rome itself, Gregory now appealed for assistance to the new ruler of the Franks, with remarkable consequences for all involved. To understand this we need to move a little further back in time, to see how the papacy became involved in a major act of regime change in Francia, not least thanks to some Anglo-Saxon missionaries.

The Frankish Connection

Although Gregory the Great had exchanged letters with the kings of the Franks around the time of Augustine's mission to Kent in 596, the loss of so much subsequent papal correspondence means we do not know how far this contact was maintained thereafter. However, the practice of the archbishops of Canterbury of coming in person to receive the *pallium,* a white woollen stole given by the popes to favoured metropolitans, was one of several ways through which the papal household kept informed about what was happening in Francia. The accounts of pilgrims coming to Rome in ever larger numbers from England and from Ireland, together with those of merchants, and the occasional diplomatic exchanges and letters from Gallic bishops and from the stewards of the papal estates in Provence, all combined to provide the papacy with intelligence on the rising power of the Frankish kingdoms.

Some of the travellers came to Rome to die close to the tombs of the Apostles, as did King Coenred of Mercia in the time of Pope Constantine I (708–715). But most visitors from Britain returned home, taking with them information about Roman practices. One frequent visitor was the Northumbrian abbot Benedict Biscop, founder of the joint monastery of Wearmouth-Jarrow in which Bede lived. He made five visits to Rome and southern Gaul, studying monastic life and buying a large number of books.

Biscop returned from his trip in 666 accompanied by Abbot John the Arch-chanter or singing master of St. Peter's in Rome, who was to introduce Roman liturgy and chant into the monasteries of Wearmouth and Jarrow. As Bede noted, the liturgical manuscripts John prepared 'have been preserved to this day in the monastery and copies have been made by many others elsewhere'.[18] So Roman forms of worship began to spread widely in England. John was also there on the orders of Pope Agatho to serve as his representative at the synod that Archbishop Theodore held at Hatfield and ensure that Anglo-Saxon theology was as sound as its singing.

Although only those in the southeast of the island had been founded by Roman missionaries, by the mid-seventh century all of the churches in the Anglo-Saxon kingdoms looked to the papacy for guidance. This was made clear at the Synod of Whitby in 664 in which adherence to the customs of Rome in calculating the date of Easter was given absolute priority by the king of the Northumbrians in a dispute between rival traditions. Clerics who then persisted in sticking with the Irish practice, which ironically was itself of older Roman origin, were expelled from the kingdom, as they would subsequently be from that of the Picts. However, in 715 the schism was ended when Iona and the other monasteries founded by Columba (died 597) in Ireland finally adopted Roman practices.

The strong Roman influence on the Anglo-Saxon churches was particularly important when they in turn began to become involved in missionary ventures on the continent from the late seventh century onwards. The main inspiration for such ventures was Irish, but the ecclesiastical authority behind them was Roman, and in the secular sphere Frankish. The peoples of the lands east of the Rhine in which the Anglo-Saxon missionaries worked had long been regarded by the Frankish kings as their subjects, even though this ceased to be a reality around 650. However, Frankish military weakness began to be reversed from 687 onwards when control passed into the hands of an aristocratic faction led by members of the Arnulfing family, later to be called the Carolingians. Several of them became interested in Christianising these territories hand in hand with their conquest, not least as this made these lands more open to Frankish cultural influences and political control.

In 690 Frisia, on the North Sea coast east of the Rhine, became the first major overseas mission field for the Anglo-Saxons, led by a Northumbrian priest called Wilibrord. He requested support from both the Arnulfing duke Pippin II, who was trying to conquer the region, and Pope Sergius I. From a visit to Rome to get papal approval, he also brought back relics of Roman martyrs for the churches he hoped to found in Frisia. From the sixth century, depositing such relics under the altar of a new church was part of the ritual of consecration. Successive popes had sent such relics to England throughout the seventh century, and Wilibrord's choice was another sign of the strong Roman influence behind these missions. In 696, at the request of Pippin II, now the political overlord of Frisia, Wilibrord was ordained archbishop of the Frisians in Rome by Sergius I, and given the old Roman fortress of Utrecht as his base.

The death of Pippin II in 714 precipitated a Frisian revolt, and as Christianity was intimately associated with Frankish overlordship, Wilibrord and his clergy had to flee. He died in his monastery at Echternach (in what is now Luxembourg) in 739, having failed to make much further headway in Frisia. However, the connections his work had established between the Frankish leaders, the Anglo-Saxon missionaries and the papacy were of enormous importance for the future, as demonstrated by the subsequent career of one of his followers. This was a West Saxon priest called Winfrith, who worked in Frisia in 716 before seeking a new missionary area for himself further south. For this he visited Rome in 719 to obtain the consent of Gregory II, and he was in Rome again in 722 to be consecrated a missionary bishop, under the new name of Boniface, given him by the pope.

He was raised to the rank of archbishop by Gregory III in 732, enabling him to restore or found subordinate episcopal sees under his authority, and was made papal vicar of Germania, using old Roman nomenclature.

The intention behind Boniface's promotion was that a new ecclesiastical province would be created east of the Rhine, following Roman traditions and free of the vices then thought to be infecting the Church in Francia. However, this depended on the maintaining of Frankish hegemony over these lands, and continued local resistance for much of the 730s and 740s made this impossible. Particularly resistant were the Saxons, who were only finally subdued by the Franks in 804. Boniface had long hoped to convert these 'Old Saxons', whom he saw as his continental cousins. In 738 Pope Gregory III even sent them a letter urging them to accept Christ through Boniface's preaching, but his Frankish backing made this impossible. Instead he turned south to Bavaria, where in 739 as papal vicar he created a network of four new dioceses for its duke, Odilo. This completed a plan made by Gregory II in 716, when Duke Theoto of the Bavarians had been the first of his dynasty to visit Rome.

Although he was committed to missionary work, Boniface's main role in the 730s and 740s was as an agent of papally inspired reform in Francia. He provided disturbing accounts to successive popes of the state of the Frankish church, noting in 742 that no episcopal synod had been held in the Frankish kingdoms for over eighty years, that 'so-called deacons have spent their lives since boyhood in debauchery, adultery and every kind of filthiness' and that 'certain bishops are to be found among them who, although they deny that they are fornicators or adulterers, are drunkards and shiftless men, given to hunting and to fighting in the army like soldiers and by their own hand shedding blood, whether of heathens or Christians.'[19] Overall, previous structures of ecclesiastical organisation in Gaul had collapsed, and there were now no metropolitans at all in the Frankish kingdoms. If Boniface exaggerated, it was only by a little. The last synod of the Frankish church of which we are aware had been held around 696, fifty years earlier, and the previous bishop of Mainz had been killed leading an attack on the Saxons. His son, Gewillib, succeeded him in office and as well as seeking revenge on the Saxons was a major obstacle to Boniface's missionary activities across the Rhine.

The key to progress was the attitude of the Frankish rulers. It is fortunate that a collection of Boniface's letters was made after his death (he was killed by pagans in Frisia in 754), as it includes several of his exchanges with the popes from Gregory II (715–731) to Stephen II (752–757), as well as messages from them to Frankish and Bavarian rulers. As so few papal letters of the period have survived in other contexts, these are especially valuable, not least for hints at yet other communications now lost. The missionary activities of Boniface and other Anglo-Saxons provided an opportunity for papal correspondence with the Arnulfings, who emerged as the de facto rulers of all of Francia after 719. That this family's new power rested on no secure constitutional foundation, requiring them to use the last kings of the Merovingian dynasty as mouthpieces for their decisions, made them more open to papal influence than had been the case in the seventh century.

Under Charles Martel (died 741) little was achieved, as his military needs took priority, and he later became unfairly notorious for his use of ecclesiastical property to reward his followers. But his sons Pippin III and Carloman were left in a stronger position by his campaigns, which had made him dominant in Francia and across the Rhine. Carloman (741–747), who inherited control over the eastern territories, proved particularly interested in revitalising the Frankish church under the direction of Boniface. Synods began to be held annually, and their decisions were sent to Rome. Boniface's own position was to be regularised, after the failure to establish a new metropolitan province east of the Rhine, by his transfer to the ancient archiepiscopal see of Cologne. This hung fire, like many of the reforms, due to inertia and opposition from vested interests, and instead in 745 he was installed in Mainz by a synod that deposed the irreconcilable Gewillib.

Carloman's brother Pippin III, who became a keen patron of the Monastery of Saint-Denis outside Paris, opened his own channel of communication with the papacy, in 747 requesting a code of canon law from Rome. What he received from Pope Zacharias (741–752) was a selection of twenty-seven canons taken from the collection of conciliar decrees and papal decretals made for Pope Hormisdas (514–523) by a monk known as Dionysius Exiguus (the Small).[20]

The same year saw major political change in Francia, when Carloman abdicated to become a monk in Italy. He left his territories to his young son Drogo, but within months Pippin III had overthrown his nephew with the backing of Boniface, among others.[21] Although still facing a variety of opponents, this coup led Pippin to another, more daring one: taking the throne in his own name. In 749 he sent the bishop of Würzburg and the abbot of Saint-Denis to consult Pope Zacharias on the legitimacy of deposing the last of the Merovingian line of kings, who had ruled the Franks since the late fifth century. According to a slightly later Frankish source, the pope ruled that 'it was better to call the one who had royal power king rather than the one who did not.'[22] Although the ensuing replacement of the last Merovingian by Pippin III depended primarily on the factional politics of the Frankish aristocracy, the papal response to the new monarch's enquiry was cited as the formal justification for it. It is highly unlikely that Zacharias thought he was authorising the resulting change of dynasty through his rather ambiguous response, but this episode would later be seen by theorists of papal power as proof of the pope's right to depose a secular ruler.

FRANKS TO THE RESCUE

Pippin III lost interest in church reform after the abdication of his brother in 747. Regular synods stopped and Boniface was sidelined. However, the papacy now needed the new Frankish monarch for other reasons. The Lombards' threat to Rome had declined during the decade, until their king Ratchis (744–749) retired to a monastery. He may have been deposed by the Lombards for failing to take Perugia in 749, possibly because Pope Zacharias asked him to lift the siege. His successor Aistulf had to prove himself more successful, which he did by conquering Ravenna and the remaining territory of the exarchate in the northeast of Italy in 751.

Other threats to the papal duchy had also been growing, with Arab raiders reported near Rome in the 730s.[23] No help could be expected from the much-weakened empire, now facing annual incursions by Arab armies and its own internal divisions. Leo III's son and successor, Constantine V (741–776), was an even more ardent iconoclast than his father and was also closing monasteries and forcing monks to marry because of their opposition to his policy. A hostile chronicler later called him 'a forerunner of the Antichrist' and claimed that when being baptised as a baby, he had defecated into the font, a sign of how much evil he would do the Church.[24] Even so, relations between pope and emperor improved in the 740s. Constantine V gave two imperial estates near Rome to the Church as a partial compensation for the lost papal lands in Sicily and the Balkans.[25] Overall, the popes remained faithful subjects of the emperors in secular matters: Their letters continued being dated by the years of imperial reigns, and gold coins were issued by the mint of Rome in the emperors' names. Gregory III and Zacharias struck small square bronze pieces bearing their own names and titles, producing what was probably the first papal coinage.[26] However, gold issues remained an imperial monopoly and their being struck in Rome in the name of the emperors was a sign of the continuing political loyalty of the papacy. Even so, some alternative military assistance was urgently needed.

Charles Martel had not responded to the appeals of Gregory III in 739, because the Lombard king had been his ally in a campaign against the Arabs in Provence, but Pippin III proved more persuadable, especially after Pope Stephen II (752–757) crossed the Alps and anointed him king with holy oil at Reims in 754. This was a reinforcement of a purely Frankish ceremony of crowning carried out in 751. Stephen's anointing of Pippin was the first time this practice, of unction or anointing with holy oil, possibly borrowed from Spanish royal initiation rites, was used in the making of French kings, and it reflected the new ruler's need for spiritual underpinning of his authority. This was also the first time that a pope travelled to France. In return Pippin invaded Italy in 755 to bring Aistulf to heel. He did so again in 756, when the Lombard king broke the agreement made the previous year. On both occasions the Lombards declined to face the Franks in open battle but capitulated when their royal capital of Pavia was blockaded.

Aistulf died later in 756, and both Pippin and Pope Stephen II claimed involvement in selecting his successor, one of the Lombard dukes called Desiderius (756–774), but thereafter the Frankish king kept out of Italian affairs. King Desiderius was more cautious than his predecessor about an open conflict with the papacy but was equally unwilling to make the restitutions of recently conquered territory agreed in the treaties. Further papal appeals to Pippin went unheeded for he was busy half-destroying Aquitaine.

CHARLEMAGNE

The death of Pippin in 768 opened a new chapter in papal-Frankish relations, as he left his kingdom divided between two sons, Charles, later known as 'the Great' (Charlemagne), and Carloman, who quickly fell out with each other. External allies became important with a threat of civil war looming, and Charles stole a march on his younger brother by arranging a diplomatic marriage with the daughter of the Lombard king. A new pope, Stephen III (768–772), was horrified that one of his Frankish protectors was about to ally with 'the perfidious and most foully stinking people of the Lombards . . . a race from which the stock of lepers is known for certain to have sprung'.[27] While this was unusually strong language, even for referring to the Lombards, the pope and his advisors had particular reasons to fear the effects of this new alliance, as the history of Lombard-papal relations in the preceding years reveals.

In 757 Stephen II, who had anointed the Frankish king Pippin, had been succeeded by his brother, Paul I (757–767). In his time the new Lombard king Desiderius gained control of the duchies of Spoleto and Benevento, effectively surrounding Roman territory. The threat of an imperial-Lombard alliance also loomed briefly, when Constantine V became enraged by papal support for opponents of his iconoclast policies in the East. He began wooing the Frankish court, sending Pippin III the exotic gift of a portable organ, and in 767 tried with some success to persuade the Franks to adopt iconoclasm. In practice none of this amounted to a serious threat, but there was an air of diplomatic desperation in Rome throughout this pontificate, with enemies seen on all sides. The only element of relief was the removal from a catacomb of what was thought to be the body and the marble coffin of St. Peter's daughter, Petronilla, with the inscription 'to Aurea Petronilla, sweetest daughter' carved on it by the Apostle's own hand. This was brought in procession to St. Peter's and placed in what had once been the mausoleum of the Theodosian dynasty.[28]

Although part of a wider papally directed programme of moving supposed relics of the martyrs out of the catacombs and into churches inside the city walls, this particular 'translation' also had a political purpose. In 757 Pippin III invited the pope to be *compater* or godfather to his new daughter Gisela. This was a much closer relationship than its modern equivalent, as it made the godparent the spiritual equivalent of the physical father or mother and formed a unique bond between them as well as with the child. For Pope Paul I this was a remarkable opportunity to forge stronger links with the papacy's Frankish protectors, and he staged an elaborate ceremony in 758 in the newly consecrated chapel of St. Petronilla, dedicating the baby's baptismal gown—she herself was not sent to Rome for baptism—which he had received from Pippin. In a letter describing the event the pope drew a parallel between the relationship of St. Peter and his daughter and that between himself and the Frankish princess. In practical terms this did little good as Pippin refused to be further drawn into Italian affairs, but the episode was part of an intense papal courtship of the Franks. In later years St. Petronilla was proclaimed the patron of treaties between the papacy and the French monarchy and the chapel itself became devoted to papal ceremonies relating to France until its demolition in 1606.

The demands of running the military and civil administration of the duchy of Rome turned the popes of the time into de facto secular rulers of a substantial territory in central Italy, including several former imperial duchies. Thus, the popes, in control of large revenues and substantial numbers of locally recruited soldiers, often had to act as secular sovereigns or face losing their authority to others. One such was Duke Toto of Nepi, whose troops controlled the northern approaches to Rome. On the death of Pope Paul I in 767, he executed a coup, using the army vote in the papal election to force through the choice of his brother, Constantine, who was still a layman but was ordained as sub-deacon and deacon before becoming pope.

Although proper procedures had been followed to the letter if not the spirit, and nothing prevented a layman being elected, this coup infuriated the leaders of the previous papal administration, especially Christopher, the *primicerius notariorum* or chief notary, head of the civil service. Needing a military counterweight to Duke Toto, he began negotiations with the Lombard king Desiderius and the duke of Spoleto, who agreed to send troops. On 30 July 768, Christopher's son Sergius staged a counter-coup in Rome with the aid of these Lombard allies, killing Toto and capturing Constantine II.

Desiderius hoped for a sympathetic pope, employing a Lombard priest called Waldipert as his agent, and another priest called Philip was their chosen candidate. He was enthroned in the Lateran by Waldipert and 'some Romans', proclaiming 'St. Peter has chosen Philip pope.' Within hours the local troops under Christopher and Sergius ejected Philip from the Lateran and returned him to his monastery. His fate was gentler than that of Pope Constantine II, who was publicly humiliated by being processed round the city 'on a horse in a saddle designed for a woman', with 'a huge weight' attached to his feet. He was then deposed by a synod in the Lateran Basilica on 6 August 768.

A section of the acts of this council has survived, stating it was presided over by the 'thrice blessed and co-angelic Pope Stephen III, supreme pontiff of the universal Church and that of this city of Rome', and attended by numerous bishops, including representatives from Ravenna and from Francia, eight priests of the Roman church, deacons and monks of both the Latin and Greek monasteries of the city, as well as by 'the nobles and also the militia', together with 'honest citizens and the general populace'.[29] The condemnation of Constantine, despite his defence that others, including the late archbishop of Ravenna, had been elected to high clerical office from the laity, was a forgone conclusion. Like all such events, this was played out with ritual drama. Constantine was 'buffeted on the neck' and literally thrown out of the basilica, before all the documents he had issued and the record of the synod that had elected him were burnt in the chancel. 'After this the holy pope Stephen with all the clergy and Roman people threw themselves on to the ground and cried out and wailed aloud *Kyrie eleison,* confessing that all of them had sinned in that they had taken communion from Constantine's hands.' It was decreed no one should be elected pope who had not risen through the ranks of the clergy 'and had not been made cardinal deacon or priest'.[30]

Constantine's brother Passibus and one of his leading supporters, Bishop Theodore, the *vicedominus* or steward of the papal palace, were blinded by 'some perverted individuals' and confined to monasteries. Constantine himself was imprisoned in the monastery of St. Saba, only to be seized by troops loyal to Christopher and Sergius, who 'gouged out his eyes and left him blind in the street'.[31] The same fate befell Waldipert, but his tongue was also cut out, with fatal effect.

The man behind this violence was Gratiosus, a relative of Christopher's, who was rewarded with Toto's duchy of Nepi. Their family thus secured Rome but needed a pope through whom to exercise their new power. For this they obtained at the synod of 6 August 768 the election of a priest of modest Sicilian origins called Stephen, who had long worked in the Lateran and had attended Paul I on his deathbed. But Stephen III soon showed he did not intend to remain the pawn of those who had manoeuvred his election, especially as there were others keen to end the dominance of Christopher and his family. Chief among these was King Desiderius, who wanted vengeance for Waldipert and was angered by the resumption of demands for territorial restitution. After his alliance with the new Frankish king Charles in 771, there was no danger that a Lombard move against Rome would provoke a reaction in Francia, and he also acquired a secret ally inside the papal court, a chamberlain called Paul Afiarta.

In the spring of 771 Desiderius approached Rome with an army, claiming he wanted to pray in St. Peter's, and requested a meeting with the pope. Christopher and Sergius barricaded themselves in the city, ready to hold out, while Stephen III slipped out to join the king at St. Peter's. Supporters of Christopher and Sergius stayed in the city, while their opponents gathered at St. Peter's on the other side of the Tiber, and the movement in one direction or the other showed who was gaining the upper hand, until even Gratiosus saw the way the wind was blowing and deserted his relatives. He and his followers broke down a gate, leaving Rome indefensible, and joined the pope and King Desiderius. Stephen III told Christopher and Sergius that their lives would be spared, but they must come to St. Peter's, before retiring into monastic life. When they did, he handed them over to be blinded that same evening by Paul Afiarta, who now shared power with the pope's brother, a duke called John. Christopher died three days later. Sergius was imprisoned in a monastery and was later murdered when Stephen III was dying.

Few other episodes in the history of the papacy in the eighth century are recorded in such detail as these lurid events. As well as indicating how violent the politics of the papal court could be at this time, they give us rare evidence of the working of the social elites. Once-fashionable ideas of divisions between lay and clerical or civil and military aristocracies fail to sustain themselves when several of the families concerned have members fitting all these categories, and in some cases moving from one to another. We also see aristocratic families with local rural power bases competing for power in the metropolis.

Within months of the overthrow of Christopher and Sergius, the alliance behind their coup fell apart. The younger of the two Frankish kings, Carloman, died in December 771, leaving only infant heirs. Rather than face a long minority, his courtiers switched allegiance to Charles, and Carloman's wife and children fled to the Lombard kingdom. No longer needing a Lombard alliance, Charles divorced Desiderius' daughter, almost in itself a declaration of war. The realignment was completed by the death of Pope Stephen III in January 772. By the terms of a new procedure for papal elections, decreed in 769, his successor was chosen by the Roman clergy alone.

Despite the efforts of Paul Afiarta to influence the outcome, they elected Hadrian I (772–795), a member of the new aristocracy.[32] His maternal uncle, who brought him up, had been a duke and then *prim-*

icerius notariorum under Stephen II and Paul. Hadrian may have been relatively young, as he had only just been made a deacon by Stephen III, but he was well connected, confident and, when required, ruthless. He got Afiarta, who commanded the papal palace guard, out of Rome by sending him on a diplomatic mission, then recalled and pardoned those who had suffered in the coup against Christopher and Sergius the previous year. Finally he had the archbishop of Ravenna arrest Afiarta on his way back from the Lombard court.

In the meantime enquiries were made about the murder of Sergius, whose body was found in a field with a rope round his neck, and a small group of clerical and military officials confessed that they had carried out the killing on Afiarta's orders. They were sent to Constantinople for sentencing, suggesting that the pope still recognised the emperor as his sovereign. Afiarta, now prisoner in Rimini, was executed. The *Liber Pontificalis* suggests that the archbishop ordered this on his own authority and that the pope's intentions were more merciful, but Hadrian was unquestionably the principal beneficiary.

In Rome blame for all of the violence of the last five years was again laid at the door of the Lombards, and Hadrian resumed demands for the return of the towns promised in the Frankish-Lombard treaty of 756. To cow the pope, Desiderius prepared to march on Rome in the spring of 773, while Hadrian sent messengers by sea to Francia to beg King Charles to intervene diplomatically if not militarily. As Desiderius had previously tried to persuade the pope to consecrate the infant son of Carloman as king of the Franks, the threat of Lombard support for a family rival made Charles open to Hadrian's appeal, despite his other commitments. Charles quickly defeated Lombard attempts to hold the Alpine passes and by late autumn of 773 was besieging Desiderius in Pavia.

Thus far the campaign mirrored those of 755 and 756, but instead of negotiating, Charles kept Pavia blockaded over the winter and in 774 went to Rome for Easter. He received the reception that would have been appropriate for an exarch, with papal officials sent to greet him thirty miles from the city, and the militia drawn up one mile from St. Peter's, where the pope waited to receive him. This may hint at the kind of role the pope hoped the Frankish king would now play in Italian affairs.

According to the *Liber Pontificalis*, Hadrian took the opportunity to 'entreat, warn and encourage' Charles to fulfil the promise made in 753 by Pippin III to Stephen II to hand over 'to St. Peter' a large swathe of cities and territory in northern Italy, stretching from Venice, Ravenna and all the lands of the exarchate in the east to the island of Corsica in the west, and extending south to include the Lombard duchies of Spoleto and Benevento. The king is said to have had a new copy of his father's grant written out, and 'with his own hands he placed it over St. Peter's body, beneath the gospels which are kissed there, as a firm security and an eternal reminder of his name and that of the kingdom of the Franks.'[33]

This is extremely significant, as the grant is often seen as founding the Papal States, the territories over which the popes would exercise sovereign authority until 1870. However, there are suspicious features to this claim, as no contemporary sources mention this donation, nor is it referred to in any of the numerous letters exchanged between Charles and Hadrian; moreover, in 753, when it was supposedly made, Pippin had no control over any part of Italy and had no intention of invading the Lombard kingdom.

It is also unclear what is meant by 'handing over to St. Peter'. Is this a cession of political sovereignty or of ecclesiastical superiority? Although Rome was the only apostolic patriarchate in the West, its metropolitan authority as opposed to its influence did not even encompass the whole of Italy. We cannot be sure who ruled Ravenna after 774, though a local source refers to its archbishop Sergius (744–769) as exercising authority 'as if he were the exarch'.[34] There is no evidence of Pope Hadrian playing such a role, and Corsica and Benevento were definitely not under papal suzerainty at this time. The full version of the 'Life of Hadrian' in the *Liber Pontificalis* was not completed until well after his death, and, as we shall see, this claim reflects papal aspirations of the 820s better than the diplomatic realities of 774.

It is clear that a number of formerly imperial military and administrative districts in central Italy were handed over to Pope Zacharias by the Lombard king Liutprand around 741.[35] They stretched from Sabina, just east of Rome, across to Ancona on the Adriatic coast. Several of them were reoccupied by the Lombards in subsequent decades but reverted to Rome during Charlemagne's siege of Pavia. At the same time the Lombard duchy of Spoleto submitted to papal suzerainty. So from 774 the pope was the overlord of these territories, which did not however include all those mentioned in Pippin III's supposed grant of 753.

Thus, the popes exercised political superiority but not sovereignty over the numerous towns, local military and civil office holders and landowners in these territories, from whom tribute was demanded on certain occasions. This helped replace revenues from the lost papal estates in Sicily, Africa and Provence and was primarily directed towards the charitable work of the *diaconiae* (diaconal centres), of which there were eighteen by the end of the eighth century, and the costs of maintaining the churches of Rome and their liturgy. Some of these, such as Santa Maria in Cosmedin, were substantially rebuilt under Hadrian I, who also funded works of urban restoration, including repairs to some of the early imperial aqueducts, to ensure the city's water supply. As for the popes' political allegiance, this remained focussed on the emperors in Constantinople, but developments in Italy were about to change that.

Returning to Pavia after Easter, Charles received the surrender of the city and of King Desiderius, who was deposed and sent with his family into monastic detention in Francia. With the consent of the Lombard dukes, Charles then proclaimed himself king of the Lombards, using that title in tandem with that of king of the Franks. This unprecedented move was justified by a Frankish claim to overlordship over the Lombards, based on treaties made in the late sixth century. Whatever the constitutional niceties, Charles substituted a benevolent and more distant Frankish rule for a Lombard regime that had been an intermittent threat to the territories controlled by the popes and to their independence of action for much of the eighth century. Both within its walls and more widely, Rome now entered into a period of greater tranquillity under Frankish protection.

The removal of the Lombard military threat enabled Hadrian to continue the re-organisation of the papal estates begun by Pope Zacharias, combining them into larger units, centred on newly constructed complexes of farmhouses, barns and stores, with churches attached. Two of these have been recently excavated, adding to the understanding of their functions.[36] The produce from these *domuscultae,* as they were called, went to the city for distribution through the network of *diaconiae* throughout Rome. These also depended on charitable gifts and were now sponsored by patrons, often members of the lay aristocracy or the papal administration. An inscription records the donations of one such patron, Theodotus, uncle of Pope Hadrian I, to the *diaconia* of St. Paul, now the Church of Sant'Angelo in Pescheria, in 755.

The material wealth of the papacy was also increased by gifts from the Frankish king. Some of these were spectacular, as in the case of the redistribution of the treasure that Charles acquired when the nomad Avar empire north of the Danube collapsed in the 790s and his generals were able to plunder the great Avar camp, known as 'the Ring', at their leisure. A further gift of treasure from Charles came as a bequest following his death in 814. The impact of better management of the papacy's own resources and Frankish largesse can be seen in the programmes of building in Rome carried out by Hadrian I and his successor Leo III (795–816), which included a substantial expansion of the Lateran Palace, and the commissioning of frescoes for several of the city's churches.

The Frankish ruler and his court, established at Aachen from 794, looked to Rome for authority in the process of *Renovatio* or Renewal in the Frankish church and society that Charles regarded as essential if divine favour was to be retained for his kingdom. His ecclesiastical advisors included the Northumbrian deacon Alcuin (died 804), whose view of Roman authority was formed by the especially close ties that had existed between the Anglo-Saxon church and the See of Peter ever since the seventh century. Rome had been a source of books for the Anglo-Saxons, and it was to the pope that Charles now turned for authoritative texts of some of the works he needed for the revitalising of the Frankish church. In particular this meant obtaining books of canon law and liturgy. The first acquisition was a much fuller and revised version of the collection of councils and papal decretals made by Dionysius the Small than the one sent to Pippin III in 747. This was presented to Charles by Hadrian I during his visit to Rome in early 774. In 785/6 Charles requested a copy of the papal Mass book known as the Gregorian Sacramentary, which was mistakenly believed to have been compiled by Gregory the Great himself. In 798 the selection of Gregory's letters described in the previous chapter was made in Rome for Charles. Similarly in Francia in 791 the king ordered the compiling of a collection of the surviving correspondence sent by the popes to his family since 739. Known as the *Codex Carolinus* or Charles's Manuscript, it contains most of the later eighth-century papal letters known today.

The importance of these 'Roman books' can be overemphasised.[37] The revised canon law collection, known from its combined origin as the *Dionysio-Hadriana,* was perhaps the most immediately important, as it became a major source of regulation for the Frankish church, especially when combined with other collections, such as the seventh-century Spanish one known as the *Hispana.* On the other hand, the Gregorian Sacramentary contained so many items that were exclusive to the popes' own special liturgy that it had to be considerably extended by a supplement compiled at the Carolingian court early in the reign of Charles's son Louis the Pious (814–840), to make it of use for Frankish bishops and priests.

The pope and the king did not always see eye to eye. A case in point was the different reactions to the condemnation of iconoclasm in the empire achieved by the regent Irene at the Second Council of Nicaea in 787. While the restoration of image veneration was warmly and unhesitatingly welcomed in Rome, reactions were less favourable in Francia. In part the problem lay in a defective Latin translation of the proceedings of the council, which had been conducted entirely in Greek, prepared in Rome and sent to Charles. This gave the impression that worship rather than reverencing of icons was being permitted. Iconoclast tendencies were strong in Francia at this time, perhaps influenced by the emperor Constantine V's propaganda campaign in the 760s. A Gothic refugee from Spain called Theodulf, later bishop of Orléans, was commissioned to produce a substantial refutation of the theology behind the decisions of the Second Council of Nicaea, to be presented to a great synod of the Frankish church that was meeting in Frankfurt in 794. Following the practice of the royal court, this had to appear the work of the king himself. Thus it is known as the *Libri Carolini*, or Charles's Books. What it was originally to be entitled is unknown, as, when almost complete, the project was suddenly abandoned, because it was discovered that Pope Hadrian had fully endorsed the decisions made at Nicaea, and an open theological rift with the papacy was not desirable.

In the secular sphere, not least in relations with the Lombard duchies of Spoleto and Benevento, the Frankish king treated the pope as his viceroy in central Italy, while on ecclesiastical issues he was keen to ensure papal approval of his doctrinal orthodoxy, for instance in the controversy over Adoptionism, which began in Spain in the 780s. Although arising from mutual misunderstanding of what was meant by Christ 'adopting' his humanity, caused by differences in the theological traditions of Rome and the former Gothic kingdom in Spain, this controversy was used by Charles to demonstrate to the pope the impeccable orthodoxy of the Church in his domain, showcased in various treatises that Alcuin was commissioned to write and in the elaborate condemnation of Adoptionism at the great synod held in Frankfurt in 794.

The complex interaction between papacy and Frankish monarchy in these years raises the question of the nature of the political relationship between them. Were the popes still politically subject to the emperors in Constantinople and did they administer their territories on behalf of those distant monarchs? Or had, intentionally or accidentally, an independent papal state come into being, with the pope as a secular sovereign in his own right? If so, when and how had this happened? These are questions that have been much debated by historians of this period. What is certain is that there was no grand moment of change, let alone of liberation. No pope ever made a declaration of independence or claimed a new secular political role. For an institution whose leaders had long been making very clear and specific statements about their responsibilities and status in the ecclesiastical sphere, the lack of clarity about their secular role is surprising.

Historians have interpreted papal attitudes and aspirations in the light of a series of often contradictory indicators. On the one hand references in letters and other documents produced by the papal administration to *Respublica Sancti Petri* have been seen as proving the existence of a papal state from around the middle of the eighth century if not before. From the Roman word *Respublica* comes our modern term 'republic', and there is a danger of treating it as having such a clear institutional significance in earlier periods, when its range of meanings was far broader and more ambiguous. More significant may be the continuing use of imperial reigns in the dating of documents and the striking of gold coins by the mint of Rome, under papal supervision, not just for Constantine V (741–775) but also for his son, Leo IV the Khazar (775–780). Both of these practices ended in 781 at the latest. Hadrian then started dating his documents by the year of his pontificate, and the mint began issuing silver coins bearing images of St. Peter and with the name and title of the pope. Similar issues were struck in the opening years of his successor Leo III up till 800.[38]

Why 781 was such a turning point is not certain. Authority in the empire was in the hands of Irene, the widow of Leo IV, regent for her infant son Constantine VI (780–797). As an Athenian, she was opposed to the iconoclast policies of her husband's family and was already working to reverse them, finally achieving this in 787. In 781 a diplomatic agreement was made between the empire and the Frankish kingdom, to be sealed by an engagement between Constantine VI and one of Charles's daughters. While the marriage would never take place, these negotiations may also have included the status of the duchies controlled by the popes. From the papal perspective the most significant feature of 781 was Charles's second visit to Rome at Easter that year, when Pope Hadrian baptised the king's second son, the four-year-old Pippin. He then anointed and crowned Pippin as king of the Lombards and his three-year-old brother Louis as king of the Aquitanians. This formed part of Charles's plans for the division of his territories amongst his sons, and perhaps a change in the allegiance of the papacy to the empire was the necessary precondition to Hadrian investing the two boys with their non-Frankish kingdoms. If so, this left the pope and his territories in something of a constitutional limbo. The pope was not a king and never aspired to be one, but he also objected to being under the secular overlordship of the king of the Lombards, even a Frankish one. One solution was the re-creation of the empire in the West.

chapter 8

JUDGING ALL MEN, JUDGED BY NONE

(799–896)

A NEW ROMAN EMPIRE

On the morning of 25 April 799, Pope Leo III departed from the Lateran palace, with the office holders of the Roman church for the annual Major Litany, asking God's blessing on the new season's crops. The route followed that of a pagan procession, the Robigalia, and would start at the Church of San Lorenzo in Lucina and end at St. Peter's. As Leo approached the starting point, he was ambushed, and his attackers tried to blind him and cut out his tongue.[1]

We do not know the reasons behind this first attempt to depose a pope by violence, but we do know that at least two of Leo's retinue were involved in the plot. It is probable that his assailants were just trying to mutilate him so he could be declared incapable of holding office. They imprisoned him in a monastery, but no attempt was made to replace him, allowing his supporters to rescue him and get him to St. Peter's. From there he escaped to Spoleto. His attackers had failed to blind him, permitting his allies to claim he had been blinded then miraculously cured.[2]

Leo III was one of the few late-eighth-century popes who was not an aristocrat. His only recent non-noble predecessor was Stephen III (768–772), whose pontificate was dominated by conflicts between aristocratic clans in the papal administration. The plot's leaders, the chief notary and the papal treasurer, were nephews of the previous pope, Hadrian I. During their uncle's pontificate, they had run the administration of Rome for him, and after his death, they secured the election of Leo III to serve as figurehead. But Leo was more independent than they had anticipated.

Leo's allies could not restore him, and so in the late summer of 799 he headed north to secure the backing of Charlemagne, who was with his army in Saxony. Ahead of him went letters from his attackers, trying to blacken his character. We know much of what happened in Saxony from letters of the Northumbrian deacon Alcuin, one of the king's leading advisors. Charles decided to reinstate Leo in Rome but also sent officials to investigate the charges made against him. One of these, Arn, archbishop of Salzburg, wrote to his old friend Alcuin giving the details. Alcuin was so shocked at the allegations that he destroyed the letter but in a letter of his own lets on that they involved adultery and perjury.[3]

These were virtually identical to the accusations made against Pope Symmachus during the Laurentian schism three hundred years earlier. So, it is appropriate that the 'Acts of Sylvester', originally forged by supporters of Symmachus, in which it was declared that the 'apostolic see is to judge but not be judged,' was now used in defence of Leo.[4] Alcuin cited it to Charlemagne to try to prevent Leo being subjected to a trial.

His accusers never challenged the authenticity of this and similar documents. They believed that the proposed alternative of Leo taking a public oath that the accusations were false would be equally effective, as they felt that he would not dare perjure himself, and so would resign.

In their discussions in Paderborn in Saxony in September 799, Leo and Charlemagne probably agreed that the king would go to Rome in 800 to be crowned emperor. However, no word of this appears in our sources, because contemporary views on how power should be acquired made it vital that Charlemagne's elevation be presented as unexpected and spontaneous. Fortunately, the various chronicles and annals that record what happened include details and contradictions revealing that the whole thing had been meticulously planned over quite some time.[5]

While in practice there had been no emperor in the West since 480, this does not mean the position was vacant. In Roman political thought the empire was universal and indivisible. When in the fourth and fifth centuries there had been separate emperors in East and West, they were seen as colleagues ruling a single empire. This view of the indivisible nature of the empire survived in eighth-century Constantinople, whose citizens still saw themselves as Romans. It was also shared by the Western kings who continued to recognize the superior status of the emperors in Constantinople. So, Charles could not be proclaimed emperor without Eastern agreement, which was unlikely to be forthcoming.

Pope Leo, however, had a solution to this constitutional issue. The young emperor Constantine VI had been blinded and killed by his mother in 797 when he tried to revive the iconoclast policies of his predecessors. She had then taken the throne for herself, the first woman to rule in her own right in the history of the Roman empire, but the uneasy nature of her position was indicated by her using the male form of the imperial title. Her regime remained weak until her overthrow in 802.[6] However, in the West in 800 the fact that she was a woman allowed it to be claimed that the imperial office was vacant, and thus no Eastern consent was needed.

Beyond that, however, it was still necessary for some explanation to be found for why the ruler of what the Romans would have regarded as a barbarian nation should be entitled to hold the imperial title. The argument was advanced, probably on papal advice, that this was justified by Charles's control of almost all the former seats of imperial government in the West: Arles, Trier, Milan, Ravenna and Rome itself.[7]

There remained the problem of the traditional refusal of power. However right conditions might be, the Frankish king could not be seen openly to claim the imperial title. Here the pope was in a unique position to help, thanks to contemporary views on what the first Christian emperor had given the papal see in what became known as the 'Donation of Constantine'. In the eighth century, Constantine was known primarily through the account of him in the legend of Pope Sylvester. In this he was incorrectly portrayed as an emperor who had persecuted Christianity until struck down with leprosy. On rejecting the suggestion of his pagan priests that he bathe in the blood of sacrificed babies, he had a vision of Saints Peter and Paul telling him to find Bishop Sylvester, who cured, healed and baptized him. Onto this core narrative was grafted the claim that when Constantine subsequently decided to leave for the East, out of gratitude he entrusted Pope Sylvester with a set of imperial regalia, including a crown, and with the authority for himself and his successors to appoint an emperor in the West should circumstances ever require it.

All this was believed to be true even before written up in a text known as the 'Constitution of Constantine', which presented itself as the official draft of the emperor's grant to the pope. This document, whose authenticity was not to be successfully challenged until 1452, was probably not written until the mid-ninth century and then in a Frankish monastery, but the ideas behind it were older and may have developed in the papal court.[8] Their widespread acceptance enabled Leo to make Charles emperor on papal authority, without it seeming the product of tyrannical ambition on the Frankish king's part.

A final requirement was that the pope be fit to consecrate a new emperor. While it had long been held that sacraments would be effective even if those who administered them were sinful, to be crowned by a man accused of perjury and fornication was a weak foundation for the legitimacy of an emperor whose title was certainly going to be challenged. So Leo had to establish his innocence by swearing that the charges made against him were false.

When Charles arrived in Rome on 30 November 800, a council of bishops and other lay and ecclesiastical dignitaries from both Francia and Italy was already assembled and formally approved his assuming the imperial title, because of *femineum imperium* or feminine rule in Constantinople. Then, Leo took his oath. The only immediately contemporary source stressed that he did this entirely of his own free will, as the doctrine that the pope was superior to all earthly justice implied there was no authority that could force him to act in this way.[9] His accusers were confounded and soon put on trial themselves.

What Charles really felt about Leo is uncertain. A letter of Alcuin reveals that Leo remained out of favor with the new emperor until sometime in the spring of 801, and Charlemagne never seems to have warmed to him personally in the way he did with his predecessor, Hadrian I, whose epitaph (still to be seen high in the wall of the narthex of St. Peter's) Charlemagne had personally commissioned and sent to Rome.[10]

Leo himself gained much from the revival of the empire in the West. He secured the involvement of the new emperor in the protection of his own person and that of Rome to a degree unknown since the fifth century. That he still had enemies in the city is clear, even after his assailants of April 799 were sentenced to death, though this was commuted to life imprisonment at his request. He was less forgiving in 815 when another conspiracy against his life was uncovered, and he had all the ringleaders killed before the Frankish ruler could intervene. When he died in 816 he was so unpopular that the populace looted his properties.

Leo's view of what happened on Christmas Day 800 was expressed visually in a new dining hall he had built in the papal palace of the Lateran, in a mosaic above his own seat, depicting both Charles and himself kneeling either side of an enthroned St. Peter, who was investing them with a military banner on a spear and a pallium or papal stole respectively. In other words, this was an alliance of equals, both in the service of the Prince of the Apostles and his Church, with the emperor working to defend its material possessions and the pope directing its spiritual welfare. Charlemagne almost certainly never saw these pictures, as he left Rome in the spring of 801 and never returned, but it is unlikely he would have approved.

In any case he was already worried about his new title of Emperor of the Romans (*not* Holy Roman Emperor, a title never used by anyone), which sounded too closely tied to the city of Rome and its inhabitants. He was also uneasy about the way it had been given to him. The events of December 800 had made the imperial office seem to be the gift either of the papacy or of a council of magnates.

Neither was an acceptable precedent as far as he was concerned, and he soon began to refer to himself as 'the emperor, crowned by God . . . governing the Roman Empire'.[11] When the time came for his own succession, he summoned his only surviving son, Louis the Pious (813–840), to a ceremony at Aachen, in which the new emperor crowned himself, a procedure that would be followed by Napoleon almost a thousand years later. In both cases the implications were obvious: The imperial office did not depend on the papacy, and a papal coronation was not required for making an emperor.

Clear as both Charlemagne and Napoleon's intentions were, virtually every other Western emperor before the sixteenth century wanted a papal coronation to legitimize his authority. Louis the Pious himself was quickly persuaded that he needed more than the ceremony at Aachen to make him a proper emperor. In 816 the new pope, Stephen IV (816–817), not only informed the emperor of his election but told him that he was coming to Francia for a personal meeting with Louis. He brought with him a so–called crown of Constantine, probably believed to be the very one referred to in the 'Donation of Constantine'.[12] The two met at Reims, the traditional place of coronation of the Frankish kings since the sixth century, and there the pope crowned both Louis and his wife Irmengard and also anointed the emperor, thus adding a further element to the ritual. This was a deliberate evoking of the anointing of Louis's grandfather as first king of the Carolingian dynasty by Pope Stephen II in 754. 'They then exchanged many gifts, celebrated splendid banquets, and established a firm friendship between them.'[13]

A similar pattern of double investiture was followed when Louis decided to share his imperial status with his own eldest son, Lothar. An initial self-coronation at Aachen took place in 817, but in 823, after Lothar had been sent by his father to rule Italy, Pope Paschal I (817–824) crowned and anointed him in Rome. In this ceremony another new element was added when Paschal invested the emperor with a sword, an act reminiscent of St. Peter giving Charlemagne a spear in the mosaic in the papal dining room. While its meaning was not made explicit in the ceremony, the act implied the papal right to invest the ruler with temporal authority. The papacy was adapting quickly to the opportunities offered by its involvement in the processes of making an emperor. After 817 the Frankish civil ceremony in Aachen was never employed again, and the only form of imperial coronation was that used in Rome in 823. Within a short time this monopoly of crowning, anointing and investing with a sword gave the papacy considerable leverage in the choice of a new emperor.

THE PAPACY UNDER FRANKISH RULE

The relationship created through Leo III's use of his own difficulties in 799 to involve the Frankish monarchy in the defence of Rome also had its drawbacks for the papacy. Since the mid-sixth century the popes had been politically subject to a distant ruler in Constantinople, whose local representatives only enjoyed limited powers to interfere in the Roman church. After 800 the political allegiance owed by the popes was diverted to Western emperors, whom they themselves consecrated, raising questions about how this new imperial authority would be exercised in Rome. This became especially urgent after 823, when Lothar I, Louis the Pious's eldest son and co-emperor, established his court at Pavia. There would be Frankish rulers based in Italy and able to interfere in the popes' control of Rome from then until 875.

Through his officials in the city, Charlemagne had intervened in Roman and papal affairs whenever he wanted and in almost any fashion in the years up to his death in January 814. Occasional complaints about the Frankish ruler's agents by Leo III were ignored. The pope only got his own way over theological issues, as in the case in 810 of the emperor demanding the addition of the word *Filioque* ('and from the Son') to the phrase in the Nicene Creed stating that the Holy Spirit 'proceeds from the Father'. This doctrine of the 'double procession' of the Holy Spirit from both Father and Son had emerged in the sixth century, appearing first in the so-called Athanasian Creed, which was mistakenly regarded as the fourth-century work of Athanasius of Alexandria but was actually composed in Spain or southern Gaul around this time.[14] Based on this spurious authority, the doctrine of the double procession became widely accepted in the West in the eighth century, but it was correctly seen, both in the East and by the papacy, as an erroneous novelty. Leo III's steadfast refusal to accept it was his only successful defiance of Charlemagne. It was not incorporated into the creeds used in Rome until the eleventh century.

During Stephen IV's visit to Francia in 816, the pope 'secured in full everything he is known to have asked for', according to the *Liber Pontificalis*. This might refer to the grant known as the *Ludovicianum*, which supposedly recognized the pope's rights to administrative control of his territories and promised that the emperor and his agents would only interfere if the pope was thought to be oppressing his subjects, or if he requested it. Papal elections were to be free, but with the proviso that the new pope must subsequently inform the emperor.

When Paschal I succeeded Stephen IV in January 817, he told the emperor that 'the papal dignity had been forced upon him not only against his will but even against his most violent resistance.'[15] As he was elected within twenty-four hours of his predecessor's death, such resistance was at best token, and the speed more suggestive of a coup. He also asked the emperor that 'the covenant made with his predecessors should also be solemnly concluded with him.'[16]

The *Ludovicianum* is, however, as controversial as Pippin III's supposed grant to Stephen II in 753.[17] In fact they may not only be related but even have been concocted together at this very time. There are no other contemporary references to the *Ludovicianum*, and only extracts from it have survived in collections of canon law dating from the eleventh and twelfth centuries. It included the territorial concessions supposedly made by Pippin in 753 and confirmed by Charlemagne in 774, but adding Sicily, actually ruled by the Eastern emperor. While such clearly anomalous additions have been seen as later interpolations, the very idea that the earlier Carolingian kings had made such sweeping concessions to the papacy could have been devised under Paschal I, and descriptions of the spurious grants of 753 and 774 inserted into the *Liber Pontificalis*'s unfinished account of Hadrian I to fabricate a justification for what was now being claimed.

What little is known of the internal politics of the new pope's reign suggests dissension within the papal court, possibly over how to handle the Frankish rulers of Italy. In the autumn of 823, soon after Lothar's coronation in Rome, the chief notary and his son-in-law, who was also a senior official of the papal administration, were blinded and then beheaded in the Lateran Palace, apparently on the orders of Pope Paschal on the grounds of being too loyal to the new emperor. Frankish investigators sent by the emperor Louis were met by a wall of silence until the pope, accompanied by the bishops of his synod, took a public oath of innocence of any involvement in the killings.

This episode cast a blight on imperial-papal relations. So, following rioting after the clearly unpopular Paschal's death in February 824, the electors were anxious to choose a new pope who would be more co-operative. Eugenius II (824–827) took an immediate oath of loyalty to the emperors, and Lothar arrived in Rome to 'order the affairs of the Roman people, which for a long time had been confused due to the wickedness of several popes'.[18] This included recalling to Rome the widows and children of Paschal I's victims and other political exiles.

In November 824 a new decree was issued on imperial oversight of the papal territories. By this, popes would be freely elected 'by all the Romans' but could not be ordained before imperial consent had been received, as had been the case up to 681. The document also declared that anyone under either imperial or papal protection could not be harmed, that the magistrates of Rome had to appear in person before the emperor for instruction in their duties and that there should be two special representatives in the city, one of whom would be chosen by the pope and the other by the emperor, who would report to the imperial court each year on how Rome was being governed. In other words there was going to be much closer supervision of what went on in the papal territories, and better protection of those loyal to the emperor.

This constitution of 824 remained the official statement of the pope's duties towards the emperors for well over a century, and infringements of it by the papal side were severely punished. When, because of a disputed election, Sergius II (844–847) was consecrated before the emperor was informed, Lothar sent his son Louis II and an army to devastate the papal estates. No redress was available to the popes, but changing political circumstances gradually reduced the emperors' ability to interfere in Rome. In 829 Lothar and two of his brothers initiated the first of a succession of civil wars with their father Louis the Pious that wracked the Frankish empire up till 843 and left it permanently divided into separate kingdoms that grew in number as the century advanced. While this offered opportunities for the papacy to ignore some of the restrictions laid down in 824, the violent conflicts between Christians and within the Carolingian ruling house were sincerely regretted by successive popes, whose needs for protection were growing.

Thus Lothar persuaded Pope Gregory IV (elected late 827 but not consecrated till May, 828–844) to accompany him into Francia in 833 after he had made another alliance with his brothers against their father. The pope hoped to prevent further bloodshed and came to negotiate an agreement on the division of territories to follow Louis's death, the principal cause of the family conflict. When the armies of the two sides confronted each other near Colmar in Alsace, Gregory began discussions, only to find that Lothar and his brothers used the time gained by the negotiations to subvert the loyalty of some of their father's key supporters. Louis's army disintegrated even as he and the pope were reaching an agreement, and the emperor was taken prisoner and deposed by his sons. Gregory IV, who realized that he had been duped, returned to Rome and took no further part in either Louis's recovery of power in 834 or the three-year civil war between the brothers that followed the old emperor's death in 840. The place where he had held his discussions with Louis in 833 subsequently came to be known as the Field of Lies.

These conflicts north of the Alps deflected the attention of the secular rulers from a growing threat in southern Italy, which was menacing papal territories at this time. Sicily, Calabria and other smaller regions in the south had remained under Eastern imperial rule when almost all of the rest of the peninsula fell into Lombard and then Frankish control. In 827, Arab forces from Tunis began the conquest of Sicily. This proved a slow process, but once they had a foothold on the island, the Arabs used it as a base for raiding up the Italian coast as far as Rome.

These Arab raids grew throughout the 830s, and Gregory IV had to defend Ostia, still the principal port of Rome. As the original Roman town was almost defenseless, with its population long in decline, he founded a new fortified settlement just to the east on the site of modern Ostia, which he called Gregoriopolis after himself. But Gregory's fortress did not long survive him, as it was captured and sacked by the Arabs in August 846, two years after his death.

Gregoriopolis was not the only target of this raid, whose primary objective was Rome itself. Its walls, now nearly six hundred years old, kept the attackers out, but outlying districts were sacked, including the two great patriarchal basilicas of St. Peter and St. Paul. This looting of the shrines of the two founding Apostles was a severe blow to the morale of both city and papacy, so much so that the story was put about that the Muslim raiders later perished in a supernatural storm, following an appearance by St. Peter foretelling their impending doom. More practically, one of the earliest acts of the next pope, Leo IV (847–855), was to construct a wall, partly visible today, around the whole area of St. Peter's, turning it into a fortified suburb known as the Leonine City. Completed in 852, this proved particularly valuable in later periods whenever the popes lost control of the rest of the city.

Leo IV defended papal territories vigorously, persuading the cities of Naples, Amalfi and Gaeta to contribute ships to a fleet, which defeated another Arab raid in a sea battle near Ostia. He installed a garrison in Rome's other port of Porto, recruited from refugees from Corsica who had been driven off the island by Arab assaults, and also moved the settlement of Centumcellae to a new fortified site, modern Civitavecchia, which he named Leopolis after himself. These increasing military costs meant that more of the papal revenues had to be diverted into paying for them and less was available for spending on churches and other buildings of Rome, despite occasional contributions from the emperor. In consequence fewer building and restoration projects were started in the city as the ninth century advanced, and gifts from the popes of liturgical vessels and silk vestments and hangings decreased in size and quantity.

While there was less disposable income available to the popes than in the days of Leo III and Charlemagne, the papacy itself was entering a significant period of reform and revival. This involved a renewed interest in its own history. The ninth-century popes became increasingly concerned with the lives of their predecessors and the traditions of their Church, employing these to justify new claims for papal authority. Artistically, this sense of the past can be seen in the way in which the early ninth-century churches, mainly constructed or rebuilt by Paschal I and Gregory IV, are modelled directly on the architectural styles of the fourth and early fifth centuries. Their surviving mosaic decorations also echo early designs and include prominent depictions of the papal patrons being presented in the court of heaven by the saints to whom these churches were dedicated. In the Church of Santa Prassede, which Paschal intended for his own place of burial, he built a chapel in honour of his mother, Theodora, giving her the title, unprecedented in Rome, of *episcopa* or female bishop.[19]

Awareness of the Christian past of Rome and the spiritual resources that lay almost untapped within it and especially underneath it had been growing since the time of Paul I (757–767). He and his successors over the next hundred years moved bodies of Christians buried in the catacombs outside the walls into the city for re-interment in its growing number of churches. The belief that those buried in the catacombs were all victims of the persecutions of the second and third centuries grew as the veneration of the relics of martyrs became increasingly popular. As we have seen, the number of early popes believed to have been martyred expanded significantly between the fourth and sixth centuries. In many cases, no record existed of the life and heroic death of the presumed saint, and legends had to be invented to provide these bones with an appropriate past.

The Arab raids added to the pressure to move such spiritual treasures out of the catacombs and into the safety of the city itself, and the pontificate of Leo IV saw the clearing out of the remaining tombs. There was also a great deal of interest beyond the city in acquiring Roman relics, especially amongst those who were building churches and monasteries in increasing numbers north of the Alps and who needed relics for the sanctification of their new foundations. Einhard (d. 836), one of Charlemagne's courtiers and author of the emperor's *Life,* wrote a detailed account of a mission he sent to Rome in 827 to try secretly to secure the bones of some early Christian martyrs, which he could place in the altar of a church he was building at Seligenstadt in the valley of the river Main. He did not mind who they were, as long as he was assured they were genuine saints, and he relied on a Roman deacon he met at the court of the emperor Louis the Pious for necessary assistance.

Einhard's narrative gives the modern reader a vivid impression of how members of the Roman clergy could work on the pious enthusiasm of wealthy foreign relic hunters, especially since the private excavating and carrying off of martyrs' bones was prohibited and local knowledge was required in finding them. As money changed hands, few seekers after relics went away disappointed. So, it is unlikely the bodies that Einhard's agents carried off were indeed those of the martyrs Marcellinus and Peter. Their basilica in Rome was restored by Pope Benedict III (855–858) without any suggestion that their relics had been stolen thirty years earlier. Only a vision of the two martyrs finally convinced Einhard that his new relics really were those of saints.

Relics from Rome also made very acceptable diplomatic gifts, as when in 850 Pope Leo IV sent some of the remains of five martyrs, including two of his papal predecessors, to the empress Irmengard, wife of Lothar I. The movement of martyr relics, both official and otherwise, opened up new interest in the city and its Church in areas that had previously not been very closely linked to Rome, as the arrival of such relics created a demand for information about their lives and deaths. The expansion eastwards of the Carolingian empire was also opening up areas across the Rhine in which there had been no early Christian presence and in consequence lacked long-established cults of local saints. Roman relics, such as those acquired by Einhard, were therefore much in demand and their presence added to the growing influence of the papacy on the Church north of the Alps.[20]

While in the early ninth century Leo III and Paschal I appear primarily concerned with the internal politics of Rome and relations with the new imperial power, their successors began reviving the papacy's claims to wider authority in the Church. Eugenius II (824–827) held a synod of Italian bishops in the Lateran Palace in November 826, which issued new rules on the educational requirements for admission to the clergy, the procedures for electing bishops, episcopal duties and the conduct of monastic life. It was intended that these canons, or ecclesiastical laws, should be obeyed throughout the Carolingian empire, and collectively they represent the most substantial papal attempt to impose standards on the Western church for over three centuries. These decrees were reaffirmed and expanded at another synod under Leo IV in 853. The papacy's sense of its unquestioned authority in matters of Church doctrine and discipline had not been affected by Frankish political oversight.

PAPAL AUTHORITY REVIVED

However, few popes of the period intervened in the affairs of churches outside Italy, except when asked, until the time of Nicholas I (858–867). Sometimes called Nicholas the Great, he proved himself to be the most significant pope between Gregory the Great (590–604) and the reformers of the later eleventh century. He and his immediate successors revived papal authority over the Church in much of Western Europe and influence on its secular rulers to a degree unmatched since the late fifth century. Their achievement proved short-lived but provided inspiration for later generations of papal reformers.

Born around 820, Nicholas was the son of a civil official in the papal administration and rose through the ranks of the clergy to become one of the deacons under Leo IV. The *Liber Pontificalis* tells us he was the closest advisor of his predecessor Benedict III (855–858) and so may have influenced his policies, which were far more robust than those of previous popes, especially in dealings with secular rulers. For example, Benedict threatened to excommunicate the brother of a queen for looting monasteries and demanded that the wife of a member of the Carolingian dynasty who had eloped with her lover be sent back to her husband. His influence again made itself felt in the family politics of the Carolingians when, on the death of Lothar I in 855, the pope intervened in the family rows that broke out over the division of the late emperor's territories between his two sons and his half-brother. Benedict III took an equally firm line in his dealings with Constantinople, reasserting the papal claims that Rome had primacy of jurisdiction and was the supreme court of appeal in all ecclesiastical matters.

In all these areas Nicholas I followed similar policies. In 862 he intervened decisively against the attempt by Lothar II (855–869) to divorce his childless wife, although this had already been approved by a Frankish synod. The queen, Theutberga, appealed to the pope, who sent representatives to a second synod, intended to justify the king marrying his long-time mistress. However, the papal agents who had been sent to veto this were instead bribed into accepting it, and the archbishops of Cologne and Trier took the synod's decrees to Rome, expecting papal consent to a fait accompli. Instead Nicholas excommunicated them both for condoning bigamy. When the emperor Louis II (850–875) then marched on Rome to force Nicholas into agreeing to his brother's divorce and pardoning his archbishops, the pope held out in the fortified Leonine City. Eventually the emperor withdrew, and Lothar had to agree to a reconciliation with his wife, with the result that he died without legitimate heirs and his kingdom was split up between his relatives in 869.

In 858 the pope also objected when the Eastern emperor Michael III deposed Ignatius, the patriarch of Constantinople. Nicholas refused to accept his successor, Photius, and sent his own agents to investigate the accusations made against Ignatius. When they reported back in favour of Photius he dismissed their findings and excommunicated the new patriarch, who responded in kind, but Nicholas died before news of this reached Rome. A further irritant was Nicholas's dispatch of missionaries to convert the Bulgars in the eastern Balkans, an area deep within Constantinople's sphere of influence.

Nicholas I was equally firm with other Church leaders. He deposed the archbishop of Ravenna in 861 for defying Roman authority and in 864 took on Archbishop Hincmar of Reims, the leading advisor to the West Frankish king Charles the Bald (840–877) and a redoubtable defender of the privileges of his see. As a controversialist, Hincmar was not above falsifying documents in support of the claims of Reims, but in this case he faced an indomitable pope and an even more impressive body of forged texts.

The collection of texts accurately but dauntingly known as the Pseudo-Isidoran Decretals is the most influential body of forgeries ever to have been produced in the Middle Ages, itself the golden age of document falsification. We shall encounter it frequently in the history of the centuries that follow. It consists of a series of ninety-three papal letters containing rulings on a wide range of issues, almost all strongly emphasizing the pope's authority and powers of jurisdiction. Of these decretals, eighty-eight are fabrications. The popes whose letters they purport to be range from Clement in the late first century to Gregory II in the early eighth, and the man who claimed to have collected them gave himself the name of Isidore Mercator. He hid his corpus of bogus texts in the middle of an otherwise genuine seventh-century collection of ecclesiastical laws of Spanish origin, known as the *Hispana*.

Mercator, who took his name from the seventh-century Spanish bishop Isidore of Seville (died 636), who had compiled the earliest version of the *Hispana*, thus carefully camouflaged his forgeries by hiding them amongst these genuine papal letters. The spurious character of these letters was never suspected, either at this time or for the rest of the Middle Ages, and consequently they were accepted by successive generations of popes, bishops and church lawyers, and appeared in different selections in all major medieval canon law collections from the ninth century onwards.

What matters is the purpose behind this daring piece of falsification. It was composed in the northern French monastery of Corbie in the 840s, whose abbot, Paschasius Radbertus (842–847), may have been Mercator.[21] One of his intentions, as the tendency of the forged texts shows, was to defend the rights of bishops against the authority of the archbishops or metropolitans who had jurisdiction over them. For Mercator, the best counterweight to the archbishops was the pope, and so, using a copy of the *Liber Pontificalis*, he concocted letters from many of the popes whose names he found in it.

When Bishop Rothad of Soissons appealed to Nicholas I against his deposition for disobedience by Archbishop Hincmar, he did so on the basis of what he had read in the Pseudo-Isidoran Decretals, a copy of which he took to Rome in 864 to put his case before the pope in person. This seems to be the first time the papacy had encountered this collection of what were supposed to be some of its own documents. Surprisingly, no suspicion was aroused by the fact that none of these letters were previously known or available in the papal archives, but the underlying tendency of the collection, extolling papal authority and rights of jurisdiction, fitted perfectly the prevailing atmosphere in the papal court, where the pope and his advisors were searching for historical precedents to justify a more active and assertive role for his office, after a period in which it had been subservient to lay rulers.

Amongst the leading members of this group of clerical advisors around Nicholas I was another of the outstanding figures of this period, Anastasius Bibliothecarius (the Librarian). He had been educated in one of the few remaining Greek monastic communities in Rome, there acquiring a good knowledge of the language, now a rare achievement in the West. He used this skill to translate several Greek texts, mainly saints' lives but also the acts of contemporary Eastern church councils, into Latin. He fell out with Pope Leo IV and was excommunicated by him when he refused to return from self-imposed exile at the court of the emperor Louis II. In 855 with imperial and aristocratic backing, an attempt was made to insert him into the papal office in place of the recently elected Benedict III, who was briefly imprisoned. But he lacked support in Rome and had to abdicate.

He was then stripped of clerical status, becoming technically the antipope Anastasius III for later generations of Church historians, although the papacy did not use the term itself before the thirteenth century. It was thereafter applied to those who claimed or exercised the office of bishop of Rome but whose election was regarded as irregular.

As will be seen, there has not always been agreement as to whom the term should be applied.

Anastasius was rehabilitated by Nicholas I and became one of his closest advisors and the author of part of the pope's biography in the *Liber Pontificalis*. He was also given the office of librarian, which included being head of the papal administration. He retained his post after the early death of Nicholas I in 867, aged less than fifty, and advised his successor Hadrian II (867–872), many of whose letters he drafted. The new pope, who was seventy-five at his accession and had actually turned down the papal office twice when elected as first choice in 855 and 858, followed the line taken by his immediate predecessors in pressing papal claims to superior jurisdiction in all disciplinary matters in the Church, and in trying to persuade the secular rulers of the time to act on Christian principles. But he proved less successful than the previous two popes, although the tone of the letters written for him by Anastasius was imperious and continued to enunciate the ideas on papal authority of Nicholas I and his circle.

But Hadrian II was generally less resolute and effective. For example, he was persuaded to lift the excommunications that his predecessor had placed on both Lothar II and his mistress Walrada when the king failed to be reconciled with his estranged wife as he had promised. When Lothar himself died suddenly in 869 leaving his kingdom to be divided, Hadrian was also unable to repeat the successful intervention made by Benedict III in 855 over the division of the lands of Lothar I. He had particularly wanted to secure a portion of Lothar II's kingdom for Rome's secular protector, the emperor Louis II, whose own territories were confined entirely to Italy. The other members of the dynasty who were carving up the kingdom firmly told the pope it was none of his business.

Similarly, Hadrian's demands that various ecclesiastical disputes in the West Frankish kingdom of Charles the Bald should be brought to Rome for judgement were completely rejected. Hincmar in particular, who never had the nerve to do so to Nicholas I, told him not to interfere where he had no authority. Hadrian then blamed Anastasius for having misrepresented him in the letters sent in his name to the West Frankish court and bishops.

Anastasius, who was obliged to write this papal missive criticizing himself, was in no position to protest, as another scandal had very nearly ended his career in 868. His brother Eleutherius, a member of the Roman secular aristocracy, had eloped with Pope Hadrian's daughter just as she was on the point of marrying someone else. When legal action was threatened against him, Eleutherius apparently murdered both the pope's wife and his daughter to prevent their testifying against him, but was convicted and executed. Hincmar claimed that Anastasius himself had advised his brother to kill the two key witnesses, but this was probably just malicious gossip, as he was reinstated in his old offices of librarian and papal secretary before a year was out. He continued to advise both Hadrian II and John VIII (872–882) up till his death in 879. This episode also indicates that the rules on clerical marriage laid down by Leo I still applied, and so there was no restriction on a married man entering the clergy and even becoming pope.

While certainly the most colourful of the group surrounding Nicholas I and his successors, Anastasius the Librarian was not unique. Others of this circle included a Roman deacon called John Hymmonides, who may have written the 'Life of Hadrian II' in the *Liber Pontificalis*. He is certainly the author of a largely unoriginal four-book *Life of Pope Gregory the Great,* which he wrote around 874 at the request of John VIII. This commission is one of several indicators of the interest of the popes of this time in the life and work of this particular predecessor.

By the time of the pontificate of John VIII (872–882), the steam was running out of the attempt to revive papal authority in the Church and in the spiritual direction of secular rulers. Several of the leading figures who had promoted this were still alive in John's reign, and so the change was less the result of a loss of confidence on the part of either the pope or his advisors and more due to the altered circumstances in which they had to operate, in particular the growing military problems faced by not only the Frankish monarchs but also the papacy itself.

The Arabs' conquest of Sicily was now in its final phase, and they had begun extending their power into parts of southern Italy. Local

Christian rulers in Naples, Amalfi, Salerno and Capua frequently allied with them against each other and against the two imperial powers also involved in the region. In 872 one of them had even taken the emperor Louis II prisoner, forcing him to swear to leave southern Italy as the price of his freedom. In consequence the Arabs were operating with even greater ease, and in 876 one of their raids devastated the area around Rome. John VIII tried to persuade the local Christian rulers in the south to cooperate against the Arabs but in 880 was obliged to excommunicate the bishop of Naples for making an alliance with the Arabs that resulted in wide-scale destruction and loss of Christian life.

The pope urgently needed an emperor who could defend Rome and the papal territories, but it would not be easy to find one. In 875 the emperor Louis II died without male heirs. The western imperial title was effectively at the disposal of the papacy, as there was now no denying that only a papal coronation legitimized an emperor. Several potential candidates existed, as the division of the kingdoms between all suitable male heirs had left the once unified Frankish empire of Charlemagne split into as many as six different realms, still ruled by his descendents. However their interests were focused north of the Alps, because of intensive Viking raiding and periods of internal conflict between the members of the dynasty themselves. John VIII on the other hand needed a new emperor to maintain a significant military presence in Italy. His first choice was the West Frankish king Charles the Bald, who came to Rome for an imperial coronation on Christmas Day 875, mirroring that of his grandfather Charlemagne seventy-five years earlier.

Charles's Italian involvement was not popular at home, not least with Hincmar of Reims, who felt his military duties in the north were more pressing, and in fact Hincmar would die in 882 while fleeing from a Viking sack of his city. Nor was it acceptable to the East Frankish kings that Charles should acquire the Italian lands of Louis II, and so one of them, Carloman, invaded Italy in 877. Charles retreated and died while crossing the Alps. The pope himself then had to take flight to West Francia, as he did not wish to be forced into crowning Carloman, but once there he could not interest Charles the

Bald's son, Louis the Stammerer (877–879), in the vacant office of emperor. Eventually, after some years of fruitless negotiation and the death of several candidates, he had no option but to give the imperial crown in 881 to Charles the Fat (881–887), by then the sole surviving adult and legitimate Carolingian. After his coronation Charles was too busy dealing with the Vikings and other problems to take an active interest in the defence of Italy. Only a revival of Eastern imperial power in the south of Italy from 880 onwards checked and partly reversed the Arab conquests.

John VIII himself died in 882. According to one version of a near contemporary German chronicle, he was beaten to death with a hammer after the failure of an attempt to poison him. Although this story is often repeated and widely believed, the fact that it appears in only a single source and this includes the further detail that the unnamed murderer himself immediately dropped dead, may throw into question its reliability. Whatever the nature of his fate, John VIII's search for a suitable emperor in 875 to 881 shows not only how closely intertwined papacy and empire had become in the years since 799 but also how changed the relationship now was. The same decades had also seen a transformation in the papacy's standing, particularly in the West. In 800 it may have been recognized that the pope was to be 'judged by none', but it took another half century or more for him to be 'judging all men'. In practice the authority achieved by Benedict III, Nicholas I and their circle of advisors and assistants did not last long in the difficult times that followed. But the ideas that inspired them and the texts through which they were expressed, especially the letters of Nicholas I and Hadrian II, survived to encourage a similar but longer-lasting movement of papal reform and revival in the eleventh century. Between the two periods, however, lay the era in the history of the papacy that has sometimes been called the Pornocracy.[22]

OUR MOTHER
THE HOLY ROMAN CHURCH

(896–999)

THE CADAVER SYNOD

In January 897, the body of Pope Formosus (891–896) was re-moved from its grave, dressed in papal robes, placed on a throne and put on trial before a synod meeting in Rome under the presidency of his successor, Stephen VI (896–897). A deacon stood beside the decomposing corpse as its legal representative in answering accusations of perjury and violation of canon law. When Formosus was found guilty, the three fingers of the right hand used in papal blessings were cut off, and the rest of the body, solemnly stripped of its vestments, was thrown into the Tiber. Thus ended the notorious Cadaver Synod, an episode that has long been regarded as marking one of the lowest points of the papacy.

Some modern discussions of the synod go no further than suggesting that Stephen's 'participation in this gruesome affair can only be explained by near hysterical hatred'.[1] But the Cadaver Synod was only the most startling of a series of interrelated events from the time of John VIII (872–882) up to the death of Sergius III in 911. Our difficulty in making sense of them lies in the evidence. The *Liber Pontificalis* ends with the death of Hadrian II in 872, and although a fragment of a life of Stephen V (885–891) survives, there follows a long gap until papal biographies began being written again from the later eleventh century onwards. For the complex events surrounding the Cadaver Synod we depend on brief references in chronicles and defences of Formosus by two priests, Auxilius and Eugenius Vulgarius.

The causes of the Cadaver Synod can be traced back to the period before Formosus was elected pope. In 864 Nicholas I made him bishop of Porto, one of the suburbicarian sees close to Rome. Since the late eighth century, the seven suburbicarian bishops took turns deputising for the pope at the Sunday liturgy in the Lateran, and three of them, those of Ostia, Porto and Albano, consecrated a new pope. They themselves could not be elected because of the decree of the Council of Nicaea of 325 forbidding the transfer of bishops from one diocese to another, which also prevented Nicholas I and Hadrian II from promoting Formosus as the first archbishop of the Bulgar kingdom, after his successful mission there in 866–867. In 875 John VIII sent him to offer the imperial title to the West Frankish king Charles the Bald.

But the following year John VIII turned on Formosus, deposing and excommunicating him in April 876 for conspiring to become pope, in defiance of a recent synodal decree forbidding all discussion of the papal succession. It may be that Formosus had persuaded Charles the Bald to support his candidacy, but with the death of the king, Formosus lost his protector and in August 878 submitted to the pope, promising to remain in permanent exile and accepting degradation to the status of layman.

John VIII died in December 882 and was succeeded by Marinus I (882–884), a leading papal advisor on relations with Constantinople. Since he was already bishop of Caere (Cerveteri), his election blatantly ignored the ban on transferring sees and was accompanied by factional violence, including the murder of a papal official, the *nomenclator* Gregory, in St. Peter's itself: 'The floor of the church was drenched with his blood as he was dragged over it.'[2] Meanwhile the new pope, who had failed to get prior imperial consent to his election, had to hurry north to meet the emperor Charles the Fat (881–887) at the monastery of Nonantula. Amongst other demands, Charles insisted on the restitution of Formosus, who was thus reinstated as bishop of Porto.

The pontificate of Marinus' similarly short-lived successor Hadrian III (884–885) saw more factional violence and score settling. He caused the blinding of a civil official, George of the Aventine, another of the exiles of the time of John VIII recalled by Marinus, and had the widow of the murdered *nomenclator* Gregory whipped naked through the streets of Rome, for reasons unknown.

One contentious issue was the succession to Charles the Fat, whose only son, Bernard, was illegitimate. By the ninth century this meant he could not succeed his father without formal legitimation, which the pope could authorise. As the only other claimant to the eastern Frankish realms was the equally illegitimate Duke Arnulf of Carinthia, Charles the Fat hoped that a gathering of lay and clerical magnates meeting under the presidency of the pope would agree to the succession of Bernard and so persuaded Hadrian III to attend an assembly in Worms. Unfortunately, the pope died on the way in September 885 and was buried at Nonantula, where thanks to the promotion of his cult by the monastery, he became the only papal saint of the two centuries between Nicholas I (858–867) and Leo IX (1049–1054).

For Charles the Fat, the death of Hadrian III was a disaster, as the next pope, Stephen V (885–891), was chosen by acclamation and consecrated without prior imperial consent. Although the emperor wanted to use the irregularity of his consecration as a pretext to depose him in favour of a more malleable candidate, the unanimity of the electors made this impossible. Stephen prevaricated about going north and instead persuaded the emperor to travel to Italy to discuss matters of common interest, including renewed threats to Rome from Arab raids. Five months later, a Viking siege of Paris forced Charles to leave Rome with little achieved. So, the scheme to legitimise Bernard stalled, and in 887 the emperor divorced his wife, in hopes of producing a legitimate heir.[3] However, in November he was incapacitated by a seizure and deposed in favour of Arnulf, dying soon after.

The supporters of Arnulf had not been the only ones opposing the legitimising of Bernard. Those with Carolingian blood through the female line might profit when the male line died out, and they included two of the four great regional magnates of northern and central Italy: Berengar, Margrave of Friuli, and Guido, Margrave of Spoleto. In 888 Berengar claimed the kingdom of Italy, which had been held in conjunction with the imperial title since 850, while Guido made an abortive bid to acquire a realm north of the Alps. When this bid failed, Guido made a counterclaim for the Italian kingdom in 889 and went to war against Berengar.

As this was likely to result in one of them dominating Rome, in 890 Stephen V tried to persuade the new East Frankish king Arnulf to take the imperial title. But the empire briefly reunited by Charles the Fat was now split between rivals scrambling for regional power, and his son Bernard was in revolt. So Arnulf could not risk the necessary journey to Rome. Instead, when Guido of Spoleto won the war with Berengar, Stephen V had no choice but to recognise him. In 891 he adopted Guido as his spiritual son and crowned him emperor in St. Peter's on 21 February. In 892 his successor Formosus re-crowned Guido and his son Lambert as co-emperors, while Rome and its territories were garrisoned by their troops.

Formosus shared his predecessor's unease at the control of Rome by the emperors of the house of Spoleto, and from 893 he began sending secret invitations to Arnulf to come and challenge them. Papal resistance to an independent and powerful kingdom of Italy (repeated a millennium later) seems short-sighted, as this could have been the best way of protecting Rome from both internal and external enemies. Ever since 876 emperors and kings of Italy had sworn to defend 'the holy Roman Church that is the head of all churches', to honour the pope and to protect 'the boundaries of blessed Peter and Paul', in other words ensure the territorial integrity of the papal estates.[4] Similarly, Guido, when crowned king of Italy in Pavia in February 889, swore first of all to preserve the honour, privileges, lands and authority of 'our mother the Holy Roman Church', as they had been granted to her 'by ancient and modern emperors and kings'. The pope was to be 'reverenced with appropriate honour by all princes'.[5] These assurances were required by the clergy, led by the archbishop of Milan, and other electors who gathered in Pavia to confer the royal title, and they show the importance of the Roman church in the eyes of the lay and clerical magnates of northern and central Italy. In consequence, several of the popes of the period came north, holding synods in Ravenna as well as Rome.

Papal fear of a dominant secular power in the peninsula went back to the time of the Lombard kingdom, and if the Frankish rulers could no longer help, there was an older defender of Rome to whom the pope might turn. Relations between Rome and Constantinople had improved markedly in the late ninth century from the time of John VIII onwards, assisted by an imperial military recovery in southern Italy in the time of the emperor Basil I (867–886). Pope Stephen V asked him to send a fleet to defend papal territories against Arab raids.

In the West, real political power was becoming increasingly localised. The military threats from Vikings, Arabs, Slavs and then Magyars, together with the structural weakness of its government, not only broke up the empire of Charlemagne but intensified the need for regional solutions for problems of defence and local order. The four Italian margraves were as wary as the papacy of losing power to kings of Italy drawn from their own number, and the dukes and princes of the south, mainly of Lombard descent, played off Eastern and Western imperial as well as Arab rulers to preserve their own independence.

Guido died in 894, but Lambert maintained his authority despite renewed conflict with Berengar until Arnulf finally invaded Italy in 896, expelling Lambert's troops from Rome in February. A few days later Formosus crowned Arnulf emperor, and the leading men of Rome swore that, saving their honour and the loyalty they owed to 'the lord pope Formosus', they would never aid Lambert and his mother, Agiltrude, or admit them into the city.[6] However, in April Formosus died and Arnulf was paralysed by a stroke, forcing his immediate return to Germany, where he died in 899.

None of the events of his pontificate explain the bizarre judicial process to which the corpse of this pope would be subjected seven months later. Formosus enjoyed a reputation for personal piety and an ascetic lifestyle. As pope he was interventionist, threatening to excommunicate the English bishops for failing to convert the Vikings, and preserving the new missionary archbishopric of Hamburg-Bremen against attempts by the archbishops of Mainz to have it reduced in status. None of the increasingly common episodes of murder and mutilation in the ranks of the papal administration are recorded under his rule.

Where he had contravened canon law was in being translated to the papal throne from the see of Porto, and thus the legitimacy of his election was questionable, affecting his status and that of the clergy he had ordained. Formosus' immediate successor, Boniface VI, was a far more dubious choice, in that he had twice been degraded in rank by John VIII for immoral conduct and had not been reinstated after the second offence, but, crippled by gout, he died after a mere fifteen days as pope.

In his place, Stephen VI (896–897), then bishop of Agnani, was elected. He had been made bishop by Formosus, so this impediment to his legitimacy as pope would be eliminated if the latter's ordinations were annulled. It was a procedural question rather than irrational hatred that brought about the Cadaver Synod. While unprecedented as an event, the thinking behind the trial shows the influence of Gregory the Great prevalent in Rome at this time.[7] In his *Dialogues* Gregory had stressed that 'those dying in a state of mortal sin who arrange to have themselves buried in a church will be condemned for their presumption' and had recounted several tales of how such bodies had been ejected from their places of burial by supernatural or other means.[8] The fate of Formosus' corpse in 897 was a re-enactment of such a Gregorian story.

So too was the sequel. According to a near contemporary, the body, although weighted down before being thrown into the Tiber, was quickly washed ashore. A monk had nocturnal visions of the dead pope telling him where to find his body, and he recovered and hid the corpse until it could be reverently re-interred in St. Peter's in November 897.

This tale had already begun circulating and casting doubt on the validity of the Cadaver Synod when, in the summer of 897, there came an even more dramatic sign of divine displeasure with Stephen VI: The Lateran Basilica was destroyed, probably by fire. Members of the Roman clergy ordained by Formosus now refused to accept annulment of their orders, and a revolt in August led to Stephen VI being imprisoned and strangled. One of his short-lived successors, Theodore II, presided over a synod that overturned the decisions of the Cadaver Synod and carried out the solemn reburial of Formosus.

At the heart of this conflict was the validity of Formosus' ordinations. Stephen VI was not alone in wanting to see these declared illegitimate, so that his election as pope would not be called into question because he was already a bishop. A Roman aristocrat called Sergius who had been appointed by Formosus to the see of Caere, willingly surrendered his office when Formosus was condemned by the Cadaver Synod and became the leader of a faction determined to uphold its decisions. In 898 he was elected pope on the sudden death of Theodore II after only a three-week pontificate but was immediately expelled from Rome by the emperor Lambert, who was determined to prevent Formosus' ordinations from being overturned.

Although Formosus had crowned Arnulf in 896, Lambert did not wish to see the former pope's decisions invalidated, as this would cast doubt on the legitimacy of his own coronation by him in 892. So he moved against Sergius III in January 898 and secured the election of an obscure former monk known as John IX (898–900). A synod then reiterated the condemnation of the Cadaver Synod, burned its acts and prohibited any future trials of the dead. Participants in the Cadaver Synod other than Sergius and a handful of his followers were pardoned if they took an oath that they had acted under compulsion, while the ordinations of Formosus were recognised, including the imperial coronation of Lambert. That of Arnulf was annulled on the spurious pretext of being secured by the threat of violence.

John IX then presided over an even larger synod of Italian bishops at Ravenna, which confirmed all the rights granted by 'pious emperors' to 'the Holy Roman Church Our Mother' since the earliest times. It also confirmed in perpetuity the decisions of the recent synod in Rome and condemned all 'illicit conjunctions' of Romans, Lombards and Franks aimed against the emperor or the pope in the 'territories of the blessed Apostle Peter, Prince of the Apostles'. Another decree urged the speedy rebuilding of the Lateran Basilica, said to have been delayed by an 'infestation of malicious men', in other words Sergius' supporters.[9] The price to be paid for Lambert's protection of the papacy was the reinstatement of the Constitution of 824 regulating papal elections, and imperial oversight of the administration of Rome and its territories. Romans 'both from the clergy and from the senate, or from any other order' were granted a right of appeal to the emperor to prevent the partisan use of papal justice.[10]

The chance of reviving the good government of Rome and Italy that had existed in the earlier ninth century was lost when Lambert was killed in a hunting accident on 15 October 898. Berengar of Friuli made another bid for power but gained limited support, and no effective central authority emerged in Italy over the next sixty years. The four margraves—of Friuli, Ivrea, Spoleto and Tuscany—proved as reluctant as the papacy to see a powerful monarchy in northern Italy and switched allegiance if their prerogatives or regional authority were threatened.

Pope Benedict IV (900–903) supported the opponents of Berengar in trying to find a new ruler from north of the Alps, and in 901 he crowned King Louis of Provence (890–928) as emperor. As a grandson of the emperor Louis II (850–875) he had a strong claim to the Italian kingdom, but Margrave Adalbert of Tuscany deserted him, and in August 902 Louis was defeated by Berengar, who made him swear to leave Italy. In 904 the same Adalbert turned against Berengar and persuaded Louis to return, only to betray him again the next year. Louis was captured by Berengar at Verona and blinded for breaking his previous oath.

THE HOUSE OF THEOPHYLACT

In the tenth century, papal Rome became a regional power, not dissimilar in size and standing to the four northern margravates, dominated by an aristocratic dynasty but retaining a unique religious status embracing all of Latin Christendom. A strong sense of local identity led to conflicts in the streets between Romans, Lombards and Franks, and alien rulers such as the emperor Arnulf were resented by the Roman populace. The terminology of senatorial rule, including women *senatrices*, reappears for the first time since the sixth century, suggesting a new group identity amongst the leading families of Rome that expressed itself through images from the city's past. Similarly, the title of consul was reused as a mark of honour for the leading members of this noble class.

Little is known of the origins of this new Roman aristocracy, which emerged from the military officials and landholders of the eighth century, with a few Frankish incomers working their way into it in the ninth. The popes of the period of Roman aristocratic origin, such as Gregory IV, Hadrian II, Stephen V and Sergius III (898/ 904–911), belonged to these 'senatorial' families, and aristocratic factional politics once again played a role in papal elections. Within the papal territories were several towns with their own local aristocracies, and factions in Rome allied themselves to them spread their influence beyond the city. The estates owned by the Church in the papal territories also depended on these local aristocracies to provide the officials needed to supervise them, as well as contribute family members to the clergy.

All these factors played a part in the turbulent events of this period. The aristocratic Benedict IV died in August 903, and his successor Leo V was a compromise candidate, a priest from outside the city with a reputation for holiness. Three weeks later he was deposed by his defeated rival Christopher and imprisoned. But in January 904 Sergius III, who had been ejected in 898 but regarded himself as the legitimate pope, seized Rome with the aid of Margrave Alberic of Spoleto.[11] In his epitaph he said he returned to the city 'with the prayers of the populace'.[12] Christopher joined Leo V in prison, and both were soon strangled—Sergius felt they should be put out of their misery. Meanwhile he reinstated the decrees of the Cadaver Synod, despite its 'eternal' condemnation in 898, and again annulled the ordinations of Formosus. His opponents took refuge in Naples, there writing the pro-Formosan pamphlets on which most of our knowledge of these events depends.

In Rome Sergius III found allies in the family of a senator called Theophylact (died c. 920) and his wife Theodora (died c. 916) and is said to have had a liaison with their fifteen-year-old daughter

Marozia, fathering by her the future pope John XI.[13] After the pope's death in 911 she married his ally, Margrave Alberic of Spoleto, bearing another son, Alberic. Through its connections with Sergius III and Margrave Alberic, the house of Theophylact acquired leadership of the dominant aristocratic faction in Rome. Theophylact was given charge of the financial administration of the Roman church and put in command of the city guard, controlling both the material and the military resources of the papacy.

As pope, Sergius III completed the external restoration of the Lateran Basilica, for the damage to which he and his supporters had been unfairly blamed by the Ravenna synod of 898; internally it was finished with a new set of frescoes under John X (914–928). Generally Sergius III was as efficient as he was ruthless. Like his predecessors he issued silver coins bearing images and symbols of St. Peter together with his own name, some of which omit that of the emperor.[14]

Sergius III's two immediate successors, Anastasius III (911–913) and Lando (913–914) faced renewed Arab threats, after a group of raiders fortified a base on the river Garigliano between Rome and Naples in 908. Under Pope Lando they destroyed the cathedral of Vescovio in Sabina, northeast of Rome, and this contributed to the election of John X (914–928). He had been archbishop of Ravenna since 905, and so his election ignored the decree against a bishop moving from another see, but John made no attempt to regularise his position. Half a century later it was claimed that he had been chosen because he was the lover of Theophylact's second daughter, Theodora the Younger, acquiring the papacy 'by a crime that outraged all law, human and divine'.[15] The more likely truth is that the Romans needed him as a man of action. As archbishop of Ravenna he had been close to Berengar of Friuli, whom he would crown emperor in December 915. As pope he put together an alliance including Berengar, Theophylact and Alberic of Spoleto, along with some Lombard princes of the south, to eliminate the Arab fortress on the Garigliano. With naval support from the Eastern empire, the Arabs were blockaded for three months before their base was destroyed in August 915 in an action in which the pope himself took part.

The years that followed are again obscure, but it is clear that Berengar, even as emperor, failed to retain the loyalty of the margraves, and in 922 there was a widespread revolt against him. Rudolf II, king of Burgundy (912–937), was invited to Italy to replace Berengar, whom he quickly defeated, and in 924 Berengar was executed at Verona. In 926 another descendant of the Carolingian emperors, Count Hugh of Arles, was persuaded to invade Italy by John X amongst others, forcing Rudolf to return to Burgundy and taking the kingdom of Italy for himself.

In Rome the death of Theophylact around 920 had left a power vacuum that was filled by the pope and Margrave Peter of Spoleto, but as non-Romans their position was insecure. In June 928 Theophylact's daughter Marozia and her second husband, Margrave Guido of Tuscany, carried out a coup in which Peter and John X were surprised in the Lateran, the margrave killed and the pope imprisoned in the Castel Sant'Angelo, the mausoleum of the Roman emperor Hadrian close by St. Peter's and now a fortress. In 929 John X was suffocated following the death of Margrave Guido, leaving the *Domina Senatrix* (Lady Senator) and patrician Marozia ruler of the city. As a Roman chronicler put it, 'Rome was subjugated by a power-wielding female hand, just as we may read in the Prophet: *the women shall dominate Jerusalem.*'[16]

By this time, John X's immediate successor, the aristocratic priest Leo VI (928–929), was also dead, replaced by the equally elderly Stephen VII (928–931). They kept the papal throne warm until it was credible to elect John XI (931–936), Marozia's son possibly by Sergius III (although if he was, he could hardly have reached the minimum age of thirty required in canon law for ordination as a bishop). His mother's regime was unstable, leading her to offer to marry King Hugh, with an imperial coronation at the hands of her son as part of the package. The marriage in 932 was not popular in Rome, least of all with Marozia's second son, Alberic, who in December led a revolt, besieging Hugh and Marozia in the Castel Sant'Angelo.[17] The king escaped, but Marozia spent the rest of her long life as prisoner of her son, who under the title of *princeps* or prince became unchallenged master of Rome until his death in 954.

THE AGE OF ALBERIC

The twenty-two-year rule of Alberic brought many benefits.[18] He and his allies took over the administration of Rome and its territories, just as if it were one of the Lombard principalities in the south or the margravates in the north, while the popes and their clerical bureaucracy dealt with the affairs of the Church, both locally and across Christendom. In some ways this was the sensible solution to a situation that had developed in a largely accidental fashion, with a bishopric gradually becoming a territorial state that could never properly defend itself.

Even in times of political turmoil or when the papal office was held by unsuitable occupants, the pope's administration continued to function and plaintiffs and pilgrims continued coming to Rome in search of justice and spiritual reward. In such contexts the personal foibles and even the name of the holder of the papal office mattered little. When Bishop Rather of Verona wrote to Rome in 965, knowing only that Leo VIII (963–965) had died, he addressed his letter 'to the Lord of the Holy Roman See whomsoever he may be . . . .'[19] Many of the documents issued in a pope's name may never have been seen by him, depending on his devotion to work. And most communications required little more than conventional replies from a long-established and self-assured bureaucracy that had its own traditions of script and of documentary forms. The documents were written by scribes called *scrinarii,* working under an *archiscrinarius,* and they would be checked and signed by the *primicerius* of the Apostolic See, the head of the papal notariate.

A succession of popes followed Alberic's short-lived half-brother John XI, and probably all were elected with the prince's approval. None of them played a major role in the secular politics of their time, though a later revision of the *Liber Pontificalis* claims that Stephen VIII was deposed for involvement in a failed conspiracy against Alberic. On the other hand the period was marked by papal support for movements of monastic reform. This was an interest shared by Alberic, who patronised monasteries such as Farfa and Subiaco, on the site of a cave in which the famous monastic founder St. Benedict (died c. 547) once lived.[20] Later in the century Alberic was described as a supporter of monasteries by the monk and chronicler Benedict of St. Andrew, whose own house on Mount Soracte was restored, fortified and liberally endowed by the 'glorious prince'.[21] These decades saw the first introduction of the *Rule* of monastic life written by St. Benedict into several of the monasteries of Rome, where it had hitherto made little impact.

The documentary records also indicate that most of the land owned by the monasteries of Rome was let out to the regional aristocracy. The monks required only limited produce for their own consumption and needed both to exploit and defend estates they did not farm directly. Thus a valuable relationship was created with the lay nobility, from the house of Theophylact downwards, who could extract what profits they were able to from these lands, while guaranteeing the monasteries a secure and regular income. Family members often joined these houses, sometimes becoming their abbots, as with the Convent of Saints Cyriacus and Nicholas in Rome, which was ruled continuously by abbesses of the house of Alberic until c. 1045.[22]

The middle decades of the tenth century saw major movements of revival and reform of monastic life in Western Europe, centred on the monasteries of Cluny in Burgundy, Fleury in the Loire Valley and Gorze in the former kingdom of Lotharingia (Lorraine). Fleury was amongst the first to seek papal protection and confirmation, obtaining a right of appeal to Rome against decisions by the local bishop as early as the eighth century. Cluny, founded in 909, received a charter of papal protection from John XI in 931 and made a point of getting papal confirmation of many gifts it received in subsequent years to ensure their protection, and its cartulary or book of legal records is a major source for the relatively few papal documents surviving from the mid-tenth century.[23] Gorze obtained its first papal privilege from Pope Leo VII, himself a monk, in June 938.[24]

This practice of monastic founders or the abbots requesting documents of papal *tuitio* or protection for their houses reflected the rapid growth and geographical spread of monasticism from the ninth century onwards. Its roots are to be found in the long-established custom of granting immunities, which freed the estates of a lord, either secular or clerical, from interference by the local officials of the king in return for their taking over responsibilities such as the administration of justice. In the mid-ninth century, diocesan bishops' attempts to limit the authority exercised by their metropolitans were reflected in the influential Pseudo-Isidoran Decretals that emphasised papal oversight of the diocesans over that of the archbishops. So, in the same way, monastic houses, wanting to free themselves from interference by local bishops in the running of their affairs, not least the choosing of their abbots, turned to the papacy for grants of *tuitio*.

The popes had no practical means of enforcing the promised protection, but they could usually find allies in kings or archbishops for whom the existence of a papal privilege was a valuable excuse for supporting the monastery against its episcopal overlord. In general this made the papacy an ever more significant institution in Western Christendom, at the very time when its own disturbed condition and the general political fragmentation of the period might have gravely weakened it.

So interested did the papacy and also Prince Alberic become in the reforms of monastic life instituted by Abbot Odo of Cluny that he was invited to Rome by Leo VII in 936 and there negotiated a peace agreement between Alberic and King Hugh of Italy, sealed by marriage between Alberic and Hugh's daughter Alda. The primary purpose for Odo's visit, however, was to introduce the Cluniac reforms into some of the monasteries of the city, beginning with San Paolo fuori le mura, which had been fortified by John VIII.[25] However, there was local resistance, especially in San Paolo. In 945 Pope Marinus II placed the monastery under the rule of the abbot of Monte Cassino, and when this failed to have much impact, monks were brought from the reforming house of Gorze by Agapitus II to replace the local ones who had refused to accept the new more austere lifestyle.

Amongst other visitors to Rome in this period was Flodoard (died 966), a priest of the diocese of Reims and a historian. He came in 936 as envoy of one of the rival claimants to the archbishopric of his city, staying nearly a year. During it he dined with Pope Leo VII and referred to his wisdom and personal charm in a long narrative poem,

De Triumphis Christi apud Italiam (The Triumphs of Christ in Italy), which incorporated a history of the bishops of Rome.[26]

Hugh of Arles's grip on the Italian kingdom appeared strong in the early 940s but was actually fragile. In 945 a confederacy of lay and ecclesiastical notables in the north threatened to transfer support to the exiled Margrave Berengar of Ivrea, forcing Hugh to abdicate in favour of his son Lothar (945–950), and withdraw to Provence, where he died in 947. Berengar of Ivrea, whose mother was the daughter of the emperor Berengar I, had Lothar poisoned in 950, taking the crown as Berengar II (950–962) jointly with his son Adalbert.[27]

Back in 937 Hugh had married Bertha, the widow of his old rival Rudolf II of Burgundy, while his son Lothar married their daughter Adelaide. Widowed by the murder of Lothar in 950, Adelaide was a highly desirable match for both her Italian and her Burgundian connections. When she refused Adalbert, Berengar II imprisoned her to make her change her mind, while she appealed to the German or East Frankish king Otto I (936–973), offering her hand to him instead. The result was the beginning of an intervention that would transform the history of Italy and the papacy.

The Carolingian dynasty had expired in eastern Francia in 911 with the death of Louis the Child, the only legitimate son of the former emperor Arnulf. The kingship then became elective between the dukes, the greater regional magnates who controlled territories thought to represent the main ethnic groups that made up the kingdom: the Saxons, Bavarians, Suabians (or Alamans) and the Franks (Franconia), together with what remained of the former kingdom of Lotharingia. The second of the kings thus elected was the Saxon duke Henry I (919–936), whose descendants inherited the monarchy until their dynasty died out in 1024. It was his son Otto I the Great who marched into Italy in answer to the former queen Adelaide's appeal in 951.

Otto easily defeated Berengar, rescued and married Adelaide and was crowned king of Italy at Pavia. He began negotiations for an imperial coronation in Rome in 952 with Agapitus II (946–955). Whatever the pope's personal inclinations may have been, Prince Alberic had no intention of allowing a powerful foreign ruler and his army into the city, and so told Agapitus to refuse. As Otto had rebellions and continuing Magyar attacks to contend with at home, he could not force his way into Rome, and instead returned to Germany in 952 with Adelaide, leaving Berengar II still holding much of the Italian kingdom.

Despite this episode, Agapitus II was keen to support the new Saxon or Ottonian dynasty in Germany. The papacy in this period was eager to assist secular rulers, and it still remained the most prestigious institution in the West. Successive popes throughout the century used their influence to sustain the much-weakened Carolingian kings in western Francia, though they could not prevent the dynasty finally being replaced by their Capetian rivals in 987. In the former eastern Frankish kingdom, popes backed royal initiatives to reform the organisation of its church, as well as supporting the monarchs against the powerful regional dukes.

JOHN XII

The most controversial pontificate of this period is undoubtedly that of John XII (955–964). Named Octavian after the first Roman emperor, he was the illegitimate son and only heir of Prince Alberic. It is claimed that in 954 Alberic on his deathbed made Agapitus II and others swear to elect Octavian as pope when the next vacancy arose.[28] The elevation of the eighteen-year-old John XII, in flagrant defiance of canon law, put an end to the separation of political and ecclesiastical authority in Rome that had so marked Alberic's rule.

What we know of him tends to be scurrilous, since it mostly comes from the pen of Bishop Liutprand of Cremona (962–972), a diplomat and propagandist for Otto I, as well as an outstanding preacher and exegete. In three consecutive texts he reports much of what we know of events in Italy from the late ninth century onwards. His loyalty to Otto, and to his previous master, King Hugh, is certain, as is his ability to weave scandalous and obscene tales about their enemies. In this he continued, with obvious relish, the classical tradition of discrediting opponents through accounts of their real or imaginary sexual excesses.

More objective sources suggest John XII shared his father's interest in monastic reform in the papal territories, and particularly favoured St. Benedict's monastery at Subiaco, where he went on pilgrimage in 958. He confirmed its properties, adding gifts of his own so that 'for the salvation of our soul and those of our successors, the priests and monks shall daily chant one hundred *Kyrie eleisons* and one hundred *Christe eleisons,* and the priests shall offer the holy oblations to God in the solemnities of the mass in three villages every week for the absolution of our soul and those of our successors.'[29] In the Lateran Basilica in Rome he built a chapel dedicated to St. Thomas.[30] Monasteries and churches across Europe continued to apply for papal protection and confirmation of their properties, and archbishops Oscytel of York (in 957) and Dunstan of Canterbury (in 960), both promoters of monastic reform in the English kingdom, came to Rome to receive the pallium in person from this pope.

In the secular sphere John XII was less adept. His attempts to conquer the Lombard principalities of Capua and Benevento were easily resisted, while papal territory to the north of Rome was overrun by an increasingly aggressive Berengar II. In 960 John had to appeal to Otto I to return to Italy, offering the inducement of an imperial coronation. By now conditions in Germany had changed considerably. A decisive victory over the Magyars on the river Lech in 955 had put an end to their threat, and the elimination of some of Otto's rivals had secured his unquestioned dominance over the regional dukedoms. So, in the summer of 961 he was able to return to Italy to take up where he had left off a decade earlier. Berengar II was no match for him and was finally captured in the fortress of Montefeltro in 963 and exiled to Bamberg in Germany, where he died in 966.

In February 962 Otto entered Rome and was crowned emperor in St. Peter's together with his wife Adelaide. He presented gifts to the Roman church and issued a charter confirming its property. This included lands either once owned by the popes and since lost, or claimed by them but never acquired, including Ravenna and the former imperial exarchate, the Pentapolis, Istria and Venetia, southern Tuscany, Naples, the duchy of Benevento and the island of Corsica as well as 'the patrimony of Sicily, if God should give it into our hands'.

The bases for this grant, known as the Ottonianum, or Pact of Otto, were the earlier agreements and territorial concessions believed to have been made by Pippin III and Charlemagne in the eighth century. Also revived was the pact of 824 regulating papal elections and the appointment of legates to oversee the proper administration of justice. This, and the statement that the emperors would be the defenders of the lands and revenues of the Roman church, made it clear that close imperial oversight of the popes was to be restored for the first time since the mid-ninth century.[31]

Otto's coronation in 962 is often taken as the foundation of 'The Holy Roman Empire', of which Voltaire famously quipped that it was 'neither holy, nor Roman, nor an empire'.[32] As we shall encounter this institution frequently in the chapters to follow and there is much confusion over its name, a few words on the subject are needed here. The full title is 'The Holy Roman Empire of the German Nation', but this only came into use at the very end of the Middle Ages. The line of emperors extends back to Charlemagne's coronation by Leo III in 800, but none of them was ever called 'Holy Roman Emperor', though 'Roman Emperor' was sometimes used from the late tenth century onwards. The term 'Roman Empire' to describe the conglomerate of territories in parts of modern Germany, Austria, Italy, Switzerland, southwest France and Eastern Europe over which the emperors exercised authority (often varying in origin, character and effect from region to region) first appears in 1034, and it was described as a 'holy empire' in 1157, but the two were not combined until 1254. To avoid confusion none of these names or titles will be used here.

The threat of more active imperial oversight or interference explains John XII's about-face in 963, when, despite the oath he had taken to Otto the previous year, he invited Berengar II's son Adalbert to come to Rome. Liutprand of Cremona attributed this to pure evil: 'Pope John hates the most sacred emperor . . . just as the devil hates his creator.' He claimed to quote a letter from the citizens of Rome to Otto listing the pope's sexual excesses, including how he had become so obsessed with the widow of one of his officials that he gave her 'the most holy golden crosses and chalices of St. Peter' and how he had had a child with his late father's mistress and an affair with her sister, with the result that 'the Lateran palace that was once the dwelling of saints is now a brothel for whores'. Female pilgrims are described as not daring to come to Rome for fear of being raped by the pope, as it was said had already happened to several of them, while the churches were said to be so neglected that rain fell onto their altars and people feared to enter them in case they might be hit by collapsing masonry.[33]

While colourful, we should not take the description at face value, as has too often been done. Liutprand was a propagandist who had no real interest in explaining what the pope's motivation was. He needed his lurid descriptions to justify what followed. When Adalbert reached Rome he and the pope began appealing for allies, sending envoys to both the Eastern emperor and the Magyars, but were not strong enough to resist Otto, who retook Rome in November 963. By then John XII and Adalbert had fled. A synod of bishops, including some from Germany, was called to depose the pope on grounds not only of immorality but also of heresy and apostasy. Liutprand, who was present, listed all those attending, including 'representatives of the princes of Rome'.

While the outcome was predictable, the issue was complicated by the existence of the well-known texts stating that there was no jurisdiction superior to that of a pope or competent to try him. As a result a whole series of accusations, some extremely bizarre, were levelled against John XII to justify his deposition. These included claims that he had ordained a deacon in a stable, that he had taken money for ordinations, had had an affair with his own niece (as well as several of the other ladies previously mentioned), had castrated and killed a subdeacon, engaged in acts of arson, appeared in public in armour, drank wine out of love of the devil, called on pagan gods for luck in games of chance and never said Matins and the canonical hours or made the sign of the Cross.[34] The council then asked John to come and reply to these charges, but he responded with a letter excommunicating all the participants if they attempted to replace him.[35] The bishops then criticised him for a grammatical error in his letter 'more suitable for a stupid child than a bishop'.

Turning to the more substantive issue of the papal prohibition on their deposing him, the bishops claimed that the powers of binding and loosing had been given by Christ to all the Apostles including Judas Iscariot. 'While Judas was a good man along with his fellow disciples, he had the power to bind and loose, but later when he committed a murder out of greed and wanted to destroy the life of all, whom could he thereafter loose that was bound or bind that was loosed other than himself, whom he strangled with the accursed noose?' John XII as the Judas of their day had thus lost any power of binding or loosing by virtue of his conduct. An ingenious but hardly convincing exegesis of Matthew 16.18, it sufficed for the bishops to ask the emperor that 'this monster that no virtue redeems from his vices be expelled from the holy Roman Church and another be appointed in his place'.[36] The ultimate responsibility was thus placed with the emperor, even if the bishops carried out the deposition at his command. Ignoring the rules restricting this to a purely Roman electorate, on 4 December 963 the synod elected the chief notary, who became Leo VIII (963–965). Being a layman at the time, he had to be raised through all the ranks of the clergy before receiving his papal ordination two days later.

Not all the participants in the synod were enthusiastic, especially the representatives of the 'princes of the Romans'. Rome had been self-governing for so long that foreign domination was resented. The strength of local support was such that John XII could hold out at Tivoli, only twenty miles from Rome. In January 964 a revolt in the city against the emperor and his new pope led to violent street fighting. Otto took hostages from the leading Roman families but was persuaded to release them by Leo VIII, who as a Roman himself thought conciliation the better policy. His error was demonstrated when John XII returned to Rome immediately after Otto left to campaign against Adalbert, forcing Leo VIII to flee to Spoleto.

In February 964 John convened a synod, attended by some of the bishops who had been present in the one that had deposed him the previous year and whose decisions were now annulled. The decrees of John's synod made masterly use of earlier papal history in condemning the way he had been tried in his absence and in defiance of the accepted belief in papal superiority to all earthly judgement. John himself died suddenly on 14 May. According to Liutprand's hardly dispassionate testimony, he had a stroke while in bed with a married woman and died refusing the last rites.[37]

THE PAPACY BETWEEN
THE OTTONIANS AND THE CRESCENTII

The Roman clergy then elected Benedict the Grammarian, a deacon known for his learning and piety, but Otto and Leo VIII blockaded the city until it surrendered in June 964. At a synod in the Lateran, Benedict V's pastoral staff was broken in two by Leo VIII and displayed to the crowd,[38] but he has never been regarded as an antipope. Degraded to the rank of deacon, he was exiled to Hamburg, and Otto refused the request of the Roman clergy that he be reinstated as pope on the death of Leo VIII in March 965.

After a five-month hiatus, John XIII (965–972), a papal librarian and then bishop of Narni (Umbria) under John XII, was elected. By this time the controversial aspect of translating a bishop from another see to the papal throne that had loomed so large in the time of Formosus was not an issue. But as an outsider and effectively the emperor's nominee, John's position in Rome was insecure. He began a reorganisation of the Church in southern Italy to promote imperial authority there, creating new archdioceses of Capua in 967 and Benevento in 989, enraging the patriarch of Constantinople, who had controlled the dioceses in Calabria and Apulia since the revival of Eastern imperial rule in those regions in the late ninth century.

John XIII's reliance on Otto I was demonstrated in 965 when he was imprisoned and then exiled in a revolt in Rome following the emperor's return to Germany. Rule in Rome was quickly seized by Crescentius, son of Theodora the Younger, the sister of the notorious Marozia. His rise to power marked the emergence of the junior branch of the family of Theophylact, though their hold on Rome and the papacy proved less secure than that of Alberic and John XII.

Otto returned to Italy in 966, soon regaining control of Rome, and negotiated with Crescentius for the safe reinstatement of John XIII.

This was part of a series of steps to establish more stable papal-imperial relations. The emperor finally put some of the Ottonianum of 962 into effect, placing the lands of the former exarchate under papal authority, though other promised territorial transfers were not made and continued contentious, and John XIII crowned Otto I's twelve-year-old son Otto II as co-emperor on Christmas Day 967, again evoking the coronation of Charlemagne. As Otto I remained continuously in Italy until 972, his pope's security was guaranteed for the time being.

On John XIII's death in September 972, Benedict, son of Hildebrand the Monk, was elected as Benedict VI, but was kept waiting for imperial consent to his consecration until January 973. Almost immediately, the death of Otto I at Magdeburg in May 973 left the new pope seriously weakened, as the young Otto II faced challenges to his authority in Germany. In June 974 Crescentius carried out a coup, imprisoning Benedict in the Castel Sant'Angelo and replacing him with the deacon Franco, son of Ferrucio, who had been his family's candidate for the papacy in 972, and now took the name of Boniface VII. When an imperial legate, Count Sicco of Spoleto, arrived to demand the release of Benedict VI, the imprisoned pope was strangled on Boniface's orders.

Boniface VII was described by a contemporary as 'a horrible monster, surpassing all mortals in wickedness' and compared with Antichrist.[39] In the summer of 974 Count Sicco forced an entry into the city, and Boniface fled with the papal treasury. The count then oversaw the election of Benedict VII (974–983), previously bishop of Sutri and, more importantly, a close relative of the family of Crescentius. A synod was assembled to proclaim the deposition of Boniface VII, who had taken refuge in Eastern imperial territory in southern Italy. Like John XIII, the new pope co-operated closely with the emperor, Otto II, approving the restructuring of the Church in Germany. He was equally dependent on imperial military backing, as Boniface VII re-established himself in Rome with local support in 980 and could not be ejected until Otto II returned to Italy in 981. His arrival was preparatory to a campaign he had planned against the Arabs in the south, also intended to make his overlordship of its Lombard principalities and duchies into a reality. Before setting out, Otto II and Benedict VII attended a synod held in St. Peter's in March 981, which forbade all forms of simony, the offence named after Simon Magus, who had offered money for spiritual authority (Acts 8. 18–24), and referring not just to any offer or demand of payment for clerical office but also to any election or investiture that involved loss of control over ecclesiastical property. This theme would be taken up with greater vigour by papal reformers of the second half of the eleventh century.

Benedict VII shared the interests of several tenth-century predecessors in monastic reform. He exchanged letters with Abbot Maiolus of Cluny (965–994) and arranged to give it control of the monastery on the Mediterranean isle of Lérins, dating from the early fifth century and once the centre of monastic life in Gaul. Like John XII, Benedict was particularly attracted to Subiaco, where he consecrated the church dedicated to St. Benedict's sister Scholastica in 980. In Rome he promoted a further monastic revival in the city with the creation in 977 of the house of Saints Boniface and Alexius on the Aventine, which he placed under the direction of the former patriarch Sergius of Damascus, who had recently fled to Rome from Muslim persecution.

In 982 Otto II's southern campaign proved a disaster. He was defeated by the Arabs and only escaped capture by swimming to one of his ships lying offshore. Returning north he had to deal with a papal election after the death of Benedict VII in July 983. The emperor made this a matter of imperial nomination, first offering the papal throne to Abbot Maiolus of Cluny and, when he refused, appointing Bishop Peter of Pavia, his long-serving chancellor of the kingdom of Italy, who was finally consecrated in early December. The new pope changed his name, becoming John XIV (983–984), because he felt it inappropriate for there to be a second Peter.

The timing was unfortunate, because Otto II died in Rome of malaria the same month, leaving as his heir the three-year-old Otto III (983–1002), whose right to the crown in Germany was quickly challenged by his relative Henry the Quarrelsome, duke of Bavaria. Otto II's widow, the empress Theophano, niece of the Eastern emperor John I Tzimisces (969–976), had to devote all her energies and diplomatic contacts to trying to secure her son on the throne. She withdrew to Pavia, leaving the new pope defenceless when Boniface VII returned to Rome from refuge in Constantinople in April 984. John XIV was starved to death in the Castel Sant'Angelo, while Boniface, who counted the years of his pontificate from 974, then ruled unchallenged with the backing of Crescentius (d. 984) and his son John Crescentius until he died in July 985. On news of Boniface's death his body was dragged out of the Lateran and exposed naked below the equestrian statue (now on the Capitoline) of the emperor Marcus Aurelius in the piazza outside, where it was stabbed and kicked by the mob. He was only finally classified as an antipope in 1904.

With the Ottonians entirely taken up by events in Germany, Rome remained firmly in the hands of the family of the Crescentii and their noble and clerical allies. In 985 it was they who chose John XV (985–996), son of a priest called Leo. John Crescentius, using the ancient title of Patrician of the Romans once given to Pippin III and Charlemagne, took control of the political life of Rome in the same way as Prince Alberic in the years 932 to 954, leaving the pope with exclusively ecclesiastical affairs. After his death in 988, his brother Crescentius II Nomentanus succeeded him.

In 991 French bishops at a synod complained to the papal legate, a Roman abbot called Leo, that their envoys were being denied access to the pope unless they bribed Crescentius. Such pressures led John XV to leave Rome in 995 and take up residence in Sutri. From there he appealed to the young Otto III to come to Rome for his imperial coronation, which he did the following year. Facing the threat of the first serious Ottonian intervention since 983, Crescentius II and his allies persuaded the pope to move back to Rome, only for him to die of malaria in March 996, when Otto had just reached Pavia. Fearing retribution for earlier ill-treatment of John XV, Crescentius asked the king to choose the new pope.

Like the Roman aristocracy, the city clergy began developing a more clearly defined corporate identity in this period. In the narratives of Liutprand of Cremona of the 960s we find frequent use of the title of *cardinalis* or cardinal applied to members of the Roman clergy, both priests and deacons. The word had long been used in the Roman church. The earliest certain evidence of it is in the acts of Pope Symmachus' synod of 499 and in some of the so-called Symmachan forgeries of the same period, in which it was used of the senior priests in the twenty-five *tituli* or parish churches of the city. The *Liber Pontificalis* attributes the creation of the organisation into *tituli* to Pope Marcellus (305/6–306/7), but this is improbable. By the late fifth century, these cardinal priests were also required to conduct baptisms, penitential rites and other services in the patriarchal or papal basilicas. As seven were assigned to each of the four basilicas, their number became fixed at twenty-eight. John VIII (872–882) gave them additional non-liturgical responsibilities, in particular to meet twice a month in their own church with their junior clergy, to scrutinise their conduct and dress, discuss issues relating to relations between seniors and juniors and also to sit as judges in disputes between members of the laity and the clergy.

The word 'cardinal' primarily indicated status within the ranks of the Roman priesthood, but some of the deacons, probably the seven who served the papal Mass in the Lateran, also used the title informally. An actual order of cardinal deacons would not appear until the end of the eleventh century, and the full College of Cardinals, as a corporate entity with three grades—deacons, priests and (suburbicarian) bishops—only emerged fully in the twelfth century. This period also saw the first appointment of a senior cleric from outside Rome to a *titulus*. In 975 Benedict VII named Archbishop Dietrich of Trier as cardinal priest of the Church of the Quattro Sancti Coronati near the Lateran. Although the precedent was slow to be followed, this began the now long-established process of assigning Roman churches to those raised to the rank of cardinal.

As we have seen, the growth in Roman local patriotism and of the sense of group identity amongst both the laity and the clergy in the city meant that popes imposed by the German emperors, even if they were of Roman origin, were unpopular and insecure. This was even more the case with Otto III's choice of the successor to John XV, who was his own cousin Bruno, aged twenty-four and a priest of the royal chapel. He was thus the first German pope, and also the first of non-Italian origin since Zacharias in the eighth century.

It was Bruno—who took the name of Gregory V (996–999) out of special reverence for Gregory the Great—who crowned Otto III emperor in St. Peter's on 21 May 996. The new emperor also received the title of Patrician of the Romans, and its former holder Crescentius II was banished, a sentence reversed at the new pope's request in a bid to win the support of the Roman elite. As had happened to Leo VIII in 984, however, such clemency seemed a sign of weakness, and after Otto III left Rome in June Gregory V became increasingly aware of his unpopularity. He failed to persuade the emperor to return, as they had fallen out when Otto had refused to confirm the Ottonianum of his grandfather Otto I. By October, when the emperor returned to Germany, Gregory's position was critical and, in a revolt led by Crescentius, he was expelled from the city and fled to Spoleto. Failing in two bids to recover Rome by force, he headed north and in February 997 held a synod in Pavia, which excommunicated Crescentius.

One of those who should have attended this synod was secretly making his way to Rome, claiming to be on pilgrimage but actually preparing to be made pope by Crescentius as John XVI. This was John Philagathos, archbishop of Piacenza since 988 and former tutor to Otto III. His close ties to the emperor made him seem a good choice if the Romans were to ward off imperial retribution, and his service to the Ottonians was long standing, as he had been chancellor of the kingdom of Italy from 980 to 982 and again in 991–992. As a native Greek speaker from Calabria, he had assisted diplomatic contacts with the Eastern empire and in 994 had been in Constantinople to try, unsuccessfully, to secure an imperial bride for Otto III.

Eastern imperial interests in southern Italy had been threatened by the rise of Ottonian power in the peninsula since 961, and there is some evidence that Constantinople was behind the choice of John XVI as pope. Letters from Bishop Leo of Synnada, envoy of the emperor Basil II the Bulgar-slayer (976–1025), reveal that he had deliberately encouraged John's papal ambitions in the hope of turning

Rome against the Ottonians, whose imperial title, like that of the Carolingians before them, was not recognised in the East.[40]

John's hopes of conciliating his former pupil were short-lived, as Otto III prepared to return to Italy to restore Gregory V. John's offers of submission were suppressed by Crescentius, and he fled to a fortress in Campania before Otto and his army arrived outside Rome in February 998. With no Eastern military aid forthcoming, the city surrendered without resistance, while Crescentius was besieged in the Castel Sant'Angelo for a further two months until it fell. He was then beheaded, and his body nailed up by the feet for public inspection. John XVI, tracked to his refuge, was brought back to Rome, and subjected to a horrific ritual of humiliation. He was blinded, and his nose, tongue and ears cut off. His much-revered fellow townsman, the saintly abbot Nilus of Rossano, had appealed to the emperor and pope for clemency and was promised that John would be released into his custody. However, in a synod in May John was subjected to ecclesiastical degradation, being enthroned in his papal robes before having them torn off him, like Formosus in the Cadaver Synod. Then he was placed backwards on a donkey and paraded around the city to be insulted by the populace. A contemporary German chronicler put the blame for this on 'the horrible Romans'.[41]

Abbot Nilus refused to accept an apology from the emperor and immediately left Rome, cursing him and the pope.[42] Gregory V, whom Nilus blamed in particular, died in February 999, like many popes, of malaria. Remembered in Germany as having 'been kept busy trying to restore canonical discipline' in Rome, Gregory had pursued reformist policies and championed papal authority with vigour.[43] His synod in Pavia in February 997 is one of the few papal councils of this period of which the decrees have survived, in a letter informing other bishops of the decisions taken. It included threatening spiritual sanctions against some of the west Frankish or French episcopate, their king Robert II and the archbishops of both Naples and Magdeburg.[44]

This was an ambitious programme for a pope exiled from Rome and relying only on a handful of northern Italian bishops. Conspicuously absent were almost all of the suburbicarian bishops, and of the three who had consecrated him only one, Albano, was present at the synod. The other two, the bishops of Ostia and Porto, were in Rome waiting to consecrate John XVI. Support for Gregory and for papal authority in general was also low amongst the French bishops, who resented his and his predecessor John XV's attempts to restore Archbishop Arnulf of Reims, who in 989 had betrayed the new Capetian dynasty in favour of a short-lived Carolingian claimant to whom he was related. They complained about the personal conduct of recent popes in 991 and at another synod in 994 declared that papal decisions contradicting the decrees of the early councils or of more recent episcopal synods should be regarded as having no authority.[45] This raised the question that would prove contentious for centuries to follow of whether higher authority lay in papal decretals or in conciliar enactments.

In reality Gregory's position was less precarious than it appeared, thanks largely to a now deeply entrenched acceptance of papal authority in Western Christendom. Widespread acceptance of the view that the pope and his synod had the right to impose the discipline of the canon law on lay rulers as well as on ecclesiastical magnates meant that in the longer term a king had to come to terms with the papacy if he was to be sure of the loyalty of the Church in his kingdom.

There were also always going to be those in any realm for whom the popes were natural allies. In France the leading reformed monasteries, already the beneficiaries of several popes' charters of protection, began to promote doctrines of papal authority over that of the bishops. Thus Abbot Abbo of Fleury (988–1004), who visited Gregory V in Spoleto in 996 and became a personal friend, compiled a canon law collection, not least from the letters of Gregory the Great, in defence of papal power.[46] He then acted as the pope's agent in enforcing the restitution of Archbishop Arnulf and in persuading King Robert to promise obedience in 997. Monastic support for papal reform policies would become even more important in the next century.

Overall, the tenth century, which has been called the Iron Century, was not as disastrous a period for the papacy as has often been thought; its bad reputation comes largely from the biased Liutprand of Cremona's saucy tales.[47] If the popes were not always masters in their own city, the administrative machinery of the Roman church continued to function and its sphere of influence expanded. Principles were rarely compromised whatever the personal circumstances or even morality of the holders of the papal office, and exactly one hundred years after the Cadaver Synod, the Synod of Pavia showed how resolute a reforming pope could be despite the precariousness of his situation. The next century would see far more radical reform and confrontation between the powers of church and state to a degree unimagined in the millennium that was drawing to its close.

~ chapter 10 ~

FREE, CHASTE AND CATHOLIC

(999–1099)

THE WAY TO CANOSSA

For three days in late January 1077, the Western emperor Henry IV knelt in the snow outside the small castle perched on a rock at Canossa in northern Italy, barefoot and dressed only in plain woollen garments, 'imploring with much weeping the aid and consolation of apostolic mercy'. Inside the fortress, owned by a staunch papal ally, the formidable Countess Matilda of Tuscany, was Pope Gregory VII, trying with 'unaccustomed hardness of mind' not to be swayed by his advisors into too quickly forgiving the apparently penitent emperor, who was undergoing his self-inflicted humiliation to try to lift a papal excommunication.[1] This scene, which for later generations became the archetypal image of the humbling of lay authority by the Church, seems far removed from the pattern of papal-imperial relations that had existed three-quarters of a century earlier, when the new millennium dawned. How so dramatic a change occurred needs some explaining.

From 998 the emperor Otto III (983–1002) lived mainly in Rome, and on the death of his cousin Gregory V in 999 he chose his own former tutor Gerbert of Aurillac as the new pope. Gerbert took the name of Sylvester II, after the predecessor who was thought to have baptised Constantine, the first Christian emperor. He is one of the best known of medieval popes thanks to his extraordinary career and the survival of 264 of his letters, though only thirty date from his papal years. A clever son of free peasants, he had been a monk in Aurillac in southwestern France until the count of Barcelona took him in 967 to further his studies in Catalonia in the Abbey of Ripoll, where he found translations of Arabic scientific and mathematical works still unknown north of the Pyrenees. This new learning made his name after the count took him to Rome on a diplomatic mission in 970. Sent from there by Pope John XIII to the Ottonian court, he was tutor to the future emperor Otto II before being given charge of the school in the Cathedral of Reims. In 980 Otto appointed him abbot of the important monastery of Bobbio in northern Italy, but he was driven out by his monks in the anti-alien backlash that followed the emperor's sudden death in December 983.

Forced to return to Reims, he was much involved in the complicated politics of the 980s relating to the succession of the child king Otto III in Germany and the replacement of the Carolingian dynasty by the Capetians in France. Gerbert's hopes of succeeding Archbishop Adalbero of Reims in 989 were crushed when King Hugh Capet gave the post to the illegitimate Carolingian prince Arnulf, but when the new archbishop was deposed by a synod in 991 for his part in a failed Carolingian revolt, Gerbert was chosen to succeed him. Arnulf's appeal to Rome was upheld by John XV, and Gerbert had to rely on royal support to hold onto his office. When this proved weak, he went to Italy to try to plead his case before the newly consecrated Gregory V, who deposed him at the Synod of Pavia early in 997. His fortunes changed when invited to become tutor to Otto III, who in early 998 persuaded the pope to appoint him archbishop of Ravenna. On 2 April 999 Otto III had him elected as Gregory V's successor.

No previous pope had been so widely travelled or enjoyed so varied a career as Sylvester II. As the author of a treatise on the astrolabe and from his writing on logic, mathematics and astronomy, he appears amongst the most learned of all popes in areas other than theology. In later legend he was seen as a magician, who secured the papal throne thanks to a pact with the Devil.

The personal ties of pope and emperor resulted in their close cooperation in promoting Western imperial overlordship, along with the conversion of the kingdom of the Magyars and the development of the Church in Moravia and Poland. But Otto III and Sylvester were not always in accord. The emperor rejected papal claims to parts of the former exarchate in northeastern Italy and is the only person known to have denied the authenticity of the 'Donation of Constantine' before the late Middle Ages. For his part, Sylvester was not uncritically obedient, in 1000 refusing the imperially sanctioned request of the Polish duke Boleslav for the title of king.

Otto III was devoted to Rome, where he resided in a new palace on the Aventine, but it proved his undoing.[2] In February 1001 a revolt led by the Crescentii forced both emperor and pope to flee the city. Soon after, Otto caught malaria and died, aged only twenty-two. His heir, his cousin Henry II (1002–1024), duke of Bavaria, first needed to establish his authority north of the Alps, and in his absence Arduin, margrave of Ivrea, was elected king of Italy at Pavia. Sylvester II had to come to terms with the Crescentii and returned to Rome to live under their rule until he died on 12 May 1003.

Under the title of Patrician of the Romans, John II Crescentius dominated the next three popes, the first two of whom were probably members of his family. The third, Sergius IV (1009–1012), the son of a shoemaker and nicknamed *Buccaporci* or Pig's Mouth, may have invented the concept of Crusade. In 1009 the increasingly erratic Shi'ite caliph of Egypt, al-Hakim (996–1021), ordered the complete destruction of the Church of the Holy Sepulchre in Jerusalem. Pope Sergius contemplated an expedition to conquer Jerusalem and restore it, but this never progressed beyond the idea.

In the West, Henry II's victory over Arduin in 1004 re-established Ottonian rule in Italy, but Crescentius was reluctant to allow Henry into Rome, recalling how his father had been beheaded and his mother gang-raped on the orders of Otto III in 998.[3] Thus, Henry's request for an imperial coronation was rejected by successive popes, until a dramatic coup occurred in Rome. Sergius IV died on 12 May 1012, and John Crescentius six days later. Even as he lay dying, his power evaporated when his candidate for the papacy was rejected in favour of Benedict VIII (1012–1024), second son of the count of Tusculum. Both the Tusculans, as they are called, and the Crescentii were descended from the Senator Theophylact who had ruled Rome in the early tenth century, through his daughters Marozia and Theodora respectively, but were bitter political rivals. Benedict, who was a layman when elected, took personal charge of military operations against the Crescentii in the Sabine hills northeast of Rome. For the first time since John XII, the pope was master of his own city, over which he installed his younger brother Romanus as governor.

In 1014 Benedict reversed Crescentius' policy towards Henry II and invited him to Rome for an imperial coronation. After the ceremony, a Roman synod agreed at the new emperor's request to accept the addition of the phrase *filioque*—'and from the Son'—to the Nicene Creed, a practice Rome had resisted since the time of Charlemagne. Benedict and Henry also met in Ravenna later the same year, where the pope presided over a synod that condemned simony, the purchasing of ecclesiastical offices. A synod held at Pavia in 1022, during Henry II's next visit to Italy, did likewise and also forbade the clergy from the level of subdeacon upwards to marry or take mistresses.

The new pope was more a man of action than a reformer or a scholar. He forcibly re-imposed papal rule throughout southern Tuscany and Campania, and in 1016, allied to the maritime cities of Pisa and Genoa, he personally commanded a fleet that defeated the Arabs and drove them out of Sardinia. He was also quick to seize the opportunity to extend papal influence in southern Italy, supporting a revolt against the Eastern emperor Basil II (969–1025) in Apulia, even though this led to his name being struck from the diptychs in Constantinople. When the rebellion was crushed, Basil's troops invaded papal territories, forcing the pope to leave Rome and seek the help of Henry II in Bamberg. There Henry renewed the Ottonianum of 961 and promised military aid. His campaign in Italy in 1022 halted the Eastern army's advance.

Benedict was succeeded by his younger brother, the consul, duke and senator Romanus, who became John XIX (1024–1032), allegedly by bribery.[4] Starting as a layman, he was elevated through all clerical grades to the rank of bishop in a day. In a less martial pontificate than that of his brother, John was reconciled with the thoroughly cowed Crescentii and supported the German king Conrad II, first ruler of the new Salian dynasty, whom he crowned emperor in 1027. The coronation was attended by King Cnut of Denmark and England (1013/16–1035), who used it to promise an annual payment, soon known as Peter's Pence, to the papacy.

A contemporary monastic chronicler in Burgundy states that in 1024 John received an embassy from the Eastern emperor Basil II the Bulgar-slayer, offering him gifts to accept that the patriarch of Constantinople was as 'universal' in his particular sphere of activity as the bishop of Rome was over the whole world. John might have been willing to agree, because 'in our time greed for riches is the queen of the world' but was persuaded otherwise by Abbot William of Volpiano. He said that the Roman emperors had once reigned over 'the whole orb of the world', but as it was now divided into many lands ruled by 'innumerable sceptres', the power of binding and loosing in both heaven and earth was confined exclusively to the holders of the chair of Peter.[5]

The monopolising of the papal office by the Tusculans continued after the death of John XIX. A third brother, Alberic, who held the office of count of Tusculum, was also administrator of the Lateran and was married with four sons, one of whom was elected in 1032 as Benedict IX. Although the contemporary chronicler Rodulf Glaber claimed he was only aged ten at the time, and that money changed hands to secure his election, at least the first of these charges was grossly exaggerated. Glaber was a Cluniac monk who wrote as an advocate of reform. His *History*, begun in 1026/7, reflected growing unease about the papacy, election to which seemed to depend upon the very simony that popes condemned. The German king Henry III (1039–1056) delayed requesting an imperial coronation because he did not want to receive it from a pope tainted by such a sin.

Even more shocking, and quite unprecedented, was the decision of Benedict IX in 1045 to abdicate. It was rumoured both that he wanted to get married and that he had put the papacy up for sale to recoup the costs of his election. The truth is harder to find, but the episode of Benedict's abdication marks a crucial transition in the history of the papacy. In September 1044 the Crescentii led a revolt that made him flee to Tusculum, and in January 1045 they secured the election of their ally John, bishop of Sabina, as Sylvester III. The rival popes excommunicated each other.

Sylvester's reign was short, as Benedict retook Rome on 10 March, forcing him to return to Sabina, where he remained under Crescentian protection still claiming to be legitimate pope. But on 1 May Benedict resigned the papacy in favour of his godfather, an elderly Roman priest called John Gratian, who was given the name of Gregory VI by popular acclamation in memory of Gregory the Great.

Although money was said to have changed hands in his election, the new pope was widely acclaimed by reformers all over Western Europe. In Burgundy Glaber ended his *History* with this event, declaring Gregory 'a most religious man and outstanding in sanctity . . . his good reputation has reformed for the better that which his predecessor had defiled.'[6] Similarly, the leading Italian reformer and ascetic Peter Damiani, prior of Fonte Avellana, wrote to congratulate the new pope and urge him to fight against the evils of simony. The changes in Rome led Henry III to request the imperial title, and a date was set for the coronation on Christmas Day 1046.

Gregory VI's accession was hailed as marking a real change in the spiritual quality of the holder of Peter's see. It is also quite likely that Benedict IX gave up office because of the growing chorus of disapproval across Western Europe and even in Rome itself not just of his personal conduct but of the style of papacy that he represented. For the previous century and a half the popes had been either members of the dominant aristocratic faction controlling the city or under its control. Their wider role in Western Christendom, as hearers of ecclesiastical appeals and issuers of charters of privilege, was secondary to their subservience to the politics of Rome. This made sense in the context of the localised structures of power that developed as the Carolingian empire had declined, but major changes were taking place across Europe as the new millennium opened, with reform ideals gaining ground throughout the Church, trade and communications improving and a more international outlook developing as states began again to grow in size and sophistication.

When pope and emperor-to-be met at Piacenza in October 1046, all seemed well, but Henry soon became aware of the rumour that Gregory had purchased his office. He was also uneasy about the co-existence of three popes, as he needed to know which was the legitimate one, and therefore the right one to crown him. To deal with these issues before the planned coronation, Henry ordered the Roman bishops and those accompanying him from Germany and northern Italy to hold a synod at Sutri, north of Rome, on 20 December, to which the rival popes were also summoned.

Sylvester III and Gregory VI both attended, but Benedict IX refused. The bishops, presided over by the king, deposed Sylvester and probably Gregory, though it was later claimed he had voluntarily resigned. Although formally sentenced to perpetual imprisonment in a monastery, Sylvester III was still serving as bishop of Sabina as late as 1062 and has never been classified as an antipope. This was due to the need to conciliate his patrons, the Crescentii. Gregory VI, however, was sent into exile in Germany.

A second meeting of the synod was held in Rome on 24 December 1046 to discuss candidates for the now vacant papal throne. The king's first choice, Archbishop Adalbert of Hamburg, declined, proposing instead his friend Bishop Suidger of Bamberg, who was consecrated as Clement II on Christmas Day. The new pope then immediately crowned Henry and his wife, Agnes.

Clement held a reforming synod on 5 January 1047, before accompanying the emperor on an expedition into southern Italy. He died in Pesaro on 9 October, and by his own decision his body was taken back for burial in his see of Bamberg, which he had never resigned. When his body was exhumed in 1942, the cause of death was identified as lead poisoning, probably from the pipes of the ancient Roman water system. His gold silk socks are amongst the treasures of Bamberg Cathedral.[7]

The sudden death of Clement II enabled Benedict IX to re-establish himself in Rome, until expelled by imperial troops in July 1048. Refusing to attend a synod in 1049 that then excommunicated him, he remained defiant in the Alban hills until his death in late 1055. One of his reformist opponents dreamed of him being reincarnated as a donkey.[8]

THE REFORM PAPACY

In Germany the emperor Henry III was looking for a replacement for Clement II and consulting many of his leading bishops. One of them, Wazo of Liège (1042–1048), surprised him with a forthright denunciation of the events of 1046. Having read through the lives of the popes, their decretals and the canons of the councils, he said there was a consensus that 'the pope, whatever his style of life, should be held in the highest honour and be judged by no-one.' He therefore explained that Gregory VI was still the legitimate pope.

Henry III refused to listen to this argument, and the exiled Gregory VI died at Cologne in late 1047. Wazo, however, was not alone in his doubts. An anonymous French cleric wrote a treatise known as the *De Ordinando Pontifice* (On the Ordination of the Pontiff), which cites a variety of texts, not least from the Pseudo-Isidoran Decretals and the letters of Gregory the Great, to claim that the pope could not be judged and that laymen, however powerful, should play no role in their election: 'the emperor, hateful to God, did not doubt he might depose someone whom he had no power to elect; he elected someone whom it was not lawful for him to depose.'[9]

Such views were still those of a minority, and Henry III proceeded to nominate a second German bishop to the papacy, the Bavarian Poppo, bishop of Brixen. Meanwhile Benedict IX had won over the margrave of Tuscany, who refused to let Poppo proceed to Rome and tried to persuade the emperor that Benedict was now legitimately reinstated with the consent of the Romans. Only the threat of Henry coming in person forced Margrave Boniface to install Poppo as Damasus II on 17 July. The new pope died three weeks later of malaria.

It took time to find a replacement, but in December the emperor settled on Bruno, a member of a family of counts from Alsace, and bishop of Toul since 1026. He agreed, on condition that he be formally elected by the clergy in Rome so that his elevation to the papal office should be procedurally correct, and in February 1049, he was. This stipulation also secured for the new pope, who took the name of Leo IX (1049–1054), the support of a Tuscan monk called Hildebrand, who had been chaplain to Gregory VI and had accompanied him into exile in the Rhineland. Hildebrand's reputation and connections in Rome made him a valuable addition to the new pope's entourage, though he had initially refused Leo's offer when it seemed he was taking office merely by imperial appointment.[10]

Leo also brought to Rome a number of his fellow Lotharingians, including Humbert (died 1061), from the monastery of Moyenmoutier, whom he made titular archbishop of Sicily in 1050 and cardinal bishop of Silva Candida in 1051; Hugh the White from the monastery of Remiremont; and Frederick of Liège, whom he appointed chancellor or head of the papal administration. Italians drawn into the new papal circle included the hermit Peter Damiani, impatient at the slow pace of reform since 1046, who later and reluctantly became cardinal bishop of Ostia. Thus emerged a group of papal advisors who rarely agreed on all issues but were similar in commitment to reform to the circle around Nicholas I in the mid-ninth century.

We may speak of Leo IX, his supporters and successors as reformers, but this was not how they saw themselves. They wanted to return the Church to a 'golden age' they thought had once existed and out of the current 'age of iron'.[11] They saw themselves correcting errors and evil customs that had been allowed to develop unchallenged in recent centuries. The past they wished to recover was largely imaginary, being derived from such spurious texts as the Pseudo-Isidoran Decretals and the conciliar acta of the Laurentian Schism, which provided seemingly authoritative evidence of papal supremacy.

The primary objective was to recover 'the liberty of the Church', or its freedom from lay domination. This was itself part of a wider move to enhance the status of the clergy over the laity and to extend the distinction between what was increasingly seen as two separate orders of society, the clerical and the lay. In the later tenth and eleventh centuries the elimination of both simony and clerical marriage were identified as vital to achieving these objectives. Although these issues had been addressed by Roman synods in 1014 and 1022, the popes of that time were regarded as simoniacs and subject to lay domination, while Leo IX and his successors saw themselves as belonging to a new generation of properly elected pontiffs.

The primary focus of reforming synods of this time in the West on simony and clerical marriage may appear restricted but makes sense when we understand what these issues were thought to involve. The attempt at prohibiting a married clergy was of relatively recent date. In 743 a Roman synod had commanded that bishops and priests should not live with women 'except perhaps with their mother or a near relative', but a letter from Pope Zacharias to Archbishop Boniface in the same year made it clear that while clergy could not marry after ordination, there was still no restriction on married men becoming priests.[12] However, in the early ninth century when more regulated and austere monastic practices were being enforced across the Carolingian empire, pressure increased for a totally celibate clergy. In part this grew out of a new sense of the need for absolute ritual purity of a priest administering the sacraments, which was thought to be threatened by any form of sexual activity. Additionally, there were fears that family concerns, especially the need to provide for heirs, could lead to the alienation or misuse of church property by its priestly custodians.

Simony too was seen as a taint that could invalidate the efficacy of the sacraments being administered by someone who had practised it. In earlier periods the papacy had endorsed the view popularised by Saint Augustine that sacraments were efficacious irrespective of the moral standing of the administrator, but by the mid-eleventh century some reformers, such as Humbert in his *Three Books against the Simoniacs,* declared all ordinations by simoniacal bishops invalid. Others such as Peter Damiani upheld the Augustinian position, which was generally preferred by the popes of the time.

In the sense of paying money for clerical office, this form of heresy, as it was defined by a Lateran synod in 1059, was relatively rare, though there were some blatant cases, not least in England after the Norman conquest of 1066. However, in their concern to liberate the Church from control by the laity, the reformers began interpreting it much more widely. Any form of agreement, exchange of property or promise of political loyalty involved in the choosing of a bishop or indeed anything interfering in the process of his free election by the clergy and people of his diocese was regarded as a form of simony. So too was any ritual of lay investiture, such as a ruler presenting a bishop with a ring and pastoral staff to symbolise the transfer of responsibility for the administrative and judicial duties of his office.

Ultimately, as Pope Gregory VII wrote in 1084, the reformers wanted to ensure that 'holy church, the bride of Christ, our lady and mother should return to her true glory, and stand free, chaste and catholic.'[13] In other words it had to be removed from any form of lay control, have an entirely celibate clergy and adhere faithfully to the doctrinal and disciplinary rules received and defended by the heirs of Saint Peter.

Behind this may be detected the influence of the monastic revival that had swept through many parts of Western Europe from the early tenth century onwards, in which celibacy and liberty from lay interference were powerful elements. Many of the leading advisors of the 'reform popes' and some of the popes themselves were monks. Leo IX had been an enthusiastic promoter and defender of monasteries in his diocese of Toul before becoming pope, and his most influential successor was Gregory VII (1073–1085), formerly the monk Hildebrand. The *Libertas Romana* or exemption from local lay and episcopal control that so many monasteries had requested from the papacy in these centuries led in turn to Rome seeking to emancipate itself from secular overlordship.

Paradoxically, the initial impetus came from the emperors, particularly Henry III, whose intervention in 1046 put an end to a century and a half's domination of the Chair of St. Peter by the Roman aristocracy and the opening up of the papal administration to ideas, personnel and practices coming from across the Alps. The imperially sponsored popes that followed were far less bound to the city itself, though wary of the danger of a reassertion of control over it by families like the Tusculans. Thus Leo IX began his pontificate by re-crossing the Alps to preside in person over synods of bishops in Reims and Mainz, claiming the authority to do so from a Pseudo-Isidoran text that ruled that such meetings could only be held with prior papal approval.

A local historian of the church of Reims reports how some bishops and abbots, including the archbishop of Sens, were worried by the possible outcome and so persuaded King Henry I of France to declare a military emergency, requiring them to lead their contingents of knights to join the royal army instead of attending the synod at Reims. However, they were excommunicated by their colleagues for failing to appear, while all of those that did were called upon to swear that they had not obtained their office by simony. Four were unwilling to do so, and one fled, only to be excommunicated by the rest, while the archbishop of Reims prevaricated, promising to come to Rome to take the oath there the following year.[14]

The synod itself issued twelve decrees that typify the reform programme. Election by clergy and people was made mandatory for all bishops, and any form of simony forbidden. No member of the laity was to hold an ecclesiastical office or a church; this decree hit at the proprietary or family-owned churches that had existed in most parts of Western Europe since Roman times. Fees for the administration of the sacraments or admittance to a church were prohibited, and clerics were ordered not to bear arms or lend money at interest (the sin of usury). Adultery, incest, stealing from the poor and assaulting clerics on their travels were similarly forbidden.[15] Most of these decrees were still more pious hopes than enforceable rules, and many would continue to be ignored with impunity, but their continued reiteration at this and similar councils gradually turned them into values widely accepted, if not always observed in practice, throughout Western society.

Leo IX's synods both in Italy and beyond the Alps drew up the blueprints for the Church's recovery of its lost golden age under papal leadership. A more practical challenge was, however, developing in southern Italy. Norman families had been moving into the region from northern France in growing numbers to serve as mercenaries, since first hired by Benedict VIII in 1018 for his failed campaign there. Since then two families in particular, those of Robert Guiscard and

Richard of Aversa, had established territorial principalities and were extending their power at the expense of the older Lombard rulers and of the Eastern emperors, who retained territories in Calabria. Threatened by a Norman conquest, the duchy of Benevento put itself under papal rule, accepting Rome's long-held claim to overlordship. In 1053 Leo IX led an army in person to defend it, only to be decisively defeated and captured by Robert Guiscard at the battle of Civitate on 18 June. He remained a prisoner of the Normans in Benevento until March 1054, just before his sudden death on 19 April.

Leo's foray into military affairs was presented as a catastrophe by contemporary chroniclers. It may also have contradicted the spirit, if not the letter, of the recent decree forbidding clerics from bearing arms, but those who perished at Civitate were regarded as martyrs and the expedition itself was described as spiritual in inspiration, serving as a further precedent for the idea of Crusade.

One consequence of the pope's involvement in southern Italian affairs was another breach with Constantinople. The patriarch, Michael Cerularius (1043–1058), was already an outspoken opponent of what were regarded as erroneous novelties in the practice of the Western Church, in particular the doctrine of the Double Procession of the Holy Spirit from both Father and Son, expressed through the addition of *filioque*—'and from the Son'—to the creed, and the use of unleavened bread in the Eucharist. The latter practice in particular led him to close all Western churches in Constantinople in 1053.

From detention Leo IX tried to negotiate a settlement, sending an embassy to Constantinople in January 1054, led by Humbert of Silva Candida. He was the most irascible member of the papal circle and quickly offended Eastern opinion by his promotion of universal papal authority, based on a revised text of the Constitution of Constantine that had been prepared for Leo IX in 1053, the authenticity of which was rightly denied in Constantinople.[16] Humbert was equally intolerant of challenges to the doctrine of the Double Procession, although only recently adopted by Rome. In his view its authority derived entirely from its acceptance by the pope.

Cerularius was similarly undiplomatic, and on 16 July, during increasingly ill-tempered negotiations, Humbert burst into the Cathedral of Hagia Sophia in Constantinople and placed a papal excommunication of the patriarch on its high altar. Cerularius anathematised the pope in a synod eight days later. While not expected at the time, the ensuing division between Eastern and Western Christendom would last for nearly a millennium, with the mutual excommunications only being lifted in 1965.

That this took so long was accidental. Cerularius soon fell from favour, and several emperors throughout the second half of the eleventh century began talks to end the rift, which was no more serious than many in preceding centuries. In Rome the attitude was generally benevolent. Constantinople was regarded as a daughter of the Roman church, and the Eastern emperor as the pope's spiritual son. The general absence of simony in the Eastern church was also favourably commented on, but the issues of clerical marriage, which was permitted in the Greek church, and *filioque* remained contentious. Each time negotiations never quite progressed far enough for reconciliation to be achieved.

Leo IX's successor was Gebhard, bishop of Eichstatt, who as imperial chancellor had dissuaded Henry III from aiding the disastrous papal campaign against the Normans in 1053. Following protracted negotiations, led by Hildebrand, now archdeacon of Rome, he was chosen by the emperor in November but only agreed to accept the office in March 1055. Under the name of Victor II (1055–1057), he was to be the last imperially appointed pope, as a result of the early death of Henry III in October 1056 and the succession of his five-year-old son Henry IV (1056–1105), fatally weakening their dynasty's hold over the papacy for the crucial decades that followed. Pope Victor hastily returned to Germany, to play a vital role in securing general acceptance of the young Henry IV under the regency of his mother, the empress Agnes, and in reconciling some of the late emperor's opponents.

These included Duke Godfrey the Bearded of Lower Lorraine, who had established an alternative power base for himself in Italy via his marriage to the daughter of Margrave Boniface of Tuscany. This union made him the dominant power in northern Italy after 1056, when the political difficulties of the regency in Germany prevented interference from beyond the Alps. An early sign of his new influence was the election of his brother Frederick, the papal chancellor of Leo IX, as abbot of Monte Cassino, and then after the early death of Victor II as Pope Stephen IX (1057–1058). After Stephen's death the support of Duke Godfrey enabled the reforming faction to choose a new pope, Nicholas II (1058–1061), from their own number at Siena in defiance of the election of the bishop of Velletri as Benedict X (1058–1059) in Rome eight months earlier. Benedict, who had the backing of the Roman aristocracy, was then ejected from Rome by the ducal army in January 1059.

The other realignment in Italian politics at this time was in papal relations with the Normans. Victor II had maintained his predecessor's hostility to them and had expected Henry III's help in launching a new campaign. But with no chance of this after 1056, the reformers began to turn to the Normans for military support against enemies closer to home. In 1059 Nicholas II held a synod at Melfi in Norman-controlled Apulia, at which he invested Richard of Aversa as prince of Capua, and Robert Guiscard as duke of Apulia and Calabria and lord of the not yet conquered island of Sicily. The Norman leaders recognised the pope and his successors as their feudal overlord and promised military aid.

The contested succession of 1058 led to new rules for papal elections being issued by a Lateran Synod in April the following year. These put the process exclusively in the hands of the cardinal bishops, the holders of the suburbicarian dioceses, who were to choose the candidate, ordain him if not already a bishop and consecrate him as pope. The clergy and people had also to give consent, without which anyone claiming the office would 'not be seen as a pope and an apostle but instead as an apostate'.[17] The election no longer had to take place in Rome, and candidates would not have to be members of the Roman clergy.[18]

The other Roman cardinals were unenthusiastic about their episcopal colleagues being given the exclusive right of choice, and this was quietly dropped. The decree of 1059 was intended mainly to provide a retrospective justification of Nicholas II's election, and at eliminating the involvement of the Roman lay aristocracy. Less easily reconciled was the German court, with the role of the emperor in papal elections being effectively ended. The 'reverence and honour' due to him was recognised in the election decree of 1059, but even this was described as something conceded by the Apostolic See.

The German bishops were increasingly irritated by the reforming decrees of the annual Roman synods, and with royal encouragement they excommunicated Nicholas II and declared his decrees invalid. On his death in July 1061 the empress Agnes, regent for her son Henry IV, convoked an ecclesiastical synod in Basel, attended by representatives from Rome and some north Italian bishops, that elected Peter Cadalus, the bishop of Parma, as Honorius II (1061–1064). This was in defiance of the leaders of the reform party, Hildebrand and Peter Damiani, who had already elected the bishop of Lucca as Alexander II (1061–1073). A partisan of the reformers ascribed the choice of Cadalus to the 'feminine presumption' of the empress and described his consecration as the work of 'his fellow fornicators and simoniacs'.[19]

Like all popes since 1046, the two rivals retained their previous episcopal sees, a practice that can only be explained by financial necessity. The lands of the Roman church were not generating enough income to support the papal administration, possibly because so many of them were in the hands of the local aristocracy, either in their own right or as tenants of monasteries and churches, and the reform party, who were almost all non-Romans, were unable to force them to pay the rents and tolls that were due.

In April 1062 Honorius II and his supporters seized Rome but the following month were confronted by Duke Godfrey and a superior force. Godfrey insisted that both popes withdraw from the city pending a final decision on their claims. In Germany the regency of the empress was replaced the same year by one led by the archbishops of Cologne and Bremen, who were far more favourable to the reformers. The expected change in royal support came at a synod held in Mantua in 1064 that recognised Alexander II and deposed Honorius, who had in any case refused to attend when denied the right of presiding. He maintained himself in Parma, still proclaiming his papal title until his death around 1071.

Once secure, Alexander II intensified papal oversight—or interference in the eyes of some—of the Western church through the use of legates, usually leading members of the papal entourage, who were sent to preside over regional synods, to ensure they promoted the reform programme, and to investigate and suppress abuses. Use of such legates had become increasingly frequent under Leo IX and his immediate successors. While there were no real historical precedents for such envoys, whose powers exceeded those of the metropolitans to whose churches they were sent, once more the Pseudo-Isidoran texts provided a justification for the papacy to claim it was only recovering its own authority.

One church causing particular papal concern was that of Milan. The cities of northern Italy had been growing in size and economic importance in the course of the century, producing social and political tensions. In particular the local dominance of their bishops, who were usually nominated by the German emperors, and who controlled the urban administration and taxation, was increasingly resented by smaller landowners and mercantile families, who began forming groups to challenge episcopal rights.

In Milan the tension became worse when in 1057 one such faction, known as the Patarini or Patarenes (probably meaning 'rag pickers'), adopted the programme of Church reform, as a way of challenging the entrenched power of the archbishop and the higher clergy. Led by a priest and a minor aristocrat, they called on the laity to boycott the services of those clerics who were living with women or were thought guilty of simony. They then created an alternative local church organisation. The archbishop appealed for papal support, and legates were sent by both Stephen IX and Nicholas II to hear the arguments of both sides and to try to broker a solution. While the sympathy of the reformers lay with the ideals of the Patarenes, they could not countenance a breach in the unity of the Church. The Lateran Synod of 1060 came out firmly behind the archbishop, but Alexander II sent a papal banner as a sign of personal support to the Patarenes.

In 1070 Archbishop Guy of Milan resigned and selected one of his priests as his successor, sending him to Henry IV, to be invested with episcopal ring and pastoral staff in the traditional manner. This broke older conciliar rules prohibiting the appointment of a new bishop while his predecessor still lived, defied recent synodical legislation demanding free election by clergy and people and ignored the reformers' opposition to lay investiture. In Milan the Patarenes and others refused to accept the new archbishop, and when Guy died in 1071, they elected one of their own with papal approval. Just before Alexander II's death in April 1073 a Roman synod excommunicated five of Henry IV's advisors for their part in the dispute.

THE GENTLE POWER OF
THE APOSTOLIC SEE: GREGORY VII

Alexander II's successor, by acclamation of clergy and people, was Archdeacon Hildebrand, who took the name of Gregory VII (1073–1085) in memory of his mentor Gregory VI and in honour of Gregory the Great, whose writings strongly influenced him. He would prove to be one of the most significant and controversial of popes. We know his policies from the decrees of the twice-yearly synods, held during Lent and in November, but also from 390 letters.[20] He is the only pope in the period 882 to 1198 whose register, the official collection of a pope's correspondence, has survived.

It includes a text headed *Dictatus Papae* (Dictation of the Pope), a list of twenty-seven propositions by the pope himself, drawn up in 1075. Although not an official decree, it reveals Gregory's ideals and something of his 'demonic zeal' in promoting them.[21] Several of the propositions stated long-accepted papal rights, such as those of hearing appeals and judging all major cases. More novel were the theses that only the pope 'can use imperial insignia' and that 'all princes kiss the feet of the pope alone.' So too were the claims that he 'is permitted to depose emperors' and 'can absolve subjects from fealty to the wicked.'[22] These derived from recent discussions in the papal circle over the conflict in Milan, and a search for such historical precedents as Pope Zacharias' role in the deposing of the

Merovingian dynasty in 751. These claims would be put to the test before a year was out.

Gregory did not inform Henry IV of his election, but the king was facing a serious revolt in Saxony and at first was keen to mend fences with the new pope, at least until the revolt was crushed in October 1075. After that he ignored papal protests, appointed Italian bishops on his own authority and called a synod of German and northern Italian bishops to meet at Worms on 24 January 1076. Here both king and episcopate denounced Gregory VII for interfering in their affairs and denying them their rights. The twenty-six bishops renounced allegiance to him, claiming he had broken a promise not to seek election to the papacy and was committing adultery with Countess Matilda of Tuscany. They complained that 'all judgements and decrees are enacted by women in the Apostolic See, and ultimately the whole orb of the Church is administered by this new senate of women' and that Gregory called his fellow bishops 'sons of whores and other names of this sort'.[23]

Their letters arrived before the opening of the Lenten synod in Rome in February, at which Gregory composed his reply: By virtue of the power 'given to me from God of binding and loosing in heaven and on earth . . . I deny to King Henry, son of the emperor Henry, who has risen with unheard-of pride against your church, the government of the entire kingdom of the Germans and of Italy, and I absolve all Christians from the bond of any oath that they have taken, or shall take, to him; and I forbid anyone to serve him as king.'[24] Henry and all the bishops who had written with him were declared excommunicate.

The king could not use force against the pope, and all hinged on whether or not Gregory's sentence on Henry would have any practical effect. To make it work, the pope resorted to the tactic he used to enforce his ecclesiastical judgements, sending copies of his decree to as many interested parties as he could reach, to make it as widely known as possible. Thus, when an archbishop was excommunicated, the pope ensured that all his suffragan bishops were informed, as the papal decision justified their defying the metropolitan.

In this case the king's weak political position in Germany proved crucial, as the Saxon aristocracy used the papal decree to justify renewing their revolt, since it invalidated their earlier submission to the king. Other discontented magnates were equally keen to use the papal ban to justify disregarding their oaths of fealty. Many German bishops, however resentful of Gregory's conduct, felt unable to reject papal authority and accepted his sentence.

So, in the course of 1076 Henry's position in Germany crumbled, while he could not coerce Gregory, who was backed by Matilda of Tuscany, the heiress of the Margrave Boniface and the wealthiest and most powerful lay magnate in northern Italy. The king attempted a spiritual riposte, asking his bishops to excommunicate Gregory VII. Only one of them would agree to do so, and he died suddenly a few weeks later, making it appear God favoured the pope.

By 16 October, when Henry met the German princes, his position had become untenable. They demanded that he get the excommunication lifted within six months or they would feel freed from their previous oaths of loyalty to him. They also invited Gregory VII to come and meet them at Augsburg in February 1077 to mediate in their disputes with the king. It was while on his way to this meeting that the pope was intercepted by King Henry at Countess Matilda's castle at Canossa in January 1077.

The road to Canossa was in many ways a short one. The conflict that produced Henry's submission was of recent origin, as were the papal reform party itself and the king's political difficulties in Germany. But the new relationship between pope and German ruler, consisting largely of friction, distrust and periodic conflict, would last for centuries to come. The traditions of more harmonious papal-imperial relations that characterised the preceding millennium effectively withered and died when the papacy ceased to be an essentially Roman institution with wider aspirations and tried instead to become a universal one with Roman connections.

The transformation in the nature of the papacy in this period reflects wider changes taking place in Western Europe. The ideal of a common Christian society of shared beliefs and culture needed an institutional structure that could no longer be provided by the emperors. In the West, the imperial office had been confined to the rulers of Germany since the mid-tenth century and was little more than a constitutional pretext for their fragile rule over its regional duchies and the overlordship of various Slav states beyond its eastern frontier. Whatever respect was accorded his title, the emperor had no authority over the other Western kingdoms and never tried to claim it. The only institution with ideologically grounded and widely accepted claims to superiority over all secular rulers was the papacy.

In political terms Canossa was less of a victory for Gregory VII than it might appear, and this may explain his reluctance to accept the royal submission. Having lifted the excommunication, the pope deprived Henry's enemies in Germany of their excuse for continued resistance, and they were less willing to rely on papal support in the future, preferring instead to elect a new king, Rudolf of Rheinfelden, in March 1077.

By 1080 Henry was able to disregard almost all the undertakings he had made to the pope at Canossa, and Gregory excommunicated him again at a synod. The impact was far weaker a second time, and on 25 June a group of twenty-seven bishops and a cardinal loyal to Henry met at Brixen in northern Italy and deposed 'the pseudo-monk Hildebrand known as Gregory VII' on charges ranging from heresy and sacrilege to arson and including claims that 'he is an open devotee of divinations and dreams, and a necromancer working with an oracular spirit.' He was also accused of murdering four previous popes, including Alexander II, and of being devoted to 'obscene theatrical shows'.[25] Having recorded these crimes with considerable relish, the bishops elected Archbishop Wibert of Ravenna as pope. He took the name of Clement III in honour of the first German pope, Clement II.

As with earlier schisms, this conflict produced a flurry of historical research into earlier papal texts supporting the claims of one side or the other, and the invention of new ones when required. Thus in the 1080s lawyers working for Clement III forged a decree of the obscure Pope Leo VIII (963–965), stating that it was the emperor who made the pope. Around 1085 an Italian bishop driven into exile by the reformers wrote to Henry IV to show that the *Liber Pontificalis* proved that bishops and popes should be appointed by kings and emperors. He further cited Otto III's mutilation of 'a certain false pope' (John

XVI) and Henry II sitting in judgement on three papal claimants at Sutri in 1046.[26] Biblical exegesis was also used to comment on the current crisis, particularly by a circle of writers patronised by Matilda of Tuscany.[27]

In 1080 Henry killed the 'anti-king' Rudolf, enabling him to intervene more effectively in Italy. In March 1084 he and his army entered Rome, while Gregory VII took refuge in the Castel Sant'Angelo. Clement III was formally elected pope by the Roman clergy and people, and then crowned Henry emperor. But in May the approach of Gregory's Norman allies, led by Robert Guiscard, made Henry and his antipope withdraw. The Normans sacked Rome and massacred those who resisted, an episode long remembered. Evidence of the destruction has been found on the Caelian where the basilicas of San Clemente and the Quattro Sancti Coronati were burned down.[28] In consequence Gregory himself was expelled by the infuriated populace when the Normans departed and took refuge with them in the south, dying in May 1085. He was canonised by Paul V in 1606.

THE BIRTH OF THE CRUSADES

Related to Gregory's attempt to create a new order within Christian society under papal leadership was his concern for its defence against external enemies. During the unstable period that followed the ending of the Macedonian dynasty in 1057, the Eastern empire was threatened by the Seljuk Turks. After their decisive defeat of the emperor Romanus IV (1068–1071) at the battle of Manzikert in 1071, Seljuk warlords overran Asia Minor and carved out new states for themselves. Unable to replace the army lost at Manzikert, the emperor Michael VII (1071–1078) asked the pope to secure military aid from the West, promising a restoration of relations between Rome and Constantinople on papal terms.

On 1 March 1074 Gregory issued a general letter 'to all who are willing to defend the Christian faith', stating that 'a race of pagans has strongly prevailed against the Christian empire . . . it has slaughtered like cattle many thousands of Christians.'[29] In a private letter to Matilda of Tuscany, he said he intended to lead the expedition in person, although expecting it would result in his martyrdom.[30] Later the same year he told King Henry IV that he hoped to form an army 50,000 strong and hinted that the Church of the Holy Sepulchre in Jerusalem would be its destination. In practice, this expedition hardly made it onto the drawing board, any more than did a proposal by the French Count Ebles de Roucy to raise an army to fight against the Muslims in Spain, which Gregory backed in 1073. His predecessor, Alexander II, may have sanctioned what in retrospect has been seen as the prototype crusade: a similar French expedition in 1064 that crossed the Pyrenees to take the fortress of Barbastro in Aragón, only to lose it again the next year.

Where Gregory had more success in the Iberian peninsula was in trying to suppress the Mozarabic liturgy, the distinctive liturgical tradition of the church in Spain, whose texts, music and ritual distinguished it from Roman and Frankish equivalents. The pope relied upon a mythical tale of a visit to Spain by seven bishops, supposedly sent by Peter and Paul themselves, to claim that 'it is sufficiently clear how great a concord Spain enjoyed with the city of Rome in religion and the ordering of the divine office.' But this uniformity in faith and worship, he argued, had been broken firstly by the spread of heresy and then by the conquest of Spain by the Goths and subsequently by the Arabs. In 1074 he demanded of King Alfonso VI of Castile (1072–1109) that he and the church in his kingdom 'recognise the Roman church as truly your mother . . . and that you receive the order and office of the Roman church, not of the Toledan or any other, but that like the other kingdoms of the west and north, you hold to that which has been founded through Christ by Peter and Paul upon the firm rock and consecrated by their blood, against which the gates of hell, that is the tongues of heretics, have never been able to prevail.'[31]

Despite argument and prevarication by both the monarch and his bishops, the Mozarabic liturgy was formally renounced at a synod held in Burgos in 1087 and replaced by the papally approved service books, which, however, were not purely Roman in origin but contained a strong admixture of Frankish elements. In reality the papal view that there had once been a uniform Latin liturgy of Roman origin used by all the churches of the West and that local variants, such as the Spanish Mozarabic rite or the Ambrosian one followed in Milan, were deviations caused by loss of communication with Rome was entirely mistaken.[32]

Gregory's death in Salerno in May 1085 left his supporters divided, and only a year later could they agree on a successor, the Lombard aristocrat Desiderius, abbot of the great monastery of Monte Cassino since 1058. Taking the name of Victor III, he was opposed not only by the antipope Clement III but also by the more uncompromising followers of Gregory, since he had once tried to broker a compromise with Henry IV. Victor was driven from Rome four days after his election by popular rioting, and withdrew to Monte Cassino, refusing to function as pope until reconfirmed by a synod of bishops meeting at Capua in March 1087. Two months later his supporters led by the Norman prince of Capua and Countess Matilda of Tuscany seized control of the Leonine City, the fortified area around St. Peter's, where he was finally consecrated on May 9. Although the antipope was expelled from Rome in June, Victor spent most of his short pontificate in Monte Cassino, dying there on 16 September.

By this time Clement III had regained Rome, and it was not until March 1088 that the reform party was able to meet at Terracina, to elect Odo de Châtillon, who became Urban II (1088–1099). A French aristocrat and former monk of Cluny, he had been made cardinal bishop of Ostia by Gregory VII in 1080 and papal legate in Germany in 1084. He was an unwavering Gregorian, writing 'in all things trust and believe in me as in my blessed lord Pope Gregory,' and thus could reconcile those who had refused obedience to Victor III.[33] He reconfirmed the reform programme through the decrees of a synod he held at Melfi under Norman protection in 1089.

Control of Rome continued to fluctuate, with Urban having to abandon the city to Henry IV and Clement III in 1090 to take refuge again with the Normans. He regained part of the city in 1093 and was triumphantly reinstalled by the army of the bellicose Matilda of Tuscany (whose armour was preserved as late as the seventeenth century) in 1096, but Clement III did not lose his last hold on Rome until 1098, when the Castel Sant'Angelo fell. Clement withdrew to his archbishopric of Ravenna, where he died in September 1100.

Just as Urban's position in Rome gradually improved throughout the 1090s so did his wider standing in Western Christendom. Compromise was necessary to bring this about, something Gregory VII would never have contemplated. No reconciliation proved possible with Henry IV, but papal relations with France recovered from threats by Gregory VII to excommunicate its king Philip I for marrying a near relative. In England Urban had to concede in 1095 that his legates would only enter the kingdom with royal consent, and he was unable to persuade King William II (1087–1100) to admit Anselm, his appointee as archbishop of Canterbury. Papal involvement in Spain was more warmly welcomed, following Alfonso VI of Castile's conquest of Toledo in 1085 and the reinstatement of its archbishopric as the primatial see for all the Iberian Peninsula by Urban II in 1088.

The principles of the reform programme, especially the removal of lay involvement in the selecting and investing of bishops, continued to be reiterated, particularly at the council Urban held at Clermont in 1095 and in his last synod in Rome in 1099. Such decrees did not provoke the frequent confrontations that had marked the pontificate of Gregory VII, not least because Urban had other more urgent objectives, notably his aim to persuade Christians in the West to join in an expedition to Jerusalem.

The loss of Urban II's letters and the text of the sermon he preached at the opening of the Council of Clermont in November 1095 make it impossible to know how he presented the objectives of what became the First Crusade. The Eastern emperor Alexius I (1081–1118), founder of the Comnenian dynasty, had sent envoys to the pope earlier in 1095, asking him to raise military aid from the West for his campaigns against the still expanding Seljuks in Asia Minor.[34] However, following the lead of Gregory VII in his plan to march to the Church of the Holy Sepulchre, Urban focussed instead on calling for an expedition to restore Christian rule over Jerusalem. And two weeks before he died, it was achieved.

chapter 11

THE SUCCESSOR
NOT OF PETER
BUT OF CONSTANTINE

(1099–1198)

THE INVESTITURE CONTROVERSY

The remarkable success of the First Crusade, in which Christian armies led by nobles from northern and southern France, Flanders and Norman Italy fought their way across Anatolia and Syria to conquer Antioch in 1098 and Jerusalem in 1099, thereby creating four Crusader States in the Near East, seemed to justify the view of Pope Urban II that the Christians had lost these lands in the seventh and eighth centuries through sinfulness. The revitalised faith of the later eleventh century under papal leadership promised to reverse these earlier losses, with further triumphs to come, but in practice this Crusade was to be the only really successful one. The Second Crusade, prompted by the fall of the newest of the Crusader States, the County of Edessa, to Zengi, the Turkish ruler of Mosul in 1145, was proclaimed by Pope Eugenius III (1145–1153) and passionately preached by the great Cistercian Bernard, abbot of Clairvaux (died 1153). Both Louis VII of France and Conrad III of Germany led armies to the Holy Land, and both suffered crushing defeats in 1147 at the hands of the Turks in Anatolia, before joining in a futile attack on Damascus, which lost the kingdom of Jerusalem one of its few allies against Zengi.

This patent failure led to criticism of those who promoted it, not least Bernard of Clairvaux and Pope Eugenius. Bernard himself saw it as a divine judgement, but drawing on the theme of papal command of both secular and spiritual power, he urged Eugenius not to be deterred: 'In this second passion of Christ we must draw the two swords that were drawn during the first passion. And who is there to draw them but you? Both of Peter's swords must be drawn whenever necessary; the one by his command, the other by his hand.'[1] The failure of the Second Crusade and the doubts it raised meant that it was not until Jerusalem fell to the Egyptian sultan Saladin in 1187 that another such expedition was launched. But this was not the only problem the papacy had to confront.

The death of the antipope Clement III in September 1100 offered a chance of resolving the long conflict between the papal reformers and the emperor Henry IV. However, several leading members of the Roman clergy owed their ordinations to Clement and were unwilling to see his legitimacy denied. So they created two successive popes from their own faction, Theoderic (1100–1101) and Adalbert (1101), while Paschal II (1099–1118), who had been elected by the majority of the cardinals, was absent from Rome. Neither could retain their precarious hold on the city, and both were deposed. Paschal faced a third antipope in 1105 when a group of Roman nobles accused him of heresy and simony, in his absence, and used this to justify elevating the archpriest Maginulf, who became Sylvester IV (1105–1111). Although quickly expelled from Rome, he survived under the protection of the count of Ancona.

Maginulf lacked imperial support, as Henry IV was beset by conflicts within Germany, culminating in a rebellion of nobles led by his sons, Henry and Conrad, in 1105. Paschal II had renewed Gregory VII's excommunication of the emperor in 1102 and now used this to justify the rebels' breaking their oaths of loyalty. However this earned him no favours when the young Henry succeeded his father as Henry V (1106–1125) and proved equally determined to resist papal demands that he take no part in selecting and investing bishops. As both King Henry I of England and King Louis VI of France had already reached agreements with the papacy on this issue in 1107,

Paschal II had fewer allies than his predecessors, but he continued to repeat the ban on lay investiture in a succession of synods.

In 1111, Henry V headed for Rome, determined to secure his imperial coronation. Lacking any means of resistance, Paschal tried to negotiate a compromise, whereby the monarch would not involve himself in electing bishops and would relinquish his right to invest them with ring and pastoral staff, while in return the bishops and abbots of the imperial territories would surrender the substantial estates and revenues of their institutions to the king, and exist instead on tithes, the obligatory annual offering of a tenth of income from the laity. This scheme would free them from the secular obligations, such as the provision of knights and foot soldiers for the royal army, which such landholding had involved, but acceptance of it depended upon the leaders of the Church in Germany and northern Italy being as idealistic as the pope.

A condition of this agreement, made at Sutri on 4 February, was that it would be announced at the forthcoming imperial coronation. Henry entered Rome a week later, greeted by the magistrates and representatives of the city's twelve regions, and twice swearing to the Romans to uphold the concessions made to them by his imperial predecessors.[2] When the following day the terms of the agreement of Sutri were publicly read out in St. Peter's, there was a riot amongst Henry's senior clergy, and Bishop Conrad of Salzburg declared he would rather be beheaded than lose the property of his see. So great was the uproar that the coronation had to be cancelled.[3] Henry may have expected this, as he had troops ready to take the pope and cardinals to the Castel Sant'Angelo, where they remained his prisoners for two months.

The king threatened to recognise the antipope Sylvester IV if Paschal continued to resist, and so a new agreement was reached, whereby the German ruler could exercise a veto over the list of candidates for a bishopric but would allow free election from it. He also retained his right to invest the bishop with ring and staff in a separate ceremony prior to his episcopal consecration. The pope agreed that no bishop could be consecrated without prior royal investiture and swore never to excommunicate Henry, whom he then crowned emperor.[4] On Henry's orders the antipope Sylvester IV then renounced his title.

This agreement, contained in a document known as the Privilege of Ponte Mammolo, of 12 April 1111, involved separate undertakings by the two parties, and Paschal II tried to publicise the new emperor's concessions while keeping his own secret. But even amongst the cardinals a group of uncompromising reformers protested that Paschal had betrayed the principles for which his predecessors had fought. Bruno of Segni, who was one of Gregory VII's appointments as cardinal bishop and the author of a biography of Leo IX, openly accused the pope of heresy for agreeing to the treaty, and in consequence was deposed from the abbacy of Monte Cassino. His colleagues were less outspoken but equally hostile.

By this time the cardinals had developed a clear institutional identity, which in the course of the century came to be known as the College of Cardinals. They had already begun to describe themselves as a new Roman Senate. The process was completed by the formation of the order of cardinal deacons in the late eleventh century. The six deacons who served in the Lateran adopted the title of cardinal under the antipope Clement III, and this privilege was extended to the twelve regional deacons of the city by Urban II. The same period also saw the emergence of a more sophisticated papal bureaucracy under the direction of the chancellor, whose office subsumed the older one of librarian. One consequence was that documents issued in the name of the pope and bearing his seal were also signed by members of the College of Cardinals. Overall, their role in papal policy making increased, something that was regretted by more absolutist pontiffs.

Faced with such bitter condemnation by this powerful body, Paschal offered to abdicate, but instead the strict reformers forced him to cancel the Privilege, which they called the *Pravilegium* (Crooked Privilege), at a synod in the Lateran in 1112. There Paschal proclaimed his adherence to the decrees of all previous holy Roman pontiffs, especially Gregory VII and Urban II: 'What they praised, I praise; what they upheld, I uphold; what they confirmed, I confirm; what they damned, I damn . . . and in these things I shall always persevere.'[5] He re-imposed the ban on investiture, and repeated it in 1116 but was then driven out of Rome by a revolt. He returned to die in the Castel Sant'Angelo in January 1118. Even to the present he is called weak by historians who would have preferred a martyr.

Time was on the side of the papacy. Although Henry V returned to Italy in 1117, primarily to secure the lands of Matilda of Tuscany, who had died without heirs in 1115, he faced growing opposition in Germany, not least from the archbishops of Cologne and Mainz, and needed to achieve a lasting settlement. Paschal II's successor was the elderly John of Gaeta, who as cardinal deacon had served as chancellor since 1089 and as such had been responsible for improvements in the drafting and script of papal documents. He was consecrated as Gelasius II, in honour of the first Gelasius, whose writings became very influential in the reform period.

Having withdrawn to Gaeta at the emperor's approach, Gelasius II refused to meet Henry or crown his wife, Matilda, daughter of Henry I of England, as empress. The emperor resorted to the tried expedient of creating a pope of his own, Maurice Bourdin, a monk of Cluny and archbishop of Braga, who had fallen out with the archbishop of Toledo and was in Rome to defend his rights. He took the name of Gregory VIII, but lacked any kind of local support once Henry V returned to Germany. In 1119 he left Rome for the fortress of Sutri, where he was captured in 1121. After public humiliation, he was consigned to a monastery until his death in about 1137.

Henry V abandoned Gregory VIII as he had Sylvester IV because he needed to settle the dispute. Gelasius II had withdrawn to France in 1118, dying at Cluny, where he was buried. The cardinals accompanying him elected an outsider, Guido, son of the count of Burgundy and archbishop of Vienne since 1088, who took the name of Callistus II (1119–1124) in honour of the early third-century papal martyr. He had already proved himself a resolute defender of his see, not above forging historical documents to support its claims, and he negotiated a new agreement with the emperor, to whom he was distantly related. This was to have been ratified at a meeting on the river Meuse in 1119, but Henry withdrew on discovering that his concessions had been redrafted by the papal notaries, ostensibly for stylistic reasons but actually to secure further advantages.

The two sides resumed discussions in 1121, when the German princes insisted that Henry come to terms with the pope. Callistus II for his part was equally keen to find a solution, as he needed imperial help to defend papal territories against the Norman leader Roger II, who had just completed the conquest of Sicily. The final settlement was similar to those agreed with the kings of England and France in 1107. By the Concordat of Worms of 1122 the emperor renounced all rights to investiture by ring and staff and any role in choosing bishops, but in Germany new bishops would be elected in the ruler's presence and receive their temporalities by being touched with the royal sceptre. In March 1123 Callistus, now installed in Rome, summoned the First Lateran Council to ratify the concordat, which it endorsed despite protests by some uncompromising reformers. The Investiture Controversy was finally over.

After the council, Callistus commissioned an artistic record of the triumph of the legitimate popes over their rivals for his new *Camera pro secretis consiliis* (room for private discussions) in the Lateran Palace. In the frescoes Alexander II, Gregory VII, Victor III, Urban II, Paschal II, Gelasius II and he himself were depicted using the antipopes—Clement III, Theodoric, Albert, Sylvester IV, and Gregory VIII—as footstools. Henry V was also depicted, standing while the pope sat enthroned, and handing to him a document containing the opening words of the concordat, likening it to a new 'Donation of Constantine'. The association recurs in a frieze showing Callistus with Saints Peter and Paul and the fourth-century Pope Sylvester I in the Lateran Basilica, where he was buried in December 1124.[6]

THE POPES AND THEIR CITY

While events on the wider stage are more dramatic, other features of the pope's daily life should not be ignored. One of these was the regular performance of the liturgy, which depended in detail on whether or not he was in Rome, where particular feasts had to be celebrated in designated basilicas. He also had duties as overlord of the patchwork of towns, monasteries, lay and ecclesiastical estates that made up the papal territories, requiring a complex diplomacy in the handling of conflicts over rights, and in numerous local power struggles. For example, in 1109 Paschal II supported the abbot of Subiaco in capturing two fortified villages that had been seized by a relative of the counts of Tusculum. One village was repossessed by the abbey, but the other, whose ownership was more contentious, was sold to the pope, and then immediately repurchased from him, to establish the abbey's legal right to it.[7]

Particularly sensitive was the pope's relationship with the city of Rome and its aristocracy. On his election in January 1118, Gelasius II had been briefly held prisoner by the noble house of Frangipani, and later in the year he was attacked by them again, causing him to flee to France. In 1124 after a majority of cardinals had elected one of themselves as Celestine II, the Frangipani burst into his consecration, forced him to resign and compelled the cardinals to chose the bishop of Ostia instead, as Honorius II (1124–1130). To understand the papacy at this time we need to know something of Rome.

The area within its walls was now dotted with clusters of habitation, divided by open spaces used for agriculture. Most occupation was in the northern half of the ancient city, in two zones that met at the bridge over the Tiber to St. Peter's. The first ran southwards along the river bank to the Aventine, the second southeastwards across the Campus Martius, the Capitoline and the Forum to the Caelian Hill, around the Lateran. There were also pockets of habitation on some of the other hills, including the Quirinal. Since the decline of the Tusculans in the mid-eleventh century, no one local noble family exercised a similar dominance in the city. Instead several newer clans controlled different parts of it, building towers, such as the still-standing Torre delle Milizie, or fortifying ancient monuments for protection and to intimidate their neighbourhoods.

Some of these families acquired their status through trade and moneylending, not least to the popes. The political turmoils made the collection of revenue from papal estates erratic, and so accommodating bankers were essential. Notable amongst them were the Pierleoni, a dynasty founded in the mid-eleventh century by a Jewish convert to Christianity, known as Benedictus Christianus, meaning both Benedict the Christian and the Blessed Christian. He was related to Gregory VII by marriage, and he and his descendents were consistent supporters of the reforming popes. From Trastevere, they took over the easily defended Tiber Island and turned the Theatre of Marcellus into a fortress. Their main rivals were the Frangipani (Breakers of Bread), first recorded in 1014, who occupied the Palatine and fortified the Colosseum during this century. Other clans included the Corsi, on the Capitoline Hill, and the Colonna, who held the Quirinal, previously the stronghold of Alberic and the Tusculans.

Handling these powerful families was a major concern of the popes when in Rome. An astute pontiff such as Callistus II used both carrot and stick, forcing the Frangipani to demolish some of their towers while promoting one of their leaders to command some papal militia. An even distribution of favours was essential, while a lack of it could be disastrous. Paschal II became too closely associated with the Pierleoni, causing the Frangipani attacks on his successor and on the conclave of 1124. Then the prospect of a Pierleoni pope in 1130 led the Frangipani into aiding a minority group of cardinals in pre-empting the election. The dying Honorius II was removed to the monastery of San Gregorio on the Caelian, within the Frangipani fiefdom, and his death kept secret until the conspirators could announce that they had elected Innocent II (1130–1143). This blatant irregularity led the majority of cardinals to elect Pietro Pierleoni as Anacletus II (1130–1138) in the Church of San Marco. These feuds were also used by factions within the papal court, as in 1124 and 1130, when the Frangipani-Pierleoni rivalry was manipulated by the papal chancellor, Cardinal Haimerich, to secure the election of popes who would keep him in office.

The distribution of the noble clans and their strongholds was only partly reflected in the division of the city into fourteen regions, which dated from the seventh century or earlier. Each had a strong sense of local identity, was represented by a leader, or *patronus,* and displayed its own banners. These were paraded by the guards provided by each region in processions such as those following a papal consecration, when the new pontiff processed on horseback across the city from St. Peter's to take formal possession of his cathedral, the Lateran Basilica. The employment of banner-bearing guards was one of the privileges specifically conceded to the popes in the spurious Constitution of Constantine. Not surprisingly, interregional rivalries added to the city's volatility, and their armed bands provided ready-made militias for any kind of conflict.

Another sense of identity derived from membership of one of the *Scholae* or schools, different groups of papal employees. At the highest social level were the *Schola Cantorum* or papal choir, and the *Adextratores,* or right-hand men, who formed the cavalry of the papal guards and were privileged to dine with the pope on the day of his consecration. There was a *Schola* of *Hostiarii,* who looked after the papal palaces, another of chamberlains *(Cubicularii)* and one of Stimulators, who kept the crowds back on the routes of papal processions. Other groups of workers and officials such as candle makers and church sweepers, and even makers of cooking pots for the papal kitchens, were similarly formed into schools, with fixed rates of pay.

The grandeur of the papal court was increased by appointing high officials, such as the Cupbearer and the Marshal, whose honorific titles were borrowed from the royal courts of the day, and who performed special services for the popes on great occasions. For example, the Prior of the Stables placed a riding hat on a new pope's head as he emerged from St. Peter's to ride to the Lateran after his consecration.

The office of *Strator* or groom in charge of the pope's horse was particularly significant, as it was one that traditionally was performed by the emperor himself whenever the two met. According to the 'Life' of Stephen II in the *Liber Pontificalis,* this was what the Frankish king Pippin III had done, 'like a groom', when the pope came to Francia in 754. Subsequent popes expected similar treatment from Pippin's heirs and successors, and this was incorporated into the Constitution of Constantine.[8] Denial of it could cause rows, as when in 1155 the English pope Hadrian IV (1154–1159) refused to rise to give Frederick I the kiss of peace because he had failed to perform the 'office of groom'. When Frederick claimed that he was not obliged to, an entire day was spent studying historical precedents and taking statements from those who had witnessed the ritual on earlier occasions, before the German princes accompanying the emperor decided that he did have to perform it.[9] In the same incident, Frederick's failure to perform the 'office of groom' had immediately been interpreted as a sign of his hostility by the pope's entourage, all of whom promptly abandoned Hadrian and took refuge in a nearby fortress. The performance or omission of ritual gestures seemed heavy with meaning in this period.

Concern for rights and duties entailed the search for precedent and historically based authority. This was the age that tried to revive the legal heritage of Rome, particularly in the form of the codifications of Justinian. Leading the way was the Bolognese jurist Irnerius, who defended Henry V's setting up the antipope Gregory VIII. Not surprisingly key statements on papal authority, such as the Pseudo-Isidoran Decretals, played a prominent part in such arguments, and their texts could be subtly modified to suit contemporary purposes. Thus a phrase in the original version of the Constitution of Constantine, conceding the pope's authority over all imperial properties on the islands of the western Mediterranean, was now rewritten to state that the islands as a whole had been so given, thus justifying the papal claim to overlordship of Sicily.[10] This was no minor adjustment, as ultimately it would permit a fifteenth-century pope to divide the Americas between Spain and Portugal.

Symbols of authority took on new importance. Amongst other privileges conferred on the papacy by the Constitution of Constantine was the right to wear a special hat, the frygium, similar to the Phrygian hat later revived as the French revolutionary cap of liberty. From this derived the mitre, the use of which was exclusive to the senior clergy of Rome until extended to all bishops by Leo IX (1049–1054). Soon after, Nicholas II (1058–1061) devised a special papal hat, in the form of a frygium within a golden crown, the first step towards the distinctive triple tiara of the popes that appears in the late thirteenth century. By the end of the eleventh century the rite of papal initiation had become a coronation rather than an episcopal consecration, and from Christmas 1075 onwards popes also wore their crowns on special occasions known as 'crowned days'.

Since the end of the Tusculan papacy, few popes had spent much of their pontificates in Rome. Alexander II and Gregory VII were the main exceptions, but the conflict with the emperors, the activities of numerous antipopes and a wide range of other military, political and pastoral obligations kept most of the popes after 1046 on the move. Although unchallenged in their overlordship of the city, they generally exercised their rule vicariously through appointed prefects, who enjoyed the strange distinction of wearing one red sock and one golden one, and rode behind the pope at the very end of the major processions. In front of them rode the prior of the subdeacons carrying the pontifical handkerchief, in case the pope should 'wish to spit or wipe his mouth'. The frequent absence of the papal court led the resident parish clergy of Rome to develop their own independent sense of identity as the *Clerus Romanus*.[11]

This period saw a revival of interest in the history and monuments of Rome, as well as of the papacy itself. Gregory VII instituted liturgical feast days for several distant predecessors, such as Sylvester I, and many of the popes of the later eleventh and twelfth centuries took the names of much earlier pontiffs, such as Anastasius, Gelasius, Innocent and Anacletus, rather than using the previously popular John, Leo, Gregory and Benedict. This period also saw the first continuations since the ninth century of the *Liber Pontificalis*, written by senior figures of the Roman church.

As Gregory VII had claimed that popes alone had the right to use imperial insignia, they took over the ancient *Adventus* ceremonies to mark formal papal entries into Rome. In these the processions passed under all the major Roman triumphal arches in the city, and new temporary ones were also erected across the route, which were then auctioned off to the city clergy for use in decorating their churches. In a similar spirit of revival, the popes processed or appeared in a series of great annual festivals wearing scarlet and bejewelled robes modelled on those of the emperors. The reverse of this appears in rituals of humiliation, as for example in 1121 when the antipope Gregory VIII was paraded backwards on a camel wearing the bloody flayed hide of a goat turned inside out so as to look like a scarlet cloak.

Other such imitations of empire included popes reusing imperial sarcophagi or coffins for their own burials. Innocent II (1130–1143) took that of the emperor Hadrian and displayed it in front of the Lateran until it was needed, and Anastasius IV (1153–1154) sent the body of Constantine's mother Helena to France as a relic when he annexed her porphyry sarcophagus for himself. The *Lupa*, an ancient bronze statue of the wolf that was said to have suckled Romulus and Remus, was also appropriated by the papacy for its symbolic value, and moved to the Lateran. There it joined the equestrian statue of Marcus Aurelius, then thought to represent Constantine, and a giant Roman statue of a hand holding a globe, which was regarded as a symbol of the world and the power to hold it.

The internationalising of the papacy in the reform period caused popes to be elected outside Rome and not always from the ranks of the cardinals, and the pontiffs, as previously mentioned, generally spent less time in the city than in earlier centuries. While the link between Rome and the popes was never questioned, it took on a more metaphysical character, expressed in the concept of *Ubi Papa ibi Roma,* or 'Rome is wherever the Pope is.'

For the Romans the physical presence of the papal court in the city provided significant economic benefit. Its financial requirements and daily needs produced work and wealth for all classes, from bankers to bakers. The growing numbers of litigants and petitioners coming to the papal court or Curia, in addition to the steady streams of pilgrims, further boosted the local economy. On the other hand, clerical dominance of the city administration and the taxes and tolls imposed under papal lordship were increasingly resented. This was not a purely Roman phenomenon, as the cities of northern Italy were becoming equally hostile to the rule of their bishops.

Feelings of local pride and economic competitiveness caused conflicts within the papal territories between the major towns, several of which had their own communal governments. Local wars were frequent especially between Rome, Tivoli and Tusculum, and became more like long-running feuds. Thus the communal revolt in Rome against Innocent II in 1143 was sparked by his refusal to let the Romans have their revenge on Tivoli, whose forces had defeated theirs the previous year. They wanted him to demolish the town's walls and impose a humiliating treaty. Later in the century Clement III (1187–1191), who had been elected in Pisa, was only allowed into Rome after promising not to interfere in the Romans' current war with Tusculum, in which they were currently ambushing Tusculans venturing beyond their town's walls and sending them back blinded.[12] In 1191 Celestine III (1191–1198) told Henry VI that he would only get a peaceful imperial coronation in Rome if he withdrew the protection he had given to Tusculum. The Romans then destroyed the town completely, and it was never restored.

While Rome had long been volatile, the schism of 1130 was the catalyst for dramatic change. Most noble families gave their support to Anacletus, in reaction to the Frangipani's pre-emptive election of Innocent II (1130–1143), who soon had to flee to Pisa and then France. Both sides courted the German king Lothar of Supplinberg (1125–1137) by offering him an imperial coronation, but the Roman backers of Anacletus insisted that he should agree to 'submit to the laws of Rome and refrain from disturbing the concord of her citizens', the first sign that the schism was being used to further the rights and independence of the Romans.[13] Unsurprisingly Lothar preferred to recognise Innocent and in 1133 forcibly reinstalled him in Rome.

Until then Anacletus II retained control of Rome and secured the backing of Roger II of Sicily, whom he recognised as king of Sicily, Apulia and Calabria, as well as overlord of the other southern duchies in September 1130. But elsewhere in the West, with the single exception of the kingdom of the Scots, Innocent II was accepted as the legitimate pope, largely through the diplomacy of his chancellor Haimerich which won him the backing of Bernard of Clairvaux and other monastic leaders. As Bernard put it: 'expelled from the City, he was welcomed by the world,' arguing that Innocent was the true pope because he was elected first, and by 'the more discreet part of those to whom the election of the Supreme Pontiff belongs'. In the propaganda war between the two parties, Anacletus II's Jewish ancestry was used against him.

For his part Anacletus emphasised both the legitimacy of his election and continuity with his reforming predecessors. In the chapel of St. Nicholas that Callistus II had built in the Lateran Palace, Anacletus commissioned an apse fresco, showing him kneeling opposite Callistus II on either side of the enthroned Virgin and Child. Beside Callistus stood Pope Sylvester I, recipient of the 'Donation of Constantine', and next to Anacletus was the pope whose name he had taken, who was said to have constructed the memorial over the tomb of St. Peter. In the level below, St. Nicholas was flanked by the two great popes of antiquity, Leo I and Gregory I, and on either side of them the recent heroes of the reform papacy: Gelasius II, Pascal II and Urban II to the left, and Alexander II, Gregory VII and Victor III to the right. After his death Anacletus' name and that of Anacletus I were replaced by those of Anastasius IV (1153–1154) and Anastasius I.

Although King Lothar and Innocent II were able to enter Rome in June 1133, they could not take the Pierleoni-controlled Tiber Island nor the Leonine City, forcing Lothar to be crowned in the Lateran. He and his pope soon left Rome, and their attempts in 1136–1137 to defeat Anacletus' ally Roger II of Sicily proved equally unsuccessful. The new emperor died on the way back to Germany, precipitating another royal election, as he lacked male heirs. But the strenuous efforts of Bernard of Clairvaux to win over the supporters of Anacletus were starting to work, and the death of Anacletus himself in March 1138 was followed by the rapid collapse of the regime of his would-be successor Victor IV.

Although the Pierleoni and other supporters of Anacletus then submitted to Innocent II, his position was weak. In 1139 he was captured by Roger II, whom he was then forced to recognise as king of Sicily, though once freed he annulled the treaty. Earlier in the year he had alienated Bernard of Clairvaux by ignoring a promise to pardon Victor IV and the cardinals who had supported Anacletus. Instead he had deposed them at the Second Lateran Council. Finally in 1143 a revolt in Rome under the leadership of Anacletus II's brother Giordano Pierleoni obliged Innocent to agree to a communal government for the city under a Senate. Based on the Capitoline, this consisted of fifty-six members—four elected from each region—under the presidency of Giordano, under the title of Patrician. This was a significant choice, because it was their status as 'Patrician of the Romans' (an office symbolised by the wearing of a special green cloak and gold headband) that was believed to give emperors the authority to oversee papal elections. In the thirteenth century and thereafter, the elected head of the city government became known as the 'Senator of Rome', sometimes ruling autocratically without a council.

The turbulence in the city continued under Innocent's two short-lived successors, as the new Senate became increasingly assertive. Having failed to get military assistance from the German king Conrad III (1138–1152), the first member of the new Staufen dynasty, Pope Lucius II (1144–1145) tried to suppress the commune by force in February 1145, attacking the Capitoline with papal guards. He was hit on the head by a rock and died of his injuries, the only pope to fall in battle. His successor, Eugenius III (1145–1153), a Cistercian abbot, was elected the day Lucius died and immediately left Rome, refusing to recognise the commune.

Around this time the commune also fell out with some of its noble supporters. Giordano Pierleoni disappears from history, and a new leadership emerged that included Arnold of Brescia, a former prior of the Augustinian order of canons in Brescia, a city ruled by a commune in frequent conflict with its count-bishop. Arnold taught that property could only be owned by the laity, and so bishops should surrender the worldly possessions of their sees to secular authorities and instead lead simple lives devoted to their pastoral responsibilities. Arnold reflects the thinking behind the *Pravilegium* of 1111, and perhaps the inspiration for his ideas came from Paschal II. In 1139 Arnold had been condemned at the Second Lateran Council and his books burned, while he himself took refuge in France with the equally controversial theologian Peter Abelard.

When Abelard himself was condemned for his views, thanks to the influence of Bernard, at the Council of Sens in 1140, Arnold continued to defend him in Paris, Switzerland and finally Bohemia, pursued by letters from Bernard warning the local authorities that Arnold was one 'who sups alone with the devil on the blood of souls' and had 'the head of a dove and the tail of a scorpion'.[14] In 1145 he finally submitted to Pope Eugenius III (1145–1153) at Viterbo and was sent by him on a penitential pilgrimage to Rome. There he was in his element, winning over the Senate and denouncing the cardinals for their 'pride, avarice, hypocrisy and many other forms of wickedness' and for turning the Church into 'a place of trade and a robbers' cave'.[15] The pope he described as 'a man of blood who imposed his authority by fire and the sword; a torturer of the churches and a beater of the innocent, who did nothing else in the world beyond eating flesh, while filling his purse and emptying those of others'.[16]

In January 1146 under his inspiration the commune drove Eugenius III out of the city again. Arnold himself was excommunicated by the pope in 1148, and in December 1149 Eugenius briefly re-entered the city, aided by Roger II of Sicily. The commune responded by telling King Conrad of Germany that the pope had formed an alliance with Roger, the Pierleoni and the Frangipani against him, and offering to surrender the Castel Sant'Angelo to him, to let him dominate the city.[17] This drove Eugenius out of Rome again.

The tide began to turn in favour of the pope in 1152. Conrad III died before he could come to Rome to be crowned, and his son Frederick I Barbarossa (1152–1191) succeeded him without the customary papal approval but immediately opened negotiations with the commune to secure Eugenius' return, as he wanted the imperial coronation promised to his father. This was agreed after elections to the Roman Senate in November 1152 in which several of Arnold's supporters lost their seats. The death of Eugenius III in July 1153, however, caused further delay.

His elderly successor, Anastasius IV (1153–1154), was himself a Roman and enjoyed better relations with the commune than any previous pope. These deteriorated again under the English abbot Nicholas Breakspeare—who became Hadrian IV (1154–1159)—when one of his cardinals was murdered by Arnold's supporters on the Via Sacra. In reply Hadrian laid the city under an interdict, which meant that the clergy were forbidden to administer the sacraments, and so baptisms could not be conducted, Mass could not be celebrated and funerals could not be performed with religious rites, thus threatening the spiritual well-being of all the inhabitants. As Easter approached, the Senate finally submitted on the Wednesday of Holy Week, agreeing to expel Arnold in return for the lifting of the interdict. Arnold took refuge in Tuscany, but Hadrian had made his capture one of the conditions for crowning Frederick emperor later in 1155. Brought back to Rome, he was hanged, his body burned and his ashes scattered on the Tiber, to prevent their being preserved as relics. The Senate's powers were reduced.

Were You Born Wearing This Mitre?

While Arnold of Brescia may have been an extreme critic of the popes and of the Roman Curia, other more established and orthodox figures within the Church were worried by the direction the papacy was taking at this time. One of the most perceptive and formidable was Bernard of Clairvaux. He addressed his five-part book *De Consideratione* (On Contemplation) to Pope Eugenius III, who had been one of his own monks at Clairvaux before becoming abbot of a Cistercian monastery near Rome. Bernard addressed him as if still his monastic superior, warning the pope that while he was 'watchman over all', he also must 'realise that you are the lowest if you think yourself supreme' and constantly remember 'you too will follow to the grave those men you have followed to the throne'.[18]

Bernard disliked the magnificence of the papal court and its rituals. Asking 'were you born wearing this mitre?', he pointed out that St. Peter had never worn silk or taken part in processions, and that 'in this finery, you are the successor not of Peter but of Constantine.' As far as Eugenius himself was concerned this was unfair, as he continued wearing his monastic habit even as pope, but Bernard's view was formed by the Cistercian tradition that stressed simplicity of life and avoidance of any form of ostentation, even in the liturgy. Bernard also stressed the collegiality of the episcopate, saying that the pope was 'not the lord of bishops, but one of them'.

Like Gregory the Great, Bernard was concerned that the pope's own spiritual well-being would suffer under the pressure of the more secular aspects of his role. He suggested that Eugenius appoint someone like a monastic prior to run the papal household, freeing him to devote himself to the spiritual needs of the Church. His only proviso was that the pope had to retain responsibility for the discipline of his following and its appearance: 'boys with luxuriously curled hair and foppish young men' did not belong in bishops' retinues, and he noted that one of the cardinals 'has promoted good-looking youths to ecclesiastical benefices [any kind of salaried or income-generating religious office] whenever he could'.[19]

The demand on papal time that Bernard particularly wanted reduced was that of hearing appeals from all over the Western church. This responsibility had existed since the papacy became the final court of appeal in ecclesiastical disputes under the fourth-century pope Damasus, but for several centuries it had been largely confined to conflicts between bishops and their metropolitans or over infringements of papal privileges. Under Innocent II, during his long period in the north, the flow of legal business coming to the papal court had increased greatly in quantity and in variety, and it continued to intensify in the decades that followed.

Bernard admitted that the rise in appeals was 'testimony of your unique primacy' but complained that many of the cases were undertaken 'lightly . . . and with evil intent' and also that the costs of having to go to Rome for a hearing were exorbitant. Essentially, he wanted Eugenius to recognise that he spent too much time listening to litigants and that many of the cases were unworthy of being heard by a pope.

Bernard was also worried by the company the pope had to keep. The Romans, he thought, were arrogant and obstinate and the papal courtiers venial, treacherous and grasping: 'They are detested on earth and in heaven, they are hostile toward both; irreverent toward God, disrespectful toward holy things, quarrelsome among themselves, envious of their neighbours, discourteous to strangers . . . they are most generous in their promises, but most sparing in their gifts;

they are fawning in flattery and biting in slander; they are blatant liars and wicked traitors.'[20]

This low view of the pope's entourage was not confined to Bernard, and criticism of the Curia as a whole and individual members of it became commonplace. Eugenius III received moral exhortations from the prophetic Abbess Hildegard of Bingen, while John of Salisbury, later bishop of Chartres, described two cardinals sent as legates to Conrad III in 1150 as 'tormenters of men and extorters of money' who 'disturbed the churches as hives are disturbed that honey may be taken from the bees'.[21] But none of the popes themselves were personally the subject of scurrilous gossip, in the way some of their tenth- and eleventh-century predecessors had been.

Criticism of the popes also came sometimes from the cardinals, who saw themselves as the defenders of the traditions of the Roman church. They stressed the pope's responsibility to his electors, telling Eugenius III, 'You must realise that being raised to the supreme power over the Church by us cardinals, around whom as its cardinal points the axis of the Church universal moves, being made by us from a private person into the father of the entire Church, you cannot henceforth belong to yourself, but rather to us.'[22]

The material concerns of the papacy became increasingly pressing as a result of the tumultuous history of the preceding decades. Revenues were down, properties mortgaged or permanently lost and rights ignored. An attempt to revive papal finances was begun by Eugenius III who commissioned the chamberlain, Cardinal Boso, to carry out a reorganisation of the papal estates, a process continued under Hadrian IV. Boso also studied old rent books and other documents in the archives of the Roman church to try to recover lost rights, and he revised the distribution of the offerings made by growing numbers of pilgrims as part of his efforts to boost papal revenues. Some of the money raised was used to buy or build fortresses within the papal territories and to hire troops, secular purposes that ignored the decree of a Roman synod of 1082 that Church resources should only be used for relieving the poor, ransoming captives and the performance of the liturgy.

In 1145 Bernard of Clairvaux had asked, 'Is not Rome at once both the Apostolic See and the capital of the Empire?'[23] Since the time of Henry IV, the German kings had been entitling themselves King of the Romans while waiting for their often long-delayed imperial coronations, but they spent little time in the city and were rarely welcome. The issue of the relative authority of pope and emperor also remained bitterly disputed. In 1157 Hadrian IV had to withdraw the suggestion made in a papal embassy to Frederick I that the empire was a *beneficium* or benefice conferred by the pope, with the implication that he was the emperor's feudal superior. One of these envoys was Cardinal Rolando Bandinelli, papal chancellor since 1153 and a supporter of the policy followed by Hadrian from 1156 of favouring good relations with the new Norman king William of Sicily over those with Frederick, who was trying to impose his authority on the cities of northern Italy.

ALEXANDER III

On 7 September 1159 Rolando Bandinelli was elected pope as Alexander III (1159–1181) by fourteen cardinals, while nine others chose Cardinal Ottaviano, who took the name Victor IV (1159–1164). Different accounts of what had happened soon circulated. In a letter, Alexander himself claimed that no sooner had he been vested in the papal robe than Victor tore it off his shoulders. When a senator snatched it back, Victor produced another one that his supporters had ready, but wore it back to front: 'even as his mind was distorted and his purpose perverse, so his mantle was put on crooked and awry, in token of his damnation.'[24] Senators supporting Victor's coup then imprisoned Alexander and his electors, but twelve days later they were freed by the Frangipani and fled the city. Alexander excommunicated Ottaviano 'the apostate and schismatic', condemning him and his supporters to the devil.[25]

Cardinals supporting Victor IV, on the other hand, claimed that they had chosen him because those backing Alexander had broken an agreement that if they could not settle the election unanimously, they would look for an outside candidate. They also claimed that Alexander had initially accepted Victor, and that his followers had only proclaimed him pope when fleeing from the city and at an ill-omened cistern in which Nero had once hidden.

Victor himself wrote to the emperor in northern Italy, warning him against the schismatic and heretical 'Roland, the former chancellor who is associated with William of Sicily in a conspiracy and plot against the Church of God and the empire'. On advice from his court clerics, Frederick determined that he had the authority, following precedents set by Constantine, Theodosius I, Justinian and Charlemagne, to call an ecclesiastical council to judge the claims of the rival popes and so summoned them both to attend one at Pavia in January 1160. Bishops were expected from England, France, Denmark, Spain and Hungary, but only fifty, all from the imperial lands, were present when the synod finally opened in February.

By this time Alexander III had announced he would not attend, stating that the emperor had 'overstepped the bounds of his office, since he has summoned a Council without the Bishop of Rome having knowledge of it and like one having power over us, has summoned us to appear'. He took his stand on the long-held principle that no one could sit in judgement on the pope: 'Is it not correct that both in prosperity and adversity it has been maintained to this day, even to the point of bloodshed if necessary, that when the occasion demanded, Peter's authority would examine and finalize matters pertaining to every church, but that its own should be subject to the judgements of none?'[26] Receiving evidence only from the partisans of Victor, the bishops at Pavia declared in his favour and 'condemned Chancellor Roland as a conspirator and schismatic who preached that discord and strife and perjury are good.'[27] Alexander responded by excommunicating the emperor.

Victor IV died suddenly in Lucca in 1164 and was buried in a local monastery (though his body was ejected from its tomb on the orders of Gregory VIII in 1187). Alexander III is said to have grieved for him—they had been fellow cardinals since 1151—and to have rebuked his cardinals for rejoicing at the news. The emperor hoped to come to terms with Alexander III, but the imperial chancellor

Rainald of Dassel, archbishop of Cologne, who had been with Victor in Lucca, pre-empted him by organising the election of a successor, who became Paschal III (1164–1168). Even in imperial territories many local churches refused to accept Paschal, but in 1165 the emperor swore at an imperial Diet, or assembly of lay and ecclesiastical nobles, held at Würzburg never to abandon him. In return Paschal canonised Charlemagne, whose cult Frederick had been promoting. In 1167 the emperor installed Paschal in Rome, expelling Alexander, who had been there since 1165, and received a second imperial coronation at his hands. But soon after he was proposing that both popes abdicate as a way of resolving the dispute.

Paschal retained his precarious hold on Rome until his death in September 1168, while Alexander III spent much of the 1160s and 1170s in France, whose king, Louis VII (1137–1180), had come out in his favour in October 1160, as had Henry II of England (1154–1189). He might even have won over Frederick I in 1169, but negotiations broke down and the emperor recognised another antipope who had been elected in Rome as Callistus III (1168–1178).

It has been said that Alexander III's papal letters are 'as colourless as they are correct'.[28] This may testify to his early legal training at the pre-eminent University of Bologna, but his position in these years was uneasy. Politically, he depended on the continued support of the French and English monarchs and financially on the diversion to his court of the contributions of Peter's Pence coming from England and the Scandinavian kingdoms. He could therefore not be as supportive of the archbishop of Canterbury, Thomas Becket, in his conflicts with Henry II as some of the latter's partisans wanted, and he was willing to be satisfied by the relatively minor penance that the king undertook following the archbishop's murder in 1170.

The determining factor in ending the schism, beyond Alexander III's durability—his being the longest of any pontificate since that of Hadrian I (772–795)—was the fortunes of a war fought in northern Italy between the emperor and several of its major cities. The core support for the Staufen dynasty, inaugurated in 1138 by Conrad III, lay in southwestern Germany, particularly in its own duchy of Swabia, and it was here and in adjacent territories in northern Italy that Frederick tried to concentrate his power. In 1158, at the Diet of Roncaglia, he claimed direct imperial rule over Italy, immediately confronting the aspirations of the citizens of Milan and other cities to communal self-government. The result was a protracted war, with pro- and anti-imperial factions appearing across the region, and the creation around 1167 of the Lombard League of cities and nobility opposed to the emperor. Other towns that had suffered from the territorial ambitions of more powerful neighbours threw in their lot with Frederick against the major cities. Sides were also taken in the papal schism of 1159, with imperialists, who came to be known as Ghibellines, supporting Frederick and his antipopes, and his opponents, called Guelphs, backing Alexander III. (The names are Italianised versions of the cries used by the Staufen and their Bavarian Welf opponents in a battle fought in 1140.)

The fortunes of war ranged from the emperor taking and sacking Milan in 1162 to his suffering a major defeat at the hands of the league at the battle of Legnano on 29 May 1176. The result of this reverse was a six-year truce, known as the Peace of Venice, signed in July 1177, by which the rebel cities retained their local self-government but accepted imperial overlordship. Frederick also recognised Alexander III and withdrew his support for Callistus III, who abdicated the following year, being rewarded by the pope with the governorship of Benevento. Alexander finally returned to Rome in 1178, only to be driven out again by the Romans the next year. A group of clerics then elected 'Innocent III', one of the cardinals of Victor IV, but he was surrendered to Alexander in January 1180 and imprisoned in a monastery. Alexander III himself died, aged over eighty, in August 1181.

Wars Near and Far

Alexander's successor was the elderly Lucius III (1181–1185), who as a cardinal since 1138, was one of the most experienced diplomats in the Curia, having negotiated various treaties, including the recent Peace of Venice, and serving as papal envoy to Sicily in 1166/7 and to Constantinople in 1167/8. In his short reign he added fifteen new cardinals to a much-diminished college of twenty-seven. This was all the more important as a revision of the electoral process in 1179 introduced the requirement, still in place today, for a two-thirds majority among the cardinals when electing a pope. However, Rome was firmly in the hands of the commune, so Lucius spent most of his pontificate in Velletri in the hills southeast of Rome and then Verona, where he was buried. His successors had to be equally peripatetic: Urban III (1185–1187) was buried in Ferrara and Gregory VIII (1187) in Pisa.

The final years of the twelfth century were dominated by two issues: the call for a new crusade and the succession to the kingdom of Sicily. The rising power of Saladin in the 1180s, uniting Egypt and much of Syria, placed the Latin Kingdom of Jerusalem under threat for the first time in decades, and appeals were sent for a new crusade to bring military assistance from the West. However, it was not until the disastrous defeat of the kingdom's army at the battle of Hattin in 1187, rapidly followed by the fall of Jerusalem, that action was taken. The Third Crusade, in which the kings of England and France participated together with the emperor, failed to recover the city, but did manage to prop up a much-reduced crusader kingdom with a new capital at Acre. One of the main victims of the campaign was the emperor Frederick I, who drowned in a river in 1190 while leading his army across Anatolia.

By this time the dominant figure in Italy was his son, who succeeded him as Henry VI (1190–1197). Frederick's requests to have Henry crowned emperor in his own lifetime had been rejected throughout the 1180s by Lucius III and Urban III, on the unhistorical grounds that there could only be one emperor. This added to existing tensions between the Staufen and the popes, including a dispute over the estates of Matilda of Tuscany (died 1115), which she had bequeathed at different times to both the papacy and the emperor. This and other issues were resolved, largely in the emperor's favour, in the Treaty of Strasbourg of 1189. By this Pope Clement III, who gained a reputation as a peacemaker, also agreed to crown Frederick's son as co-emperor and in return was restored to possession of the papal territories, most of which had been annexed by Henry in 1186 in an attempt to coerce Urban III.

The main diplomatic worry of the popes at this time was with the succession to King William II of Sicily (1166–1189). He was childless, and the heir to the kingdom was his aunt Constance, who became engaged to the Staufen prince Henry in 1185. This situation threatened the succession of a Staufen to both the empire and the kingdom of Sicily, whereas ever since the days of Gregory VII the papacy had looked to one to balance the other. In practice the Sicilians were not keen on a German king, even if ruling in right of his wife, and in 1190 they chose another member of the family, Count Tancred of Lecce, as king. Henry failed to impose himself at first attempt and then had to secure his position in Germany, before making a second and successful attempt to take over Sicily in 1194.

Celestine III (1191–1198), who had been a cardinal since 1144, crowned Henry as emperor in 1191 but then tried to stir up opposition to him in Germany and invested Tancred (who died in 1194) with the kingdom of Sicily, a papal fief since its first granting to Roger I by Urban II. When Henry took the Sicilian crown in November 1194 he refused to swear allegiance to the pope, but there was no formal breach, as Celestine wanted to persuade Henry to launch a new crusade, and the emperor was keen to have the pope baptise his infant son Frederick, heir both to the empire and to Sicily.

The contentious issue of royal control of the Church in Sicily—resulting from a permanent grant of papal legatine authority to the ruler of the kingdom by Urban II—also featured in the negotiations that were still underway when Henry died suddenly in September 1197. Celestine, now in his nineties, offered to abdicate if the cardinals agreed to elect a candidate he favoured, but they unanimously refused, saying there was no precedent for a pope abdicating.[29] He died in early January 1198, to be followed by the best known of medieval popes.

chapter 12

LESS THAN GOD BUT GREATER THAN MAN

(1198–1294)

A TRICKY CASE

On 15 August 1202 the monks of the monastery of Evesham in the west of England faced a dilemma. Their abbot, Roger, who had embezzled the money for the monks' food, let the monastery decay so badly that the rain came in, gave away its property to his relatives and was 'in the habit of keeping his concubines in his chamber from morning to night'.[1] Some of the monks supported him, but most complained twice to the new archbishop of Canterbury, Hubert Walter. Roger was reprimanded both times, but quickly returned to his old ways. And so the bishop of Worcester, in whose diocese Evesham was situated, decided to hold a visitation, a formal inspection of the monastery, during which the monks could present their complaints against the abbot.

The monks of Evesham considered Bishop Mauger of Worcester (1200–1212) 'a just, god-fearing man' with 'the depth of understanding of a cardinal of the Roman Church'. But they decided not to receive him, thanks to the arguments of one of their number, Thomas of Marlborough, who had studied arts in Paris and theology in Oxford, where he had also taught. He had used some of that time to study Evesham's history. He had a reputation of being 'knowledgeable in the law' and told the monks that the monastery was only answerable to the pope, through his legate, currently the archbishop of Canterbury. To allow the bishop of the diocese to conduct a visitation was to recognise that he had authority over them, and thus deprive them of their freedom. According to Thomas, the special ties of the abbey to the papacy meant that 'the pope would never pass judgement against himself.'[2]

The monks locked their buildings and refused to appear before the bishop in the chapter house, although Abbot Roger slipped away in the night to one of the abbey manors. After a week of negotiation Bishop Mauger excommunicated them (but not the elusive abbot), as they continued to insist they could be visited only by the papal legate. Thomas then went to the archbishop to request lifting the bishop's sentence, telling him, 'it is your cause for which we stand.' Archbishop Hubert played for time, ordering representatives of both parties to appear before him for a day at a time in three different locations, while he reported the details to Rome. Soon after, a papal mandate arrived delegating the enquiry to the abbots of Malmesbury, Abingdon and Eynsham. Such panels, of usually three ecclesiastics, normally bishops or abbots, carried out local enquiries into a case. These papal 'judges delegate' did not pass sentence but sent their findings to the pope, who, in consultation with cardinals meeting with him in a consistory, would make the final judgement.

The choice of these three abbots seemed too favourable to Evesham, and so the bishop appealed directly to the pope. Because any such appeal to a higher ecclesiastical court immediately inhibited the jurisdiction of the lower one, both parties had to send representatives to Rome, at some considerable expense.

In Rome the bishop's appeal was first heard by the Court of Auditors, a recently created institution that dealt with minor cases or, as with this one, the opening stages of more complex ones. The presiding cardinal's report on the hearing resulted in papal mandates being sent to yet another panel of judges delegate in England to investigate and report back. They were also empowered to reach a temporary decision and did so in favour of the bishop. Meanwhile, the parties were required to send proctors to the Curia along with the evidence they were relying on, for the pope himself to make the final judgement.

Above left: *Popes first appear in art in the sixth century, normally shown carrying a model of the church they have built. Here, in a mosaic of c. 625 in the apse of Sant'Agnese, Honorius I presents one to the patron saint of the church, St. Agnes* (akg-images / Andrea Jemolo)

Above right: *Few pictures exist before the later twentieth century of a future pope as a child, but here in a fresco of the family of Duke Theodotus in Santa Maria Antiqua, painted in the 740s, is his nephew, who became Hadrian I.* (Roger Collins)

Right: *Around 820, Pascal I built a chapel in the basilica of Santa Prassede, in the mosaic decoration of which uniquely he included a portrait of his mother, Theodora Episcopa. The square halo signifies that she was still alive at the time.* (akg-images / Tristan Lafranchis)

Grants of papal protection to monasteries were ways of extending the authority of the papacy, which the recipients then promoted. John XIX (1024–1032) presents a charter to a church dedicated to St. Laurence, here personified as receiving it. (copyright © 1990 Scala Archives, Florence / Vatican)

Papal grants could be the most important documents in a monastery's archive. Here the text of Innocent III's bull for the monastery of Subiaco was painted into a fresco in 1210, along with a portrait of the pope himself. (akg-images)

From the 12th century popes expected emperors to perform 'groom service' when they met, as represented in this fresco from the Church of the Quattro Sancti Coronati in Rome of c. 1330, depicting Constantine leading Pope Sylvester I's horse. (Roger Collins)

Nicholas III (1277–1280) commissioned frescoes of all his predecessors for the upper level of the nave of San Paolo Fuori le Mura, but only four of the paintings survived the fire of 1823. This one depicts Anacletus I. (akg-images / Nimatallah)

Above: *While earlier papal tombs were covered by large, elegantly carved inscriptions, by the 13th century life-size sculptures of the dead pope were standard, as with the tomb of Honorius IV (1285–1287) in the church of Santa Maria in Aracoeli in Rome.* (akg-images / Andrea Jemolo)

Right: *Boniface VIII became notorious for the life-size sculptures of himself erected during his pontificate, to symbolise his authority. This one, in the Vatican, was carved for the Jubilee Year of 1300 by Arnolfo di Cambio.* (akg-images)

Above: *The papal palace at Avignon still dominates the city. After the expulsion of Benedict XIII in 1403 it never again served as a papal residence, but was the seat of a succession of cardinal legates until finally annexed by France in 1791.* (akg-images / Bildarchiv Monheim)

Left: *Benedict XIII (1394–1423) was anathematised and deposed by the Council of Constance in 1417, an event illustrated here in a contemporary chronicle. He refused to recognise its authority.* (akg-images)

In the fifteenth century the cardinals played a number of roles, not least as papal diplomats, of which Cardinal Niccolò Albergati (died 1443) was the outstanding example. His travels resulted in his portrait being painted in 1431 by Jan Van Eyck. (akg-images / Erich Lessing)

Other cardinals served as generals of papal armies—for example, Ludovico Trevisano (died 1465), legate in Romagna, victor over the Milanese at the battle of Anghiari, and admiral of the papal fleet, here portrayed by Andrea Mantegna. (copyright © 2005 Scala Archives, Florence / Staatliche Museen, Berlin)

A folded bull of Sixtus IV (1471–1484) of 1479 for a church in Worms. It would have been wrapped in its string and closed by its lead seal, which thereby authenticated the document. (Roger Collins)

Bartolomeo Platina, the papal librarian, is here shown kneeling before Sixtus IV in this fresco by Melozzo da Forlì in the Vatican. Standing in front of the pope are his nephews, including the future Julius II and Count Girolamo Riario of Imola. (akg-images)

Pope Leo X and his cousin, Cardinal Giulio de' Medici, later pope Clement VII, are shown with their relative Cardinal Innocenzo Cibo (died 1550), in a painting of 1517 by Raphael. (akg-images / Erich Lessing)

Paul III used his pontificate to transform his family into territorial princes. Here the pope is shown with his grandsons: Cardinal Alessandro Farnese (died 1583) and his brother Ottavio, Duke of Parma (1547–1586), in a painting of 1546 by Titian. (akg-images / Erich Lessing)

The Council of Trent, which opened under Paul III in 1545, is here shown in session on 13 July 1563 in an anonymous Italian painting of the time. It completed its work in December of that year. (akg-images / Andre Held)

Julius III (1550–1555), a distinguished canon lawyer, appears with his secretary in an anonymous contemporary portrait. He reconvened the Council in May 1551, but had to suspend it in April 1552. (copyright © Sotheby's / akg-images)

Pius V published the authoritative versions of the Catechism, Breviary and Missal, tasks left to the pope by the Council. His retaining his white Dominican habit may have created the tradition of the popes always wearing a white soutane. (akg-images / Pirozzi)

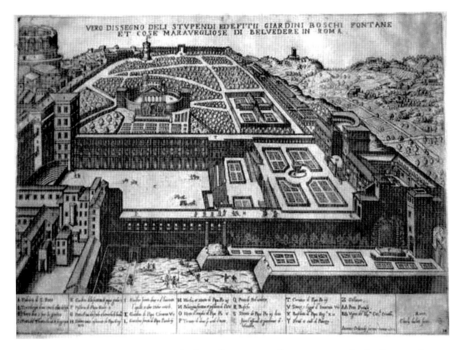

The Vatican palace expanded in the sixteenth century to include a series of gardens and pavilions. This view dates from 1579. The dome of the new basilica of St. Peter's is not yet finished. (Roger Collins)

Annual medals issued by the popes often publicised new building projects, such as Bernini's colonnade in St. Peter's Square on this one issued by Alexander VII of 1662. The plan was modified to leave the approach from the city side open. (Stoyan Spassov)

From the late sixteenth century papal tombs became increasingly grandiose. This one was commissioned for the short-reigned Leo XI (April 1605) by his family from Alessandro Algardi in 1642/4. Only Gregory XIV insisted on a simple tomb. (akg-images)

Prominent painters and sculptors were also called upon to depict papal relatives, as in this remarkable marble bust of Donna Olimpia Maidalchini, sister-in-law of Innocent X, carved by Antonio Algardi c. 1650. (akg-images / Pirozzi)

This joint portrait of Benedict XIV and Cardinal Silvio Valenti Gonzaga (1690–1756) by Pierre Subleyras, emphasises the centrality of the relationship between pope and secretary of state, upon which effective papal government depended. (akg-images / Andre Held)

The transformation of part of the Vatican palace into the museums that draw most visitors to Rome today began under Clement XIV and was continued by Pius VI, here depicted in the catalogue of the Vatican's classical sculptures by Giambattista Visconti. (Roger Collins)

Pius IX's embracing of papal infallibility never obscured his essentially kindly and jovial nature; here, a photograph of him in old age. (Mary Evans Picture Library)

Pope Pius X (1903–1914) was described as having 'hands inert and cold' and 'being sulky and morose', but he became the first papal saint of modern times. (Roger Collins)

'The King of Awesome Majesty' was what Pius XI was called by his eventual successor Paul VI. Here, in 1922, the newly elected pope is simultaneously having his portrait painted and a bust sculpted by artists in full court dress. (Mary Evans Picture Library)

The coronation of Pius XII in 1939 was the last great manifestation of a largely nineteenth-century ancien régime papacy of noble guards, fan bearers, chair carriers and the like that his successors would reduce and abolish. (akg-images)

Above: *The closing session of the Second Vatican council on 8 December 1965 shows how much greater had been the attendance than at the Council of Trent (see earlier image), but which will be the more influential is an open question.* (akg-images)

Right: *The image of Pope John Paul II (1978–2005), photographed in 1981, typifies the less grandiose but more morally absolute style of papacy that emerged in his pontificate.* (akg-images / ullstein bild)

This time it was Thomas and the abbot who went on behalf of the abbey, swearing an oath of mutual loyalty for the duration. Thomas was clearly becoming unpopular, as his advice had landed the monks with this increasingly costly dispute, and he assured them he would not come back if he did not win.

In Rome, Thomas tried to obtain a letter of revocation from the pope to suspend the interim verdict of the panel of judges delegate back in England. In this kind of ecclesiastical litigation, there was almost no stage before a final papal judgement in which it was not possible to request a higher court to have the decision of a lower one suspended or reversed, pending a further appeal or enquiry. If successful this would have put the onus back on the bishop to try to recover possession of the rights he was claiming. Having been promised such a letter of revocation, Thomas gave the pope, Innocent III (1198–1216), a silver cup but was told the letter would not be issued until Abbot Roger arrived.

Roger had been arrested in France, and by the time he had bought his freedom and reached Rome, he and Thomas found it was too late to reverse the decisions made by the judges delegate in England, and so had to pin their hopes on the final papal hearing. An urgent requirement was more money, and they arranged a loan with which they presented the pope with 'a gift worth a hundred pounds of silver coin, and the cardinals and the Curia with gifts worth a hundred marks'[3]. Presumably the bishop's proctor made a similar donation.

As nothing more could happen until the report from the judges delegate back in England arrived, after six weeks in Rome the abbot returned home while Thomas, at the pope's suggestion, went to spend the next six months in the famous law school in Bologna, preparing for the case and attending daily lectures on civil and ecclesiastical law. He returned to Rome around the beginning of October 1205, over three years after the dispute began, and the long-awaited report finally arrived in late November.

With it came three representatives of the bishop, who to Thomas's amazement requested a final hearing. As the bishop had secured the interim adjudication of the judges delegate in his favour, it was in his interests to delay, rather than press for a definitive judgement, which might go against him. Thomas then hired the four best lawyers in Rome, much to his opponents' annoyance. They complained to the pope, who joked that the one thing there was never a shortage of in Rome was lawyers. The professional advocates, though, only attended to advise on matters of law, as the case had to be argued by the proctors for the two parties.

The bishop's proctor began with a long and learned preamble, but this was a court that prized brevity, and he was cut short by the pope: 'We don't want all this introduction; get to the point of your argument.' Forewarned, Thomas quickly moved to the documentary evidence, giving an account of the royal foundation of his monastery in the early eighth century and of the two letters of Pope Constantine I (708–715) exempting it from episcopal oversight. He then cited documents from Innocent II (1130–1143) to Celestine III (1191–1198) that confirmed Evesham's rights because they had been granted by Pope Constantine.

Everything hung on the authenticity of the two papal letters, or bulls, dated 709 and 713 that Evesham claimed to possess. The bishop of Worcester's proctor claimed they were forgeries, because 'the writing material, the style, the thread, and the bulla of Constantine's privileges are completely unknown in our land.' He also argued that some of the more recent papal documents were also the work of a notorious forger, Nicholas of Warwick.

Documents like these were written on papyrus or parchment, with lead seals bearing the name of the pope issuing them, known as *bulla*—hence the documents themselves being called 'bulls'—attached to them by cords of hemp or silk, which could be used to tie up the document after it was signed, so its contents remained secret until opened by the recipient. The seal was regarded as vital for the authentication of a papal letter. Other tests could be applied, such as the literary style of a papal document whose authenticity was being challenged.[4]

In the Evesham case, everything hinged on the bulls. Pope Innocent ordered Thomas to give him two letters.

He took them in his own hands and pulled between the seal and the document to see if he could separate the seal from the cord. Scrutinizing them very carefully, he then handed them to the cardinals to scrutinize, and when they had gone the rounds of them all they came back to the pope. Holding up the privilege of Constantine, he said 'Privileges of this kind which are unknown to you are very well known to us, and could not be forged'; then holding up the letters, he said 'These are genuine.'[5]

Although Innocent III was deeply interested in the detection of forgery and issued several decretals on the subject, in this case he was quite wrong. The very thing that validated the Evesham privileges in his eyes proves they were forgeries. Genuine documents of Pope Constantine I (708–715) would not have had seals that appeared genuine in the early thirteenth century. Although papal documents had carried seals since at least the time of Agapetus I (535–536), for several centuries they just bore the name of the issuing pope. Not until Alexander II (1061–1073) was an image placed on a papal seal, that of St. Peter receiving the keys.

Paschal II introduced what became the definitive style when he replaced this with busts of Saints Peter and Paul side by side, with the name of the issuing pope and his number on the reverse side. With some infrequent changes in artistic style, this has remained the practice right up to the present.[6] Innocent III himself imposed an alteration, increasing the number of dots in the beard of St. Peter and lines in that of St. Paul, so as to make a subtle distinction between his seal and those of his immediate predecessors, but did not realise that an authentic seal of Constantine I would be entirely different in appearance and content. Furthermore genuine documents of that pope would have been written on papyrus and not on parchment. The latter is first found being used by the papal notariate in 1007, and it took over entirely from the more fragile papyrus in 1057.[7] It is only fair to Thomas to add that he was not the forger of these documents, which he had found during his historical researches in the monastery archive. They had almost certainly been fabricated during an earlier legal dispute in the 1120s.[8]

After the inspection and misplaced authentication of the abbey's documents, the parties broke for dinner. The hearing then rumbled on for several more sessions while the two sides argued over the precise meaning of the wording of the spurious documents, but the pope finally gave judgement in favour of the abbey in January 1206. This was not entirely the end of the matter, and Thomas, who became abbot of Evesham (1229–1237), wrote a history of the monastery and of his great legal battle in Rome to advise his successors should the case ever be reopened.

And then there was the abbey's substantial debt to Roman moneylenders for the costs of travel, gifts, lawyers and the maintenance of its proctors over the best part of two years. Innocent III forbade Thomas and two monks with him to take the verdict in favour of the monastery home until they had paid the bankers, but they ignored him and slipped out of Rome; the irate lenders pursued them to England but did not get repaid until 1214.

While this case involved purely ecclesiastical participants, lay litigants could also use the church courts if a cleric or clerical property was involved. To take an example from later in the century, an English knight accused the bishop of Lichfield of fornicating with the appellant's stepmother and assisting her in poisoning his father. He also alleged that the bishop frequently worshipped the devil and kissed his backside. While this was investigated, the bishop was suspended and summoned to Rome, but the knight never appeared at the final hearing. His charges were clearly malicious and probably intended to be vexatious, as the bishop had been suspended from office by this time for the best part of three years. Even so, Pope Boniface VIII did not just let the case lapse. To be reinstated, the bishop was required to take an oath proclaiming his innocence and to find twenty senior clerics to support him.

THE LAWYER POPES

With the growing emphasis on their legal activity, it is hardly surprising that most of the popes of this period were trained lawyers and were concerned about codifying the ever growing body of laws that the papacy itself was generating. Thus, Honorius III (1216–1227) issued the first authorised collection of papal decretals, which he had circulated to the universities that were then starting to appear in Italy, France, England and Spain. One of Innocent III's cousins, who became Pope Gregory IX (1227–1241), authorised in 1234 an official collection of papal decretals in five books, compiled for him by his confessor, Raymond of Peñaforte. Another of Gregory IX's advisors, Sinibaldo Fieschi, was elected pope as Innocent IV (1243–1254) and published three collections of his own decretals and a commentary on those of Gregory. Clement IV (1265–1268) had been a civil judge before being ordained after the death of his wife.

Those in search of justice were not the only ones arriving in growing numbers at the papal Curia in this period. Penitents and petitioners also came. Although penances for most sins were imposed locally, by the early thirteenth century, penitents were sent to the papal court for sentence if they had committed a 'reserved sin', such as assaults on the clergy or members of the monastic orders, forging of papal letters and arson. Some cases could be serious, as when in 1200 a servant of the earl of Orkney cut out the tongue of the bishop of Caithness, but the penalties were far milder than with civil justice, and never involved capital punishment, even for murder. The increasing number of penitents led Innocent III to create the office of cardinal penitentiary to handle all but the most serious cases, and he soon had to delegate some of the mounting workload to assistants, the minor penitentaries.

Even penitential issues not related to the 'reserved sins' could come to the pope. For example, in 1200 a priest of the diocese of Lincoln went to explain to Innocent III how he had accidentally killed a baby. Suffering from an ailment that had deprived him of appetite and sleep, he had decided that a ride might help. His horse bolted when a rein broke, fatally crushing a child. The priest had suspended himself from saying Mass, but the pope ordered him to resume his ministry, as the death had been accidental. In such cases the pope was acting as what canon lawyers called the Universal Ordinary. An Ordinary was the ecclesiastical superior of a designated area or jurisdiction, such as a bishop in his diocese, but the pope was now regarded as the universal superior, to whom all could appeal.

Along with litigants and penitents, and many types of petitioner, senior members of the Church hierarchy from all over Western Europe regularly visited the Curia. Elections of bishops and abbots required confirmation, which might have to be secured in person. The pope could quash any ecclesiastical appointment with or without an appeal for him to do so, and if an impediment in canon law existed that would prevent a candidate being chosen, he had to 'postulate', or appeal in advance for a papal dispensation to allow his election.

Thus, when Mauger of Worcester, formerly Richard the Lionheart's personal physician, was chosen bishop by the chapter of Worcester in 1200, he immediately confessed to the archbishop of Canterbury that his parents had never been married. Although both the archbishop of York and the bishop of Salisbury at the time were also illegitimate, canon law texts made this a bar to high office in the Church. So Mauger went to Rome, where Innocent III was impressed by 'his learning, his honesty, his virtuous life and his personal reputation', as well as by his decision to 'confess his defect rather than mount the episcopal throne with guilt on his conscience'. While ruling that a decree of the Third Lateran Council of 1179 invalidated the original election, which he then quashed, he also allowed the electors to vote again for Mauger and 'postulate' for a papal dispensation from the taint of bastardy.[9]

The papacy could require senior clerics to visit the Curia for its financial advantage. In 1257 a newly elected abbot of Bury St. Edmunds sent messengers to inform Alexander IV (1254–1261) of his appointment, but he was ordered to come in person, as all abbots of houses exempt from episcopal oversight were obliged to do. While it had been possible to buy an exemption from this rule, in 1257 Alexander began applying the rule in full. In Rome the new abbot had to pay £2,000 for the privilege of confirmation, later called the 'service tax', on top of the costs of his journey and maintenance awaiting his papal audience.[10]

Alexander IV also created the requirement that still exists for bishops to make *ad limina* visits, to come 'to the threshold of the Apostles' in Rome or wherever else the pope might be. These also involved the distribution of suitable gifts to pope and cardinals. The financial outlay required for almost anything involving attendance at the Curia became increasingly notorious, and some of the popes of this period were placed in Purgatory or even Hell by Dante for Avarice, notably Nicholas III, who appears in the *Inferno* on top of several of his predecessors: 'Beneath my head are pushed down all the others who came, sinning in simony, before me, squeezed tightly in the fissures of the rock.'[11]

As Hildegard of Bingen and Bernard of Clairvaux recognised, the papacy's legal workload threatened not only the spiritual well-being of individual popes but also that of the institution itself. Becoming a great international court that charged fees for justice made it less a source of spiritual leadership and renewal just when this was increasingly sought. Instead, its main concern seemed to be making money. As the renowned preacher Friar Hugh of Montpellier put it in the 1240s: 'The Roman Curia does not take care of the sheep that has no wool,' and, making a pun on the cases in Latin grammar 'if you go to the Curia in the accusative, you will get nowhere if you do not have something in the dative' (i.e., to give).[12]

Similarly, the seemingly endless litigation of the monastic houses and higher clergy, often requiring them to be more concerned about increasing their revenues and exploiting their financial rights than carrying out their pastoral responsibilities, added to the sense that the institutional church was failing the faithful. This in turn prompted interest in alternative forms of piety that either rejected the organised church as a whole or those parts of it that seemed in the service of Mammon. In the early 1170s a merchant of Lyon, Peter Waldo, began taking literally the Gospel injunction to give away his property and lead a life of apostolic poverty (as St. Francis of Assisi would also do in 1209). He acquired a growing following of pious laypeople keen to lead lives on scriptural principles and received papal approval from Alexander III in 1179. This, however, was conditional upon him and his supporters not preaching without prior approval of their diocesan bishops. When this command was flouted, they were condemned as heretics by Lucius III in 1184 and again by the Fourth Lateran Council in 1215. In 1211 at Strasbourg, eighty of them were convicted of heresy by an episcopal inquisition and burned.

More threatening to the established order than the Waldensians, as they became known, were the Cathars, also called the Albigensians (from the town of Albi), who from the early eleventh century became deeply entrenched in the society of southwestern France, in lands ruled by the counts of Toulouse and the kings of Aragón. Their ideas came from the teachings of the Manichees, who had been influential in the Roman and Persian empires in the third to fifth centuries and who believed good and evil, light and dark, material and immaterial, were evenly balanced, intermingled and in permanent conflict. They saw Christ as pure spirit, as matter was equated with evil. The papacy regarded them as irremediably heretical, but they included many of the leading magnates of the region amongst their number and so could largely ignore papal legations and the condemnation of their ideas at the Third Lateran Council in 1179.

DEFENDER OF THE FAITH: INNOCENT III

A nephew of Clement III and of Roman noble birth, trained in theology and canon law and the author of two theological treatises, Innocent III (1198–1216) was younger than any of his immediate predecessors when elected pope.[13] While widely regarded as the greatest of medieval popes, his achievements owe something to luck as well as to skill. Rome was relatively tranquil, and in most years of his pontificate he was able to appoint the Senator and the civil government of the city himself. He was elected soon after the death of a potentially dangerous opponent, Henry VI, who had been on the point of making Staufen control of both the empire and the kingdom of Sicily a reality. His heir was the infant Frederick II, whose mother, the heiress to the Sicilian kingdom, herself died late in 1198, placing their son under the guardianship of the pope. Although Henry had already made the German princes take an oath to the infant Frederick, political necessity required a stronger ruler than a two-year-old.

The imperial title normally passed from father to son, but in circumstances like these election by the princes—the great lay and ecclesiastical magnates of the empire—took on real significance, rather than just being a formality. The electors declined to endorse Frederick and even considered candidates from outside the empire, such as Richard I of England (1189–1199) and Philip Augustus of France (1180–1223), before settling on Philip, duke of Swabia, the brother of Henry VI, and Otto of Brunswick of the rival Welf family, whose strength lay primarily in Saxony. Both were elected by their own partisans, and the kingdom remained divided until Philip was assassinated in 1208. During this time Innocent III acted to preserve the young Frederick's rights in Sicily while generally supporting Otto IV, as he became, against Philip of Swabia in Germany, so as to prevent the two kingdoms being reunited.

In Italy the war of succession led to many of the unpopular German local governors and military commanders submitting to the pope or returning home. A group of them tried to take over the Sicilian kingdom but were defeated by an alliance of papal and local forces in 1204. In these highly favourable circumstances, Innocent III was able to impose his personal rule over most of central Italy, an achievement seen by some as creating the papal state.

For the first time there was a unified body of territory over which the pope was the sole acknowledged ruler, answerable to no political superior and with full monarchical power over the numerous subordinate lordships and towns into which these lands were divided. Since the eighth century, popes had exercised overlordship over territories in central Italy, such as the duchy of Rome, on the strength of delegation of authority by the Eastern emperors. To these in the ninth century had been added lands conceded by the Carolingian rulers, though not all had ultimately come under papal control. But even within the original nucleus of papal territories there remained towns, such as Tivoli, and property-owning institutions, such as the Abbey of Farfa near Rome, over which the feudal superior was the emperor and not the pope.

In the twelfth century there had been frequent arguments over the lands that the martial Countess Matilda of Tuscany, who died in 1115, had bequeathed both to the emperors and to the popes. Under Frederick I and Henry VI the imperial claim was generally recognised, though the papal one was not abandoned. In the time of Pope Hadrian IV (1154–1159) those territories under papal overlordship had been reduced to the area of the former duchies of Rome and of Spoleto, but under Innocent III, with little effective imperial opposition in Italy, they expanded to limits that would be retained almost intact until the annexation of the Papal States by the kingdom of Italy in the 1860s.

On his election in 1198 one of Innocent III's priorities had been promoting a new crusade. The Third Crusade had failed to recover Jerusalem, and a fresh attempt was required. However, the conflict in the empire over the succession to Henry VI and war that broke out between the French and English kings in 1199 meant that any such expedition would lack royal leadership. Instead, various magnates of the second rank answered the pope's call, and an army was assembled, led from 1200 by the Marquis Boniface of Montferrat. From its composition, it has been deduced that the intended purpose was an attack on the Nile delta, as control of Egypt was seen as the key to the security of the kingdom of Jerusalem. However, the crusaders had raised just over half of the money they had pledged the Venetians for transporting the army. So Venice imposed its own conditions, diverting the Crusade to the conquest of Zadar on the Croatian coast, which it had once owned but which was now tributary to the king of Hungary. Next the expedition was sidetracked into assisting the restoration of the deposed Eastern emperor Isaac II (1185–1195, 1203–1204), in return for promises of financial assistance. Although this was achieved in 1203, the restored Isaac II and his son Alexius IV were unable to pay and locally so unpopular because of their Western allies that they were quickly killed. A new emperor, Alexius V, refused to honour their pledges, and in April 1204, urged on by the Venetians, the crusaders took Constantinople, setting up one of their leaders, Count Baldwin of Flanders, as emperor of a new Latin state of Romania, which survived until 1261. Three-eighths of the territory conquered in 1204 was ceded to Venice.

Innocent III was furious that the Crusade had turned into a prolonged assault on fellow Christians, but although he reprimanded his legates accompanying the army, he recognised the new emperor, Baldwin, who died in 1205. He also instituted a Latin patriarch of Constantinople, whose status as second in the Church to the pope was confirmed at the Fourth Lateran Council in 1215. The success of the Fourth Crusade, against Christians who were not in communion with Rome, also planted the idea that such expeditions could legitimately be directed at heretics as well as non-Christians. Innocent III had made the conversion of the Cathars a priority from the start of his pontificate, but local preaching, in which the new Dominican order took the lead, was not achieving the desired result. So, the Fourth Crusade may have inspired him in 1208 to issue the call for a crusade against heresy in southwestern France.

The immediate cause was the murder in January of a papal legate, Pierre de Castelnau. Count Raymond VI of Toulouse was held responsible, as he had been excommunicated the previous year for supporting the Cathars. In response to the papal call, an army was assembled in northern France under Simon de Montfort to be used against Raymond and other southern lords thought to be protecting heretics. There followed over two decades of fighting in the southwest, marked by several massacres and mutilations of the civil population of besieged towns, starting at Béziers in 1209. Little attempt was made to distinguish between Cathars and the non-Cathar population. When King Peter II of Aragón intervened in 1213 to aid his vassals in the region from attack by the crusaders, he was defeated and killed at the battle of Muret. His descendents would have their revenge on the papacy when they acquired the kingdom of Sicily in 1282. After the death of Simon de Montfort, crushed by a mangonel ball during an unsuccessful siege of Toulouse in 1218, French royal interest in securing more control of the south led Louis VIII (1223–1226) to become involved. A council of French bishops at Bourges in 1225 proclaimed another crusade against the new count of Toulouse, Raymond VII, soon ended by Louis's death from dysentery.

The wars in southern France finally concluded when Raymond VII of Toulouse ceded many of his territories both to the papacy and to the kingdom of France in 1229. They had transformed the nature of the crusading ideal, if that be the right word for it by this time, making it an instrument to be directed against almost anyone who could be presented as an enemy of the Church. Before the century was out, Innocent III's successors were using crusading bulls to try to raise armies to attack non-heretical Christian rulers whose ambitions were thought to threaten papal rights. It could be suggested that if the papacy created the concept of Crusade, it also corrupted it.

The year 1208 ushered in new problems for Innocent III in the empire. After the murder of Philip of Swabia that year, Otto IV was less dependent on papal support, especially after being accepted as emperor by a Diet of the leading magnates of the empire in November. The following year he requested a coronation from the pope, agreeing to give up the imperial claim to both the lands of Matilda of Tuscany and to Ravenna and the Romagna, which the papacy still claimed on the basis of Pippin III's supposed donation. In return he was crowned in St. Peter's on 4 October 1209. However, he began 1210 by seizing the papal territories of Ancona and Spoleto and then invaded the kingdom of Sicily to try to dispossess Frederick II. The pope excommunicated him in November and the following year persuaded some of the imperial electors to switch their allegiance to Frederick. In 1212 Frederick came of age and was crowned emperor at Aachen in 1215. By the time Otto died in 1218, he had been driven out of most of his lands, and once again the empire and the kingdom of Sicily were in the hands of the same ruler.

In April 1213 Innocent III issued a bull calling the Fourth Lateran Council, which opened in November 1215, attended by seventy-one archbishops and patriarchs, 412 bishops and over 900 heads of monastic houses. Although the Greek church was only represented by the recently installed and papally appointed Latin patriarchate of Constantinople, it was regarded as an ecumenical council, the twelfth in the Roman numbering of such assemblies. It included practical objectives, such as discussion of plans for a new crusade, the Fifth, which was launched in 1217, along with the proclamation that those who had taken crusading vows to fight heretics would receive the indulgences granted to those who fought to regain the Holy Places. It issued rules for the conduct of the clergy, including prohibitions on their visiting taverns, hunting and gambling. It firmly restated the ideal of clerical celibacy. It ensured that the clergy received their income from their parishioners: The payment of tithes, the tenth due to the church, was decreed to take precedence over secular taxes. It proscribed various forms of tithe-evasion. The council remains notorious for its insistence that Jews and Muslims wear distinctive dress, 'lest by error Christians might unite with the women of the Jews or of the Saracens, or Jews or Saracens with the women of the Christians'.[14]

The Fourth Lateran Council also issued a ban on the founding of new religious orders. Papal approval had already been given to both the Franciscans and the Dominicans, and the draft constitution for the latter was discussed by the pope and its founder, the Spanish canon Domingo de Guzmán, at the council. We have already noted that the inspiration behind Peter Waldo and his movement that the council declared heretical was very similar to that behind Francis of Assisi and his order. The essential difference was that Francis persuaded both the bishop of Assisi and Pope Innocent that he and his followers were entirely obedient to papal authority. Overall, issuing seventy canons and the decrees on the crusade, this was the most important of all the medieval councils of the Roman church. Of Innocent III, it was recalled later in the century that 'the Church had been vigorous and powerful in his time, holding firm its lordship over the Roman Empire and over all the kings and princes of the earth.'[15] Such a time would not last long.

A Turbulent Age

Innocent III was succeeded by Honorius III (1216–1227), formerly the Roman aristocrat Cencio Savelli, a cardinal since 1193 and chancellor under Celestine III. In 1192 he had compiled the first version of the *Liber Censuum* (Book of Taxes), a record of the financial assets and expected annual revenues of the papacy. As pope he approved the rules of both the newly founded orders of Friars—the Dominicans in 1216 and the Franciscans or Friars Minor in 1223—and appointed Cardinal Hugo, who would succeed him as pope, as the Franciscans' official protector.

Amongst his other duties before his election, Honorius had been tutor to young Frederick II when he had been a papal ward in Rome. The personal ties this created helped limit subsequent conflict between pope and emperor, and when the Lombard League was revived in 1226, Frederick persuaded Honorius to mediate between him and the rebel cities. The principal friction resulted from the failure of the Fifth Crusade of 1217–1221, for which both Frederick II and the papal legate, Cardinal Pelagius, were blamed, and Honorius threatened to excommunicate Frederick if he did not launch a new crusade by 1227.

When he was Cardinal Hugo in 1221, Gregory IX (1227–1241) had preached the Crusade in Italy. Now, as pope he was more suspicious of the emperor, putting the threatened excommunication into effect when Frederick seemed to be prevaricating over his promise to lead it. He was overhasty, as the expedition set out, and the excommunicated Frederick regained control of Jerusalem in 1228, albeit by negotiation with the ruler of Egypt rather than by battle. In the meantime the pope had authorised an invasion of the kingdom of Sicily before agreeing to a truce.

It was now that the Albigensian Crusade came to an end, with the Treaty of Meaux of April 1229. Catharism remained strong in southwest France, despite the damage and loss of life inflicted on the region in the Albigensian Crusade, and in November Gregory IX established the Inquisition in Toulouse to carry on the suppression of heresy. Since the 1180s diocesan bishops had exercised the right to set up inquisitorial panels to investigate suspected heretics, but these were limited in their powers and geographical reach. This was the first such enquiry to be established under papal authority, and, as would become the norm, was largely run by members of the Dominican Order, one of whose original purposes had been preaching against Catharism. While the friars and other inquisitors carried out the interrogation of suspected heretics, those convicted were handed over to the local secular authorities to carry out the sentence, usually that of being burned alive.

Relations between pope and emperor improved in 1232 when Frederick reinstated Gregory in Rome, after he had been expelled in a communal revolt led by the Senator Luca Savelli, a nephew of Honorius III and the father of Honorius IV. The pope returned the favour in 1234, mediating on the emperor's behalf with the Lombard League, and excommunicated Frederick's son Henry when he rebelled against his father. However a decisive victory over the league in 1237 restored imperial dominance in Italy, and in 1238 Frederick installed one of his illegitimate sons as king of Sardinia without Gregory's consent, although it was a papal fief.

Friction turned to open conflict when Frederick entered into secret correspondence with some of the cardinals in 1239 to persuade them to depose Gregory, with some of the letters falling into the pope's hands. He excommunicated the emperor again and began a new alliance with the northern cities. Frederick then called for a general council of the Church to be summoned to hear charges against the pope, and Gregory retorted by calling such a council to meet in the Lateran. However, the emperor's control of much of Italy enabled him to arrest those making their way to the papal council, and in April 1241 he besieged Rome, where Gregory IX held out until his death on 22 August.

By this time there were only twelve cardinals, two of whom were prisoners of the emperor. Although Innocent III had created thirty-two new cardinals, popes now generally relied on a small inner group of half a dozen or so for the daily running of the Curia. Financial and political considerations also militated against too many cardinals, as they received a share of papal revenues and could form factions. So Gregory IX let the numbers decline. From the later twelfth century, popes also tended to appoint some of their own relatives as cardinals, to create a body of support in the college. Innocent III had been the nephew of Clement III and made cardinals of three relatives. Innocent IV (1242–1254) was particularly notorious for his promotion of family members.

In August 1241 the ten available cardinals were divided over how to treat Frederick II and unable to agree on a new pope. Since 1198, papal elections had been held in the Septizonium, a late Roman structure on the southwestern approach to the Palatine Hill that had later been turned into a monastery. It had the advantage of being easily defensible, but in 1241 this was used against the cardinals in what became known as the Conclave of Terror. The Senator, Matteo Rosso Orsini, one of whose duties was guarding the conclave, kept the cardinals prisoners in the Septizonium for two months, after they failed to agree on a new pope. He also refused to let them elect a non-cardinal. One cardinal died before the nine survivors finally settled on Celestine IV on 25 October. Two days later he fell ill, probably as a result of his own electoral process, and died, unconsecrated, on 10 November. By then the surviving cardinals had fled Rome to avoid another such conclave.

As there were now only eight cardinals at liberty and no way of creating more without a pope, an eighteen-month vacancy followed, while they tried to secure the release of their two colleagues held by the emperor. Once that was achieved, a conclave was held in the town of Anagni in the papal territories, which led to the election of Innocent IV (1242–1254). Son of an imperial tax collector and himself a former papal vice chancellor (the office of chancellor remained unfilled after 1216), he was highly experienced in both curial administration and civil government.

As the emperor still controlled the approaches to Rome, Innocent IV held a general council in Lyon in 1245. This was a politically divided city, most of which was in imperial territory (only becoming French in 1307), but a section of it belonged to the kingdom of Louis IX (1226–1270) of France, under whose protection the council met, marking the start of a much closer French involvement in papal affairs.

Although its discussions focussed on church reform and plans for what became the Seventh Crusade (1248–1254), this First Council of Lyon was amongst the most politically assertive of such assemblies. Under papal direction it deposed Frederick II and asked the German princely electors to choose a new emperor. In justification, Innocent IV claimed that the papacy possessed supreme secular as well as ecclesiastical authority. To achieve this in practice he supported several unsuccessful challengers to Frederick in Germany, commissioned the orders of friars to preach a crusade against him and even plotted his murder. It was later claimed that the cardinals' distinctive large red hats with long tassels were first worn at this council, as a symbol of their willingness to shed their blood in defence of the Church.[16]

Despite all this Frederick survived to die of natural causes in 1250, but Innocent was determined that his son, Conrad IV, crowned king of the Romans in 1237, should not succeed him as emperor. The papal insistence that no Staufen should come to power in either Germany or Sicily reflects how seriously relations had deteriorated from the time of Frederick I onwards. Innocent IV returned to Italy in 1251 and, after the failure of all German challenges to the Staufen, began seeking a foreign prince to become king of the Romans and eventually emperor. The leading candidate was Richard of Cornwall, younger brother of the English king Henry III, but no serious opponent to Conrad IV could be put in the field before he died in 1254.

Manfred, an illegitimate son of Frederick II, acknowledged papal overlordship of the kingdom of Sicily following the death of Conrad, hoping thereby to secure his own confirmation as king. Although this would have separated Germany and Sicily, Innocent IV was determined to prevent a Staufen succession to either and declared the kingdom annexed to the papacy. Manfred rebelled, defeating the pope's army at Foggia, just as Innocent himself was dying in Naples.

Although the cardinals accompanying him wanted to return to Rome, the mayor of Naples, elated at the honour, forced them to hold a conclave in his city. They quickly elected a nephew of Gregory IX, who took the name Alexander IV (1254–1261). He had been made a cardinal in 1227 in one of the three most significant consistories of the century. Of the six cardinals then appointed, three were subsequently elected pope. Similarly, in 1261 three out of seven newly appointed cardinals would later occupy the papal throne, as would three of the five elevated in 1273, unusually high percentages for any period.[17]

Failing to reach an agreement with Manfred, Alexander IV devoted himself to finding alternative candidates for both the empire and the Sicilian kingdom. Alfonso X the Learned of Castile (1252–1284) was keen to challenge Richard of Cornwall, who had now been elected king of the Romans but not emperor, and Henry III of England had already agreed with Innocent IV that he would pay to have his younger son invested with the kingdom of Sicily. A papal grant to the king of the right to impose a ten-percent tax on clerical incomes for a five-year period, ostensibly to fund a crusade, was intended to help him with this payment.[18] In other words money from the English church was diverted to the papal coffers to enable Prince Edmund to be made king of Sicily. This fuelled discontent in England with both king and pope, but the deal was cancelled in 1258, when it was clear Henry could not complete his side of the bargain, though money already paid was not returned.

Manfred proclaimed himself king the same year, and rapidly conquered much papal territory, including Spoleto, the Romagna and the March of Ancona. In 1261 he was even elected Senator of Rome by the citizens. Alexander IV had to remain in the hill town of Viterbo, where a new papal palace began being built in 1257, which would be the setting for the conclaves that elected most of his immediate successors.

Alexander IV failed to appoint any cardinals, and so there were only eight of them when he died in 1261. After three months of debate they settled on Jacques Pantaléon, the son of a shoemaker, who had risen through his studies in Paris to become a master in the university and thence to higher office in the Church in France. He served as papal legate in Eastern Europe and as titular patriarch of Jerusalem. He took the name of Urban IV (1261–1264), in honour of the French pope Urban II, and quickly appointed fourteen new cardinals, six of whom were French.

Similar patriotic sentiments may have influenced his decision to offer the kingdom of Sicily firstly to King Louis IX and then to his brother, Charles, count of Anjou, but in any case the French royal house was best placed to assist the papal programme. Charles accepted the pope's offer in 1263, paying 50,000 marks down and promising a further 10,000 ounces of gold per annum once he became king. He also swore not to accept election as emperor. Urban was unable to decide between the rival claims of Richard of Cornwall and Alfonso X of Castile to the imperial title but forbade the election of Conradin, son of Conrad IV and last legitimate Staufen. He also failed to gain control of Rome, having to spend his pontificate in Orvieto and then Perugia, where he was buried.

The rising French influence in the Curia expressed itself in the election of one of Urban IV's new cardinals, the archbishop of Narbonne, who became Clement IV (1265–1268). He was also the last pope to have legitimate children, two daughters from an early marriage. He returned the Curia to Viterbo, where the palace was completed in 1267, while awaiting the outcome of Charles's attempt to conquer Sicily.

Charles and his army reached Rome in 1265, where he was elected Senator and invested with the kingdom of Sicily by five cardinals acting on the pope's behalf, before defeating and killing Manfred in battle near Benevento the next year. The only challenge to his conquest of Sicily and dominance of much of Italy came in 1268, when the eighteen-year-old Conradin arrived in Italy. Warmly received in Rome, he was immediately excommunicated by Clement IV and then defeated by Charles at the battle of Tagliacozzo. As one of the offices that Charles had been invested with by papal mandate was that of imperial vicar in Tuscany, which gave him powers of capital punishment over disturbers of the peace, he used this to execute Conradin. No objection was raised by Clement.

Following the pope's death the same year, the cardinals in Viterbo were more divided than ever, meeting in a conclave that lasted for two years and ten months, the longest ever. Eventually they were locked into the palace and their food rations gradually reduced to force them to decide, which at last they did in favour of Teobaldo Visconti, an Italian archdeacon, then on crusade with Edward I of England (1272–1307). He did not reach Viterbo until two months after his election, then proceeding to Rome to be enthroned as Gregory X (1271–1276).

Although 'unquestionably very holy, extremely hostile to the infidel, and obsessed with the recovery of the Holy Land', Gregory also recognised the need to create a political counterweight to Charles of Anjou, who was becoming more of a threat to the independence of the papacy and to its territories than the Staufen had ever been, and so he tried to revive the stalled process of finding a new emperor.[19] The death of Richard of Cornwall in 1272 provided the opportunity, and the following year the landgrave of Alsace, Rudolf of Hapsburg, was elected to replace him as king of the Romans. An appointment for him to be crowned emperor in February 1276 fell through when the pope died the month before.

In 1274 Gregory had called another general council to meet in Lyon, to formalise a reunion of the Latin and Greek churches, essentially on papal terms. The Eastern empire had regained control of Constantinople in 1261 and faced the threat of attack from the ejected Westerners, now allied to Charles of Anjou. To prevent this the emperor Michael VIII Palaeologos (1259–1282) opened negotiations with Gregory X for a reconciliation of the churches. Papal envoys insisted that this involved acceptance of the *filioque* clause in the Nicene Creed, the use of unleavened bread in the Mass and the recognition of the pope's universal primacy, the issues that had caused the breach in 1054. While the Eastern bishops and monks were generally opposed to any concessions, not least after successful resistance to Western rule in Constantinople, the emperor was willing to compromise to secure peace. At the council his envoys accepted the papal conditions, but resistance from the Eastern church meant they could not be put into effect.

The council imposed a tax of a tenth on ecclesiastical incomes, including those of monasteries, to fund a new crusade. Such clerical taxation was becoming increasingly unpopular, and a monastic chronicler tartly commented on reporting the death of Gregory X that the man who had imposed the tenths *(decimas)* had himself been decimated.[20] The council enacted a new electoral decree to prevent any future conclave lasting as long as that of 1268–1271 requiring the cardinals to assemble within ten days of a pope's death and remain together without contact with the outside world, with their food and other comforts being gradually diminished the longer they took. The cardinals themselves objected to this proposal, but Gregory forced it through with the support of the bishops attending the council.

Facing these conditions at the conclave in January 1276, the cardinals quickly elected a French Dominican friar, Pierre of Tarentaise, as Innocent V (January to June 1276). He had been the provincial, or head of the French province of his order, and a noted scholar, before being appointed archbishop of Lyon (1272) and then cardinal bishop of Ostia (1273) and cardinal penitentiary. In a very short pontificate, Innocent reversed his predecessor's policy towards Charles of Anjou, confirming him as Senator of Rome and imperial vicar in Tuscany, delaying the coronation of Rudolf of Hapsburg and supporting the idea of a crusade against Constantinople. His demand that the Greek clergy all swear to accept *filioque* and recognise papal primacy threatened to undermine the tentative reunion agreed at the Second Council of Lyon.

His early death threw the cardinals into disarray. As Senator, Charles of Anjou oversaw the ensuing conclave and applied the new rules when it began to drag on. In the height of the Roman summer several of the participants came down with heat stroke before they could agree on Ottobono Fieschi, a nephew of Innocent IV, who took the name Hadrian V. As one who had suffered from its effects, he immediately suspended the new electoral decree but fell ill and died at Viterbo just over a month after his election, without being ordained priest or crowned pope.

DANGEROUS INHERITANCES

Hadrian's successor was one of the few popes of the period to be placed in Paradise by Dante and is the only one from Portugal. Pedro Julião was the son of a doctor and himself taught medicine in the newly created University of Siena. He wrote a work on ophthalmology, a medical self-help guide entitled *The Poor Man's Treasury* and works on philosophy. Having been introduced to Gregory X by Cardinal Fieschi (later Pope Hadrian V), he became papal physician, titular archbishop of Braga then cardinal bishop of Tusculum. He took the name John and was persuaded his number was XXI. The diligent reader may feel cheated of a John XX, but there had been no Pope John since the nineteenth, who died in 1032, and since then confusion developed over the numbering.

Even when pope, John XXI preferred to devote himself to scholarship in the palace at Viterbo, and papal policy was largely directed by Cardinal Giangaetano Orsini, son of the Senator, Matteo Rosso

Orsini. According to a contemporary, the cardinal was so thoroughly 'composed in his manner, that many called him *el composto*'.[21] As he would himself be elected as Nicholas III (1277–1280), there is considerable continuity between the two pontificates, except for the six-month conclave that followed John XXI's death, when the ceiling of his new study collapsed on him in May 1277. That human agency was not suspected is surprising: When the former archbishop of Canterbury Robert Kilwardby died in 1279, a year after being made cardinal, many in England immediately assumed that he had been poisoned at the Curia.[22]

Resistance to electing Orsini in the conclave of 1277, which was attended by only seven cardinals, came from three partisans of Charles of Anjou. Under John XXI the papacy had distanced itself from him again, not confirming him as Senator or imperial vicar in Tuscany, and Nicholas III forced him to renounce both offices. At the same time negotiations continued with Rudolf of Hapsburg over imperial claims to the Romagna region, which he eventually renounced in 1279, allowing it to be completely integrated into the Papal States. This concession proved too late for Rudolf, as Nicholas III died of a stroke the following summer and was succeeded by another French pope, more supportive of the house of Anjou and less interested in creating a new German emperor. So, Rudolf died in 1291 still uncrowned.

Neither John XXI nor Nicholas III could make a reality of the reunification of Greek and Latin churches promised at the Second Council of Lyon, nor were they able to launch a new crusade, despite exploring the possibility of using the Mongols as allies against the Muslims. Similar in many ways, Nicholas III differed from John XXI in being consigned to Hell by Dante for his nepotism. In other respects, though, he had been a very effective pontiff.

Nicholas's death opened the way for cardinals sympathetic to Charles of Anjou to elect a pope more favourable to his interests. Two Orsini cardinals, relatives promoted by Nicholas III, were imprisoned by Charles, but it still required a six-month conclave to secure another French pope, Simon de Brion, former chancellor of the kingdom of France, who took the name of Martin IV (1281–1285) in honour of the much-revered French saint Martin of Tours (died 397). Although residing mainly in Orvieto, he was elected Senator of Rome for life, a unique distinction for a pope (although in principle anyone could be elected Senator), but then gave the title to Charles of Anjou, rejecting a decree of Nicholas III that it should never again be held by a foreign prince.

He supported Charles's planned expedition against Constantinople that Nicholas III had previously thwarted, and facilitated the king's alliance with Venice to provide the necessary shipping. He excommunicated the emperor Michael VIII in 1281 as another preliminary, leading to the formal renunciation the following year by the latter's successor, Andronicus II (1282–1328), of the agreement on reunion reached at the Second Council of Lyon. The launch of Charles's campaign was planned for 1283, but the whole project was scuppered when he and his henchmen were ejected from the kingdom of Sicily in 1282 in what is called the Sicilian Vespers, a rising of the populace against the hated French king and his countrymen.

The Sicilians then offered homage directly to the pope, recognising the kingdom as a papal fief, but he demanded that they return to their allegiance to Charles. Instead, they began seeking a new monarch, and in 1283 found one in King Peter III of Aragón (1276–1285). Although immediately excommunicated by the pope, Peter was able to establish himself as king of Sicily, in successful defiance of both Martin IV and Charles of Anjou, both of whom who died in 1285.

The ensuing conclave at Perugia was unusually brief, resulting in the election of the Roman aristocrat Giacomo Savelli five days after his predecessor's death. Taking the name Honorius IV (1285–1287) in honour of his great-uncle Honorius III, he was well established in Rome, where his family dominated the Aventine Hill and the Theatre of Marcellus, and was immediately elected Senator for life, an office that he delegated to his brother Pandolfo. He followed the preference of Nicholas III for the Vatican Palace over the Lateran but also had built for his family a new fortified palace on the Aventine, parts of which are still visible.

The new pope did not repudiate Martin IV's policy over Sicily, regarding the Sicilians' political self-determination an affront to papal overlordship, and so supported a crusade against the island planned by the French king Philip III (1270–1285). Philip's death prevented it, and the passing of Peter III in the same year saw an unchallenged Aragonese succession, when the latter's younger son James II (1285–1295) took over the Sicilian monarchy, while the elder son, Alfonso III (1285–1291), inherited Aragón. Both Aragonese kings were promptly excommunicated, but the overuse of papal excommunications too blatantly serving the interests of the House of Anjou was now devaluing their spiritual currency.

Honorius' death was followed by a vacancy of eleven months, from April 1287 to February 1288, when six cardinals died of disease during that summer and others fell ill. The survivors fled Rome but subsequently decided to elect the only one of their number who had stayed in the city, Cardinal Girolamo d'Ascoli, a Franciscan friar who had succeeded St. Bonaventura as general of the order in 1274. He was made cardinal in 1278 and bishop of Palestrina in 1279. In Rome, although named Senator for life, he was less sure-footed than his predecessor, giving too much papal backing to the Colonna, one of the leading aristocratic families of the city, when a more even-handed distribution of favour was required.

He followed the line of his predecessors on Sicily, fomenting an alliance of France and Castile against Aragón in 1288 and crowning Charles of Anjou's son Charles of Salerno (died 1309) as titular king of Sicily (in reality Naples) in 1289. This move proved counterproductive, as the Aragonese and Sicilians took the war into southern Italy and began making conquests there. When James II succeeded his brother as king of Aragón as well as Sicily in 1291, the failure of the papacy's pro-Angevin policy seemed absolute.

These internecine struggles between Christians coincided with the final collapse of the Crusader States in the Near East, marked by the fall of Tripoli in 1289 and of Acre in 1291 to the Mameluke Sultan Baybars of Egypt. New appeals for crusades were hardly heeded. In the circumstances, the twenty-seven-month-long conclave that followed Nicholas IV's death in April 1292 marked a low point in papal prestige, far removed from its high standing at the beginning of the century. Popular hopes and those of the handful of cardinals themselves ultimately came to rest on the possibility that, with the choice they eventually made in July 1294, they had at last found the long-anticipated Angelic Pope of prophetic expectation.

FALSE GUILT-LADEN BABYLON

(1294–1378)

THE ANGELIC POPE

Early in the morning of 7 September 1303, armed men crept into a hill town forty miles east of Rome, intending to capture or kill the pope. Their leaders were a Roman aristocrat, Sciarra Colonna, and Guillaume de Nogaret, chief minister of King Philip IV the Fair of France. The sound of troops moving towards the papal palace woke the residents of Anagni.[1] As the church bells rang, the town's leading citizens gathered in the main square, while others began looting the papal treasury and the houses of cardinals loyal to the pope and raiding their wine cellars. Three cardinals fled through a sewage drain. Two cardinals and several guards remained with the pope, Boniface VIII (1294–1303).

The conspirators demanded that Boniface abdicate, surrender the papal treasury and free two imprisoned cardinals of the Colonna family. By evening Boniface VIII was a prisoner in his chamber. Sciarra, brother of the two imprisoned Colonna cardinals, threatened to kill the pope, but de Nogaret stopped him. His orders were to take Boniface to France for trial by a general council of the Church, charged, inter alia, with murdering Celestine V (1294), his predecessor, the Angelic Pope.

Nine years before, in Perugia, a small and bitterly divided body of cardinals elected as pope the eighty-five-year-old Peter of Morrone,

chapter 13

taking the name Celestine V.[2] The son of a peasant, Peter had been a Benedictine monk in his youth, before becoming a hermit in the Abruzzi, living in a cave in Monte Morrone. His reputation as a holy man and healer drew so many disciples and lay visitors that he withdrew to a more solitary location. But he also organised his disciples into a community that was officially recognised as part of the Benedictine order by Urban IV in 1263 and taken under papal protection by Gregory X in 1274. In 1293 Peter gave up the direction of his community, later to be called the Celestines, to retreat to a tiny cave high up in Monte Morrone.

Not as remote from the world as his career might suggest, Peter had founded and led a new religious order, directing two of its monasteries and presiding over its first general chapter, and from his remote hermitage he followed what was happening in the Church. It was his letter to one of the cardinals warning of God's wrath at their failure to choose a new pope that led to his own election in 1294.

Celestine's career was intimately linked with the teachings of Joachim of Fiore (1135–1202), a Calabrian hermit, mystic, and monastic leader who had prophesied the coming of the Angelic Pope and the Age of the Holy Spirit, when the Eternal Gospel would be revealed and the existing organisation of the Church give way to rule by the Order of the Just, with humanity communicating directly with God in a time of universal love. In 1200 Joachim had submitted his writings for examination by Innocent III but died before approval was given. His message spread, though some of his teaching was condemned by the Fourth Lateran Council in 1215. He was placed in Paradise by Dante, whose own ideas he influenced.

Around 1250 one of his followers, Gerard of Borgo San Donnino, claimed that the Franciscan friars were the Order of the Just of the prophecy.[3] The Franciscans themselves were bitterly divided over their ownership of property, an issue exacerbated by their rising popularity and the goods, lands and churches they were being given. The more austere faction in the order, soon known as the Spirituals, wished to renounce all its property, and so warmly embraced the Joachimite message and subsequently Celestine V. This conflict amongst the Franciscans led Alexander IV to appoint a commission to investigate Joachim's teachings, resulting in his condemnation as a heretic in 1263, but a compromise was reached with the Spirituals in 1279 when Pope Nicholas III put all Franciscan property under papal control, to use on their behalf.

Expectations of a new and more spiritual age were not confined to the followers of Joachim and the Franciscans. In Milan, for example, a small community of lay and religious developed around a mysterious ascetic called Guglielma (died 1281), whom her followers believed was the Holy Spirit in female form. She appointed the nun Maifreda da Pirovano, a relative of the Visconti lords of Milan, as her pope and Lord Vicar. Believers expected that in the year 1300 Maifreda would publicly celebrate Mass at Easter and Pentecost, causing Guglielma to return, ushering in a new Age of the Spirit. The Inquisition, however, arrested Maifreda and others, interrogated and burned them before the second Mass could be said.[4]

Despite the condemnation of Joachim of Fiore and the persecution of the Guglielmites, many Christians, including some of the higher clergy, longed for and expected a new age. The cardinals' eventual choice of Peter of Morrone in July 1294 reflected this atmosphere. Having initially resisted election, he entered the town of L'Aquila on a donkey, to be crowned in a church of his own order. He granted the Spiritual Franciscans the status of an independent association as the Poor Hermits of Pope Celestine, and on 18 September he appointed the significant, symbolic number of twelve new cardinals, perhaps to inaugurate a 'monastic age of the Holy Spirit'.[5] They were not all monks, numbering the archbishops of Lyon and of Bourges, the chancellor of the diocese of Paris, the papal vice-chancellor and the chancellor of the kingdom of Sicily amongst them.

And then, on 13 December 1294, for reasons that were not explained, Celestine abdicated, the first pope to do so since Benedict IX in 1045. Cardinal Benedetto Caetani, who was suspected of influencing his decision, was unanimously elected to succeed him as Boniface VIII on 24 December. Celestine wanted to return to his hermitage on Monte Morrone, but Boniface feared he might become a tool of the new pope's numerous enemies. While accompanying Boniface to Rome for his coronation in January 1295, however, Celestine escaped and was hunted across southern Italy, before being captured in June trying to reach the Eastern empire. Boniface confined him to a castle near Anagni, and there he died on 19 May 1296.

WOLF, LION OR DOG: BONIFACE VIII

The new pope had a very exalted view of his office. He elaborated the papal liturgy, and elongated the papal tiara, adding a second crown to it, and an enormous ruby, which was lost during the coronation of one of his successors. Statues of him wearing this expanded tiara were set up in Rome, Orvieto and Anagni, enabling his enemies to claim that he had erected images of himself for the people to worship.[6]

Boniface was also keen to advance the interests of his family, the Caetani, promoting some to high clerical office, and expanding the estates of others. His nephew Peter, who became marquis of Ancona in 1296, was given control of the Torre delle Milizie in Rome, and turned the huge tomb of Caecilia Metella on the Appian Way into a fortified palace. Peter's sons were helped by gifts of land and marriages to wealthy heiresses. Other popes earlier in the century had been criticised for favouring their families, but Boniface was the first to pack the College of Cardinals with his own relatives, four out of the fifteen cardinals appointed during his pontificate.

While learned and forceful, Boniface was also imperious and arrogant at a time when other qualities were called for. The papacy could no longer rely upon the effect of purely spiritual weapons such as excommunication and lacked a powerful lay protector. In fact, the most likely candidate for such a role, the king of France, became the pope's most determined opponent.

The clergy had been freed from lay jurisdiction in both England and France in the early twelfth century. Clerics were also exempt from being taxed by their secular rulers by decree of the Fourth Lateran Council of 1215, but they could be obliged to pay a tenth of their revenues to the papacy in support of crusades.[7] The purposes served by crusades had expanded since 1095, and they were called more frequently in the thirteenth century. Papal 'crusading tenths' became increasingly common and were often extended for more than a single year. Their proceeds were frequently split, with the Curia keeping some, but the bulk being granted to the lay ruler of the kingdom, to assist him in fulfilling his crusading vows.

None of this was popular with the clergy being taxed, and although legates were sent from the Curia to oversee the collection, the process became increasingly protracted, with much passive resistance. Thus, the tax on the French clergy imposed in 1266 by Clement IV to help cover the costs of Charles of Anjou's expedition against Manfred of Sicily, which had been declared a crusade, was only finally collected in 1274. Ambitious lay rulers also began regarding clerical taxation as a source of revenue that should be theirs of right, because of their role as defenders of the Church. In 1294, in the absence of the new archbishop of Canterbury in Italy, Edward I of England called a convocation of his leading clergy to demand that they pay him half of their annual revenues. He rejected an offer of twenty percent, and threatened those who refused with the removal of his protection, leaving them and their property undefended by the law. He proposed to do the same again in 1296. Across the Channel, Philip IV of France was taking similar measures, ignoring the need for prior papal authorisation and arguing that his realm was in danger of invasion by the English.

In February 1296 Boniface VIII issued the bull known from its opening words as *Clericos laicos,* intended to stop such royal raids on clerical incomes. Stating that 'history teaches us that the laity are generally hostile to the clergy,' this forbade the clergy from paying tax on clerical property without prior papal consent, and ordered members of the laity not to collect it on pain of excommunication that would not be lifted until their dying day. In both England and France royal reaction was vigorous.

King Edward indicated to the leading clergy of his kingdom that there would be severe consequences if they obeyed the papal command. When in January 1297 they decided that they 'feared the Eternal more than him who was king for the time, and the peril of their souls more than the hazards of worldly affairs', he outlawed the clergy, removing all legal protection for their lives and property. As this was followed by the seizure of Church estates and clerical revenues, total submission to the royal will quickly followed.

In France in August 1296 Philip IV forbade the export of bullion, jewels and any other form of negotiable currency from his kingdom, preventing payments from the Church in France being sent to the pope. As all such regular revenues were normally pledged long in advance by the papacy to Italian bankers in return for immediate funds, this threatened to undermine the system of credit upon which papal finances rested, at a time when Boniface was paying for a long and ultimately unsuccessful war to remove the Aragonese king from Sicily.

As a threat of excommunication of the French king issued in September 1296 lacked effect and financial disaster loomed, the pope backed down in February 1297, indicating that *Clericos laicos* was only a statement of general principle and that in periods of immediate danger a monarch might tax his clergy without prior papal approval. He did not indicate who decided when such a situation had arisen, but King Philip wanted the decision to be his alone and sent his chief minister to get the pope to agree. Meanwhile Boniface speeded up the diplomatically useful canonisation of the king's grandfather, Louis IX.[8]

In Italy Boniface's attempts to expand his family's estates led to a conflict with his former allies, the Colonna, who also resented the pope's growing favour to their Roman rivals, the Orsini, two of whom had recently been made cardinals. The two Colonna cardinals, who had voted for him in 1294, began expressing doubts about the legality of Boniface's replacement of Celestine V, and in May 1297 a group of Colonna retainers seized a papal wagon train transporting treasure. In negotiating for its return, Boniface demanded the Colonna cardinals recognise his authority, hand over their brother who had led the raid and to surrender three key fortresses. Instead they fled and issued the first of the Colonna Manifestoes, stating that Boniface was a usurper and simoniac, since it was not legal for a pope to abdicate. They had already taken the opinion of leading canon lawyers in the University of Paris, the pre-eminent centre of learning in Western Europe at the time, and now demanded that Boniface be suspended until a council of the Church could decide the issue.

One of the Colonna cardinals had ties to the Spiritual Franciscans, who now came out in their support. The Spirituals had been shocked by the fate of Celestine V and by Boniface VIII's cancellation of all of his predecessor's decrees, including revoking their independent status. The Franciscan mystic and poet Jacopone da Todi joined the Colonna in revolt in their town of Palestrina and drew up charges against Boniface, who was now alleged to have murdered Celestine.[9] A skull with a nail hole in it was produced as proof, while Boniface promised crusader privileges and indulgences to those who took up arms against the Colonna.

Envoys from the rebels had already encountered Philip IV's first minister on his way to see Boniface and had offered to make common cause with him, leading the pope to decide he should compromise. Late in 1297 he exempted France from the terms of Clericos laicos and conceded that clerical taxation might be imposed by the king whenever he decided the necessity existed. With Philip pacified, Boniface could deal with the Colonna, storming Palestrina in 1298 and completely destroying the town except for its cathedral.

The high point of Boniface's pontificate came in 1300, which was the focus of many messianic and apocalyptic expectations, and which he declared, using an Old Testament term, to be a Jubilee Year, the first of what would become a succession of Holy Years, in which pilgrims coming to receive the sacraments in the patriarchal basilicas of Rome would thereby receive a new plenary indulgence. So many pilgrims made the journey and so substantial were their donations that a contemporary recorded that two clerics stood by the high altar in San Paolo fuori le mura day and night raking the huge offerings of coins into piles.[10] This influx of offerings recharged papal finances, greatly reduced by the conflicts of 1296 and 1297, and made Boniface less conciliatory when conflict with the king of France was renewed the next year.

In 1301 Bernard Saisset, the bishop of Pamiers, a new diocese south of Toulouse, created in 1295, was charged with treason and

heresy and tried before the king, in defiance of canon law. His real offence may have amounted to little more than incautious criticism of
the royal government, but the political situation in southwest France
was sensitive, and King Philip determined to make a public example
of an apparent dissident.[11] The bishop was briefly imprisoned, and
Philip wrote to Boniface for his approval, noting that the bishop had
described the pope as the devil incarnate.

Boniface responded by demanding his release, revoked the concessions made in 1297 and threatened excommunication. He issued a
bull, approved by the College of Cardinals, condemning the king for
offences against the Church and against his own subjects. But this
failed to win the sympathy of the French clergy because the royal
court suppressed the real text of the decree and instead circulated a
totally fictitious one, making the outrageous claims that the papacy
had complete authority over the kingdom in all temporal as well as
spiritual affairs, thus treating France as a papal fief like Sicily. This
offended the national pride that had been gradually developing
throughout the thirteenth century, which hailed the robust retort the
king was said to have sent to the pope, calling him 'Your Stupidity'.[12]

Boniface VIII then summoned the French episcopate to a council
to meet in Rome in November 1302, but the king prohibited them
from leaving the kingdom and ordered them instead to attend a
meeting of prelates, barons and other faithful subjects in April, which
was later seen as the first meeting of the Estates General, the nearest
France came to a representative forum before 1789.[13] There the
French nobles refused to recognise Boniface as legitimate pope, while
the bishops asked him to abandon his supposed claim to temporal
authority over the kingdom. Boniface and his cardinals denied that
this had ever been made, recognising it came from a forgery, but they
also restated the position that a pope could intervene in the temporal
affairs of a kingdom to suppress or prevent sinfulness. The other request of the French bishops, that the council being called to Rome in
November be cancelled, was refused, but only half of them braved
royal displeasure to attend it, and it achieved little.

Boniface, infuriated by the failure of his council, issued a new bull,
Unam sanctam, on 18 November 1302, concerning papal primacy

over secular rulers, stating that as there had been one Ark, so there was one Church, and of this there was one head: Christ, represented on earth by his vicar, the successor of Peter. He added that 'if the earthly power err, it shall be judged by the spiritual power . . . but if the supreme power err it can only be judged by God, not by man.'[14]

In France plans were laid to call a general council of the Church to try Boniface on a series of charges, including heresy, which derived from the claim that he had said that he would rather be a dog than a Frenchman. As dogs were held to have no souls, his remark was taken to imply that neither did the French. More serious were accusations relating to the abdication and death of Celestine V, and also claims of sexual misconduct. Just as the Colonna manifestoes of 1297 had precipitated a rash of treatises on the subject of papal abdication, so now canon lawyers and theologians began writing substantial works on the relationship between the royal and papal authority. Especially notable were *On Christian Government* by James of Viterbo, *On Ecclesiastical Power* by Giles of Rome and *On Royal and Papal Power* by John of Paris, which all appeared in 1302/3, the two former supporting the papal position and the latter the royal one.

Boniface VIII prepared to issue another bull on 8 September 1303, declaring all foreign alliances of the French king null and void and releasing his subjects from their allegiance, effectively encouraging them to revolt and hostile neighbours like Edward I of England to invade France. It was no coincidence that on the day before this bull was to be promulgated, the conspirators entered Anagni and seized Boniface.

Had they removed him from the town at once, their plan might have worked, but on the 9th, while they were still arguing over what to do, the citizens of Anagni freed the pope and expelled his captors, as they feared the town would be placed under interdict, with its priests forbidden to administer the sacraments and that 'all Christendom will rise against us.'[15] The liberated pope publicly forgave the commune, including those who had stolen his personal property, and was given an armed escort back to Rome, but his health was undermined by what came to be known as the Outrage at Anagni, and he died a month later. As an English chronicler put it, 'As a wolf he entered, as a lion he ruled, as a dog he finished.'[16]

THE MOVE TO AVIGNON

The crucial question for his successor was how to handle the aftermath of the Outrage. The cardinals unanimously elected the Dominican Benedict XI (1303–1304), who had stood by Boniface since 1298 and was supported by Charles II of Naples. He tried to follow a delicate policy of compromise, releasing the two Colonna cardinals from excommunication but not restoring them to the College and absolving Philip IV of France from any blame for the Anagni affair. He was, however, determined to punish those personally involved in the assault, setting a date for them to appear before him for trial or face excommunication, but he died of dysentery, though poison was suspected, at Perugia before the time expired.

After Benedict XI no cardinal could command sufficient support in the College to be elected, as they were now divided over relations with France and the rehabilitation of the Colonna. Eleven months of wrangling led to the election in June 1305 of an outsider, Bertrand de Got, archbishop of Bordeaux. His recently deceased brother had been one of Boniface VIII's cardinals, and although on good terms with Philip IV, he was born in Gascony and thus a subject of Edward I of England, duke of Aquitaine.

With Clement V (1305–1314), as he became, begins the period of the Avignon papacy that lasts till 1378, but it was not his initial intention to reside permanently outside Italy.[17] He was in his archdiocese when elected and was crowned at Lyon, though not in the cathedral but in a church in the French-ruled section of the city west of the Rhône. Conditions in Italy remained tumultuous, so Clement settled in the Comtat-Venaissin, one of eight provinces ceded to the papacy by Raymond VII of Toulouse in 1229 but not fully brought under papal overlordship till 1274. Several of its towns, notably Avignon, were owned under the popes' suzerainty by the Angevin kings of Naples, who were also counts of Provence.

Clement V fell ill soon after his election, probably with the stomach cancer that would eventually kill him, and was frequently incapacitated by it throughout his pontificate. Although declaring he intended to go to Italy, he continued moving his court around the Comtat-Venaissin, spending a few months in Avignon in 1309, 1311 and the winter of 1312/3. His main concern was to hold a general council, called to meet at Vienne in October 1310, but then postponed for a year. At the same time a posthumous judicial process on Boniface VIII was being prepared at the insistence of Philip IV. The king claimed that his title and descent—he was *Rex Christianissimus,* the Most Christian King, and grandson of St. Louis—gave him a divine obligation to act against a pope who had fallen into heresy, while papal officials worked to stall the hearings until a negotiated settlement could be reached, avoiding any judicial condemnation of a former pope. This was finally achieved in 1311, with all previous papal concessions to France being reinstated, and a token penance imposed on Guillaume de Nogaret in return for the lifting of his excommunication. The trial of Boniface was then suspended *sine die*.

Canon lawyers from the mid-twelfth century onwards had been debating and adding glosses to collections of papal decretals, thus creating a large body of literature interpreting them. One of the topics that had interested them was that of papal superiority to all earthly jurisdiction, and they developed the argument that a pope could indeed be deposed, but only for heresy.[18] However, because he was not subject to any court, no enquiry could be made into a pope's beliefs. Only if he declared publicly that he believed doctrines that had already been condemned by his predecessors could he be regarded as a heretic. Even then, as nobody could sit in judgement on him, it had to be further argued that by admitting himself to be a heretic he automatically ceased to be pope. No allowance could be made for a lay power claiming the right to bring a pope to trial who had not openly confessed to being a heretic and thus abdicating.

The French king had two additional objectives: the canonisation of Celestine V and papal agreement to the trial of the knights of the Order of the Temple. Both of these appear cynical moves, in the first case to further discredit Boniface and in the second to enrich the royal treasury by taking over the property of an extremely wealthy military order whose crusading function was now minimal. But other influential interests, including the Spiritual Franciscans, and the order which Celestine himself had founded, as well as several members of the College of Cardinals also pressed for Celestine's canonisation.[19] Popular opinion was favourable, and, although Clement protracted the process, he conceded it in 1313 on the recommendation of a commission set up during the Council of Vienne. However, the new saint was proclaimed as St. Peter of Morrone, and not as St. Celestine V, ignoring his papal status.[20]

The case of the Templars has been well documented.[21] On 13 October 1307 about 15,000 individuals associated with the order were arrested in a surprisingly efficient sweep throughout France. Contemporary observers assumed prior papal approval, as the Templars were an exempt Order, that is, not answerable to any lay or ecclesiastical superior other than the pope. This was an impression Philip IV was keen to promote, but Clement only heard of the arrests two weeks later, and wrote complaining that in laying hands on persons and property under papal protection the king's 'hasty act is seen by all, and rightly so, as an act of contempt towards ourselves and the Roman Church'.[22]

The issue was resolved by the confessions of the Grand Master and 133 other Templar knights to several of the charges laid against them, including denying Christ and spitting on crucifixes. However obtained, and officially it was said that no violence had been used, these confessions enabled Clement to write to other kings, several of whom had been outraged by Philip IV's action, instructing them secretly to arrest the Templars in their kingdoms and secure their property. This turned the process into a European-wide one led by the papacy, instead of one driven by the king of France.[23]

In 1305 Clement V began the process of transforming the College of Cardinals from a body that was predominantly Italian into one that was largely French, appointing ten new members, nine of whom were French. By 1314, when he died, there were twenty-four French cardinals and only six Italians. Even more remarkably, eight of them were the pope's relatives. Others were fellow Gascons. They continued to use the titles of the Roman priestly and diaconal churches but had no real connection with them. There was disapproval that most of the new cardinals were canon lawyers by training, and Dante lamented the replacement of spiritual values by legal ones, commenting dryly, 'And so the Gospels and Great Doctors lie neglected, and the Decretals alone are studied, as their margins testify,' in reference to the lawyers' practice of writing interpretative glosses in the margins of legal texts.[24]

While contemporaries thought that Philip IV of France had a hand in selecting the new cardinals, Clement was creating a body of advisors and assistants with whom he felt comfortable. The papacy was becoming more the personal possession of the holder of the office, imitating a dynastic monarchy but without hereditary succession. Clement distributed other ecclesiastical offices and rewards to his family, friends and fellow countrymen at will, though when he died his Gascon servants absconded with the baggage, leaving his body unburied.[25]

He bequeathed the greater part of the papal treasure to his own relatives and to the kings of England and France. Of just over a million florins that had been accumulated by the end of his pontificate by the papal financial department, known as the Camera—because it had originally been based in the pope's private chamber *(camera)*—320,000 went to the two monarchs, and a further 300,000 was given to the pope's nephew, the viscount of Lomagne, supposedly to support crusading activity, but 200,000 florins were distributed as gifts to other family members. Only 70,000 florins were left as a specific bequest to the next pope.[26] No objection was raised to treating of the treasury as a personal possession by the incumbent pope, as the canon lawyers had established that it was impossible for a pope to commit simony, since the Church's money was his to dispose of.

After Clement's death at Carpentras, the cardinals divided into Gascon, Provençal and Italian factions, with none securing the necessary majority. When Gascons led by the former pope's nephew attacked the conclave, the cardinals took refuge in Avignon under the protection of King Robert the Wise of Naples (1309–1343), son of Charles II. It took another two years for them to elect a former bishop of Avignon as John XXII (1316–1334). Already in his early seventies, he had been chancellor of both Charles II and Robert of Naples, and his election resulted from French royal pressure on the cardinals meeting in Lyon. He was as great a nepotist as his predecessor, but his favours went to those from his home region of Quercy. Of twenty-eight cardinals he appointed, six were relatives, two were Italians, one a Spaniard and the rest French. No new English cardinal would be chosen until 1368, and none from the empire until 1378.

THE AVIGNON POPES

The new pope expected to return the Curia to Rome once the situation in Italy had stabilised. In the papal state the absence of the Curia and the incompetent government of Gascon administrators appointed by Clement V allowed more and more of its towns to fall under the control of local potentates or popular communes. Elsewhere war was endemic between two rival alliances, prolonging the Guelph-Ghibelline or pro- and anti-papal conflicts of the preceding centuries, but by now the issue had much less to do with rival ideologies and was more centred on local power struggles.[27] Thus opposing factions could associate themselves with the Guelph or Ghibelline names according to which best served their immediate purposes. The Guelph alliance, which enjoyed papal approval and had existed since 1266, included the Angevin kings of Naples and the dominant faction in the city of Florence. Ranged in opposition to them were the Visconti lords of Milan, the cities of Pisa and Lucca and the Aragonese kings of Sicily. The emperors had taken little interest in Italian affairs in recent decades but generally favoured the Ghibellines.

The emperor Henry VII died suddenly in 1313, soon after he had been excommunicated by Clement V for attempting to depose Robert of Naples, and anti-papalists suggested he had been poisoned by his confessor on the pope's orders. Clement V, however, used Henry's death as the opportunity to proclaim that during such imperial vacancies the empire would be directly subject to the pope and that the oath taken by an emperor at his coronation was in itself recognition of papal suzerainty.[28] His own death soon after and the subsequent papal two-year *sede vacante* meant this claim was not tested in practice, but it remained a bone of contention for the future. In the imperial election of 1314 conflict broke out between the two rival claimants, Ludwig of Bavaria and Frederick of Austria. John XXII supported the Austrian duke, only for him to be decisively defeated and captured by the Bavarian at Mühldorf in 1322. John then demanded, in the light of Clement V's decree, that Ludwig must accept the status of papal vassal to be confirmed as emperor, causing him to support the anti-papal conflicts in Italy and patronise scholars who wrote in defence of imperial authority against that of the pope.

Amongst the best of these was the physician Marsilius of Padua (died before 1343), who ridiculed papal claims in his monumental *Defensor Pacis* (Defender of the Peace) of 1324, wherein he denied that St. Peter ever held any authority superior to that of the other Apostles or over the Church, and claimed that the emperor had the power to appoint, depose or otherwise punish the pope. John XXII condemned Marsilius in 1327 and was unrelenting in attempts to hunt him down, while in 1343 Clement VI described his work as the worst example of heresy he had ever encountered.[29]

John XXII created other enemies in his pontificate through his treatment of the Spiritual Franciscans. The conflict over the proper lifestyle for the Franciscan Order had grown increasingly bitter ever since the failure of Celestine V's attempt to form the Spirituals into a separate body. In 1312 Clement V, who was broadly sympathetic, issued a decree refusing to countenance a split in the order but accepting several of the Spirituals' interpretations of how the 'life of poverty' should be led.[30] The more authoritarian John XXII fell out with some of them early in his pontificate over the storing of food in Franciscan houses. Four friars refused to accept his ruling that retaining of supplies for future use, in defiance of the Gospel injunction to 'take no care for the morrow' (Matthew 6.34) was legitimate and proclaimed the pope 'a heretic and destroyer of the evangelical life',[31] but it was they who were burned as heretics, at Marseille in 1318. A wider rift followed a heresy trial in Narbonne in 1321 in which the accused stated that Christ and the Apostles had not owned property. When a Franciscan intervened to say that was a perfectly orthodox belief, and this was confirmed by a council of the Spirituals in Perugia the next year, the question was referred to the pope. Although he tried to be accommodating, he eventually condemned their view as heretical, and revoked the agreement of 1279 by which the property of the order had been taken over in trust by the papacy.[32]

When some of the Spirituals then denounced him as a heretic, he set the Inquisition on them and eventually ordered their complete suppression in 1326. A few were burned, others submitted, but several of their leaders took refuge with the emperor and gave their services in his propaganda war against the pope. The most distinguished of these was the theologian and philosopher William of Ockham (c. 1285–c. 1347), who wrote *A Short Discourse on Tyrannical Government over Things Divine and Human but especially over the Empire and those subject to the Empire, usurped by some who are called Highest Pontiffs* on the proper relationship between spiritual and secular authority. His shorter works included *A Dialogue on the Rights of the Roman Empire* and *Eight Questions on the Power of the Pope,* and in his arguments he quoted St. Bernard's comment to Eugenius III that in the abundance of wealth the papacy had accumulated it was the successor not to Peter but to Constantine.[33] Although both Ockham and Marsilius of Padua lost influence once the emperor began seeking a negotiated settlement with the papacy after the death of John XXII, their writings survived to take on greater importance in the early fifteenth century.

The emperor, excommunicated by the pope in 1324, still needed an imperial coronation and in 1328 went to Rome, where he proclaimed John XXII to be a heretic and thus self-deposed, and oversaw the election of a Franciscan, who took the name of Nicholas V (1328–1330). He was recognised by William of Ockham and other opponents of John XXII, but the emperor took the unprecedented step of having his own coronation carried out by representatives of the Roman commune, headed by none other than Sciarra Colonna, who had led the attack on Boniface VIII in 1303. This secular ceremony put into practice the theories of the anti-papalists, who denied that the pope had a necessary part in either choosing or crowning an emperor. Ignored even by his own emperor, Nicholas V submitted to

John XXII when Ludwig IV withdrew from Italy in 1330 and lived his last three years as a pensioner of the legitimate pope.

In the winter of 1331/2 John preached four sermons in which he expressed a view of the Beatific Vision, or the soul's view of the Godhead after death, entirely at odds with orthodox belief. When consulted, theologians at the University of Paris and elsewhere rejected his interpretation, giving fresh ammunition to his many enemies, who again denounced him as a heretic and called for a general council to judge him. He is reported to have changed his mind on his deathbed, but the ideas he had advanced were categorically condemned by his successor in 1336.[34]

It was probably the fear of a council being called to sit in judgement on John XXII's teaching that led the cardinals at Avignon to agree immediately upon the election of Benedict XII (1334–1342). He is one of the few medieval popes familiar to modern readers, because as Jacques Fournier he is the anti-hero of Emmanuel Le Roy Ladurie's *Montaillou*, which uses the Inquisition records of 1318–1325 to reveal detailed aspects of village life in southwestern France in this period. As bishop of Pamiers, Fournier, a Paris-trained theologian and former Cistercian abbot, oversaw the investigation of suspected Cathar heretics in his diocese. He took the three registers of depositions with him when made cardinal in Avignon in 1327, one of which survived.

As an experienced inquisitor, he avoided the theological thickets that had mired his predecessor. Contemporary accounts of him agree in describing him as 'hard' and as 'a fervid opponent and stern persecutor of heretics'.[35] His pontificate was, however, more devoted to diplomatic efforts to secure peace than hunting for heresy. He attempted unsuccessfully to mediate in the conflict that broke out between the kings of England and France in 1337 that became the Hundred Years War. Despite the supposedly French leanings of the papacy, Benedict himself was even-handed. When in 1340 English envoys to his court were kidnapped and given to the French by the marshal of his court, he used ecclesiastical sanctions to secure their release and hanged the marshal outside their lodging.[36] He also tried to act as honest broker in conflicts between England and Scotland,

Castile and Navarre, the rival kings of Sicily, and the Orsini and Colonna in Rome.

Like his predecessors, Benedict expected to return the papacy to Italy if not Rome and planned to move his court to Bologna. When that city remained hostile, he began turning Avignon into a long-term papal residence. John XXII had lived in its episcopal palace, having assumed the office of bishop of the town, but Benedict began work on a new palace on the site, compensating the bishop with another. His was an austere building with cloister and chapel, modelled on a monastery, but with the papal chambers in a massive tower.[37] The costs were high, at a time when receipts from Italy and elsewhere were declining thanks to war in the peninsula. Benedict also paid for the complete restoration of the roof of St. Peter's in Rome and work on the Lateran, as well as distributing 100,000 florins to the College of Cardinals, whose own finances were decaying.[38]

He rejected the nepotism of his predecessors, refusing to advance his own relatives either in the Church or lay society and revoking gifts and appointments made by previous popes. Legates were sent out to deal with abuses such as the 'infinite number' of Spanish priests living with concubines.[39] Benedict also imposed more austere lifestyles on the Benedictine monks and on his own Cistercian Order, arousing hostility, not least from one anonymous commentator who claimed that the pope was mean, hated the friars, regarded all the cardinals as liars and drank more than any of them, giving rise to the toast *Bibamus papaliter*—'Let's drink like a pope!'[40] Others reported miracles at his tomb and the great sadness of both Curia and Church at his passing.[41]

The cardinals voted for a very different successor. Chroniclers hailed the advent of Clement VI (1342–1352) and joked that his name lived up to his nature. Others were equally pleased. Philip VI of France had sent his son to persuade the conclave to choose his former chancellor and archbishop of Rouen, Pierre Roger, only to find him already elected. The new pope reversed his predecessor's monastic reform and his moratorium on granting benefices, with the result that Avignon was soon swarming with petitioners, as many as 100,000 in the first year, according to one source. Proclaiming that no one should leave his presence discontented, he needed to acquire more to give to make this a reality and in 1344 proclaimed the reservation of all churches, benefices, ecclesiastical offices and dignities to the Holy See, effectively dispossessing all other patrons of their rights but providing himself with a vast store of patronage.

In 1343 he was persuaded by the Romans to proclaim 1350 as another Jubilee, rather than restricting such events to once a century as Boniface VIII had intended. They anticipated that Rome would benefit economically from the influx of pilgrims and hoped it might also lure the pope back to the long-neglected and decaying city. Clement, however, had no intention of moving, much to the annoyance of Italians in the Curia. Amongst them was the poet Petrarch (1304–1374), then a clerk in papal service, whose views on Avignon as the 'fountain of anguish, the dwelling place of wrath, the school of errors, the temple of heresy, once Rome, now the false guilt-laden Babylon, the forge of lies, the horrible prison, the hell upon earth', became increasingly jaundiced as a result.[42] Others who shared his feeling that the papacy must return to Rome included the Swedish noblewoman, visionary and monastic founder Birgitta Birgersdotter (1303–1373), three times canonised as St. Bridget of Sweden (in 1391, 1415 and 1419 by different parties in the Great Schism). In the 1340s she began warning Clement about his failure to move to Rome, where she arrived herself in 1349, to await the pope's coming.

Clement, meanwhile, was transforming Benedict XII's austere monastic palace into something grander and more luxurious, which became the setting for a lavish succession of court festivals, balls and tournaments. In 1348 he bought Avignon from Queen Joanna of Naples, the granddaughter and successor of Robert the Wise. The costs, together with other building projects, put an enormous strain on papal finances, the effects of which would be strongly felt during the pontificates of his successors. This was at a time when the Anglo-French war was reducing contributions from the Church in France, already protesting at papal financial demands, and when revolt and disorder in the Papal States were cutting revenues from Italy.

The 1350 Holy Year took place in the aftermath of the Black Death, which had swept across Europe, devastating Avignon in 1348. A letter from a friend of Petrarch's claimed half the city's population had died. Clement reacted with the generosity for which he was famed, paying for doctors and gravediggers for the citizens, and purchasing a field to serve as a communal cemetery, in which over 11,000 people were buried between 14 March and 27 April. Some blamed the Jews for poisoning water supplies, and the pope intervened to protect them from lynching. In the aftermath, it was widely felt the plague had been divine punishment, and popular religious movements of an extreme penitential kind, involving self-flagellation, began spreading. So threatening did these become that Clement ordered their suppression in 1349.

Politically Clement VI's pontificate had mixed results. The Anglo-French war continued, but the death of Ludwig IV in 1347 was followed by the election of a new emperor, Charles IV of Bohemia, who established much better relations with the popes, as he was far less interested in Italian affairs than his predecessors. In Italy the old quarrel over the kingdom of Sicily subsided, but more serious threats to papal possessions emerged with the rise of ambitious urban tyrants like the Visconti in Milan and of local potentates and communes in the towns of the Papal States. In Rome in 1347 there was a populist rising against the noble factions that had long dominated the city, in which many of them were killed, and a former notary, Cola di Rienzo, was installed as virtual dictator under the extraordinary title of 'the one Baptised by the Holy Spirit, the knight, the severe and clement liberator of the City, the zealous lover of Italy and the world, and the august Tribune'.[43] There is a hint of the promised 'New Age of the Spirit' in his titles, and his excommunication by the pope did not weaken him, but in 1350 he was ejected and sent to Avignon for trial.

Clement's generosity extended particularly to his own family and friends. Eight of the twenty-five cardinals he appointed were his relatives, the last being a nephew aged only twenty, whom one sycophantic chronicler was sure 'will be the glory of his father'.[44] Petrarch claimed to be an eyewitness to papal dalliances, and some chroniclers thought the pope's death in 1352 the result of a dissolute lifestyle, though it was more likely caused by a tumour.[45]

The conclave that followed was the first in which the College of Cardinals tried to restrain the actions of whomsoever they elected by drawing up a prior capitulation or list of agreements to which they then all swore. When elected, Innocent VI (1352–1362) was the first of many popes to repudiate such a contract, on the grounds that it infringed the papal 'plenitude of power'. Like his predecessor he had been a French royal official, before becoming a bishop in 1348, and was also a fervid nepotist, though on a smaller scale. He imposed new rules, requiring cardinals to be resident with the pope and limiting the additional benefices they could accumulate.

Innocent's most important goal was to re-establish his authority in the Papal States, preparatory to returning the papacy to Rome, through appointing Cardinal Gil de Albornoz (died 1367) as his vicar and legate in 1353. Archbishop of Toledo since 1338, Albornoz had fallen out with King Pedro I the Cruel of Castile (1350–1369) and moved to Avignon in 1350. He proved himself to be a soldier of genius, restoring order in the Papal States and resisting the expansionary ambitions of the Visconti lords of Milan, who had gained control of the papal city of Bologna. The local rulers of Rimini, Fermo and Forlì were also forced back into papal obedience. His Aegidian Constitutions of 1357 (*Aegidius* being the Latin for Giles) drew together several existing local constitutions to create a blueprint for the government of the Papal States that continued in use for nearly five centuries.

Innocent nearly lost these gains in 1357 by taking a bribe from the Visconti to replace Albornoz by the less competent abbot of Cluny but reversed the decision the next year. In a second phase of campaigns Albornoz re-imposed papal authority over Bologna in 1360 and defeated the Visconti, before being finally replaced in 1365.[46] The pope's attempt to do something about the city of Rome by sending Cola di Rienzo back as Senator in 1354 was less effective, as he was killed within weeks in a riot. Charles IV was crowned in Rome in 1355 by the cardinal bishop of Ostia by papal mandate.

Ill, elderly and increasingly indecisive, Innocent marked time in his last years, though he helped facilitate the Treaty of Brétigny of 1360, which created a short lull in the Anglo-French war. The treaty had unintended consequences, though, as large companies of mercenaries no longer employed by the kings began roaming southern

France, looting and extorting protection money. Avignon itself had to be defended with walls in 1360 after marauding companies besieged the town until bought off. Under a new pope the palace itself was fortified.

THE RETURN TO ROME

Urban V (1362-1370) has been called 'a man of meticulous routine, a scholar, and perhaps the most spiritual of the Avignon popes', who liked 'in the evenings to stroll along the covered walks of the papal palace and the gardens which he had enlarged'.[47] He was abbot of the Cluniac monastery of Saint-Victor in Marseille when elected by a conclave in which rival French factions of cardinals had neutralised each other. As an outsider, he was more sympathetic than they to the rising demand across Western Europe that the papacy return to Rome. A further motive was created by the offer of the Eastern emperor John V Palaeologus to discuss reuniting the Greek and Latin churches on papal terms and to plan a new crusade, for since the Ottoman Turks established a foothold in Europe in 1356, the threat to Constantinople was mounting. For Urban V such a meeting could only properly be held in Rome.

A crucial preliminary was securing peace in northern Italy by buying off the Visconti and recovering papal rule over Bologna in 1364 through costly treaties. In Rome the Lateran had been severely damaged by a fire in 1360, and so the Vatican Palace had to be renovated to serve as papal residence when the move to the city was finally agreed in 1365. Two more years passed before the papal party left Avignon on 30 April 1367, entering Rome on 16 October. Here the pope received the Western emperor Charles IV in 1368 and the Eastern emperor John V in 1369.

The results proved ephemeral. Although John V declared an end to the long schism, submitting to all papal demands, his bishops refused to follow suit. The planned crusade never materialised, and political conditions in Rome deteriorated even as papal resources were being exhausted trying to repair its decayed churches and palaces. Like many of his predecessors, Urban V found himself ejected from the city and forced to take refuge in Viterbo. Perugia rebelled and the Visconti broke the truce, while back in France the Hundred Years War had resumed in 1369. To the unconcealed delight of the French cardinals, Urban V ordered a return of his court to Avignon. Bridget prophesied that this would lead to his early death, as it did just two months after he re-entered Avignon in September 1370.

A brother of Clement VI had declined election in 1362, and in 1370 it was a nephew of the former pope who was elected as Gregory XI (1370–1378). Made a cardinal at the age of nineteen, he was now only forty but in poor health. He had never held a bishopric but was a notable scholar and has been described as the first humanist pope.[48] Less of a nepotist than his uncle, he only appointed three more of the family as cardinals. He was also as determined as his predecessor on the need to return the papacy to Rome, to which he continued to be urged by Petrarch and by St. Bridget in a stream of visionary messages until just before her death in 1373. To her voice was added that of another visionary, the Dominican nun Catherine of Siena (1347–1380; canonised 1461), who wrote urging the pope to come to Rome 'with the Cross in your hand like a meek lamb', to reform the Church and preach a crusade.[49] Gregory shared this view that the crusade should be his priority, but in the meantime lack of aid from the West led John V into making a truce with the Ottoman sultan in 1373.

Gregory XI had announced to the cardinals in 1372 his intention of returning to Rome but was persuaded to delay the move. The Curia was strongly opposed, and the king of France urged him to remain. Money was even shorter than before, after the failure of the attempt to return under Urban V. Meanwhile the military and diplomatic problems of Italy again needed solving, to prepare the way for the papal journey. The revolt in Perugia was crushed in 1371, but war with the Visconti continued from 1371 to 1375. When this ended, a large contingent of mercenaries under their notorious English commander Sir John Hawkswood began intimidating the main towns of Tuscany into paying not to be attacked.

This so annoyed the Florentines that they determined that the cost of this protection money should be covered by the local bishops and clergy, on the grounds that it was the papacy's fault. Their taxing of the Church provoked a papal interdict on the city, to which Florence responded by encouraging a widespread revolt across the Papal States, even including Rome for a while. This conflict was known as the War of the Eight Saints after the eight-man commission set up in Florence to recoup the city's costs from its clergy. It put an end to the old Guelph alliance, in which Florence had been a mainstay of support for the papacy, and also increased the strain on overstretched papal finances. Catherine of Siena, who failed to persuade Lucca and Pisa not to join the anti-papal league, suggested to Gregory XI that he should just move to Rome, make peace and channel all Christian military efforts instead into a great new crusade.[50]

In these circumstances the pope's decision in 1376 to carry out the return of the Curia to Rome was courageous, not least as he made the journey in the depth of winter, finally entering the city on 13 January 1377. He was more cautious than his predecessor, leaving more of the papal administration and several of the cardinals in Avignon, to follow later if all went well. Conditions in Rome proved uncomfortable and tense, so much so that the French cardinals persuaded Gregory to promise to return to Avignon, but he died of 'an unbearable pain in his bladder' before he could.[51]

The Avignon papacy has a bad reputation, not least because a homesick Italian bureaucrat who became the most famous poet of his age called it a new Babylon. There were certainly periods of hedonism and extravagance, but also some of austerity and reform. The residence in Avignon began by accident, and only two popes of the period did not contemplate a return to Italy if not Rome. Individually the popes were rarely the poodles of the French kings that some, especially the English, believed.[52] On the other hand papal influence could do little to stop the Anglo-French wars, which sometimes extended to the Spanish kingdoms, and appeals for new crusades went largely unanswered, even as the last areas of Christian rule in the East were extinguished and the Turks gained a first foothold in Europe.

Papal leadership of Western Christendom was a memory at best, reflecting a declining regard for the holders of the See of St. Peter and a search for other forms of Christian leadership. Nepotism, pluralism, abuse of the rights of provision and ever-increasing financial demands fuelled a rising tide of criticism most clearly expressed in the writings of dissident academics, such as William of Ockham and the Oxford theologian John Wyclif (c. 1330–1385), who argued for a more Scripturally based Christianity. In 1377 Gregory XI condemned eighteen of Wyclif's arguments, including several highly critical of papal authority, and in 1381 he was formally silenced by an order not to preach or publish such views, but his ideas survived to be taken up in wider and more popular movements of protest in the years that followed.[53]

chapter 14

THREE BISHOPS
ON ONE SEAT

(1378–1449)

THE GREAT SCHISM

The cardinals, of whom only three were now Italians, had hoped to be safely back in Avignon before another conclave was needed, but the death of Gregory XI on 28 March 1378 made them hold one in Rome. Their first thought was to place all their personal goods and the papal treasure in the Castel Sant'Angelo. Amidst cries from the streets that 'By God's nailing we shall have a Roman and no other', the Senator warned the cardinals in the Vatican that they had better elect a local pope or at least an Italian one if they valued their lives.

Left to themselves the cardinals agreed they could not possibly elect either of the two Roman cardinals: It would look as if the election were made under duress. The majority-French contingent was divided between cardinals from Limoges—mostly relatives or compatriots of Gregory XI and his uncle Clement VI, who were determined to elect another Limousin—and cardinals from elsewhere in France who wanted anyone but a Limousin.

And so on 8 April the cardinals chose a Neapolitan, the vice chancellor, Bartolomeo Prignano. Short, squat and sallow, he had been a curial official and titular archbishop of Bari since 1363 and appeared to be a competent, unobtrusive administrator of lowly social origin, whom the cardinals expected to dominate. Soon after Prignano had been crowned as Urban VI (1378–1389), they found that he was a very different man as their master than as their servant. He began insisting on reforming the Curia, ordering the cardinals to eat only a single-course lunch. He also gave vent to a violent temper that had hitherto been well concealed, turning red in the face when he abused the cardinals for their self-indulgent lifestyles, calling them fools and liars. They in turn reacted by openly sneering at him behind a thin façade of deference, and circulated stories about how much he drank. As relations deteriorated and rows became more violent, the French and Spanish cardinals asked the pope's permission to leave for Anagni, to avoid the summer heat in Rome. Urban VI and the three Italian cardinals took up residence in Tivoli, in the hills east of Rome.

Urban alienated many whose support he needed. He denounced bishops working for the Curia in Rome as hirelings who had deserted their flocks, refused to repay a large debt owed by Gregory XI to Count Onorato Caetani of Fondi and threatened that he would depose Queen Joanna of Naples for immorality and put her in a convent. As a result the count offered his troops to the cardinals, who were now trying to persuade Urban to join them in Anagni, to imprison or assassinate him. He refused to come and sent the Italian cardinals to negotiate, but all three defected when each was secretly promised he would be elected pope once Urban had been deposed. Ignoring their previous acceptance of him, in August the now united cardinals proclaimed his election had been unlawful, as it had been conducted under threat of violence.

Moving to Fondi in the kingdom of Naples, on 20 September the cardinals elected as pope their most socially distinguished member, Robert, son of Count Amadeus III of Geneva and related to the French royal family, who took the name Clement VII (1378–1394). Immediately afterwards the cardinals' mercenaries marched on Rome and were only prevented from taking the city by the intervention of Queen Joanna, but a few weeks later she recognised Clement as pope and entertained him in Naples before he departed for Avignon in June 1379. By then Urban VI had gained the upper hand in the Papal States, from Ferrara and Bologna to the frontier with Naples, hiring mercenaries of his own who defeated those of his rival and taking the

Castel Sant'Angelo, which had been in the hands of the cardinals since the conclave. In September 1378 he appointed an entirely new college of twenty-five cardinals, mostly fellow Neapolitans, but including for the first time a Hungarian and a Bohemian, and then excommunicated Clement, proclaiming a crusade against him.

Urban VI's legitimacy was affirmed by Catherine of Sweden, abbess of Vadstena and daughter of St. Bridget, who was in Rome campaigning for her mother's canonisation, and even more vehemently by Catherine of Siena, who had prophesied that reform would provoke schism: 'I maintain that as soon as the pope tries to improve the moral standard of the clerics, they will cause immense dissension within the Church, which will be divided . . . by a heretical pestilence.'[1] Her view of the schismatic cardinals was robust: 'I have heard that these devils in human form have made an election. They have not chosen a vicar of Christ but an anti-Christ', and she wrote to them denouncing them all as liars, fools and simoniacs 'a thousand times worthy of death'.[2]

The Great Schism, which would become the longest and bitterest such dispute in the history of the papacy, was rooted in tension between the claims of the popes to an absolute authority derived from their plenitude of power and those of the cardinals, the 'Senate of the Roman Church', to advise and approve papal decisions.[3] The Avignon popes had been more autocratic than consensual, and with the election of Urban VI the cardinals chose someone they expected to control, but Urban held a magisterial view of the authority of his new office and believed strongly in the need to reform the Church, starting with the Curia.

The conflict extended itself over the whole of Western Europe because of existing political fault lines. King Charles V of France (1364–1380) looked favourably on a papal claimant who was related to him and who returned the papacy to Avignon. England, hostile to France, recognised Urban, while Scotland, long at odds with England, backed Clement. In 1381, John of Gaunt, the dominant figure in the court of the young Richard II of England, launched a claim to the throne of Castile in the name of his wife, so the incumbent king, Henry I of Trastámara, recognised the French pope. Portugal, threatened by

Castile and newly allied to England, promptly switched its support to Urban.

In some states allegiances to one or other of the two 'obediences', as they were called, shifted as political conditions changed, while others remained constant. Countries with strong centralised governments such as England could impose uniformity, depriving partisans of what to them was the antipope of their benefices, imprisoning his agents and refusing admission to his envoys.[4] But much of the empire was split according to the personal choices made by local rulers as to which side to support, although the newly elected emperor Wenzel (Wenceslas) IV of Bohemia (1378–1400; died 1418) and the kings of Poland and Hungary remained loyal to the Roman pope.

None of the forty-three cardinals whom Urban VI appointed were his relatives. Scrupulously avoiding nepotism in church appointments, he pursued it vigorously, however, in the secular sphere. In return for the promise of a Neapolitan principality for his nephew, he deposed Queen Joanna of Naples and replaced her with one of her distant cousins, Charles III (1381–1386), who had her strangled in 1382. Such a move set a precedent for papal politics in the next centuries. Popes were rarely of aristocratic birth but could use the enormous power of their office to raise the social level of their families, securing them advantageous marriages, estates and titles in the highest levels of Italian society. The noble houses, in return, enjoyed the substantial benefits of an alliance with the pope.

The new king, however, was slow to carry out his side of the bargain, so Urban, 'blazing like a lamp', turned on him, only to be besieged by the Neapolitan army at Nocera and see the kingdom revert to the Clementine obedience. Urban's new cardinals found him as difficult as those who had elected him and began asking for legal advice on what action they could take against a pope incapable of ruling. Urban had six of them interrogated, and it was said that he walked in his garden reading his breviary out loud to drown out the screams as one of them was being tortured in the cellar below.[5] Five were secretly executed while the sixth, the Englishman Adam Easton, was only spared by the intervention of King Richard II (1377–1399), whose support the pope needed.

RIVAL POPES

Urban VI, who had become unpopular in Rome, died in 1389, possibly poisoned, while Clement VII survived until 1394. Both were replaced by popes elected by their respective cardinals. In Avignon the choice fell on the Aragonese Pedro de Luna, who took the name of Benedict XIII (1394–1422), while the Roman obedience elevated the Neapolitan cardinal Pietro Tomacelli as Boniface IX (1389–1404). He proved far more politically adept than Urban VI, regaining the adherence of Naples by backing the winning side in the civil war that followed the murder of Charles III in 1386. But he also lost the support of the Aragonese-ruled kingdom of Sicily and the city of Genoa.

Boniface became notorious for his nepotism, while his constant shortage of money, a problem shared by his rivals in Avignon, led to serious abuse of the system of papal provisions, with benefices and Church titles being openly granted to petitioners in return for substantial gifts, in addition to the usual payment of a percentage of the appointee's first year's revenues. Together with heavy increases in clerical taxation by both obediences, such measures only added to widespread discontent with the contemporary papacy across all of Western Europe.

Offers made by one pope to the other to try to settle the issue were infrequent and always rejected. Eventually Charles VI of France (1380–1423) tried to impose a solution by withdrawing his recognition of Benedict XIII and besieging Avignon from 1398 to 1403, ultimately forcing Benedict to flee the city disguised as a monk and take refuge in Marseille and then in Genoa. In 1408 he was abandoned by most of his cardinals and had to retire to his native Aragón, establishing a new papal court at Peñiscola in 1415, where he remained irreconcilable until his death.

Boniface IX's most important achievement was his re-establishment of papal control over the city of Rome,[6] but this did not last beyond his death, and his successor, Innocent VII (1404–1406), was unable to prevent King Ladislas of Naples (1386–1414) from imposing a communal government on Rome in 1404. In the conclave that elected Innocent, all the cardinals of the Roman obedience swore that if elected they would devote themselves to ending the schism, even if it meant their own abdication. Innocent went as far as convening a council in Rome in 1405 to discuss the issue, but it achieved nothing concrete.

Innocent VII was succeeded by the elderly Gregory XII (1406–1415), a Venetian nobleman and theologian of repute, also committed to ending the schism. His pre-election pledges had included promises to begin negotiations within three months and to abdicate if Benedict XIII was willing to do likewise. Laborious diplomacy led to an agreement that the two claimants would meet in Savona by 1 November 1408, but the town supported Benedict, which made Gregory fear for his safety, and under pressure from his nephews and from the king of Naples, who were reluctant to see him abdicate, he constantly delayed the meeting, which Benedict XIII was equally reluctant to attend. So exasperated did Gregory's cardinals become, especially when he appointed two more of his nephews to the college, that all but three of them renounced their obedience to him in July 1408 and took refuge in Pisa, where they were joined by four of Benedict's cardinals. Together they appealed to the leading Christian rulers and called for a council to meet in the city in May 1409.

Those who attended saw their aim as not just ending the schism but also 'the necessary reform of the many ills that have oppressed the Universal Church of God, both in itself and in its members for so many years'.[7] For this they drew up twenty proposals which received the approval of a new pope, who was elected during the council, after the participants decided they could legitimately depose the existing popes.

As both Gregory XII and Benedict XIII had refused to attend, and as the right of any general council to depose a pope other than for manifest heresy had never been established, this decree deposing them was ignored by both. In electing the Franciscan archbishop of Milan, Cardinal Peter of Candia, who took the name Alexander V (1409–1410), the council added a third, a Pisan, obedience to the existing two.[8]

While the kings of England, France and Bohemia recognised the new Pisan pope, the emperor-elect Rupert remained committed to

Gregory XII, as for the time being did King Ladislas the Magnanimous of Naples, who was also titular king of Jerusalem and claimant to the kingdom of Hungary. Alexander V remained in Bologna, while Rome was captured for him in January 1410 by forces led by the most influential of his cardinals, the Neapolitan Baldassare Cossa, whose earlier career was said to have included piracy as well as general drunkenness and debauchery.[9] Four months later, Alexander V was dead, poisoned by Cossa, it was rumoured. Whatever the truth of that, Cossa was elected at Bologna as John XXIII (1410–1415), largely through the influence of Florence and of the claimant to Naples, Louis II of Anjou (died 1417).

John proclaimed a crusade against Ladislas and backed Louis in the renewed war in the kingdom of Naples, only to see his candidate decisively defeated in 1412. Not least because he was committed by the undertakings made by his predecessor to hold a reforming council in Rome later the same year, he had to recognise Ladislas as the legitimate king, as the only way of gaining admission to the city. This council completed the condemnation of the writings of John Wyclif initiated by Alexander V but accomplished little else, and in 1413 John was ejected from Rome by Ladislas and forced to take refuge in Florence. The king then proceeded to overrun most of the Papal States until his death in 1414.

THE COUNCIL OF CONSTANCE

No military aid against Ladislas could be expected from France, where civil war was raging, and so John XXIII appealed to the king of the Romans, Sigismund (1410–1437), who made his assistance conditional upon the pope calling a council to meet at Constance in southern Germany to try to end the schism. The participants gathered in November 1414. They divided themselves into five groups according to their political allegiances and discussed and voted on issues in these national blocs. John himself had hoped to take personal charge of the war to recover the Papal States after the death of King Ladislas, but his cardinals insisted he attend the council. There he expected to preside over the assembled prelates, but they favoured making a clean sweep of all three papal claimants and choosing an entirely new pope. In March 1415, failing in a bid to break up the council by force, John XXIII escaped from Constance in disguise but was quickly captured by imperial soldiers.

He was deposed by the council for being 'a notorious simoniac, a notorious destroyer of the goods and rights not only of the Roman church but also of other churches' and 'an evil administrator and dispenser of the church's spiritualities and temporalities', who 'notoriously scandalised God's church and the Christian people by his detestable and dishonest life and morals, both before his promotion to the papacy and up to the present time'. Although his deposition defied the ancient tradition of papal superiority to all earthly jurisdiction, John accepted the council's decree. He was held prisoner in the Rhineland until June 1419, when in return for a very large ransom he was released and reinstated as cardinal by a new pope, Martin V (1417–1431), only to die six months later. His tomb by Donatello and Michelozzo is in the baptistery of Florence Cathedral.

The Council of Constance, whose sessions continued for nearly four years, saw the end of the other surviving popes of the Great Schism. Gregory XII had taken refuge with Carlo Malatesta, lord of Rimini, in 1411. Now ninety, he was willing to accede to the demand for his abdication but indicated that he could not recognise the legitimacy of a council that had been called by one whom he (and now they) regarded as an antipope, the recently deposed John XXIII. So, it was agreed that the council would be re-convoked under his authority, and with his cardinals merging with those of the former Pisan obedience, so that he could offer it his abdication. This preserved the papal authority to convoke such a council. Once Gregory's proctors had presented his resignation to the assembly, he was appointed cardinal bishop of Porto and legate of the March of Ancona, retaining these offices until his death in October 1417.

Even though the king of Aragón formally withdrew recognition of him in 1416, Benedict XIII remained in Peñiscola, defiant, refusing to accept the council which deposed him in 1417 and continuing to appoint his own cardinals. He died in 1422, the last survivor of the conclave of 1378 which had given rise to the Great Schism. But this was still not the end of it. Following an oath they had sworn to Benedict on his deathbed, three of his four surviving cardinals elected a successor, who took the name Clement VIII (1423–1429). The fourth refused to recognise this election, claiming it was the product of simony, and on his own authority appointed yet another pope, Benedict XIV, a sacristan in the town of Rodez, of whom nothing more is known.

Clement VIII remained secure in Peñiscola for as long as it suited the king of Aragón, who, however, never recognised him as pope. In 1429 when that usefulness finally ended, he abdicated, requiring his handful of cardinals to elect the legitimate pope Martin V in his place. In return he was invested with the archbishopric of Mallorca, which he kept until his death in 1446. Thus ended the Great Schism.

Even so, some time would pass before a definitive verdict emerged on which of the three obediences represented the legitimate line of the successors of Peter. At first the honour was accorded to the Pisan popes, largely because it was the last of them, John XXIII, who called the Council of Constance, something only a legitimate pontiff could do.[10] If, despite his deposition, he was regarded as an antipope then the acts of the council, and most importantly its election of a new pope in the person of Martin V, would lack legitimacy. As time passed and the conciliar ideal waned, preference was given instead to the Roman obedience, which is now held to be the true one, but in 1724 the next pope to choose the name Benedict had to be persuaded to call himself XIII and not XIV, because he thought the fourteenth-century Benedict XIII had been legitimate. Many of the papal names of this period were not used again for a century or more because of this uncertainty, and there would not be another pope John until 1958: the second John XXIII.

The Council of Constance is famous or notorious for another episode, the burning of the Czech reformer Jan Hus, due to his criticisms of both the theory and practice of papal authority in the Church. He was a priest and master in the University of Prague, and his writings were strongly influenced by the ideas of John Wyclif, whose works were becoming increasingly influential in Central Europe; largely thanks to contacts with England resulting from the marriage of Richard II (1377–1399) and Anne of Bohemia. Hus had already taken a leading role in shaping his university's neutral attitude to all three papal claimants, and it was to counter his influence that the archbishop of Prague had asked Alexander V to decide on the orthodoxy of those works of Wyclif not already condemned by Gregory XI in 1377.

The ensuing papal condemnation led to the public burning of Wyclif's writings and to the excommunication of Hus when he appealed to the pope to reverse his decision. However, he retained the backing of the former king of the Romans, Wenzel IV of Bohemia, and of his university, allowing him to continue teaching and preaching freely in Prague that all doctrines and hierarchies must derive from Scripture alone, and that the Church was a body of equals, made up of the elect predestined to salvation. A pope would not qualify for salvation merely by virtue of his office: 'if the pope is evil, and especially if he is predestined to damnation, then he is a devil like Judas the Apostle.'

When John XXIII called a crusade against King Ladislas of Naples in 1411, Hus reacted by attacking indulgences like those in the crusading bull that offered a reduction of time in Purgatory in return for payments for the war effort. Hus argued that neither pope nor bishop should be involved in promoting warfare, and that forgiveness of sin was only possible by repentance and never through money. In general he criticised the ethical standards of the contemporary Church, and the sale of its sacraments. These ideas attracted support in all levels of Bohemian society and spread into neighbouring states. Although the ecclesiastical authorities found themselves powerless against Hus, three of his followers were executed for describing the papal indulgences as fraudulent.

In 1414 the new king of the Romans, Sigismund, invited Hus to attend the Council of Constance under his protection to debate his ideas. Within a few weeks of his arrival Hus was imprisoned in a monastery and by June 1415 the debate had turned into a trial. Although Sigismund was furious at the violation of his promise of protection, he was persuaded that his intervening would cause the collapse of the council. Hus himself admitted his veneration of Wyclif and refused to recant any of his ideas unless they could be confounded by arguments from Scripture. Amongst his propositions cited as heretical was the claim that 'the papal dignity originated with the emperor.' Hus was condemned on 6 July 1415 as 'a disciple not of Christ but of the heresiarch John Wyclif', stripped of his priestly vestments and handed over to the secular authorities to be burned alive.

The council also condemned 300 propositions from the writings of Wyclif. Several contained absolute denials of papal authority more extreme than those of Hus: 'the pope is Antichrist made manifest. Not just the present one, but all popes from the time of the foundation of the church, all cardinals, bishops and their other accomplices, make up the composite, monstrous person of Antichrist.' Wyclif allowed that there had been some good popes, Gregory the Great in particular, but denied that their repentance had been enough to save them. Wyclif's bones were ordered to be dug up and scattered outside consecrated ground.

The execution of Hus caused uproar in Bohemia, where he enjoyed powerful support, leading to attacks on the clergy and on monks, many of whom were expelled from the kingdom. Nobles influenced by him formed a league to protect Hussite preachers, and King Wenzel IV gave them open backing until 1418. His attempt then to re-establish bishops loyal to Rome led to revolt, with the result that the Hussites controlled the kingdom unchallenged until 1434, when the rise of a more extreme faction, the Taborites, alienated more moderate opinion, but even thereafter papal authority was rejected in most of Bohemia.

While men like Wyclif and Hus, who were precursors of the Protestant Reformation, are the best-known critics of the papacy in this period, there were others who did not doubt that 'the Apostolic See and the Roman Curia are the root and foundation of the entire Church' but insisted on a need for reform.[11] Matthew of Cracow, bishop of Worms (1404–1410), wrote that the Curia was devoting too much time to administrative matters, especially dealing with petitions for benefices, and giving them to the wrong sort of people. He was not alone, in an age of renewed and intense lay piety, in complaining that the papacy had become little more than a great bureaucratic and fiscal machine and was failing to provide spiritual leadership for a society increasingly craving it.

At the Council of Constance the participating bishops and cardinals themselves wanted certain specific reforms in the structure of authority in the Church. The schism had raised serious doubts in the minds of canon lawyers and theologians, not least about the proper form of government for the Church. The existence of rival popes was not just a scandal that threatened the faith of clergy and laity alike, it also called into question the continuance of papal leadership. For example, the influential canon lawyer Cardinal Francisco Zabarella argued that, as there was no one pope who could command the allegiance of all Christians, then the see of Peter was in effect vacant, and leadership therefore rested with the Congregation of the Faithful, represented by a general council.[12]

Advised by Zabarella and others, the assembled prelates decided after John XXIII's flight in March 1415 that his departure did not dissolve the council, even though he had called it, and that it should remain in session until the schism was fully healed. The council claimed 'authority immediately from Christ, and that all men of every rank and condition, including the pope himself, are bound to obey it in matters concerning the Faith, the abolition of the schism and the reformation of the Church of God in its head and in its members'.[13]

The council condemned and forbade such features of papal government as the reservation of benefices to be filled only by nomination by the pope and the taking of 'spoils', the personal possessions of dead bishops whose sees had been awarded by papal provision. The council's most significant decisions involved papal authority and the processes of election. Henceforth, all future popes were required to take an oath confirming their adherence to the decrees of a series of general councils, from I Nicaea in 325 to Vienne in 1311, and it was stipulated that another general council should meet five years after this one ended, and another seven years after that. Thereafter they would be held regularly every ten years, and the pope was required to name the place of meeting for the next council a month before the ending of the current one. He was thereafter only allowed to change the location in case of emergency, and with the consent of two-thirds or more of 'his brothers' the cardinals. Similarly, he could bring forward the date of a meeting with their consent, but under no circumstances could it be postponed.

In the event of a schism, the next scheduled council would be advanced to a date exactly one year after a rival pope was proclaimed, to meet at the previously agreed location. No papal summons was required for this, and each claimant had to announce the holding of the council within a month of learning of the existence of his rival, on pain of being automatically disqualified from being selected by the council as the rightful holder of the office. All claimants would be considered suspended from the day the council opened and none of them might preside.

Recalling the events of 1378, the Council of Constance also decreed that if a conclave was held under threat, the cardinals involved should not carry out a second election on pain of being deprived of their offices, but should instead retire to a safe place and announce that they had acted under duress. This would trigger the bringing forward of the next regular council, just as if there were rival popes. The overall intention was that while the popes might return to running the day-to-day administration of the Church, their authority would henceforth be subordinated to that of the regular councils.

MARTIN V, EUGENIUS IV AND THE COUNCILS

In November 1417 the council appointed a commission of twenty-two cardinals and thirty other representatives of the five 'nations' to elect a new pope. After three days sufficient votes were cast for Cardinal Oddo Colonna, a member of the Roman noble family, who took the name Martin V (1417–1431). He was made to swear to uphold all decisions taken 'in a conciliar manner' by the council, which then dissolved itself on 22 April 1418, while the new pope moved to Florence, before trying to regain control of the Papal States.

Martin was able to establish himself in Rome in 1420, with the aid of the new ruler of Naples, Queen Joanna II (1414–1435). Making papal authority a reality in its own states was a much harder and longer task, as it required subduing several well-entrenched local lords. The communal movements that had once been the main source of opposition to the popes' rule in the towns had given way in the fourteenth century to lordships, created by local magnates whose landed wealth enabled them to hire private armies to dominate their cities. Some of these *Signori* also offered their services as mercenary captains who could be hired or receive a contract or *condotta*—hence *condottieri*—to fight for a paymaster, a system increasingly used by the popes for their military needs. The most powerful of these was Braccio di Montone, whom Martin V had to accept as lord of Perugia, until he could put together an alliance to crush him, as he did in 1424.

Beyond the frontiers of the Papal States the same phenomenon could be witnessed in the emergence from the later thirteenth century in northern Italy of powerful dynastic dictatorships, often cloaked in constitutional disguises, which replaced previous more democratic or oligarchic forms of local government. The best known of these are the Medici in Florence and the Visconti, followed by the Sforza, in Milan, but most other cities of any significance produced equivalents, like the Malatesta in Rimini, the Scaligeri in Verona and the Este in Ferrara.[14] Several of these, and the republic of Venice, cast ambitious glances at papal territory whenever the popes were in difficulties.

Martin V was the first pope since the thirteenth century to live permanently in Rome. The intervening years had been hard on the city, despite occasional efforts to restore some of the major ecclesiastical buildings. The Lateran Palace was uninhabitable, and Martin turned the Vatican into the principal papal residence. He also began an intensive programme of reconstruction and new building, paid out of revenues from the gradually recovered Papal States and the resources of his own family. Only one of his relatives was made a cardinal, in 1426, but the appointment was kept secret until 1430. This was one of the first nominations *in pectore,* the process begun by Martin whereby the pope could create a cardinal secretly or 'in his breast'.

Despite his electoral oath, Martin V was unenthusiastic about implementing the policies of the Council of Constance relating to papal financial practices and the calling of regular councils. He reintegrated the curial administrations of the former Roman and Avignon obediences and in spring 1418 carried out a number of reforms, including giving up the papal right to the revenues of vacant dioceses. However, he did not relinquish provision to reserved benefices, which would have meant a serious loss of revenue. In 1423 he convoked a council to meet in Pavia, in conformance with the rule decreed at Constance, but only two cardinals and twenty-five bishops attended, and after it relocated to Siena, it was dissolved the following year without results. Seven years later, under some pressure from the cardinals, Martin called another council, to meet in Basel under the presidency of Cardinal Cesarini, his legate in Germany. He himself did not plan to attend it, any more than he had the one at Pavia, and in any case he died in January 1431.

His successor was Gabriele Condulmer, a Venetian and nephew of Gregory XII, who had made him a cardinal in 1408 and whom he succeeded as governor of the March of Ancona. He took the name Eugenius IV (1431–1447). The fourteen cardinals attending the conclave of 1431 had resented Martin V's increasingly autocratic style, as well as his rewarding of his relatives. So they all swore an oath that the one elected would respect the rights of the college, pay half of the papal revenues to the cardinals, and only reform the Curia with their consent. They also insisted on being consulted about the venue for each future general council.[15]

Eugenius' immediate concern was trying to recover key fortresses south of Rome that Martin V had given his Colonna relatives, as these controlled communications with Naples. At the first hint of this threat, the Colonna attacked Rome in April 1431, and when Queen Joanna II of Naples sent a mercenary army to aid the new pope, they bribed its commander into changing sides. Other lords in the Papal States took the opportunity of the chaos to ignore papal authority. By August, Eugenius was paying the huge sum of 13,000 florins a month to hire his own mercenaries, just for the ordinary soldiers; their commanders received further unrecorded payments. With more reliable assistance from the queen, the papal commanders forced most of the Colonna to submit in September, taking their castles.

In the meantime the Council of Basel was slowly starting. Only the abbot of Vézelay had arrived by the time it was due to open in March, and he was joined in April by another abbot, one bishop and three academics from the University of Paris. The council finally began on 23 July, but without its president. Cardinal Cesarini, having just been defeated by the Hussites in Bohemia, arrived the next month and was anxious to invite them to send representatives to Basel to try to secure a peaceful settlement. The prospect of Hussites attending it only added to Eugenius' feeling that the council should be quickly dissolved or relocated somewhere it might be less open to radical influences.

A further reason for him to want to move it came from an embassy sent by the Eastern emperor, John VIII Palaeologus, whose now much-diminished state was under continuing threat from the Ottomans. He wanted to make another effort to achieve reunion with the West in the hope of securing military assistance and offered to come in person to attend a meeting. His secretary said that Basel seemed rather too remote but agreed on Bologna. In November Eugenius sent Cesarini a private letter suggesting the council be suspended and reassemble in Bologna in eighteen months, and in December he issued a formal bull ordering it to disband because of its invitation to the Hussites.

Even before this arrived, rumours were circulating of the pope's intention to close the council, and the participants, several of whom had felt they had been duped by the sudden dissolution of the Pavia/Siena council in 1424, announced that they would not accept such a decision. They drew up a circular letter to Western rulers, blaming not the pope but the cardinals advising him. Cardinal Cesarini also urged the pope to reconsider, as he saw negotiation with the Hussites as the only way to stop their ideas spreading into Germany. When the bull arrived ordering its suspension, the council rejected it and in February 1432 re-enacted the decree of the Council of Constance affirming the superiority of conciliar to papal authority. The cardinals in Rome were warned that they had to 'persuade the pope to support the council by all opportune means, getting rid of obstacles of every kind'.[16]

Reconvening in April the council now ordered the cardinals not yet present to come to Basel within the next three months and the pope himself to attend or send a proctor. When on June 6 a copy of this was nailed to the door of St. Peter's, the cardinals still in Rome panicked, as it threatened them with deprivation of their offices.

That the Church needed reform from the top down was widely felt, and a general council was seen as the best forum in which to achieve this. Sigismund, king of the Romans, who had been kept out of Bohemia by the Hussites since his brother Wenzel IV's death in 1418, declared himself to be the protector of the Council of Basel. Other secular rulers, including the kings of England, Scotland, France and Castile and the Visconti dukes of Milan, sent delegations. So, in any confrontation the council was likely to triumph over the pope. Many of the cardinals in Rome decided to obey the summons, even when Eugenius denied them permission to leave the city; only five of them remained with him.

Eugenius offered to compromise, but his envoys were refused admission for six weeks while the council debated if their letters of introduction contained sufficient recognition of the superiority of conciliar to papal authority. Furthermore, as one of the cardinals supporting the council had been excluded from the conclave of 1431, he claimed that the ensuing election was invalid, and the council began threatening to depose Eugenius on those grounds.

By September 1432 more than three-quarters of the cardinals had arrived in Basel, and those who had not sent written declarations were now proclaimed contumacious, along with the pope himself. In December decrees were issued limiting papal patronage and giving curial officials sixty days in which to repudiate Eugenius or lose their offices. By February 1433 a mass exodus of curialists from Rome was under way, despite the pope locking the city gates in a vain effort to prevent it.

Eugenius IV was at heart a tough Venetian aristocrat and not easily daunted. In 1433 he offered some concessions to the council, including withdrawing his bull of dissolution but also began trying to alter the balance of forces. He encouraged more bishops to attend the council, offering to pay their travel expenses, and arranged for King

Sigismund to come to Rome for the coronation for which he had been waiting since 1411. When the council appointed a new governor for Avignon, Eugenius sent one of his loyal cardinals to evict him and take over the city.

For its part the council threatened to depose Eugenius if he did not appear within two months, insisting it could only be dissolved by a two-thirds majority of its own members and transferring all curial business to Basel. The pope was also deprived of his right of nomination to benefices, and free election to bishoprics was granted, as 'there will never be complete harmony between the pope and the prelates' unless the rights of the bishops were secured.[17] The council also attempted separate negotiations with the Eastern empire, offering to send representatives to a reunion synod in Constantinople rather than Italy. The threat of a new schism was in the air, making some of the prelates assembled in Basel uneasy.

A further setback in 1434, when Eugenius was driven from Rome by another popular revolt and established his court in Florence until 1443, may have also worked to his advantage, as it advanced his plans for a meeting with the Greeks. While the delegates assembled in Basel wanted the proceedings to be held there, or alternatively in Avignon, the Easterners always preferred a venue in northern Italy and in 1437 accepted the pope's proposal that a reunion council should meet in Ferrara, where it opened under the presidency of a papal legate in January 1438. In the meantime Eugenius IV sent a bull to Basel ordering the council meeting there to reconvene in Ferrara. This was a high-risk strategy, as it reversed his previous concessions and challenged the council's own doctrine that it could only be transferred or dissolved with the consent of a majority of its own members. If they opted not to move, a schism was inevitable.

Fear of that and the hope of an end to the ancient rift with the Greeks led many of the bishops in Basel to move to Ferrara and thence to Florence, where Eugenius' council transferred in January 1439. A determined minority remained in Basel and voted for the suspension of Eugenius in January 1438, just as his council was opening in Ferrara, but took no further action until it was too late. It was not until June 1439 that the much-reduced assembly declared him deposed but then waited until November to elect a successor, by which time the papal council now in Florence had achieved the re-union of Greek and Latin churches entirely on the papacy's terms. Enshrined in the decree *Laetantur Caeli* (Let the Heavens Rejoice) of 6 July 1439, the agreement included recognition of papal primacy and the use of *filioque* in the creed and of unleavened bread in the celebration of the Mass by the Greeks.

The rump Council of Basel's choice of replacement for Eugenius was a layman, Duke Amadeus of Savoy, who took the name of Felix V (1439–1449). He had ruled Savoy as count and then duke until going into a retreat in a castle on Lake Geneva in 1434 with a monastic military order, the Knights of St. Maurice, which he had founded. While his personal reputation for holiness was high, his election was largely the work of the French cardinal Louis Aleman (died 1450), who chaired the commission set up to find a new pope. He was recognised as legitimate by a number of states, including Scotland, Aragón and the duchy of Milan, but the new king of the Romans, Frederick III (1440–1493), and the rulers of England, France and Castile refused to do so. In 1440 Felix appointed thirteen new cardinals, including Dutch, Polish, Spanish and Walachian ones as well as French, German, Italian and Savoyard, marking a further stage in the internationalising of the College of Cardinals, but some refused to accept office at his hands.

Felix V's relations with the Council of Basel were not harmonious, as he was reluctant to accept further limitations on papal authority. Distancing himself from it, he maintained a learned court and developed an interest in the life-extending properties of drinking gold.[18] In 1442 he withdrew from Basel to install himself in Lausanne and then Geneva in his former duchy, now ruled by one of his sons. In the same year almost all of the states in his obedience other than Savoy withdrew their recognition.

In 1446 secret negotiations were opened with the backing of King Charles VI of France to end both council and schism. In Rome, the election of a new pope, Nicholas V (1447–1455), made compromise easier, and in 1449 an assembly at Lyon saw both the formal dissolution of the Council of Basel and the abdication of Felix V. He was appointed as papal legate in his own former duchy until his death in 1451. Some of his cardinals, including Louis Aleman (beatified in 1527), were also reinstated in their rank after submitting to Nicholas V. The Age of Schism seemed to be over.

chapter 15

A LEADER OF THE WORLD, NOT OF THE CHURCH

(1449–1513)

THE 'DONATION' IN QUESTION

In the winter of 1439, Lorenzo Valla, Latin Secretary to King Alfonso I of Naples, was busy writing a new book. His aim was to discredit the text on which papal overlordship of all islands depended, for his master was also King Alfonso V of Aragón and Sicily (1416–1458), who was fighting a rival claimant, backed by Pope Eugenius IV, to the Sicilian throne. Valla (1406/7–1457), a former university teacher who had once wanted to be a missionary in China, was already famous for questioning received wisdom, having faced the Inquisition for arguing against the orthodox view that each of the Apostles had contributed to the Creed that bears their name. He would subsequently debunk the supposed letter of Christ to King Abgar of Edessa and accuse St. Augustine of heresy.

He was not the first to deny the authenticity of the 'Constitution of Constantine', the text of the donation supposedly made by the emperor Constantine I to Pope Sylvester I. The emperor Otto III questioned it in the 990s, and it had been called a 'lie and a heretical fable' by a follower of Arnold of Brescia in 1152.[1] Most recently it had been described as apocryphal by the German canon lawyer Nicholas of Cusa (1401–1464), a participant in the Council of Basel, who in 1433 had written *De Concordantia Catholica* (The Catholic Concordance), a substantial defence of imperial over papal authority.[2] He argued that the popes had been subordinate to emperors in the West even after the time of Constantine and that the claim that the papacy had transferred the imperial dignity 'from the Greeks to the Germans' in the time of Charlemagne was unhistorical.[3]

Using coins and inscriptions, as well as previously neglected historical texts, Valla's far more detailed historical and linguistic analysis exposed the Constitution's numerous errors and textual anachronisms.[4] Renaissance enthusiasm for the recovery of the 'pure' Latin of antiquity gave Valla philological tools to detect grammatical forms and items of vocabulary in the text that could only belong to periods much later than the fourth century.[5]

Even so, Valla's work was not widely known. For example, as late as the 1520s, Henry VIII of England still accepted the historicity of the 'Donation', and the papacy tried to repress criticism of it.[6] This was satirized in an anonymously written dialogue, 'Julius Excluded from Heaven,' between St. Peter and Pope Julius II (1503–1513):

> JULIUS: . . . they do say that someone called Constantine transferred the whole majesty of his empire to the Roman pontiff Sylvester. . . .
>
> PETER: Are there any reliable records of this splendid gift?
>
> JULIUS: Nothing but one interpolation included among the decretals.
>
> PETER: Perhaps it's all a hoax.
>
> JULIUS: I sometimes think that myself. What sane man would give up such a magnificent empire, even to his father? But it pleases us greatly to believe it, and we've used threats to impose absolute silence on the snoopers who try to disprove it.[7]

NICHOLAS V AND THE END OF CONCILIARISM

A growing confrontation in the time of Eugenius IV between the papacy and the new learning that was being pursued in many parts of Italy turned itself into a courtship under his successor, Nicholas V (1447–1455). Born Tommaso Parentucelli in 1397, he was the orphaned son of a doctor and worked as a tutor to the children of noble families to fund his studies in Bologna, before joining the household of its bishop, the Carthusian Niccolò Albergati (d. 1443).

Albergati, who was made a cardinal in 1426, was a leading papal diplomat, who presided over the Council of Ferrara for Eugenius IV in 1438.[8] Parentucelli assisted him for over twenty years, and his value was recognised by his appointment to the see of Bologna as Albergati's successor. In 1446 the further reward of a cardinal's hat resulted from his success in helping persuade the imperial assembly or Diet in Frankfurt to recognise the legitimacy of Eugenius IV over Felix V.

A surprise choice in the conclave of 1447, largely thanks to the need to block the election of Colonna relatives of Martin V, Parentucelli took the name Nicholas V (1447–1455) in honour of his former mentor, Cardinal Albergati. As pope his two main passions were books and buildings. He formed a collection of twelve hundred manuscripts that became the starting point of the Vatican Library. Equally important were his efforts at restoring his city.

Rome had suffered nearly two centuries of neglect while the Curia resided elsewhere, and even the most important of its churches and monuments had decayed. The city depended for its economic prosperity on the presence of the papal court, and because of its absence, by the early fifteenth century the population had sunk to 20,000. Most of these lived in the walled Leonine City, or the Borgo, as it was also called, close to St. Peter's and along the Tiber from there to Trastevere, with only a few pockets of habitation surviving across the river within the original walled city. The urban environment was squalid. As Martin V noted with displeasure in 1425, 'many inhabitants of Rome have been throwing . . . entrails, viscera, heads, feet, bones, blood, and skins, besides rotten meat and fish, refuse, excrement, and other fetid and rotting cadavers into the streets.'[9]

In the 1420s Martin had begun restoration work on the Lateran Basilica and St. Peter's, but Eugenius IV's ejection from Rome in 1433 left urban renewal suspended. So it was Nicholas V who started the transformation of Rome, making the Vatican Palace the permanent papal residence. Located within the Borgo and incorporating the Castel Sant'Angelo, the Vatican was more secure than the semi-ruined Lateran Palace. Nicholas began fortifying as well as restoring the Vatican, but the city remained volatile and a plot to murder him and set up a communal government was sternly suppressed in 1453. Fear of further of as well as ill-health clouded his last years.

Amongst his plans was a new street system in the Borgo, which was not completed by the time of the next Jubilee, in 1450. Despite vile weather and an outbreak of plague, numerous pilgrims came to Rome for the first time in a century. A tragedy on the bridge over the Tiber into the Borgo, the Ponte Sant'Angelo, in which two hundred pilgrims were crushed or drowned in a crowd surge, led to further improvements both to the bridge and the district, providing a grander and safer approach to St. Peter's, which became the site of the last imperial coronation held in the city, when Frederick III (1440–1493) was crowned by the pope in 1452.

As well as collecting books, Nicholas V also commissioned new ones, persuading Lorenzo Valla to translate both Herodotus and Thucydides into Latin. This papal patronage was far removed from the scholar's experiences under Eugenius IV, when he had had to escape from Rome by sea in 1444 to avoid prosecution for heresy, and is typical of the new directions taken by Nicholas V. In 1448 he made Nicholas of Cusa, the former advocate of imperial supremacy, a cardinal, and he advanced the career of Aeneas Sylvius Piccolomini, another prominent figure at the Council of Basel and formerly secretary to the antipope Felix V, making him bishop of Trieste and then of Siena. The pope's own accommodating attitude also facilitated the ending of the schism in 1449, allowing Felix (died 1451) to stand down in return for appointment as cardinal. Most of the few surviving cardinals appointed by Felix were also reappointed by Nicholas or otherwise compensated.

The realignment in these years of so many of the former partisans of the Council of Basel with the papacy and the almost total loss of enthusiasm for conciliarism are remarkable. However, not only had the conciliar mechanism proved cumbersome, it also failed to generate the reforms that were widely demanded. Instead, national church assemblies, backed by secular rulers, achieved much of what was being sought. For example, in 1438 the French church, encouraged by Charles VII, had promulgated a Pragmatic Sanction of Bourges that rejected papal rights of appointment to reserved benefices and the taking of annates, the first year's income of those presented.

Such a repudiation of papal authority would have provoked excommunications of king and bishops and the threat of interdict on the kingdom in earlier centuries, but the standing of the papacy had declined so strongly and resentment risen so high amongst the clergy of the kingdoms of Western Europe that the deployment of such spiritual sanctions was no longer effective.

This vulnerability was recognised in the flurry of diplomatic activity between the Curia and the royal courts in the decades after the end of the Great Schism in 1417. On the papal side concessions had to be made. Negotiations with the emperor-elect and the German Diet led to restrictions on papal rights and financial exactions in the empire similar to those the French clergy had imposed in 1438. In 1442, Eugenius IV finally accepted Aragonese rule in Naples, recognising Alfonso I as king.

In England legal powers to limit appeals to Rome and stop papal provisions and the payments of annates already existed, thanks to a series of parliamentary statutes in the 1350s and early 1390s. In practice, they were not fully applied and their main purpose may have been to give the English rulers a bargaining chip in negotiations with the Curia.[10] Similarly, the offer to repeal or the threat to reinstate the Pragmatic Sanction of Bourges provided the French kings with a powerful weapon in their diplomatic dealings with the papacy well on into the sixteenth century. In such circumstances it is not surprising that effective diplomats, such as Cardinal Albergati and Aeneas Sylvius Piccolomini, were amongst the most prized and rewarded of papal servants in this period. Such skills included the ability to fit into the learned and artistic culture of the royal and princely courts of the time. Hence scholars, able to write in the new classicising style and satisfy the taste for antiquity in their speeches, came into demand as royal and papal secretaries, administrators and envoys. For some the Curia offered particularly good opportunities, including in the cases of Nicholas V and Pius II (1458–1464) the route to the throne of Peter itself.

Another nail in the coffin of the conciliar movement had been the prospect of the reunion of the Latin and Greek churches after four centuries of schism. Eugenius IV's establishing of the council attended by the emperor John VIII Palaeologus in Ferrara and then Florence had been crucial, and the summons to attend in 1437 made Nicholas of Cusa break with the Council of Basel and led to his subsequent opposition to conciliarism. In practice, the agreements reached in Florence in 1439 proved ephemeral, as the emperor was unable to enforce them in his much-diminished realm, and the anticipated Western military aid for which he had made his concessions scarcely materialised.

Some Western states, notably the Republic of Genoa, even assisted the Ottoman Turks in defeating a papal and Hungarian crusade at Varna in 1444. Others such as the equally trade-oriented republic of Venice were unwilling to antagonise the Turks as long as their own territories remained secure. Little attention was thus paid in the West to the parlous state of the tiny remnant of the Roman empire, as its inhabitants still called it, in its few remaining days, until it was entirely extinguished by the Turkish conquest of Constantinople in 1453.

This event caused a profound shock, and not just to those who were rediscovering the Roman past or realised the significance of the Eastern empire to the papacy through renewed interest in works such as the *Liber Pontificalis*.[11] The Ottoman Turks had been extending their hold in southeastern Europe since the late fourteenth century, initially as allies of the emperor.[12] Most of the eastern Balkans was already theirs, and the fall of Constantinople was followed by the conquest of almost all the western half. Athens fell in 1456, most of the Peloponnese in 1460, Bosnia in 1463 and Epiros by 1479, when the Turks began the conquest of Albania. To the north lay the kingdom of Hungary, which now became the front line against Turkish expansion.

THE SCHOLAR POPE: PIUS II

The conclave following the death of Nicholas V in March 1455 began with the cardinals agreeing that whoever was elected should devote himself to organising a crusade. In the circumstances, the choice of the austere seventy-six-year-old Aragonese cardinal Alfonso de Borja (italianised as Borgia), who became Callistus III (1455–1458), was surprising. He was another of those rewarded for diplomatic achievements, being made bishop of Valencia for persuading the antipope Clement VIII to abdicate in 1429, and a cardinal in 1444 for his part in securing the recognition of Eugenius IV by Alfonso V of Aragón and Sicily. As the first Spanish pope, he typified the wider geographical range from which the College of Cardinals was now drawn.

His election was intended to prevent that of the Greek Cardinal Bessarion (d. 1472), titular archbishop of Nicaea and an outstanding scholar, one of several distinguished refugees in Rome from lands overrun by the Turks. A cardinal since 1439, he was widely regarded as the outstanding candidate to succeed Nicholas V, whose interests he shared, but prejudice, focussed on his beard, which was a distinguishing feature of the Greek as opposed to the Latin clergy, gave his opponents the means to wreck his chances.[13]

Callistus held firm to his pre-election commitment to launch a crusade to recover Constantinople. He halted Nicholas V's building works in Rome, selling treasures and diverting funds to hiring galleys and mercenaries and ordered the preaching of the crusade, for which he also imposed a tithe on clerical incomes, an increasingly unpopular means of raising money. In France the jurists of the University of Paris resurrected the threat of a general council to restrict papal financial autonomy yet further, and there were similar mutterings in the empire.

Although this opposition never led to anything, and the money raised was used for military operations against the Turks, resulting in a victory at Belgrade (1456) and the defeat of one of their fleets off Lesbos (1457), the pope could not persuade any of the major powers of Western Europe to commit themselves to the project. Even in Italy

King Alfonso gave priority to a war with Genoa over the papal call to crusade, leading Callistus to oppose the succession of the king's illegitimate son Ferrante (1458–1494) to the kingdom of Naples while Sicily reverted to the Crown of Aragón.

As an alternative candidate he considered one of his own nephews, rather than one of the now redundant Angevin claimants, typical of Callistus' obsession with inserting his family into the power structures of the Roman church and Papal States. A consistory in September 1456 saw the appointment of three new cardinals, all in their early twenties, two of whom were papal nephews. One of them, Rodrigo Lanzol Borja y Borja, was made vice chancellor of the Roman church in 1457, holding this crucial office for the next thirty-five years before becoming pope as Alexander VI (1492–1503). A second consistory in December added six new cardinals, mainly Italians, including Aeneas Sylvius Piccolomini, who would be elected pope in August 1458.[14]

Aeneas Sylvius, the son of an impoverished Sienese noble family, is one of the most engaging as well as best recorded of popes before modern times, largely thanks to his own autobiographical writings, which he called *Commentaries*, in imitation of those of Julius Caesar and similarly written in the third person. As well as a separate work devoted to his experiences serving the Council of Basel in 1438 and 1439, he wrote a twelve-book narrative covering his whole life, from his birth in 1405 up to the end of 1463, and continuing this into a thirteenth that reaches July 1464 at the time of his death.[15] This was in addition to a substantial body of other works in prose and verse.

Trained in the arts and in civil law in the universities of Siena and Florence, he took service with a succession of clerics attending the Council of Basel, including Cardinal Niccolò Albergati, through whom he met the future Nicholas V. On behalf of the council, Albergati sent him on a secret diplomatic mission to Scotland in 1435, to persuade King James I to raid the English frontier and thus induce the government of Henry VI to make peace with France. He describes how he was frostbitten on a barefoot pilgrimage to a Marian shrine to give thanks for being saved from shipwreck, how he fathered the first of his illegitimate children while in Scotland—none survived infancy—and how returning in disguise through northern England he was given shelter in a village, whose menfolk all took refuge in a pele tower for fear of Scots raiders, leaving the women outside, because 'they think the enemy can do their women no wrong, as they do not consider rape a crime.'[16] No other pope has been so candid a chronicler of his life and times.

His continued adherence to the Council of Basel, when others were abandoning it, led to his appointment in 1439 as secretary to the antipope Felix V, about whom he was far from enthusiastic. Describing the effects of Felix shaving off the beard he had grown as a hermit, Aeneas remarked that 'the barber's razor had removed what had been a real and becoming ornament . . . when he appeared without it, with his insignificant face, slanting eyes (for he squinted) and flabby cheeks he looked like a very ugly monkey.'[17] In 1442 he obtained Felix's reluctant consent to his transferring to the court of the emperor Frederick III, of whom he would later write a history and by whom he had recently been crowned a poet laureate.

Although receiving some of his income from ecclesiastical benefices, Aeneas Sylvius had long resisted ordination. But in 1445 he went as imperial envoy to Eugenius IV, to whom he made a personal apology for his long adherence to the Council of Basel and was reconciled with friends in Rome who had submitted much earlier, bringing about a dramatic change in his views and lifestyle. In 1446 he was ordained deacon and under Nicholas V became bishop of Trieste only three weeks into the new pontificate, before being translated to Siena in 1451.

As a cardinal of recent creation, his election as pope in 1458 resulted more from divisions in the college than from any established body of support. With the Italian cardinals split between the Orsini and the Colonna, but united in determination to keep out the leading French candidate, Guillaume d'Estouteville, his stock rose. At least in retrospect, he himself was surprisingly confident of the outcome, writing that 'most men foretold that Cardinal Aeneas of Siena would be pope.'[18]

His account gives the fullest record of any conclave up to that time. As well as describing how the cardinals met in the lavatories to discuss their voting intentions, he tells how in the final stages, when only he and the French cardinal were still in the running, with nine and six votes respectively, some of the latter's supporters wanted to transfer their backing to him through the process of *per accessum*, giving him the necessary two-thirds majority for election. This involved individuals openly declaring a change in their vote rather than waiting for another secret ballot. This was not without self-interest, as by playing such a pivotal role they could expect to be rewarded by the elected candidate. Cardinal Rodrigo Borgia was the first to do so, but when a third cardinal rose to provide the crucial majority, two of the others tried unsuccessfully to drag him out of the room before he could speak. Aeneas also bitterly records how by tradition the attendants of the cardinals then looted the possessions of the newly elected pope, stealing all his books and clothes.[19]

Although the popes of this period tended to take names of predecessors of much earlier periods instead of the Johns, Benedicts and Clements of more recent times, Aeneas Sylvius' choice of Pius II was an academic joke. It played on Virgil's references to 'Pious Aeneas' in the *Aeneid* rather than commemorating the obscure Pius I (c. 142– c. 155). There was also a change of style in the way cardinals were referred to, reflecting how many of them now held episcopal or archiepiscopal sees outside of the Papal States, and thus not always attending the papal court. It was by these offices rather than by their titular churches in Rome that they were known. Aeneas Sylvius, for example, had been known as the Cardinal of Siena, rather than the Cardinal of Santa Sabina.

Although he shared the scholarly tastes of Nicholas V, Pius II (1458–1464) inherited the primary concern of his pontificate, the crusade, from Callistus III. This was not continuity for its own sake, as he quickly reversed his predecessor's opposition to the succession of Ferrante of Naples (1458–1494) and supported him against yet another Angevin claimant invited in by rebel barons. Pius was also firm in repudiating his own earlier convictions, issuing the bull *Execrabilis* (Detestable) in 1460, prohibiting on threat of automatic excommunication any appeal from a papal decision on a legal or theological issue to a general council.[20]

Pius was more at ease with his past in his patronage of scholars trained in the arts and classical learning. He promoted such Humanists, as they came to be known, in the papal administration and was supportive of the Roman Academy founded by Giulio Pomponio Leto around 1457. This served as a forum for discussion amongst the scholars increasingly being drawn to Rome to study the remains of its classical past, and by the employment opportunities of the papal bureaucracy.[21] He established a College of Abbreviators for the papal notaries and drafters of decrees. However, he had little time and few resources to devote to the rebuilding of Rome itself or the promotion of projects such as the Vatican Library.

He did, however, in 1462 transform his birthplace, the Tuscan hilltop village of Corsignano, transferring to it the seat of an established bishopric, building both new papal and episcopal palaces and requiring all of the curial cardinals to construct houses of their own in this new town, which he renamed Pienza (loosely, Piusville) after himself. He intended his court to spend part of each year in Pienza and while there relished leading the somewhat unenthusiastic cardinals on long and often muddy hikes and picnics in the local woods and hills.

Pienza aside, Pius's energies and money were put to recruiting troops and ships for a new crusade and to trying to persuade the leading powers of Europe to take part. To this end he called a congress to meet in Mantua in 1459, which he himself and the cardinals attended despite the pleas of the Romans that they should not leave the city. The absence of the papal court threatened its prosperity and raised fears of fresh political disturbances.

The outcome of the congress was disappointing. The emperor Frederick III and the king of France, who had been expected, never appeared, and a substitute imperial delegation was sent back, because its leaders were of insufficiently high status. Francesco Sforza, the duke of Milan (1450–1466), did turn up briefly but left before any agreements had been reached. The Congress of Mantua, which extended into 1460, only confirmed how little interest the rulers of Western Europe had in a new crusading venture, let alone taking part in person.

Ever determined, Pius II, like the elderly Callistus III, proclaimed his intention of accompanying the crusade he himself was calling. Money became less of an issue following the discovery in papal territory of a source of alum, an essential flux needed for the dyeing of wool, which had hitherto only been available through trade with the Turks. The mine that was then established at Tolfa near Civitavecchia with the backing of the Medici bank gave the papacy a monopoly on alum in the West, and Pius issued a bull in 1463 urging Christians to buy it only from him.[22]

In the summer of 1464, with promises of ships from Venice, an expeditionary force assembled at Ancona. Thither the now physically frail pope was carried, to lead an expedition that was already disintegrating as he approached. He died in Ancona on 15 August 1464, and the venture collapsed.

THE RENAISSANCE PAPACY

Pius's authoritarian style had rankled with the cardinals, the senate of the Church, who expected a more consensual and consultative attitude from the pope. As his successor they elected in a single ballot, thanks to some *per accessum* declarations, Pietro Barbo, a Venetian nephew of Eugenius IV.[23] It was suggested that because he was proud of his own appearance he wanted to take the name Formosus (Handsome) II, and only changed his mind when the cardinals started sniggering, both at the meaning of the name and the memory of what had happened to its first holder at the Cadaver Synod. Whatever the truth of this story (his numerous portraits do not suggest he was eye-catching), he took the name Paul II (1464–1471), the first use of it since the eighth century.

In the conclave the cardinals had agreed to an eighteen-clause capitulation, including swearing to use the revenue from the alum monopoly to promote a new crusade and pledging to call a general council within three years. Paul rejected it after his election, though several European rulers including the emperor urged the new pope to convoke a reforming council. His fear that this would be directed at limiting papal primacy was justified by threats from Louis XI of

France and the University of Paris during contentious negotiations over the liberties claimed by the French church.

As well as alienating the cardinals, in 1466 Paul dismayed the civil service by abolishing the College of Abbreviators, established by his predecessor, leading one of them, the later papal librarian Bartolomeo Platina (1421–1481), to comment that Paul hated all the acts and decrees of Pius II and deliberately set about undoing them.[24] In 1468 he suppressed the Roman Academy, accusing its members of paganism and of conspiring with the Turks against him. Several, including Platina, were imprisoned in the Castel Sant'Angelo and tortured to make them confess. Paul also forbade the study of pagan poets in Roman schools, adding to his largely undeserved reputation as uncultured.

His interests lay more in the collecting of art and antiquities, many of which were displayed in the palace he had built adjacent to the Church of San Marco (the patron saint of Venice) of which he had become cardinal priest in 1451. He not only ensured that the palace was defended during the conclave of 1464, preventing the crowd from looting the residence of the new pope as was customary, but he also continued living there in preference to the Vatican. Construction of the palace and the adjacent Piazza Venezia, on the southern edge of the inhabited part of the old city, represented an important step in the urban regeneration of this sector of Rome. Paul revitalised civic life through his taste for public entertainments, feasts and ceremonies, beginning with those marking his election, and also decreed that Jubilees would henceforth be held every quarter century, but did not live to see the one he planned for 1475.

His successor, Francesco della Rovere, was a Franciscan professor and famous preacher, who had risen to become general of the order in 1464 and a cardinal in 1467, with the support of Cardinal Bessarion. Taking the name Sixtus IV (1471–1484), he returned to the cultural agenda of Nicholas V, allowing the re-establishment of the Roman Academy and dedicating rooms in the Vatican to a new library, increasing its holding of manuscripts, and appointing Platina as its first librarian in 1475. He constructed a new, larger papal chapel in the Vatican that became known after him as the Sistine, for which he commissioned frescoes from such leading artists as Perugino, Ghirlandaio and Botticelli, and built a new bridge over the Tiber, the Ponte Sesto. Other commissions included an extensive fresco cycle for the paupers' hospital of Santo Spirito in the Borgo, founded by Innocent III. These depicted Sixtus' mother receiving a vision of his future status, and various episodes of his life, concluding with his being admitted to Paradise by St. Peter as a reward for his charity to the inmates of the hospital.[25]

Like Paul II, Sixtus quickly repudiated a conclave pact, which in his case would have prevented the appointment of his relatives to the College of Cardinals. In December 1471 he made two of his nephews cardinals and did the same for four more in the course of his pontificate, out of a total of thirty-four new appointments. He was also known generally to favour those from his own native region of Liguria in the papal household and the Curia. This resurgence of nepotism to levels not seen since the end of the Avignon papacy reflected a more seigniorial style of papal government, similar to that of the courts of the leading Italian princes.

Popes relied increasingly on their relatives, including those not in clerical orders, for advice and counsel, rather than the cardinals, who could be hostile and factional. Family members were also frequently entrusted with the security of the pope's person, by means of appointments as prefect of Rome and governor of the Castel Sant'Angelo and with control of the papal armies, exercised through the two offices of captain general and *gonfalioner* (standard bearer) of the Church. While this provided the popes with advisors and military commanders committed to their personal interests, it also meant that papal policy became increasingly dominated by family concerns and dynastic advancement, often involving the acquisition of regional territorial power.

A striking example of where this might lead occurred under Sixtus IV. One of the few diplomatic successes of Paul II had been what was called the Pax Paolina (Pauline Peace), a defensive alliance made in 1470 between the leading powers in Italy—the kingdom of Naples, the duchy of Milan, Medici-dominated Florence, the republic of Venice and the papacy. This was undermined by the Pazzi conspiracy of April 1478, a failed coup in Florence in which the two sons of Cosimo de Medici were to be murdered while worshiping in the cathedral, and the Pazzi family and other aristocratic allies exiled from the city restored. Giuliano, the younger Medici brother, was killed, but Lorenzo survived, and his supporters quickly captured most of the conspirators, who were promptly hanged from the windows of the Palazzo Vecchio. As the anti-Medicean archbishop of Pisa was one of those summarily despatched, papal censure quickly followed, with an interdict placed on the city and war declared.[26]

One of the leading figures in the conspiracy was Girolamo Riario, a nephew of Sixtus IV (who had made him count of Imola) and who was married to a sister of the duke of Milan. The Pazzi had already replaced the Medici as papal bankers in 1474, following a decline in revenue from the alum monopoly caused by overproduction. Girolamo, by now Sixtus' close advisor in political matters, expected financial advantage for the papacy from the grateful Pazzi and revenge on the Medici who had opposed his acquiring Imola, close to the Florentine borders. Although unproven, it is generally assumed that the pope himself was aware of the plot and had given his consent.

The outcome was disastrous. Not only did the conspiracy fail, but the ensuing war from 1478 to 1480 achieved little and drove Florence into an alliance with Louis XI of France, with whom the papacy had been in dispute for most of the previous two decades. Even worse, the Turks took advantage of these events to capture Otranto and massacre its inhabitants, raising the threat of a Muslim conquest of Italy. This forced a hasty political reconciliation, followed by a crusade to recapture Otranto and exterminate its Turkish garrison.

General war broke out again in 1482, and in 1483 Girolamo Riario was also responsible for persuading his uncle to turn against another former ally, the republic of Venice, because of its ambitions in the Romagna, in which his county of Imola was located. The following year the leading Italian states combined to impose a peace, on which the papacy was scarcely consulted. These bitter wars of Sixtus IV's last years consumed resources still theoretically intended for crusading and necessitated tax increases in the Papal States, prompting riots and local revolts, along with intensified sale of offices and indulgences, further fuelling demands for reform. To these issues we must briefly turn, but not before noting that in 1488 Girolamo Riario was murdered in Imola, the victim of Medici vengeance.[27]

The restrictions imposed by the Councils of Constance and Basel, and then copied by the national churches, on the methods used by the papacy to raise its revenues made its financial position increasingly difficult. It has been calculated that in the later fifteenth century nearly seventy percent of papal income came from taxation of the Papal States. Curial offices and other appointments in the popes' gift had long been conferred only in return for prior payments from the recipient. So weakened did Sixtus IV leave papal finances that his successor, Innocent VIII (1484–1492), had to pawn the jewelled papal tiara in 1484 for 100,000 ducats and created many new and unnecessary curial offices just in order to be able to sell them. Purchasers could hope to reimburse themselves through fees or bribes from petitioners and litigants.

The doctrine of indulgences had been developed by medieval theologians, notably the Dominicans Albert the Great (d. 1280) and Thomas Aquinas (d. 1274), and was reasserted by the Council of Constance in 1415 against Wyclif's denunciation of it. An indulgence has been defined as 'the extra-sacramental remission of the temporal punishment due, in God's justice, to sin that has been forgiven, which remission is granted by the Church in the exercise of the power of the keys'.[28] Indulgences were not a means of obtaining forgiveness or replacing penitence: Instead they granted a reduction in the time a soul might have to spend in Purgatory, the existence of which was only formally defined in 1254.

In the typical scholastic argument of the period, it was held that the remission obtained by an indulgence derived from 'the treasury of merit' accumulated by the Church, above all through Christ's self-sacrifice on the Cross: 'wishing to enrich his sons with treasure, that so men might have an infinite treasure, and those who avail themselves thereof are made partakers of God's friendship', as Clement VI put it in his bull *Unigenitus* (The Only-begotten) of 1343 proclaiming this doctrine. This infinite treasure, which was to be distributed 'through blessed Peter, bearer of heaven's keys, and his successors as vicars on earth', was augmented by the life of the Virgin Mary and the merits of the saints.[29]

Bishops had been limited to issuing indulgences lasting only for a single year by the Fourth Lateran Council of 1215. Papal right to grant indulgences had no such limitation because it derived from the 'plenitude of power'. Amongst the earliest uses of indulgences had been the promotion of crusading, and they could also be earned by pilgrimage to Rome during the Jubilees, attending the liturgy and venerating the saints in the patriarchal basilicas and other specified churches of the city. Although indulgences were never sold, the requirement for an offering in return blurred the distinction.

War was not the only drain on papal finances, as the growing number of building projects in Rome required funding. These included the need for work on the basilica of St. Peter's. Constantine's original church still stood, with later additions such as a papal blessing loggia on its west face, but despite periodic repairs over the centuries it now required major restoration, or total replacement. Although work on repairing it commenced under Nicholas V, a decision was subsequently made by Julius II around 1505 to build an entirely new church. While ruinously expensive, this project typified the way the papacy was now trying to present itself.

After the centuries of absence and neglect, this involved a renewed emphasis on the ties between the popes and their city of Rome. The Rome this envisioned was not the scruffy and diminished city to which Martin V had returned in 1420 but an idealised amalgam of the ancient capital of the Roman empire and a new papal city. From this arose not only the grandiose building projects that required the services of the leading architects of the day and which employed styles revived from classical antiquity but also the patronage of scholars recovering both the literature and the material remains of the ancient Roman past, upon which the new constructions might be modelled. Amongst these was Flavio Biondo of Forli (died 1463), who was secretary to all the popes from Eugenius IV to Pius II and is regarded as the father of archaeology. His *Roma Ristaurata* (Rome Restored) was the first attempt at a topology of the city, combining both its monuments of antiquity and its principal Christian remains. He also wrote a history covering the whole span from the end of the Roman empire up to 1440.

Although the wife of Count Girolamo Riario was governing the Castel Sant'Angelo when Sixtus IV died in August 1484, the family had no hope of seeing its leading ecclesiastical representative, Cardinal Giuliano della Rovere, succeed him. So unpopular had Sixtus' regime become that the family properties and those of his Genoese favourites were sacked by a Roman mob. In the conclave, the first to be held in the new Sistine Chapel, Cardinal della Rovere worked to secure the election of the amiable but lightweight Giovanni Batista Cibo as a candidate acceptable to all factions in the conclave. Duly elected, Cibo took the name Innocent VIII. Born in Genoa, he had been brought up in Naples, where his father had been a diplomat and where he produced two illegitimate children, before proceeding to a career in the higher clergy as bishop in 1467 and cardinal in 1473.

Innocent VIII broke with Cardinal della Rovere after being persuaded by him into a disastrous attempt to support rebels against King Ferrante of Naples in 1485. This resulted in the loss of the annual tribute due from the kingdom and a disadvantageous peace in 1486, prompting Innocent to ally himself instead with the Medici, enemies of the della Rovere. He married one of his own sons to a daughter of Lorenzo de Medici (died 1493), now the undisputed master of Florence, and also made the latter's son Giovanni a cardinal in 1489, although he was only aged thirteen. This was kept secret, until he was sixteen, now the legal age at which the office could be held. Equally astute was a treaty in 1489 with the Turkish Sultan Bayazid II (1481–1512), who sent him the relic of the Holy Lance, said to have been used in the Crucifixion, and an annual payment of 40,000 ducats for keeping hostage his younger brother Cem, who had taken refuge in Christian territory following defeat in a succession struggle. Thus papal finances were enhanced, while Innocent's introduction of a new apostolic secretariat improved the working of the administration.

THE BORGIA POPE: ALEXANDER VI

A lengthy illness, in which he was said to have consumed only human milk, preceded the death of Innocent VIII in July 1492, the year of the fall of Granada and Columbus's first voyage to the Americas. The ensuing conclave saw Cardinal Rodrigo Borgia elected as Alexander VI (1492–1503), although he was the only non-Italian in an electorate of twenty-three cardinals, of whom eight were nephews of former popes. Thirty-five years as cardinal had provided him with much wealth, numerous offices and several palaces, all of which were offered to fellow members of the college in return for their votes in the conclave.[30] He held sixteen bishoprics in Spain alone, and his office of vice chancellor was the most lucrative post in the Curia.

His pontificate has long been regarded as the most scandalous and dissolute of any pope, certainly since the tenth century. His conduct came in for criticism in his own lifetime, but this was as nothing to how it was regarded in the centuries that followed. He and members of his family were accused of murdering many who stood in their way, and the pope's death in August 1503 and the simultaneous illness of his son Cesare were quickly attributed to a botched attempt on their part to poison one of the cardinals.[31]

They were also seen as habitually corrupt and dissolute, treating faith with scorn and devotion with cynicism. Around 1655 a later pope ordered the destruction of a painting by Pinturicchio, depicting Alexander VI kneeling before the Madonna and Child, because it was rumoured that the model for the Virgin Mary had been Alexander's mistress, Giulia Farnese. Two fragments of this were reported as still in existence in the 1940s, one of which, depicting the infant Jesus, has recently been rediscovered.[32]

For the Catholic Church in the centuries following, almost anything that might have to do with the Borgias was treated with the utmost caution, as likely to involve elements of scandal that could be used by Protestant controversialists and anticlericals. Thus, the tower and apartments added to the Vatican Palace by Alexander VI and wonderfully decorated for him by Pinturicchio were long excluded from tourist itineraries. In 1885, the unexpected discovery of the register of official letters of Alexander by a group of Austro-Hungarian scholars, who had obtained permission to visit the then entirely neglected archive in the Lateran, led to its immediate closure on the orders of Pope Leo XIII, with armed guards being placed on the doors and the rapid transfer of all the documents to the greater safety of the Vatican's Secret (i.e., private) Archive.[33]

The knowledge that there existed a manuscript diary by Johann Burchard, the master of ceremonies of the papal court for most of the pontificates of Innocent VIII and Alexander VI, expected to contain all sorts of intimate details and startling revelations, was another cause for scholarly excitement and Vatican apprehension. The book was 'kept under lock and key like some demon it was dangerous to let loose'.[34] Although a fascinating source, what it describes are the processions, diplomatic receptions and liturgical ceremonies in which its author was involved, often recording his objections to breaches in protocol.[35] Apart from mention of the presence of fifty naked courtesans at a banquet in the pope's presence hosted by his son Cesare in 1501, there is little in the diary to cause even the slightest shock.[36]

Burchard's narrative illustrates the increasing ceremoniousness of the papal court in this period, with great attention to protocol and careful stage managing of events to emphasise the different ranks of the participants and the symbolic significance of each gesture and movement. Music, especially vocal, took on a greater part in both liturgical ceremonies and court entertainments, and the size and magnificence of Sixtus IV's new papal chapel allowed for larger numbers of choristers and more elaborate forms of worship in the palace as well as in the great basilicas of the city.

If Alexander VI was rare amongst popes in continuing to live openly with his mistresses and in producing nine illegitimate children during his years as cardinal and pope, this did not detract from his attention to his ecclesiastical duties, which he took seriously, if with a love of show and magnificence. Burchard records how Alexander chose to wait outside St. Peter's for half an hour while the Holy Door, a bricked-up entry into St. Peter's only used in Jubilee years, was fully opened to mark the proclamation of the Holy Year of 1500, rather than knock out a few token bricks and then proceed into the basilica through the normal door.[37] His personal tastes, including a fondness for sardines, were frugal.

Politically, his pontificate was marked by his reaction to French intervention in Italy and by his efforts to establish his children in positions of power in Italian society. With strong Aragonese ties of his own, he was far more favourable than his immediate predecessors to the kings of Naples and recognised the succession of Ferrante's son Alfonso II (1494–1495). He also used their friendship to advance his children, for example, by marrying his son Joffre, who thereby became prince of Squillace, to an illegitimate daughter of King Alfonso.

The claim to the kingdom of Naples of the displaced Angevin line had been inherited by the senior branch of the French royal house of Valois, and in 1494 Charles VIII (1483–1498) led an army into Italy to pursue it. Encouraging the jovial but not very able French king was Cardinal Giuliano della Rovere, whose own ambitions were threatened by the Borgia papacy and who had gone into exile at Charles's court early in Alexander's pontificate. The noble factions of the Orsini and the Colonna in Rome also conspired with Charles, and again there was talk of a general council to depose the pope.

No Italian state was strong enough by itself to resist the French king, who was also allied to the duke of Milan. The French army had to be allowed to pass through the Papal States and Rome without resistance, though Alexander took the precaution of moving into the Castel Sant'Angelo, where he had new palatial apartments constructed, during the royal visit. His son, Cesare, then a cardinal, was taken as a hostage but quickly escaped as the French overran Naples with little resistance. Alfonso II fled, abdicating in favour of his illegitimate son Ferrantino (1495–1496). Meanwhile, however, papal diplomacy had been putting together an alliance that became known as the Holy League, consisting of the new emperor, Maximilian I (1493–1519), the kingdoms of Castile and Aragón, the duchy of Milan and the republic of Venice. Faced with this, Charles VIII had to withdraw rapidly from Naples and fight his way back over the Alps, before dying three years later after hitting his head on a doorpost.

Charles's claim and his kingdom were inherited by his more effective and ruthless cousin, Louis XII (1498–1515), who invaded Italy in 1499 to pursue the claim to Naples and for revenge on Lodovico Sforza the Moor, the duke of Milan (1494–1499), who had deserted Charles VIII in 1495. The duchy fell quickly and remained in French hands until 1511. In the circumstances the pope had no option but to consent to annul the king's marriage, as Louis demanded, and permit him to marry his predecessor's widow so as to strengthen his claim to the throne, despite the ludicrous and obscene grounds on which the case was based.

The Holy League of 1495 no longer functioned, and by the Treaty of Granada of 1500, Louis XII and King Fernando II of Aragón, ruler of Sicily, agreed to divide the kingdom of Naples. In this Alexander VI was given no say, and the last independent king was dispossessed by the Franco–Spanish alliance in 1501. Then, after a falling out between them, the Spanish easily overran the whole kingdom in 1504, reuniting it with Sicily. This was formalised by papal recognition in 1510. Thereafter the kingdom was ruled from Spain through viceroys until 1714. These events mark the end of the troubled legacy resulting from the papal investiture of the house of Anjou with the kingdom of Sicily in 1266.

In the later years of his pontificate, Alexander VI became more concerned with the inheritances of his children. For his daughter, the unfairly notorious Lucrezia (1480–1519), subject of much scurrilous and largely ill-founded gossip, this was to be achieved through marriage, ultimately to the heir to the duchy of Ferrara. In 1497 Alexander gave the papal fiefs of Benevento and Terracina as heritable property to his eldest son, Juan, who also held the Aragonese title of duke of Gandia. However, Juan was murdered in Rome later that year; gossip attributed responsibility to Cesare, who was also blamed for the killing of one of his sister's husbands in 1499, but neither charge was proven. Cesare did use his brother's death to resign as cardinal and was thereafter his father's principal military commander, as captain general of the Church.

The Papal States now consisted of four distinct territories, with a few detached additions. Firstly, there was the original Patrimony of St. Peter around Rome, while, secondly, to the west of this lay the duchy of Spoleto. Both of these fronted to the south onto the kingdom of Naples, which contained some small papal enclaves such as Benevento. Thirdly, north and east of Spoleto, on the other side of the Apennines from Rome, was the March of Ancona, and, fourthly, north of that lay the Romagna, extending up to Ravenna, of which papal as opposed to imperial overlordship had been achieved in the fourteenth century. Romagna had acquisitive neighbours, Florence to the west and Venice to the north, and was the most volatile as well as distant of papal lands.

Within these four larger territories were numerous smaller political and administrative units, including major cities such as Bologna, whose local rulers paid tax to Rome but ignored papal lordship whenever possible. They were formally incorporated into the papal administration by being appointed as vicars for the lands and settlements they controlled but could never be fully trusted. Alexander VI and his son's ambition was to turn the Romagna into a heritable duchy for Cesare, through the elimination of these vicars.

By the ruthless methods later applauded by Niccolò Machiavelli in *The Prince* (1532), this is what Cesare had almost achieved by the time malaria laid low him and his father in August 1503. The pope died, and his son was too ill to manipulate the ensuing conclave, which elected an elderly and ailing nephew of Pius II, who became Pius III, but his death less than a month later opened the way to a second conclave, from which emerged the Borgias' most formidable opponent, Cardinal Giuliano della Rovere, as Julius II (1503–1513).

THE TERRIFYING POPE: JULIUS II

The death of his father completely undermined Cesare Borgia, who soon had to take refuge in Spain, where he was killed in 1507. Other members of the family suffered less, though the Borgia estates in the Romagna became papal property and an anti-Spanish reaction briefly gripped Rome. The new pope, whose own parentage was a matter of gossip, followed his predecessor's methods. He made advantageous marriages for his daughter Felice, one of three born while he was a cardinal, and a branch of the family inherited the duchy of Urbino in the Papal States in 1508, holding it until 1631.[38] Although he forbade offering financial incentives in conclaves, it was rumoured that his own election had been secured by bribery, and he ignored a conclave pact to call a general council within two years.

Julius II is now best remembered as the patron of Michelangelo, who worked on the pope's tomb in the Church of San Pietro in Vinculis. He also commissioned Donato Bramante to start work in 1506 on a new St. Peter's to replace the Constantinian basilica, and hired Raphael to decorate parts of the Vatican, not least with a fresco of Gregory IX with the facial features of Julius II issuing his collection of decretals. Raphael also painted a remarkable portrait of a bearded Julius which seemed so lifelike that after his death visitors were frightened that he had come back from the dead.[39]

Julius, who became known as *il papa terribile*, was determined to restore the frontiers of the Papal States to their fullest extent, in particular to reimpose papal rule on Perugia and Bologna, and recover territories in the Romagna overrun by Venice in 1503. He put himself at the head of his armies, even when simultaneously afflicted with gout and syphilis, and by diplomacy and military action drove the Venetians out of the Romagna by 1508. In 1506 he expelled the Bentivoglio dynasty from Bologna and regained control of Perugia.

Aiming next to end French control of Milan, he reversed his alliances in 1510, recognising Spanish sovereignty over Naples and joining with Venice and Spain in a new Holy League in 1511. Louis XII reacted by reissuing the Pragmatic Sanction of Bourges, limiting papal rights over the French church and supporting a small group of dissident cardinals who called a general council at Pisa in 1511 to depose Julius, electing one of themselves as Martin VI, though he was never recognised by any secular power. As their call for a reform council was viewed sympathetically by the emperor Maximilian, Julius pre-empted it by calling the Fifth Lateran Council. Attended almost entirely by Italians, this condemned the Concilabulum (the little talking shop) of Pisa and annulled the Pragmatic Sanction.[40]

The authority of the rival councils depended entirely on the fluctuating military and diplomatic situation. A weakening of French power in northern Italy forced the Council of Pisa to move to Milan, and finally to Lyon.[41] The five cardinals who supported it were excommunicated, and in December 1513, after Julius's death, Louis XII repudiated it, repealed the Pragmatic Sanction and recognised the Fifth Lateran Council, which remained in session until 1517, and finally prohibited the use of bribery in papal elections.[42]

Julius's last years saw the Papal States expand, with the capture of Modena (1510) and Parma and Piacenza (1512), and the French ejected from Italy. While making papal rule a reality in the Papal States, Julius's campaigns, in which he took a vigorous part to the end of his life, attracted growing criticism across Europe from those who felt this was not the kind of leadership expected of a pope. In the satirical dialogue 'Julius Excluded from Heaven', quoted early in this chapter, the pope, arriving at the gates of Heaven with twenty thousand soldiers killed in his wars, boasts to St. Peter of his achievements:

> JULIUS: You must still be dreaming of that ancient church in which, with a few starving bishops, you yourself, a pontiff shivering with cold, were exposed to poverty, sweat, dangers and a thousand other trials. But now time has changed everything for the better . . . if you could only see life in Rome today: all the cardinals in purple, attended by whole regiments of retainers, the horses more than fit for a king, the mules decked in fine cloth, gold and jewels, some even shod with gold and silver! If you could catch a glimpse of the supreme pontiff, carried aloft in a golden chair on the shoulders of his men, while the people on all sides pay homage at a wave of his hand; if you could hear the thunder of the cannon, the blare of the cornets, the blasting of the horns, see the flashes of the guns, and hear the applause of the people, the cheers, the whole scene lit by gleaming torches, even the greatest princes barely permitted to kiss

the blessed foot . . . if you could see and hear all this, what would you say?

PETER: That I was looking at a tyrant worse than any in the world, the enemy of Christ, the bane of the church.[43]

When St. Peter refuses to admit Julius into Heaven, the pope threatens to storm Heaven and expel Peter. Criticisms like this of the contemporary papacy were mild compared with those to come.

chapter 16

BEAUTIFUL AS A DOVE

(1513–1572)

THE PAPACY AND THE HAPSBURGS

The Sistine Chapel in the Vatican had been the venue for all conclaves since 1484. The cardinals were housed inside the chapel itself in specially constructed cubicles ranged along the wall, but later in the sixteenth century when the college had increased in size, these were erected in the corridors next to the chapel, where the voting itself took place, as it still does. In the ballot for cubicles it was thought particularly lucky to get the one underneath the fresco by Perugino depicting Christ handing the keys to St. Peter. This was occupied by Julius II in the conclave of 1503, and would be similarly fortunate for Clement VII in 1523 and Paul III in 1534, though it did not guarantee a successful pontificate.

Julius II was the last pope able to play an effective independent military role in Italy, and even he had been successful as much through diplomacy as siegecraft. The early sixteenth century saw France and the empire struggling for control of northern Italy. The succession of a grandson of the emperor Maximilian I to the kingdoms of Castile (1506) and Aragón (1516) brought Spain and its growing empire in the New World together with the kingdoms of Sicily and Naples under Hapsburg rule. Despite a Franco-papal attempt to find an alternative candidate, the same young man would also be elected emperor of the Holy Roman Empire of the German Nation in 1521, securing his family's de facto monopoly of the imperial title until its abolition in 1806.

The new emperor, Charles V (1521–1556), was determined on preventing his French rival, Francis I (1514–1547), from securing his claim to Milan and on imposing imperial suzerainty over most states of northern Italy. The result was a succession of conflicts between the two that continued intermittently until France became engulfed in civil wars from 1562 onwards. Long before then, the question of dominance in northern Italy had been settled in the Hapsburgs' favour at the battle of Pavia in 1525, after which Francis I had become the emperor's prisoner, and had to be ransomed.

What had been the papacy's political nightmare in the thirteenth century became a reality in the sixteenth, with empire and *regno* (the unified kingdom of Sicily and Naples) united for the first time since 1254. In the circumstances this was far less of a threat to the independence of the papacy than in the earlier period, but since the time of the Great Schism the emperors had been amongst the foremost advocates of general councils for the reform of the Church, and thus closely associated with conciliarist theory and attempts to impose limits on the papal plenitude of power.

On the other hand, two powerful shared interests should have prompted close cooperation between pope and emperor in the 1520s. The first of these was containing the rapid spread of the new ideas of Martin Luther and Huldrich Zwingli on the reform of religion that were having their strongest impact at this time in imperial territories. The second was the seemingly unstoppable Ottoman conquests menacing the eastern borders of the empire. Belgrade fell in 1521, in 1526 the Hungarians were decisively defeated at the battle of Mohács and in 1529 Vienna was besieged for the first time. In fact, Vienna marked the limit of the Ottoman expansion, but nobody could have known that at the time. Unavailingly, successive popes planned crusades and appealed to the rulers of Western Europe to make peace amongst themselves so as to focus on the Islamic threat, but papal diplomacy itself contributed to the disunity of Christendom.

A surprisingly speedy conclave in 1513 saw the election of the first Florentine pope, Giovanni de' Medici, the son of Lorenzo the Magnificent, who took the name of Leo X (1513–1521) to signal that he would be a reformer and defender of the Church like Leo IX

(1049–1054). He had also been ruler of Florence since his family returned from an eighteen-year exile in 1512, and preserving Medici control of the city was a major objective for him. It was a concern shared by his cousin Giulio, whom he made a cardinal and vice chancellor of the Roman church, and who in 1519 became ruler of Florence, as well as its archbishop. Narrowly failing to be elected on Leo's death, Giulio became pope as Clement VII (1523–1534) in the bitterly fought conclave that followed the brief pontificate of Hadrian VI (1522–1523).

Both Medici popes hoped short-lived French interventions in Milan would produce a counterweight to Hapsburg power in Italy, and also feared that failure to support Francis I could lead to his helping the exiled leaders of the Florentine republic of 1494–1512. Leo X was the more astute in his shifting alliances, joining Charles V, Aragón and England against France in 1513, then coming to terms with Francis I in 1515, before finally switching back to an imperial alliance in 1521. Hadrian VI, who had been Grand Inquisitor in Spain was consistently pro-Hapsburg, but Clement VII took the papacy back into alliance with Francis I in 1524, changed sides after the French defeat at the battle of Pavia in 1525, but then joined a new alliance of France, Venice and Milan against Charles V in 1526, just when the emperor was trying to cope with the Turkish victory in Hungary.

The last of these diplomatic realignments proved fatal. The new alliance, known as the League of Cognac, provided no assistance when imperial troops, mostly Swiss and German mercenaries with some Spanish contingents, besieged Rome. Although their commander was killed by a stray shot, they broke into the city in July 1527 and sacked it. There was an immediate massacre, only ended when the soldiers realised it was more profitable to keep their victims alive for ransom. How many died is uncertain, but a Spanish soldier remembered supervising the burial of over 10,000 corpses along one bank of the Tiber.[1] The population of Rome is thought to have been halved.

The ensuing occupation of the city until August 1528 allowed prolonged looting and further killing, sometimes exacerbated by religious differences, as many of the Swiss and German soldiers supported the new Protestant reform. The Sapienza University, founded by Boniface VIII in 1303, was left in ruins, as was some of the papal palace. The Vatican Library only survived because it was used for accommodation by the officers of the occupying army. After it was over, a contemporary diarist wrote, 'Hell itself was a more beautiful sight to behold.'[2]

Clement had taken refuge in the Castel Sant'Angelo, but in June 1528 agreed to pay the huge ransom of 400,000 ducats. He raised most of this with difficulty, before fleeing bankrupt from Rome in December 1528. Although Charles was shocked by reports of the sack, he increased the sufferings of the city by refusing to pay his soldiers, until they too began to starve and die of disease in the summer heat.

A short papal-imperial rapprochement followed, allowing Charles's coronation at Bologna in February 1530, the last crowning performed by a pope. Later in his pontificate, Clement resumed his independent diplomacy, entering into secret negotiations with Francis and in 1533 visiting France to attend the wedding of his great niece, Catherine de' Medici, to the king's son and eventual successor, Henry II (1547–1559). But he resisted French suggestions of removing the papacy once more to Avignon. In general Clement's reputation has suffered from the disastrous results of his diplomacy, and he has been called 'without doubt the most ill-fated pontiff that ever sat on the papal throne'.[3]

Subsequent popes generally accepted Hapsburg dominance in Italy, especially as France became less viable as an alternative. Spaniards were often the focus of popular dislike in Rome, with memories of the sack of 1527 still strong, and the Neapolitan pope Paul IV (1555–1559) resented not only their rule in his homeland but felt he had been personally slighted when serving as legate in Castile. This led him to enter another of the recurring Franco-Hapsburg wars and try to eject the Spanish from Naples, with disastrous results. His small army was quickly defeated and the Spanish viceroy, the duke of Alba, invaded the Papal States. The resulting peace treaty was generous only because of the new Spanish king Philip II's respect for the papal office.

After this conflict, known from Paul IV's family name as the Carafa war of 1555/6, and the outbreak of the civil wars in France, papal reliance on Spain became almost absolute until the end of the century, not least because of shared views on the need to contain the spread of Protestantism. It was fortified by growing economic dependence as the population of Rome mushroomed. Estimated at around 20,000 in the late fifteenth century, it had risen to about 100,000 by the end of the sixteenth. This was not self-sustaining, especially in the frequent years of poor harvests in the 1580s and 1590s. Then, the city had to rely on shipments of grain from Spain and Spanish-ruled Sicily, Naples and Sardinia, adding to Philip II's leverage over the papacy.[4]

PAPACY AND REFORMATION

Papal revenues were decreasing almost as quickly as new expenditure on wars, construction projects in Rome and the lifestyle of the papal court was rising. In particular Leo X had inherited the grandiose project of Julius II for a new St. Peter's and was desperate to raise money for a crusade against the Turks. Equally short of funds was Albrecht of Brandenburg (died 1545), archbishop of Mainz and Magdeburg and administrator of the see of Halberstadt. In 1517 he owed his bankers the huge fees he had given the pope for the dispensations needed to hold this plurality of benefices, and so was keen to promote the special indulgence recently proclaimed by Leo X towards funding the building of St. Peter's, as he could keep half the revenue from it raised in Germany for himself.

Earlier qualms about selling indulgences and care in defining their purposes had now given way to high-pressure salesmanship, with fixed tariffs replacing voluntary offerings. By the instructions Archbishop Albrecht issued to the Dominican friar Johann Tetzel (d. 1519), in charge of preaching the new indulgence, lay rulers were to pay twenty-five gold guilders per indulgence, as were bishops. Abbots, counts and barons would be charged ten and lesser nobles and clerics six. Ordinary members of the laity should pay either one or half a guilder depending on income.[5] Tetzel himself was later accused of claiming that indulgences would provide remission even for a sexual assault on the Blessed Virgin Mary and could be bought to gain forgiveness for sins not yet committed.

Some of the German princes, such as the Elector Frederick of Saxony, refused to let indulgence sellers into their states, and it was in the Saxon university of Wittenberg that on 31 October 1517 the Augustinian canon and theology professor Martin Luther (1483–1546) posted on the door of its cathedral ninety-five theses for debate that were critical of the theory and practice of the indulgence. These included the propositions that 'if the pope knew the exactions of the preachers of indulgences he would rather have St. Peter's basilica reduced to ashes than built with the skin, flesh and bones of his sheep' (thesis 50), that the pope would willingly sell St. Peter's 'to give of his own to the poor' (51) and that the pope's wealth so far exceeded that of the richest of other individuals that he could 'build one single basilica of St. Peter out of his own money, rather than out of the money of the faithful poor' (86).⁶ It was the particular misfortune of the papacy in this period that it had engaged in a programme of promoting itself through magnificence for which it could not pay and so had to rely on the very expedients that idealists such as Luther thought it would never condone.

If Luther believed that the pope, once properly informed, would justify his optimistic expectations, he was quickly disabused. Albrecht of Brandenburg, now a cardinal, sent a report on Luther's theses to Leo X. As the doctrine of indulgences was almost impossible to defend, it was decided that Luther should be charged with heresy, for questioning papal authority. He was summoned to a Diet of the states of the empire in Augsburg in October 1518, where the papal legate Cardinal Thomas Cajetan (1468–1534) ordered him to recant, and on his refusal Luther was smuggled out of the city by night for fear of arrest.

In November 1518 Luther issued an appeal to a general council and began studying the history of the papacy and contemporary polemical pamphlets such as 'Julius Excluded from Heaven', for arguments on the superiority of conciliar authority to that of the pope. Resort to conciliarism had long been the standard response for those in dispute with the papacy, but Luther took a more radical position after a debate at Leipzig with the Dominican Johan Eck in July 1519. When taunted by Eck with sharing the ideas of Jan Hus, who had been burned for heresy by the Council of Constance in 1415, Luther became convinced that general councils could also fall into error, and that Scripture was the only reliable source of authority, as Hus and Wyclif had argued. In 1520 he wrote, 'We are all Hussites without knowing it.'[7]

In the same year Luther published tracts, such as *Address to the Christian Nobility of the German Nation,* in which he attacked 'the Romanists' and argued that the Church in Germany could only be saved by the complete destruction of papal authority, and in particular the abolition of indulgences, dispensations, excommunications, the payment of annates, clerical celibacy, Jubilee years and Masses for the dead. He criticised the wealth of the cardinals and urged the reform of the university curriculum, away from medieval scholastic theology and in favour of study of the Bible. Throughout he adopted a strongly nationalist tone, and often revisited episodes in the German past to expose the damage inflicted by the papacy, as in his tract *Against the Roman Papacy, an Institution of the Devil* (1545), where he depicts a diabolically inspired Clement IV beheading with his own hands the praying Conradin, last of the Staufen dynasty.[8]

Protection by his own ruler, the elector Frederick III the Wise of Saxony (1486–1525), was vital for Luther's survival and the spread of the movement of reform to which his writing and preaching gave rise. In 1494, the Dominican friar Girolamo Savonarola (1452–1498) had become de facto leader of a new Florentine republic thanks to his preaching against clerical abuses, including the sale of indulgences, and immorality. He too demanded the return to a more scripturally based faith, but his attack on pleasures such as gambling, music and fine clothes—symbolised by a 'bonfire of the vanities' in 1497—alienated popular opinion in the city and led to his being handed over to the Inquisition for burning.[9]

Luther's support in many parts of Germany, as well as his native Saxony, was more firmly grounded than that of Savonarola. On 15 June 1520 Leo X issued the bull *Exsurge Domine* (Arise O Lord) condemning forty-one of Luther's theses, ordering his writings to be burned and giving him two months in which to submit or face excommunication. Luther's response was equally dramatic: holding a burning of his own at Wittenberg in which books of canon law and papal decretals were consigned to the flames, along with a copy of the pope's bull. He declared that Leo X had condemned the Gospels. His excommunication followed in January 1521, but he and his growing number of followers were beyond the power of Rome.

Although often seen primarily through the dramatic clash of ideas and personalities represented by Luther and his opponents in the years from 1517 to 1521, the Reformation in Germany was clearly more deeply rooted than a narrative focussed on the contribution of a single individual would suggest. Luther's contemporary Huldrich Zwingli (1484–1531) in Zurich claimed independent inspiration for his theological ideas and a similar programme of reform. The widespread support that Luther received in many parts of Germany from all sectors of society also argues for deep dissatisfaction with the contemporary state of the Church and the role played in it by the papacy.

In part the problem lay with the direction the papacy had taken ever since the twelfth century. It had become an increasingly large and complex legal, financial and administrative organisation in which the pastoral and spiritual priorities once advocated by Gregory the Great and Bernard of Clairvaux played little part. The laity could not look to the papacy for that kind of leadership, nor did it play a role in popular piety. No pope since Leo IX (1049–1054) had been venerated for his sanctity, except for Gregory X (1271–1276), who enjoyed a purely local cult around Arezzo. Most of the few medieval popes now recognised as saints would not be so proclaimed until the late nineteenth century.[10]

The papacy's conflicts with secular rulers, often seen by their subjects as embodying their national identity, caused tensions between political and ecclesiastical loyalties. These conflicts increasingly resolved themselves in favour of the king rather than the pope. Such was especially the case in France, but German patriotism was the most potent source of princely and popular backing for Luther when he was confronted by the popes and the predominantly Italian cardinals. Crusading taxes, such as that of 1502, which were never spent on their intended purpose, became a particular source of discontent. Even the clergy, whose superiority to the laity had been established and guaranteed by the papacy from the time of Gregory VII, were increasingly alienated by its taxation, scandals and bureaucratic abuses. The grandiose papal building programmes in Rome since the end of the Great Schism, knowledge of which was spread by the rising flow of visitors to the city, only added to a mistaken belief that this was an institution rolling in money.

A rather similar situation had existed in the early thirteenth century, which had witnessed a rise in popular piety that went hand in hand with growing criticism of the conduct and privileges of the clergy. In some areas this led to the spread of movements such as the Waldenses and the Cathars that offered their members stricter more devout lives, even if the theology behind them was not orthodox. At that time the newly established Inquisition, faith in the ideals of crusade and the rise of the mendicant friars, the Dominicans and Franciscans, helped contain the lay discontent.

In the early sixteenth century the wealthy monastic orders were once again the object of popular derision, especially the longest established of them, and even the friars fell under suspicion of being avaricious and uninterested in the pastoral care of the laity. Their involvements as inquisitors and indulgence sellers added to popular distaste. In his *Praise of Folly* of 1511 the Dutch scholar Desiderius Erasmus (d. 1536) satirised 'those who are popularly called "Religious" or "Monks". Both names are false, since most of them are a long way removed from religion'.[11] New lay communities provided an outlet for piety that the orders were no longer thought capable of satisfying.

Lay piety was becoming ever more intense. A movement known as *Devotio Moderna* (Modern Devotion) spread from Holland in the late fourteenth century to become influential in many parts of Germany and in Italy. It stressed the importance of the interior life for clergy and laity alike, not least through intense reflection on the sufferings of Christ, called for a more spiritual priesthood and criticised reliance on purely external acts as the route to salvation. Its best-known literary product was the widely read *Imitation of Christ* by Thomas à Kempis (died 1471), and its spiritual ideals are reflected in paintings showing contemporaries participating in scenes from the life of Christ, particularly the Nativity and the Passion. Lay communities, known as the

Brethren of the Common Life, formed under its influence and founded schools, one of which had a powerful influence on the upbringing of the austere Dutch pope Hadrian VI (1522–1523).

A backlash was also underway against the theology and philosophy long taught in the universities of Western Europe. The dominant Scholasticism of the age of Thomas Aquinas (1225–1274) and Duns Scotus (1266–1308) was under attack for its dogmatic certainties and mechanical methods of argument, out of fashion in an age that valued interior spirituality and intellectual exploration. Recovery of the classical past also included new interest in earlier Christian authors. Bernard of Clairvaux, not least in his criticism of the papal court, was an influence on Luther, but even more so was St. Augustine (d. 430).[12] He was one of many authors to benefit from the printing revolution, with numerous editions of his works being published from the 1470s onwards for a growing readership. His ideas on the unearned nature of divine grace as the sole requisite for salvation undermined the dominant emphasis of the late medieval church on the need for good works and the provision of remedies, such as indulgences, pardons and dispensations to wipe away sins that in the Augustinian scheme were indelible without grace. Added to a reading of Paul, above all *The Epistle to the Romans,* this led Luther to his conviction that justification, that is to say salvation, could be obtained through faith alone.

Search for reform and revival in religious life was far from being a predominantly northern European phenomenon. The new piety led to the forming of oratories, groups mainly of aristocrats meeting for regular prayer, in several Italian cities including Rome. These decades also saw the founding of new religious orders such as the Theatines (1524), Capuchins (1528) and Barnabites (1530) for men and the Ursulines (1535) for women, but in their early stages such associations could be suspected of Protestant tendencies or of seeking direct 'illumination' from the Holy Spirit in defiance of the authority structures and sacramental practices of the Church. Thus one of the founders of the Barnabites, St. Anthony Zaccaria (canonized 1897), was twice investigated for heresy, as was Countess Ludovica Torelli, the patroness of the new order.[13] This was a sign of things to come, with the rulers of the Church perturbed by lay enthusiasm that was not firmly regulated by the clergy, and by extremes of reforming zeal in the religious orders that criticised authority.

Particularly significant amongst the new orders of the mid-sixteenth century was the Company of Jesus, the Jesuits. Formed in 1539 by the Basque nobleman Ignatius Loyola (1491–1556), this developed from a group of six disciples in Paris, who followed a set of spiritual exercises of his devising and who agreed either to go to Palestine to try to convert Muslims or to put themselves at the disposal of the pope. On 27 September 1540, Paul III established them as a society for 'the propagation of the faith', whose fully professed members had to take a 'Fourth Vow, which made Jesuits available for missions from the pope', on top of the normal three monastic vows of poverty, chastity and obedience.[14] Two of the original six appeared amongst the most forthright defenders of papal authority in the Council of Trent, and by the 1580s the Jesuits were being called the 'black horsemen of the pope'.

We have seen how the papacy of the age of Alexander VI and Julius II attracted criticism. Erasmus was explicit in condemning such popes and their Curia in *Praise of Folly*:

> a grain of the salt Christ spoke of would suffice to rid them of all their wealth and honours, their sovereignty and triumphs, their many offices, dispensations, taxes and indulgences, all their horses and mules, their retinue and countless pleasures. In place of all this it would bring vigils, fasts, tears, prayers, sermons, study, sighs and a thousand unpleasant hardships of that kind. Nor must we overlook what this will lead to. Countless scribes, copyists, clerks, lawyers, advocates, secretaries, muleteers, grooms, bankers and pimps . . . would be left to starve.[15]

THE CATHOLIC REFORMATION

The focusing of the Protestant reformers' criticisms of the current state of the Church on its papal leadership led those who opposed their view into rallying to its defence. The papacy came to be valued and extolled by one side the more it was reviled by the other, and as attitudes hardened and the divide became irreconcilable, so did writings about the authority of the holder of the papal office become more effusive. For example, in the preface to his *De Auctoritate et Potestate Romani Pontificis in Ecclesia Dei* (On the Authority and Power of the Roman Pontiff in the Church of God) of 1555, Bishop Tommaso Campeggi, son of one cardinal and brother of another, told Paul IV,

> Because of truth, mercy and justice, the right hand of the Lord has miraculously led you, O Paul, Best and Greatest of Pontiffs. His justice and judgement are in the preparation of your seat. The Lord has gone before you in blessings and has placed upon your head the crown of precious stones. The Lord has dressed you in the vestments of salvation, and with the raiment of justice has he surrounded you; like a bride he has adorned you with a crown and like a spouse ornamented you with his jewels.[16]

But not all were ready to go as far as Campeggi in allowing unlimited authority to the pope.

Several leading cardinals of the first half of the sixteenth century were prepared to challenge old certainties. These included Luther's interrogator, Cardinal Thomas Cajetan, who was a committed papalist but also held that divorce should be permitted, doubted the material existence of Hell and supported the use of vernacular liturgy. Other cardinals wished to enlarge their role in church government, making the popes more dependent on their council and consent. The college was again spoken of as the senate of the Church, but the influence of the cardinals was diminished by a dramatic increase in their numbers.[17] In 1517, following a dispute over a promotion, an embittered Cardinal Alfonso Petrucci (1491–1517) plotted with a papal doctor to poison Leo X. When indiscreet letters were intercepted, he was imprisoned in the Castel Sant'Angelo, confessed and was strangled, but Leo suspected that other cardinals were involved and so created the unprecedented number of thirty-one new cardinals, a figure not exceeded in a single consistory until 1946. This more than doubled the size of the college, which was never thereafter reduced. Sixtus V (1585–1590) established a maximum of seventy members, which would not be increased until 1959.

Other developments, such as assigning individual cardinals to act as protectors of the interests of the states in obedience to Rome also tended to divide the members of the Sacred College, as it now became known, and limit their cooperation, thus advancing papal absolutism. The enhanced power of the greater Catholic rulers also gave them more leverage in proposing cardinals from their own subjects, reinforcing the divisions in the college based on political allegiances. Sixtus V's creation in 1588 of fifteen congregations, effectively specialist ministries to which cardinals resident in Rome were assigned, helped split it further. Thus, parties and factions amongst the cardinals became increasingly common, especially as a series of short pontificates in the sixteenth century produced clearly defined groups of cardinals appointed by the successive popes, who generally thereafter remained loyal to their particular benefactor's family and who tended to act in concert in conclaves.

This tendency of the college to divide into such political or family-oriented factions was reinforced by the formalising of the role of the cardinal nephew *(cardinal nipote)*. Large-scale nepotism had been prevalent since the thirteenth century. From the mid-sixteenth century until the practice was abolished by Innocent XII (1691–1700), it became normal for the first cardinal appointed by a pope to be a close relative, usually a nephew, who received the official title of Cardinal Nephew, and through whom most day-to-day business of the papacy would be conducted, and to whom questions for decision would first be referred. One or more lay nephews would also usually be entrusted with command of the papal army and control of the Castel Sant'Angelo, the pope's refuge in time of danger and place of imprisonment for his enemies.

This system was created for someone incapable of running it. In 1550 a long and bitter conclave resulted in the election of a compromise candidate, Julius III (1550–1555). Earlier in his career he had become fond of a Neapolitan street urchin called Innocenzo, whom he persuaded his brother to adopt and who, at age eighteen, was his first appointee as cardinal, directing that all papal diplomatic and administrative affairs be sent to Innocenzo in the first instance. So incompetent did Innocenzo prove, but so devoted to him did Julius remain, that a new office of secretary of state had to be created, to enable another cardinal to carry out the actual work for him. This title was merged with the role of cardinal nephew under Paul IV (1555–1559). Innocenzo, although never stripped of the rank of cardinal, was subsequently accused of two murders and two rapes and spent several years in monastic confinement, until his death in 1577.[18]

His was not the only example of a style of curial life reminiscent of the late fifteenth century. Some long-lived cardinals survived from that colourful period. Amongst these was Alessandro Farnese, born in 1468, whose sister had been the last mistress of Alexander VI and by whom he was made a cardinal in 1493, thereafter nicknamed the petticoat cardinal. Like his benefactor he had a daughter and three sons of his own, one of whom together with a grandson were made cardinals when Farnese was elected pope as Paul III (1534–1549), and he always retained his affection for the Borgias, sending a cardinal's hat to Alexander's thirteen-year-old great-great-grandson in Spain in 1537 (who, unfortunately, died during the visit of the legation presenting it).[19] He followed their precedent in alienating papal territory to create a state for his family, installing his son Pierluigi (murdered in 1549) as duke of Parma and Piacenza in 1545. He also commissioned Michelangelo to remodel the Campidoglio, the piazza on the Capitoline formerly the seat of civil government in Rome, and design the grandest of all the noble palaces in the city, the Palazzo Farnese.

Paul III was famous for the elaborate liturgical ceremonies he developed as well as for reviving the Roman Carnival in 1536. These public spectacles and popular entertainments, together with his building and decorative programmes, were part of a deliberate scheme to enhance the uniqueness of Rome and emphasise its sacral character.[20] Plans were also made to update the fortifications of the city, after a Turkish fleet sailed into the mouth of the Tiber in 1535, but they proved too expensive to pursue. If Paul III was the last of the

Renaissance popes, he also initiated a new phase in papal history, as the promoter of the Catholic Reformation.[21]

The term is a significant one, as it implies that what has been more generally called the Counter-Reformation was not just a reaction to the criticisms made by the Lutherans and Calvinists but was instead a genuine movement of renewal of the Church from within, with older and deeper roots than the Protestant Reformation of 1517.[22] The main difficulty about initiating such a programme of internal renewal was the long-held view that fundamental reforms could only be proposed by a general council, which itself would only be legitimate if called by the pope. The popes, however, were extremely wary of councils after their experiences with those of Constance, Basel and Pisa.

The emperor Charles V, although personally unwavering in his very traditional faith, needed religious consensus or at least tranquillity within the different states of the empire, especially when facing the Turkish threat. He and many of the princes of the empire wanted a reform council, but to be credible for them it had to be held in imperial territory. France was not keen on such a venue, and Rome resisted, as it felt such a council should be held in the Papal States or at least in Italy, so that its proceedings could be properly directed and not allowed to get out of hand, as had happened with the previous imperially sponsored councils.

Attempts to hold a council in Mantua in 1537 and Vicenza in 1538 had to be abandoned, when representatives from Germany refused to attend. A solution was found with the suggestion that it be held in Trento, in Italy but also imperial territory. A first meeting there in 1542 failed because the French refused to appear, but the Council of Trent, the longest assembly of its kind in the history of the Church, finally opened in December 1545. Initial attendance was small, with only five cardinals and thirty bishops attending, but by the third sitting in 1562–1563 over two hundred bishops were present, making it much harder to control.

The event depended upon the participants, and here too Paul III played a decisive role. In twelve consistories in the course of his pontificate he appointed seventy-one new cardinals, four of whom would later become pope.[23] As was now standard, many of these cardinals were nominees of the emperor (who was also king of Spain) or of the king of France, but others included a group of reformers, closely involved with the new monastic orders and the Oratory of the Divine Love in Rome, founded in 1516. Amongst the most important of these were a group known as the *Spirituali* that included the Venetian aristocrat Gasparo Contarini (1483–1542), the English nobleman Reginald Pole (1500–1558), who was a cousin of King Henry VIII, Jacopo Sadoleto (d. 1547), Marcello Cervini (the future Marcellus II) and Gianpietro Carafa, who became Paul IV, and was one of the co-founders of the Theatine Order. Associated with them were the Neapolitan poet Vittoria Colonna (1490–1547?), a friend of Michelangelo, and the nun Giulia Gonzaga, countess of Fondi (d. 1566).

In 1536 Paul III commissioned this group of cardinals to draw up a report, submitted the next year and entitled *Concilium de Emendenda Ecclesia* (Advice on Reforming the Church). This was a blueprint for far-reaching institutional and theological change, which emphasised the need for a well-educated clergy to provide clear moral leadership for the laity and proposed curbing curial personnel and malpractices. Above all, inspiration, direction and example had to come from the top, in the hope that, as they told the pope, 'under your leadership, we may see the Church of God purged, beautiful as a dove.'[24] However, Paul III was uncertain how far to let reform develop, and disagreements developed over rival policies of conciliation and confrontation in dealing with the Protestants.

Several of the cardinals responsible for *de Emendenda Ecclesia* had been led by their reading and discussions to a view on justification through faith similar to that of Luther but without sharing his rejection of papal primacy or his reduction of the seven sacraments of the Church to the two—baptism and the Eucharist—he felt were scripturally authorised. This common ground led the most intellectually influential of the *Spirituali*, Cardinal Contarini, into discussions with leading Lutherans at Regensburg in 1541. While a formula on justification by faith was agreed, no progress could be made on the question of the sacraments, and the meeting ended in discord. This gave those opposed to compromise greater influence with the pope.

In 1542 Cardinal Carafa, whose fear of heresy had now divorced him from his earlier sympathies, persuaded the pope to revive the dormant Inquisition, with himself and five other cardinals as inquisitors general, to try to suppress the spread of Lutheran and Calvinist ideas by force. Carafa later declared that he would willingly gather the wood to burn his own father if proved to be a heretic. Given powers of arrest, distraint and execution that could only be overridden by the pope himself, the new Roman Inquisition's remit was confined to parts of Italy, as other states, including Spanish-ruled Sicily and Naples, would not permit a papal institution to operate independently within their borders. Only about a dozen people were executed for heresy by the Roman Inquisition between 1542 and 1555, though the numbers then increased under Paul IV (1555–1559) and especially under Pius V (1566–1572).[25]

This hardening of attitudes did not mark the end of a search for compromise. When the Council of Trent assembled in 1545, the papal legates sent to direct it included cardinals Pole and Cervini, who had both contributed to *de Emendenda Ecclesia*. Pole travelled in disguise, fearing assassins sent by Henry VIII, who had already executed his mother and elder brother in revenge for his published rejection of the king's new religious policy.[26] Lutheran representatives were expected at the council but never arrived.

Charles V had hoped that disciplinary matters could be discussed at the council before the more contentious doctrinal ones, but Paul III insisted that the order be reversed. A compromise was reached in the council itself, which debated doctrinal and disciplinary questions in turn. In any case, the delegates, almost all of whom were Italians, and their more numerous theological advisors were generally more conservative than their presidents. Using one of the earliest justifications for papal authority, they decreed that truth had been revealed both in scripture and through tradition passed down from the Apostles. They also pronounced that the Vulgate, the Latin version of the Bible that was largely the work of St. Jerome (d. 419), was true and authoritative, in defiance of recent criticisms of its text. Even the formula that Contarini had agreed with the Lutherans at Regensburg on justification was rejected in favour of one insisting on a combination of faith and works. Argument over this led to Pole's nervous collapse in December 1546.

The dangers of such councils from the papacy's perspective were realised in Trent's decrees that insisted that bishops be resident in their sees and forbidding the accumulation of benefices. No allowance was made for papal dispensation from these requirements, which was an embarrassment as there were around eighty to one hundred senior officials then working permanently in the Curia who were paid by the dioceses of which they were the nominal bishops. Taking fees to be allowed to hold multiple benefices was another vital papal financial strategy. To bring the council to heel, Paul III used an alleged outbreak of typhus in Trento in 1547 to order his legates to transfer it to Bologna in the Papal States. Fourteen imperial bishops, backed by Charles V, refused to move, and it was eventually accepted that the delegates in Bologna might continue discussions but could not issue decrees. Not surprisingly the pope suspended the whole council in February 1548.

The long and bitter conclave that began in November 1549 and lasted until February 1550 was the product of political divisions in the college, with factions of cardinals devoted to either French or imperial interests refusing to accept a candidate favoured by their opponents. Theological issues arising from the attempts to negotiate with the Protestants added a further dimension of conflict. Pole, who had argued strongly against the interference of secular rulers, was denounced as a heretic by Carafa when it looked as if he might be elected. As the Venetian ambassador reported, Roman bookmakers were by then giving him the shortest odds to be the next pope.[27] Regarded as acceptable to the emperor, he lost his chance by a principled refusal to be proclaimed *per adorationem* by his supporters in the middle of the night. In the ballot the next day, he was one vote short of a majority, and the arrival in Rome of more French cardinals put him out of the running for good.

The conclave, which Pole called a 'comedy, let me not say tragedy', was marked by flagrant disregard of the rules. The cardinals were attended by their cooks and their barbers, as well as their lay and clerical advisors, *conclavisti,* who acted as go-betweens with the outside world. Several *conclavisti* wrote narratives of the conclaves in which they had participated or prepared elaborate briefing papers for their employers, few of which have ever been published, that provide most of our information on these events. Feasts were held by the factions to try to win more votes, and the imperial ambassador climbed onto the roof of the Sistine Chapel to discuss the election with supportive cardinals. In the end the stench of the drains and thousands of burned candles proved so overpowering that the bloc of cardinals loyal to the Farnese family of Paul III agreed with the pro-French faction to elect Giovanni Maria Ciocchi del Monte, who took the name of Julius III (1550–1555) in honour of Julius II, whose chamberlain he had once been.[28]

Under pressure from Charles V, the new pope re-convoked the Council of Trent in 1551, despite the objections of Henry II of France. Lutheran and Calvinist representatives were invited but would only attend if the question of Scripture and tradition was re-opened. The council proceeded to issue decrees on transubstantiation and the real presence in the Eucharist but postponed discussing the question of communion in two kinds, consecrated wine as well as bread being given to lay communicants, on which German Protestants had long insisted, in the hope of their arriving to participate in the debate. Then a revolt of German princes against Charles V and fear that the army of the Lutheran Duke Maurice of Saxony was approaching the town led to the council being suspended in summer of 1552.

One of the leading *Spirituali* cardinals, the scholar and former cardinal librarian Marcello Cervini, was elected as Marcellus II in a short but heated conclave in April 1555. Like Hadrian VI he kept his own name, and like John Paul I in 1978 appeared a harbinger of real change in the papal office. He cut the costs of his coronation, planned economies in the papal court and began drafting a reform decree. A critic of nepotism under his predecessor, he instructed members of his own family not to come to Rome. The parallel with John Paul I extends to the fact that both died within a month of their election. Appropriately their tombs face each other in the grotto under St. Peter's. The premature death at age fifty-four of Marcellus was pivotal as far as the future direction of the papacy is concerned, as the conclave of May 1555 elected another reform-minded pope, but of a very different sort: the seventy-nine-year-old inquisitor, Cardinal Gianpietro Carafa, who took the name Paul IV (1555–1559).

Personally austere, he was more authoritarian than his predecessors and totally opposed to any compromise on matters of doctrine or discipline in the interests of conciliating the Protestants. It was said that sparks flew from his feet as he walked, so fierce and determined was he, and Ignatius Loyola, founder of the Jesuits, who had fallen foul of him as inquisitor in Venice in 1537 declared 'every bone in my body trembles at the news' of Carafa's election.[29] His only weakness was nepotism: the traditional over-reliance on his two nephews, one of whom he made cardinal secretary of state, while the other received a dukedom and led him into a disastrous alliance with France and military defeat by Spain.

Paul's dislike of the Hapsburgs combined with his distrust of councils made him refuse to restart the Council of Trent, preferring instead to set up a reform commission of sixty bishops in Rome, working under immediate papal supervision. In 1557 he authorised publication by the Sacred Congregation of the Inquisition of the first Index of Prohibited Books *(Index Librorum Prohibitorum)* to apply to the whole Church—there had been previous local equivalents in the Netherlands (1529), Venice (1543) and Paris (1551). This was a list of those works or parts thereof that Catholics should not read, and which it was an offence to possess, together with advice on how they might be emended. This provoked outrage but also derision, as it included numerous classics of Italian literature, such as the writings of Dante. But over 10,000 books on the Index were burned in a single day in Venice.[30]

Paul IV's anti-Hapsburg bias and doubts about the orthodoxy of his former friends amongst the *Spirituali* led to his falling out with England's Queen Mary I (1553–1558), married to Philip II of Spain, and with her archbishop of Canterbury, Cardinal Pole, who together had just restored the kingdom to obedience to Rome. He revoked Pole's commission as papal legate in 1557 and awaited his return to have him subjected to investigation by the Inquisition. Another liberal cardinal, Giovanni Girolamo Morone, was stripped of his rank and imprisoned in the Castel Sant'Angelo by the pope the same year on the charge of being a Lutheran. Pole prepared a lengthy defence document but wisely remained in England until his death in 1558, two days after that of the queen.

The unpopularity of the repressive measures taken by Paul IV, which included confining the Jews of Rome to a ghetto, led to a violent reaction in the city on his death on 18 August 1559, when the headquarters of the Roman Inquisition that he himself had purchased in 1542 were destroyed and its prisoners released. More institutionalised vengeance was taken on his two nephews, whom he had dismissed from their offices for maladministration early in 1559. Both were now accused of crimes ranging from heresy to murder, tried by a commission of eight cardinals and executed in the Castel Sant'Angelo. Such a fate for papal nephews was unprecedented, but they had offended many interests, lost a war and most crucially of all had forfeited their late uncle's support, so the eighteen other cardinals of his creation did not stand by them.[31]

The now regular political complications led to another lengthy conclave before the election of Pius IV (1559–1565) on Christmas Day 1559. In some respects he was a throwback to an older papal style, owing his advance to the Farnese family into which his brother had married and being one of the last popes to have children of his own. However, his cardinal nephew, Carlo Borromeo (1538–1584), who would be canonized in 1610, was a powerful influence on the side of reform. The activities of the Inquisition were restricted, and a new, less drastic, version of the Index was issued in 1564.

There was debate over the reform council as both the emperor Ferdinand I (1558–1564), brother of Charles V, and the French court wanted an entirely new council. This would enable all previous discussions to be reopened, as the Protestants demanded. In both France and the empire, Calvinism and Lutheranism had been growing steadily. In the empire the agreement reached at Augsburg in 1548 let each state follow the religious persuasion of its ruler, but in France, now under the regency of Catherine de' Medici, politics was dominated by intensifying conflict between Catholic and Protestant factions that would lead to civil war in 1562. So, religious reconciliation was seen as essential to political stability in both states.

It was Philip II of Spain (1556–1598) who thwarted these efforts and ensured that the Council of Trent resumed. His perspective differed from that of his uncle, the emperor, as the few Protestants in Spain were ruthlessly hunted down by the Inquisition, especially after a group was discovered and burned in the royal capital of Valladolid in 1559. Many more bishops attended this third phase of the council, especially from Spain, and with reform stalled since 1552, there was more criticism of the papacy. The superiority of a general council to the pope was again proclaimed, and equally vigorously contested, especially by the Italians.[32]

Demands that diocesan bishops be resident were reiterated, causing so much dissension that the council seemed on the verge of collapse. Only the appointment of the recently liberated Cardinal Morone as legate-president in 1563 led to a resolution, and the decree against non-residency began to be applied in practice in the Curia from 1564, under the influence of Carlo Borromeo and a group of like-minded reforming cardinals. Borromeo, who was the first archbishop of Milan to reside in his archdiocese for many decades, also put into practice the precepts of the Council of Trent that bishops should preach frequently, closely oversee their clergy and the monastic houses of their dioceses and hold regular provincial synods. His cousin Mark Sittich von Hohenems, Cardinal Altemps (1533-1595), followed a similar programme in the diocese of Constance, as did another member of the group, Cardinal Paleotti (1522-1597), in Bologna.[33]

The decrees of the council were formally confirmed by Pope Pius IV on 26 January 1564 and began to be circulated in printed editions, though complete publication of all its documents and debates would not occur until the twentieth century.[34] Outside of Italy, reception of the decrees depended on the attitude of secular rulers. The kings of Spain and France refused to give up the right to nominate their own bishops. In Spain all the decisions of Trent were received in 1564 but could be applied only with royal consent. In France its decrees were admitted by some regional synods of bishops, but the whole Church in the kingdom did not agree to them until 1615. Likewise the emperor Maximilian II (1564–1576), who needed to preserve harmony between the Catholic and Protestant princes, would not automatically accept the conciliar decrees.[35]

Under the influence of his nephew Carlo Borromeo, Pius IV issued a series of decrees in 1561/2 reforming the running of most of the administrative departments of the Curia. The problem of how to pay the papal bureaucracy when no longer permitted to divert the revenues from foreign bishoprics was solved by increasing taxes in the Papal States, but at the cost of considerable resistance and unrest.

In the conclave of January 1566 Cardinal Borromeo and his group secured the election of the extremely ascetic Michele Ghisleri, a former shepherd, Dominican friar and professor of theology. In 1557 he had been made Perpetual Supreme Inquisitor by Paul IV, to whose memory he remained devoted, but he took the name of Pius V (1566–1572) as a sign of goodwill towards Borromeo and the cardinals of Pius IV. He appointed a cardinal nephew of his own, but otherwise was strongly opposed to nepotism. In particular he issued a bull forbidding alienation of any part of the Papal States, to prevent his successors benefiting their families in this way. More controversially he rehabilitated the Carafa family and executed the author of a satire on the late Pope Paul IV. He even contemplated renewing the inquisitorial process on Cardinal Morone and destroying the classical statues that had been collected in the Vatican since the mid-fifteenth century, but was dissuaded by the cardinals.[36]

His pontificate saw the publication of a revised catechism (1566), breviary (1568) and missal (1570), completing projects the council had asked the pope to undertake when it dissolved itself in 1563. Pius V shared Paul IV's enthusiasm for the Inquisition, giving it a new headquarters to replace the one whose destruction in 1559 was thought to have strengthened the 'northern heretics'.[37] A new Index had been issued in 1564, and in 1571 Pius V set up a permanent Congregation of the Index to update it regularly and supervise its implementation. He also issued decrees imposing new or more severe punishments for sodomy, blasphemy and clerical concubinage, and had to be talked out of making adultery a capital offence. He expelled prostitutes from Rome, which had long had the reputation of being 'the European capital for prostitution' (known as 'the French vice'), and he imposed taxes on nobles' carriages and their wives' jewellery.[38]

His bull *Regnans in Excelsis* (Ruling in Heaven) of 1570 excommunicating Queen Elizabeth I of England and freeing Catholics from political allegiance to her was in keeping with the confrontational approach the Holy See was now adopting towards Protestantism, but it created serious difficulties for English Catholics, whose political and religious loyalties were pulled in opposite directions. They also became objects of now seemingly justified suspicion to the royal government, and Catholic priests were pursued as traitors, and many tortured and executed.

The year 1571 saw the removal of a long-term fear, when after the making of a new Holy League between the pope, Spain and Venice, the allied fleet decisively defeated the Turks at the battle of Lepanto on 7 October 1571. Pius V was said to have announced the hour, the day and the outcome of the event in advance, and this became one of the miracles accepted in support of his canonisation in 1712 (the other being the miraculous provision of a supply of wheat to a convent of Dominican nuns in Prato).[39] In 1572 he celebrated Lepanto by creating a new liturgical Feast of Our Lady of Victory on 7 October.[40]

Between the era of Pius V and that of Paul III the papacy had experienced a sea-change, symbolised but not created by the Council of Trent, which had been constantly monitored from Rome with deep suspicion. In the end, what came from the council was more or less what one party in the Church wanted. Along the way, another more humane and liberal group had failed, and the opportunities they represented were lost. There may be similarities with the Second Vatican Council of 1962–1965 and its implementation. From 1555 onwards authority, centralisation, uniformity and control were in the ascendancy. Resistance to change and opposition to novelty became instinctive, leaving the Church apparently strengthened, but ill-adapted to face the intellectual challenges that lay ahead in 'the age of science'.

chapter 17

SUNDIAL OF THE CHURCH

(1572–1676)

THE GALILEO AFFAIR

Addressing the Pontifical Academy of Science in November 1979, Pope John Paul II noted how the seventeenth-century Italian scientist Galileo Galilei (1564–1642) had 'suffered much . . . at the hands of the men and the institutions of the Church'[1] and referred to a 1965 constitution of the Second Vatican Council deploring attitudes that had 'misled many into opposing faith and science', that is, thinking of them as opposites.[2] John Paul then appointed a special commission to investigate and publish the historical evidence relating to Galileo's two trials, the second of which had led to his imprisonment, the burning of his books and a ban on future publication.[3] Only in 1820 had the Congregation of the Holy Office, as the Inquisition was called after 1586, reversed this verdict.[4]

Central to the dispute were the ideas of the Polish priest and diplomat Nicholas Copernicus (1473–1543) that the earth and the planets rotated around the sun, published in 1543 in a book dedicated to Pope Paul III. While Copernicus' arguments contradicted the orthodoxy based on Aristotle and the Greek geographer Ptolemy that saw an unmoving earth as the fixed centre of the universe, they caused little concern to Catholic theologians at the time. Indeed, the Copernican thesis was welcomed, as it solved certain problems of calculation that then made possible the revision of the calendar under Pope Gregory XIII in 1582, hence known as the Gregorian calendar.[5] Protestants demanding a literal reliance on Scripture, were more hostile, and Luther declared Copernicus' theory insane, because it contradicted a story in the Book of Joshua.[6]

This implicit tolerance of the Copernican system by Catholic theologians was endangered by Galileo, the court mathematician of Grand Duke Cosimo II de' Medici of Florence (1609–1620). Using the telescope he created, Galileo became one of the first scientists to try to prove theoretical arguments by empirical evidence, and his well-publicised disputes with other scholars brought his views to a wider and less sophisticated readership. In December 1614 in a sermon in Florence, an ambitious Dominican denounced mathematicians in general and Galileisti in particular for adhering to the Copernican view of the universe. He also denounced Galileo to the Inquisition, resulting in his first trial in 1616.

Rome was at the time amongst the foremost intellectual and artistic centres of Europe, home to the Jesuit Collegio Romano, the Accademia de Lincei and the Sapienza University, and several of the cardinals were as interested in the arguments of the mathematicians as in patronising painters and architects. Galileo was well known and respected in such circles. But because of conflicts with Protestants over the interpretation of Scripture and the history of the early Church, Pope Paul V (1605–1621) was distrustful of anything that might create division between Catholics. As the Florentine ambassador told his grand duke, this was not a good time 'to come to Rome and argue about the moon'.[7] However, Galileo's hearing in Rome in 1616 was generally supportive, thanks not least to Cardinal Maffeo Barberini, who would become Pope Urban VIII (1623–1644). Galileo was just required to make some corrections to his latest book, to emphasise the hypothetical nature of the Copernican system.

At the conclusion of the enquiry Galileo was presented with a precept ordering him to 'abstain from teaching or defending, or treating in any way' Copernicus' view that the sun was the immobile centre of the universe, on pain of imprisonment.[8] Such a document would normally be signed by the recipient and by witnesses, but seventeen years later, when Galileo faced another enquiry, a signed version of this document could not be found, and he declared that he had no memory of any such stringent restrictions being placed upon him.[9]

In the meantime Cardinal Barberini had become pope. In 1630 Galileo asked him to accept the dedication of a new book he was writing on tidal forces. The necessary arrangements for this were made in Rome by the Master of the Sacred Palace, who was responsible for licensing all new books, and by the office of the Inquisition in Florence, where publication would take place. *A Dialogue Concerning the Two Chief World Systems* was published in 1632, with official approval, but because of a series of accidents and an outbreak of plague, which quarantined all items in transit between Florence and Rome, it had not been closely scrutinised by the appropriate authorities.

The book was denounced by Galileo's academic opponents, including the Jesuits of the Collegio Romano with whom he had recently fallen out over the nature of comets, for treating the Copernican view as true. Urban VIII, who had a violent temper, was furious. For one thing an argument he himself had once advanced was in the book attributed to a comic character called Simplicius (Simpleton). Furthermore, the pope had recently been threatened with that perennial papal nightmare, a general council, to investigate his stewardship of his office and had been implicitly criticised in a sermon by a pro-Spanish Jesuit for tolerating heresy. Additionally, the pope was informed of the precept that Galileo was believed to have signed in 1616, and so Urban regarded the new book as a deliberate defiance of papal authority.[10]

It was the pope's personal insistence that propelled the enquiry before the cardinals of the Congregation of the Holy Office in April 1633, despite his being advised to adopt a slower approach, and the seventy-year-old Galileo petitioning for a delay due to ill health. It was also Urban who authorised the threat of torture, not normally used by the Inquisition on the elderly, should there be any indication that Galileo was being evasive.[11]

It had not been expected that Galileo would be treated harshly.[12] He might have received a sentence like that of 1616, with publication of the *Dialogue* being delayed until corrected, but instead it was burned and Galileo imprisoned on the pope's command, applying the penalties threatened in the precept. It was with papal consent that the sentence also proclaimed the Copernican view of the earth circling the sun to be heretical. When in 1634 Galileo petitioned to be allowed to retire to the countryside on account of his poor health, the pope personally refused and ordered the inquisitor of Florence to tell him not to submit any future such request, on pain of 'being recalled to the prison of the Holy Office'.[13] The kindly intervention of the archbishop of Pisa eventually secured Galileo a more comfortable final decade of life.

That this second trial and subsequent harsh treatment of Galileo were driven by the pope in person is not as surprising as it may seem. Despite some resistance, the absolute nature of papal rulership had grown considerably during the second half of the sixteenth century, as the relationship with the Protestants in northern and central Europe moved from one of attempted accommodation to one of confrontation and suppression. A willingness to compromise or at least discuss gave way to a determination to preserve the essentials of the faith and to prevent any further threat of schism. Although some papal practices and the conduct of some individual popes had contributed to the calls for reform in the late medieval Church, the standing of the office had been enhanced by the decisions of the Council of Trent and the acceptance of more authoritarian leadership, expressed in the Index, the Inquisition and the 1566 catechism.

THE PAPAL COURT

Once elected the popes were absolute rulers within the city of Rome and the Papal States. As we have seen, the role of the cardinals as papal advisors declined as their number increased, and consistories in which they met as a body with the pope became less frequent. Several cardinals holding bishoprics elsewhere rarely came to Rome, as the Council of Trent had encouraged them to concentrate on their diocesan responsibilities, while the resident, or palatine, cardinals were primarily concerned with the work of the various congregations to which they were assigned. Their status in the city was second only to that of the pope, though precedence amongst themselves was a permanent source of concern, and their palaces and entourages grew in size and magnificence.

The grandeur of their mini-courts was as nothing to the aura of majesty surrounding the person of the pope. To be received by him required the kissing of the papal foot, though bishops kissed his knee. Letters to the pope concluded with similar reverence: 'Most humbly I kiss your holiness's holiest feet.'[14] In the palace and in the liturgy, elaborate ceremonial emphasised the superiority of the pope and the Roman church. In the Sistine Chapel titular patriarchs of Alexandria, Antioch, Jerusalem and Constantinople, who were all papal appointees, sat not only below the level of the pope, now sometimes called Patriarch of the Whole World, but also beneath that of the Roman cardinals. Kings or the emperor (not that they ever attended) would be seated between the cardinal deacons and the cardinal priests.[15]

The papal court, hierarchically organised in the Sistine Chapel, was seen as a mirror of the court of Heaven, and as the greatest locus of the holy on earth. For the direction of a renewed Church and for combating heretics, powerful leadership was required. This was explained in the catechism of 1566 in terms of 'a visible head being necessary to establish and preserve unity in the Church'.[16] The anti-papal rhetoric of the Protestants from Luther onwards elevated the importance of the pope for those who opposed them, and it was argued that heresy itself was primarily a product of the non-recognition of the pope's headship.

In the sermons, previously vetted and not permitted to exceed twenty minutes in length, that were preached before the pope in the Sistine Chapel on nineteen annual occasions, emphasis was placed on this papal leadership of the Church and the special relationship between pontiff and city.[17] In one favoured metaphor, the pope, said not to be able to err in faith or morals even if he wished to, was described as 'the sundial of the Church'.[18] As well as 'infallible' and being worthy of adoration, the pope could be described as 'a Vice-God', and Gregory XIII (1572–1585) was even hailed as 'a mortal God . . . greater and more excellent than a man'.[19] The unique standing of the pope reflected upon the city in which he lived: In a memorial speech for Sixtus V in 1591, the holiness of Rome was described as entirely dependent on that of the pope.[20]

The city itself enjoyed a less savoury reputation, reflected in the popular saying *Veduta Roma: perduta fede* (See Rome and lose your faith!).[21] The Renaissance papacy had promoted the discovery and study of the ancient city, not least accumulating its own collections of classical sculpture that reformist popes wanted to give away or destroy. Such interests were not merely antiquarian, as Rome's classical past was held to add lustre to its present. However, in the later sixteenth century, undue emphasis on pagan antiquity was deemed improper, and the triumph of the Church in the city was now regarded as the only suitable subject for commemoration.

This had mixed results, for example in the efforts at rediscovering Rome's early Christian heritage in what has been called a 'great palaeochristian revival'. Gregory XIII (1572–1585) restored buildings rightly or wrongly associated with Constantine and deliberately replicated the actions of Gregory the Great, building granaries, distributing alms and founding new churches on the sites of miracles.[22] Early 'Fathers of the Church' such as Basil of Caesarea (died 369), Gregory of Nazianzus (died c. 389), Jerome and Gregory the Great were commemorated in papally commissioned art, and new editions of the works of several of them were published. Felice Peretti, the future Sixtus V (1585–1590), devoted a long period of disgrace under his predecessor to re-editing the writings of Ambrose of Milan (d. 397), anachronistically replacing all their original biblical quotations with ones taken from the Vulgate, which had been proclaimed the infallible Latin version of the Bible by the Council of Trent. Sixtus' own hastily produced edition of the Vulgate, published during his pontificate, had to be suppressed on his death because of its numerous errors 'so as to prevent accusations that the Holy Word had been falsified by the Pope himself'.[23] It was replaced by an authorised edition in 1592.

More successful was the writing of a multi-volume history of the early Church up to 1198 by the Vatican librarian and later cardinal, Cesare Baronio or Baronius (1538–1607), at the request of Pope Gregory XIII and intended to combat the treatment of the subject by a team of Protestant authors known as the Magdeburg Centuriators. Baronius, who was nearly elected pope in 1605, also produced an authoritative edition of the Roman martyrology (1589), listing the recognised martyrs and their feast days, and had completed twelve volumes of his history before his death.[24]

For the city the new priority meant a far less reverential treatment of the relics of antiquity. Sixtus V tore down the late-second-century Septizonium on the Palatine to reuse the stone in his rebuilding of the Lateran Palace. Although he was later seen as a ruthless destroyer of the classical city, his aims were as much ideological as practical, as the remains of pagan Rome were redeployed in the service of its Christian present.[25] Thus, he placed statues of Saints Peter and Paul on top of the columns of Trajan and Marcus Aurelius, and re-erected three Egyptian obelisks on new sites, after exorcism and placing crosses on their tips. Pagan landmarks were thus Christianised or made to play a part in the renovation of the city. Stone from several ancient aqueducts were sold off or redeployed, but to build a new one that brought water onto the Esquiline and the Quirinal, allowing these parts of the city to be repopulated. He named it the Aqua Felice—Happy Water, or Felice's Water—after himself, Felice Peretti.

Sixtus, like Clement VIII (1592–1605) after him, was keen to underline the length and continuity of Rome's Christian history, in contrast to the Protestants, whose recent campaigns of image smashing emphasised their radical break with the traditions of the Church.[26] Rebuilding also permitted the reuse of newer constructions no longer suitable in the reformed Rome of the Counter-Reformation. Thus Sixtus destroyed the theatre and jousting arena created by Bramante for Julius II in the Belvedere attached to the Vatican Palace, so as to rehouse the Vatican Library, which he decorated with frescoes depicting both the great libraries of antiquity and the ecumenical councils.

Papal residences became grander, more elaborate and more numerous in this period. The Vatican saw the construction of new pavilions and formal features in its large gardens, including the *casino* or summer house built there for Pius IV, which has been described as 'the most thoroughly pagan of papal villas', albeit decorated entirely with biblical imagery.[27] Gregory XIII (1572–1585) began work on a summer palace on the Quirinal Hill. Although little more than a mile from the Vatican, it enjoyed a higher elevation and cooler breezes in the hottest part of the year. His successor, Sixtus V (1585–1590), who detested him, preferred to rebuild the Lateran Palace on the Caelian Hill, but so comprehensively covered its rooms with his own initials and emblems that subsequent popes abandoned it in favour of the Quirinal Palace.

Under Paul V (1605–1621) this became the main papal residence for most of the year, while in 1613 his nephew Cardinal Scipione Caffarelli-Borghese (1576–1633) built him a summer villa near Frascati in the hills east of Rome, which had become a favoured region for papal vacations. Popes from Gregory XIII on often imposed themselves on the hospitality of cardinals with villas in the area, until Urban VIII created one of his own in 1626 at Castel Gandolfo, which has remained the papal summer retreat up to the present.[28]

The greater attention to etiquette, ceremony and precedence in papal Rome was common to many of the royal courts of Europe in this period. Like the king of Spain, the pope ate alone, even if on public occasions under the gaze of numerous courtiers and attendants. However, many of the popes of these decades were genuinely ascetic in their personal lifestyles. Some, such as Pius V and Sixtus V, were friars who retained the discipline and the dress of their orders, and all of them up to the time of Urban VIII wore the full clerical tonsure, in which the whole top of the head was completely shaved, other than for a thin circle of hair. Several popes, not least Paul V and Urban VIII, while presiding over magnificent if not profligate courts, preferred simpler daily routines for themselves, and liked to avoid the lavish entertainment that was part of the diplomatic round. Here the cardinal nephew was useful, as he could host such events on the pope's behalf.

Although the tradition began with Julius III's scapegrace favourite, Innocenzo, it was under Pius IV (1559–1565) that the role of cardinal nephew, also known as the *cardinale padrone* (cardinal boss), became properly institutionalised. Pius V (1566–1572) and Gregory XIV (1590–1591), who otherwise tried to prevent their relatives benefitting from their election, appointed cardinal nephews. Innocent X (1644–1655) was the first pope not to have a permanent cardinal nephew, but only after his one nephew resigned as cardinal in 1647 to get married and ensure the continuity of the family. One effect of his resignation was for the secretary of state, hitherto responsible for the papal correspondence, again to take over directing the administration of the Curia and become principal advisor to the pontiff.[29]

In the court of Innocent X there existed an even more influential figure. This was the elderly pope's sister-in-law (and rumour had it, his mistress), Donna Olimpia Maidalchini. An heiress in her own right and married to the pope's brother, this formidable lady took charge of transforming the family's social and economic status, by, for example, taking over responsibility for licensing the brothels of Rome from the papal administration, which she said was an entirely inappropriate activity for the Church. Thereafter the licences that appeared over their doorways bore her arms, earning her the nickname of La Pimpessa.

So much influence did she have over her brother-in-law that ambassadors were reported as calling on her before being received in the Vatican, gaining her the further unofficial title of La Papessa. So embarrassing did she become that her influence declined from around 1649 until the final years of the pontificate. On Innocent's death she showed the stuff of which she was made:

> After three days during which the pope's remains were laid out in St. Peter's no one could be found to take upon himself the task of burial. A message was sent to Donna Olimpia asking her to provide coffin and grave-clothes; but she replied that she was only a poor widow. None of his other relatives or nephews bestirred themselves, and the body was removed to a chamber where the masons engaged upon repairs stored their building material. . . . Monsignor Segni, a canon of St. Peter's, who had once been Innocent's majordomo and had been dismissed, rewarded evil with good by paying five dollars for his burial.[30]

This story was one of the numerous slanders circulating after the pope's death, which provided material for a scurrilous *Life of Donna Olimpia Maidalchini* by the renegade priest Gregorio Leti. However, it is clear that Innocent's relatives were unwilling to lavish money on his funeral and memorials once he was gone. Shrewd pontiffs such as

Sixtus V arranged their own burials. He constructed his own funerary chapel in Santa Maria Maggiore, into which he also transferred the remains of his revered predecessor Pius V. Similarly Urban VIII commissioned his own flamboyant tomb in St. Peter's from Bernini in 1627, very soon after his election. The same sculptor was approached by Innocent X's family, the Pamphili, after his death, but despite Bernini producing a dramatic design for a tomb, the project drifted due to their parsimony, and a far less magnificent one was only completed the following century, by which time his remains had been (temporarily) lost.[31]

After the pope's death in 1655 it was also Donna Olimpia who served as the leader of the faction of the cardinals he had appointed, and she was even permitted to address the enclosed conclave before the voting, one of very few members of the laity and the only woman ever to do so. However, the next pope exiled her from Rome, and she died of plague in Viterbo. Even so, allied by marriage to the ancient Genoese noble house of Doria, her family continued to prosper across the centuries to follow.

The pope responsible for her exile was Fabio Chigi, a highly regarded diplomat who had led the papal delegation to the peace talks ending the Thirty Years War and who had served as Innocent X's secretary of state from 1652. So magnificent were the ceremonies surrounding his coronation that his biographer claimed that several Protestant visitors to Rome were converted on the spot, exclaiming, 'we are beasts; where so much of the divine is made apparent, there God must be also.'[32] He took the name of Alexander VII (1655–1667) in honour of the twelfth-century pope Alexander III, a fellow citizen of Siena. He also commissioned Bernini's most grandiose papal tomb in St. Peter's.

As the leading Catholic nations saw papal nepotism as a scandal, putting Rome at a disadvantage in dealings with non-Catholic states, Alexander VII continued his predecessor's practice of giving his secretary of state, Cardinal Rospigliosi, more influence than his cardinal nephew, named Flavio Chigi. Although he initially ordered his own family not to come to Rome, in 1656 he was persuaded to change his mind by the cardinals and some of the ambassadors, who found the lack of the usual channels of influence provided by a papal family bewildering and preferred returning to a system they understood.[33]

John Bargrave, an English exile then living in Rome, recorded the ensuing transformation:

> In the first months of his elevation to the Popedom, he had so taken upon himself the profession of an evangelical life that he was wont to season his meat with ashes, to sleep upon a hard couch, to hate riches, glory and pomp, taking a great pleasure to give audience to embassadors in a chamber full of dead men's sculls, and in the sight of his coffin, which stood there to put him in mind of his death. But so soon had he called his relations about him he changed his nature. Instead of humility succeeded vanity; his mortification vanished, his hard couch was turned into a soft featherbed, his dead men's sculls into jewels, and his thoughts of death into ambition— filling his empty coffin with money as if he would corrupt death, and purchase life with riches.[34]

While not untainted by prejudice, Bargrave's rhetorical account of how the pope began enriching his relatives is confirmed in more detail by modern investigation.[35] The family continued to flourish after the pope's death, becoming in 1721 the hereditary marshals of the papal conclaves (responsible for locking in the cardinals), a post they have retained to the present.

Behind all such papal nepotism lay the basic principle that looking after one's family was a sacred obligation, and it was said, 'as Italians our cardinals owed their first allegiance to their families and familiars; as cardinals they owed their first allegiance to the church. When these allegiances clashed, our cardinals tended to act as Italians.'[36] However, the cardinals as a body also felt the pope needed one trusted advisor and saw a close family member as best suited for this role.

In the earlier seventeenth century the role of the cardinal nephew was not dissimilar to that of the royal favourite, or *valido,* found in many of the royal courts of Europe at the time. Once seen as a symptom of monarchical weakness or incompetence, the favourite is now

understood in terms of the heavy administrative burden he shoul-
dered for his monarch, who was constrained by the demands of rigid
etiquette and could not be seen to be personally responsible for fail-
ures. Such favourites could amass great wealth and power, but their
tenure of it rested entirely on continued royal support, and they
could be dismissed if a scapegoat was needed.

The essential difference was that the papal office, now as absolute
as many of the secular monarchies of Europe, was not hereditary.
Furthermore the pope's courtiers, apart from the holders of a few titular offices reserved for the lay nobility, were all clerics. While a king
had a wide range of choice in the selection of a minister, a pope
needed a nephew of suitable age. Clement VIII (1592–1605) appointed two nephews and shared offices and responsibilities between
them until it became clear that one was more competent than the
other. As in this case, a cardinal nephew could prove himself an able
administrator and politician, capable of leading the faction of other
cardinals appointed by his uncle after the pontiff's own death.

Statistically a papal tenure could be expected to be brief, in some
cases spectacularly so. Up to the late eighteenth century the average
length of a papal reign was roughly six and a half years. Some periods
saw a more rapid turnover, with five different popes in office between
August 1590 and January 1592, including Urban VII, who is the
shortest reigned of all, dying twelve days after his election. The seventeenth century saw a shift towards longer pontificates, in some cases
because younger men, in their fifties, were chosen to prevent the frequent conclaves that were required in 1590/1 and again in 1605.

Even so, the time available for the families of a new pope to take
advantage of the opportunities his election afforded them was short.
To some extent the system depended on this, as a long pontificate
gave rise to such an extended monopoly of power and influence as to
create serious resentments, as happened during the twenty-one-year
tenure of Urban VIII (1623–1644) of the Barberini family.

It has been calculated that the annual receipts of the papacy around
1625 amounted to roughly 2.5 million *scudi,* on top of which existed
a reserve of 2.8 million more. (While it is difficult to suggest modern
equivalents for these figures, the annual salary of a construction

worker was about fifty to sixty *scudi*.) However, there were also debts owed to papal bankers, amounting to sixteen million *scudi*, the interest payments on which swallowed up two-thirds of the annual income. By 1629 this debt had risen to twenty million *scudi*, despite highly unpopular increases in the taxes on meat, salt and wine. Thus, the actual disposable annual income of the papacy was far less than the estimated 2.5 million. Yet at the same time, Urban VIII, who as pope had absolute control of the papal revenue, gave 14,000 *scudi* in 1630 to his nephew Taddeo, prefect of Rome, 'for swaddling clothes' for a newborn son, and another 30,000 in 1632 to help pay for work on his palace. In 1635 Taddeo received a further 15,000 *scudi* from his uncle for a hunting party.[37]

Such casual gifts were not the only way in which the resources of the Roman church were used to benefit papal relatives. By the late sixteenth century most popes came from middle-ranking provincial families and had risen through their education and their diplomatic or administrative service to the Church. Some were from very poor origins: Sixtus V was the son of a farm labourer, and Pius V had been a shepherd before joining the Dominicans. Generally, their background was in trade, banking, the law or the minor aristocracy, and they mainly came from Naples or the north, with little connection to Rome. As it was very rare for two members of a family to be elected pope, acquisition of the office provided the unique opportunity for social transformation.

Various strategies were followed, but the more extreme measures attempted in the past were no longer practicable. Paul III was the last pontiff to be able to turn his family, the Farnese, into independent territorial princes by making them rulers of one of the component parts of the Papal States. Any such alienation had been strictly forbidden by Pius V. But marriage into the upper ranks of the Roman aristocracy was an attractive alternative, followed by the Aldobrandini relatives of Clement VIII, the Pamphili of Innocent X and the Rospigliosi of Clement IX, amongst others. The wealth and patronage at the disposal of a pope made such an alliance with his family highly advantageous.

Diplomacy provided another route, especially for popes who were on good terms with the kings of Spain, who as rulers of Naples had numerous estates and titles that could be given to papal relatives. The most outrageous procedure, in the straitened state of the papacy's finances, was to use its resources to buy status outright. In 1629 Urban VIII spent 575,000 *scudi* buying the principality of Palestrina in the Papal States from the Roman noble house of Colonna for his nephew Taddeo, whom he had already paid to marry into their family two years earlier.[38] By 1632 Taddeo's properties and estates were said to be worth four million *scudi*.[39] But it was upon him that the family's future depended. The sons of his marriage to Anna Colonna enabled the Barberini to become one of the leading aristocratic dynasties of the city in the generations that followed.

The ambitions of relatives could be a dangerous influence on papal policy. After a close brush with death in 1637, a much-weakened Urban VIII became increasingly reliant on the advice of his nephews, who persuaded him in 1641 into a foolish war with the Farnese duke of Parma over the duchy of Castro, a papal fief which they had been trying to acquire for themselves since 1635. The results of the three-year War of Castro were disastrous.[40] A league of northern Italian states, backed by France, forced the pope into the humiliating Treaty of Venice in 1644, in which he gained nothing, and the costs of the war, estimated as five million *scudi*, were ruinous to the already enfeebled papal finances. Highly unpopular taxes went up, even on basics such as wheat and wine, and it was widely suspected in Rome that the Barberini nephews had pocketed some of the funds raised for the war.[41]

This catastrophe produced an unexpected reaction on the death of Urban VIII later that year. Normally the depredations of a papal or 'reigning' family were accepted without question, and the length of his pontificate meant that Urban had appointed some seventy-four new cardinals.[42] Traditionally such cardinals regarded the pope who chose them as their patron and would act together in ensuing conclaves and generally in support of his family. However, so unpopular had the Barberini become that the faction of cardinals they relied on disintegrated, allowing for the election of a new pope, Innocent X, who was determined to make them disgorge their profits.[43]

At the time it was suggested the Barberini had received about 105 million *scudi* from the papal treasury during their uncle's pontificate; a modern estimate is closer to twelve million *scudi*. Even this is an extraordinary amount when seen in relation to papal annual income and the level of debt with which it was burdened. In practice nothing came of the planned prosecution, as France, governed by Cardinal Mazarin in the name of the young Louis XIV, threw its diplomatic support behind the Barberini, solely because Innocent X was felt to be too pro-Spanish.

War and Diplomacy

Just as the Carafa war in the 1550s showed that in military terms the papacy was no match for one of the greater powers of Western Europe, so now the War of Castro demonstrated it had difficulty holding its own against even some of the minor states of northern Italy. In 1642 the Duke of Parma had been able to invade the Papal States and bring his not very strong army to within a hundred miles of Rome, causing panic in the city, the mobilising of a rag-tag militia and the pope's moving from his favoured Quirinal Palace to the better-fortified Vatican. The Venetian republic and other allies backed the duke because the Barberini papacy had recently seemed so acquisitive, with the della Rovere duchy of Urbino being absorbed into the Papal States in 1626, and the war with Parma over Castro was regarded as evidence of further expansionary ambitions. The outcome dispelled such illusions.

Papal spiritual armament had by this period become equally ineffectual. Early in his pontificate Paul V (1605–1621) had a confrontation with Venice over the rights of the Church. The republic had decreed that new churches could only be built with the consent of the state and was also trying two priests in its own courts, in defiance of the long tradition of clerical immunity from secular jurisdiction. When papal protests were ignored, in April 1606 Paul placed the republic under an interdict and excommunicated its governing body, the Venetian Senate.

While such methods had often worked in the past, they depended upon the collaboration of the local clergy. In this case Venice declared the interdict unlawful and expelled the Jesuits, who were the only ones likely to obey it. The Venetian clergy almost entirely ignored it and supported their government against the pope. Numerous treatises and pamphlets were published by both sides, deploying historical arguments in favour of their claims, and there was a danger that Venice might withdraw its obedience from Rome entirely. A settlement was finally agreed in April 1607, largely through French intermediacy, by which the two imprisoned priests were released and the interdict lifted. However, the issue of principle was not resolved and the Jesuits remained barred from Venetian territory until 1656. It was in practice a significant defeat for papal authority and left the threat of interdict as little better than a bluff. Papal animosity towards Venice remained strong, and on his deathbed Urban VIII referred to the Venetians as *becchi futtuti*, 'fucked goats', meaning cuckolds.[44]

After the vigorous and combative papacy of the later sixteenth century, that of the seventeenth looks anxious and lacking in self-confidence. From the time of Paul IV (1555–1559), the popes almost entirely abandoned any interest in or expectation of reconciling the Protestants and set about creating a more clearly defined, reformed and tightly controlled Church. By the time of Paul V (1605–1621) this firm, even aggressive, stance had transformed itself into one more resembling timidity. The cause of this was a fear that if thwarted, disagreed with or otherwise opposed by the papacy, hitherto good Catholic rulers of Europe might ally with the Protestants, or even become Protestants, not from theological conviction but out of sheer pique. Venice played this card in 1606/7 but was not alone in doing so.

An awareness of this new timorousness started making itself felt in the late sixteenth century, when Philip II of Spain (1556–1598) began interfering in papal elections by having his ambassador in Rome inform the cardinals of the names of those of their number who would not be acceptable to him as pope, because they were thought not to favour or be actively opposed to Spanish interests. The practice started with one or two such names being given, but in the conclave following the death of Urban VII in 1590, the Spanish ambassador produced a list of thirty cardinals whom his master would not wish to see elected. When political stability was restored in France under the former Protestant Henry IV (1589–1610), the French monarchy insisted on the same right of veto in papal elections as enjoyed by Spain. These rulers also began demanding that the pope should appoint cardinals whom they suggested.

Many of the cardinals were not happy about these de facto royal rights of exclusion and nomination but did not dare take a stand against them. During the conclave of 1644, the curial theologians were consulted on the practice of exclusions and came to the lawyerly conclusion that while there were no theological or legal grounds upon which they could be based, there also existed an important principle that nothing should be done that might cause a schism by thwarting a powerful king. Bluntly put, it was better to let the Catholic monarchs have their way, though preferably only in the form of excluding just a handful of candidates each, than face any possibility that they might break their ties with Rome if they did not. Not surprisingly, the Hapsburg emperor also began sending in lists of exclusions. In 1691 the right of exclusion by the leading Catholic monarchs was formally recognised, surviving until abolished by Pius X after the conclave of 1903.

There was some flexibility in the system. If a pope was known to be dying, then there was time for a Catholic monarch to inform his ambassador of his list of exclusions, but sometimes a papal vacancy occurred unexpectedly, and the news might arrive in Madrid, Paris or Vienna too late for the appropriate instructions to be issued. Thus the new pope could have been elected by the time the royal exclusions were known, as happened with Innocent X in 1644, who was chosen before a French veto arrived. In some conclaves cardinals representing a particular national interest tried to insinuate that one or more of the candidates was unacceptable to their royal patron, but lacking the ambassadorial lists, the others could ignore such protests.

While the leading Catholic rulers of Europe were concerned to secure the election of acceptable popes, they were disinclined to let popes play a significant role in what they saw as their own affairs. During this period religious divisions started to matter far less in international relations, a situation that the papacy found hard to come to terms with. The civil wars that rent France between the 1560s and 1590s were articulated primarily in religious terms but were really more to do with competition to control a succession of weak or under-age kings. When Henry IV succeeded the assassinated Henry III in 1589, he had been excommunicated by Sixtus V as a Protestant, but his subsequent conversion cleared the way for his excommunication to be lifted by Clement VIII, a process that His Catholic Majesty, Philip II of Spain, did everything in his power to prevent, as the last thing he wanted to see was the re-emergence of a strong albeit Catholic French monarchy. Similarly, Clement VIII was dismayed to find that the price of a revived France, a useful counterweight to an obtrusively dominant Spain, was the acceptance of Henry IV's Edict of Nantes of 1598, which guaranteed religious tolerance to the Protestant Huguenots, whose massacre in Paris on St. Bartholomew's Eve in 1572 Gregory XIII celebrated with a *Te Deum* and the striking of a special medal. Clement wrote to the king that it was 'the most cursed edict that I could imagine . . . whereby liberty of conscience is granted to everyone, which is the worst thing in the world.'[45]

Since the death of Charles V, the emperors had remained personally faithful to Rome but had shown little or no interest in pursuing policies that might reignite religious conflict within the empire. In 1609, for example, the emperor Rudolf II (1576–1612) had guaranteed freedom of religion in Bohemia. However, 1617 saw the election of the Hapsburg heir apparent, Ferdinand II, as the new king of Bohemia. In his previous role as archduke of Styria and Carinthia, he had shown himself a zealous Catholic and active persecutor of heretics, and so when the following year he moved against the liberties guaranteed in 1609 to the Protestant majority in Bohemia, some of his officials were thrown out of a window in Prague Castle (the so-called Defenestration of Prague), though landing safely in a heap of manure (later hailed as a miracle). The crown was then offered by the rebels to the Protestant Frederick Count Palatine of the Rhine, and probably unwisely it was accepted by him. The result was the Thirty Years War.

Beginning as a war over religious allegiances, it gradually transmuted itself as other factors came into play. Initially it promised to be a triumph for Ferdinand, who was elected emperor in 1619 and whose armies quickly gained control of Bohemia and of the Rhineland palatinate, expelling the Winter King, as the Count Palatine Frederick became known from his brief tenure of the Bohemian crown. One consequence was the effective elimination of Protestantism in the Czech-speaking lands after two centuries of Hussite tradition, a process overseen by a papal nuncio. From the emperor's rapid victory over Frederick, the papacy received a gift of the great library of medieval manuscripts assembled in Heidelberg by the Counts Palatine, which, apart from a selection later returned as a goodwill gesture, remain today as the *Codices Palatini* in the Vatican Library. However, it was while taking part in a liturgical procession to celebrate the defeat of count-king Frederick that Paul V was incapacitated by a stroke that was followed by a second, fatal, one in January 1621.

The war did not long remain one-sided, as the Swedish king Gustavus Adolphus (1611–1632) entered on the side of the Protestant princes when it looked as if the Hapsburgs were going to crush them. Nor did the sides remain long-defined by religious allegiance. In 1631 a militarily revitalised France allied with Sweden and in 1635 declared war on both Spain and the empire. The personally Francophile and anti-Hapsburg Urban VIII did little more than urge the French government, directed by Cardinal Richelieu (1585–1642), to try and keep the peace, and refused material assistance to the emperor. The death of Gustavus Adolphus and the Swedish withdrawal in 1632 had already tilted the balance back a little in favour of the Hapsburgs, but eventually the war was ended by agreement formalised in the Peace of Westphalia in 1648.

A papal delegation led by the nuncio in Cologne, Cardinal Chigi, the future Alexander VII (1655–1667), took part in the negotiations in Münster, but he refused to talk face-to-face with heretics and was unable to prevent concessions being made to the Protestant states that eventually led Innocent X to denounce the resulting treaty. However, this papal repudiation of the agreement was tacitly ignored: The papacy now seemed as insignificant diplomatically as it was militarily when it came to the decisions that needed to be taken by the secular rulers of Europe, and it had no way to enforce its displeasure.

GALLICANISM

Ever since the popes had stopped residing in Avignon, France had taken an often abrasive and high-handed attitude in its dealings with the Holy See. This was justified and reinforced by the independent traditions of the French church, known collectively as Gallicanism, which the monarchs themselves encouraged whenever it suited their purposes. Claiming ancient precedents and privileges going back to the early Church and to the time of Charlemagne, the French clergy insisted that they enjoyed particular freedom from papal oversight and interference. In the seventeenth century, with both empire and Spain weakened by the Thirty Years War, the France of Louis XIV emerged as the dominant power in Western Europe, more than willing to throw its weight around in its dealings with Rome.

Paul V (1605–1621) had formally condemned the claim of the French church to its special Gallican liberties in 1613, after a spate of pamphleteering had included outright attacks on papal authority, but it was under Alexander VII (1655–1667) that Franco-papal relations became seriously strained.[46] Some of the problems stemmed from a personal hostility between the pope, who had become anti-French during his involvement in the negotiations for the Treaty of Westphalia in 1648, and Cardinal Mazarin (1602–1661), first minister to Louis XIV. Alexander objected to the French being allied to Protestant Sweden, and in 1654 as secretary of state he had given refuge in Rome to Cardinal de Retz (1613–1679), leader of the French aristocratic revolt known as the Fronde. At the same time Mazarin felt France was not strongly enough represented in the College of Cardinals—of the forty chosen by Innocent X only three were French—and so wanted a pope who could be relied on to appoint more. This prompted a French veto on Alexander in the eighty-day-long conclave of 1655, which was withdrawn when it became clear that the candidate they favoured instead could not gain enough votes.[47]

The kingdom and the papacy thereafter tended to take opposing sides on almost every major issue of the day. France supported the Farnese in trying to reclaim Castro, while Alexander VII promoted the election of the emperor Leopold I (1658–1705) against attempts led by Mazarin to persuade the electors to choose a non-Hapsburg candidate. France then excluded the papacy from its traditional role as intermediary in conflicts between major Catholic powers in the negotiations leading to the Treaty of the Pyrenees in 1659, which ended the long-running war with Spain.

In Rome the French ambassador had been instructed by his king to create as many difficulties as possible, manipulating issues of etiquette and precedence. Amongst these was a demand that a unit of the city's Corsican guard (distinct from the pope's Swiss ones) should not pass in front of the ambassador's official residence, the Palazzo Farnese. In August 1662 a brawl between Corsican guards and some of the ambassador's men led to one of his wife's pages being killed as she was returning home from church. The result was a major diplomatic incident that ideally suited French purposes. Louis XIV severed diplomatic links with the papacy and invaded Avignon.

As neither Philip IV of Spain, who was the French king's father-in-law, nor the emperor Leopold I, a better composer of religious music than statesman, were willing to intervene, Alexander VII had to accept the king's humiliating terms, set out in the Treaty of Pisa of February 1664. A monument was to be erected in Rome proclaiming the guilt of the Corsican guard, the pope's nephew Cardinal Flavio Chigi was required to present a personal apology to the king and the pope himself agreed to accept royal suggestions on the appointment of French bishops, giving Louis rights of nomination.

THE FLYING SQUADRON

In this era of increasing interference by the Catholic monarchies, with rising tensions leading to diplomatic slights and a decline in papal influence in secular affairs, a group of cardinals began discussing a programme of reform. Their intentions were to restore the independence of the papacy by putting an end to exclusions in conclaves and by ensuring that it adopt an even-handed approach to diplomatic relations with the rival lay powers, and thus not be susceptible to influence or threats. Admittedly this was to some degree self-interested, in that cardinals might then be courted and rewarded by all sides rather than just be expected to promote the cause of one of the lay powers.[48]

This group of cardinals, drawn from the ranks of those appointed by Innocent X, became known from a nickname given them by the Spanish ambassador as the *Squadrone Volante,* the Flying Squadron, and was the first such faction to be formed in the college that was not based upon ties of patronage. Other factions, usually led by the former cardinal nephews, consisted of cardinals who were all the appointments of previous popes. By the late sixteenth century these chronological factions had even established a gentleman's agreement that a new pope would be chosen from the ranks of the cardinals appointed by the pontiff before the one who had just died. Thus Gregory XIII (1572–1585) was a cardinal of Pius IV, Sixtus V (1585–1590) of Pius V, Gregory XIV (1590–1591) of Gregory XIII, Clement VIII (1592–1605) of Sixtus V and so on.

As a faction the *Squadrone Volante,* led by cardinals Pietro Ottoboni (later Pope Alexander VIII), Decio Azzolini (1623–1689) and Francesco Albizzi (1593–1684), was united by policy rather than by partisanship. With eleven members, they were never more than a minority in the college, which was normally close to its full strength of seventy, but their cohesion gave them an influence above their number. Their first success came with the election of Alexander VII in 1655, as this was achieved in defiance of various exclusions issued by the Spanish and French courts. Cardinal Albizzi had declared that his group's intention was of only electing a candidate who was 'prudent, learned and pious' and that they were willing to give up their lives for this ideal.[49]

The *Squadrone* had a lay patron in the person of Queen Christina of Sweden (1626–1689), the daughter and successor of Gustavus Adolphus, who had abdicated in favour of her cousin in 1654. Following her departure from Sweden she had announced her conversion to Catholicism and so had been received in Rome with enormous enthusiasm when she arrived in 1656, not least by Alexander VII. A patron of artists and scholars—Descartes had died of influenza at her court—an author herself and a prodigious collector of books and manuscripts, she was one of the most learned and influential figures of her day.

Her choice of Rome as her new home proved something of a mixed blessing. She was often in financial difficulties, from which successive popes occasionally had to save her, and diplomatically she was a loose cannon. She conspired with the French to be made ruler of Naples if they could eject the Spanish, and in a visit to France in 1657 she executed in a particularly brutal and shocking way one of her entourage who was actually a papal subject, causing diplomatic waves in both Paris and Rome.[50] She became a close friend of Cardinal Azzolini soon after her first arrival in Rome, and her residence, the Palazzo Riario, became a headquarters for the *Squadrone*.

Their real triumph came in 1667, with the election of the saintly Clement IX (1667–1669), who had long been friendly with the queen.[51] A former professor of canon law, Giulio Rospigliosi had been advanced in the Curia by Urban VIII and the Barberini, for whose courts he wrote numerous plays.[52] Indeed he has been hailed as the founding father of comic opera, as well as the author of the first libretto on a historical subject. He was equally highly regarded as a diplomat, serving as nuncio in Madrid, before being appointed secretary of state by Alexander VII in 1655, in direct succession to himself, and then a cardinal in 1657.

As pope he restricted the benefits his family were allowed to enjoy. Despite his earlier Spanish connections, he had strong pro-French sympathies and was able to maintain good relations with both powers during his brief reign. This included a revival of the papal role as mediator in bringing an end to the short War of Devolution between them by the Peace of Aachen in May 1668. He had appointed Cardinal Azzolini his secretary of state, but the French ambassador noted that the pope preferred 'to do everything his own way and doesn't easily accept counsel or the opinion of others'.[53] This included his long-harboured hope of helping Venice recover Crete, possibly the last crusading venture. As with so many earlier ones, divided counsels amongst the leaders of the joint Hapsburg and French naval expedition that he managed to organise resulted in failure, and the last Venetian strongholds were lost. The news caused a decline in the pope's health, leading to his death from a stroke in December 1669.

Queen Christina and the *Squadrone*, which was starting to lose cohesion, were unable to replicate their success of 1667 in the ensuing conclave.[54] The late pope had only appointed a handful of cardinals, and the faction of his predecessor, Alexander VII, was still numerous. Spanish and French parties also tended to balance one another, resulting in a protracted conclave with many of the cardinals receiving votes. Not until April 1670 did consensus form around a most unlikely candidate, a sign of how divided they had been. This was Emilio Altieri, who was nearly deaf, would be eighty in May and had only been a cardinal for a month before the conclave. He took the name of Clement X (1670–1676) in honour of his predecessor, who had appointed him. He gave the office of cardinal nephew to a relative by marriage, whose family proved to be amongst the most rapacious of all.

His pontificate was marked by a further downturn in relations with France, including a major diplomatic incident when in 1675 the French ambassador pushed the pope back into his chair when he tried to cut short an audience. This happened during one of several attempts to persuade the pope to appoint more cardinals from the main Catholic states. In the course of the sixteenth and seventeenth centuries, the papacy had become extraordinarily insular. No non-Italian had been elected pope since 1522, and there were few non-Italian cardinals in the much-expanded college, and relatively few of these were resident in Rome. They were thus little known to their Italian colleagues and were increasingly regarded as unelectable because they might favour the interests of the state from which they came and thus upset the others. The papacy had become essentially Italian and Roman, to a degree unparalleled since the mid-eleventh century.

~ *chapter 18* ~

THE LAST POPE

(1676–1774)

PAPAL REFORMERS

As the seventeenth century drew to a close, the standing of the papacy was high, largely thanks to the reforms of two outstanding popes, Innocent XI (1676–1689) and Innocent XII (1692–1700), but the international situation was becoming threatening. The last of the Hapsburg kings of Spain, Charles II (1665–1700), was close to death. The product of generations of in-breeding between the Spanish and Austrian branches of the dynasty, he lacked children, even though the Inquisition had burned the witches held responsible for his plight. Because of the marriage policies of his predecessors, those with a claim to succeed him included members of both the rival Austrian Hapsburg and French Bourbon dynasties. Partitioning the Spanish empire, which included vast territories in South and Central America, the Spanish Netherlands and most of Italy, apart from Venice and the Papal States, as well as Spain itself was unacceptable to Madrid. When the dying king was persuaded to bequeath it all to the Bourbon candidate, a grandson of Louis XIV, other powers both Catholic and Protestant prepared for war to support the Hapsburg claimant or force a division, rather than see the whole Spanish empire go to a French monarch.

While the papacy was the natural mediator in such a conflict, individual popes were suspected of favouring one side or the other. Franco-papal relations had been contentious under Innocent XI, who in 1678 tried to stop the autocratic Louis XIV expanding his control over the Church in his kingdom. The response came in an assembly of the French clergy in 1682 that with royal encouragement issued four Gallican Articles, denying the pope any kind of secular authority and once more subordinating his office to a general council. For historical justification Louis looked to the works of scholars like the Jesuit Louis Maimbourg, who addressed the king as Louis the Conqueror and warned him that papal interference had undermined the empire of Charlemagne.[1] Maimbourg's books were placed in the Index of Forbidden Books, and Innocent denounced the Gallican Articles, refusing to ratify royal nominations to French bishoprics, with the result that thirty-five remained vacant by 1685.

Pope Alexander VIII (1689–1691) tried to mend fences with France, which itself was now more conciliatory, as Louis's principal opponent in northern Europe, William of Orange, had just acquired the English throne. Avignon was returned to the papacy, but the Gallican Articles were not withdrawn. This Franco-papal rapprochement caused alarm in Vienna, which intensified when Innocent XII reached a new accord with France in 1693, through which French bishops were freed from subscribing to the Gallican Articles, and those waiting for papal confirmation of their appointments were now ordained.

When war came over the Spanish succession in 1700, the papacy was economically and administratively in better shape than it had been for decades. It had been about 50 million *scudi* in debt in 1676 when Innocent XI commissioned Giovanni Battista di Luca (appointed cardinal in 1681) to calculate how much revenue had been diverted to papal relatives since the beginning of the century. When di Luca came back with the staggering figure of 30 million *scudi*,[2] Innocent drafted a bull limiting the benefits available to a pope's family, but he faced strong opposition from the cardinals, who argued that the magnificence of the 'ruling family', as it was called, reflected that of the pope himself.[3]

That Innocent XI did not publish his bull is symptomatic of the more collegial style of papal government in the later seventeenth century. The popes of the period consulted their cardinals more frequently, and tended to be swayed by their opinion. A 'Manual of

Practice' for the cardinals published in 1680 by Innocent XI's counsellor di Luca made an elaborate comparison between the Roman Republican Senate and the Sacred College, which he depicts as the senate of a 'new republic', downplaying the monarchical role of the pope.[4] Instead he presents the pope as First Senator.

Innocent's own austere lifestyle and the limits he placed on his family meant that nepotism was never a cause of scandal in his pontificate. A revival of it under his successor, Alexander VIII (1689–1691), was intensified by his relatives' fear that they only had a short time to profit from his tenure of the papal office, as he was seventy-nine when elected: 'The twenty-third hour has already struck,' he warned them. This return to the bad old days made a solution imperative, and one of the earliest measures of Alexander's successor, the Neapolitan aristocrat Antonio Pignatelli, who became Innocent XII, was the bull *Romanum decet Pontificum* (It Is Appropriate That the Roman Pontiff . . .) of 1692, which strictly limited the offices and perks available to members of a pope's family. Although sometimes described as abolishing nepotism, his decree actually stopped papal 'ruling families' enriching themselves from the wealth of the Church. Popes continued to appoint nephews or occasionally brothers as cardinals, but the formal role of cardinal nephew was not revived, and the office of secretary of state became the most important of curial posts in the hands of the runner-up in the conclave of 1676, Cardinal Aderano Cibo (1613–1700), who described himself as the pope's 'First Minister with all the authority'.[5] Amongst Cibo's achievements were the numerous economic and administrative reforms of the pontificate of Innocent XII (1691–1700).

Innocent XI, when Cardinal Benedetto Odescalchi, had been a founding member of the *Squadrone Volante*, but subsequently transferred his support to another faction nicknamed the *zelanti* or zealots. They shared many of the *Squadrone*'s aims of reducing secular interference in conclaves but were more concerned that popes be chosen for their moral and spiritual qualities rather than their political or diplomatic ones. The election of Innocent XI himself in 1676 marked the first success of this faction, and it achieved another with that of Clement XI (1700–1721). As Secretary of Apostolic Briefs,

Clement had drafted his predecessor's bull against nepotism. When unanimously elected, after news of the death of Charles II of Spain galvanised a hitherto protracted and divided conclave into a decision, he refused election, saying he did not want to have to refuse his own nephews the benefits of office. Three days of theological argument convinced him that resistance to unanimous election was defiance of the Holy Spirit. His elevation also marked a change of style: He became the first beardless pope since Clement VII stopped shaving in 1527 following the sack of Rome, setting a trend followed by all his successors.

Relations with the warring Catholic states dominated much of Clement XI's pontificate. Like his immediate predecessors he was thought by everyone other than the French to be pro-French. The Austrian Hapsburgs conquered Naples in 1707, adding to friction caused by their incursions into the Romagna, the northeastern section of the Papal States, leading Clement to declare war, with catastrophic results. A 20,000-strong papal army had to surrender at Ferrara in November 1708, and the Austrians advanced on Rome, threatening another sack of the city. In January 1709 Clement capitulated, agreeing to demilitarise the Papal States and allow Hapsburg forces free passage from Milan to the kingdom of Naples. He also had to abandon his neutrality in the ongoing War of Spanish Succession and recognise the Hapsburg claimant as king, creating an immediate schism, as the Bourbon candidate had long since been accepted as Philip V (1700–1746) in most of Spain. The Spanish church remained out of communion with Rome until the war ended in 1714.

THE JANSENIST CONTROVERSY

For a pope who has been characterised as indecisive, Clement XI's decisions had dramatic if unexpected results.[6] One of them concerned an earlier theological controversy affecting the Church in France and the Netherlands. In trying to combat the Protestants on their own ground, a Dutch Catholic bishop, Cornelius Jansen (1585–1638), argued, in his book on the theology of St. Augustine, that the need for divine grace in salvation was being ignored in favour of individual freedom and responsibility. This was sensitive ground as Augustine had influenced the thinking of Luther and even more so of Calvin, and the book threatened to reopen the 'faith or works' debate settled by the Council of Trent. In consequence five of Jansen's propositions had been condemned by Urban VIII and Innocent X.

However, his views also attracted some influential support, as contemporary piety tended away from the good-works-oriented religiosity of the age of the Counter-Reformation, towards a more pessimistic view of human nature and an internalised spirituality. Movements such as Quietism, advocating the annihilation of the self through absorption into the divine, were popular and even influenced Innocent XI. As viewed by the Congregation of the Holy Office (formerly the Holy Inquisition), these were disturbing developments.

Supporters of Jansen, known as Jansenists, who regarded his ideas as orthodox and salutary but also accepted papal authority, had claimed that the five condemned propositions were not actually to be found in his book *Augustinus,* but Alexander VII rejected this. The Jansenists fell back into a state of 'respectful silence', disagreeing but without saying so. The issue continued controversial in France, where Jansen's views had been taught in the schools attached to the fashionable Cistercian convent of Port-Royal des Champs, whose pupils included the playwright Jean Racine (1639–1699) and the mathematician and philosopher Blaise Pascal (1623–1662), who had answered Jesuit criticisms of Jansen in his *Provincial Letters* of 1657.

Louis XIV, the Sun King, who wanted 'his' church to appear united, persuaded the new pope to end the controversy. A bull of Clement XI in 1705 condemning 'respectful silence' gave Louis justification for suppressing Port-Royal. Its nuns were forcibly removed in 1709 and its buildings razed the next year. Further measures followed when complaints were made to the Holy Office about the highly popular *New Testament in French with Moral Reflections on Each Verse* published in 1693 by the Jansenist Pasquier Quesnel (1634–1719), who had already fallen foul of the Vatican for questioning papal inerrancy and primacy and lived in exile in Protestant Amsterdam.[7]

In 1713 Clement XI issued a bull entitled *Unigenitus* (The Only Born), in which 101 propositions from the *Moral Reflections* were condemned,[8] creating an enormous storm even in England, where several translated editions had been published.[9] In France, Cardinal de Noailles, the archbishop of Paris and several other French bishops appealed to the pope to withdraw *Unigenitus* and resisted it passively until 1728. Others claimed that the bull lacked force without the prior approval of the French episcopate, and in 1717 four of them appealed to a general council. This group, known as the Appellants, were excommunicated by Clement XI in 1718 but their numbers grew to include over twenty bishops and three thousand lesser clergy, and they continued to defy Rome until the last one died in 1754. Similarly, in what is called the Old Catholic schism, a group of Dutch Jansenist clergy formed a break-away communion in 1723, known as the Dutch Old Catholic Church that still exists.

There was wider concern because several of the passages from *Moral Reflections* marked down for condemnation in *Unigenitus* seemed to be pure Augustinian thought, as in the statement that 'Grace is the operation of the hand of the omnipotent God, which nothing can impede or retard.'[10] As Augustine had been as strong an influence on Thomas Aquinas as on Luther or Calvin, the Dominicans feared their own intellectual tradition was being called in question and lobbied for withdrawal or modification of the bull. This might have occurred when a Dominican became pope as Benedict XIII (1724–1730), but while assuring the friars of the unimpeachable orthodoxy of both Augustine and Aquinas, he also commanded that *Unigenitus* 'be observed in full . . . by all of whatever condition and rank'. Those clergy or members of religious orders 'who did not have good feelings about or spoke ill' of it were to be corrected by their bishop or provincial and if necessary sent to Rome, as should all books criticising it.[11]

The main opponents of the Jansenists in France had been the Jesuits, who in turn had been criticised for their supposed failings by Pascal in his *Provincial Letters,* in which he accused them of 'moral laxism' and a 'pagan morality'.[12] By this he meant that they were able to accommodate themselves to all opinions and to all men, and he criticised their use of casuistry, a form of reasoning that avoids absolute principles. Their status as the favoured confessors of the powerful, including most of the European Catholic monarchs, gave them influence thanks to their flexible approach to assessing sinfulness and the light penances they imposed, with the result that they 'governed Christendom today'.[13] The wide readership of Pascal's book led to the Jesuits being seen as secretive, manipulative and a law unto themselves. None of this would have mattered much if they had retained the support of the one authority to which they had to answer, the pope. But a new controversy now threatened this vital bond.

THE CHINESE RITES

Papally sponsored missionary contacts with the Far East began in the middle of the thirteenth century, but were broken off after the Mongols, amongst whom the most converts had been made, were expelled from China by the Ming dynasty in 1368. The Chinese mission revived in the mid-sixteenth century, thanks to maritime contacts via the new Portuguese trading stations in Goa and Indonesia. The task was entrusted to the Jesuits, whose founders had been committed to mission. One of Ignatius Loyola's six original companions, Francis Xavier (canonised by Gregory XV in 1622), obtained permission to evangelise in Indonesia and then Japan, and was on his way to create a new missionary field in China when he died in 1552.

His most significant successor was Matteo Ricci (1552–1610), who in 1582 arrived in Macao, where he learned to speak and write Chinese, eventually translating the *Analects* of Confucius and other classical texts into Latin. His skills as mathematician and map maker were prized by various Chinese provincial governors, and he was eventually admitted to the imperial court, though not to an audience with the emperor. Adopting Chinese dress and much of the lifestyle of a Buddhist monk, his willingness to fit in with the cultural norms of his hosts and his Western scientific skills made him acceptable to a society traditionally suspicious and disdainful of outsiders.

The ensuing success of the Jesuits in China was largely due to this willingness to adopt features of Chinese thought and custom and to limit contact with other Westerners. Hence the significance of the Chinese Rites introduced by Ricci, by which Chinese converts to

Christianity could preserve such traditional practices as burning incense in honour of their ancestors and venerating Confucius. The Dominicans in particular objected that this was idolatrous, but those better acquainted with Chinese society recognised that these were not forms of worship and that Confucius was not regarded as a divine being.

In Rome the Congregation for the Propagation of the Faith *(Congregatio de Propaganda Fide)*, founded by Sixtus V in 1588, was suspicious, and other religious orders involved in missionary work did not follow the Jesuit lead, resulting in lively debate about the appropriateness of the Rites. In 1645 Innocent X approved a decree of the Congregation condemning them, but in 1656 Alexander VII permitted the Rites and recognised them as being non-religious ceremonies. He also approved Chinese clergy reading the daily office in their own language. In the same year Pascal claimed the Jesuits allowed their Chinese converts 'to practice idolatry, by the ingenious idea of getting them to hide under their clothes an image of Christ, to which they are taught to apply mentally the worship paid publicly to the idol Chacim-Choan and their Keum-fucum' [Confucius].[14] But for the next half a century the issue rested where Alexander VII had left it, with the critics of the Chinese Rites quiescent but not quelled.

The issue came to the fore at the start of the pontificate of Clement XI in 1700 through appeals to the Congregation from the Franciscans. The Jesuits' independence, answerable only through their general to the pope, and their educational and evangelising methods had aroused both envy and unease in various quarters, from the College of Cardinals downwards, and the Chinese Rites promised to constitute an issue in which they might be found vulnerable. Opponents argued that the Jesuits in China lacked sufficient supervision and were not as responsive to direction from Rome as they should be.

In response, Clement XI sent a legate to the Chinese court in 1702 to try and establish a permanent diplomatic presence in Beijing, to monitor the activities of the Jesuit missionaries. At the same time the issue of the Rites was reopened, with the Jesuits submitting a defence of their position to the Congregation, but it ruled against them in 1704. The Jesuits then appealed to the pope, but in 1715 he issued the bull, *Ex illa die* (From That Day on . . .), prohibiting the Chinese Rites and forbidding the use of the Chinese words *Shang di* (supreme emperor) and *Tian* (heaven) as translations of 'God'.[15] The Jesuits ignored the pope's prohibition, until this was discovered in the time of his successor, Innocent XIII (1721–1724), who was already prejudiced against them. He forbade them from receiving any more novices, threatening the continued survival of the order itself, and giving them three years in which to convince him of their absolute obedience. In 1742 Benedict XIV ordered the Jesuit missionaries in China to swear not to use the Rites.

This episode brought about a fundamental change in the attitude of the Chinese rulers towards Christian missionaries in their empire. The emperor Kangxi (1660–1722) had used Jesuit priests trained in Western medicine, mathematics, music, astronomy and cartography, though regarding their knowledge as different rather than necessarily superior. He was tolerantly amused by the diplomatic and linguistic errors of the papal legate, Charles Thomas Maillard de Tournon (d. 1710), titular patriarch of Antioch but was suspicious of his purposes: 'he was a biased and unreliable person, who muddled right with wrong.'[16]

Brushing aside the legate's arguments in favour of a permanent legation—'China has no matters of common concern with the West'—and warning the court Jesuits that de Tournon was hostile to them, Kangxi raised the subject of the Chinese Rites. He was annoyed by some of the foreigners' misunderstanding of Chinese society and found them strangely quarrelsome: 'in this Catholic religion, the Society of Peter quarrels with the Jesuits, Bouvet quarrels with Mariani, and among the Jesuits the Portuguese want only their own nationals in the church while the French want only French in theirs.'[17]

Because he regarded the Rites as recognition of the values of Chinese culture, he insisted that they be preserved. As a further mark of commitment, future missionaries would only be admitted if coming to China for long periods, preferably for life, and the emperor made it clear that he did not intend to lose those already established at his court and versed in Chinese ways. He told the court Jesuits in jest that he would not permit them to return to the West and that if the pope declared them guilty of anything, he would cut their heads off and send them back so the pope could 're-form' them. He also began restricting the movements of Christian preachers by confining them to towns, starting a process that led to the repression of all missionary activity under his successors. When de Tournon issued a legatine decree in 1707 ordering the Jesuits to obey the ban on the Rites issued in Rome in 1704, the emperor imprisoned him in Macao until his death.

Ultimately, Clement XI's decisions on the Chinese Rites, not reversed until 1939, proved fatal to the continuing success of the missions in China, and led to a weakening of the ties between the papacy and the Society of Jesus. The Jesuits convinced themselves that they were right to follow practices they believed necessary despite explicit papal prohibition, and the memory of this defiance led some popes and cardinals later in the century to regard the Society as less than entirely loyal and to give ear to a growing body of criticism of it. This mattered all the more as friction between the papacy and the Catholic powers continued to grow.

THE HAPPIEST OF TIMES

These conflicts were not of the papacy's making. The popes of the eighteenth century have collectively been described as 'humane, comfortable, paternal, considerate . . . good men; not heroic men usually, but open-hearted, friendly, trying to do what little they could to smile upon the world of men to make the human race happy and well-doing and better prepared for eternity'.[18] One of them, Clement XIV (1769–1774), expressed a similar sentiment when he described his predecessors as 'good chaps'.[19]

Some were unworldly, notably Benedict XIII (1724–1730), a member of the Orsini family, who was seventy-five when elected and previously a cardinal for over fifty years. As pope he retained the archbishopric of Benevento, which he had held since 1686, because he was so fond of the city, still visiting it just a few months before his death. As archbishop and pope he observed the rule of the Dominican order, which he had joined in 1669, and always treated its general as his superior, kneeling when he wrote to him. Given to mystical ecstasies, he preferred to devote himself to pastoral duties, preaching, hearing confessions, consecrating churches and visiting hospitals, rather than the administrative and diplomatic affairs that normally took up so much papal time. A contemporary observer described him as 'a good man, very pious, very weak and very simple, who had no greater pleasure in the world than making saints'.[20] He convoked a synod of the bishops of the Roman province in 1725, which pursued the policy of the Council of Trent in insisting that seminaries be established in every diocese and existing ones improved.

Unfortunately for him the papacy was a monarchy based upon personal rule and dependent upon the competence of its monarch. Benedict delegated matters of state and of papal finance to a Beneventan confidant, Niccolò Coscia (1681–1755), who had been his secretary and whom he made titular archbishop of Traianopolis in 1724 and a cardinal the next year. Coscia proved a mixture of rogue and fool, selling offices and taking bribes, and his six-year tenure led to serious losses in papal finances and the growing unpopularity of the pope himself with the citizens of Rome. Coscia tried to distance the pope from the cardinals and to control key appointments, notably to the crucial post of secretary of state. When the news of Benedict's death was announced in the Rome opera, the audience shouted, 'Good. Now all that remains is to burn Coscia!' and rushed out to loot his house.[21] He was imprisoned in the Castel Sant'Angelo and stripped of his cardinal's office by Clement XII (1730–1740), while the once-favoured Beneventans were hounded out of Rome.

One of the most embarrassing episodes of Benedict's pontificate cannot be blamed on Coscia, however. In 1728 the pope's personal enthusiasm for his distant predecessor Gregory VII (1073–1085), who had been canonised in 1606 but whose liturgical feast was observed only in Rome, led him to make it mandatory for the whole Church. This involved creating some new liturgy, one of whose texts referred to Gregory's excommunicating the emperor Henry IV, depriving him of his kingdom and releasing his subjects from their obedience. This reminder of the never-relinquished papal claim to authority over secular rulers was entirely out of step with the mood of the times, in which religion carried less weight than reason and priestly rule seemed an anachronism. And so, these few words in a minor text produced a short-lived diplomatic uproar, with various governments either protesting to the pope or preventing it being printed and circulated.

This episode added weight to growing royal distrust of the Jesuits, seen as the leading promoters of the pope's right to interfere in secular matters. Thus the French monarchy vetoed Cardinal Carlo Alberto Guidobono Cavalchini in the conclave of 1758 when he was close to being elected because of his known support for the campaign to canonise Robert Bellarmine (1542–1621), the first Jesuit cardinal, who had argued that a pope could depose a king if it were necessary for the good of his subjects' souls. His canonisation would only be achieved in 1930.

Cardinal Coscia was temporarily released from detention to take part in the four-month-long conclave that would elect the pope who would deprive him of his rank. The change of pontiff in 1730 only put a stop to the harm he had done but hardly reversed it. Once noted as a patron of the arts and 'one of the best violins in Italy', Clement XII, a member of the Florentine noble house of Corsini, was seventy-eight on his election, and in poor health.[22] He tried to maintain personal control over the papal administration, despite the ambitions of a nephew he made cardinal, but went blind in 1732 and suffered from serious memory loss before being completely incapacitated in the final year of his pontificate.

Papal treasurer from 1695 to 1707, and a former member of ten different Vatican Congregations, Clement was experienced in government and well aware of the problems he had inherited from his predecessor. He tried various expedients to deal with the massive papal debt, now amounting to sixty million *scudi,* introducing a national lottery in 1732 and issuing a paper currency. He also attempted to improve the economy of the Papal States through the encouragement of trade, for example, making Ancona a free port in the same year. But as his disabilities grew, his capacity for leadership waned and his last years saw the papacy entirely lacking direction, both in its internal affairs and in diplomatic relations.

The only major doctrinal decision of the period was the condemnation of freemasonry as a form of heresy in April 1738, largely because of the secret nature of the societies and their proceedings. As the pope said in an encyclical—an authoritative papal letter issued either to the episcopate as a whole or to a particular group of bishops—

> We, Commander of the family of the Lord, like the faithful and prudent Servant, should teach with Divine Eloquence that vigilance must be preserved by day and night, in case men of this type break into the house like thieves, and in case, like foxes attempting to destroy the vineyard, they corrupt the hearts of the simple, and shoot the innocent with arrows.[23]

Diplomatically the papacy's position was weakened by Clement XII's resistance to the restoration of Spanish rule over Sicily and Naples. The treaties that had ended the War of Spanish Succession resulted in the emperor Charles VI (1711-1740) acquiring Naples in 1714 and Sicily in 1720, but the outbreak of another conflict involving most of the major European powers, the War of Polish Succession, gave the Spanish Bourbons the chance to conquer both in 1735. The pope, still accepted as feudal overlord of the two kingdoms, was reluctant to recognise this change of rule, and a serious diplomatic row broke out between Rome and Madrid that was only resolved in 1737 by a new concordat or agreement, which also regulated royal control over the Spanish church. In 1738 one of the sons of the Spanish king was finally invested as ruler of Naples and Sicily by Clement XII, but the episode had generated a lot of anti-papal feeling in the Bourbon courts in both Spain and Italy.

Clement's successor, Prospero Lambertini, who became Benedict XIV (1740–1758), was the outstanding pope of the eighteenth century, both for his practical and for his intellectual achievements. Cardinal Ganganelli, later to be Pope Clement XIV, described the years of Benedict's pontificate as 'the happiest time in history'.[24] The new pope was elected at the end of a six-month conclave, the longest in recent centuries. A French observer drew pen portraits of the participating cardinals, describing one as 'without manners, decency, intelligence or judgement', another as 'a rogue of the first class' and the Camerlengo and dean of the college as 'without faith or principles . . . the most evil man in Rome'.[25] But he was kinder to Cardinal Lambertini, whom he called 'good, easy, amiable and without arrogance; something very rare in those of his sort'.[26]

Aged sixty-five at his election, Benedict XIV was younger than most of his predecessors. He had already proved himself a very competent administrator, serving from 1720 as secretary of the Congregation of the Council, 'the most powerful of curial offices', before becoming archbishop of Ancona and then Bologna.[27] He was also a distinguished church lawyer. His four-volume work on the history and law of canonisation is still the standard work on the subject, as is his book on diocesan synods.[28] The new pope was also assisted by one of the ablest secretaries of state, Cardinal Silvio Valenti Gonzaga (1690–1756), who developed the work begun by Clement XII improving the trade and economy of the Papal States.

Benedict is said to have advised his fellow cardinals in the conclave: 'if you want a saint, take Gotti; if you want a statesman, take Aldovrandi; if you want a good fellow, take me.' This, appropriate to the tradition of eighteenth-century popes, was indeed what they got, but more besides. Unlike most of his immediate predecessors, he was a major figure on the European stage. In 1741 Voltaire dedicated his play *Fanaticism or Mahómet the Prophet* to the pope, and the two men exchanged correspondence over Virgil's testimony on whether the vowel in the Latin word *hic* should be long or short.

In 1745 Benedict created an academy of twenty-five outstanding scholars from the Papal States, who became known as the Benedettini, and included Laura Maria Bassi (1711–1778), appointed at the age of twenty-one as the first female professor of anatomy (at the University of Bologna) and who was one of the earliest teachers of Newtonian physics in Italy. Not everyone was convinced of his merits. The historian of classical art Johann Winckelmann, who lived in

Rome from 1748 until his murder in 1768, called him a clown, and he was notorious for the obscenity of his language, said to be 'more suitable for a grenadier than a pontiff'.[29]

Benedict tried to lessen the friction that had marked so many diplomatic exchanges between the papacy and the Catholic power in previous decades by negotiating new concordats with virtually all of them, ensuring that relations between church and state were based on agreements. As in the concordat made in 1737 with Spain, most concessions came from the papal side, and some of those by the monarchies were never fully implemented. Other reforms included a radical remaking of the *Index*, which had hitherto been organised by Christian names of the condemned authors and was full of errors. For example, only the Latin translation of Thomas Hobbes's *The Leviathan* of 1651, whose final section was devoted to the question of how the Roman church could be likened to the Kingdom of the Fairies, was included, and not the English original. Its author's name had also been catalogued as Thomas Gobes.[30] The list was pruned, and Copernicus amongst others was finally removed. Benedict also abolished some of the canon law obstacles to Catholics marrying non-Catholics. His appointment as cardinal in 1747 of the younger son of James VIII and III, the Stuart claimant to the British crown, did irreparable harm to the Jacobite cause, associating it firmly in British public opinion with the Catholic Church.[31] Cardinal Henry Stuart (1725–1807) became the longest-serving member of the college.

Useful as these agreements and reforms were, the flurry of diplomatic activity in Benedict's pontificate was another sign of that anxiety with which the papacy increasingly viewed the Catholic states. This was fuelled by the scarcely veiled threats some of them used to suggest that if they did not get their way this might lead to schism on the often-cited precedent of Henry VIII of England.

'I HAVE CUT OFF MY RIGHT HAND'

For many centuries the papacy had been able to play off the rivalries of the lay powers that could either protect or threaten it. Thus France and the Hapsburg empire had long been counterweights to each other. However, by 1735 four kingdoms—Spain, France, Naples and Sicily—were under the rule of three different branches of a single dynasty, the Bourbons, who retained a stronger sense of family unity and more frequently acted together than had the Hapsburgs.

By the middle of the eighteenth century, the rise of the kingdom of Prussia added a new factor to the diplomatic equations. Yet another major European conflict, the War of Austrian Succession (1740–1748), revealed Prussia's ability to take on the Hapsburg emperors in a contest for dominance over the smaller states of northern Germany. As a result, from 1748 the empire became less willing to fall out with the Bourbon monarchies, for fear they would ally with Prussia against it. Rome thus had no powerful friends to turn to when the Bourbon states wanted to bully her. This is the essential diplomatic background behind the papal suppression of the Society of Jesus in 1773.

The Jesuits already suffered from distrust of their motives. Works by disenchanted former Jesuits painted them in lurid colours as fabulously wealthy or as inveterate conspirators, and their roles as confessors and providers of education in schools and colleges across Catholic Europe added to the fear of the nebulous but malevolent influence they were thought to exercise. Add to this their loyalty to their general, 'the black pope', and there appears the stuff of conspiracy theories: a secret church within a church. While these vague and ill-grounded perceptions fed a widespread but by no means universal prejudice, the Jesuits' political opponents were inspired by practical objectives.

The first battleground was the kingdom of Portugal, which was treated with growing respect in Rome throughout the eighteenth century—thanks to its possession of Brazil, across the southwestern frontiers of which Jesuit missionaries had established large reservations known as Reductions for some of the indigenous population of the Spanish-ruled region of Paraguay. From these they excluded both colonists and slavers, thereby making influential enemies.

A treaty between Spain and Portugal in 1750 adjusted the frontier between Paraguay and Brazil, requiring the relocation of seven out of the thirty Reductions. The Jesuit fathers protested that this was in practice impossible, and when local uprisings against the Portuguese led to a savage war in 1752, the Jesuits were blamed for inspiring it. In 1758 in the first formal move to have them suppressed, the Portuguese ambassador in Rome told the ailing Benedict XIV that the Jesuits needed either to be reformed or abolished. The pope agreed to appoint a commission to investigate, under the presidency of a Portuguese cardinal with close ties to the government in Lisbon.

Benedict's death in May 1758 halted this process, as his successor Clement XIII (1758–1769) had been educated by the Jesuits, and, although not a member of the Society himself (no pope has ever been), was a staunch defender of it. In consequence in 1759 the Portuguese government resorted to other measures, confiscating all Jesuit property in the kingdom and expelling or imprisoning its members on charges of having fomented the war in Paraguay and of plotting to assassinate the king. The Inquisition, which as in Spain was controlled by the state, was also turned on them. A first consignment of 133 Portuguese Jesuits landed in the Papal States in October 1759, with several hundred more following soon after, while another forty-five of them were imprisoned without trial near Lisbon for the next nineteen years.

If confined to Portugal, the controversy over the Jesuits might have had no wider implications, but soon after they came under attack elsewhere for other reasons. The Jesuit community in the French West Indies had become heavily and initially profitably involved in trade with mainland France, but the loss of a flotilla of their ships to the English at the start of the Seven Years War (1756–1763) caused the bankruptcy of their Paris agents in 1756, leaving debts of around three million *livres*. The superior of the French Jesuits denied responsibility for the actions of the West Indian branch, but protracted litigation lasting until 1761 went against him, by which time the debt had risen through accumulated interest to five million *livres*.

This sum was beyond their ability or that of the headquarters of the Society in Rome to pay, and in April 1762 the Jesuits' French property was sequestrated to meet what was owed. This was accompanied by an order for the closure of their schools and houses and the expulsion of the members. Nearly 3,000 French Jesuits were deported to Avignon, still papal territory. When Clement XIII issued a brief describing the actions of the Parlement de Paris, the French supreme court, as a persecution, the French bishops refused permission for its publication. The pope's subsequent bull declaring the Parlement's sentence null and void merely increased the friction without improving the lot of the ejected Jesuits.

By this time anti-Jesuit propaganda and prejudice across many parts of Western Europe had become so intense that almost anything could be blamed on them, making them useful scapegoats for any internal difficulties a government might face. The cases of France and Portugal also showed that their properties could be confiscated with impunity. Thus when in 1766 riots broke out in Madrid over an attempt by the Bourbon regime to impose French forms of dress on the Spanish population, this resistance was immediately blamed on the Jesuits, and King Charles III (1759–1788) ordered their expulsion and the confiscation of their property in February 1767.

In April an appeal by Clement XIII to Charles III, whose installation as king of Sicily and Naples had been delayed by papal opposition thirty years earlier, was immediately rejected. Faced with the prospect of as many as 20,000 Jesuit refugees being shipped from Spanish territories in Europe and South America to the Papal States, the pope, advised by the general of the Jesuits, then told the king he would not admit them. When the first consignments of exiled Jesuits tried to land at Civitavecchia near Rome they were turned back. The same happened when they tried to disembark in Genoese-ruled Corsica, and they remained at sea until permission to land was granted five months later. When in May 1768 Corsica was ceded to France, the Jesuit refugees were shipped to Genoa by the new French administration, and made their way in bedraggled condition to the Papal States.

In the third Bourbon state, the joint kingdom of Sicily and Naples, the government was still dominated by the king's minister, Bernardo Tanucci, who was hostile to the Jesuits and dismissive of Rome. Here the excuse for ridding the kingdom of the Jesuits was even more bizarre, as they were blamed for causing an eruption of Mount Vesuvius in 1767 and expelled.

Clement XIII remained unwavering in support of the Jesuits and in January 1765 issued a bull expressing his confidence in them.

However, he was not expected to live long, and the Bourbon powers anticipated that the next conclave would produce a pontiff who might be persuaded to suppress the Society. Then a further incident exacerbated the already high level of tension between Rome and the Catholic monarchies.

On 16 January 1768 the Bourbon duke of Parma forbade the clergy of the duchy from making legal appeals to Rome. As the papacy had never recognised the loss of its sovereignty over Parma, which had changed hands between the Bourbons and the Hapsburgs several times since 1714, this move by the ruler of what Clement XIII regarded as 'our duchy' was deeply offensive. Two weeks later he issued a bull declaring the duke's edict null and threatening excommunication to any of his subjects who tried to apply it. The French ambassador immediately declared that 'the Pope is a fool and his Secretary of State [Cardinal Luigi Maria Torreggiani] an ass.'[32] Enlightened Europe was shocked at the prospect of an ecclesiastical potentate trying to overturn the laws of a civil sovereign. Voltaire criticised the whole notion of the papacy having temporal sovereignty and Edward Gibbon, author of *The Decline and Fall of the Roman Empire,* who had visited Rome during a tour of Italy in 1764-5, proudly recorded that he had 'departed without kissing the foot of Rezzonico [Clement XIII], who neither possessed the wit of his predecessor Lambertini, nor the virtues of his successor Ganganelli'.[33]

When in October 1768 Clement refused the demand of all the Bourbon states that he withdraw his bull, they took action to coerce him. France invaded Avignon and the Comtat-Venaissin, while Naples annexed Benevento, threatening further dismemberment or loss to the Papal States. The three monarchies then demanded in January 1769 that the Society of Jesus be dissolved. On February 2 the pope died. The British minister to the Hapsburg-ruled grand duchy of Florence, Sir Horace Mann, wrote to Horace Walpole, Earl of Orford,

The Pope's death so *à propos* may put a stop to the inconveniences which were still to be apprehended from his perseverance to support what he had done with regard to Parma and to protect the

Jesuits in defiance of the Bourbon Courts, who had peremptorily demanded the suppression of that society. . . . In short nothing but his death could produce a new system in that Court conformable to the times and save the temporals [earthly possessions] of that state from ruin.[34]

Everything depended on the conclave. Defenders of the Jesuits tried to rush through an election before the foreign cardinals could arrive, to secure a pope 'devoted to their interest', but were warned by the French ambassador that 'if they alone make a pope of their own, they alone would enjoy him, by which he gave them to understand that such a step would infallibly produce a schism.'[35] Faced by such a threat, the resident cardinals had no option but to wait several weeks for the arrival of the cardinals from the Bourbon kingdoms. In the meantime they had to continue going through the required process of twice-daily balloting in the conclave, while ensuring that no vote was decisive. As Sir Horace Mann remarked in another letter to Horace Walpole: 'I greatly pity the poor old cardinals, who will be confined for so long, and who must twice a day play at choosing a pope, though their only care must be not to choose one by inadvertency.'[36] On 11 May, Walpole himself wrote suggesting the conclave might see the election of 'the last pope', anticipating the institution itself might be destroyed by the row over the Jesuits.[37] On 19 May a new pope was elected.

Clement XIV (1769–1774), formerly Cardinal Lorenzo Ganganelli, was a Franciscan and a distinguished theologian, who had twice refused election as general of his order and had shown himself a friend to the Jesuits, dedicating one of his works to the memory of their founder, St. Ignatius Loyola. However, in the conclave, in which his chances had originally not been highly rated, he made it clear that he did not regard their suppression as unthinkable. With so many other candidates vetoed or regarded as unsuitable, this willingness to consider the possibility was enough for him to be elected.

The new pope assured the Bourbon kingdoms that he would address the Jesuit question and re-established diplomatic relations with Portugal before the year was out. However, he and his new secretary of state, Cardinal Lazaro Opizio Pallavicino (1719–1785), who as a former nuncio in Madrid enjoyed good relations with the Spanish court, hoped that such gestures, allied to procrastination, might suffice to prevent the issue being brought to a head, especially as it was by no means clear that the abolition of the Jesuits would be accepted by the devout Hapsburg empress Maria Theresa (1740–1780), who ruled with her son Joseph II (1765–1790). However, in 1770 she made it clear that her position on the matter was now neutral, and under unremitting pressure from the Bourbon monarchies a decision on abolition became unavoidable. One Protestant divine gleefully recalled earlier prophecies of how 'in the end, God to justify his law, shall suddenly cut off this society, even by the hands of those who have most succoured them and made use of them; so at the end they shall become odious to all nations.'[38] Enlightenment thinkers hastened to congratulate the pope, though he himself is said to have declared, 'I have cut off my right hand,' by ordering the suppression.[39]

On 21 July 1773 in Santa Maria Maggiore, Clement XIV issued the bull *Dominus ac Redemptor Noster* (Our Lord and Redeemer) abolishing the Society of Jesus. A second decree on 6 August appointed a commission of cardinals, under the virulently anti-Jesuit Mario Marefusco, to supervise the process. *Dominus ac Redemptor Noster,* a long and rather rambling document, was quickly translated into French, German and English. It devotes much space to providing historical examples of how earlier popes had suppressed a variety of other orders.[40] What surprises is the lack of anything like a reasoned justification for the action being taken. The bull's main concern is to underline the pope's authority to take such a step and to prevent any criticism of it. The failure of the Jesuits to act on earlier warnings is mentioned, but the nature of their supposed offences is left entirely obscure, and any form of discussion in print or in conversation of the papal decree was strictly forbidden.

Rumours abounded. It was said that the Jesuit general Lorenzo Ricci (1703–1775) had ordered his followers to ignore the bull because the pope's election was simoniacal and thus Clement was not a true pontiff. Although it was discovered that someone else was behind this rumour, Ricci was imprisoned in the Castel Sant'Angelo and died there. Inquisitors searching the Jesuit archives were also said to have found a document proving that the Society had been behind the Gunpowder Plot of 1605, aimed at blowing up the English Houses of Parliament, and the British government ordered its man in Rome to get a copy.[41]

Clement XIV himself developed an obsessive fear that Jesuit plots were being hatched to assassinate him and became increasingly reclusive, allowing the papal government to be dominated by what the imperial ambassador called a 'little band of incompetent and unscrupulous favourites', who plunged it deeper into debt.[42] A symptom of Clement's growing secretiveness was the unprecedented way in which he made so many appointments of cardinals *in pectore*, without revealing their names until a few years later. This process was often used when papal finances were too straitened to afford the stipend due to a new cardinal, but could also be employed to ensure the loyalty of the secret appointee. In his final consistory in April 1773 Clement XIV kept the names of eleven out of thirteen new cardinals secret. As he died without ever revealing them, their appointments remained officially unrecognised.

Thanks to his suppression of the Jesuits, Clement became the toast of non-Catholic Europe and would later be known as the Protestant Pope. After his death an anonymous 'Life' and two volumes of his letters (some possibly spurious) became best sellers and were quickly translated into English and French. He died suddenly at the height of his fame in September 1774, and it was rumoured that his drinking chocolate had been poisoned by former Jesuits, a belief strengthened by the rapid decomposition of his body.

During the ensuing conclave a Venetian observer drew up a humorous list of the vices of the various peoples and rulers of Europe, criticising the English for 'fighting everyone' and the Dutch for 'buying everything'. Of the popes he said they were 'afraid of everything'.[43] If the affair of the Jesuits shows that his comment had some truth in it, no one at the time could have predicted the far greater reasons for fear that lay ahead.

chapter 19

THE LAST GREAT THING
LEFT TO ITALY

(1774–1878)

THE AGE OF REVOLUTION

A t the start of the year 1799 it was possible the papacy would not survive till the end of it. Rome had been a republic since being occupied by French troops the previous February, and the eighty-year-old Pius VI was a prisoner in France, where he died in August. The cardinals were scattered, with little hope of being allowed back into Rome for a conclave. Some contemporary commentators regarded the papal office as an anachronism, an institution that had outlived its usefulness. In France, religion itself had been proscribed, and from the Catholic powers little help could be expected. Spain was militarily too weak to intervene, and the empire had just been defeated by a French army commanded by the new first consul, Napoleon Bonaparte.

In the same year in Rome a thirty-four-year-old monk, Mauro Cappellari, published a book, *The Triumph of the Holy See and of the Church over the Assaults of the Innovators, Combated and Defeated with Their Own Weapons,*[1] which gave a new systematic presentation to arguments supporting papal infallibility, the belief that a pope's pronouncements on issues of doctrine and conduct were incapable of being wrong. It was hardly the best time for claiming greater authority for a papacy whose very survival was in question, but just over thirty years later Cappellari would be elected Pope Gregory XVI

(1831–1846) and forty years after that the doctrine of papal infallibility would be proclaimed at the greatest ecumenical council since Trent. In the intervening decades the papacy and the Catholic Church took on many of the characteristics that have distinguished them up to the present.

The suppression of the Jesuits had not ended the Catholic monarchies' attempts to reduce the papacy to an ornamental function. Pressure came primarily from Vienna, where Joseph II exercised absolute rule after the death in 1780 of his pious mother, the empress Maria Theresa (known to Frederick the Great of Prussia as the Apostolic Hag). As a sovereign determined to be rational and enlightened, Joseph proposed to eliminate all institutions and practices that hindered the efficient running of his empire. The Church was an obvious target for such improvement, and the emperor imposed reforms, such as the creation of a new parish structure, without consulting Rome. All monasteries were put under the jurisdiction of the local bishop, irrespective of papal grants of immunity, and some religious orders were suppressed by imperial decree. In October 1781 the emperor issued an edict of religious toleration, causing alarm in Rome, as did the presence of science and agriculture in the imperially devised curriculum for the new state seminaries that replaced the diocesan ones.

Influencing the emperor's thinking was a treatise of 1763 by the German bishop Johann Nikolaus von Hontheim (1701–1790), who under the pen name Justinus Febronius argued that the pope should have no authority in the secular sphere.[2] Hontheim, a noted antiquarian, was indebted to the more rigorous and sceptical historical scholarship of the age, personified by Ludovico Muratori in Italy, Edward Gibbon in England and Lenain de Tillemont in France, which challenged the certainties on which the papacy's own view of its past rested.

He urged Clement XIII, to whom his book was dedicated, to abandon the papacy's unhistorical claims to absolute authority, and to return to an earlier more collegial style of primacy, which might end the schism with the Protestant churches. This involved recognising not only the superiority of general councils but also the rights of secular princes, who should be able to reform their own national churches on the advice of their bishops. Hontheim also argued that the pope could not be infallible in the definition of doctrine, and that Rome did not have to be the papal see. Although forced to retract his views in 1778, his model for church-state relations, referred to as Febronianism, was much admired in Enlightenment circles.

The emperor's adaptation of Hontheim's ideas, which became known as Josephism, was also imposed in Hapsburg-ruled territories in northern Italy by Joseph II's brother Leopold, grand duke of Tuscany. In January 1786 Leopold sent a circular letter to all Tuscan bishops suggesting fifty-seven reform proposals aimed at increasing episcopal authority at the expense of papal and including regular diocesan synods, reducing monastic privileges and eliminating legendary saints.

This programme was enthusiastically embraced by Scipione de' Ricci, bishop of Pistoia and Prato (1780–1790), who called a diocesan synod in September 1786 in which he encouraged his 246 clergy to speak freely.[3] Their decisions, strongly influenced by Jansenist and Febronian ideas, included statements that the Church should exercise no secular authority, had no right to introduce new dogmas and could only be infallible in so far as it conformed to Scripture and tradition. Although the restriction of papal primacy to the purely spiritual sphere was not specifically demanded, it was implied by these decrees.

The clergy of Pistoia also showed themselves hostile to new and 'enthusiastic' forms of piety, such as the cult of the Sacred Heart of Jesus. They wanted images of the saints replaced by pictures of biblical scenes and the number of feast days of saints reduced. They voted to encourage the laity to read the Bible, recommending the use of the Jansenist Pasquier Quesnel's 1693 *Moral Reflections,* despite its papal condemnation, and demanded vernacular liturgy that congregations could understand.

More radical were the plans for the religious orders in the diocese, which were all to be amalgamated and follow a single monastic rule. No town would be permitted to have more than one monastery. The distinction between choir monks and lay brothers (the often illiterate members of the community who performed the manual labour) was to be abolished and no monk would take permanent vows and so could leave the order at will. Nuns would be permitted to take them, but only once they reached the age of forty.

Elsewhere in the Hapsburg domains even the higher clergy were resisting papal interference in their affairs. In 1786 the German archbishops united to refuse to allow a new papal nunciature to be established in Munich, capital of the kingdom of Bavaria. The authority of nuncios, as papal representatives with both precedence and authority over often very long-established regional archbishoprics, was resented. Thus with France committed to the Gallican Articles and the other Bourbon monarchs already limiting papal oversight of their national churches, the Hapsburg reforms threatened to leave the pope as little more than Catholicism's spiritual figurehead, the 'Grand Lama of the Vatican' in another of Frederick the Great's trenchant phrases.[4] Hoping that a personal intervention might make the emperor change his mind, the new pope, Pius VI, visited Vienna in 1782 and was shocked when the imperial chancellor shook his hand instead of kissing it. After the pope's departure, the chancellor commented that they had given him a black eye.

PIUS VI

To succeed Clement XIV was always going to be difficult, and the conclave of 1774/5 took nearly five months to settle on Giovanni Angelo Braschi, who took the name of Pius VI (1775–1799). At the age of fifty-eight he was younger and more vigorous than most of his predecessors, and as former secretary to Benedict XIV and apostolic treasurer under Clement XIII he was experienced in both curial administration and politics. He broke with the long tradition of using the names Benedict, Clement and Innocent to honour instead the last papal saint, Pius V, and thereby promise a change in values.

However, his personal reputation with later generations of historians has not been high. In part this is due to the remarks of a Scottish doctor and novelist, John Moore, who was present in Rome when the pope inaugurated the Holy Year of 1775, and whose ironic book *Society and Manners in Italy with Anecdotes relating to some Eminent*

Characters was much read in the years before the French Revolution. He shared the view widely held in the Protestant world that Clement XIV 'was a man of moderation, good sense and simplicity of manners, and could not go through the ostentatious parade which his station required, without reluctance, and marks of disgust.'[5] Pius VI, on the other hand, he believed was chosen as

> a firm believer in all the tenets of the Roman church, and a strict and scrupulous observer of all its injunctions and ceremonials. As his pretensions, in point of family, fortune and connections, were smaller than those of most of his brother cardinals, it is the more probable that he owed his elevation to this part of his character, which rendered him a proper person to check the progress of abuses that had been entirely neglected by the late pope; under whose administration free-thinking was said to have been countenanced, and Protestantism in general regarded with diminished abhorrence.[6]

His comments on Pius's appearance at the Christmas liturgy at St. Peter's lies behind every modern reference to the pope's vanity:

> His Holiness went through all the evolutions of the ceremony with an address and flexibility of body, which are rarely to be found in those who wear the tiara; who are, generally speaking, men bowing under the load of years and infirmities . . . his present Holiness is not insensible of the charms of his person, or unsolicitous about his external ornaments.[7]

Less cynical may be Dr. Moore's view that the new pontiff was elected in reaction to the policies of his predecessors. Although for much of the eighteenth century the popes had been pressured and intimidated by lay Catholic rulers and had had to accommodate them on several issues, something of a counter-current was building up in its final decades. Throughout the century some cardinals, the *zelanti* or zealots, believed that the spiritual values of the Church must never be compromised and distrusted those of their brethren, the *politicanti,* who gave priority to maintaining good relations with secular rulers.

This was a view shared by many of the laity. To see the eighteenth century primarily as an age of reason is to view it through the eyes of a small number of philosophers, historians and other thinkers. It was also a period marked by emotional if theatrical piety, reflected in its music and in its religious art. New devotional practices such as following the Stations of the Cross and veneration of the Sacred Heart were widely used, despite the scorn of Enlightened clergy, and popular enthusiasm led to the canonisation of many new saints.

How far Bishop Ricci of Pistoia and other clerical 'rationalists' were out of tune with many of the laity, especially in the countryside, can be seen in his own fall from grace. A synod of all the Tuscan bishops in April 1787 rejected the decrees of his synod, with only three voting in favour. His position in his own diocese became untenable, as Pistoia was already mutinous over his attempts to modernise its Dominican church, by removing the body of a fourteenth-century friar, locally venerated as a saint but which Ricci insisted was not a true relic. Then Prato erupted in 1787 when it was rumoured that he was planning to demolish the altar housing the revered relic of the Blessed Virgin Mary's girdle. As peasants poured into the town, the bishop's palace was sacked, the state seminary overrun and order had to be restored by the army. Ricci resigned after his protector Grand Duke Leopold left to become emperor in 1790.

Despite the plans of reformers to rationalise monastic orders, during this century many of the major monasteries of Catholic Europe were physically transformed, with their medieval churches and conventual buildings being swept away, to be replaced by more ornate new ones in the fashionable Rococo and then from the 1770s Neoclassical styles. In Rome during the final quarter of the century several large-scale projects, including completing the work on St. Peter's with a vast new sacristy and canons' residence, were carried out for Pius VI. There was renewed interest in the city's past and in antiquity more generally, as wealthy aristocrats and others on the Grand Tour bought classical sculpture and other antiquities, sometimes newly faked, to take home. So much of Rome's heritage began being exported that Pius VI forbade further unauthorised excavations and the removal of ancient sculpture. Instead he promoted a project started by his predecessor of forming a papal collection of classical art, to be displayed to select visitors in the Vatican Palace in a museum later called the Pio-Clementino, whose contents were catalogued in four mighty double-folio volumes. This first papal museum was supplemented by others devoted to Egyptian and Etruscan art under Gregory XVI (1831–1846).

While Rome was the best source for classical antiquities, the city also had a unique early Christian heritage to be exploited and reflecting on this served to reassure the papacy in troubled times about its mission and authority. Excavations in sacred sites took on a dual importance, as antiquarian interest allied itself to the hope of reanimating the spiritual riches of the city's past. In 1729 excavations in the Church of Santa Prassede, close to the Basilica of Santa Maria Maggiore, had led to the discovery of relics of over two thousand presumed martyrs transferred there from the catacombs by Paschal I (817–824) and also the body of the 'Santo Papa' himself, whose tomb was opened in the presence of Benedict XIII.[8] Although even more dramatic results might follow from excavations in St. Peter's, no pope dared make the attempt.[9]

The changing atmosphere of the later part of the century was reflected in a new paper, the *Giornale ecclesiastico di Roma*, founded in July 1785, which devoted itself to the defence of traditional Catholic values and of papal authority. The French Revolution of 1789 also gave the remaining Catholic monarchies something more menacing to worry about than the supposed conspiracies of the Jesuits or the archaic nature of the papacy. In August 1794 Pius VI took the offensive in his bull *Auctorem Fidei* (Author of Our Faith) annulling the decrees of the Synod of Pistoia.

Developments in France, however, had already proved more threatening to Rome than the 'enlightened despotism' of Joseph II. The Revolutionary assembly had turned its attention to the reform of the Church in 1790, voting for the Civil Constitution of the Clergy, which turned all French churchmen into salaried officials of the state.

Pius VI only reacted in March 1791, when an oath of loyalty was demanded from the French clergy. He then threatened that priests who took the oath would be suspended from their orders and condemned both the Civil Constitution of the Clergy and the Declaration of the Rights of Man, issued in 1789.

This papal decree led to diplomatic relations between Paris and Rome being broken, and to what became the permanent French seizure of Avignon and the Comtat-Venaissin. Pius VI responded by backing the alliance of monarchies opposing the revolutionary government in France, and supporting French royalist exiles in the Papal States. Members of the French clergy, brought up on Gallicanism and Febronianism and in some cases approving the ideals of the Revolution, found themselves torn in their loyalties.

In 1796 Napoleon defeated the Austrians at the battle of Lodi and occupied the duchy of Milan. Despite having minimal forces of his own, Pius VI refused to back down, and so the French army invaded the Papal States, which quickly submitted. The Peace of Tolentino was signed on 19 February 1797, requiring the papacy to pay a large indemnity and surrender numerous valuable manuscripts and works of art to the victor. Most of the northern sections of the Papal States, known as the Legations because they were governed by papal legates, were transferred to the new Cisalpine Republic, whose capital was Milan, which had just been created under French protection.

Rome and its immediate hinterland stayed under papal rule, but the situation remained tense, with French forces nearby. The death of a French general in a riot in Rome in February 1798 provided the excuse for their army to march in. A Roman Republic was proclaimed, with the enthusiastic backing of many in the city, and Pius himself was deposed as head of state and exiled to Sardinia. The renewal of war in Europe caused him to be taken instead into France, where he died at Valence on 29 August 1799.

THE PAPAL PRISONER: PIUS VII

By this time, after Napoleon made himself first consul, the situation in Italy had changed. The army of the emperor Francis II (1792–1834) counter-attacked in 1799, briefly regaining the Hapsburg duchies. Granting leave for his successor to be elected outside Rome had been one of Pius VI's last acts, and so the cardinals held a conclave in Venice in December. As the city had been in Hapsburg hands since 1797, pressure was put on them to elect a pope acceptable to Vienna, but *zelanti* cardinals feared the permanent loss of the northern Papal States, which Francis had just occupied. For them the continuing existence of the States of the Church, as they were now called, was the sole guarantee of the political and economic independence of the papacy. They were opposed by cardinals supporting the imperial interest and by others of a liberal persuasion, who felt that some accommodation was needed with the revolutionary ideals planted in Italy by the French.

The outcome was a protracted conclave that produced a candidate acceptable to all factions, the fifty-eight-year-old monk Barnabà Chiaramonti, formerly confessor to Pius VI, in whose honour he named himself Pius VII (1800–1823). He was so small that none of the sets of papal vestments, prepared ahead of the conclave, fitted him, and even his pontifical slippers had to be stuffed with straw.

The new pope had liberal leanings. As a professor in Parma he was one of twenty-seven citizens to subscribe to Denis de Diderot's great *Encyclopédie,* and he read the philosophical and historical works of John Locke, Muratori and de Tillemont. These tastes aroused official suspicion when he was transferred to the College of San Anselmo in Rome in 1775, and in 1797 at the height of the threat from revolutionary France he preached a sermon telling the congregation, 'Be good Christians and you will be excellent democrats.'

The Hapsburgs, whose own candidates had been rejected, were annoyed by his election and refused to let him be crowned in the cathedral of Venice. They were further displeased by his insistence on returning to Rome, where the French-backed republic had just been crushed by the Bourbon king of Naples. There he augmented the much-diminished Sacred College, making twenty-four new appointments in February 1801. But if wary of the Hapsburgs, Pius was no friend of revolutionary France. In his first encyclical he likened the recent treatment of Pius VI to that suffered by Martin I at the hands of the emperor in the seventh century, and he praised those French bishops who were refusing to compromise with the demands of the state.

Together with his new secretary of state, Cardinal Ercole Consalvi (1757-1824), Pius VII tried to improve the running of the Papal States, which economically and administratively were falling further and further behind the rest of Italy, let alone other parts of Western Europe. When Pius VI had come to the throne in 1774, he was said to have inherited 'an empty treasury, an almost non-existent commerce overburdened by tolls, and a heavy and inequitable system of taxation'.[10] He had taken some steps, including draining the Pontine Marshes to create new farmland, though this was not completed, and debasing the currency, which only created inflation. Government throughout the Papal States remained a clerical monopoly resented by the local aristocracy, many of whom welcomed the republics of 1796–1799. The economic backwardness of the Papal States meant there were no urban middle classes other than for certain professionals such as doctors and civil lawyers.

Pius VII proclaimed an amnesty for political offences committed up to the restoration of papal rule, and four new congregations were created in Rome to oversee reforms, which included recalling Pius VI's debased currency and issuing a new one with proper metallic value, as well as freeing commerce from tolls. For the first time, some administrative positions were opened to laymen, as well as military ones in the papal army. A Noble Guard was created in Rome in May 1801 for the protection of the pope, made up of members of the aristocracy, who guarded the papal apartments, and accompanied the pontiff during public ceremonies and on his travels. It was abolished in 1970, leaving the Swiss Guard, re-established by Pius VII in 1800, as the last papal military unit.

There was no hope that the pope's army could take on Napoleon, who had again driven the Austrians out of northern Italy, following his victory at Marengo on 14 June 1800. The pope and the Papal States were at the victor's mercy, and to prevent the imposition of a new republic a concordat was signed with France in 1801. By this it was accepted that Catholicism was 'the religion of the majority of the

French people' and their freedom of worship was guaranteed, 'subject to police regulation'. What this meant in practice was not made clear until the concordat was published in France in February 1802, along with seventy-seven Organic Articles, which included the further restrictions that papal bulls and nuncios would not be admitted to France without prior agreement of the state. A papal protest was ignored.

Other terms of the concordat of 1801 brought up to date those agreed between Leo X and Francis I in 1516, including the right of the secular ruler to appoint all bishops, who would then be instituted by the pope. The bishops remained responsible for ordaining priests, who had to be acceptable to the government. Both bishops and priests became salaried officials of the French state. Property already confiscated from the Church was not to be returned, and nothing was said about the restoration of monastic life. This had been obliterated early in the Revolution, with many monasteries being demolished and their lands sold.

The pope also agreed to help reconstruct the hierarchy of the French church, by requesting that the bishops cooperate. The process involved forty-eight of them being asked to resign, of whom thirty-seven refused on principle. Pius VII then declared their sees vacant. While most then accepted his decree, the others went into schism, forming a small break-away church that survived for several decades.

As a sign of goodwill, Pius appointed five French cardinals in 1803, including Napoleon's uncle, Joseph Fesch (1763–1839), who in 1804 persuaded Pius to travel to Paris to attend the impending imperial coronation, against the advice of a majority in the Sacred College, many of whom were also hostile to the pope's recent administrative reforms. There the pope blessed the imperial crown, but the new emperor placed it on his own head. Pius did at least persuade Napoleon to marry the empress Josephine before their imperial coronation could proceed.

More serious strain was placed on Franco-papal relations by Napoleon's unilateral decision in February 1806 to create a Feast of St. Napoleon and place it in the liturgical calendar on 15 August, the date of the Feast of the Assumption of the Blessed Virgin Mary. He also asked leaders of Jewish communities across Europe to come to Paris to form a new Sanhedrin, something only the Messiah could summon.

While such displays of incipient megalomania might be ignored, Napoleon soon presented more material threats to the papacy. In 1805 the Italian Republic (which had changed its name from the Cisalpine Republic in 1802) turned itself into a monarchy, in order to offer its crown to Napoleon. His proclamation as King of All Italy, justified the annexation of the kingdom of Naples in February 1806, which he bestowed on his brother Joseph without reference to the papal suzerainty that had been recognised, however formally, by the Bourbons.

In October 1806 Napoleon occupied the port of Ancona in the Papal States, ostensibly to protect it from the English and the Turks. In reply to papal protests earlier in the year, he had told Pius VII that 'all of Italy will be subject to my law. I will never threaten the independence of the Holy See . . . on condition that your Holiness will have for me in temporal affairs the same respect I have for him in spiritual affairs. . . . Your Holiness is sovereign of Rome, but I am the emperor. All my enemies must be yours.'[11]

On the same day, he wrote to his envoy in Rome, his uncle Cardinal Fesch, instructing him to ensure that British and Neapolitan agents be expelled from papal territory and that its ports be closed to their shipping. He was also to make the pope realise that 'I am Charlemagne, the sword of the church, and must be treated as such . . . if he does not acquiesce, I shall reduce the papacy to the state that it occupied before Charlemagne.'

Late in 1807 Pius VII refused Napoleon's command to close papal ports to British ships and join the Continental Blockade aimed at breaking Britain's trade with Europe, as he regarded this as an act of war, something he could not condone. In reply, the emperor demanded that the pope renounce all temporal power, giving up his authority over what remained of the Papal States. When Pius refused, French forces invaded Rome again in February 1808, and the pope became a virtual prisoner in the Quirinal Palace, the main papal residence since the time of Benedict XIV and now the only part of the city left to him. A stand-off ensued until May 1809, when an imperial decree abolished the pope's temporal sovereignty entirely.

Pius VII responded by excommunicating all those involved in dispossessing the papacy of its states. Although Napoleon was not explicitly named, he fell within its purview. The bull was posted on the doors of all the patriarchal basilicas, but in secret, as the pope feared those carrying out his orders 'would certainly be condemned to death, and I should be inconsolable'.[12] Napoleon was enraged, declaring in a letter to his viceroy in Italy, Marshal Joachim Murat, that the pope was 'a dangerous madman who must be restrained'.

This seemed to Murat to justify ordering the arrest of the pope, though whether Napoleon intended this remains debatable. French troops broke into the Quirinal Palace during the night of the 5th of July. Carrying only his breviary and rosary, Pius VII was taken away into exile at Savona on the Ligurian coast close to the French frontier, where he was held in the bishop's palace, with a monthly pension and the use of three carriages. As Napoleon later commented, 'The pope is a good man but an uninformed fanatic.'[13]

The emperor commissioned grandiose plans for the urban transformation of Rome, which he wished to make into the second city of his empire under the titular rule of his infant son, Napoleon II, born 1811. Mercifully these were never put into execution as they involved the wholesale destruction of existing buildings as well as the obliteration of the most important parts of the ancient city so far unexcavated. In the meantime he pursued a plan inspired by the Concordat of 1801. If the Catholic Church was to be the religion of his subjects, then its headquarters would have to be that of the empire itself. In 1810 Napoleon ordered the twenty-seven surviving cardinals to be brought to Paris, together with all the Vatican archives. With some exceptions, the cardinals proved less pliant than he had expected, as thirteen of them refused to attend the emperor's marriage to the Austrian princess Marie Louise, since he had not received a papal dispensation for his divorce from his first wife, the empress Josephine. They were sent into exile for their resistance, leaving only the cooperative ones free.

Protracted negotiations were also under way with Pius VII for a revision of the concordat, when in January 1811 police in Paris claimed they had found evidence of a papally inspired plot to create a popular uprising. The emperor used this to justify appointing a commission of French bishops under Cardinal Fesch to replace papal authority, but it refused to deprive the pope of his right to institute bishops and was therefore dissolved by the infuriated emperor. After its members had been individually intimidated, it was reconvened and this time declared the pope had no power in temporal matters and could not use spiritual sanctions such as excommunication against lay rulers and their servants.

Pressure was also put on Pius VII to moderate his stand. In poor health and lacking his advisors, he consented to the proposed new system of institution by metropolitan in all regions except in the Papal States. When Napoleon demanded it apply there too, Pius withdrew his consent to the whole idea. In 1812 he was taken from Savona to the palace of Fontainebleu. However, by the time he arrived in June, Napoleon had departed for his disastrous Russian campaign.

It would not be until 1813 that the pope was browbeaten into agreeing to a new concordat in six days of face-to-face talks with Napoleon himself, including physical shakings by the emperor, who regularly did this to officers who annoyed him. By the resulting treaty all bishops throughout the empire, except in the area around Rome, would be nominated by the emperor and instituted by the pope, or by their metropolitans if he had not done so within six months. The pope was further required to condemn those cardinals who had refused to acknowledge Napoleon's second marriage, and he himself agreed to live in Avignon on a state pension. He also had to accept the complete loss of the Papal States, which had been formally annexed as two new *départements* of France in February 1810; as Napoleon saw it, 'I have reunited Rome to the Empire.'[14] In consequence, all monasteries and convents in Rome were closed in April 1810, and about 10,000 monks were put onto the streets throughout the Papal States.

The military situation in Europe, however, had turned decisively against Napoleon, and Cardinal Consalvi persuaded the pope to renounce the newly signed concordat. As Napoleon's armies and allies were defeated or deserted him, he sent the pope back to Savona, but in March 1814 Pius was allowed to return to Rome as the Napoleonic regime collapsed. By the time he arrived in May the emperor had abdicated.

The final years of Pius VII's pontificate were devoted to picking up the pieces. His own earlier liberal leanings were undermined by his experiences and the influence of a group of *zelanti* cardinals, who wanted to turn the clock back to 1796. Recent events reinforced the pope and his cardinals in their belief that full possession of the Papal States was the only way the pontiff could remain free from control by secular powers. Thus, on 11 May 1814 all the Napoleonic administrative reforms were abolished along with the use of the French Civil Code. At the urging of the *zelanti*, the Society of Jesus was fully restored on 7 August, although some more liberal cardinals such as Consalvi, now reinstated as secretary of state, argued against the move. At the same time negotiations began in Paris, led initially by the nuncio Archbishop Annibale della Genga and then by Consalvi, for a new Concordat which accepted that Avignon and the Comtat-Venaissin were now irrevocably part of France.

In 1814 only a small allowance was offered by the new French government of Louis XVIII to cover the costs of transporting the papal archives back to Rome, and the whole process was cancelled during Napoleon's brief return to power, resuming after his fall in 1815. The French state archivist, an ardent anticlerical and former priest, persuaded his Vatican counterpart that it would save money to destroy or sell off those parts of the papal archives that were of no practical use. In 1816 Cardinal Consalvi sent a circular around the Congregations, asking them to consider if they actually wanted their documents back. Fortunately, most of them said they did, but by this time some items had already been burnt or sold for reuse of the parchment. The return of the surviving archives was only completed in December 1817. As 3,239 chests of documents left Rome in 1810 and only about 2,200 returned ten years later, about a third of the total perished or were dispersed.[15]

In the meantime more high-level negotiations had been taking place, leading to the Treaty of Vienna, which amongst other things redrew the boundaries of many of the states of Western Europe. Thanks to the diplomatic efforts of Cardinal Consalvi, this included the restoration to papal sovereignty of all of the lands of the Legations south of the river Po and recognition of the pope's rule over the Romagna. Benevento and Pontecorvo, the papal enclaves in the kingdom of Naples (or the Kingdom of the Two Sicilies, as it became in 1816), were also recovered.

In a consistory on 8 March 1816 Pius VII named thirty-one new cardinals, including his two immediate successors. Although several were politically conservative, Consalvi persuaded the pope to consent to administrative reforms in the Papal States, including the abolition of a whole series of feudal customs, and to take steps to improve the economy. His introduction of vaccination, and street lighting and a fire service in Rome were vehemently opposed as 'useless innovations' by the *zelanti*, who demanded their abolition at the next conclave.[16] Moreover, the clerical monopoly of government remained unchallenged, and what has been called its *rigidification sacrale* continued.[17]

Serious challenges to this were already being felt. The Napoleonic republics, the French law codes and administration and the philosophical and other literature that lay behind the revolutionary fervour of the recent decades had all influenced political ideals throughout Italy, especially amongst the urban middle classes and local aristocracies. However benign in its intentions, undemocratic clerical government that lacked representative institutions appeared ever more of an anachronism. In the Romagna in particular, taking orders from distant Rome was resented, all the more so when communications were so slow and difficult. There was also a strong strain of anticlericalism, intensified by the revolutionary assaults on religion, which focussed opposition on the rule of the papal legates as civil governors.

THE INTRANSIGENT POPES

At the same time forces were working to extend this political resistance. Freemasonry, condemned by Clement XII in 1738, had been driven underground in Italy, and had as a result acquired a more radical and anticlerical character. Needing to maintain secrecy, it also developed a cell structure. During the Napoleonic period a number of secret political societies came into being in southern Italy. Collectively their members became known as *carbonari* (charcoal burners) after one of the most famous of these societies, which, however, varied greatly in their aims and methods. Those in Sicily are the ancestors of the modern Mafia.

Some of the earliest were cells of resistance fighters against the French occupation of the kingdom of Naples, but others were inspired by radical political ideals. After 1814 such clandestine groups spread more widely, especially in the Romagna and the Marches region around Ancona, and took the lead in stirring up resistance to papal rule. All such societies were condemned, along with Freemasonry, in a bull of 21 September 1821. Similarly, Protestant Bible Societies had been denounced in 1816 as an active arm of heresy, because they disseminated free Bibles with interpretative glosses in their margins that contradicted Catholic teaching.

On 16 July 1823 the late-fourth-century church of San Paolo fuori le mura, till then the best preserved if most neglected of the great patriarchal basilicas, was almost totally destroyed by fire.[18] The news was kept from the ailing eighty-year-old Pius VII, who had spent much time there during his early years in Rome, as it was feared that it would hasten his death, which followed on 23 August.

Without waiting for non-resident cardinals to arrive, the ensuing conclave was dominated by the *zelanti,* even if their first choice of candidate was excluded by Hapsburg veto. A second was then dropped when they recognised that Consalvi was voting for him and so assumed to have secret liberal tendencies. Their third choice, Annibale della Genga, was elected with just the stipulated minimum of two-thirds of the votes, despite his appeals to his colleagues not to elect him because 'they were voting for a corpse.'[19] Although he suffered from ulcerated legs and haemorrhoids, he survived for nearly six years, taking the name Leo XII in honour of Leo I the Great, of whom he called himself a 'humble client, the most insignificant inheritor of so great a name', and close to whom he chose to be buried.[20]

Although one of the least well known of popes, his pontificate is important for the lead he gave to the anti-liberal stance of the majority of cardinals.[21] He had been chamberlain and secretary to Pius VI, and subsequently served as a papal diplomat, attending the Diet of Regensburg in June 1806 at which, under Napoleonic prompting, the so-called Holy Roman Empire had been formally dissolved and replaced by a Germanic Confederation. As an envoy he was renowned for his elegant dress and witty conversation, and his following amongst the court ladies. Even as pope he enjoyed shooting birds in the Vatican Gardens, much to the disapproval of the cardinals.

In 1814 he had been blamed by Consalvi for the failure to save Avignon for the papacy in the negotiations in Paris at which he had been late in arriving. So, it was no surprise that one of his first acts as pope was to remove the cardinal from his post of secretary of state on the very day of his election. In keeping with his historically minded outlook, Leo XII also moved the papal court back from the Quirinal Palace, where even the conclaves now took place, to the long-deserted Vatican.

As ruler of Rome, Leo was austere, limiting public festivities and imposing new restrictions on the city's Jewish community, who had been forced back into living in the traditional ghetto by Pius VII in 1814. In the Papal States he abolished Consalvi's reforms, restoring the judicial processes that had been in place before 1798, and dividing the lay consultative councils into separate noble and bourgeois sittings. Firm action was taken against brigandage, which had revived in the turbulent last years of the Napoleonic period. Many of those caught or suspected were executed, as were some members of the *carbonari,* against whom new apostolic letters were issued in 1825. Freemasonry was again condemned, and Catholic rulers were warned that Masons not only wanted to undermine religion but also to overthrow royal government.[22]

On the wider stage Leo XII issued his first encyclical in May 1824 condemning Indifferentism, or religious relativism, and initiating what he saw as the restoration of true religion. As he put it, 'God, according to St. Augustine, has placed the doctrine of truth on the chair of unity', that is to say the throne of Peter.[23] There could thus be no picking and choosing amongst the precepts of the faith as laid down by Rome. A modern judgement sees him as 'the last pope of the Ancien Régime, prisoner of an unshakeable attachment to the old order and to a reactionary project for the reconstitution of the States of the Church and the holy city that ran contrary to all the aspirations of their inhabitants and of the century itself. It was thanks to him above all that the Catholic Church of the nineteenth century embarked on the road towards an intransigent restoration of its discipline and traditions.'[24]

The conclave following his death saw the election of Francesco Castiglione, whom Pius VII had appointed Grand Penitentiary and Prefect of the Congregation of the Index, and who had been his personal choice as successor. He took the name Pius VIII in honour of his old patron. Although he owed much to the *zelanti* in the past, he had shown himself a moderate on many issues, and in 1829 was the preferred choice of the Austrian imperial chancellor, Prince Klemens von Metternich (1773–1859), because he was thought to be politically conservative but nothing like as reactionary as Leo XII.

This was a vital distinction. Metternich was worried that the rising levels of unrest in the Papal States and papal unwillingness to institute reform could lead to revolts, which in turn might inspire larger-scale upheavals elsewhere in Europe, not least in France, where the regime of Charles X (1823–1830) was deeply unpopular. At the same time, more liberal tendencies were equally undesirable, for fear that overenthusiastic reform might produce the same effect. So, Metternich and his allies wanted a conservative reformer as pope, which is what they found in the sixty-eight-year-old Pius VIII.

His twenty-month pontificate was too short to make a difference, and on religious issues he was as uncompromising as his predecessor. His first encyclical contained a furious denunciation of Indifferentism, also known as religious tolerance: 'Among these heresies belongs that foul contrivance of the sophists of this age who do not admit any difference among the different professions of faith and who think that the portal of eternal salvation opens for all from any religion.' It again denounced Protestant Bible Societies and the copies of the Scriptures they gave away for free: 'They skilfully distort the meaning by their own interpretation. They print the Bibles in the vernacular and, absorbing an incredible expense, offer them free even to the uneducated. Furthermore, the Bibles are rarely without perverse little inserts to insure that the reader imbibes their lethal poison instead of the saving water of salvation.'[25]

However, Pius VIII and his secretary of state, Cardinal Giuseppe Albani (1750–1834), coped with the political turmoil affecting much of Western Europe during this time. This included the predominantly Catholic southern provinces of the Netherlands breaking free to form a new Kingdom of Belgium, and a revolution in France in 1830 that saw the autocratic regime of Charles X replaced by the liberal monarchy of Louis Philippe, the Citizen King (1830–1848). Against the advice of his nuncio in Paris, the pope ordered the French clergy to remain in post, thus recognising the legitimacy of the new government, and he accorded the king the hereditary but papally granted, French royal title of 'Most Christian'.

The revolutions of 1830 threatened trouble in the Papal States. When Pius VIII died suddenly in November, Metternich was anxious for a quick election, before radical groups took advantage of the immobilising of the papal government always produced by conclaves. He was thwarted by his own agent, Cardinal Albani, who was determined to secure the election of a pope who would retain him as secretary of state. He used every means to prevent the speedy decision sought by Vienna, even hinting untruthfully that he had an Austrian veto against the leading candidate. Only when word finally reached Metternich about what was happening were his machinations exposed, and the conclave elected Mauro Cappellari on 2 February 1831. He took the name of Gregory XVI in honour of Gregory the Great, of whose monastery on the Caelian Hill he was abbot. Two days later a *carbonari*-inspired revolt broke out in the Romagna, and a provisional commission seized control of Bologna.

The new pope had been vicar general of the austere Benedictine order of Camoldolesian monks, which had suffered badly in recent years, with all their houses other than those in Rome and Venice being suppressed under Napoleonic rule. By 1830 only seventy-six of the monks remained. As shown by his book of 1799, *The Triumph of the Holy See,* which now enjoyed a reprint and translations into German and Spanish, Gregory was uncompromising in his commitment to papal authority, and completely opposed to concessions to liberalism or to reforms that might weaken his hold on the Papal States, the possession of which he saw as the only guarantee of the independence of the Roman church.

Modest reforms of the political system and an amnesty for the rebels was precisely what Metternich wanted him to concede, as an Austrian military intervention to put down the revolt risked a diplomatic breach with the new liberal regime in France that had threatened war if this happened. The long-standing rivalry between France and the empire (since 1806 the Austrian empire) over territory and influence in northern Italy remained as strong after the revolution of 1830 as before.

Austrian involvement was also something that Gregory XVI and his secretary of state, Cardinal Tommaso Bernetti (1779–1852), who had held the same office under Leo XII, were anxious to avoid, remembering Hapsburg annexations of papal territory in the Romagna in the 1790s. Bernetti tried instead to create a counter-revolutionary militia from the devout peasantry to supplement regular papal units that were already deserting or being incompetently led. But it soon became clear that Austrian military intervention was the only way to end the revolt, which spread south into Umbria. Hapsburg forces were therefore admitted into papal territory, crushing the rebellion by the end of March 1831, while some astute diplomatic negotiation warded off the threatened French reaction.

A longer-term solution depended upon political reforms, especially allowing greater lay involvement in government and the creation of representative institutions. Western states, both liberal like England and France after 1830 and conservative like the Austrian empire, found it hard to support a papal regime that depended upon an undemocratic clerical monopoly of power. In 1831 France and Austria combined to demand that the pope carry out constitutional reforms. Gregory's prompt refusal to allow any elected assemblies led to renewed revolts, and thus to military intervention by both Austria and France in the Romagna and the Marches respectively. Most of the Papal States outside Lazio, the area around Rome, remained under their occupation for the next seven years. For the brief period left of their existence the popes' rule over the States of the Church relied entirely upon external protectors willing to maintain it.[26] Internally, order depended on an enlarged and much-feared police force, including secret units and informers. Punishments for political conspiracy were harsh and included execution as well as hard labour in the galleys.

In his first encyclical, issued on the Feast of the Assumption 1832, Gregory XVI solemnly denounced the 'absurd and erroneous' principle of liberty of conscience—'which spreads ruin in sacred and civil affairs'—and 'that harmful and never sufficiently denounced' freedom to publish. On the latter he lamented: 'We are horrified to see what monstrous doctrines and prodigious errors are disseminated far and wide in countless books, pamphlets, and other writings which, though small in weight, are very great in malice.'[27] To these he added condemnations of liberalism in general, of all arguments in support of the separation of church and state and of the activities of the London Bible Society. Its American equivalent, the New York Christian Alliance, received the same treatment in May 1844 in the encyclical *Inter praecipuas machinationes* (Amongst the Foremost Machinations). Its members were accused of plotting to spread 'the insanity of Indifferentism' amongst the people of Rome and Italy, and Italian bishops were warned to keep a close watch on all ports to prevent this subversive literature from being smuggled in.

Politically, the pope was equally conservative, largely on theological grounds. He took a firmly Pauline view of the need for obedience to the civil power (Romans 13.2), even where relations between Catholic subjects and non-Catholic rulers were concerned. Thus he was critical of the Polish bishops for supporting the failed nationalist uprising against Russia in 1832, and he urged the Irish clergy not to become involved in the movements for Catholic Emancipation and the repeal of the Act of Union with Britain.

The pope's conservatism did not prevent him taking a more radical line in humanitarian issues, notably in his condemnation of slavery in 1839. From the time of Paul III (1534–1549) onwards, several pontiffs had denounced the enslaving of Indians in the New World, but no account was taken of the African slave trade. It was this that Gregory XVI addressed in his encyclical:

> We warn and adjure earnestly in the Lord faithful Christians of every condition that no one in the future dare to vex anyone, despoil him of his possessions, reduce to servitude, or lend aid and favour to those who give themselves up to these practices, or exercise that inhuman traffic by which the Blacks, as if they were not men but rather animals, having been brought into servitude, in no matter what way, are, without any distinction, in contempt of the rights of justice and humanity, bought, sold, and devoted sometimes to the hardest labour.[28]

The Papacy and the *Risorgimento*

Near one end of the platform at Spoleto station is a monument commemorating the opening of the line from Rome to Ancona through the patronage of Giovanni Maria Mastai-Ferretti, archbishop of Spoleto (1827–1832). Creating a rail link between Rome and his diocese was a daring step in the age of Gregory XVI, who told the French ambassador that *chemins de fer* (railroads) would be better called *chemins d'enfer* (roads of Hell), as they allowed the faster spreading of dangerous ideas. But when Gregory died in June 1846 it was Mastai-Ferretti who was elected to succeed him, taking the name of Pius IX in honour of Pius VII.

He was elected in an unusually quick conclave lasting only two days, as the candidate of a majority of cardinals who wanted change, although not too much of it. Unusually, the new pope had experience extending not only outside of Italy but beyond Europe, having taken .part in a papal embassy to Peru and Chile in 1819, and he had earned a good reputation as bishop of Imola since 1832. Suspicions of his liberal leanings during the previous pontificate helped raise expectations of him as pope.

Other forces were at work in Italy at this time with ambitions beyond regional independence or reform of local institutions. The Napoleonic kingdom of Italy had been a model for those who now hoped to see the whole peninsula united and free of domination by external powers. Several of the secret political societies adopted this ideal, and a growing body of literature extolled it. There were numerous rival plans as to how it might be achieved and what form the hoped-for independent state might take.

One of the most influential of these blueprints was the hefty *Il primato morale e civile degli Italiani* (The Moral and Civil Primacy of the Italians) of the Piedmontese priest and politician Vincenzo Gioberti (1801–1852), published in 1843. The future Pius IX himself read it in 1845, and when going to the conclave the next year he promised the friends who gave him his copy that he would make sure that whoever was elected would read it too.[29] Through a study of Italy's history and its numerous foreign occupations, Gioberti had reached the conclusion that the ideal model for its future would be a federation of the historic states of the peninsula under the presidency of the pope. He called the papacy 'the last great thing left to Italy'. Ironically, his works were placed on the Index, because of his criticism of the Jesuits.

Gioberti was not alone in thinking that papal Rome should play a central role in what came to be known as the Risorgimento, the Awakening or Rebirth of Italy. But other nationalists, not least those of anticlerical persuasion, felt that the kingdom of Piedmont-Savoy, the only significant Italian state not under foreign rule, should take the lead. This was certainly the expectation of the king of Piedmont's first minister, Count Camillo Cavour (1810–1861), whose policies were firmly directed to bringing this about. In any event, the unification of Italy would have serious implications for Rome and the Papal States, as it was inconceivable that the centre of the peninsula could be excluded from whatever model of government was adopted.

The genial snuff-taking Pius IX seemed to be the kind of liberal and nationalist pope many had been waiting for. He was known to refer to 'the Italian nation', and he issued an amnesty for those involved in recent revolts soon after his coronation. He quickly began introducing political reforms, including consultative councils at both city and state level. In March 1848 he even authorised the setting up of a two-chamber assembly as a kind of parliament for the Papal States.

However, in matters of faith and of papal authority he did not waver from the position taken by Gregory XVI and his predecessors, denouncing Indifferentism, Protestant Bible Societies and the 'unspeakable doctrine of Communism' in his first encyclical. Here too he made clear his view of infallibility:

> God Himself has set up a living authority to establish and teach the true and legitimate meaning of His heavenly revelation. This authority judges infallibly all disputes which concern matters of faith and morals, lest the faithful be swirled around by every wind of doctrine which springs from the evilness of men in encompassing error. And this living infallible authority is active only in that Church which was built by Christ the Lord upon Peter, the head of the entire Church, leader and shepherd, whose faith He promised would never fail. This Church has had an unbroken line of succession from Peter himself; these legitimate pontiffs are the heirs and defenders of the same teaching, rank, office and power. And the Church is where Peter is, and Peter speaks in the Roman Pontiff, living at all times in his successors and making judgment, providing the truth of the faith to those who seek it.[30]

A new wave of revolts swept across Western Europe in 1848, sparked by the overthrow of the regime of Louis Philippe in France, engulfing Austria. Metternich fled and the emperor abdicated. It also prompted a revolt against Austrian rule in Italy that was backed by Piedmont. Pius IX refused to commit the Papal States to the cause, saying he could take no part in a war against a Catholic state, dashing the hopes held of him by some nationalists. In consequence his own government became a target, and his recently appointed lay minister, Count Pellegrino Rossi, was assassinated on 15 November. Nine days later a revolt broke out in Rome, and the pope fled to Gaeta disguised as a priest. On 9 February 1849 a Roman republic was proclaimed.

By this time order had been restored across Europe, and even governments that had been created by the revolutions of the previous year had little taste for turmoil in the Papal States, especially after the pope issued an appeal to the Catholic powers to secure his restoration. The French Second Republic, already dominated by Louis Napoleon, who would make himself the emperor Napoleon III in 1852, was most eager to assist. The Roman Republic was forcibly suppressed, and the pope returned to Rome on 12 April 1850, with his face firmly set against Italian nationalism. In the revolts of the 1830s Rome had remained consistently loyal to the pope, but from now on even here foreign military assistance was needed to preserve what survived of the temporal power of the papacy.

In the meantime Piedmont, ruled along with Sardinia by the kings of the house of Savoy, was moving towards a unification of the peninsula by military and diplomatic means, with the backing of most nationalists. Its policies became increasingly anticlerical, and included the suppression of monasteries in 1854. In 1859 with French assistance it launched a war against Austria that led to the conquest of Milan and the grand duchy of Tuscany. At the same time a revolt broke out in papal Bologna, which justified Piedmontese intervention there to restore order. Nationalists in the northern Papal States, including the Romagna and Parma, were encouraged to hold plebiscites that voted in favour of uniting with Piedmont. In reply Pius IX excommunicated the Piedmontese king Victor Emmanuel II and issued an encyclical condemning those wanting to 'become subject to that Italian government which for these last years has acted as an adversary to the Church and its legitimate rights and sacred ministry', but he could do nothing to prevent loss of his territories. Like so many of his predecessors over the centuries, he believed that 'temporal power is necessary to this Holy See, so that for the good of religion it can exercise spiritual power without any hindrance.'[31]

In 1860 the strongly anticlerical nationalist Giuseppe Garibaldi (1807–1882) and his 'red shirt' volunteer army invaded the Bourbon Kingdom of the Two Sicilies, completing its conquest the following year. Victor Emmanuel II used this and the ensuing local revolts in papal towns to justify sending his army into Umbria and the Marches, claiming again that they were there to restore order and protect the papacy from Garibaldi. This time the pope ordered his army, including Catholic volunteers from France and Belgium, to resist, but it was overwhelmingly defeated in the last battle it ever fought, on 16 September 1860 at Castelfidardo. The remainder of the Papal States other than for Rome and a small area around the city then followed the northern parts in voting for union with Piedmont.

Rome itself was preserved thanks to the protection of Napoleon III. His alliance with Piedmont included a guarantee of papal independence, ensured by the presence of a French garrison in the city. So Victor Emmanuel, who was proclaimed first ruler of a new kingdom of Italy in 1861, had to head off Garibaldi as he advanced from Naples determined to 'liberate' Rome. But any change in the French stance would spell the end for papal rule. On 19 July 1870 war broke out between France and Prussia, leading to Napoleon III's decisive defeat at Sedan and abdication the following year. But even from the start the emperor needed all his military resources, and in August 1870 the French garrison was pulled out of Rome.

On 10 September a Piedmontese envoy told the pope that his king was ready to occupy the city and offered terms: Pius would be recognised as a sovereign with full rights over the Leonine City—the walled area extending from the Vatican to the Castel Sant'Angelo and the Tiber—and receive a financial compensation for his lost territories. So furious was the papal response that the ambassador nearly fell out of a window trying to withdraw. The following day the Piedmontese army marched on Rome, arriving on the 19th. Pius IX had ordered his remaining troops to resist, hoping that an Italian assault on the supreme pontiff would create a diplomatic backlash in his favour, but when the royal army broke through the Porta Pia into the city on the 20th, he allowed his men to surrender, and he locked himself in the Vatican. Two weeks later a referendum of the citizens came out overwhelmingly in favour of Rome joining the new Italian state. The Quirinal, whose keys the pope refused to surrender, became the new royal palace.

Pius remained in the Vatican, 'a prisoner' as he described himself, until his death in 1878, refusing to recognise or negotiate with the Italian government, and turning down a financial settlement that was far more generous than the one eventually agreed in 1929. Without papal participation, a one-sided resolution was imposed by the new Italian kingdom in the Law of Guarantees, drawn up in December 1870. This formalised the loss of the Papal States, and even the Vatican was declared state property. On the other hand the pope was granted the honours and legal immunity of a sovereign, allowed a personal guard, and was permitted to occupy the Vatican and Lateran palaces and the summer residence at Castel Gandolfo. He was also offered an annual grant of three and a half million lire.

As Pius continued denying the legitimacy of the Italian kingdom, hoping that an outside power would restore his rule over the Papal States, he refused the money. But there was no support inside Italy or beyond for a return of clerical rule and enormous opposition to it. However, the pope's spiritual authority would be enhanced just as his temporal sovereignty was finally extinguished.

INFALLIBILITY AND THE FIRST VATICAN COUNCIL

Pius VII had gained celebrity status throughout Europe for his long resistance to Napoleonic bullying, and this reflected on his office as well as his person. At the same time, the experience of a state-run church, as had existed in France under the revolutionary and Napoleonic regimes, made several influential French Catholics regard Gallicanism as a dangerous inheritance and a threat to the faith, as it was seen as closely associated with the scepticism and rationalism of the Enlightenment. The conclusion they reached was that if the Church was to be kept from lay control, it needed to recognise the supreme and unquestionable authority of the papacy. As the latter was based in Rome, beyond the Alps, this programme and its supporters came to be labelled Ultramontane—'across the mountains'.

The intellectual origins of French Ultramontanism can be traced to a book by a Jesuit-educated diplomat from the kingdom of Sardinia, Count Joseph de Maistre (1753–1821). In his *Du Pape* (On the Pope) of 1819 he argued that the pope had sovereign authority over the Church, exercised through his role as teacher. As a characteristic of sovereign power is that its decisions cannot be appealed to a higher jurisdiction, it therefore follows that papal teaching is infallible and should be obeyed without question. He further proposed that, as the recent wars had shown, individual nations needed to recognise some authority superior to their own, capable of resolving their conflicts, and for this he suggested that of the pope.

Equally influential were the works of the Breton priest Félicité de Lamennais (1782–1854), who published anonymously a book on the state of the French church in 1808, which was quickly suppressed by the police. He followed this with attacks on Gallicanism (1814) and Indifferentism (1817), arguing against religious tolerance and in favour of Ultramontane Catholicism, and which earned him a substantial readership, especially amongst a younger generation of priests. It was later suspected that he might even have been the cardinal named *in pectore* by Leo XII in 1826, whose identity was never revealed but who was said to be a scholar whose works had strongly defended true religion.

However, the line that he and a band of supporters took, particularly in the newspaper *L'Avenir* (The Future) that they founded in 1830, arguing for a complete separation of church and state, was not appreciated in Rome, where such an approach seemed to question the pope's right to temporal sovereignty over his states, a topic of extreme sensitivity for the papacy. In politics Lamennais was also becoming increasingly liberal and outspokenly democratic, which further alienated the staunchly conservative and monarchist church hierarchy. His final breach with the papacy came over Gregory XVI's criticism of the Polish bishops for their support of the revolt against the czar, and his ideas were condemned in the encyclical *Mirari vos* (You may wonder why) of 1832, as belonging with those of the Waldensians, Wyclifists and 'other sons of Belial'. Here he and those who shared his views were described as 'shameless lovers of liberty' who 'desire vehemently to break the mutual concord between temporal authority and the priesthood'.[32] Although he died unreconciled and refused to be buried with religious rites, Lamennais's earlier books and essays continued to aid the growth of Ultramontane sentiment that soon extended beyond France.

In England, where Catholics had been given the right to vote in 1829 and where a system of Catholic dioceses was re-established by Pius IX in 1850, a strong Ultramontane tendency also developed. This was furthered by the hostility with which the restoration of the hierarchy was greeted by Queen Victoria, her prime minister, Lord John Russell, and *The Times* newspaper amongst others and by a growth in the number of enthusiastic converts who did not feel their new faith should be tepid and cautious.[33] Amongst the most distinguished of these was Henry Manning (died 1892), Anglican archdeacon of Chichester, whose conversion in 1851 was in part influenced by a case in which the British Privy Council upheld the rights of a vicar against his bishop, as well as by the anti-Catholic riots that accompanied the re-establishment of the hierarchy. His resentment at secular interference in matters of ecclesiastical discipline made him a natural Ultramontane once accepted into the Catholic Church, in which he rapidly prospered.[34] As archbishop of Westminster from 1865 (cardinal in 1875), he promoted the growing campaign for a declaration of the doctrine of papal infallibility and then played a leading role in the council in which this was to be defined.

When Pius IX first had the idea of calling an ecumenical council is not known. The earliest mention was in a conversation with some of the cardinals in December 1864, and it was not until 29 June 1868 that he issued the bull *Aeterni Patris* (Of the Eternal Father), convoking such a council to meet in the Vatican on 8 December the following year. Approximately 750 bishops attended it.

Although now most famous for its declaration on papal infallibility, this topic had not originally been part of the business intended for discussion by what became the First Vatican Council. It was too controversial a subject to be openly included in advance of the meeting, not least because it was diametrically opposed to one of the Gallican Articles to which the French church was still pledged. This was

Article 4, which stated that 'although the Pope has the chief voice in questions of faith, and his decrees apply to all churches and to each particular church, yet his decision is not unalterable unless the consent of the Church is given.'[35] It was to eliminate such views that the Ultramontane supporters of the papacy hoped to use the general council he was calling to establish once and for all papal superiority to any council.

The promotion of the doctrine of infallibility was driven not so much by the Vatican itself, where habitual caution reigned, as by enthusiastic lay and clerical papalists in France and Italy. On 6 February 1869 it was stated in an article in *La Civiltà Cattolica* that papal infallibility would be proclaimed a doctrine of the Church by spontaneous acclamation by the participating bishops. Whether this was a ploy by the journal to get the issue of infallibility onto the agenda or whether it had received leaked information that this was indeed going to happen is unknown. It certainly created the widespread controversy it had probably been intended to provoke. Several leading lay and clerical opinion formers in both France and Germany argued hotly over the issue.

When the council itself met in Rome in December a majority of bishops were in favour of the doctrine, not least as a means of outlawing the Gallicans, Febronians and others who wanted to see papal authority restricted and made subject to conciliar supervision. Others agreed with the principle but felt this was not a good time in which to transform it into a fully defined article of faith, not least out of fear of the adverse reactions both from elements of the laity and from some governments. In the outcome their fears were justified, but they represented a small minority—107 out of over 700 archbishops and bishops present, including twenty-seven of the forty-four from the United States.

Although the topic was not included in the official order of business, it was introduced at the stage in the proceedings, in late January 1870, in which petitions or *postulata* (postulations) were submitted to the pope by the bishops attending. Over four hundred of these requested that the doctrine of papal infallibility be proclaimed. To this Pius IX eventually agreed on 1 March, appointing a committee to draw up a text for a full discussion in the council, which took place from the 13th to the 16th of July, before a vote on the 18th. Although the more extreme Ultramontanists such as Manning would have preferred to see almost all papal pronouncements accorded the status of being infallible, concerns raised by others led to the context in which such an infallible statement could be made being precisely delineated.

The decree defining the doctrine was finally accepted in the middle of a great thunderstorm by 533 votes to 2, though a number of opponents had withdrawn from the council early, so as not to have to take a public stand against it. Amongst these were several representatives from Eastern churches following the Roman rites, who saw the enhancement of papal superiority as yet another bar to reconciliation with the Orthodox and were themselves unhappy at the increasing Latinization of their own traditions.

The text accepted by the council was then published in the dogmatic constitution *Pastor Aeternus* (Eternal Shepherd). It is divided into four chapters. The first states that primacy of jurisdiction had been given to Peter directly by Christ and did not come to him through the Church, with the implication that the Church as represented by a general council had no right to limit or in any way interfere with the exercise of that jurisdiction. The second chapter asserts that papal primacy is eternal. In the third, the nature of that primacy is defined, and it is stated explicitly that an ecumenical council cannot alter a papal decree. Finally, the fourth chapter comes to the heart of the matter in laying down the conditions in which the pope speaks *ex cathedra* (from the throne). These are that firstly he be explicitly making the pronouncement by virtue of his 'office of Pastor and Teacher of all Christians'. Secondly, it has to be on a question of faith or morality. Thirdly, it has to be addressed to 'the Universal Church', and fourthly, it must be expressed in terms making it clear that this is a definitive statement of truth. With these conditions met, 'such definitions of the Roman Pontiff of themselves and not by virtue of any consent of the Church are irreformable.'[36] Although a remarkable recognition of papal teaching authority within this carefully prescribed context, it was far removed from the aspirations of those who saw the pope as 'the vice-God of humanity' or who said 'when the pope thinks it is God who is thinking in him.'[37]

There was enormous popular enthusiasm for the decree, but also some strong criticism. Theologians, especially in the German-speaking world—worried about its effect on relations with the non-Catholic governments—denounced it. Several of them met in Munich in September of 1871 to discuss it, though with little effect. Lay opposition to *Pastor Aeternus* was particularly strong in Switzerland, where a schismatic Christian Catholic Church was formed. Several German states prohibited the publishing of the acts of the Vatican Council, the Austro-Hungarian empire renounced a concordat made in 1855, and in the new German empire (proclaimed 1871) it gave rise to Chancellor Otto von Bismarck's *Kulturkampf* (Battle for Civilisation) of 1871–1878. This was an ultimately unsuccessful attempt to eliminate Catholic political parties and schools, not least as these were seen as being hostile to the predominantly Prussian Protestant and secularist traditions the German chancellor wanted to promote. In England, the Prime Minister W. E. Gladstone spoke out strongly against the Vatican decrees.

On his death in 1878, after a thirty-two-year pontificate, the longest ever, Pius IX was buried in Santa Maria Maggiore, but in 1881 his body was moved to San Lorenzo fuori le mura, with which he had been closely associated. So much of a hate figure did he remain for liberals and nationalists that a mob tried to break up the cortège and throw his body into the Tiber. Although this failed, it is suspected that he was buried not in the sarcophagus bearing his name but secretly elsewhere in the basilica to prevent a further assault. His long and troubled pontificate, together with his strong Marian devotion, endeared his memory to his successors. John XXIII (1959–1963) had hoped to achieve his canonisation, but this was still too controversial at the time of the Second Vatican Council.

However, in 2000, together with the far more liberal John XXIII himself, Pius IX was beatified, as the first step to full canonisation as a saint, by John Paul II, who said of him in the homily marking the event:

Amid the turbulent events of his time, he was an example of unconditional fidelity to the immutable deposit of revealed truths. Faithful to the duties of his ministry in every circumstance, he always knew how to give absolute primacy to God and to spiritual values. His lengthy pontificate was not at all easy and he had much to suffer in fulfilling his mission of service to the Gospel. He was much loved, but also hated and slandered.[38]

With twelve hundred years or more of tradition behind him, it is not difficult to understand why Pius IX had felt the loss of the Papal States so keenly. Possession of them had seemed to be the only way that the papacy could preserve its independence from lay control, so hard-won in the eleventh and twelfth centuries, and it was their defence that had led the popes into innumerable political alliances and wars over the intervening years. Foreign powers had been brought into Italy and sometimes expelled from it in the interest of preserving papal sovereignty. Much blood had been spilt and not just in Italy over the defence of these territories. The events of 1870 showed that in fact the papacy could survive without them, and that the forces within nineteenth-century Catholicism that combined to achieve the declaration on infallibility in the First Vatican Council would give it far greater authority over the Church and influence in the world in the decades ahead.

chapter 20

THE PRISONER OF
THE VATICAN

(1878–1939)

AN EXPANDING CHURCH

W hile Pius IX lamented the loss of the Papal States, the worldwide standing of the papacy had risen dramatically during his pontificate. He was the best-known holder of his office since St. Peter thanks to the growing readership of newspapers across Europe, Asia and the Americas. Pictures of him were everywhere, and he appeared in cartoons, on cameos and medals, in photographs and on a range of pious memorabilia for the faithful. The political difficulties he confronted with courage and dignity in his last years added to his renown. As with John Paul II, who would beatify him a century after his death, the demeanour of the pope in a final period of suffering wiped away memories of earlier criticism.

Both popes also shared deeply felt personal devotion to the Blessed Virgin Mary that led Pius IX to define the doctrine of the Immaculate Conception in 1854, by which Mary being born without the taint of original sin became a necessary item of belief for Catholics. It ended centuries of debate between theologians and encouraged an already rising tide of Marian piety. In 1830 the French nun Catherine Labouré had a vision of the Blessed Virgin Mary standing on a globe and crowned with stars, within a frame bearing the inscription 'O Mary, conceived without sin, pray for us who have recourse to you.'[1] She was told that all who wore medals depicting the Virgin in this form would receive special graces.

When Catherine's vision was declared valid by the local Church authorities, such medals began being made in large numbers and widely distributed. They helped build up a wave of popular devotion and a growing number of appeals to the pope, especially from France, to define the dogma. In 1848 Pius IX appointed a commission of theologians to advise him on whether he should do so, and in exile the next year he issued an encyclical to the bishops requesting their views.

While some thought it too divisive a step to take, the majority were enthusiastically in favour, and the pope proceeded to issue the definition, but stressing it was done on his authority and not because of episcopal approval. The papal definition quickly seemed to receive a sign of heavenly approval, when in 1858 a French peasant girl, Bernadette Soubirous (1844–1879), had eighteen visions of the Virgin Mary at Lourdes in the Pyrenees, in the sixteenth of which the Virgin said to her, 'I am the Immaculate Conception,' words which Bernadette herself apparently did not understand. The whole episode added to the widespread enthusiasm for papal infallibility, defined in 1870. Marian devotion was advanced by Pius's successor Leo XIII (1878–1903), eleven out of whose eighty-six encyclicals encouraged the use of the Rosary, with its repetition of the prayer 'Hail Mary' and Paternosters, as an aid to meditation.

By connecting to this rising tide of lay piety, *Pio Nono* made himself into the first really popular pope in history, and in so doing made the papal office far more significant to ordinary Catholics and more central to their sense of religious identity than ever before. This was despite his never travelling outside Rome after 1850. The definition of infallibility at the First Vatican Council added to the sense of the unique significance of the papal office, and has been seen as giving 'the Roman pontiffs an enormous moral and spiritual authority over the world-wide Roman Catholic church', making possible 'the practice of increasingly frequent public interventions by the popes in a wide variety of subjects of importance to the clergy and laity'.[2]

It was not just the role of the pope as a public figure that developed during these decades; Catholicism itself was spreading fast. Gregory XVI, obscurantist in terms of European politics, gave enormous impetus to missionary activity. In 1845 he had approved the creation of diocesan organisations in the major mission fields, which included West Africa, India and the Pacific as well as South America, responsibility for which was assigned to different religious orders. Two hundred bishops were ordained for work in the mission field during his pontificate, and the new dioceses were largely served by indigenous clergy, in defiance of the tendency to treat native Christians as inferiors, but in line with the pope's own declaration against slavery of 1839.

In the United States, where British penal laws had been in force till 1776, a small Catholic population, at first concentrated in Maryland, increased enormously through Irish immigration, especially following the famine of 1846–1849. This rise in the number of Catholics created cultural conflicts later in the century when the clergy were accused of trying to isolate their congregations from contact with their non-Catholic fellow citizens and thus keep them separate from the rest of American society. Such suspicions prompted anti-Catholic riots. Gregory XVI created ten new dioceses in the United States and four in Canada. By around 1850 there were 1.75 million Catholics in the United States and thirty-one dioceses, with Baltimore, founded in 1789, being the primatial see. There were also four apostolic vicariates in states in which dioceses had not yet been approved. Numbers continued to rise, and sixty-seven Catholic bishops from the United States and Canada attended the First Vatican Council in 1869/70. This compared with just over forty from Asia and eighteen from the South Seas.

The colonial conquests of the European powers opened the way to further expansion, as they encouraged or at least protected missions. France's annexation of Tunisia and parts of Southeast Asia, Italy's seizure of Somalia and the notorious private empire created by the Belgian king Leopold II (1865–1909) in the Congo all provided opportunities for evangelising, with mixed results, and the creation of dioceses. As Leo XIII (1878–1903) wrote in an encyclical in 1880:

'new routes have been opened, in consequence of more complete exploration of places and populations, towards countries hitherto accounted impracticable; numerous expeditions of the soldiers of Christ have been formed, and new stations have been established; and thus many labourers are now wanted to devote themselves to these missions, and contribute seasonable help.'[3] He encouraged the formation of parochial and other organisations in Europe and the United States that would raise money for and support particular missionary ventures, adding to the sense of a worldwide and interconnected Catholic community.

In the same decades, as the Western powers began intimidating China and forced Japan to open up to commercial and cultural exchange, the Vatican requested freedom of movement and protection for its missionaries and their converts. In 1885 Leo XIII wrote to the Japanese emperor Meiji pointing out the advantages of having Catholic subjects, including their readiness to obey the law and their inbuilt respect for the civil power. But papal reliance on European states could create problems where issues of national prestige were concerned. In 1886 Leo XIII sent a nuncio to Beijing, but was forced to withdraw him at the insistence of France, which claimed that the Catholic Church in China was under its protection, and it could not tolerate this being undermined by direct contacts between the Vatican and the Chinese court.

The possibilities of reunification of the churches first began to be explored in the later nineteenth century and have been under discussion ever since. More effort was directed at trying to heal the rift with the Orthodox churches in the East than that with the Protestant ones in the West, and some genuine concessions were made to try to achieve this. Leo XIII reversed his predecessor's policy of trying to impose Latin liturgy and Western practices on the Uniate churches, those Eastern communions that recognised papal primacy and Catholic dogma, and in 1882 he gave up the practice, that had given offence since started in the sixteenth century, of bestowing Eastern patriarchal titles on Roman cardinals and archbishops. In 1888 reunification with the Armenian Orthodox church seemed possible, but negotiations broke down over the requirement from the Catholic side that papal authority be recognised as superior to that of ecumenical councils.

There were also hopes at the time amongst high church or Anglo-Catholic members of the Church of England that communion with Rome might be restored, if not full reunification. This depended upon a mutual recognition of the validity of holy orders, meaning in practice Rome's acceptance of the Anglican priesthood. Papal letters were sent, intended 'to hasten the day of a happy reconciliation', but the first flush of enthusiasm was doused by the encyclical *Apostolicae Curae* (Apostolic Cares) of September 1896.

Apostolicae Curae followed the report of a special commission Leo XIII had appointed to examine the question of the validity of Anglican orders, to determine whether or not an unbroken line of ordination had existed stretching back to an Apostolic origin. This was not necessarily affected by the English church's breach with Rome under Henry VIII, for if bishops consecrated before that event had ordained successors in proper sacramental form who in turn had done the same 'according to the accustomed Catholic rite', then a chain of ordinations, extending back to Peter's consecration of Linus, remained unbroken. Thus the two churches might be in schism, but each would possess what the other could recognise as a valid priesthood.

The problem faced in 1896 related to what had happened in England under Edward VI (1547–1553), when the influence of continental reformers was at its height, and new forms of service had been introduced, especially in the second Edwardian Prayer Book of 1552. The commission was instructed 'to re-examine all documents bearing on this question which were known to exist in the Vatican archives, to search for new ones, and even to have at their disposal all acts relating to this subject which are preserved by the Holy Office'. This doomed the project, as during the brief restoration of Catholicism under Mary I (1553–1558), Cardinal Pole had reported on the deficiency of Anglican orders as administered under the Edwardian Prayer Book, and both Julius III and Paul IV had proclaimed them to be lacking sacramental validity. Rome was not going to recognise the Anglican priesthood.

The geographical spread of the Catholic Church had its counterpart in the way that popes from Leo XIII onwards saw involvement in social and economic relations as a new and urgent responsibility. The starting point was Leo's encyclical *Rerum Novarum* (Of New Things) of May 1891, which addressed the 'Rights and duties of capital and labour'. Its context was the dramatic changes of recent decades:

> That the spirit of revolutionary change, which has long been disturbing the nations of the world, should have passed beyond the sphere of politics and made its influence felt in the cognate sphere of practical economics is not surprising. The elements of the conflict now raging are unmistakable, in the vast expansion of industrial pursuits and the marvellous discoveries of science; in the changed relations between masters and workmen; in the enormous fortunes of some few individuals, and the utter poverty of the masses; the increased self-reliance and closer mutual combination of the working classes; as also, finally, in the prevailing moral degeneracy.[4]

A powerful motive was the fear of political instability. The pope noted how inequalities of wealth had intensified across the century and traditional defences of labour, such as craft guilds, had declined or disappeared. He saw socialists, who would abolish private ownership of property, as a threat, describing them as 'emphatically unjust, for they would rob the lawful possessor, distort the functions of the State, and create utter confusion in the community'.[5] He emphasised that private ownership of property was a right to which everyone was entitled 'in accordance with the law of nature'. However, he was also prepared to support the rights of workers to form themselves into unions, hoping these would be predominantly Catholic. He was also keen to limit the degree to which the state could interfere with individual families and households and claimed instead a unique role for the Church in trying to regulate socio-economic relations according to Christian principles. This involved advising the rich of the transitory nature of earthly goods and their responsibilities for caring for those less fortunate than themselves.

Although in terms of social and political theory this encyclical and others that followed were hardly radical, papal involvement in such questions was welcomed by Catholic labourers who were warned off socialism and the rhetoric of class warfare by their clergy, and by employers who anticipated it would produce a more docile workforce. When Leo XIII died in 1903 he was mourned, for example, in Argentina as 'the Vicar of the Divine Artisan of Nazareth . . . who established and sustained the rights and duties of employers and labourers . . . and who wished to be called the Father of the Working Class'.[6] This was said of an aristocrat who never spoke a word to the coachman who served him for a quarter of a century.[7]

THE CAMPAIGN AGAINST MODERNISM

Rerum Novarum was a reaction to a new threat to the social order and was an attempt at a positive alternative to what were seen as the dangerous ideas of socialism. Over the decades that followed, social teaching would take on ever greater importance in the popes' directing of the faithful. But in other respects 'new things' had been a source of worry to the papacy for much of the preceding two centuries, as papal authority had been eroded and its territorial power declined and was lost during the Enlightenment, the Revolutionary era and the age of Romantic nationalism. Novelty was always a threat, as it had been in the theological disputes of the early Church or during the Reformation, against which a stand had to be made in the name of unchanging tradition.

In 1899 Leo XIII wrote to Cardinal James Gibbons of Baltimore and the American episcopate, warning them of

a greater danger and a more manifest opposition to Catholic doctrine and discipline in that opinion of the lovers of novelty, according to which they hold such liberty should be allowed in the Church, that her supervision and watchfulness being in some sense lessened, allowance be granted the faithful, each one to follow out more freely the leading of his own mind and the trend of his own proper activity. They are of opinion that such liberty has its counterpart in the newly given civil freedom which is now the right and the foundation of almost every secular state [and so] we are not able to give approval to those views which, in their collective sense, are called by some 'Americanism.'[8]

This charge referred indirectly to the cardinal's successful efforts to encourage the large and ever growing Catholic population to become more fully involved in the political, social and cultural life of the country. But so indirect was the criticism that Gibbons was able to accept the papal encyclical without reservation, because he said that none of the dangers the pope warned against were currently threatening the church in the United States. 'Americanism' thus came to be seen as 'the phantom heresy'.[9]

Fear of novelty and independent thinking dominated the pontificate of Pius X (1903–1914), whose first encyclical, *E Supremi* (From the Chair of the Supreme Apostolate), of October 1903 began with a lamentation on 'the disastrous state of human society today'. 'Who', the pope asked, 'can fail to see that society is at the present time . . . suffering from a terrible and deep-rooted malady which, developing every day and eating into its inmost being, is dragging it to destruction?' This included 'every effort and every artifice being used to destroy utterly the memory and knowledge of God', and he speculated that 'there is good reason to fear lest this great perversity may be as it were a foretaste, and perhaps the beginning of those evils which are reserved for the last days, and that there may already be in the world the "Son of Perdition" of whom the Apostle speaks (2 Thess. 2.3).'[10]

Such apocalyptic rhetoric was not the usual stuff of papal pronouncements but indicates the seriousness of the threat that Pius X and his advisors thought modern ideas presented to the survival of 'relations between man and the Divinity'. He identified the particular duties of his pontificate as restoring the honouring of the Gospels and the teachings of the Church on such issues as marriage, education, 'the possession and use of property, the duties that men owe to those who rule the State', and 'equilibrium between the different classes of society according to Christian precept and custom'. He had particular words of warning for members of the clergy who might be 'drawn to the snares of a certain new and fallacious science, which savoureth not of Christ, but with masked and cunning arguments strives to open the door to the errors of rationalism and semi-rationalism'.

For most subsequent generations of Catholics, Pius X has been the model pastor, the pope who popularised the more frequent taking of communion and who lowered the age at which it was first received from the mid-teens to seven, generating the special place that 'First Communion' has since enjoyed in family and parish. In 1985 John Paul II declared that 'in him one era of Church history came to an end, and another began that would lead to Vatican II.'[11] He is the subject of books for children in several languages, telling the story of *The Farm Boy Who Became Pope*[12]. His election in the conclave of August 1903 had been deliberately intended to produce a different style of pontificate to that of his predecessor.

The son of a postman and a village seamstress, Giuseppe Sarto, the future Pius X, came from a social background unlike that of the aristocratic Leo XIII, and the two enjoyed contrasting ecclesiastical careers. Leo completed his training at the Academy of Noble Ecclesiastics in Rome founded by Clement XI, had been a chaplain to Gregory XVI and was rising through the Vatican diplomatic service until an intervention on the side of the bishops against the royal government when nuncio in Belgium led to his recall and relegation to the diocese of Perugia, where he remained in obscurity thanks to the hostility of Pius IX's long-serving secretary of state, Cardinal Giacomo Antonelli (1806–1876). He was elected in 1878 because of his lack of ties to the previous pontifical regime, but had not been expected to live long because of his frail appearance. Resembling Voltaire in more than looks, he surprised his electors by enjoying one of the longest tenures of the papal throne.[13]

On the other hand Pius X was chosen because the cardinals wanted a pope 'who had grown old in the care of souls . . . who would above all be a father and a shepherd'.[14] He had served several years as a curate and priest in his native northern Italy, before becoming director of the seminary at Treviso and then bishop of Mantua in 1884. His noted success in this diocese led to his appointment as patriarch of Venice in 1893. He would be the first of three twentieth-century popes to be elected from that office (the others being John XXIII and John Paul I), and all three were highly regarded for their pastoral qualities.

Pius X allowed people to sit in his presence while Leo XIII had always made them stand, and he laid down new rules for sacred music for the liturgy, promoting the revival of Gregorian chant in parish and monastic churches. As well as his campaign for early and frequent communion, he himself conducted catechism classes on Sunday afternoons in Rome. It was the same strong pastoral imperative that made him a formidable foe of novelty and innovation, preferring to see his worldwide flock protected from the threats posed by new ideas, not just in the social and political arenas but also in more abstract intellectual fields.

BATTLE FOR THE BIBLE

Since the sixteenth century, Rome had been a centre of scholarship in the Near Eastern languages needed for the study of biblical texts, but the papacy was less keen on versions of the Scriptures in Western vernaculars that the laity could actually read without clerical instruction. This distrust lay behind the frequent denunciations of the Protestant Bible Societies and their freely distributed 'self-interpreting' Bibles in nineteenth-century papal encyclicals. An exception had been made for the Douay-Rheims Bible, an English translation of the Latin Vulgate, carried out in the English College at Douai (New Testament in 1582, Old Testament in 1609–1610), which was intended to provide recusant Catholics in Britain with a text to oppose to those of the Protestant vernaculars.

The Council of Trent had declared the Vulgate version, deriving from the work of St. Jerome, to be 'inerrant', and this epithet could be applied more forcefully once an official text of it had been issued in 1592 under Clement VIII. This obligatory reliance on an essentially fifth-century Latin translation of earlier Hebrew, Aramaic and

Greek originals created scholarly problems where the study of the text was concerned, but until the nineteenth century Protestant vernacular versions were hardly any more accurate. The situation changed with the discovery of manuscripts preserved in monasteries in Egypt and elsewhere of considerably earlier date than any containing the Vulgate text.

In 1844 in the monastery of St. Catherine in Sinai a German biblical scholar, Constantine Tischendorf (1815–1874), came upon 'a considerable number of sheets of a copy of the Old Testament in Greek, which seemed to me to be one of the most ancient I had ever seen', waiting in a heap to be burned.[15] In 1859 he obtained (in controversial circumstances) what remained of what is now called *Codex Sinaiticus,* which dates from the first half of the fourth century. To this and a handful of other early manuscripts, such as the fourth-century *Codex Vaticanus,* have been added countless fragments of other biblical and related codices, not least from the ancient rubbish dumps in Oxyrhynchus and the Fayyum in Egypt, some of which are even earlier in date.[16] A modern critical edition of the New Testament is based on readings from literally hundreds of manuscripts and papyrus fragments.[17]

This quiet revolution in the study of the text of the Bible began to be felt in the Vatican. In 1893 Leo XIII permitted the Dominicans to create a centre for biblical research, the École biblique, in Jerusalem, and in 1902 he established the Pontifical Bible Commission in Rome. His own outlook was scholarly, if conservative. In 1881 he had opened the Vatican archives to scholars irrespective of their religious affiliations, and he had personally encouraged a revival of interest in the theology of Aquinas, founding the Academy of St. Thomas in Rome in 1879. But this turned into an instrument of control when in 1892 Leo instructed Catholic professors of theology that some of Aquinas' theological propositions were definitive and that their views needed to be in close accord with those of 'the Angelic Doctor', leading to what has been called 'ossified orthodoxy'.[18]

The improved quality of the biblical text, challenging the reliance on the Vulgate, was not the only way that modern scholarship impinged on orthodoxy. Archaeological study in the Holy Land and

Egypt produced discoveries that could challenge the evidence of Old and New Testaments. More threatening was the development of new forms of literary analysis that enabled biblical texts to be interpreted in other than a purely literal fashion. Issues of authorial intention, structure and genre began to be raised that distanced the historical narratives from the events they purported to describe. Contradictions in biblical texts were examined for the evidence they gave of authorship and date. Unsound but traditional certainties were undermined. All of this could seem frightening or exciting depending on perspective.

A leader in this field of applying modern methods of literary analysis to biblical texts was the French priest and theologian Alfred Loisy (1857–1940). As professor of Hebrew at the Institut Catholique in Paris from 1881 he argued that the opening of the book of Genesis did not provide a literal account of Creation, and that the Pentateuch had not been written by Moses, not least because it describes his own death. All of these seemed at the time extraordinarily radical propositions, and in 1899 Loisy had to resign his chair but obtained a new teaching post in the extremely prestigious École pratique des hautes études (Institute for Advanced Studies).

Here he wrote a series of books to show how doctrine had developed over time, and that there was no way of trying to bypass the tradition of the Church to get back to a historical Jesus, directly accessible through a literal reading of Scripture. This argument was intended to controvert traditional Protestant reliance on biblical authority and the rejection of tradition as advocated by the German theologian Alfred von Harnack (1851–1930). However, Loisy caused more concern in Rome than in Germany, and in 1908, because of his book on the synoptic gospels (Matthew, Mark and Luke), Pius X excommunicated him *vitandus,* meaning that Catholics were forbidden to speak to him for the rest of his life.

The pope had been growing increasingly worried about the sceptical tendency of biblical scholarship, fearing it would undermine trust in religious truth, and his view of his pastoral responsibility was that he had to put a stop to it. We have already seen that in his encyclical *E Supremi* of October 1903 he was worried about 'the disastrous state of human society today'. Even so, he was happy to 'praise those young priests who dedicate themselves to useful studies in every branch of learning the better to prepare to defend the truth and refute the calumnies of the enemies of the faith', but by 1907 he was determined to set limits to 'ecclesiastical and literary erudition'.

On 3 July 1907 Pius issued the decree *Lamentabili Sane* (With Truly Lamentable Results), warning Catholic scholars who 'go beyond the limits determined by the Fathers and the Church herself', that 'in the name of higher knowledge and historical research (they say), they are looking for that progress of dogmas which is, in reality, nothing but the corruption of dogmas'. The decree contains a list of sixty-five propositions judged worthy to be condemned and proscribed.[19] Among them were the views that because the Bible was not divinely inspired it could contain errors (clause 11), that the Gospel texts did not become fixed until the canon of the New Testament was fully established (15), that 'the divinity of Jesus Christ is not proved from the Gospels' (27), that 'the doctrine of the expiatory death of Christ is Pauline and not evangelical' (38) and that 'when the Christian supper gradually assumed the nature of a liturgical action those who customarily presided over the supper acquired the sacerdotal character' (49). Most of the propositions would today be taken as self-evidently true by biblical scholars of almost any denomination.

For Pius X, biblical criticism was one facet of a wider threat to 'the deposit of faith delivered by the saints' posed by modern philosophical, political and psychological theories. He saw the times as especially dangerous, warning in the encyclical *Pascendi* of 1907 that 'although there had always been "vain talkers and seducers" (Titus I. 10) . . . it must be confessed that the number of the enemies of the cross of Christ has in these last days increased exceedingly, who are striving, by arts, entirely new and full of subtlety, to destroy the vital energy of the Church, and, if they can, to overthrow utterly Christ's kingdom itself.'[20] He declared that 'the partisans of error are to be sought not only among the Church's open enemies; they lie hid, a thing to be deeply deplored and feared, in her very bosom and heart.' In consequence he launched what has been described as 'a reign of terror'.[21]

This involved the detecting, silencing, sacking or expelling from the Church of those Catholics, especially theologians, scholars and journalists, who were suspected of promoting modernist thinking, a process likened to 'the Church devouring its own children'.[22] Vigilance councils were established in every diocese to monitor teaching in schools and seminaries, and diocesan censors were chosen to approve or ban works by Catholic writers that were now being published in quantities too great to be vetted in Rome alone. Those denounced for teaching or publishing what were called the heretical ideas of Modernism could expect to be disciplined and their books put onto the Index. Little latitude was allowed: As Pius X put it, 'kindness is for fools', and of the Modernists he said that 'they want to be treated with oil, soap and caresses. But they should be beaten with fists.'[23] His favour was reserved for Integralists, the good Catholics who accepted without question all that the Church taught and the pope decreed.

In Rome his chief instrument was Monsignor Umberto Benigni, a former professor of ecclesiastical history in the Seminary of Rome, who was made undersecretary of state for extraordinary affairs in 1906. In an article Benigni published in 1904, he may have invented the term Modernism as a catch-all for the various schools of thought worrying the Vatican of Pius X.[24] Once inside the Curia, he persuaded the Anglo-Spanish secretary of state, Cardinal Rafael Merry Del Val (1865–1930), to let him lead a propaganda campaign against the *Modernisti*, starting his own paper, briefing Catholic journalists and issuing a regular newsletter. He also distributed false information to the liberal press, while Merry Del Val arranged with the Italian post office for the correspondence of bishops and priests suspected of Modernist leanings to be opened and read.

Benigni also operated through a pious brotherhood, the Sodalitium Pianum, which he set up in honour of that inquisitorial saint, Pius V. Its members reported seminary staff and parish clergy for signs of Modernist heresy and sometimes tried to persuade them to incriminate themselves by expressing sympathies with such views themselves. Denunciations were frequent, even of some of the cardinals, and it is thought that Pius X's successor, Benedict XV (1914–1922), when archbishop of Bologna, was amongst those accused of Modernist tendencies, explaining why he was not made a cardinal until 1914, less than six months before he was elected pope.

The culmination of the campaign was the imposition on 1 September 1910 of the Oath Against Modernism, which thenceforth had to be taken by all members of the clergy, religious superiors and seminary professors and which continued to be enforced until abolished in 1967. It required affirmation of five propositions including belief that 'the Church was built upon Peter, the prince of the Apostolic hierarchy, and his successors for the duration of time' and total rejection of 'the heretical misrepresentation that dogmas evolve'. The oath-taker also swore complete adherence 'with my whole heart' to Pius X's decree *Lamentabili* and encyclical *Pascendi* of 1907, and repudiation of 'that method of judging and interpreting Sacred Scripture which, departing from the tradition of the Church, the analogy of faith, and the norms of the Apostolic See, embraces the misrepresentations of the rationalists and with no prudence or restraint adopts textual criticism as the one and supreme norm'. A final commitment was 'to hold to my dying breath the belief of the Fathers in the charism of truth, which certainly is, was, and always will be in the succession of the episcopacy from the apostles.'

The effect of all this was to condemn Catholic scholarship in many theological and biblical fields to half a century of intellectual sterility and serve as a restraint on independent thought in the Church long after the other repressive mechanisms of control of the time of Pius X had been dismantled. These retreats from 'the reign of terror' included the gradual fall from favour of Benigni after 1911 and the closure of his paper, the immediate acceptance of Cardinal Merry Del Val's resignation as secretary of state by Benedict XV in 1914 and his refusal to give any further apostolic benedictions to the Sodalitium Pianum. On hearing that Cardinal Della Chiesa, who became Benedict XV (1913–1922), had secured the necessary votes for election, Merry Del Val whispered to a neighbour in the conclave 'But this is a calamity!' To which the other cardinal replied, 'For Your Eminence, evidently it is.'[25]

This was not the last of the Modernist heresy, and although Benedict XV changed the way in which it was handled, he did not disagree with his predecessor's view that much of modern thought was a threat to the immutable tradition of faith. In his first encyclical in November 1914 he insisted 'that Catholics should shrink from the errors of Modernism, but also from the tendencies of what is called the spirit of Modernism' on the grounds that 'those who are infected by that spirit develop a keen dislike for all that savours of antiquity and become eager searchers after novelties in everything.' But he was determined that priests and theologians should no longer be vilified by their opponents as Modernists, as if they were adherents of a heretical sect.[26] He also declared that 'the era of secret denunciations is over.'[27]

It is said that when Pius XII promoted the cause of the sanctification of Pius X in 1949, considerable shock was felt in the Vatican when the treatment of several prominent Catholics during the anti-Modernist crusade was brought to light during the process. Only the pope's determination to secure the canonisation of a predecessor he revered, and whose ideas and outlook he increasingly shared in the last years of his pontificate, led to its achievement in 1954. A similar process begun for the beatification of Cardinal Merry Del Val was never completed.

THE ROMAN QUESTION

Pius X was also combative on the international front, opposing anticlerical measures taken by the government of the French Republic in 1905. His own appointing of Integralist bishops and abbots rather than professional Vatican diplomats as envoys did not make relations smooth with foreign powers. The Roman Question, the papacy's continuing demand for the return of its States, was the source of particular difficulties. The existence of the Italian state and monarchy was not recognised by the popes or by the traditional aristocracy of Rome, many of whose families had intermarried with those of successive popes over the centuries, and included some of the oldest

Roman noble houses, such as the Orsini and the Colonna, who were still squabbling over precedence in the 1890s.

In the same decade this papal or 'black' aristocracy, as it was called, suffered a gradual social and economic decline in comparison with the 'white' aristocracy that supported the royal house of Savoy, making its members ever more dependent on largesse from successive popes.[28] In the time of Leo XIII this came from money kept in an iron chest under the pope's bed.[29] Meanwhile the impasse caused by the papacy's refusal to accept the loss of its states led to endless difficulties in both protocol and diplomacy. For example, when Kaiser Wilhelm II had an audience with Leo XIII, the German ruler came from the Prussian embassy in a carriage and horses brought specially from Germany, so that technically he 'arrived in the Vatican from Prussian territory'.[30]

The Roman Question had peculiar ramifications. It was revealed in the press after his death that Leo XIII had secretly continued paying for the water supply to the Quirinal Palace, the home of the Italian monarchy since 1870, because it might strengthen his hand in a legal claim to the building.[31] Slights were exchanged. King Umberto I (1878–1900) remarked that the clergy should all be castrated, and Leo XIII created difficulties about giving him a Christian burial, causing offence in return. All the monarchs of the house of Savoy were openly anticlerical, and in 1919 Victor Emmanuel III (1900–1944) threatened to abdicate if his government entered into negotiations with the Vatican to settle the Roman Question.[32] By this time it was the papacy that wanted a solution, for several reasons.

The determination of Pius IX and his immediate successors not to give up their claims to the Papal States had seriously restricted the Vatican's diplomatic influence on the world stage at a time when it might have been able to play a mediating role. The refusal to recognise the kingdom of Italy meant that the Vatican could not be allowed to become involved in any negotiations in which Italian participation was required. At the same time, international diplomacy was one area in which the papacy could assert its survival as an independent state, albeit one without territory. Thus when in 1898 the Tsar of Russia proposed a major international conference at the Hague, Leo XIII and his secretary of state were determined to secure an invitation and kept working at it long after it was clear that both Italy and Germany had made the Vatican's exclusion a condition of their attending. The same happened in 1918 with the peace conference at Versailles after the end of the First World War, as Italy had secured agreement from the other allied powers when it came into the war in 1915 that the Vatican would not be allowed to participate in any such discussions.

The continuing grievance also made it difficult for the papacy to be regarded as a neutral party in international affairs, even in the First World War, which coincided with the first half of the pontificate of Benedict XV. Because of its supposed hostility to the Italian government and its earlier dependence on Austrian support, there was an ingrained suspicion amongst the allies that the Vatican favoured Austria-Hungary and therefore the Central Powers. In France this was reinforced by the strongly anticlerical stance of the Republican government. In Britain it was suspected that the Vatican was plotting to win over both Italy and France to its own ends and turn the war into one against the Protestant British and the Orthodox Russians.[33] Italian military intelligence became convinced that the pope was secretly being controlled by a sinister triumvirate located in Switzerland that included the general of the Jesuits and the bishop of Chur, and the Germans exaggerated the significance of any sign that the pope might favour them and their allies.

In the spring of 1917 the German chancellor discussed the possibility of a negotiated settlement with the papal nuncio, Cardinal Eugenio Pacelli, the future Pius XII. Inspired by this, Benedict XV put forward a peace plan in August 1917 in which all parties would retire to their original frontiers with no reparations being made by either side. For this he was denounced in France as 'the Boche pope' and it was rumoured in Italy that the Germans had offered to restore the Papal States to him. There actually had been a plan floated briefly in 1915, whereby Austria-Hungary would cede some Italian-speaking territories on its frontiers to the papacy, in return for its securing Italy's neutrality. The ceded districts would then be offered to the Italian kingdom in return for its allowing an independent papal state around the Vatican, with a corridor of land to the sea.

However, the papacy never sided with the Central Powers, despite the German government allowing 'Peter's Pence', the voluntary contributions from its Catholic congregations, to continue to be sent to Rome, using Swiss banks as intermediaries. By the end of the war the papacy was dangerously isolated on the world stage. In 1914 it had enjoyed formal diplomatic relations with only Austria, Germany and Russia amongst the major world powers, as well as with Spain and Belgium.[34] In 1918 Russia was in the hands of the communists and the Austro-Hungarian and German empires had been dissolved.

A solution to the Roman Question was essential if the papacy hoped to act as a moral force in international affairs. Fortunately the issue started to lose heat once the Vatican began seeing the Italian government as an ally against the more serious menace of socialism. As early as 1904 Pius X had lifted his predecessor's ban on Italian Catholics standing for election or voting, enabling them to form parties and become involved in the political life of the kingdom.

Economic conditions in the peninsula prior to its unification, with large numbers of landless labourers migrating for seasonal work and a relatively small middle class, primarily located in the northern cities, gave left-wing political ideologies an appeal in Italy that has never since been lost. Secret societies had been endemic since the eighteenth century, and several, notably the Freemasons, had been such consistent targets of papal hostility that they became institutionally anticlerical. Some of the newer political movements, such as communism, were also inherently anticlerical, and the general alignment of the Church with the landowners, as well as its own substantial property holdings, made it a target for redistributive policies and rhetoric.

The Russian Revolution and communist seizure of power under Lenin in 1917 added to the unease, especially as a new pope, Pius XI (1922–1939), had experienced some of the effects at first hand. One of the outstanding popes of the century, if now rather neglected, he has been described as being 'more richly endowed with gifts' and 'of a personality more complex and impressive than either his two predecessors or his successor'.[35] He was in some ways an unusual choice.

Born near Milan in 1857, Achille Ratti was a distinguished scholar of medieval church history and paleography, with several doctorates, who became the librarian of the Biblioteca Ambrosiana in Milan, before being called to the Vatican to serve in its library, of which he was appointed prefect in 1914. His spare time was devoted to mountaineering, on which he wrote a book.

A gifted linguist, but without any previous diplomatic experience, he was sent by Benedict XV to Poland as Apostolic Visitor in 1918 and raised in rank to nuncio and archbishop the next year. While there he experienced the revival of Soviet power which the Poles and their Western allies thought had been crushed. Archbishop Ratti refused to abandon his post when the Russian forces besieged Warsaw in August 1920, and the experience convinced him of the danger posed by communism. The following year he was recalled to Italy to be made archbishop of Milan and a cardinal.

He had only held his new rank for a few months when elected pope on the eighteenth ballot in February 1922. The conclave was amongst the most contentious of modern times, as a group of cardinals close to Pius X were determined to prevent the election of another liberal, as they regarded Benedict XV. It is said that both Cardinals Merry Del Val and Gaetano De Lai were temporarily excommunicated during the conclave, the latter for offering his votes to Cardinal Ratti in return for a promise not to keep Benedict's secretary of state, Cardinal Pietro Gasparri, in office.

Pius XI had carefully avoided Vatican politics during his years in the library and now showed his independence of mind by giving the *Urbi et Orbi* blessing for the first time since 1870 and appearing in public again on the day of his coronation. These prefigured the opening up of the Vatican that took place during his pontificate, including his own former fiefdom of the library that granted greater access for scholars. On a wider stage came diplomatic moves to put relations with several states on a better footing through new concordats, including ones signed with Latvia and Bavaria in 1924, Poland in 1925, Romania and Lithuania in 1927, Prussia in 1929, Austria in 1933 and the kingdom of Yugoslavia in 1935.

The particular value of these treaties to the Vatican was that they usually included agreement that national bishops be appointed by the pope rather than by the state. This was in addition to the long-standing right of the popes to confirm episcopal elections. Since the abolition of papal provision at the end of the Middle Ages, the papacy had few rights of direct appointment outside Italy. This only began to change when in 1831 the constitution of the new kingdom of Belgium gave the pope responsibility for selecting its bishops.[36] As part of the centralising of authority after the First Vatican Council, securing control of the processes of appointing bishops in all states with Catholic communities became a major policy objective for successive popes and was, for example, a central issue in discussions over the re-establishment of diplomatic relations between the Vatican and the People's Republic of China in 2000.

The most significant of these agreements made by Pius XI, from a papal perspective, was the one known as the Lateran Treaty that was made with the Italian state, now directed by Benito Mussolini, in February 1929. This stated that the Roman Question was definitively settled.[37] A small independent Vatican state just over 108 acres in size was created around St. Peter's. Added to this were the Lateran Basilica, the papal summer retreat at Castel Gandolfo and a number of institutes, palaces, and the Gregorian University in the city, which were all carefully mapped out and were to enjoy 'the privilege of extraterritoriality and exemption from expropriation and taxation'.[38] Monetary compensation was now finally accepted for the loss of the Papal States and other parts of the so-called Patrimony of St. Peter, but this had to take account of 'the financial situation of the State and the economic condition of the Italian people, especially since the war'.[39] The agreed sum was 1,750 million lire, but nearly half of it came in government stocks.

There had been doubts in the Curia over the wisdom of this treaty and criticism of the size of the payment, but Pius XI was not one to put up with that. Normally charming, he was notorious for his terrifying rages when crossed or facing procrastination by the Vatican bureaucracy. He tolerated nothing less than total obedience. People could emerge quaking from an audience with him, and a French ambassador noted that 'Pius XI's personality was so strong that everyone around him disappeared behind him.'[40]

The Concordat or Lateran Treaty of 1929 put the finances of the Vatican back on a sound footing. The loss of the revenues from the States of the Church had been counterbalanced by a rise from the 1860s in the voluntary offerings, known as 'Peter's Pence' or the *Obolo,* from Catholic churches around the world.[41] Much of this was invested, largely through a network of Catholic banks, in a building boom that took place in Rome itself between 1870 and 1914. Then the First World War seriously curtailed the inflow of funds, while inflation in Italy rose 300 percent during the war. It has been calculated that the Vatican lost forty percent of its capital in these years, through distribution of relief and in trying to prop up the Catholic banks during a succession of crises, plunging it into a financial crisis of its own in 1919.[42]

In the post-war years Vatican finances and in particular a series of major building projects initiated by Pius XI depended primarily on the generous influx of offerings from Catholic churches in the United States; for example $100,000 from the archdiocese of Chicago alone in 1920.[43] American Catholics replaced those in Germany as the main donors (a situation that repeated itself in 2004, when the American Catholic community's contributions constituted twenty-five percent of the Vatican's annual budget of $260 million[44]).

The Lateran Treaty of 1929 ensured that 'after 60 years of uncertainty and difficulty, the papacy was now financially secure, it would never be poor again'. But there had been a political price to pay to achieve it, in the form of the destruction of the Catholic Partito popolare italiano (Italian Popular Party), which had been founded at the end of the First World War with the approval of Benedict XV and was led by a priest, Luigi Sturzo.[45] Following the appointment of Mussolini as prime minister by Victor Emmanuel III in October 1922, it became clear that other political parties would not long be tolerated and that the elimination of the PPI was a precondition to a good working relationship with the new fascist government. So, in

1923 Sturzo was forced to resign under pressure from the Vatican, and the following year priests were instructed not to join political parties. By the end of 1926 the PPI had disintegrated.

Pius XI famously described Mussolini as 'a man sent by Providence' and at the time no doubt felt it, as the solution of the Roman Question had been essential, and he thought he had secured the future in Italy of Catholic Action, an umbrella title for a whole range of Catholic lay non-political organisations, which had begun as the Italian Catholic Youth Society in 1867. It had been promoted by Pius X in an encyclical in 1905, and was the subject of the first of those of Pius XI. He was extremely keen on it and encouraged the formation of new branches throughout the world.

Fascism, however, was genuinely totalitarian and so would not easily tolerate the existence of educational and social organisations separate from its own. Soon after the Lateran Treaty was signed, Mussolini began to attack Catholic Action, closing, sometimes violently, its youth organisations and associations of Catholic students. This provoked Pius XI into issuing his firmly worded encyclical *Non abiamo bisogno* (We have no need) in June 1931, denouncing the behaviour of the paramilitary fascists and 'the inventions, falsehoods and real calumnies diffused by the hostile press of the party, which is the only press which is free to say and to dare to say anything'.[46] The result was an agreement by Mussolini to lay off Catholic Action so long as it confined itself to essentially religious activities.

Pius XI had been almost as keen to see a proper relationship restored with France as with the Italian government, and as willing to take unpopular steps to achieve it. Here the stumbling block was an intransigent Catholic organisation called Action française that was rabidly opposed to the Third Republic. It was led by a journalist, the anti-Semitic monarchist and later supporter of the Vichy regime Charles Maurras, whose work had been much admired by Pius X. In 1925 Pius XI placed the organisation's journal of the same name and all of Maurras's works on the Index and in 1927 excommunicated its supporters. The French Jesuit Cardinal Louis Billot, who wrote a sympathetic letter to Maurras, was immediately required by the pope to resign for so doing, the only cardinal to renounce his rank in the twentieth century.

In 1930 Eugenio Pacelli, cardinal since the previous year, succeeded Gasparri as secretary of state. A curial insider, whose cousin had been the main financial advisor and banker to Leo XIII, he had taken over from Umberto Benigni as undersecretary of state for extraordinary affairs in 1911 and was able to keep in with all shades of opinion in the Vatican. In 1917 he was sent as nuncio to Bavaria and to Berlin in 1920, beginning a long and close association with Germany. An even longer one would be with Sister Pasqualina Lehnert (1894–1983), a Bavarian nun who became his housekeeper in 1917 and remained so until his death in 1958. Her influence, said to have been much resented by members of his family, would lead to her being called La Papessa.

Probably the most important of Cardinal Pacelli's responsibilities was negotiating a concordat with the German government under its newly elected chancellor, Adolf Hitler. As with the Lateran Treaty, this involved the removal of support for a Catholic political party, the Deutsche Zentrumspartei, resulting not least in the transfer of its leader, Monsignor Ludwig Kaas, to Rome and his subsequent involvement with the search for the bones of St. Peter. Before that, the Zentrumspartei voted for the enabling act in the Reichstag in March 1933 that gave the National Socialist government its legislative powers, in return for guarantees of its continued existence, and freedom for the Catholic Church and its educational institutions. This was followed by an offer by the new government to the Vatican of a *Reichskonkordat,* a national agreement to supplement the regional ones that already existed between the papacy and Bavaria, Prussia and Baden. The resulting concordat, which remains in force to the present, was signed in Berlin on 20 July 1933 and ratified in September.

Amongst its conditions was the dissolution of the Zentrumspartei, in defiance of earlier promises, and this was carried out a fortnight before the signing of the concordat with the agreement of Pacelli and Kaas. German bishops were required to take an oath of loyalty to the state, and no clerical participation in politics, including membership of parties, was to be permitted. In return, free communication between the Vatican and German Catholics was guaranteed, and the payment of the church tax was guaranteed. This was a system created in 1919 whereby the state collected a proportion of income from self-declared members of particular religious denominations to pass on to their church. A secret annexe also exempted Catholic clergy from military call-up.

As with relations with the fascists in Italy, early optimism soon gave way to annoyance at frequent violations of the concordat by the state. Over thirty diplomatic notes of protest were sent by the Vatican to Berlin between 1933 and 1936, but with little effect, leading Pius XI to issue in 1937 another denunciatory encyclical, *Mit brenender Sorge* (With deep anxiety), which had to be secretly distributed in Germany. In this the pope made plain what he feared would have happened if he had not accepted the concordat on Hitler's terms: 'despite many and grave misgivings, We then decided not to withhold Our consent for We wished to spare the Faithful of Germany, as far as it was humanly possible, the trials and difficulties they would have had to face, given the circumstances, had the negotiations fallen through.'[47] This was also the view of Cardinal Pacelli, who said: 'I had to choose between an agreement and the virtual elimination of the Catholic Church in the Reich.'

It is clear that by this stage the ailing eighty-year-old pope had lost hope of improvement in relations with the Nazi regime. In *Mit brenender Sorge* he had stated explicitly that 'humanity comprises a single great universal human race', an indication of his concern at the racial policies being put into ever more horrible effect in Germany at the time. This was a topic on which he was prepared to speak out, and, despite his declining health, he ordered three priests to draft a new encyclical that he intended to issue early in 1939, which was to be entitled *Humani Generis Unitas* (The Unity of the Human Race), which was a robust rebuttal of all forms of political totalitarianism. It warned of the dangers of relying too heavily on the state as the defender of the unity of humanity, of the depersonalising of human life by economic and social forces and of the resulting pressures towards uniformity. All of these combined to produce

'Mechanical-Totalitarian' systems of government in which rights of association were suppressed, individuality was eroded through state control of education and the media, a false nationalism was engendered and outsiders and non-conformists were persecuted.[48] Unfortunately, Pius XI died on 10 February 1939, before the new encyclical could be issued, and Cardinal Pacelli, immediately promised Mussolini's envoy to the Vatican that it would not be released and 'will remain a dead letter'.[49]

chapter 21

THE IMPREGNABLE
ROCK OF PETER

(1939–2008)

Pius XII

All the popes of the second half of the twentieth century are currently being considered for canonisation, and the causes of some are very well advanced. Maybe those decades were so remarkable that an unbroken line of saints was needed at the helm of the Church to steer it through them. A more mundane reflection would be to wonder what impact the development of mass communication has had on public interest in the personalities and actions of the popes of this time, as there is an almost exact correlation between the rise of television and these pontificates.

Popes have been seen in the flesh or on screen by people all around the world to a degree entirely unprecedented. Conclaves, marked by the drama of the white and grey smoke signals from the chimney in the Sistine Chapel and the first appearance of the new pope, have been televised since 1958. From the 1970s the popes themselves have been travelling the world, attended by press and television, in a way their predecessors could never have imagined. The overall effect is that modern popes have lived in the minds of the faithful in ways entirely unknown in the past.

Of those popes being considered for canonisation, by far the most popular cause is that of John Paul II, but the only controversial one is that of Pius XII (1939–1958), thanks to questions about his failure to condemn the treatment of Jews in Nazi Germany. This debate is not going to be settled easily, especially as materials in the Vatican archives are currently accessible only up to the end of the pontificate of Pius XI, itself a recent advance from the previous cut-off date of 1922. Criticisms of his conduct, including his time in Germany negotiating the concordat of 1933, have raised legitimate questions, but the case against him is far from proven. Rather more serious may be the less well aired charges that the Vatican was unwilling to intervene to prevent Catholics from taking part in the ethnic cleansing of Orthodox Christians and of Jews in Croatia in 1941. In the events of these years Pius XII was at the very least constrained by the habitual caution that made him a good Vatican diplomat rather than a natural leader of men in time of crisis.

That such a time was upon them must have been evident to the fifty-three cardinals who assembled in the Vatican after the death of Pius XI. As in the conclave of 2005, their instinct was to favour continuity. Cardinal Pacelli had been the closest collaborator of the previous pontiff throughout the decade and may have been his preferred successor. His family had close ties with the Vatican, he had been a professor of ecclesiastical diplomacy and his experience of it in practice was extensive, including visits to France, Hungary, Britain, Argentina and the United States, and made him an obvious choice when international relations would be a new pope's most pressing concern. Described as 'a very gentle, cultured, shy, very controlled, very prayerful, lonely man with a yearning Christian heart', he was elected on the third ballot on the very first day of the conclave on 2 March 1939.[1]

The decision not to publish the encyclical that Pius XI had prepared on 'the unity of the human race' was the product of the new pope's characteristic restraint, but he may also have preferred that the first such document of his pontificate should be his own. It was not until 20 October 1939, two months after the start of the Second World War, that he issued *Summi Pontificatus* (Of the Supreme Pontificate), in which he identified the cause of the current conflict as 'the poisoned source of religious and moral agnosticism'.[2] While the subject of the encyclical was 'the Unity of Human Society', and the pope spoke of the 'marvellous vision which makes us see the human race in the unity of one common origin in God', he avoided the explicit condemnation of totalitarian government that his predecessor had hoped to make. This would set the style to be adopted in the Vatican during the ensuing years of war, regretting the conflict and seeing its causes as lying in 'the abandonment of that Christian teaching of which the Chair of Peter is the depository and exponent'.[3] The discovery of what appeared to be the bones of St. Peter at this very time seemed a remarkable affirmation of this analysis but for the pope's cautiousness about revealing it prematurely.

During the period of 'the phoney war', before fighting actually broke out in Western Europe in the spring of 1940 and Belgium and France were overrun, the Vatican became a centre of secret diplomatic activity and conspiracy. One of the most significant episodes involved an approach by a group opposed to the Nazi regime within the Abwehr, the German army's intelligence unit, represented in Rome by a former lawyer, Captain Josef Müller. He made contact with Monsignor Ludwig Kaas, former leader of the Zentrumspartei and now Prefect of the Fabric of St. Peter's, and they used visits to the excavations under the basilica as a cover for their discussions. These concerned the possibility of the pope acting as go-between with the Allies to discover what their reaction would be if the conspirators in the Abwehr could get rid of Hitler. Similar contact was made through a German Jesuit professor, Robert Leiber, who was a close friend of the pope.

How realistic the Abwehr group's plans for eliminating Hitler actually were remains uncertain. The British government was suspicious, as it had recently lost agents lured to a meeting with supposed anti-Nazis, and so refused to take the approach seriously during the months before open war broke out in 1940. Because there had been so many previous false alarms, they also refused to believe a genuine warning sent to them from the group via the Vatican that the blitzkrieg would be launched in May that year, as it was. When war became a reality the Abwehr group broke off contact, and the Vatican withdrew into a stance of concerned neutrality.[4]

It is unlikely that Mussolini would have gone beyond cancelling the Lateran Treaty of 1929 had the Vatican taken a stronger line in condemning his German ally, but a different situation arose when he was dismissed by the king in July 1943. This precipitated the German occupation of Rome and most of central and northern Italy in September, aimed at holding back the Allied advance from the south. While a papal denunciation of Mussolini's regime during the previous stages of the war might have seemed unpatriotic to many Italians, open opposition to the deeply resented German occupation would certainly have been popular. However, Pius XII had always feared that a public stand against the Nazis would make them take reprisals on the Catholic Church in Germany, and in 1943 he believed it might lead to the Germans seizing the Vatican. Suitcases were kept packed in case a quick escape was needed, and the colonel of the papal bodyguard, the Swiss Guard, was told not to try to resist if the Germans broke in.[5]

In fact, Hitler had already talked of doing so and of 'getting out the whole lot of swine' when planning the seizure of Rome but had been persuaded not to by Goebbels and Joachim von Ribbentrop, his propaganda and foreign ministers, because of the likely impact on international opinion.[6] Remembering Pius VII's treatment by Napoleon, the pope himself had kept a letter of resignation ready since the outbreak of the war, so that if he were imprisoned the cardinals could elect a successor.

Pius XII admitted numerous refugees into the Vatican when the Germans invaded Rome in September 1943. How far he personally was aware of the way some of the clergy and Vatican officials were protecting the Roman Jews and helping Allied military personnel in the city to hide or escape during the final stages of the war is unknown, though these activities would certainly have been much harder had he forbidden them. His removal to Germany was likely if his involvement was proved, and the Gestapo are said to have been gathering evidence of the Vatican infringing its neutrality right up to the time the city was liberated by the Allies in June 1944.[7]

The post-war years of Pius XII's pontificate saw a revival of the spirit of the age of Pius X. He had always had something of a siege mentality, like his newly sainted predecessor, when it came to the menace of modernity. In his first encyclical in 1939 he had written of 'the indissoluble unity of the Catholic Church rallying all the closer to the impregnable Rock of Peter, to form around it a wall and a bulwark as the enemies of Christ become bolder'.[8] Despite the war, Pius XII always saw communism as a far greater threat than fascism, both because it was overtly anti-religious and because the ideology of class warfare militated against the message of social harmony preached by popes from Leo XIII onwards. The destruction of churches and religious objects and the death and exile of those thought to stand in the way of utopian progress in Russia had been all too obvious since 1917, and there was a strong feeling that the political triumph of communism elsewhere would produce similar results. So in 1949 a decree was issued threatening excommunication for any Catholic who supported communism. As the Communist Party became influential in Italian politics after the war, this produced local confrontations of Church and party throughout Italy, as humorously depicted in the Don Camillo stories of Giovanni Guareschi that first appeared in 1946.

In the 1950s Pius XII issued twenty-five encyclicals in eight years, on subjects ranging from 'combating atheistic propaganda throughout the world' to the persecuted condition of the Church in China after the communists took power, which resulted in the breaking off of diplomatic relations with Beijing in 1951. Not all were on topics of such contemporary importance. One was devoted to the Anglo-Saxon missionary St. Boniface (martyred in 754), through whose work 'a new era dawned for the German people', and another to St. Bernard of Clairvaux, whose 'teaching was drawn, almost exclusively, from the pages of Sacred Scripture and from the Fathers, which he had at hand day and night in his profound meditations: and not from the subtle reasonings of dialecticians and philosophers, which, on more than one occasion, he clearly held in low esteem.'[9] Bernard was here being enrolled as an anti-Modernist.

This period also saw the only occasion to date in which a pope has made an infallible proclamation. In 1950 Pius XII defined the doctrine of 'the bodily Assumption into heaven of Mary, the Virgin Mother of God'. As he indicated, there was a theological connection between this newly defined doctrine and that of the Immaculate Conception on which Pius IX had pronounced almost exactly a century earlier: If the corruption of the body comes through the working of sin, then as Mary had been born without the taint of it, there would be no need for her to receive a purified material form upon resurrection, and so she could be envisaged being immediately enthroned in Heaven upon her death. In its way it is a rather abstract and theoretical doctrine, required to complete the logic of an earlier one, but it was hailed with enormous enthusiasm by Catholics, and was followed four years later by the encyclical *Ad coeli Reginam,* which proclaimed Mary as the Queen of Heaven. This developed from the instituting of the liturgical feast of Christ the King by Pius XI in 1925.

Pius XII in his numerous encyclicals, apostolic constitutions and letters became extremely communicative, excessively so in the eyes of some commentators. He liked television and had he lived a bit later would probably have used it more than some of his successors. He recognised that it posed dangers, including the risk of provoking family squabbles, and one of his last documents, issued in August 1958, was an apostolic letter instituting St. Claire, the sister of St. Francis of Assisi, as Heavenly Patron of Television, to 'prevent its defects and support its honest use'.[10] She was chosen because she once had a vision of the Nativity so clear and precise she could almost have been present in person.

The shy and reclusive Pius XII, who had to control a stammer when speaking, was devoted to a small band of people, but whose influence on him was distrusted. They included his German housekeeper, Sister Pasqualina, who had even attended him during the conclave of 1939, and his doctor, Riccardo Galeazzi-Lisi, and there was criticism of the favours he gave his nephews in the later part of his pontificate. Like Pius XI, he rarely summoned the non-curial cardinals to Rome, and he allowed several of the major offices of state to remain vacant. For example, he had no permanent secretary of state after 1944, and there was no *camerlengo* in post when he died, requiring the cardinals immediately to elect one to take charge of the papal palaces and organise the conclave.

Influence mattered, especially when accusations of liberal tendencies could be used to block the rise of a rival or undermine a successful career. Giovanni Battista Montini, the later Paul VI, had worked in the Secretariat of State since 1924 and was one of Pius XII's closest advisors during the war years, before becoming one of two acting, or pro-, secretaries of state in 1952, but two years later was sent to Milan as its archbishop. While a distinguished position, it was a surprising appointment for someone who had hitherto been a curialist, with a retiring personality.

That it marked something of a disgrace was made clear by his not receiving the elevation to the rank of cardinal that almost invariably accompanied it. As Pius XII held his second and last consistory for the appointment of cardinals in 1956, the intention of preventing Montini being a candidate in the next conclave seemed clear. It was suggested that Montini's exile was the result of the hostility of Sister Pasqualina, but his liberal sympathies at a time in which the papacy of Pius XII was becoming increasingly conservative may be a more attractive explanation. In any case it was a good omen for the future pope, as Leo XIII and Benedict XV had also endured 'wilderness years' under their predecessors.

Pius XII's trust in his doctor was clearly unaffected by the misidentification of the bones from the Vatican excavations, as he agreed to being injected by Galeazzi-Lisi with a serum made from the glands of foetal lambs, intended to prolong his life. The didactic tendencies of Pius's last years, reflected in the outpouring of documents on so many topics, indicate his sense of having much to say, while the useless serum suggests an equally strong awareness of the shortness of time. Following his death at Castel Gandolfo in October 1958, the doctor used a preservative process of his own to delay the decomposition of the pope's body during its journey back to Rome, but it had the opposite effect. It was said 'no pope had ever so occupied the public gaze as did Pius XII; yet no pontiff of modern times had so lonely an end as he, or one so surrounded by unfitting drama.'[11]

A TURNING POINT?

Ten years after, the result of the conclave of 1958 was hailed as 'the irrevocable end of an epoch' in the history of the papacy.[12] But what once seemed seminal may look less so half a century later, as change is measured over time, and the effects of what was once a seismic shift may diminish to that of a tremor. There is no denying that the

election of John XXIII on 28 October 1958 produced dramatic results and by papal standards very quickly, but it may be wondered
how much of what was achieved through the Second Vatican Council
has survived intact, and how much has been reversed. Even four
decades later, it is too early to know for sure what the real long-term
legacy of the council will be. Its shorter-term effects and consequences can be more easily appreciated.

The conclave that followed the death of Pius XII was the first to
have its opening televised. Faster, more frequent flights made it possible for cardinals to arrive for the proceedings from all over the world
including Australia.[13] This meant that more non-Italians took part in
the election than ever before, but because of the many curial cardinals
and the large number of archbishoprics in Italy whose holders were
normally made cardinal, the Italians remained the largest single bloc
within the conclave, though not necessarily united. It had been impossible even to think of electing a non-Italian in the conclaves of 1914
and 1939 when the world was at war or on the edge of it, as this
would seem to take sides in the conflict. One non-Italian was considered in 1958, but as he was an Armenian residing in Rome he was unlikely to be the candidate for breaking a tradition going back to 1523.

Once assembled, the cardinals still had to live in temporary accommodation created in the corridors around the Sistine Chapel,
something that only changed when a hostel in the grounds of the Vatican was first used in 2005. The conclave itself was preceded by the
Mass of the Holy Spirit and a traditional Latin speech delivered by
the curial official known as the Secretary of Briefs to Princes on the
subject of *de eligendo pontifice* (How a Pontiff Should Be Chosen).

The electoral process in the chapel remained essentially as laid
down in the bull of Gregory XV (1621–1623) and confirmed by Urban VIII in 1626. This required the cardinals to take an oath only to
vote for a worthy candidate, eliminated election by adoration and instituted the use of a secret ballot, held usually but not necessarily
twice every morning and twice every afternoon, in which a voter was
forbidden to vote for himself. Special election slips were devised on
which the cardinal entered his name and that of the candidate he was
voting for, who did not himself have to be a cardinal, though the

printed form on which they wrote contained the phrase *Eligo in Summum Pontificem Rv.mD. meum D. Cardin.* (I elect as Supreme Pontiff the most reverend Lord my Lord Cardinal). The cardinals were expected to disguise their handwriting but identify themselves with a private motto, such as *Gloria in excelsis,* to prevent them voting in the name of their colleagues.[14]

In the conclave of 1958 at least two votes were given to the non-cardinal, Archbishop Montini of Milan, to whom Pius XII had denied the promotion since 1954. Amongst those representing continuity with the policies of the previous pope, Cardinal Giuseppe Siri, archbishop of Genoa since 1947, was the favourite as the particular protégé of Pius XII, but several traditionalists did not vote for him because he was only fifty-two and might enjoy too long a pontificate, blocking the papal hopes of others and raising fear of stagnation.[15] As was said of the very long-lived Leo XIII, 'We elected a Holy Father, not a Father Eternal.'[16]

After three days but eleven ballots, the necessary majority was achieved by Angelo Roncalli, the patriarch of Venice. He was essentially the first choice of those wanting change—less rigidity and a stronger sense of the pastoral rather than the magisterial responsibilities of the papal office—but he was also acceptable to the traditionalists as a compromise candidate, being in many ways quite conservative. The new pope was 'a serious Church historian' and an experienced Vatican diplomat, though not a curialist, having served as apostolic delegate to Bulgaria, Greece and Turkey before and during the Second World War, and then nuncio in France from January 1945.[17] From Paris he was transferred to the patriarchate of Venice in 1953.

His encounters with non-Catholic Christians in Turkey and Bulgaria and with Marxists in France had given him an enthusiasm for dialogue and for reunification of the churches, but aged seventy-seven in 1958, he was not expected to enjoy a long pontificate. His choice of John as papal name, for the first time since 1410, was thought to be a deliberate recognition of this, as none of its previous holders had lived long, but he said he chose it because it was his father's name and that of the saint to whom his baptismal church was dedicated.

This sense of the shortness of time added to his determination to use it to good purpose. He held his first consistory for naming new cardinals on 15 December 1958, appointing twenty-three of them, with Giovanni Battista Montini of Milan being the first. This brought the membership of the college to seventy-four, taking it beyond the limit set by Sixtus V. Then on 25 January 1959, the feast of the Conversion of St. Paul, in the Basilica of San Paolo fuori le mura John XXIII made three announcements: Firstly, a new ecumenical council was to meet in September 1962. Secondly, it was to be preceded and prepared for by a synod of the bishops of the Roman metropolitanate, the first such to be summoned since the Middle Ages. And thirdly, a revision of the *Corpus Juris Canonici* (Code of Canon Law) would be undertaken. The previous version of the *Corpus,* commissioned by Pius X, and published in 1917 by Benedict XV, had produced the first systematic organisation of canon law, becoming in the process what has been called 'probably the greatest instrument of centralisation and Romanization in this period'.[18] John XXIII's proposed new version was intended to include the decrees of the forthcoming council.

The choice of venue and date for these announcements was not accidental, as John XXIII intended the council would meet in San Paolo and be *Concilium Ostiensis* (Council on the Ostia Road), not the Second Vatican. This was the first signal that the pope wished to break with some associations of the past and indicate a new openness to dialogue with both Protestant and Orthodox churches.[19] The Pauline rather than Petrine context for both announcement and council implied a concern for unity and spreading the word to the 'Gentiles', and less of an emphasis on authority and obedience. The change of location to the Vatican, for reasons of greater practicality, was one of the early victories for the curial cardinals, who had received the original announcement in complete silence, and who, when they saw the pope could not be deflected, determined to control the council's agenda. This they did through themselves chairing the ten commissions and two secretariats set up in 1960 to plan the conciliar business, staffing them with their own people.

What prompted John XXIII to call an ecumenical council is not clear. He said, 'The first conception of this council came unexpectedly into our mind,' and the next step that he mentions was the proclamation in San Paolo.[20] He recalled those present on that occasion being suddenly and deeply moved, as if illuminated by a supernatural ray of light, a kindly interpretation of their shocked silence.

Anticipation of major change as a result of the council was high amongst liberal Catholics, looking for a loosening of authority and reforms to modernise views on hierarchy, contraception, clerical marriage, the role of women in the Church, liturgy in the vernacular and the life of the religious orders, amongst many other topics. Traditionalists recognised that changes were needed in some far more limited areas but were doubtful about the conciliar route to obtaining them. One commented, 'I suppose the greatest reform of our time was that carried out by St. Pius X: surpassing anything, however needed, that the Council will achieve.'[21]

A month before the council convened on October 11 1962, the pope was diagnosed with terminal cancer but refused an operation, so as to be present. The opening of its second session was delayed from May to September 1963 because of the expectation that he would die that year. There was concern in curial quarters that if this happened while the council was in session, the assembly of some two and a half thousand bishops might interfere in the process of selecting the next pope, citing the election of Martin V by the council of Constance in 1417 as precedent. A similar fear had prompted Pius IX in 1869 to decree that his death would automatically terminate the First Vatican Council, to prevent its members trying to elect his successor. The Second Vatican Council had already proved itself hard for the curia to control, overturning much of the agenda designed for it by the cardinals and the curial commissions.

By the time the council reconvened in September 1963, it was under the presidency of a new pope, Paul VI (1963–1978), the former Giovanni Battista Montini. The polarising of opinion in the Sacred College into liberal and traditionalist groupings was even more accentuated by the recent work of the council. The college itself now consisted of eighty-one cardinals and would have been even larger if three names reserved *in pectore* had been revealed before John XXIII's death. He publicly appointed fifty-two cardinals in four years, altering the balance in the college. However, the Italians remained the largest bloc, and the favoured candidates from liberal and traditionalist sides, Montini and Siri, were Italian. Larger numbers of cardinals from North and South America and Africa were present than ever before. An abusive pre-election sermon by one of the more conservative cardinals containing 'ridicule of the late pope's simplemindedness' only hardened opinion in favour of Montini, who was elected on the fifth ballot in a conclave that lasted less than two days.[22]

Terms like liberal and traditionalist are relative, and there was little that was radical about Paul VI beyond his choice of name, which was in honour of the Apostle and fitted John XXIII's original conception for his council. When the council reconvened under his presidency, he showed how much he shared his predecessor's concern for dialogue by inviting non-Catholic and non-Christian observers to attend. This followed a pre-conciliar encounter, when in December 1960 Geoffrey Fisher became the first archbishop of Canterbury to be received by the pope since the Reformation.

By training and experience, and even by temperament, Paul VI was more of a curialist than a pastor. Shy and scholarly, with a personal library of six thousand books, he had worked in the papal Secretariat of State from 1924, and became substitute Secretary for Ordinary Ecclesiastical Affairs in 1937, giving him particular responsibility for Catholic Action and similar organisations. He was closely involved in the Vatican's relief programmes during the war and providing assistance to refugees and captured combatants. Together with Domenico Tardini, who would become John XXIII's first secretary of state, he was Pius XII's closest curial advisor, until sent to Milan in 1954.

Paul broke with tradition in abandoning use of the three-crowned papal tiara after his own coronation, replacing it in the liturgical contexts in which it would normally be worn by an episcopal mitre. He sold his own tiara for charity, much to the annoyance of traditionalists, and his successor John Paul I declined to be crowned at all, and instead received the pallium as the sign of the pope's universal authority, as have his successors ever since. Paul VI stopped using other traditional trappings of papal magnificence such as the *sedia gestatoria,* the portable throne in which a pope was carried on the shoulders of members of a special corps of *sediari pontifici* on formal occasions, accompanied by others bearing *flabelli,* long liturgical fans once intended to cool the pontiff and keep the flies away while processing in the open. In 1970 Paul also abolished the Pontifical Noble Guard, along with the papal police body, founded in 1816 and known since 1851 as the Pontifical Gendarmerie.

The rejection of the trappings of power did not, however, involve the abandonment of its realities. Paul VI put limits on the topics which the Second Vatican Council could address, excluding for example contraception and clerical celibacy, which had even been on the agenda of the Council of Trent. While keen to promote what in his first encyclical he called 'the Church's heroic and impatient struggle for renewal' and encourage dialogue with other Christian communions, he was equally determined not to allow these to diminish papal primacy.[23]

When close to the end of the council he instituted 'a special Council of bishops, with the aim of providing for a continuance after the Council of the great abundance of benefits that We have been so happy to see flow to the Christian people during the time of the Council as a result of Our close collaboration with the bishops', its purely consultative and subordinate role was made clear in the text of the decree calling it into existence: 'on our own initiative and by Our apostolic authority, We hereby erect and establish here in Rome a permanent Council of bishops for the universal Church, to be directly and immediately subject to Our power.'[24]

In 1966 Paul VI finally abolished the Index of Prohibited Books, which had last been updated in 1948. However, Catholics were still expected not to read or circulate books that they were authoritatively advised would endanger their faith or morality. The writings of Catholic theologians continued to be monitored by the Congregation for the Doctrine of the Faith. Works of theirs submitted for preliminary examination were subjected to fuller enquiry if 'certain errors and imprecisions' were found in them. If these books were enjoying widespread readership or were in use in seminaries, this might be expedited into 'the process of urgent examination'. The author would be informed of the 'erroneous or dangerous propositions' found in his work and be asked to respond to the points raised. If this was thought not to go far enough in the direction indicated by the congregation, it might issue a Notification, an official statement approved by the pope in person, pointing out in detail where the book contains 'notable discrepancies with the faith of the Church'. The most recent such Notification was issued in November 2006.[25] In cases where an author's work is judged to contain 'serious doctrinal errors contrary to the divine and Catholic faith of the Church', the ruling may state that 'until his positions are corrected to be in complete conformity with the doctrine of the Church, the Author may not teach Catholic theology.'[26]

Within the Vatican, Paul VI was responsible for ordering the most thorough reorganisation of its administrative structures since the pontificate of Sixtus V in the late sixteenth century, though following on from changes carried out by Pius X. He also introduced the rule that cardinals over the age of eighty be ineligible to vote in a conclave, and limited the number below that age in the Sacred College, which had grown further in size in recent years, to 120. His appointments totalled 143 new cardinals. Although John Paul II would make a greater number of cardinals, 231 in all, this was a smaller annual average than that of Paul VI. His appointments put an end to the numerical dominance of the Italians, making the choice of a non-Italian pope in a subsequent conclave all the more likely.

The international interests of Paul VI, which made him the first pope to travel beyond the boundaries of Europe, in visits to India, the United Nations, South America, Uganda and Australia, again prefigure the even more extensive and frequent travels of John Paul II, and helped make this a regular and expected feature of pontifical activity. It was Paul VI too who pursued contacts made between John XXIII and Patriarch Athenagoras, leading to the lifting of the mutual excommunications that had been pronounced by both Rome and Constantinople in 1054. This was achieved on 7 December 1965, and two years later Paul VI became the first pope since 710 to visit the former Eastern imperial capital, long since renamed Istanbul. While contact and occasional dialogue has continued, no further real progress has been achieved in reunification of Catholic and Ortho-dox, not least because of irreconcilable differences concerning the primacy of papal authority over that of ecumenical councils.

In recent years the Congregation of the Doctrine of the Faith, for-merly the Inquisition, over which Cardinal Joseph Ratzinger, now Pope Benedict XVI (2005–), presided from 1981 to 2005, has been issuing 'doctrinal documents' intended to clarify or reinterpret the meaning of some of the decrees of the Second Vatican Council. One of these, issued in June 2007, deals with 'the authentic meaning of some ecclesiological expressions', that is to say the status of Christian bodies not in full communion with Rome. In the case of the Ortho-dox, the document states that the council used the term 'Churches' in reference to them because they 'have true sacraments and above all—because of the apostolic succession—the priesthood and the Eu-charist, by means of which they remain linked to us by very close bonds'. However, they are also regarded as defective 'since commun-ion with the Catholic Church, the visible head of which is the Bishop of Rome and the Successor of Peter, is not some external complement to a particular Church, but rather one of its internal constitutive principles'. In other words, without acceptance of Roman primacy, there can be no reunion. Viewed from the Rock of Peter, the Ortho-dox are in a better condition than the Protestants and others, who merely enjoy 'ecclesial Communities', because they 'do not enjoy apostolic succession in the sacrament of Orders' and therefore 'be-cause of the absence of the sacramental priesthood have not pre-served the genuine and integral substance of the Eucharistic Mystery'.[27] Pope Benedict XVI gave his formal approval to the Con-gregation's document in July 2007, arousing indignation in some ec-umenical quarters.

As this episode suggests, the results of the Second Vatican Council have divided opinion over the decades that followed, pleasing some in the Church and offending others, and requiring interpretations to make them conform to papal understanding of the meaning of the conciliar decrees. The replacement of the Latin Mass by liturgy in the vernacular, accompanied by changes reflecting new views of the na-ture of worship, for example the celebrant facing the congregation across the altar rather than standing with his back to the laity, may have caused the greatest upset. The refusal of the French archbishop Marcel-François Lefebvre (died 1991) to accept the abolition of the Latin Mass and his consecration of clergy to perform it was the first open defiance of major decrees of the council. Paul VI suspended the archbishop in 1976. Lefebvre in turn refused to acknowledge the outcomes of the two conclaves of 1978 because of the denial of voting rights to cardinals aged over eighty and continued to support the ultra-traditionalist Society of St. Pius X, which he founded in 1970 and for which he un-canonically ordained four bishops in 1988. For this John Paul II declared him to be automatically excommunicated. The Society is held not to be schismatic but 'in a state of separation' from the Church.

Although in July 2007 Benedict XVI reinstated the Latin Mass as a permitted alternative to the vernacular liturgy, this in itself may not heal the rift as Lefebvrist bishops and clergy have referred to Vatican II in terms not dissimilar to those used by the Monophysites for the Council of Chalcedon, and are unlikely to accept its legitimacy. In 1983 nine priests in New York broke away from the Society of St. Pius X to form the Society of St. Pius V, because they objected to the 1962 Missal, which Archbishop Lefebvre had accepted in place of that of 1570, and because they claimed that the papal throne had been vacant since 1958, a view not shared by their erstwhile colleagues.

Paul VI's own hesitancy in pursuing the kind of change that many wanted to see in the Church after the closure of the council was made clear in his encyclical *Humanae Vitae* of 25 July 1968 on the subject of birth control, a topic he had already kept from conciliar debate but one over which he himself long agonised before issuing this document. The opening sections lay out some of the issues making this an urgent subject for change, notably 'a new understanding of the dignity of woman and her place in society, of the value of conjugal love in marriage and the relationship of conjugal acts to this love' and a recognition 'that not only working and housing conditions but the greater demands made both in the economic and educational field pose a living situation in which it is frequently difficult these days to provide properly for a large family'.[28] There follows an account of the work of a commission on this subject set up by John XXIII in 1963, but Paul VI decided its conclusions 'could not be considered by Us as definitive and absolutely certain, dispensing Us from the duty of examining personally this serious question'.[29]

In reaching his own conclusions on this issue Paul VI was influenced by the advice of Karol Wojtyla, archbishop of Kraków, whom he had made a cardinal two months earlier. While explained at length in the encyclical, the papal decision was clear:

> The right and lawful ordering of birth demands, first of all, that spouses fully recognize and value the true blessings of family life and that they acquire complete mastery over themselves and their emotions. For if with the aid of reason and of free will they are to control their natural drives, there can be no doubt at all of the need for self-denial. Only then will the expression of love, essential to married life, conform to right order. This is especially clear in the practice of periodic continence.[30]

Opposition or disappointment was expected: 'It is to be anticipated that perhaps not everyone will easily accept this particular teaching. There is too much clamorous outcry against the voice of the Church, and this is intensified by modern means of communication.' But 'the Church is convinced that she is contributing to the creation of a truly human civilization. She urges man not to betray his personal responsibilities by putting all his faith in technical expedients.'[31] The expected outcry was actually far greater than anticipated, and the encyclical itself contributed to a feeling amongst liberals that the principles of the Second Vatican Council were being betrayed by this and other decisions from Rome. On the other side the traditionalists claimed that the council had betrayed the Church.

Faced with such a tension between two powerful bodies of opinion the hesitant Paul VI lapsed into virtual silence. After *Humanae Vitae* he issued no more encyclicals during the remaining ten years of his pontificate, and his enthusiastic announcement of the discovery of the bones of St. Peter in 1968 may have been inspired by the feeling this was a sign around which all shades of opinion in the Church might unite in rejoicing. For once hesitancy might have been the wisest course.

The conclave that followed Paul VI's death was notable for some changes resulting from his 1975 electoral decree. The personal followings of conclavists the cardinals had for centuries brought with them were now replaced by a seventy-strong support staff, and electronic countermeasures were used to prevent bugging and other illicit communication between the conclave and an outside world more interested than ever in what went on in the Sistine Chapel. It was not just the public but also governments that were concerned with the outcome, especially the communist regimes of Eastern Europe, whose acrimonious contacts with the Vatican had been increasing since 1958.

Once more it was Cardinal Siri who was the standard bearer of the traditionalist wing, leading in the first ballot, only to be overtaken by Cardinal Albino Luciani, patriarch of Venice. By the fourth ballot Luciani had ninety-six votes, and took the name John Paul I, a complete break with previous papal nomenclature, to honour both his immediate predecessors and to symbolise his hopes of harmonising the contradictory features of their respective legacies. His appearance on the balcony from which the papal benediction was always pronounced, captured on television, was remarkable for the warmth of his smile, and he became known as 'the laughing pope'. After fifteen years of the pensive, worried looks of Paul VI, this in itself seemed to promise a new style of papacy, confirmed by his abandonment of the traditional coronation.

John Paul I's sudden death after a pontificate of thirty-three days caused consternation in many quarters, as there had not been a papal reign so short since the twenty-six days of Leo XI in 1605. In the conflict over the legacy of the Second Vatican Council, the brevity of John Paul I's reign provided ammunition for traditionalists who objected to Paul VI's exclusion of the votes of cardinals aged over eighty. Some questioned if the election of John Paul I were the work of the Holy Spirit, while the followers of Archbishop Lefebvre suggested he had been poisoned by the Freemasons. Other conspiracy theorists argued that he had been murdered by sinister figures in the Vatican to stop him exposing a financial scandal relating to the Vatican Bank's involvement with the Banco Ambrosiano, an issue then coming into the open and which would cloud the early years of the pontificate of John Paul II. However, a meticulous enquiry by the English Catholic historian John Cornwell revealed that the Curia had been unaware of the precarious state of the new pope's health, as his medical records were still with his personal physician in Venice, and that when he was found around dawn by the nun who usually woke him, the Vatican released contradictory accounts of his death out of embarrassment at the fact that he had died earlier in the night, unattended, probably in considerable pain, and without benefit of the last rites. The cause of the death of John Paul I was nothing more sinister than a weak heart, though the fatal attack may have been provoked by the pressure of work the new pope was trying to master.[32]

The most significant outcome of the untimely demise of John Paul I was the election in October 1978 of John Paul II, who would enjoy the second longest recorded pontificate, after that of Pius IX. It is still too soon for its mixed legacy to be assessed, not just because much of the documentary evidence is inaccessible but even more importantly because it is difficult at this distance in time to see what its real and lasting outcomes may be. The pope's poor health in his last years, stemming from the effects of the assassination attempt on him in 1981, revived the question of papal abdication, as there appeared a danger of his becoming completely incapacitated. John Paul II had recognised this as a possibility, but despite occasional flutters of speculation in the Curia it was not a route he himself ever wished to follow. Nor may his advisors have encouraged it, as his growing physical weakness allowed the Curia greater control of the levers of power in Vatican policy making than would be tolerated by a pope in full command of his faculties. His very visible suffering in those last years, always bravely borne and often compared to a personal Calvary, only increased the great popular affection and sympathy with which he was regarded around the world.

Features of John Paul II's pontificate that are positive must include his extraordinary range of travels throughout the pontificate, with the huge crowds and enormous enthusiasm they inspired (though his extended absences were not always popular in the Curia), and his role in inspiring Polish resistance to communist rule. The precise extent of his contribution to the collapse of communism in Eastern Europe will be long debated, but that he had a vital part to play cannot be denied. John Paul II's doctrinal conservatism, Eastern European piety and stern morality generated more of a mixed reaction, arousing enthusiasm in some and repelling others. His absolute rejection of the possibility of women being admitted to the priesthood and of the use of contraception as a means to combat the worldwide AIDS epidemic have been strongly criticised. So too was his intransigent stand on most issues relating to ecumenism and the reunification of churches other than on the Vatican's terms. Theologians were silenced by the Congregation of the Doctrine of the Faith, presided over from 1981 to 2005 by Cardinal Ratzinger, now Benedict XVI, to a degree unparalleled since the Modernist controversy.

John Paul's canonisation of eighty-five and beatification of about 400 new saints exceeded the total number proclaimed by all of his predecessors since the time of Innocent III in the thirteenth century. It redressed the balance as far as Eastern Europe was concerned and included several prominent and remarkable religious figures such as Mother Teresa of Calcutta (died 1997), Padre Pio (died 1968)—to whom the devil once appeared disguised as Pius X—and Josemaría Escrivá de Balaguer (died 1975), founder of Opus Dei.[33]

John Paul II's almost silent reaction to the various scandals of paedophile abuse by members of the clergy and the attempts by some of their bishops to protect the perpetrators in Europe and the United States that were uncovered in the later years of his pontificate betrayed a clerical mind-set reminiscent of the Middle Ages: The clergy are by their ordination set apart from and above the laity and not answerable to secular justice. The stories of abuse, in some cases going back five decades, first emerged in 2000, and many more have since come to light. While issues of compensation to the victims have been dealt with at the archdiocesan level and have led to settlements involving payment of hundreds of millions of dollars by the Church, it must have surprised the numerous victims that no thunderous denunciation of what they suffered emerged from the Vatican. Instead certain low-key papal statements created the impression that the victims were the real culprits for serving as objects of temptation to the clergy.[34] This occurred at a time of 'increasing uncertainty over just who was in charge at the Vatican', and the apparent lack of concern for the victims was reversed when Benedict XVI spoke openly about the issue on several occasions during his visits to the United States in April and to Australia in July 2008.[35]

THE SWEET CHRIST ON EARTH

For a small minority of Catholics the outcome of the Second Vatican Council has been little more than a disaster, a mass apostasy or a betrayal. Even if popes from Paul VI onwards reinterpreted the conciliar decisions in a more conservative way than the bishops who voted for them may have intended, ultra-traditionalists viewed many of the council's decrees as unacceptable compromises with modernity.

For them Pius X's denunciation of Modernism as a heresy provided the justification for defying his successors. By embracing the modern ideas that he, the last canonised pope, had condemned, his successors from John XXIII onwards could be accused of being heretics. Even John Paul II, a more traditional and authoritarian pope, is tainted because he stands in a line of succession from predecessors whose legitimacy was lost by their falling into heresy. The papal throne, by this line of argument, has remained vacant since the death of Pius XII in 1958.

Ultra-traditionalist groups have devised different ways of choosing new popes for themselves. These have ranged from the election of Michael I by himself, his parents and three others above a store in Kansas to the self-appointment (or mystical coronation by Christ) of a Spanish insurance broker, Clemente Domínguez y Gómez (died 2005), following a series of visions in which he was promised the succession to Paul VI, whom he believed was being kept a prisoner in the Vatican by the cardinals.[36] He became Gregory XVII in 1978, when the seat of the Petrine succession was also transferred from Rome to Palmar de Troya near Seville. His successor is Peter II.

Not all these break-away papacies have founded themselves on the *sede vacante* argument. Amongst the most inventive of the alternatives is the claim that Cardinal Siri (1906–1989), archbishop of Genoa, was actually elected pope in the conclave of 1958, only for the vote to be overturned by the cardinals because of mysterious threats. He was supposedly elected again in both 1963 and 1978 with the same outcome. A small band of believers recognised him, under the name Gregory XVII, as 'the Red Pope' whose coming was foretold in one of the visions of the Augustinian nun Anne-Catherine Emmerich (1774–1824), who was beatified by John Paul II in 2004.

While Cardinal Siri is said to have been so enraged at the prospect of the liberal Paul VI being elected in the 1958 conclave 'that he slammed his fist on the table and smashed his episcopal ring', there is no certainty that he ever encouraged the idea that he was really Gregory XVII.[37] However, those who accepted him as the true pope believe that he has a secret successor, elected by unnamed cardinals that Siri had appointed, thereby fulfilling the terms of yet another prophecy, this time by a French shepherdess called Melanie Calvat (c. 1850), who is reported to have said, 'The Church will be eclipsed. At first, we will not know which is the true pope.' After five centuries without them, we find ourselves in a world once more full of antipopes.

For these traditionalist groups, the mainstream Catholic Church is the 'Apostate Vatican II sect' or the *Novus Ordo* or 'New Order' Church, a mocking reference to John XXIII's statement that 'in the present state of human events, in which humanity seems to be entering into a New Order of things, I would see instead the mysterious plans of Divine Providence.'[38] Prophecy plays a central role in many of the justifications for their breaking with Rome, and in their expectations for what lies ahead. Here, though, they do not entirely part company with the mainstream tradition of the papacy itself, which since the end of the Enlightenment has embraced the message of prophecy, as in the case of 'the third secret of Fatima'.

In 1917 three peasant children in Fatima, Portugal, experienced visions of the Virgin Mary, which were only written down over twenty years later, by which time two of them had died. The third wrote several accounts in the early 1940s at the request of the local bishop.

From these it was officially deduced that the first two secrets referred to 'the Second World War, and . . . the immense damage that Russia would do to humanity by abandoning the Christian faith and embracing Communist totalitarianism'.[39] The third part was written down in 1944 and placed in a sealed envelope, before being read by John XXIII in August 1959. He 'decided to return the sealed envelope to the Holy Office and not to reveal the third part of the "secret".'[40] Paul VI did likewise in 1965. John Paul II read it in the summer of 1981, while recovering from the assassination attempt made on him in St. Peter's Square on 13 May 1981. He decided in due course to publish the text, having already in June 1981 consecrated 'the world to the Immaculate Heart of Mary', as the first two secrets had suggested.

In the third vision, of 13 July 1917, the children had seen

> a Bishop dressed in white—we had the impression it was the Holy Father. Other Bishops, Priests, men and women Religious going up a steep mountain, at the top of which there was a big Cross of rough-hewn trunks . . . on his knees at the foot of the big Cross he was killed by a group of soldiers who fired bullets and arrows at him, and in the same way there died one after another the other Bishops, Priests, men and women Religious, and various other peoples of different ranks and positions.[41]

John Paul II understood this third vision to refer to the attempt by a Turkish gunman to assassinate him in May 1981, and in gratitude presented the bullet to the shrine at Fatima. Although the assassination attempt was possibly instigated by an Eastern European power worried by the pope's influence on the growing resistance to communist rule in his native Poland, the assassin's motives have never been established. But for some in curial circles, 'The twentieth century was one of the most crucial in human history, with its tragic and cruel events culminating in the assassination attempt on the "sweet Christ on earth"'.[42]

In more measured fashion, in the 'Theological Commentary' by the then prefect of the Congregation for the Doctrine of the Faith,

Cardinal Joseph Ratzinger, the significance of the vision is broadened to embrace the whole twentieth century:

> In the *Via Crucis* of an entire century, the figure of the Pope has a special role. In his arduous ascent of the mountain we can undoubtedly see a convergence of different Popes. Beginning from Pius X up to the present Pope, they all shared the sufferings of the century and strove to go forward through all the anguish along the path which leads to the Cross.[43]

Benedict XVI's own pontificate has seen a move both away from what was starting to look like a papal cult of personality and towards a greater measure of episcopal collegiality. Symbolically this has been expressed in the replacement of the tiara in the pope's arms by a simple episcopal mitre. Notable too is his dedication of the year 2008 to St. Paul, like John XXIII emphasising the Apostle symbolic of mission, but interpreting his significance both in the context of his own period when 'a crisis of traditional religion was taking place' and as inspiration to Catholics of today: 'to learn from St. Paul, to learn faith, to learn Christ, and finally to learn the way of upright living.'[44]

This does not mean there has been any less emphasis on Peter, the Apostle representative of authority. Benedict XVI, like many of his predecessors back to Pius IX, has shown himself distrustful of synods, or national bishops' conferences as they are now called. In part this is the traditional papal fear that such meetings can be too independent, but his personal preference is for reform to come about as a result of the inner transformation of the individual Christian rather than through changes at the institutional level.[45] It is thus something to be achieved in the sphere of morality and the spiritual life rather than in administrative and organisational structures.

Other features of the pontificate include some distancing from the intense populism that was so marked a feature of that of John Paul II. The present pope has been initially less willing to travel as extensively or as frequently as his predecessor, but this has added to the impact of those visits he has made, not least his trip to the United States in April 2008. It is still too early to tell what real differences may emerge between the two pontificates, let alone the direction the papacy will really take in the first century of the third millennium. That it will still exist at the end of the one, and even of the other, is something its previous history suggests, but this will depend upon the nature of its responses to old and new challenges. One of the latter comes in the recognition by Benedict XVI that the Christian heritage of Europe is under threat, no longer from the menace of communism that had so worried his predecessors but from the spread of Islam. The military form this once took ended with the failure of the last Turkish siege of Vienna in 1685 and the subsequent long decline of the Ottoman empire, but it is now represented by the very different forces of immigration and conversion.

The papacy in the twentieth century was more defensive on its impregnable rock than at almost any other time in its past, and more disturbed by changes in human society and in thought than at any previous period, at least since the Reformation. The latter remains the great turning point in its history. Recent decades have, on the other hand, put the person of the pope at the forefront of the Catholic sense of identity to an unparalleled degree, and focussed popular piety upon it. At the same time there have been losses, both of vocations and of faith, more in some parts of the world than others, as expectations of change, reform and leadership have been disappointed. The papacy may need to adapt to the changing circumstances and demands of the new millennium, but if its history suggests anything, this will be done slowly, reluctantly and with a firm denial that anything of the kind is happening.

In his book interpreting the figure of Jesus in the New Testament, completed in 2006, Benedict XVI writes, 'Everyone is free then to contradict me. I would only ask my readers for that initial goodwill without which there can be no understanding.'[46] That final sentiment seems a good note on which to close this enquiry.

LIST OF POPES

(The first twelve popes to Victor I are from Irenaeus' list, with modern suggested dates. Antipopes are in italics.)

Linus: c. 70

Anacletus: c. 85

Clement I: c. 95

Evaristus: c. 100

Alexander I: c. 110

Sixtus I: c. 120

Telesphorus: c. 130

Hyginus: c. 140

Pius I: c. 145

Anicetus: c. 160

Eleutherus: c. 180

Victor I: c. 195

Zephyrinus: 198/9–217

Callistus I: 217–14 October 222

Urban I: 222–18 May 230

Pontian: 230–28 September 235

Anteros: 22 November 235–
3 January 236

Fabian: 10 January 236–
20 January 250

Cornelius: 251–253

Lucius: 26 June 253–5 March 254

Stephen I: May 254–2 August 257

Sixtus II: 30 August 257–6 August 258

Dionysius: 22 July 260–
26 December 267

Felix I: January 268–30 December 273

Euthychian: 4 January 274–
7 December 282

Gaius: 17 December 282–22 April 295

Marcellinus: 295–Autumn 303

Marcellus I: 305/6; died 308

Eusebius: 8 April 308–September 308

Miltiades: July 310–10 January 314

Sylvester I: 31 January 314–
31 December 335

Marcus: January 336–7 October 336

Julius I: 6 February 337–12 April 352

Liberius: 17 May 352–24 September 366

Felix II: 355–22 November 365

Damasus I: 1 October 366–
11 December 384

Ursinus: September 366–November 367

Siricius: December 384–
26 November 399

Anastasius I: 27 November 399–
19 December 401

Innocent I: 21 December 401–
12 March 417

Zosimus: 18 March 417–
26 December 418

*Eulalius: 27 December 418–
3 April 419; died 423*

Boniface I: 28 December 418–
4 September 422

Celestine I: 10 September 422–
27 July 432

Sixtus III: 31 July 432–19 August 440

Leo I: August/September 440–
10 November 461

Hilarus: 19 November 461–
29 February 468

Simplicius: 3 March 468–10 March 483

Felix III: 13 March 483–1 March 492

Gelasius I: 1 March 492–
21 November 496

Anastasius II: 24 November 496–
19 November 498

Symmachus: 22 November 498–
19 July 514

*Laurentius: 22 November 498–February
499; 501–506; died 507/8*

Hormisdas: 20 July 514–6 August 523

John I: 13 August 523–18 May 526

Felix IV: 12 July 526–22 September 530

*Dioscorus: 22 September 530–
14 October 530*

Boniface II: 22 September 530–
17 October 532

John II: 2 January 533–8 May 535

Agapitus I: 13 May 535–22 April 536

Silverius: 8 June 536–
11 November 537;
died 2 December 537

Vigilius: 29 March 537–7 June 555

Pelagius I: 16 April 556–3 March 561

John III: 17 July 561–13 July 574

Benedict I: 2 June 575–30 July 579

Pelagius II: 26 November 579–
7 February 590

Gregory I: 3 September 590–
12 March 604

Sabinian: 13 September 604–
22 February 606

Boniface III: 19 February 607–
12 November 607

Boniface IV: 15 September 608–
8 May 615

Adeodatus I: 19 October 615–
8 November 618; *also known as*
Deusdedit

Boniface V: 23 December 619–
25 October 625

Honorius I: 27 October 625–
12 October 638

Severinus: 28 May 640–
2 August 640

John IV: 24 December 640–
12 October 642

Theodore I: 24 November 642–
14 May 649

Martin I: 5 July 649–17 June 653;
died 16 September 655

Eugenius I: 10 August 654–2 June 657

Vitalian: 30 July 657–27 January 672

Adeodatus II: 11 April 672–17 June 676

Donus: 2 November 676–11 April 678

Agatho: 27 June 678–10 January 681

Leo II: 17 August 682–3 July 683

Benedict II: 26 June 684–8 May 685

John V: 23 July 685–2 August 686

Conon: 21 October 686–
21 September 687

Theodore: 687

Paschal: 687; died 692

Sergius I: 15 December 687–
9 September 701

John VI: 30 October 701–
11 January 705

John VII: 1 March 705–18 October 707

Sisinnius: 15 January 708–
4 February 708

Constantine: 25 March 708–
9 April 715

Gregory II: 19 May 715–
11 February 731

Gregory III: 18 March 731–
28 November 741

Zacharias: 3 December 741–
15 March 752

Stephen II: 26 March 752–26 April 757

Paul I: 29 May 757–28 June 767

Constantine: 5 July 767–6 August 768

Philip: 31 July 768

Stephen III: 7 August 768–
24 January 772

Hadrian I: 1 February 772–
25 December 775

Leo III: 26 December 795–
12 June 816

Stephen IV: 22 June 816–
24 January 817

Paschal I: 24 January 817–
11 February 824

Eugenius II: 5? June 824–
27? August 827

Valentinus: August–September 827

Gregory IV: end 827–
25 January 844

John: January 844

Sergius II: January 844–
27 January 847

Leo IV: 10 April 847–
17 July 855

Benedict III: 29 September 855–
17 April 858

Anastasius: August–September 855

Nicholas I: 24 April 858–
13 November 867

Hadrian II: 14 December 867–
November/December 872

John VIII: 14 December 872–
16 December 882

Marinus I: 16? December 882–
15 May 884

Hadrian III: 17 May 884–
17 September 885

Stephen V: September 885–
14 September 891

Formosus: 3 October 891–
4 April 896

Boniface VI: April 896

Stephen VI: April/May 896–August 897

Romanus: August–November 897

Theodore II: December 897

John IX: April 898–May 900

Benedict IV: May/June 900–
July/August 903

Leo V: August–September 903; died 904

*Christopher: September 903–
January 904*

Sergius III: 29 January 904–
September 911

Anastasius III: September 911–
October 913

Lando: late November 913–
late March 914

John X: April 914–June 928; died 929

Leo VI: June 928–early January 929

Stephen VII: January 929–
late February 931

John XI: March 931–January 936

Leo VII: January 936–July 939

Stephen VIII: July 939–late October 942

Marinus II: late October 942–
early May 946

Agapitus II: 10 May 946–
December 955

John XII: 16 December 955–
14 May 964

Leo VIII: 4 December 963–
March 965

Benedict V: late May–late June 964

John XIII: 1 October 965–
6 September 972

Benedict VI: 19 January 973–
late June 974

*Boniface VII: late June 974–
late July 985*

Benedict VII: October 974–
7 July 983

John XIV: September 983–
20 August 984

John XV: August 985–March 996

Gregory V: April 996–18 February 999

*John XVI: February 997–
May 998; died 26 August 1001*

Sylvester II: 9 April 999–
12 May 1003

John XVII: 16 May 1003–
6 November 1003

John XVIII: 25 December 1003–
June/July 1009

Sergius IV: 31 July 1009–
12 May 1012

Benedict VIII: 17 May 1012–
9 April 1024

Gregory VI: May 1012

John XIX: 19 April 1024–
20 October 1032

Benedict IX: 21 October 1032–
1 May 1045/16 July 1048;
died 1056

*Sylvester III: January 1045–
March 1046; died 1062/3*

Gregory VI: 1 May 1045–
20 December 1046

Clement II: 24 December 1046–
9 October 1047

Damasus II: 17 July 1048–
9 August 1048

Leo IX: 12 February 1049–
19 April 1054

Victor II: 13 April 1055–28 July 1057

Stephen IX: 2/3 August 1057–
29 March 1058

Benedict X: 5 April 1058–April 1060

Nicholas II: 24 January 1059–
20 July 1061

Alexander II: 30 September/
1 October 1061–21 April 1073

*Honorius II: 28 October 1061–
31 May 1064*

Gregory VII: 22 April 1073–
25 May 1085

*Clement III: 25 June 1080–
8 September 1100*

Victor III: 24 May 1086/9 May 1087–
16 September 1087

Urban II: 12 March 1088–
29 July 1099

Paschal II: 14 August 1099–
21 January 1118

Theodoric: September 1100–
January 1101; died 1102

Albert: 1101

Sylvester IV: 11 November 1105–
12/13 April 1111

Gelasius II: 24 January 1118–
29 January 1119

Gregory VIII: 3 March 1118–
April 1121

Callistus II: 2 February 1119–
14 December 1124

Celestine II: 16 December 1124

Honorius II: 16/21 December 1124–
13 February 1130

Innocent II: 14 February 1130–
24 September 1143

Anacletus II: 14/23 February 1130–
25 January 1138

Victor IV: March–May 1138

Celestine II: 26 September 1143–
8 March 1144

Lucius II: 12 March 1144–
15 February 1145

Eugenius III: 15 February 1145–
8 July 1153

Anastasius IV: 12 July 1153–
3 December 1154

Hadrian IV: 4 December 1154–
1 September 1159

Alexander III: 7 September 1159–
30 August 1181

Victor IV: 7 September 1159–
20 April 1164

Paschal III: 22 April 1164–
9 September 1168

Callistus III: c. 20 September 1168–
28 August 1178; died 1180

Innocent III: 29 September
1179–January 1180

Lucius III: 1 September 1181–
25 November 1185

Urban III: 25 November 1185–
20 October 1187

Gregory VIII: 21 October 1187–
17 December 1187

Clement III: 19 December 1187–
28 March 1191

Celestine III: 10 April 1191–
8 January 1198

Innocent III: 8 January 1198–
16 July 1216

Honorius III: 18 July 1216–
18 March 1227

Gregory IX: 19 March 1227–
22 August 1241

Celestine IV: 25 October 1241–
10 November 1241

Innocent IV: 25 June 1243–
7 December 1254

Alexander IV: 12 December 1254–
25 May 1261

Urban IV: 29 August 1261–
2 October 1264

Clement IV: 5 February 1265–
29 November 1268

Gregory X: 1 September 1271–
10 January 1276

Innocent V: 21 January 1276–
22 June 1276

Hadrian V: 7 July 1276–
18 August 1276

John XXI: 8 September 1276–
20 May 1277

Nicholas III: 25 November 1277–
22 August 1280

Martin IV: 22 February 1281–
28 March 1285

Honorius IV: 2 April 1285–
3 April 1287

Celestine V: 5 July 1294–
13 December 1294; died 1296

Boniface VIII: 24 December 1294–
11 October 1303

Benedict XI: 22 October 1303–
7 July 1304

Clement V: 5 June 1305–
20 April 1314

John XXII: 7 August 1316–
4 December 1334

Nicholas V: 12 May 1328–
25 July/25 August 1330

Benedict XII: 20 December 1334–
25 April 1342

Clement VI: 7 May 1342–
6 December 1352

Innocent VI: 18 December 1352–
12 September 1362

Urban V: 28 September 1362–
19 December 1370

Gregory XI: 30 December 1370–
27 March 1378

THE GREAT SCHISM

The Roman Obedience

Urban VI: 8 April 1378–
15 October 1389

Boniface IX: 2 November 1389–
1 October 1404

Innocent VII: 17 October 1404–
6 November 1406

Gregory XII: 30 November 1406–
4 July 1415; died 18 October 1417

The Avignon Obedience

Clement VII: 20 September 1378–
16 September 1394

Benedict XIII: 28 September 1394–
29 November 1422

Clement VIII: 10 June 1423–
26 July 1429

The Pisan Obedience

Alexander V: 26 July 1409–
3 October 1410

John XXIII: 15 May 1410–29 May
1415; died 27 December 1419

AFTER THE GREAT SCHISM

Martin V: 11 November 1417–
2 February 1431

Eugenius IV: 3 March 1431–
23 February 1447

Felix V: 5 November 1439–7 April
1449; died 1 January 1451

Nicholas V: 6 March 1447–
24/25 March 1455

Callistus III: 8 April 1455–
6 August 1458

Pius II: 18 August 1458–
14 August 1464

Paul II: 30 August 1464–26 July 1471

Sixtus IV: 9 August 1471–
12 August 1484

Innocent VIII: 29 August 1484–
25 July 1492

Alexander VI: 11 August 1492–
18 August 1503

Pius III: 29 September 1503–
18 October 1503

Julius II: 1 November 1503–
20 February 1513

Leo X: 11 March 1513–
1 December 1521

Hadrian VI: 9 January 1522–
14 September 1523

Clement VII: 19 November 1523–
25 September 1534

Paul III: 13 October 1534–
10 November 1549

Julius III: 8 February 1550–
23 March 1555

Marcellus II: 9 April 1555–1 May 1555

Paul IV: 23 May 1555–18 August 1559

Pius IV: 25 December 1559–
9 December 1565

Pius V: 7 January 1566–1 May 1572

Gregory XIII: 13 May 1572–
10 April 1585

Sixtus V: 24 April 1585–
27 August 1590

Urban VII: 15 September 1590–
27 September 1590

Gregory XIV: 4 December 1590–
16 October 1591

Innocent IX: 29 October 1591–
30 December 1591

Clement VIII: 30 January 1592–
5 March 1605

Leo XI: 1 April 1605–27 April 1605

Paul V: 16 May 1605–28 January 1621

Gregory XV: 9 February 1621–
8 July 1623

Urban VIII: 6 August 1623–
29 July 1644

Innocent X: 15 September 1644–
7 January 1655

Alexander VII: 7 April 1655–
22 May 1667

Clement IX: 20 June 1667–
9 December 1669

Clement X: 29 April 1670–22 July 1676

Innocent XI: 21 September 1676–
12 August 1689

Alexander VIII: 6 October 1689–
1 February 1691

Innocent XII: 12 July 1691–
27 September 1700

Clement XI: 23 November 1700–
19 March 1721

Innocent XIII: 8 May 1721–
7 March 1724

Benedict XIII: 29 May 1724–
21 February 1730

Clement XII: 12 July 1730–
6 February 1740

Benedict XIV: 17 August 1740–
3 May 1758

Clement XIII: 6 July 1758–
2 February 1769

Clement XIV: 18 May 1769–
22 September 1774

Pius VI: 15 February 1775–
29 August 1799

Pius VII: 14 March 1800–
20 August 1823

Leo XII: 28 September 1823–
2 February 1829

Pius VIII: 31 March 1829–
30 November 1830

Gregory XVI: 2 February 1831–
1 June 1846

Pius IX: 16 June 1846–7 February 1878

Leo XIII: 20 February 1878–
20 July 1903

Pius X: 4 August 1903–20 August 1914

Benedict XV: 3 September 1914–
22 January 1922

Pius XI: 6 February 1922–
10 February 1939

Pius XII: 2 March 1939–
9 October 1958

John XXIII: 28 October 1958–
3 June 1963

Paul VI: 21 June 1963–6 August 1978

John Paul I: 26 August 1978–
28 September 1978

John Paul II: 16 October 1978–
2 April 2005

Benedict XVI: 19 April 2005–

ABBREVIATIONS

AAS: *Acta Apostolicae Sedis* (Vatican City).

AF: *The Apostolic Fathers*, ed. and trans. Kirsopp Lake (2 vols. LL, 1912).

Bettenson: *Documents of the Christian Church*, trans. Henry Bettenson (New York and London, 1947).

CBCR: *Corpus Basilicarum Christianarum Romae*, ed. Richard Krautheimer, Spencer Corbett and Alfred K. Frazer (5 vols. Vatican City, 1936–1977).

COD: *Conciliorum Oecumenicorum Decreta*, ed. Giuseppe Alberigo, Giuseppe L. Dossetti, Perikles-P. Joannou, Claudio Leonardi and Paolo Prodi (2nd edn. Bologna, 2002).

Coll. Av.: *Epistulae Imperatorum Pontificum Aliorum inde ab A. CC-CLXVII usque ad A. DLIII Datae Avellana quae dicitur Collectio*, ed. Otto Guenther (2 vols. CSEL XXXV 1898).

Coustant: *Epistolae Romanorum Pontificum et quae ad eos scriptae sunt, a S. Clemente I usque ad Innocentium III, vol. 1 ab anno Christi 67 ad annum 440*, ed. Pierre Coustant (Paris, 1721).

CSEL: *Corpus Scriptorum Ecclesiasticorum Latinorum* (96 vols. to date, Vienna, 1866–2006).

CT: *Theodosiani Libri XVI cum Constitutionibus Sirmondianis et Leges Novellae ad Theodosianum pertinentes*, ed. Theodore Mommsen and Paul M. Meyer (3 vols. Zurich, 1904–1905).

EE: *Enchiridion delle Encicliche (1740–1998)* (3rd edn. 8 vols. Bologna, 2002).

ICUR: *Inscriptiones Christianae Urbis Romae septimo saeculo antiquiores*, ed. Giovanni Battista de Rossi (2 vols. Rome, 1861–1868); *Nova series* ed. Angelo Silvagni, Antonio Ferrua (3 vols. Rome, 1922–).

Jaffe-Wattenbach: P. Jaffe, *Regesta Pontificum Romanorum ab condita ecclesia ad annum post Christum natum MCXCVIII*; 2nd edn. revised by W. Wattenbach (2 vols. Leipzig, 1885; reprinted Graz, 1956).

JThS: *Journal of Theological Studies* (n.s. = new series).

Levillain: Philippe Levillain (ed.), *Dictionnaire historique de la Papauté* (Paris, 1994).

LL: Loeb Library (Cambridge, Mass. and London).

LP: *Liber Pontificalis*, ed. Louis Duchesne (2nd edn. 3 vols. Paris, 1955); English trans. by Raymond Davis, 3 vols. (Liverpool, 1989–1995).

Mansi: *Sacrorum Conciliorum Nova et Amplissima Collectio*, ed. Giovanni Dominico Mansi (31 vols. Florence, 1759–1798).

MGH: Monumenta Germaniae Historica series:

AA: *Auctores Antiquissimi*
Const.: Constitutiones
Dipl.: Diplomata
Epp.: Epistolae
Epp. sel: Epistolae selectae
Libelli: Libelli de Litis
Schrift.: Schriften
SRG: *Scriptores Rerum Germanicarum*
SS: *Scriptores*

Pastor: Ludwig Pastor, *A History of the Popes* (English trans. 31 vols. London, 1908–1940).

PG: *Patrologia Graeca*, ed. J.P. Migne
PL: *Patrologia Latina*, ed. J.P. Migne

PLRE: *Prosopography of the Later Roman Empire*, ed. A.H.M. Jones, J.R. Martindale, and J. Morris (3 vols. Cambridge, 1971–1992).

PP: *Päpste und Papsttum* (published Stuttgart).

SC: *Sources Chrétiennes* (published Paris).

Thiel: *Epistolae Romanorum Pontificum Genuinae et quae ad eos scriptae sunt a S. Hilaro usque ad Pelagium II*, ed. Andreas Thiel (Braunsberg, 1867–1868, reprinted Hildesheim, 2004).

Vatican website: www.vatican.va

VPA: *Vitae Paparum Avenionensium*, ed. S. Baluze, revised G. Mollat (4 vols. Paris, 1916).

NOTES

CHAPTER I

1. For all of these events see John Curran, 'The Bones of St. Peter?', *Classics Ireland* 3 (1996), 18–46.

2. Carlo Falconi, *The Popes in the Twentieth Century* (English trans. London, 1967), 325.

3. John Cornwell, *Hitler's Pope: the Secret History of Pius XII* (London, 1999), 105–156, and 351; see also *http://www.dhm.de/lemo/html/bio grafien/KaasLudwig/*

4. Venerando Correnti, 'Relazione dello stato compiuto su tre gruppi di resti scheletrici umani gia rinvenuti sotto la Confessione della Basilica Vaticana', in Margharita Guarducci (ed.), *Le Reliquie di Pietro sotto la Confessione della Basilica Vaticana* (Rome, 1965), 83–160, and Luigi Cardinio, 'Risulto dell'esame osteologico dei resti scheletrici di animali', *ibid.*, 161–168.

5. B.M. Apollonj Ghetti, A. Ferrua, E. Josi, E. Kirschbaum, *Esplorazioni sotto la Confessione di San Pietro in Vaticano* (2 vols. Rome, 1951); see also Angelus De Marco, *The Tomb of Saint Peter: A Representative and Annotated Bibliography of the Excavations* (Leiden, 1964).

6. Jocelyn Toynbee and John Ward Perkins, *The Shrine of St. Peter and the Vatican Excavations* (London, New York and Toronto, 1956), vii.

7. *http://www.vatican.va/holy_father/ paul_vi/audiences/1968/documents/hf _p-vi_aud_1*

8. Margharita Guarducci, 'Pietro in Vaticano. Commento ad una recensione del p. Antonio Ferrua', *Archaeologia Classica* 36 (1984), 266–298.

9. R. Ross Holloway, *Constantine and Rome* (New Haven and London, 2004), 120–155.

10. Margharita Guarducci, *Le Reliquie di Pietro in Vaticano* (Rome, 1995), 5.

11. *The Oxford Annotated Bible* (New York, 1962).

12. *ibid.*

13. Suetonius, *Vita Divi Claudii* 25.4; Peter Lampe, *From Paul to Valentinus: Christians at Rome in the First Two Centuries* (English trans. Minneapolis, 2003), 11–16.

14. Daniel W. O'Connor, *Peter in Rome: The Literary, Liturgical and Archaeological Evidence* (New York and London, 1969), 3–7.

15. *I Clement* 5.4: AF 1, 16–17.

16. *ibid.*, 5. 5–7, 16–17.

17. R.P.C. Hanson, 'The Eucharistic Offering in the Pre-Nicene Fathers', in his *Studies in Christian Antiquity* (Edinburgh, 1985), 89.

18. *Ignatius to the Romans* 4.3: AF 1, 230–231.

19. Irenaeus 3. 3. 2–3, trans. Robert M. Grant, *Irenaeus of Lyons* (London and New York, 1997), 125.

20. Henry Chadwick, *The Church in Ancient Society, from Galilee to Gregory the Great* (Oxford, 2001), 119–120.

21. Jean-Pierre Martin, 'Sixte Ier', in Levillain, 1588.

22. Joseph A. Jungmann, *The Mass of the Roman Rite* (English trans. New York, 1980), 7–18.

23. Campenhausen, Hans von, *Ecclesiastical Authority and Spiritual Power in the Church of the First Three Centuries* (English trans. Peabody, Mass., 1997), 124–148.

24. e.g. *Ignatius to the Ephesians* 4. 1–2; *Ignatius to the Magnesians* 7. 1–2; *Ignatius to the Smyrnaeans* 8. 1–2 etc., AF 1, 176–179, 202–203, 260–261.

25. Paul's Epistle to the Romans 16.3; Lampe, *From Paul to Valentinus*, 187–195.

26. Ute E. Eisen, *Women Officeholders in Early Christianity* (English trans. Collegeville, Minn., 2000), 116–142, 158–198.

27. Peter Lampe and Ulrich Luz, 'Post-Pauline Christianity and Pagan Society', in Jürgen Becker (ed.), *Christian Beginnings: Word and Community from Jesus to Post-Apostolic Times* (English trans. Louisville, 1993), 242–280, especially 245–250.

28. Hermas, *The Shepherd*, vision 2, 4.3, ed. Kirsopp Lake, AF 2, 24–25.

29. Lampe, *From Paul to Valentinus*, 397–408.

30. Allen Brent, *Hippolytus and the Roman Church in the Third Century: Communities in Tension before the Emergence of a Monarch-Bishop* (Leiden, 1995).

31. Kurt Rudolph, *Gnosis: The Nature and History of Gnosticism* (English trans. San Francisco, 1984), 10–25.

32. Bruce M. Metzger, *The Canon of the New Testament* (Oxford, 1987), 75–112; Geoffrey Mark Hahneman, *The Muratorian Fragment and the Development of the Canon* (Oxford, 1992), 73–131.

33. Elaine Pagels, *The Gnostic Paul* (Philadelphia, 1975), 1–10.

34. Rudolph, *Gnosis*, 34–52; Elaine Pagels, *The Gnostic Gospels* (New York, 1979), 13–32.

35. *ibid.* 62–64; Karen L. King, *What is Gnosticism?* (Cambridge, Mass., and London, 2003), 164–190.

36. Michael Allen Williams, *Rethinking Gnosticism* (Princeton, 1996), 23–26.

37. Acts 12.2, 15. 13–22, Galatians 1. 19, 2.9 etc.

38. Eusebius, *Historia Ecclesiastica* 3. 19–20, quoting Hegesippus, ed. Kisopp Lake, 2 vols. LL, 1, 236.

39. Udo Schnelle, 'The Writings of the Johannine School', in his *The New Testament Writings* (English trans. London, 1998), 434–538.

40. Andrew Chester and Ralph P. Martin, *The Theology of the Letters of James, Peter, and Jude* (Cambridge, 1994), 87–133.

CHAPTER 2

1. Tacitus, *Annales* XV. 43, trans. Michael Grant, *Tacitus: the Annals of Imperial Rome* (Harmondsworth, 1959), 354.

2. Eusebius, *Historia Ecclesiastica* 2. 25. 5–8, and 4. 23. 9–10.

3. T.D. Barnes, 'Pre-Decian *Acta Martyrum*', JThS n.s. 19 (1968), 509–531; Gary A. Bisbee, *Pre-Decian Acts of Mar-*

tyrs and Commentarii (Philadelphia, 1988).

4. Lucy Grig, *Making Martyrs in Late Antiquity* (London, 2004).

5. Victor Saxer, *Morts, martyrs, reliques en Afrique chrétienne aux premiers siècles* (Paris, 1980).

6. Michele Renee Salzman, *On Roman Time: the Codex-Calendar of 354 and the Rhythms of Urban Life in Late Antiquity* (Berkeley, 1990), 42–50 and 279–282.

7. Grig, *Making Martyrs*, 136–141.

8. J.A. Cerrato, *Hippolytus between East and West* (Oxford, 2002), 3–5.

9. R.E. Heine, 'The Christology of Callistus', JThS n.s. 49 (1998), 56–91.

10. Bettenson, 19.

11. J.B. Rives, 'The Decree of Decius and the Religion of Empire', *Journal of Roman Studies* 89 (1999), 135–154.

12. Eusebius, *Historia Ecclesiastica* 6. 43. 11; Georg Schwaiger, 'Cornelius', in *Dictionary of Popes and the Papacy* (Eng. trans. New York, 2001), 29–30.

13. Cyprian, *De catholicae ecclesiae unitate*, 4, trans. Bettenson, *Documents*, 101.

14. Cyprian, *epistulae* 71–73, ed. Wilhelm Hartel, CSEL 3 (3 pts. 1868–1871), 771–799.

15. *ibid.*, 799.

16. *ibid.*, 810–827; trans., 413, 418.

17. S.G. Hall, 'Stephen I of Rome and the One Baptism', *Studia Patristica* XVII (Oxford, 1982), 796–798.

18. Eusebius, *Historia Ecclesiastica* 7. 30. 18–19.

19. *Chronographus Anni CCCLIIII*, ed. Theodore Mommsen, MGH AA 9, 71.

20. Lucy Grig, 'The Paradoxical Body of St. Agnes', in Andrew Hopkins and Maria Wyke, *Roman Bodies: Antiquity*

to the Eighteenth Century (London, 2005), 111–122.

21. *Liber Genealogus*, ed. Theodore Mommsen, MGH AA vol. 9, 196.

22. Raymond Davis, 'Pre-Constantinian Chronology: the Roman Bishopric from AD 258 to 314', JThS n.s. 48 (1997), 439–470, at 461.

23. A. Amore, 'Il preteso "Lapsus" di Papa Marcellino', *Antonianum* 32 (1957), 411–426.

24. ICUR IV. no. 10183; Nicolai, Vincenzo et alii, *The Christian Catacombs of Rome* (English edn. Regensburg, 1999), 165 and fig. 167.

CHAPTER 3

1. Lactantius, *De Mortibus Persecutorum* 44. 5, ed. and trans. J.L. Creed (Oxford, 1984), 62–63.

2. Eusebius, *Vita Constantini* I. 27–32, trans. Averil Cameron and Stuart G. Hall (Oxford, 1999), 79–82; Timothy D. Barnes, *Constantine and Eusebius* (Cambridge, Mass. and London, 1981), 43.

3. John Curran, *Pagan City and Christian Capital* (Oxford, 2000), 43–69.

4. Coll. Av., 1.6, 3.

5. G.W. Bowersock, 'Peter and Constantine', in William Tronzo (ed.), *St. Peter's in the Vatican* (Cambridge, 2005), 5–15.

6. Coll. Av. 3, 46–47.

7. R. Ross Holloway, *Constantine and Rome* (New Haven and London, 2004), 112–115.

8. Curran, *Pagan City*, 76–90.

9. Marina Magnani Cianeri and Carlo Pavolini (ed.), *La Basilica Constantiniana di Sant'Agnese* (Rome, 2004).

10. Richard Krautheimer, *Rome: Profile of a City, 312–1308* (Princeton, 1980), 3–31.

11. Ugo Fusco, 'Sant'Agnese nel quadro delle basiliche circiformi di etá constantiniana a Roma', in Cianeri and Pavolini (ed.), *Basilica Constantiniana di Sant'Agnese*, 10–28; 12 and 21, note 10.

12. CBCR 5.

13. LP XXXIV, 3–32: 1, 170–187; trans. Davis, 16–26.

14. LP XXXV: 1, 202; trans. Davis, 27.

15. LP XLVII: 1, 239; trans. Davis, 38.

16. Possidius, *Vita Augustini* 19. 1–5, ed. Michele Pellegrino, *Vita di S. Agostino* (n.p., 1955), 110–115.

17. Eusebius, *Historia Ecclesiastica* 10. 5. 18–20; Optatus of Milevis, *De Schismate Donatistarum Libri Septem* 1. 22–24, ed. C. Ziwsa, CSEL 26 (1893); W.H.C. Frend, *The Donatist Church* (Oxford, 1952), 148–150.

18. H.A. Drake, *Constantine and the Bishops: the Politics of Intolerance* (Baltimore and London, 2000), 218–219.

19. Carl Joseph von Hefele, *Histoire des Conciles* (3 vols. Paris, 1907–1909), vol. 1/1, 552.

20. Stephen J. Davis, *The Early Coptic Papacy* (Cairo and New York, 2004), 47–50.

21. Julius I, *ep.* 4, ed. Coustant, 403–404.

22. Athanasius, *Historia Arianorum* 75, PG 25, col. 784.

23. R.H. Barrow, *Prefect and Emperor: the 'Relationes' of Symmachus A.D. 384* (Oxford, 1973), 1–19.

24. Theodoret, *Historia Ecclesiastica* 2. 14, PG 82, col. 1041.

25. Optatus 2.4; trans. Mark Edwards, *Optatus: Against the Donatists* (Liverpool, 1997), 34–35.

26. CT 16. 5.2, 855.

27. LP XXXVII: 1, 207; trans. Davis, 28.

28. LP XXXVIII: 1, 211; trans. Davis, 29.

29. James T. Shotwell and Louise Ropes Lomis, *The See of Peter* (New York, 1927), 595–596.

30. Malcolm R. Green, 'The Supporters of the Antipope Ursinus', JThS n.s. 22 (1971), 531–538.

31. Coll. Av. 1.5, 2.

32. Coll. Av. 1.7, 3.

33. Ammianus Marcellinus, *Res Gestae* 27. 3. 13, ed. J.C. Rolfe (revised edn. London and Cambridge, Mass., 1952), 3, p. 18.

34. Coll. Av. 5, 7, 13, pp. 48, 49–50, 55.

35. Roman synod of 378: Mansi 3, 624.

36. Coll. Av. 35, 28–30.

37. Coll. Av. 1. 9, 4.

38. CT 16. 2. 20, 841.

39. *Nov. Marciani* 5: CT 3, 193–196.

40. Jerome, *ep.* 15. 2, Bettenson, 113.

41. Charles Pietri, *Roma Christiana* (Rome, 1976), 90.

42. Michele Renee Salzman, *The Making of a Christian Aristocracy* (Cambridge, Mass., and London, 2002).

43. *Relatio* 3.9, ed. Barrow, *Prefect and Emperor*, 40.

44. Peter Brown, 'Pelagius and his Supporters: Aims and Environment', JThS n.s. 19 (1968), 93–114.

45. *Vita Melaniae* 15–19, ed. Denys Gorce, *Vie de Sainte Mélanie* (Paris, 1962), 156–167.

46. J.N.D. Kelly, *Jerome* (London, 1975), 104–115.

47. A. Ferrua (ed.), *Egigrammata Damasiana* (Vatican City, 1942), 21–35.

48. *ibid.*, 7–13; Carlo Carletti et alii, *Damase et les martyrs romains* (Vatican City, 1986).

49. CT 16. 1.2, 833.

50. I Constantinople, c. 3: COD, 32.

51. Francis Dvornik, *Byzantium and the Roman Primacy* (New York, 1966), 44–47.

52. Neil B. McLynn, *Ambrose of Milan* (Berkeley and London, 1994), 288.

53. Coll. Av. 13, 54–58.

CHAPTER 4

1. Robert Cabié (ed.), *La lettre du pape Innocent 1er a Décentius de Gubbio* (Louvain, 1973), 18–21.

2. Zosimus, *ep.* 1: Coustant, 935–938.

3. Charles Duggan, quoted in Detlev Jasper and Horst Fuhrmann, *Papal Letters in the Early Middle Ages* (Washington, D.C., 2001), 13.

4. Jean Gaudemet, *Les sources du droit del'Eglise en Occident du IIe au VIIe siècle* (Paris, 1985), 57–64.

5. Jasper and Fuhrmann, *Papal Letters*, 11–12.

6. Siricius, *ep.* 1: Coustant, 623–639.

7. Leo, *ep.* 16, ed. P. and J. Ballerini, *Sancti Leonis Magni Romani Pontificis Opera* (3 vols. Venice, 1753–1757), 1, 715–723; trans. Edmund Hunt, *St. Leo the Great: Letters* (New York, 1957), 68–69.

8. Leo, *ep.* 14, ed. Ballerini, 1, 682–691; trans. Hunt, 66.

9. Siricius, *ep.* 1. 20: Coustant, 637.

10. Innocent I, *ep.* 6: Coustant, 796.

11. J.M. Huskinson, 'Concordia Apostolorum': *Christian Propaganda at Rome in the Fourth and Fifth Centuries* (Oxford, 1982), 96–98.

12. Walter Ullmann, 'Leo I and the theme of papal primacy', JThS n.s. 11 (1960), 25–51.

13. Gerald Bonner, *Augustine and Modern Research on Pelagianism* (Villanova, Pa., 1972), 35–52.

14. In general, Otto Wermelinger, *Pelagius und Rom* (Stuttgart, 1975).

15. Peter Brown, 'The Patrons of Pelagius: the Roman Aristocracy between East and West', JThS n.s. 21 (1970), 56–72.

16. J.N.D. Kelly, *Golden Mouth: the Story of John Chrysostom, Ascetic, Preacher, Bishop* (London, 1995), 211–285.

17. Christoph Baumer, *The Church of the East* (London, 2006), 42–50.

18. Council of Chalcedon canon xxviii: COD, 100; trans. Henry R. Percival, *Library of Nicene and Post-Nicene Fathers* XIV (reprinted Grand Rapids, 1971), 287.

19. Leo, *ep.* 19, ed. Ballerini, 1. 731–735; trans. Hunt, 77–80.

20. Basilius 13: PLRE 2, 217.

21. Patrick T. R. Gray, *The Defense of Chalcedon in the East (451–553)* (Leiden, 1979), 28–34.

22. Stephen J. Davis, *The Early Coptic Papacy* (Cairo and New York, 2004), 88–98.

23. Thiel, *Epistolae*, 447.

24. LP LI: 1, 255; trans. Davis, 42–43.

25. Cyrille Vogel, *Introduction aux sources de l'histoire du culte chrétien au Moyen Age* (Spoleto, 1981), 48–57.

26. Thiel, 285–613.

27. Gelasius, *ep.* 12: Thiel, 350–351.

28. Jasper and Fuhrmann, *Papal Letters*, 61–65; Johannes Fried, *Donation of Constantine and 'Constitutum Constantini'* (Berlin and New York, 2007), 90.

CHAPTER 5

1. LP LII: 1. 258; trans. Davis, 43.

2. Dante, *Divina Commedia: Inferno* XI. 8–9.

3. Jerome, *Contra Ioannem Hierosolytanum* 8, ed. Dominico Vallarsi, *Sancti Eusebii Hieronymi Stridonensis*

Presbyteri Opera 2/1 (2nd edn. Venice, 1767), 415.

4. Ugo Falesiedi, *Le Diaconie: i servizi assistenziali nella Chiesa antica* (Rome, 1995), 65–88.

5. Henry Chadwick, *Boethius: The Consolations of Music, Logic, Theology and Philosophy* (Oxford, 1981), 32.

6. Ed. Erich Caspar, *Theoderich der Grosse und das Papsttum* (Berlin, 1931), 20–29; there dated to 502.

7. Mansi, 3, 624ff.

8. Ennodius, *Libellus pro synodo* 93, ed. Vogel, MGH AA 7, 61; ed. Caspar (note 6 above), 49.

9. LP LVIIII, ed. Duchesne 1. 287–288; trans. Davis, 52.

10. *Chronicon Paschale Olympiad* 328, trans. Michael Whitby and Mary Whitby (Liverpool, 1989), 128.

11. LP LX:1. 290–293; trans. Davis, 54.

12. *ibid.*, trans. Davis, 53.

13. *ibid.*, trans. Davis, 56; Procopius, *Anecdota* I. 14 and 27, ed. H.B. Dewing, LL, Procopius (7 vols.) 6, 8 and 14.

14. LP LXI, ed. Duchesne, 1. 296–299; trans. Davis, 57.

15. Coll. Av. 83, 318.

16. *Ep.* 5, ed. G.S.M. Walker, *Sancti Columbani Opera* (Dublin, 1970), 36–56.

CHAPTER 6

1. Josep Vilella Masana, 'Gregorio Magno e Hispania', in *Gregorio Magno e il suo tempo* (2 vols. Rome, 1991), 1, 167–186.

2. Paul Meyvaert, 'A Letter of Pelagius II Composed by Gregory the Great', in John C. Cavadini (ed.), *Gregory the Great: A Symposium* (Notre Dame and London, 1995), 94–116.

3. Ugo Falesiedi, *Le Diaconie* (Rome, 1995), 96–116.

4. *Codex Theodosianus* 15. 12.1 of 325 AD, but cf. 15. 12.2 of 357, which presupposes their continuation.

5. A.W.J. Holleman, *Pope Gelasius I and the Lupercalia* (Amsterdam, 1974), chs. 1–3.

6. Edmund Bishop, *Liturgica Historica* (Oxford, 1918), 128–130.

7. cf. Walter Ullmann, *The Growth of Papal Government in the Middle Ages* (2nd edn. London, 1962), 36–41.

8. Leo Santifaller, *Liber Diurnus* (Stuttgart, 1976), 1–13.

9. e.g., Coll. Av. 41 from Innocent I, 96: *et alia manu*; cf. the imperial *ep.* 11, 53.

10. Roger Collins and Judith McClure, 'Rome, Canterbury and Wearmouth-Jarrow: Three Viewpoints on Augustine's Mission', in Simon Barton and Peter Linehan (ed.), *Cross, Crescent and Conversion* (Leiden and Boston, 2008), 17–42.

11. LP LXVII: 1. 315; trans. Davis, 62.

12. Guy Ferrari, *Early Roman Monasteries* (Vatican City, 1957), 159–162 and 242–253.

13. Bede, *Historia Ecclesiastica Gentis Anglorum* II. 17, ed. B. Colgrave and R.A.B. Mynors (corrected edn. Oxford, 1991), 194.

14. Andrea Augenti, *Il Palatino nel Medioevo: Archeologia e topografia* (Rome, 1996).

15. LP, Deusdedit and Boniface V, trans. Davis, 63.

16. Braulio of Saragossa, letter 21, trans. Claude W. Barlow, *Fathers of the Church*, vol. 63, 52.

17. *Relatio Motionis*, ed. and trans. Pauline Allen and Bronwen Neil, *Max-*

imus the Confessor and His Companions (Oxford, 2002), 55.

18. M.D. O'Hara, 'A Find of Byzantine Silver from the Mint of Rome for the Period A.D. 641–752', *Swiss Numismatic Review* 64 (1985), 105–139; and http://www.byzconf.org/1988abstracts .html, see section VII A.

19. Bede, *Historia Ecclesiastica, IV.* 18, ed. Colgrave and Mynors, 388.

20. Michael McCormick, *Origins of the European Economy: Communications and Commerce 300–900* (Cambridge, 2001), 483–488.

21. Giuseppe Cremascoli, 'Le lettere di Martino I', in *Martino I Papa (649–653) e il suo tempo* (Spoleto, 1992), 243–258.

22. Allen and Neil, *Maximus the Confessor and His Companions,* 49 and 51.

23. Bede, *Historia Ecclesiastica* IV. 17, 386.

24. trans. Henry R. Perceval, *The Seven Ecumenical Councils of the Undivided Church* (reprinted Grand Rapids, Mich., 1971), 331.

25. *ibid.,* 332.

26. LP, trans. Davis, 77.

27. Perceval, *Seven Ecumenical Councils,* 343.

28. Jaffe-Wattenbach, no. 2118 (Latin version).

Chapter 7

1. LP LXXXI, iv: 1, 350; trans. Davis, 74.

2. LP LXXXIIII, v and LXXXV, v: 1, 367, 369; trans. Davis, 81–82.

3. LP XC, x: 1, 392 ; trans. Davis, 92.

4. LP LXXXVI, vi–ix: 1, 372–374; trans. Davis, 85.

5. LP LXXXVI, ix: 1, 372; trans. Davis, 85.

6. LP LXXXVIII, v–vi: 1, 385–386; trans. Davis, 89.

7. Sabine G. MacCormack, *Art and Ceremony in Late Antiquity* (Berkeley, 1981), 62–89.

8. LP XC, xi: 1, 392; trans. Davis, 91.

9. André Grabar, *Les voies de la création en iconographie chrétienne* (Paris, 1979), 59–82.

10. Averil Cameron, 'The *Theotokos* in Sixth Century Constantinople', JThS n.s. 29 (1978), 79–108.

11. Rodolfo Lanciani, *The Destruction of Ancient Rome* (English trans. London, 1901), 180–197.

12. Jaffe-Wattenbach, 2180, 253.

13. *ibid.,* 2182, 252–253.

14. *ibid.,* 252.

15. Theophanes, *Chronicon* AM 6221, trans. Cyril Mango and Roger Scott, *The Chronicle of Theophanes Confessor* (Oxford, 1997), 565.

16. LP XCII, i: 1, 415; trans. Davis, 19.

17. LP XCII, iii: 1, 416; trans. Davis, 20.

18. Bede, *Historia Ecclesiastica* IV. 18, ed. Betram Colgrave and R.A.B. Mynors (Oxford, 1991), 389.

19. Boniface, *ep.* 50, ed. Michael Tangl, MGH *Epp. sel.* (Berlin, 1955), 80–86; trans. Ephraim Emerton, *The Letters of Saint Boniface* (New York, 1940), 80.

20. *Codex Carolinus* 3, ed. W. Gundlach, MGH *Epp.* I, 479–487.

21. Roger Collins, 'Pippin III as Mayor of the Palace: the Evidence', in Matthias Becher and Jörg Jarnut (ed.), *Der Dynastiewechsel von 751* (Münster, 2004), 75–91.

22. *Annales Regni Francorum* s.a. 749, ed. F. Kurze, MGH SRG.

23. Boniface, *ep.* 27, ed. Tangl, 48.

24. Theophanes, *Chronicon* AM 6211, trans. Mango and Scott, 551–552.

25. LP XCIII, xx: 1, 433; trans. Davis, 46 and n. 78.

26. Allen G. Berman, *Papal Numismatic History* (2nd edn. South Salem, NY, 1991), 48–49.

27. *Codex Carolinus, ep.* 2 (770), trans. P.D. King, *Charlemagne* (Lancaster, 1987), 271.

28. LP: XCV: 1, 464; trans. Davis, 81.

29. LP: 1 483, note 46.

30. LP XCVI, xx: 1, 476; trans. Davis, 99.

31. LP XCVI, xii and xiv–xv: 1, 471–473; trans. Davis, 93 and 95.

32. LP XCVII, i–ii: 1, 486; trans. Davis, 123.

33. LP XCVII, xliii: 1, 498; trans. Davis, 142. For what follows, see Mario Costambeys, *Power and Patronage in Early Medieval Italy* (Cambridge, 2007), 311–323.

34. Agnellus, *Liber Pontificalis Ecclesiae Ravennatis* 159, ed. Claudia Nauerth (Freiburg im Breisgau, 1996), 552.

35. LP XCIII, ix: 1, 428.

36. N. Christie and C.M. Daniels, 'Santa Cornelia: the Excavation of an Early Medieval Papal Estate and a Medieval Monastery', in Neil Christie (ed.), *Three South Etrurian Churches* (London, 1991), 1–209.

37. Rudolf Schieffer, '*Redeamus ad fontem*: Rom als Hort authentischer Überlieferung im frühen Mittelalter', in *Roma—Caput et Fons* (Opladen, 1989), 45–70.

38. Philip Grierson and Mark Blackburn, *Medieval European Coinage*, vol. 1: *The Early Middle Ages* (Cambridge, 1986), 560–563; Berman, *Papal Numismatic History*, 56–64.

CHAPTER 8

1. LP XCVIII, xi–xiii: 2, 4–5.

2. LP XCVIII, xiv: 2, 5.

3. Alcuin, *ep.* 179, ed. E. Dümmler, MGH *Epp.* 4, 296–297.

4. *ibid.*

5. Roger Collins, 'Charlemagne's imperial coronation and the Annals of Lorsch', in Joanna Story (ed.), *Charlemagne: Empire and Society* (Manchester, 2005), 52–70.

6. Steven Runciman, 'The empress Irene the Athenian', in Derek Baker (ed.), *Medieval Women* (Oxford, 1978), 101–118.

7. *Annales Laureshamenses Breves s.a.* 801, ed. Eberhard Katz, *Laureshamensium Editio Emendata Secundum Codicem St. Paulensium* (St. Paul, in Lavanttal, 1889), 44.

8. Johannes Fried, '*Donation of Constantine*' and '*Constitutum Constantini*' (Berlin and New York, 2007), 53–114.

9. *Annales Lauershamenses, s.a.* 800, ed. Katz, 44.

10. Angelo Silvagni, *Monumenta Epigraphica Christiana I: Roma* (Vatican City, 1943), tab. II. 6.

11. *Divisio imperii* of 8th February 806.

12. Ermoldus Nigellus, *In honorem Hludowici*, lines 1076–1077, ed. Edmond Faral (Paris, 1964), 84.

13. *Annales Regni Francorum, s.a.* 816, ed. F. Kurze, MGH SRG, 144; trans. Bernhard Scholz, *Carolingian Chronicles* (Ann Arbor, 1972), 101.

14. J.N.D. Kelly, *The Athanasian Creed* (London, 1964), 109–124.

15. *Annales Regni Francorum, s.a.* 817, ed. Kurze, 144–145; trans. Scholz, 102.

16. *ibid.*

17. A. Hahn, 'Das Hludowicianum', *Archiv für Diplomatik* 21 (1975), 15–135.

18. *Annales Regni Francorum, s.a.* 824, ed. Kurze, 166; trans. Scholz, 117.

19. Ute E. Eisen, *Women Officeholders in Early Christianity* (English trans. Collegeville, Minn., 2000), 200–205.

20. Julia M.H. Smith, 'Old Saints, New Cults: Roman Relics in Carolingian Francia', in *eadem* (ed.), *Early Medieval Rome and the Christian West* (Leiden, 2000), 317–339.

21. Klaus Zechiel-Eckes, 'Ein Blick in Pseudoisidors Werkstatt', *Francia* 28/1 (2002), 37–90, and *idem*, 'Zwei Arbeitshandschriften Pseudoisidors', *Francia* 27/1 (2001), 205–210.

22. *Cambridge Medieval History* vol. III: *Germany and the Western Empire* (Cambridge, 1922), 151.

CHAPTER 9

1. J.N.D. Kelly, *Oxford Dictionary of the Popes* (Oxford, 1986), 115.

2. *Annales Fuldenses s.a.* 883, trans. Timothy Reuter, *The Annals of Fulda* (Manchester and New York, 1992), 94.

3. Simon MacLean, *Kingship and Politics in the Late Ninth Century* (Cambridge, 2003), 169–191.

4. Pavia Capitulary of the Emperor Charles II, February 876, clauses 1–3: Claudio Azzara and Pierandrea Moro (ed.), *I capitolari italici* (Rome, 1988), 224–227.

5. Election Capitulary of Guido, *ibid.*, 232–233.

6. Oath of the Romans to the Emperor Arnulf, February 896, *ibid.*, 242–243.

7. LP CXII, xi, xvi, xvii, xx: 2, 194–196; trans. Davis, 303–307.

8. Gregory *Dialogues* IV. 55, ed. A. de Vogué, SC vol. 265, 182.

9. Azzara and Moro (ed.), *I capitulari italici*, 246–251.

10. *ibid.*, cl. 2, 246.

11. Liutprand of Cremona, *Antapodosis* I. 30, ed. Joseph Becker, MGH

SRG, 23, says it was Adalbert of Tuscany, but Auxilius, *In defensionem* 1.1 is to be preferred.

12. ICUR II. 212.

13. Liutprand, *Antapodosis* II. 48, ed. Becker, 59.

14. Philip Grierson and Mark Blackburn, *Medieval European Coinage*, vol. 1 (Cambridge, 1986), 262–266 and plate 49.

15. *Antapodosis* II. 47, trans. F.A. Wright, *Liutprand of Cremona: The Embassy to Constantinople and Other Writings* (London, 1993), 56.

16. Benedict of St. Andrew, *Chronicon* 30, MGH SS 3, 714.

17. *ibid.*, 32, 715.

18. Pierre Toubert, *Les structures du Latium médiéval* (Rome, 1973), 974–998.

19. Fritz Weigle (ed.), *Die Briefe des Bischofs Rather von Verona* (MGH, Munich 1981), *ep.* 21, 112.

20. L. Allodi and G. Levi (ed.), *Il Regesto Sublacense* (Rome, 1885), docs. 16, 17, 24.

21. Benedict of St. Andrew, *Chronicon* 33, 716.

22. L.M. Hartmann (ed.), *Ecclesiae S. Mariae in Via Lata Tabularium* (Vienna, 1895), xiii.

23. Jaffé-Wattenbach, nos. 3584, 3585, 3588, 3598–3600, 3603, 3605, etc.

24. *ibid.*, 3609.

25. Marina Docci, *San Paolo fuori le mura* (Rome, 2006), 74–75.

26. PL 135.

27. Giuseppe Sergi, 'The Kingdom of Italy', *New Cambridge Medieval History*, vol. 4, 352–355.

28. Benedict of St. Andrew, *Chronicon* 34, 717.

29. Jaffe-Wattenbach 3684, 595–885.

30. Krautheimer, CBCR 5, 11.

31. *Ottonianum*: MGH *Dipl.* 1, 322–327; trans. Boyd Hill Jr. *Medieval Monarchy in Action* (London and New York, 1972), 149–152.

32. Voltaire, *Essai sur l'histoire générale et sur les moeurs et l'esprit des nations* (Paris, 1756).

33. Liutprand, *Historia Ottonis* ch. 4, ed. Joseph Becker, MGH SRG, 161.

34. *ibid.*, ch. 10, ed. Becker, 167; cf. Benedict of St. Andrew, *Chronicon* 34–37, 717–718.

35. Liutprand, *Historia Ottonis* chs. 12–13, ed. Becker, 168–169.

36. *ibid.*, chs. 14 and 15, 170 and 171–172.

37. *ibid.*, ch. 20, 173–174.

38. *ibid.*, ch. 22, 175.

39. H.P. Lattin, *The Letters of Gerbert* (New York, 1961), 36 note 6.

40. P.E. Schramm, 'Neun Briefe des byzantinischen Gesandten Leos', *Byzantinische Zeitschrift* 25 (1925), 89–105.

41. Thietmar of Merseburg, *Chronicon* IV. 30, ed. Werner Trillmich (Darmstadt, 1985), 146; also John of Venice, *Chronica Venetum*, ed. G. Monticolo, *Cronache Veneziane antichissime* (Rome, 1890), 155.

42. *Vita Nili*, ed. G. Waitz, MGH SS 4, 616–617.

43. Hermann of Reichenau or *Hermannus Contractus*, *Chronicon*, s.a. 997, ed. Aemilianus Ussermann, *Germaniae Sacra Podromus* (St. Blasien, 1792), vol. 1, 194.

44. *Epistola de Synodo Papiensi*, ed. G.H. Pertz, MGH SS 3, 694.

45. Richer, *Historia* IV. 89, ed. Robert Latouche, *Richer, Histoire de France* (2 vols. Paris, 1930; reprinted 1967), 2, 288.

46. PL 139, cols. 473–508.

47. Harald Zimmermann, *Das dunkle Jahrhundert* (Graz/Vienna/Cologne, 1971).

CHAPTER 10

1. Gregory VII, *epp.* 4. 12, trans. H.E.J. Cowdrey, *The Register of Pope Gregory VII* (Oxford, 2002), 221–222.

2. See Gerd Althoff, *Otto III* (English trans. University Park, Pa., 2003), 132–148.

3. Arnulf of Milan, *Liber Gestorum Recentium* 1. 12, ed. Claudia Zey, MGH SRG 67 (Hanover, 1994).

4. Rodulf Glaber, *Historiarum Libri Quinque* 4.4, ed. John France, Neithard Bulst and Paul Reynolds, *Rodulfus Glaber, Opera* (Oxford, 1989), 176; cf. 5. 26, 252.

5. *ibid.*, 4.2–3, 172–174.

6. *ibid.*, 5.26, 252.

7. *Heiliges Römisches Reich Deutscher Nation, 962 bis 1806* pt.1: Katalog (Dresden, 2006), III. 20, 144.

8. Peter Damiani, *epp.* 4. 72, PL, 144.

9. H.H. Anton (ed.), *Der sogenannte Traktat 'De ordinando pontifice'* (Bonn, 1982), lines 279–280, 83.

10. Bruno of Segni, Sermon on Simoniacs 2, ed. Ernst Sackur, MGH *Libelli* 2, 543–562.

11. William of Hirsau, letter to Herman of Salm, quoted by I.S. Robinson, *Papal Reform of the Eleventh Century* (Manchester, 2004), 2.

12. Boniface, *ep.* 51, ed. M. Tangl, MGH *Epp. sel*, 1, 87–88.

13. Gregory VII, *Epistolae vagantes* 154, ed. H.E.J. Cowdrey, 133.

14. Anselm of Reims, *Historia dedicationis Remensis ecclesiae*, chs. 8–9, 14–15, PL 149.

15. *Acta* of the Council of Reims, 1049, ed. Mansi.

16. *Constitutum Constantini*, ed. H. Fuhrmann, MGH SRG, 15–17.

17. Lateran synod of 1059, canon 1, ed. Carl Mirbt, *Quellen zur Geschichte*

des Papsttums und des römischen Katholizismus (3rd edn. Tübingen, 1911).

18. *Decretum* of Nicholas II: *Corpus Iuris Canonici* vol. 1, ed. E. Friedberg (Leipzig, 1879), cols. 77–79.

19. Benizo of Sutri bk. VI, trans. Robinson, *Papal Reform*, 206.

20. Cowdrey, *Register*, xi–xvii.

21. H.E.J. Cowdrey, *The 'Epistolae Vagantes' of Pope Gregory VII* (Oxford, 1972), xvii.

22. Cowdrey, *Register* 2.55a, 149–150.

23. *Imperial Lives and Letters*, trans. Theodor E. Mommsen and Karl F. Morrison (New York, 2000), 149.

24. Gregory VII, *Register* 3.6*, trans. Cowdrey, 181.

25. Decree of the Synod of Brixen, trans. Mommsen and Morrison, *Imperial Lives and Letters*, 157–160.

26. Benzo of Alba, To Emperor Henry, Book 7.1–2, trans. I.S. Robinson, *The Papal Reform of the Eleventh Century*, 364–368.

27. Beryl Smalley, *The Bible in the Middle Ages* (3rd edn. Oxford, 1983), 48–49.

28. Rodolfo Lanciani, *The Destruction of Ancient Rome* (London and New York, 1901), 159–166.

29. Gregory VII, *ep.* 1. 49, trans. Cowdrey, *Register*, 54.

30. *Epistolae vagantes* 5, ed. H.E.J. Cowdrey, *The 'Epistolae Vagantes' of Pope Gregory VII* (Oxford, 1972), 10–13.

31. *Ep.* 1.63, trans. H.E.J. Cowdrey, *The Register of Pope Gregory VII 1073–1084* (Oxford, 2002), 68.

32. Roger Collins, 'Continuity and Loss in Medieval Spanish Culture: the Evidence of MS Silos, Archivo Monástico 4', in Roger Collins and Anthony Goodman (ed.), *Medieval Spain: Culture, Conflict and Coexistence* (Basingstoke and New York, 2002), 1–22.

33. Ed. Robert Somerville, *Pope Urban II, the 'Collectio Britannica' and the Council of Melfi (1089)* (Oxford, 1996), 45.

34. Bernold of St. Blasien, *Chronicon* s.a. 1095, MGH SS vol. 5, 462; also Stephen Runciman, *History of the Crusades*, vol. 1 (Cambridge, 1951), 101–108.

CHAPTER 11

1. St. Bernard, *ep.* 399, trans. Bruno Scott James, *The Letters of St. Bernard of Clairvaux* (London, 1953), 471.

2. *Relatio registri Pascalis II*, ed. L. Weiland, MGH *Const.* 1 (1893), no. 99, 147–148.

3. Gerhoh von Reichersberg, *De investigatione Antichristi* ch. 25, ed. E. Sackur, MGH *Libelli* 3 (1897), 333–334.

4. *Privilegium Paschalis II de investituris*, ed. Weiland, MGH *Const.* 1, no. 96, 144–145.

5. *Concilium Lateranense s.a.* 1112, *ibid.*, no. 399, 571.

6. Mary Stroll, *Symbols as Power: the Papacy following the Investiture Contest* (Leiden, 1991), 16–35.

7. *Chronicon Sublacense*, ed. Raffaello Morghen (Subiaco, 1991), 174–175.

8. LP XCIIII, xxv: 1, 447; *Constitutum Constantini* 16, lines 257–258, ed. Fuhrmann, 92.

9. *Vita Adriani IV; Adrian IV The English Pope*, ed. Brenda Bolton and Anne J. Duggan (Aldershot, 2003), 220–223.

10. *Constitutum Constantini* 13, line 206, ed. Fuhrmann, 86.

11. Tommaso di Carpegna Falconieri, *Il clero di Roma nel medioevo* (Rome, 2002), 37–82.

12. Roger of Howden, *Annales* II s.a. 1191.

13. Richard Krautheimer, *Rome: Profile of a City, 312–1308* (Princeton, 1980), 152.

14. Bernard, *epp.* 250 and 251, trans. Scott James, 330 and 331.

15. John of Salisbury, *Historia Pontificalis* xxxi, ed. Marjorie Chibnall (London, 1956), 64–65.

16. *ibid.*, 65.

17. Otto of Freising, *Gesta Friderici Imperatoris* i. 29; trans. C.C. Mierow, *The Deeds of Frederick Barbarossa* (New York, 1953), 61–62; Martene and Durand, *Veterum scriptorum et monumentorum . . . amplissima collectio* (Paris, 1724), II, 399–400, 554–557.

18. *De Consideratione*, 65; *Ep.* 205, trans. Scott James, 280.

19. Bernard, *ep.* 355, trans Scott James, 431.

20. Bernard, *De Consideratione* 4.4, trans. John D. Anderson and Elizabeth Kennan, *St. Bernard of Clairvaux: Five Books on Consideration* (Kalamazoo, 1976), 114–115.

21. John of Salisbury, *Historia Pontificalis* xxxviii, ed. Chibnall, 76.

22. Rahewin's continuation of Otto of Freising, *Gesta Friderici* i. 60, trans. Mierow, 99.

23. Bernard, *ep.* 320, trans. Scott James, 394.

24. Otto of Friesing, *Gesta Friderici* 4. 61, trans. Mierow, 291.

25. *ibid.*, 294.

26. *Boso's Life of Alexander III*, trans. G.M. Ellis (Oxford, 1973), 49.

27. Rahewin 4. 79, trans. Mierow, 320.

28. Beryl Smalley, *The Becket Conflict and the Schools* (Oxford, 1973), 139.

29. Roger of Howden, *Annales* II s.a. 1198.

CHAPTER 12

1. Thomas of Marlborough, *History of the Abbey of Evesham*, III. v, 480, ed. Jane Sayers and Leslie Watkiss (Oxford, 2003), 455.

2. *ibid.*, III. ii. 203, p. 211.

3. *ibid.*, III. iii. 273, p. 275.

4. *Selected Letters of Pope Innocent III concerning England*, ed. C.R. Cheney and W.H. Semple (London, 1953), xvii.

5. Thomas of Marlborough III. iii. 300, p. 299.

6. Fernando J. de Lasala S.J., 'Typology of the Papal Seals' (Rome, 2003): http://www.unigre.it/pubblicazioni/lasala/Papal%20Seals.pdf

7. http://asv.vatican.va/en/dipl/docfirstperiod.htm

8. Thomas of Marlborough III, xxviii–xxxix.

9. *Selected Letters of Pope Innocent III*, ep. 6, 16–22.

10. *Chronicle of Bury St. Edmunds 1212–1301*, ed. Antonia Gransden (London, 1964), 21–22. In 1279 the amount dropped to 1,675 marks, ten shillings and nine pence: *ibid.*, 70.

11. Dante, *The Divine Comedy* I: *Inferno*, XIX. 73–75, trans. Mark Musa (rev. edn. New York and London, 1984), 242.

12. Salimbene de Adam, *Cronaca,* trans. Giuseppe Tonna (Reggio, 2006), 112.

13. *The Deeds of Pope Innocent III*, trans. James M. Powell (Washington, D.C., 2004), 3.

14. Fourth Lateran Council, canon 68, COD, 266.

15. Salimbene de Adam, *Cronaca*, 4.

16. D.S. Chambers, *Popes, Cardinals and War* (London, 2006), 18–19.

17. 1227: the future Celestine IV, Innocent IV and Alexander IV; 1261: the future Clement IV, Martin IV and Honorius IV; 1273 the future John XXI, 'Gregory XI' (not counted as he died a day after his election), Innocent V.

18. *Chronicle of Bury St. Edmunds* s.a. 1253, ed. Gransden, 19.

19. Leonardo Bruni, *History of the Florentine People* III. 46, ed. James Hankins, vol. I (Cambridge, Mass. and London, 2001), 281.

20. *Chronicle of Bury St. Edmunds* s.a. 1276, ed. Gransden, 61.

21. Ptolemy of Lucca, quoted in Francisco Hernández and Peter Linehan, *The Mozarabic Cardinal* (Florence, 2004), 174 note 99.

22. *Chronicle of Bury St. Edmunds* s.a. 1279, ed. Gransden, 70.

CHAPTER 13

1. Henry G.J. Beck, 'William of Hundleby's Account of the Anagni Outrage', *Catholic Historical Review*, vol. 32 (1947), 190–220.

2. Antonia Gransden (ed.), *Chronicle of Bury St. Edmunds* (London, 1964), s.a. 1294, 122 suggested he was aged over a hundred.

3. Marjorie Reeves, *The Influence of Prophecy in the Later Middle Ages. A Study in Joachimism* (rev. edn. Notre Dame and London, 1993), 60–62, 187–190.

4. Barbara Newman, *From Virile Woman to Woman Christ. Studies in Medieval Religion and Literature* (Philadelphia, 1995), 182–192; Stephen Wessley, 'The thirteenth-century Gugliemites: salvation through women', in Derek Baker (ed.), *Medieval Women* (Oxford, 1978), 289–303.

5. Peter Herde, 'Celestine V', *Dictionary of Popes and the Papacy* (English trans. New York, 2001), 20.

6. Marina Righetti Tosti-Croce (ed.), *Bonifacio VIII e il suo tempo* (Milan, 2000), 133–138 and ills. 70–74.

7. *Chronicle of Bury St. Edmunds* s.a. 1292, ed. Gransden, 104–113, for an example of an assessment.

8. *Codex Constitutionum quas Summi Pontifices ediderunt in Solemni Canonizatione Sanctorum* (Rome, 1729), 109–116.

9. On whom see *Jacopone da Todi e l'arte in Umbria nel suo tempo* (Milan, 2006).

10. Chronicle of Asti s.a. 1300, ed. Ludovico Muratori, *Rerum Italicarum Scriptores*, vol. XI, 191.

11. Joseph R. Strayer, *The Reign of Philip the Fair* (Princeton, 1980), 262–266.

12. Pierre Dupuy, *Histoire du différend d'entre le Pape Boniface VIII et Philippe le Bel Roy de France* (Paris, 1655), 44.

13. A.R. Myers, *Parliaments and Estates in Europe to 1789* (London, 1975), 66.

14. *Unam sanctam*, trans. Bettenson, 161–164.

15. William of Hundleby, trans. Beck, 203.

16. William Thorne's *Chronicle of Saint Augustine's Abbey Canterbury*, trans. A.H. Davis (Oxford, 1934), 385.

17. See Sophia Menache, *Clement V* (Cambridge, 1998) for this pontificate.

18. Gratian I. xl. 6, *Corpus Iuris Canonici*, ed. A. Friedberg, vol. I (Leipzig, 1897), 146; Walter Ullmann, *Medieval Papalism* (London, 1949), 156–158.

19. *Vita Prima Clementis V*, VPA 1, 1 and 20.

20. *Codex Constitutionum in Solemni Canonizatione Sanctorum*, 117–121.

21. See Malcolm Barber, *The Trial of the Templars* (rev. edn. Cambridge, 1993), and Menache, *Clement V*, 205–246.

22. Menache, *Clement V*, 207 and n. 171.

23. *ibid.*, 216–217.

24. Dante, *Paradiso* IX. 133–135, quoted by Menache, *Clement V*, 45.

25. *Vita Prima Clementis V*, VPA 1, 23.

26. Menache, *Clement V*, 51–54.

27. George Holmes, *Florence, Rome and the Origins of the Renaissance* (Oxford, 1986), 163–203.

28. *Vita Prima Clementis V*, VPA 1, 22.

29. George Garnett, *Marsilius of Padua and 'the Truth of History'* (Oxford, 2006), 18–21.

30. See David Burr, *The Spiritual Franciscans. From Protest to Persecution in the Century after Saint Francis* (University Park, Pa., 2001), 111–158.

31. *Vita Prima Johannis XXII*, VPA 1, 117.

32. Patrick Nold, *Pope John XXII and His Franciscan Cardinal* (Oxford, 2003), 1–24.

33. William of Ockham, *The Work of Ninety Days*, trans. John Kilcullen, in Arthur Stephen McGrade and John Kilcullen, *William of Ockham: A Letter to the Friars Minor and Other Writings* (Cambridge, 1995), 105.

34. Christian Trottman, *La Vision Béatifique, des disputes scholastiques à son définition par Benoit XII* (Rome, 1995), 417–743.

35. *Vita Prima Benedicti XII*, VPA 1, 206: *fervidus hereticorum expugnator et rigidus persecutor*; *Vita Quarta Benedicti XII, ibid.* 223: *justus et durus erat*.

36. *Vita Quarta Benedicti XII, ibid.*, 224.

37. Dominique Barthélemy and Philippe Contarmine, 'The Use of Private Space', in Georges Duby (ed.), *A History of Private Life*, vol. 2 (English trans. Cambridge, Mass. and London, 1988), 470–475 for the papal palace.

38. *Vita Secunda Benedicti XII* and *Vita Tertia Benedicti XII*, VPA 1, 213 and 216.

39. *Vita Prima Benedicti XII, ibid.*, 202.

40. *Vita Octava Benedicti XII, ibid.*, 236.

41. *Vita Prima Benedicti XII*, and *Vita Sexta Benedicti XII, ibid.*, 211 and 232.

42. Quoted in Ludwig Pastor, *The History of the Popes* (English trans. London, 1906), vol. 1, 64.

43. *Vita Sexta Clementis VI*, VPA 1, 307.

44. *Vita Tertia Clementis VI*, VPA 1, 285.

45. *Historia di Matteo Villani Cittadino Fiorentino* (Venice, 1562) Book III, ch. 39, 154; G. Mollat, *Les Papes d'Avignon* (9th edn. Paris, 1949), 91.

46. F. Filippini, *Il cardinale Egidio Albornoz* (Bologna, 1937).

47. Kenneth Fowler, *Medieval Mercenaries vol. 1: The Great Companies* (Oxford, 2001), 118.

48. Yves Renouard, *The Avignon Papacy 1305–1403*, trans. Denis Bethell (London, 1970), 62.

49. S. Nofke (trans.), *The Letters of St. Catherine of Siena* (Binghamton, 1988), vol. 1, 212 (*ep.* 69).

50. F. Thomas Luongo, *The Saintly Politics of Catherine of Siena* (Ithaca and London, 2006), 157–201.

51. Leonardo Bruni, *History of the Florentine People* VIII. 125, ed. and

trans. James Hankins, vol. 2 (Cambridge, Mass. and London, 2004), 523.

52. Mollat, *Papes d'Avignon*, 393–409; but also A.M. Barrell, *The Papacy, Scotland and Northern England, 1342–1378* (Cambridge, 1995), 158–159.

53. Gordon Leff, 'John Wyclif: the Path to Dissent', *Proceedings of the British Academy*, vol. 52 (1966), 143–180; K.B. McFarlane, *John Wycliffe and the Beginning of English Nonconformity* (London, 1952).

CHAPTER 14

1. Odoricus Raynaldus, *Annales Ecclesiastici*, 398–399, trans. Walter Ullmann, *The Origins of the Great Schism* (London, 1948), 60–61.

2. Ludwig Pastor, *The History of the Popes* (English trans. London, 1906), vol. 1, 130.

3. Brian Tierney, *Foundations of the Conciliar Theory* (Cambridge, 1955), 68–84; John A. Watt, 'The Constitutional Law of the College of Cardinals: Hostiensis to Joannes Andreae', *Medieval Studies*, vol. 33 (1971), 127–157.

4. Ullmann, *Origins of the Great Schism*, 102–142.

5. Dietrich of Niem or Nieheim, *De Schismate* I. lii. 94, quoted by E.F. Jacob, *Essays in the Conciliar Epoch* (3rd edn. Manchester, 1963), 33.

6. *Annales Forolivienses*, quoted by Peter Partner, *The Papal State under Martin V* (London, 1958), 16.

7. *De Concilio Pisano*, rev. edn. Jürgen Miethke and Lorenz Weinrich, *Quellen zur Kirchenreform im Zeitalter der grossen Konzilien des 15. Jahrhundert* vol. 1 (Darmstadt, 1995), 166.

8. Jacob, *Essays in the Conciliar Epoch*, 39.

9. Theodoricus de Niem, *Historia de Vita Iohannis XXIII Pontificis Romani* (Frankfurt-am-Main, 1620), 1–2.

10. Francis Oakley, *The Conciliarist Tradition* (Oxford, 2003), 91–92.

11. Matthew of Cracow, *De Squaloribus Curie Romane*, ed. Miethke and Weinrich, *Quellen zur Kirchenreform*, 62.

12. Ullmann, *Origins of the Great Schism*, 191–231; appendix on Zabarella.

13. Decree *Sacrosancta*, trans. Bettenson, 192.

14. Daniel Waley, *The Italian City Republics* (London, 1969), 221–239.

15. Joseph Gill, *Eugenius IV: Pope of Christian Union* (London, 1961), 39–40.

16. *Monumenta conciliorum generalium saeculi decimi quinti*, vol. 2, 93–94, trans. C.M.D. Crowder, *Unity, Heresy and Reform 1378–1460* (London, 1977), 149.

17. *ibid.*, 155, translating a memorandum from an Italian abbot.

18. Chiara Crisciani, *Il papa e l'alchimia: Felice V, Guglielmo Fabri e l'elixir* (Rome, 2002).

CHAPTER 15

1. Gerhard Laehr, 'Die Konstantinische Schenkung in der abendländische Literatur des Mittelalters bis zur des XIV Jahrhunderts', *Historische Studien* vol. 166 (1926), 1–188; Alfred Hiatt, *The Making of Medieval Forgeries* (London and Toronto, 2004), 142.

2. Hiatt, *Making of Medieval Forgeries*, 159–161.

3. Nicholas of Cusa, *The Catholic Concordance*, ed. Paul E. Sigmund (Cambridge, 1991), book III. 294–324, pp. 216–227.

4. Roberto Weiss, *The Renaissance Discovery of Classical Antiquity* (2nd edn. Oxford, 1988), 59.

5. *The Treatise of Lorenzo Valla on the Donation of Constantine*, ed. and tr. Christopher B. Coleman (Yale, 1922; reprinted Toronto, 1993), 100–115.

6. Hiatt, *Making of Medieval Forgeries*, 170–172.

7. *Julius Exclusus de coelis*, trans. Michael J. Heath in A.H.T. Levi (ed.), *Collected Works of Erasmus*, vol. 27 (Toronto, 1986), 192 ; on its authorship see 156–163.

8. On his portrait (in the Kunsthistorisches Museum, Vienna) see Otto Pächt, *Van Eyck and the Founders of Early Netherlandish Painting* (English edn. London, 1994), 111–112 and pl. 9.

9. Loren Partridge, *Art of the Renaissance in Rome 1400–1600* (Upper Saddle River, N.J., 1996), 19.

10. A.D.M. Barrell, *The Papacy, Scotland and Northern England, 1342–1378* (Cambridge, 1995), 141–159.

11. Christopher Tyerman, *God's War: A New History of the Crusades* (London, 2006), 847.

12. e.g., Nicholas of Cusa, *Catholic Concordance* III, 296–297, ed. Sigmund, 217–218.

13. It has been suggested that Carpaccio's famous depiction of St. Augustine becoming aware of the Sack of Rome represents a portrait of Bessarion: see Peter Humfrey, *Carpaccio* (London, 2005), pl. 25, 91–92.

14. A fresco of 1503, commissioned by his nephew Pope Pius III depicts his investiture: Scarpellini, Pietro and Maria Rita Silvestrelli, *Pintoricchio* (Milan, 2003), 268.

15. Denys Hay and W.K. Smith (ed.), *De Gestis Concilii Basiliensis Commentariorum Libri II* (revised edn. Oxford, 1992); Florence A. Gragg and Leona C. Smith (tr.), *The Commentaries of Pius II* in *Smith College Studies in History* vols. XXII 1–2, XXX, XXXV and XLIII (Northampton, Mass., 1937–1951), now being replaced by an edition in the I Tatti Renaissance Library (see note 16 below).

16. Commentaries I. 6 in Margaret Meserve and Marcello Simonetta (ed.), *Pius II Commentaries*, vol. 1 (Cambridge, Mass. and London, 2003), 25.

17. Florence A. Gragg (trans.), *Secret Memoirs of a Renaissance Pope* (London, 1988), 216.

18. R.J. Mitchell, *The Laurels and the Tiara: Pope Pius II, 1458–1464* (London, 1962), 121.

19. Gragg, *Secret Memoirs*, 74–82.

20. C.M.D. Crowder, *Unity, Heresy and Reform 1378–1460* (London, 1977), 179–181 for a translation.

21. John F. D'Amico, *Renaissance Humanism in Papal Rome* (Baltimore and London, 1983), 89–102.

22. Mitchell, *Laurels and the Tiara*, 192–193.

23. Frederic J. Baumgartner, *Behind Locked Doors: a History of Papal Elections* (New York and Basingstoke, 2003), 78–79.

24. Bartholomaeus Platina, *Vitae Pontificum* (Venice, 1479): Paulus II (unpaginated).

25. Eunice D. Howe, *Art and Culture at the Sistine Court* (Vatican City, 2005), 220–248, figs. 18–48.

26. Lauro Martines, *April Blood: Florence and the Plot against the Medici* (London, 2003), 174–196.

27. *ibid.*, 7–12.

28. *Catholic Encyclopedia*, art. *Indulgences*.

29. *Unigenitus*, trans. Bettenson, 259–260.

30. Baumgartner, *Behind Locked Doors*, 84–85.

31. Johannes Stella, *Vite ducentorum et triginta sumorum pontificum a beato Petro Apostolo usque ad Julium secundum modernum Pontificem* (Basel, 1507), n.p.

32. Franco Ivan Nucciarelli, *Pinturicchio: Il Bambin Gesù delle Mani* (Perugia, 207), 46–55.

33. Owen Chadwick, *Catholicism and History: The Opening of the Vatican Archives* (Cambridge, 1978), 110–116.

34. *ibid.*, 111.

35. E. Celani (ed.), *Johanni Burckardi Liber Notarum ab anno 1483 usque ad annum 1506*, 2 vols. (Città di Castello, 1906); Geoffrey Parker (trans.), *At the Court of the Borgia* (London, 1963) provides a selection.

36. Evidence discussed in Michael Mallett, *The Borgias* (London, 1969), 205–206.

37. Parker, *At the Court of the Borgias*, 173–177.

38. Caroline P. Murphy, *The Pope's Daughter* (London, 2004).

39. Cecil Gould, *Raphael's 'Portrait of Pope Julius II': the Re-emergence of the Original* (London, n.d.), 1.

40. See N.H. Minnich, *The Fifth Lateran Council* (Aldershot, 1993); R. J. Schoek, 'The Fifth Lateran Council: its Partial Success and Its Larger Failure', in G.F. Lytle (ed.), *Reform and Authority in the Medieval and Reformation Church* (Washington, D.C., 1981), 99–126.

41. Renaudet, A., *La Concile gallican de Pise-Milan* (Paris, 1922).

42. Baumgartner, *Behind Locked Doors*, 92.

43. *ibid.*, 193.

CHAPTER 16

1. Judith Hook, *The Sack of Rome* (2nd edn. Basingstoke and New York, 2004), 177.

2. Marino Sanuto, *I Diarii* vol. XLV, 219 (Venice, 1902), quoted in Hook, *Sack of Rome*, 167.

3. Leopold von Ranke, *History of the Popes* (English trans. 3 vols. London, 1913), vol. 1, 100.

4. Thomas James Dandelet, *Spanish Rome 1500–1700* (New Haven and London, 2001), 84–87.

5. Henry Bettenson, *Documents of the Christian Church* (New York and London, 1947), 261.

6. *ibid.*, 267 and 270.

7. quoted in Owen Chadwick, *The Reformation* (rev. edn. London, 1972), 51.

8. Reproduced in Heiko A. Oberman, *Luther: Man Between God and the Devil* (English trans. New Haven and London, 1989), 258.

9. Lauro Martines, *Scourge and Fire: Savonarola and Renaissance Italy* (London, 2006), chs. 13–19.

10. Saints (with date of canonisation): Gregory VII (1606), Celestine V (1313); Blesseds: Victor III (1887), Urban II (1881), Eugenius III (1872), Innocent V (1898), Benedict XI (1736), Urban V (1870).

11. Erasmus, *Praise of Folly*, ch. 54, trans. Betty Radice (Harmondsworth, 1971), 164.

12. Oberman, *Luther*, 68–70.

13. P. Renée Baernstein, *A Convent Tale: A Century of Sisterhood in Spanish Milan* (New York, 2002), 57–78.

14. J. Carlos Coupeau, 'Five Personae of Ignatius of Loyola', in Thomas Worcester (ed.), *The Cambridge Companion to the Jesuits* (Cambridge, 2008), 37.

15. Erasmus, *Praise of Folly*, ch. 59, trans. Radice, 179.

16. *Opus Thomae Campegii Bononiensis Episcopi Feltrensis De Auctoritate et Potestate Romani Pontificis et alia opuscula* (Venice, 1555), f. 2r.

17. Hubert Jedin, *A History of the Council of Trent*, vol. 1 (English trans. Edinburgh, 1957), 76–100.

18. Burkle-Young, Francis A. and Michael Leopoldo Doerrer, *The Life of Cardinal Innocenzo del Monte: A Scandal in Scarlet* (Lewiston, N.Y., 1997).

19. Alois Uhl, *Papstkinder. Lebensbilder aus der Zeit der Renaissance* (Düsseldorf and Zurich, 2003), 129–142.

20. Charles L. Stringer, 'The Place of Clement VII and Clementine Rome in Renaissance History', in Gouwens and Reiss (ed.), *Pontificate of Clement VII, especially* 182–184.

21. Michael A. Mullett, *The Catholic Reformation* (London and New York, 1999), 1–28.

22. John W. O'Malley, *Trent and All That: Renaming Catholicism in the Early Modern Era* (Cambridge, Mass., and London, 2000) for the arguments.

23. Julius III, Marcellus II, Paul IV and Pius IV.

24. *de Emendanda Ecclesia*, trans. Coleman J. Barry, *Readings in Church History* (Westminster, Md., 1965), quoted by Mullett, *Catholic Reformation*, 35.

25. William Monter, 'The Roman Inquisition and Protestant Heresy Executions in 16th Century Europe', in Agostino Borromeo (ed.), *L'Inquisizione* (Vatican City, 2003), 539–548.

26. W. Schenk, *Reginald Pole, Cardinal of England* (London, 1950), 111–112.

27. *Calendar of State Papers, Venetian*, ed. R. Brown, vol. V, 596.

28. Schenk, *Reginald Pole*, 115–118.

29. Marcia B. Hall, *After Raphael: Painting in Central Italy in the Sixteenth Century* (Cambridge, 1999), 268 and note 28.

30. Chadwick, *Reformation*, 271.

31. Thomas V. Cohen, *Love and Death in Renaissance Italy* (Chicago and London, 2004), 125–170 for another dimension of this affair.

32. e.g., Francesco Cattani da Diacetto, *Discorso del autoritá del Papa sopra'l Concilio* (Florence, 1562).

33. *Constitutiones et Decreta Synodalia Civitatis et Dioecesis Constantiensis* (Dillingen, 1569).

34. *Concilium Tridentinum: Diariorum, Actorum, Epistolarum, Tractatuum* (13 vols. Freiburg-im-Breisgau, 1901–2001).

35. Paula Sutter Fichtner, *Emperor Maximilian II* (New Haven and London, 2001), 115, 144–145.

36. Paul F. Grendler, *Critics of the Italian World (1530–1560)* (Madison, Wis., 1969), 47–48.

37. Cardinal Giulio Antonio Santorio (d. 1602), *Deploratio calamitatis suorum temporum*, quoted in Frederick J. McGinness, *Right Thinking and Sacred Oratory in Counter-Reformation Rome* (Princeton, 1995), 177.

38. Coupeau, 'Five Personae of Ignatius of Loyola', 37.

39. *Codex Constitutionum quas Summi Pontifices ediderunt in Solemni Canonizatione Sanctorum* (Rome, 1729), 501.

40. Bonnie Blackburn and Leofranc Holford-Strevens, *The Oxford Companion to the Year* (Oxford, 1999), 406.

CHAPTER 17

1. Speech in Italian, French and Portuguese versions on the Vatican website: *http://www.vatican.va/holy_father/john_paul_ii/speeches/1979/november/documents/hf_jp-ii_spe_19791110_einstein_it.html*

2. Clause 36 of the Constitution *Gaudium et Spes* of 7th December 1965: *Vatican Council II. The Conciliar and Post Conciliar Documents*, ed. Austin Flannery (Leominster, 1975), 935.

3. Sergio M. Pagano (ed.), *I Documenti del processo di Galileo Galilei* (Vatican City, 1984).

4. Mario d'Addio, *The Galileo Case: Trial/Science/Truth* (English trans., Rome, 2004).

5. *ibid.*, 19–25.

6. Book of Joshua 10. 12

7. Stillman Drake, *Galileo* (Oxford, 1980), 63.

8. *Documenti del processo di Galileo*, ed. Pagano, doc. 20 (25th February 1616) from Archivio Segreto Vaticano, 101.

9. D'Addio, *The Galileo Case*, 123–129.

10. *ibid.*, 107–117, and Drake, *Galileo*, 76–77.

11. Pagano, *Documenti del processo di Galileo*, doc. 17 (16th June 1633) from Archivio della Sacra Congregazione per la Dottrina della Fede, 230.

12. *Letters to Father: Suor Maria Celeste to Gallileo, 1623–1633*, ed. and trans. Dava Sobel (New York, 2001), 222–227.

13. Pagano, *Documenti del processo di Galileo*, doc. 25 (23rd March 1634), 234.

14. e.g., *Le Lettere del Signor Gio. Francesco Peranda* (1601; edition used, Venice, 1610), 294 (letter to Gregory XIII, 3rd July 1577).

15. Niels Krough Rasmussen, 'Maiestas Pontificia: A Liturgical Reading of Etienne Dupérac's Engraving of the Capella Sistina from 1576', *Analecta Romana Instituti Danici* vol. 12 (1983), 109–148; Frederick J. McGinness, *Right Thinking and Sacred Oratory in Counter-Reformation Rome* (Princeton, 1995), 87, and 260 notes 4 and 5.

16. *ibid.*, 141.

17. *ibid.*, 87–107.

18. *ibid.*, 157.

19. *ibid.*, 105, 140.

20. *ibid.*, 172.

21. *ibid.*, 177.

22. Nicola Courtright, *The Papacy and the Art of Reform in Sixteenth-Century Rome* (Cambridge, 2003), 20, and 18–27 generally.

23. B. Rekers, *Benito Arias Montano (1527–1598)* (London and Leiden, 1972), 67.

24. Irena Backus, *Historical Method and Confessional Identity in the Era of the Reformation* (Leiden and Boston, 2003).

25. Rodolfo Lanciani, *The Destruction of Ancient Rome* (London and New York, 1901), 235–244.

26. Marcia Hall, *After Raphael: Painting in Central Italy in the Sixteenth Century* (Cambridge, 1999), 258–267.

27. *ibid.*, 200.

28. Tracy L. Ehrlich, *Landscape and Identity in Early Modern Italy: Villa Culture at Frascati in the Borghese Era* (Cambridge, 2002), 68–112.

29. Antonio Menniti Ippolito, 'The Secretariat of State as the Pope's Special Ministry', in Gianvittorio Signorotto and Maria Antonia Visceglia (ed.), *Court and Politics in Papal Rome, 1492–1700* (Cambridge, 2002), 132–157.

30. 'Contemporary account' quoted by Ferdinand Gregorovius, *The Tombs of the Popes* (English trans. Westminster, 1903), 135–136.

31. Aidan Weston-Lewis (ed.), *Effigies and Ecstasies: Roman Baroque Sculpture and Design in the Age of Bernini* (Edinburgh, 1998), item 118, 152–154.

32. Sforza Pallavicino, *Vita di Alessandro VII* (Milan, 1843), vol. I, 262–263, cited in Marie-Louise Rodén, *Church Politics in Seventeenth-Century Rome* (Stockholm, 2000), 133.

33. Rodén, *Church Politics in Seventeenth-Century Rome*, 133–144.

34. John Bargrave D.D., *Pope Alexander the Seventh and the College of Cardinals*, ed. James Craigie Robertson (London, 1867), 7.

35. Marco Teodori, *I Parenti del Papa. Nepotismo pontificio e formazione del patrimonio Chigi nella Roma Barocca* (Padua, 2001), 58–136.

36. Barbara McClung Hallman, *Italian Cardinals, Reform and the Church as Property* (Berkeley and London, 1985), 167.

37. Frederick Hammond, *Music and Spectacle in Baroque Rome: Barberini Patronage Under Urban VIII* (New Haven and London, 1994), 9, and 284 note 21.

38. Judith A. Hook, 'Urban VIII: The paradox of a spiritual monarchy', in A.G. Dickens (ed.), *The Courts of Europe. Politics, Patronage and Royalty, 1400–1800* (London, 1977), 213–232, at 222.

39. Report of the Venetian Ambassador to the Papal Court, quoted in Ludwig Pastor, *History of the Popes*, vol. 28, 44–48.

40. Laurie Nussdorfer, *Civic Politics in the Rome of Urban VIII* (Princeton, 1992), 205–227.

41. *ibid.*, 211–212, and 218.

42. Renata Ago, *Carriere e clientele nella Roma barocca* (Rome and Bari, 1990), 67–68.

43. Maria Antonietta Visceglia, 'Factions in the Sacred College in the Sixteenth and Seventeenth Centuries', in Signorotto and Visceglia (ed.), *Court and Politics in Papal Rome*, 99–131, at 121–131.

44. Hammond, *Music and Spectacle*, 286–287, note 13, quoting a contemporary diarist.

45. Owen Chadwick, *The Reformation* (revised edn. London, 1972), 167.

46. Joseph Bergin, *Crown, Church and Episcopate under Louis XIV* (New Haven and London, 2004), 23 and 194–198.

47. Frederic J. Baumgartner, *Behind Locked Doors: A History of the Papal Elections* (New York and Basingstoke, 2003), 155–157.

48. Gianvittorio Signorotto, 'The *squadrone volante*: "independent" cardinals and European politics in the second half of the seventeenth century', in Signorotto and Visceglia (ed.), *Court and Politics in Papal Rome*, 177–211, at 180–187; Rodén, *Church Politics in Seventeenth-Century Rome*, 89–112.

49. Signorotto, 'The *squadrone volante*', 181.

50. Veronica Buckley, *Christina Queen of Sweden: The Restless Life of a European Eccentric* (London and New York,

2004), 311–324 for the Monaldeschi incident.

51. Pierluigi Guiducci, '*Aliis non sibi clemens': spiritualità e pastoralità di Giulio Rospigliosi (Clemente IX, 1667–1669)* (Pistoia, 2000).

52. Hammond, *Music and Spectacle,* 202–203.

53. Signorotto, 'The *squadrone volante',* 197–198 and note 64.

54. Rodén, *Church Politics in Seventeenth-Century Rome,* 221–226.

CHAPTER 18

1. Louis Maimbourg S.J., *Histoire de la Decadence de l'Empire aprés Charlemagne et des Differends des Empereurs avec les Papes au sujet des Investitures et de l'Indépendence* (Paris, 1681).

2. Pastor, 14, 961.

3. Marie-Louise Rodén, *Church Politics in Seventeenth-Century Rome* (Stockholm, 2000), 286–289.

4. Gio: Battista di Luca, *Il Cardinale della S.R. Chiesa, Pratico* (Rome, 1680), 1–13.

5. Rodén, *Church Politics in Seventeenth-Century Rome,* 284 and 306 note 8.

6. Owen Chadwick, *The Popes and European Revolution* (Oxford, 1981), 277.

7. *Leo I Magnus: Opera Omnia,* ed. Pasquier Quesnel (Paris, 1675).

8. *Clementis Undecimi Pontificis Maximi Bullarium* (Rome, 1723), item LXIV, cols. 313–334.

9. *A short history of the famous Constitution or Bull Unigenitus thundered out by Pope Clement XI against that incomparable work called Moral reflexions upon the New Testament* (London, 1720).

10. *Unigenitus,* proposition 10, col. 327.

11. *Concilium Romanum in Sacrosancta Basilica Lateranensi celebratum Anno Universalis Jubilaei MDCCXXV a Sanctissimo Patre et Domino Nostro Benedicto Papae XIII* (Rome, 1725), canon 2, 3–4.

12. Blaise Pascal, *The Provincial Letters,* trans. A.J. Krailsheimer (Harmondsworth, 1967), Letter 5, 76.

13. *ibid.,* 84.

14. *ibid.,* 76.

15. *Clementis Undecimi . . .5Bullarium,* item LXXVIII, cols. 425–436.

16. Jonathan D. Spence, *Emperor of China: Self-portrait of Kang-Hsi* (London, 1974), 75.

17. *ibid.,* 81.

18. Owen Chadwick, *The Popes and the European Revolution* (Oxford, 1981), 256.

19. *Lettres intéressants du Pape Clément XIV,* vol. 1, 34.

20. *Lettres d'Italie du Président de Brosses,* ed. Frédéric d'Agay (2 vols. Mesnil-sur-l'Estrée, 2005), vol. 2, 139.

21. *ibid.,* vol. 2, 149.

22. Jean Boutier, 'Clément XII', in Philippe Levillain (ed.), *Dictionnaire historique de la Papauté* (Paris, 1994), 391, quoting de Brosses.

23. Encyclical *In eminenti* of 26th April 1738.

24. *Lettres intéressants du Pape Clément XIV (Ganganelli)* (2 vols. Paris, 1776), vol. 1, 244.

25. *Lettres d'Italie du Président de Brosses,* vol. 2, 486, 488.

26. *ibid.,* 488.

27. Chadwick, *The Popes and the European Revolution,* 296.

28. *De Servorum Dei Beatificatione et Beatorum Canonizatione* (Bologna, 1734–1738), and *De Synodo Diocesana Libri Tredecim* (Rome, 1748).

29. Carl Justi, *Winckelmann und seine Zeitgenossen* (4th edn. Leipzig, 1943), vol. 1, 693; *Lettres d'Italie du Président de Brosses*, vol. 2, 524.

30. Chadwick, *The Popes and the European Revolution*, 327.

31. Frank McLynn, *Charles Edward Stuart, a Tragedy in Many Acts* (London and New York, 1991), 327–333.

32. Jean-Jacques Rousseau, quoted by Chadwick, *The Popes and the European Revolution*, 365.

33. *The Autobiography of Edward Gibbon*, edited by Lord Sheffield (London, 1907), 159.

34. Letter from Sir Horace Mann Friday 24th February 1769: *Horace Walpole's Correspondence with Sir Horace Mann*, ed. W.S. Lewis, Warren Hunting Smith, and George L. Lam (London, 1967), vol. VII, 88–89.

35. *ibid.*, 89–90.

36. *ibid.*, 90.

37. Letter of 11th May 1769 in *ibid.*, 117.

38. Andrew Meagher ('Formerly a Priest of the Church of Rome . . . but now of the established Church of Ireland'), *The Popish Mass Celebrated by Heathen Priests* (Limerick, 1771), 318–319; a prophecy ascribed to George Brown, Archbishop of Dublin in 1551.

39. Quoted from N. Atkin and F. Tallett, *Priests, Prelates and People: a History of European Catholicism since 1750* (Oxford, 2003), 35.

40. *Bulle du Pape Clément XI, Touchant la Suppression de la Société de Jesus, en Latin et en François* (?Paris, 1773).

41. *Horace Walpole's Correspondence with Sir Horace Mann*, vol. VII, 517–518, 526–527 and 532.

42. Pastor, 39, 1.

43. Quoted in Jeffrey Collins, *Papacy and Politics in Eighteenth-Century Rome* (Cambridge, 2004), 7.

CHAPTER 19

1. Mauro Cappellari, *Il Trionfo della Santa Sede e della Chiesa contro gli assalti dei Novatori* (Rome, 1799; new edition Venice 1832, with translations into German [1833], and Spanish [1834].

2. Justinus Febronius Juriscultus, *De statu Ecclesiæ et legitima potestate Romani Pontificis liber singularis, ad reuniendos dissidentes in Religione Christianos compositus* (Frankfurt-am-Main, 1763) (On the State of the Church and the Legitimate Power of the Roman Pontiff).

3. On the Synod see Charles A. Bolton, *Church Reform in 18th Century Italy (the Synod of Pistoia, 1786)* (The Hague, 2001).

4. Letter from D'Alembert to Voltaire, 13 May 1768; quoted in Owen Chadwick, *The Popes and the European Revolution* (Oxford, 1981), 366.

5. John Moore M.D., *A View of Society and Manners in Italy* (5th edn. 2 vols. London, 1790), II, 21.

6. *ibid.*, 24–25.

7. *ibid.*, 42–44.

8. *Relazione* of Benigno Aloisi (1729), ed. Caterina-Giovanna Coda, *Duemilatrecento corpi di martiri* (Rome, 2004), 17–78, at 49–53.

9. Pietro Zander, 'La tomba di San Pietro e la necropoli vaticana: dalle prime esplorazioni ai recenti restauri', in *Pietro. La storia, l'immagine, la memoria* (Milan, 1999), 215.

10. Antonio Nodari, *Vitae Pontificum Romanorum Pii VI, Pii VII, Leonis XII, Pii VIII* (Pavia, 1840), 12.

11. Letter of Napoleon dated 13th February 1806, quoted in Robert Asprey, *The Rise and Fall of Napoleon Bonaparte* (2 vols. London, 2001), vol. 2, 18.

12. Memoirs of Cardinal Pacca, quoted by Susan Vandiver Nicassio, *Imperial City: Rome, Romans and Napoleon, 1796–1815* (Welwyn Garden City, 2005), 196.

13. Letter of 6th August 1809: Asprey, *Rise and Fall of Napoleon*, vol. 2, 175.

14. *ibid.*, 198, letter of 16th July 1811.

15. Owen Chadwick, *Catholicism and History: The Opening of the Vatican Archives* (Cambridge, 1978), 14–18.

16. Alan J. Reinerman, *Austria and the Papacy in the Age of Metternich*, vol. 1 (Washington, D.C., 1979), 119–120.

17. Philippe Boutry, 'Pie VII', in Levillain, 1334–1342, at 1341, quoting Adolfo Omodeo (1889–1946).

18. CBCR 5, 131–146 for the 'graphic evidence' for its state before the fire.

19. Frederic J. Baumgartner, *Behind Locked Doors: A History of the Papal Elections* (New York and Basingstoke, 2003), 187.

20. Nodari, *Vitae Pontificum Romanorum*, 157.

21. For the best likeness: *Papi in Posa* (Rome, 2005), 159.

22. Encyclical *Quo graviora* of 13th March 1836, clause. 7: http:www.papalencyclicals.net/Leo12/l12quogr.htm

23. Philippe Boutry, 'Léon XII', in Levillain, 1031–1035, at 1033.

24. *ibid.*, 1035.

25. Encyclical *Traditi Humilitati* of May 24th 1829, clauses 4 and 5: http:www.papalencyclicals.net/Pius08/p8tradit.htm

26. Alan J. Reinerman, *Austria and the Papacy in the Age of Metternich*, vol. 2 (Washington, D.C., 1989), 10–34.

27. Encyclical *Mirari vos* of 15 August 1832, clauses 4 and 5, EE 2, 26–53.

28. Encyclical *In supremo apostolatus* of 3rd December 1839, EE 2, 920–927; trans. http:www.papalencyclicals.net/Greg16/g16sup.htm

29. E.E.Y. Hales, *Pio Nono* (London, 1954), 36.

30. Encyclical *Qui pluribus* of 9th November 1846, chapters 10 and 16, EE 2, 152–182; trans: http:www.papalencyclicals.net/Pius09/p9quiplu.htm

31. Encyclical *Qui nuper* of 18th June 1859, EE 2, 424–427.

32. Encyclical *Mirari vos* of 15th August 1832, chapter 20, EE 2, 48.

33. J.D. Holmes, *More Roman Than Rome: English Catholicism in the Nineteenth Century* (London, 1978).

34. Dominic Aidan Bellinger and Stella Fletcher, *Princes of the Church: A History of the English Cardinals* (Stroud, 2001), 124–130.

35. Gallican Declaration, ch. 4, Bettenson, 379.

36. *Pastor Aeternus* 4, *ibid.* 383; Dominique Le Tourneau, 'Infaillibilité' in Levillain (ed.), *Dictionnaire historique de la Papauté*, 865–871.

37. Vidler, *The Church in an Age of Revolution* (Harmondsworth, 1961), 154; Eamon Duffy, *Saints and Sinners: A History of the Popes* (2nd edn. New Haven and London, 2001), 297.

38. Homily of 3rd September 2000: http:www.vatican.va/holy_father/john _paul_ii/homilies/2000/documents/ hf_jp-ii_hom_20000903_beatification _en.html

CHAPTER 20

1. E.E.Y. Hales, *Pio Nono* (London, 1954), 147.

2. John F. Pollard, *Money and the Rise of the Modern Papacy* (Cambridge, 2005), 8.

3. Encyclical *Sancta Dei Civitas* of 3 December 1880, clause 8, EE 3, trans. Vatican website.

4. Encyclical *Rerum Novarum* of 15 May 1891, clause 1, EE 3: trans. Vatican website; also *I Documenti sociali della Chiesa* (Vatican City, 1991), 7.

5. Encyclical *Rerum Novarum* of 15 May 1891, cl. 4.

6. Gilded medal issued in Buenos Aires, dated 20 July 1903.

7. Eamon Duffy, *Saints and Sinners* (3rd edn. New Haven and London, 2007), 318.

8. Encyclical *Testem Benevolentiae Nostrae* of 22 January 1899, EE 3: http:www.papalencyclicals.net/Leo13/l13teste.htm

9. Alec R. Vidler, *The Church in an Age of Revolution* (Harmondsworth, 1961), 245.

10. Encyclical *E Supremi* of 14 October 1903, EE 4, 18–39.

11. Quoted in Peter Hebblethwaite, *In the Vatican* (Oxford, 1987), 26.

12. e.g., Walter Diethelm, *St. Pius X: The Farm Boy Who Became Pope* (Fort Collins, Col., 1994) and three volumes of *'Beppo': Pape Saint Pie X* by Guillaume Hunermann (Paris, 2005–2006).

13. Carlo Falconi, *The Popes in the Twentieth Century* (English trans. London, 1967), 2.

14. Cardinal François-Désiré Mathieu, quoted in H. Daniel-Rops, *A Fight for God, 1870–1939* (London, 1965), 51.

15. T.S. Pattie, *Manuscripts of the Bible: Greek Bibles in the British Library* (revised edn. London, 1995), 18.

16. Keith Elliott and Ian Moir, *Manuscripts and the Text of the New Testament* (Edinburgh, 1995), 14–15.

17. Nestle-Aland, *Greek-English New Testament* (8th edn. Stuttgart, 1994), 684–718.

18. Duffy, *Saints and Sinners*, 314.

19. EE 4, 772–787.

20. Encyclical *Pascendi Dominici Gregis* of 8 September 1907, EE 4, 206–309; trans. Vatican website.

21. Duffy, *Saints and Sinners*, 328.

22. Carlo Falconi, *The Popes in the Twentieth Century* (London, 1967), 35.

23. *ibid.*, 54.

24. Alec R. Vidler, *The Modernist Movement in the Roman Church* (Cambridge, 1934), 270–271.

25. F.A. MacNutt, *A Papal Chamberlain* (London, 1936), 313.

26. Encyclical *Ad Beatissimi Apostolorum* of 1 November 1914, clauses 24–25, EE 4, 484–486; trans. Vatican website.

27. David Alvarez, *Spies in the Vatican* (Lawrence, Ks., 2002), 115.

28. MacNutt, *Papal Chamberlain*, 217 and 221; Pollard, *Money and the Rise of the Modern Papacy*, 62.

29. Pollard, *Money and the Rise of the Modern Papacy*, 60.

30. MacNutt, *Papal Chamberlain*, 146.

31. Denis Mack Smith, *Italy and its Monarchy* (New Haven and London, 1989), 166.

32. *ibid.*, 267.

33. Alvarez, *Spies in the Vatican*, 120–121.

34. John F. Pollard, *The Unknown Pope* (London and New York, 1999), 59.

35. Falconi, *Popes in the Twentieth Century*, 151.

36. Owen Chadwick, *A History of the Popes 1830-1914* (Oxford, 1998), 16–17.

37. *Conventiones inter Sanctam Sedem et Italiae Regnum*, in AAS XXI/6 of 7 June 1929, 273.

38. *ibid.*, 227.

39. *ibid.*, 273.

40. Quoted in Owen Chadwick, *Britain and the Vatican During the Second World War* (Cambridge, 1986), 56.

41. Pollard, *Money and the Rise of the Modern Papacy,* 33 gives the figures.

42. *ibid.*, 112–121.

43. *ibid.*, 136.

44. David Gibson, *The Rule of Benedict* (San Francisco, 2006), 283.

45. Pollard, *Unknown Pope,* 171–173.

46. Encyclical *Non abbiamo bisogno* of 29 June 1931, clause 12, EE 5, 804–805, trans. Vatican website.

47. Encyclical *Mit brennender Sorge* of 14 March 1937, clause 3, EE 5, 1076; trans. Vatican website.

48. Georges Passelecq and Bernard Suchecky, *L'Encyclique cachée de Pie XI* (Paris, 1995), 219–310.

49. Quoted in Chadwick, *Britain and the Vatican,* 34.

CHAPTER 21

1. Owen Chadwick, *Britain and the Vatican During the Second World War* (Cambridge, 1986), 52.

2. Encyclical *Summi Pontificatus* of 20th October 1939, clause 34, EE 6; trans. Vatican website.

3. *ibid.*, clauses 38 and 29.

4. See David Alvarez, *Spies in the Vatican* (Lawrence, Ks., 2002), 173–184.

5. *ibid.*, 187.

6. Ian Kershaw, *Hitler, 1936–1945: Nemesis* (London, 2000), 596.

7. William Simpson, *A Vatican Lifeline '44* (London, 1995), 186.

8. Encyclical *Summi Pontificatus* clause 14, EE 6.

9. Encyclicals *Ecclesiae Fastos* of 5th June 1954, clause 16, and *Doctor Mellifluus* of 24th May 1953, clause 3, EE 6.

10. http:www.vatican.va/holy_father/pius_xii/apost_letters/documents/hf_p-xii_apl_21081958_st-claire_fr.html

11. Carlo Falconi, *The Popes in the Twentieth Century* (English trans. London, 1967), xi.

12. *ibid.*, 303.

13. Frederic J. Baumgartner, *Behind Locked Doors: A History of the Papal Elections* (New York and Basingstoke, 2005), 209–210 and 215.

14. *S.D.N. D. Urbani Divina Providentia Papae VIII, Confirmatio Bullae Gregorii XV de electione Romani Pontificis* (Rome, 1626).

15. Baumgartner, *Behind Locked Doors*, 216.

16. Falconi, *The Popes in the Twentieth Century*, xi.

17. Peter Hebblethwaite, *In the Vatican* (Oxford, 1987), 34.

18. John F. Pollard, *Money and the Rise of the Modern Papacy* (Cambridge, 2005), 12.

19. Hebblethwaite, *In the Vatican*, 327–328, citing Mgr. Pericle Felici.

20. *Discorso per la solenne apertura del SS. Concilio,* 11 October 1962, para. 3.1: AAS 54 (1962), 785–795.

21. J.R.R. Tolkien, letter to Michael Tolkien of 1st November 1963, in Humphrey Carpenter (ed.), *The Letters of J.R.R. Tolkien* (London, 1981), 339.

22. Baumgartner, *Behind Locked Doors*, 221.

23. Encyclical *Ecclesiam suam* of August 6th 1964, clause 11, EE 7.

24. Motu Proprio *Apostolica Solicitudine* of 15th September 1965: http:www.vatican.va/holy_father/paul_vi/motu_proprio/documents/hf_p-vi_motu-proprio_19650915_apostolica-sollicitudo_en.html

25. Congregation for the Doctrine of the Faith, *Notification on the works of Father Jon Sobrino S.J.*, 26 November 2006. (Vatican website, English version).

26. *ibid.*, *Notification on the book 'Jesus the symbol of God' by Father Roger Haight S.J.*, 13 December 2004. (Vatican website).

27. ibid., *Responses to questions regarding certain aspects of the Doctrine of the Church*, 29 June 2007, questions 4 and 5. (Vatican website).

28. Encyclical *Humanae Vitae* of 25 July 1968, clause 2. Original version in AAS 60 (1968), 481–503; trans. Vatican website.

29. *ibid.*, clause 6.

30. *ibid.*, clause 21.

31. *ibid.*, clause 18.

32. John Cornwell, *A Thief in the Night: The Death of Pope John Paul I* (London, 1989), 184–190.

33. http:www.padrepio.catholicwebservices.com/ENGLISH/The_Devil.htm

34. John Cornwell, *The Pope in Winter: the Dark Face of John Paul II's Papacy* (London, 2004), 218–233.

35. David Gibson, *The Rule of Benedict: Pope Benedict XVI and his Battle with the Modern World* (New York, 2006), 38.

36. See their websites: http:popemichael.homestead.com/whoispope-michael.html, and http:www.geocities.com/Area51/Lair/7170/ibio1.htm

37. Baumgartner, *Behind Locked Doors*, 215. See http:www.thepopeinred.com/

38. *Discorso per la solenne apertura* 4.3.

39. Tarcisio Bertoni, 'Introduction' to *The Message of Fatima* (Vatican City, 2000), 3.

40. *ibid.*, 4.

41. *The Message of Fatima* (Vatican City, 2000), 21.

42. *ibid.*, 3.

43. *ibid.*, 41–42.

44. Benedict XVI, address during the General Audience of Wednesday 2nd July 2008: http:www.vatican.va/holy_father/benedict_xvi/audiences/2008/documents/hf_ben-xvi_aud_20080702_en.html

45. Gibson, *Rule of Benedict*, 302–303.

46. Pope Benedict XVI, *Jesus of Nazareth* (English trans. London, 2007), xxiii–xxiv.

SELECTED BIBLIOGRAPHY

General

Barraclough, Geoffrey, *The Medieval Papacy* (London, 1968).

Duffy, Eamon, *Saints and Sinners: a History of the Popes* (3rd edn. New Haven and London, 2006).

Enciclopedia dei Papi (3 vols. Rome, 2000).

Eno, Robert B., *The Rise of the Papacy* (Wilmington, Del., 1990) [origins to 6ᵗʰ century]

Fliche, Augustin and Victor Martin (ed.), *Histoire de l'Eglise* (21 vols. Paris, 1946–1952).

Jalland, T.G., *The Church and the Papacy* (London, 1944).

Kelly, J.N.D., *Oxford Dictionary of the Popes* (Oxford and New York, 1986).

Levillain, Philippe (ed.), *Dictionnaire historique de la Papauté* (Paris, 1994).

Norman, Edward, *The Roman Catholic Church: An Illustrated History* (London, 2007).

Schimmelpfennig, Bernhard, *Das Papsttum. Von der Antike bis zur Renaissance* (3rd edn. Darmstadt, 1988); English trans. *The Papacy* (New York, 1992).

Steimer, Bruno and Michael G. Parker (ed.), *Dictionary of the Popes and the Papacy* (English trans. New York, 2001).

Tronzo, William (ed.), *St. Peter's in the Vatican* (Cambridge, 2005).

Ullmann, Walter, *The Growth of Papal Government in the Middle Ages* (2nd edn. London, 1962).

Ullmann, Walter, *A Short History of the Papacy in the Middle Ages* (London, 1972).

Walsh, Michael, *Pocket Dictionary of Popes* (London, 2006).

Source Studies and Guides

Blouin, Francis X, and others, *Vatican Archives: an Inventory and Guide to the Historical Documents of the Holy See* (New York and Oxford, 1998).

Boyle, Leonard E., *A Survey of the Vatican Archives and of its Medieval Holdings* (Toronto, 1972).

Chadwick, Owen, *Catholicism and History: the Opening of the Vatican Archives* (Cambridge, 1978).

Duchesne, Louis (ed.), *Le Liber Pontificalis* (2nd edn. 3 vols. Rome, 1955).

Fabre, Paul, *Etude sur le Liber Censuum de l'Eglise Romaine* (Paris, 1892).

Foerster, Hans (ed.), *Liber Diurnus Romanorum Pontificum* (Bern, 1958).

Frenz, Thomas, *Papsturkunden des Mittelalters und Neuzeit* (2nd edn. Stuttgart, 2000).

Fuhrmann, Horst, *Einfluss und Verbreitung der pseudoisidorischen Fälschung: Von ihrem Auftachen bis in die neuere Zeit* (3 vols. MGH Schriften, 1972–1974).

Gualdo, Germano (ed.), *Sussidi per la consultazione dell' Archivio Vaticano* (Vatican City, 1989).

Hack, Achim Thomas, *Codex Carolinus* (2 vols. Stuttgart, 2007).

Jamme, Armand and Olivier Poncet (ed.), *Offices, Ecrit et Papauté (XIIIe–XVIIe siècle)* (Rome, 2007).

Lohrmann, Dietrich, *Das Register Papst Johannes VIII* (Tübingen, 1968).

Lunt, William E., *Papal Revenues in the Middle Ages* (2 vols. New York, 1934).

Natalini, Terzo, *Archivio Segreto Vaticano* (Vatican City, 2000).

Pitz, Ernst, *Papstreskripte im frühen Mittelalter* (Sigmaringen, 1990).

Poole, R.L., *The Papal Chancery* (Cambridge, 1915).

Rabikauskas, Paul, *Die römische Kuriale in der päpstlichen Kanzlei* (Rome, 1958).

Santifaller, Leo, *Liber Diurnus* (Stuttgart, 1976).

Sayers, Jane E., *Original Papal Documents in England and Wales from the Accession of Pope Innocent III to the Death of Pope Benedict XI (1198–1304)* (Oxford, 1999).

Tu es Petrus: il tempio di Pietro nelle medaglie dei papi: Catalogo della mostra (Vatican City, 2007).

CANON LAW

Brundage, James A., *Medieval Canon Law* (London and New York, 1995).

Gaudemet, Jean, *Les sources du droit de l'Eglise en Occident du IIe au VIIe siècle* (Paris, 1985).

Gaudemet, Jean, *Eglise et Cité. Histoire du droit canonique* (Paris, 1994).

Gilchrist, John, *The Collection in Seventy-Four Titles: a Canon Law Manual of the Gregorian Reform* (Toronto, 1980).

Jasper, Detlev and Horst Fuhrmann, *Papal Letters in the Early Middle Ages* (Washington, D.C., 2001).

Kuttner, Stephan, *Medieval Councils, Decretals and Collections of Canon Law: Selected Essays* (London, 1980).

Somerville, Robert and Bruce C. Brasington, *Prefaces to Canon Law Books in Latin Christianity: Selected Translations, 500–1245* (New Haven and London, 1998).

Somerville, Robert, with Stephan Kuttner, *Pope Urban II, the 'Collectio Britannica' and the Council of Melfi (1089)* (Oxford, 1996).

Winroth, Anders, *The Making of Gratian's Decretum* (Cambridge, 2000).

Ziólek, Ladislao, *Sede vacante nihil innovetur* (Rome, 1966).

CHAPTER 1

Apollonj Ghetti, B.M. *et alii*, *Saecularia Petri et Pauli* (Vatican City, 1969).

Brown, Raymond E., Karl P. Donfried, and John Reumann (ed.), *Peter in the New Testament* (Minneapolis, 1973).

Campenhausen, Hans von, *Ecclesiastical Authority and Spiritual Power in the Church of the First Three Centuries* (English tr. Peabody, Mass., 1997).

Curran, John, 'The Bones of St. Peter?', *Classics Ireland* 3 (1996), pp. 18–46.

Donati, Angela (ed.), *Pietro e Paolo. La storia, il culto, la memoria nei primi secoli* (Milan, 2000).

Donfried, Karl P. (ed.), *The Romans Debate* (revised edn. Peabody, Mass., 1991).

Donfried, Karl P. and Peter Richardson (ed.), *Judaism and Christianity in First-Century Rome* (Grand Rapids, Mich., and Cambridge, 1998).

Eisen, Ute E., *Women Officeholders in Early Christianity* (English tr. Collegeville, Minn., 2000).

Faivre, Alexandre, *Naissance d'une hiérarchie: les premières étapes du cursus clérical* (Paris, 1977).

Fiocchi Nicolai, Vincenzo and Jean Guyon (ed.) *Origine delle catacombe Romane* (Vatican City, 2006).

Gnilka, Joachim, *Petrus und Romi Das Petrusbild in den ersten zwei Jahrhunderten* (Breisgau, 2002).

Guarducci, Margherita, *Le Reliquie di Pietro in Vaticano* (Rome, 1995).

Il Primato del Successore di Pietro: Atti del Simposio Teologico (Vatican City, 1998).

King, Karen L., *What Is Gnosticism?* (Cambridge, Mass., and London, 2003).

Lampe, Peter, *From Paul to Valentinus: Christians at Rome in the First Two Centuries* (English tr. Minneapolis, 2003).

Meeks, Wayne A., *The First Urban Christians* (New Haven and London, 1983).

Murphy-O'Connor, Jerome, *Paul: A Critical Life* (Oxford, 1996).

O'Connor, Daniel W., *Peter in Rome: the Literary, Liturgical and Archaeological Evidence* (New York and London, 1969).

Pani Ermini, Letizia and Paolo Siniscalco (ed.), *La comunità cristiana di Roma, la sua vita e la sua cultura dalle origini all'alto medioevo* (Vatican, 2000).

Perkins, Pheme, *Peter, Apostle for the Whole Church* (Edinburgh, 2000).

Pietro e Paolo. Il loro rapporto con Roma nelle testimonianze antiche (Rome, 2001).

Toynbee, Jocelyn and John Ward-Perkins, *The Shrine of St. Peter and the Vatican Excavations* (London, 1956).

Williams, Michael Allen, *Rethinking Gnosticism* (Princeton, 1996).

Chapter 2

Barnes, Timothy D., *Tertullian, a Historical and Literary Study* (Oxford, 1971).

Bowersock, G.W., *Martyrdom and Rome* (Cambridge, 1995).

Burns, J. Patout, *Cyprian the Bishop* (London and New York, 2002).

Davis, R., 'Pre-Constantinian Chronology: the Roman Bishopric from AD 258 to 314', *Journal of Theological Studies* new series vol. 48 (1997), pp. 439–470.

Finney, Paul Corby, *The Invisible God: the Earliest Christians on Art* (Oxford, 1994).

Fiocchi Nicolai, Vicenzo, Fabrizio Bisconti, and Danilo Mazzoleni, *The Christian Catacombs of Rome. History, Decoration, Inscriptions* (Regensburg, 1999).

Frend, W.H.C., *Martyrdom and Persecution in the Early Church* (Oxford, 1965).

Grant, Robert M., *Irenaeus of Lyons* (London, 1997).

Grig, Lucy, *Making Martyrs in Late Antiquity* (London, 2004).

Matthews, Thomas F., *The Clash of Gods: a Reinterpretation of Early Christian Art* (Princeton, 1993).

Musurillo, Herbert (ed. and tr.), *The Acts of the Christian Martyrs* (Oxford, 1972).

Reekmans, Louis, *La tombe du pape Corneille et sa région cémétériale* (Vatican City, 1964).

Reekmans, Louis, *Le complexe cémétérial du pape Gaius dans la Catacombe de Callixte* (Vatican City, 1988).

CHAPTER 3

Barnes, Timothy D., *Athanasius and Constantius* (Cambridge, Mass., and London, 1993).

Curran, John, *Pagan City and Christian Capital: Rome in the Fourth Century* (Oxford, 2000).

Drake, H.A., *Constantine and the Bishops* (Baltimore and London, 2000).

Ferrua, Antonio (ed.), *Epigrammata Damasiana* (Vatican City, 1942).

Geertman, Herman, 'Hic Fecit Basilicam': Studi sul 'Liber Pontificalis' e gli edifici ecclesiastici di Roma di Silvestro a Silverio* (Leuven and Paris, 2004).

Holloway, R. Ross, *Constantine and Rome* (New Haven and London, 2004).

Huskinson, J.M., *Concordia Apostolorum: Christian Propaganda at Rome in the Fourth and Fifth Centuries* (Oxford, 1982).

Pietri, Charles, *Roma Cristiana. Recherches sur l'Eglise de Rome, son organisation, sa politique, son idéologie de Miltiade à Sixte III (311–440)* (2 vols. Rome, 1976).

Saecularia Damasiana (Vatican City, 1986).

Shotwell, James T. and Louise Ropes Loomis, *The See of Peter* (New York, 1927).

CHAPTER 4

Cabié, Robert, *La lettre du Pape Innocent I à Décentius de Gubbio* (Louvain, 1973).

Frend, W.H.C., *The Rise of the Monophysite Movement* (Cambridge, 1972).

Grillmeier, A. and H. Bacht (ed.), *Das Konzil von Chalkedon: Geschichte und Gegenwart* (3 vols. Würzburg, 1953–1962).

Holleman, A.W.J., *Pope Gelasius I and the Lupercalia* (Amsterdam, 1974).

Jalland, Trevor, *The Life and Times of St. Leo the Great* (London, 1941).

Sellers, R.V., *The Council of Chalcedon* (London, 1961).

Ullmann, Walter, *Gelasius I (492–496)* (Stuttgart, 1981).

Wessel, Susan, *Cyril of Alexandria and the Nestorian Controversy* (Oxford, 2006).

CHAPTER 5

Blair-Dixon, Kate, 'Memory and authority in sixth-century Rome: the *Liber Pontificalis* and the *Collectio Avellana*', in Kate Cooper and Julia Hillner (ed.), *Religion, Dynasty and Patronage in Early Christian Rome* (Cambridge, 2007), 59-75.

Gray, Patrick T.R., *The Defense of Chalcedon in the East (451–553)* (Leiden, 1979).

Grillmeier, Alois, *Christ in Christian Tradition*, vol. 2.2 (English trans. London and Louisville, 1995).

Moorhead, John, *Theoderic in Italy* (Oxford, 1973).

Noble, Thomas F.X., 'Theoderic and the Papacy', in *Theoderico il grande e i Goti d'Italia* (Spoleto, 1993), 395–423.

Richards, Jeffrey, *The Popes and the Papacy in the Early Middle Ages, 476–752* (London and Boston, 1979).

Sotinel, Claire, 'Autorité pontificale et pouvoir impérial sous le règne de Justinien: le pape Vigile', *Mélanges de l'Ecole française d'Athènes et de Rome* 104.1 (1992), 439–463.

Sotinel, Claire, 'Emperors and Popes in the Sixth Century: The Western View', in Michael Maas (ed.), *The Cambridge Companion to the Age of Justinian* (Cambridge, 2005), 267–290.

CHAPTER 6

Azzara, Claudio, *L'ideologia del potere regio nel papato altomedievale (secoli VI al VIII)* (Spoleto, 1997).

Cavadini, John C. (ed.), *Gregory the Great: a Symposium* (Notre Dame and London, 1995).

Dagens, Claude, *Saint Grégoire le Grand. Culture et expérience chrétienne* (Paris, 1977).

Fontaine, Jacques, Robert Gillet and Stan Pellistrandi (ed.), *Grégoire le Grand* (Paris, 1986).

Gregorio Magno e il suo tempo (2 vols. Rome, 1991).

Gregorio Magno nel XIV centenario della morte (Rome, 2004).

Homes Dudden, F., *Gregory the Great: his Place in History and Thought* (2 vols. London, 1905).

Llewellyn, Peter, *Rome in the Dark Ages* (London, 1971).

Marcus, Robert, *Gregory the Great and his World* (Cambridge, 1997).

Richards, Jeffrey, *Consul of God: the Life and Times of Gregory the Great* (London, 1980).

Straw, Carole, *Gregory the Great: Perfection in Imperfection* (Berkeley and London, 1988).

CHAPTER 7

Arnaldi, Girolamo, *Le origini dello Stato della Chiesa* (Turin, 1987).

Bertolini, Ottorino, *Roma di fronte a Bisanzio e ai Longobardi* (Bologna, 1941).

Bertolini, Ottorino, *Scritti scelti di storia medioevale* (2 vols. Livorno, 1968).

Brown, T.S., *Gentlemen and Officers. Imperial Administration and Aristocratic Power in Byzantine Italy A.D. 554–800* (Rome, 1984).

Duchesne, Louis, *The Beginnings of the Temporal Sovereignty of the Popes A.D. 754–1073* (English trans. London, 1908).

Fritze, Wolfgang, *Papst und Frankenkönig* (Sigmaringen, 1973).

Hallenbeck, Jan T., *Pavia and Rome: the Lombard Monarchy and the Papacy in the Eighth Century* (Philadelphia, 1982).

Marazzi, Federico, 'Il conflitto fra Leone III Isaurico e il papato e il "definitivo" inizio del medioevo a Roma', *Papers of the British School at Rome* 59 (1991), 231-257.

Marazzi, Federico, I *'Patrimonia Sanctae Romanae Ecclesiae' nel Lazio (secoli IV–X)* (Rome, 1998).

Noble, Thomas F.X., *The Republic of St. Peter: the Birth of the Papal State 680–825* (Philadelphia, 1984).

Zanini, Enrico, *Le Italie Bizantine* (Bari, 1998).

Chapter 8

Angenendt, Arnold and Rudolf Schieffer, *Roma—Caput et Fons* (Opladen, 1989).

Cammarosano, Paolo, *Nobili e re. L'Italia politica dell'alto medioevo* (Rome-Bari, 1998).

Carlo Magno a Roma (Rome, 2001).

Classen, Peter, *Karl der Grosse, das Papsttum und Byzanz* (Sigmaringen, 1985).

Costambeys, Mario, *Power and Patronage in Early Medieval Italy: Local Society, Italian Politics, and the Abbey of Farfa, c. 700–900* (Cambridge, 2007).

Fried, Johannes, *'Donation of Constantine' and 'Constitutum Constantini'* (Berlin and New York, 2007).

Roma e l'etá carolingia. Atti delle giornate di studio 3–8 Maggio 1976 (Rome, 1976).

Smith, Julia M.H. (ed.), *Early Medieval Rome and the Christian West* (Leiden and Boston, 2000).

Chapter 9

Arnaldi, Girolamo, *Natale 875. Politica, ecclesiologia, cultura del papato altomedievale* (Rome, 1990).

Bacchiega, Mario, *Papa Formoso* (Foggia, 1983).

Dümmler, Ernst, *Auxilius und Vulgarius* (Leipzig, 1866).

Gerbert l'Européen. Actes du Colloque d'Aurillac (Aurillac, 1997).

Hamilton, Bernard, *Monastic Reform, Catharism and the Crusades* (London, 1979), items I–VI.

Johrendt, Jochen, *Papsttum und Landeskirchen im Spiegel der päpstlichen Urkunden (896-1046)* (Hanover, 2004).

Lapôtre, Arthur, *De Anastasio Bibliothecario* (Paris, 1885).

Zimmermann, Harald, *Das dunkle Jahrhundert* (Graz/Vienna/Cologne, 1971).

Chapter 10

Blumenthal, Uta-Renate, *Gregory VII. Papst zwischen Canossa und Kirchenreform* (Darmstadt, 2001).

Cowdrey, H.E.J., *The Cluniacs and the Gregorian Reform* (Oxford, 1970).

Cowdrey, H.E.J., *The Age of Abbot Desiderius* (Oxford, 1983).

Cowdrey, H.E.J., *Pope Gregory VII 1073–1085* (Oxford, 1998).

Cushing, Kathleen G., *Papacy and Law in the Gregorian Revolution* (Oxford, 1998).

Cushing, Kathleen G., *Reform and the Papacy in the Eleventh Century* (Manchester and New York, 2005).

Di Carpegna Falconieri, Tommaso, *Il clero di Roma nel medioevo* (Rome, 2002).

Falkenstein, Ludwig, *La papauté et les abbayes françaises aux XIe et XIIe siècles: exemption et protection* (Paris, 1997).

Guarneri, Valeria, *I Conti di Toscolo (999-1179). Caratteri delle vicende familiari, dell'assetto patrimoniale e del loro Adelspapsttum* (Rome, 1997).

Herrmann, Klaus-J., *Das Tuskulanerpapsttum (1012–1046)* (Stuttgart, 1973).

Robinson, Ian, *The Papacy 1078–1198: Continuity and Innovation* (Cambridge, 1990).

Robinson, Ian, *Henry IV of Germany, 1056–1106* (Cambridge, 1999).

Robinson, Ian, *The Papal Reform of the Eleventh Century* (Manchester, 2004).

Steigmann, Christoph and Matthias Wermhoff (ed.), *Canossa 1077. Erschütterung der Welt* (2 vols. Munich, 2006).

Szabó-Bechstein, Brigitte, *Libertas Ecclesiae. Ein Schlüsselbegriff des Investiturstreits und seine Vorgeschichte* (Rome, 1985).

Violante, Cinzio, '*Chiesa feudale' e riforme in Occidente (sec. X–XIII)* (Spoleto, 1999).

CHAPTER 11

Bolton, Brenda and Anne J. Duggan (ed.), *Adrian IV the English Pope (1154–1159)* (Aldershot, 2003).

Cantarella, Glauco Maria, *Il costruzione della verità. Pasquale II, un papa alle strette* (Rome, 1987).

Classen, Peter, *Gerhoch von Reichersberg. Eine Biographie* (Wiesbaden, 1960).

Gleber, Helmut, *Papst Eugen III (1145–1153) unter besonderer Berücksichtigung seiner politischen Tätigkeit* (Jena, 1936).

Pacaut, Marcel, *Alexandre III* (Paris, 1956).

Stroll, Mary, *The Jewish Pope: Ideology and Politics in the Papal Schism of 1130* (Leiden and New York, 1987).

Stroll, Mary, *Symbols as Power: The Papacy following the Investiture Contest* (Leiden and New York, 1991).

Stroll, Mary, *The Medieval Abbey of Farfa: Target of Papal and Imperial Ambitions* (Leiden and New York, 1997).

Stroll, Mary, *Callixtus II (1119–1124): a pope born to rule* (Leiden and Boston, 2004).

Twyman, Susan, *Papal Ceremonial at Rome in the Twelfth Century* (London, 2002).

CHAPTER 12

Baiello, Laura, *Il Papa e la città: papato e comuni in Italia centro-settentrionale durante la prima metà del secolo XIII* (Spoleto, 2007).

Birch, Debra J., *Pilgrimage to Rome in the Middle Ages* (Woodbridge, 1998).

Bliss, H.W., *Calendar of Entries in Papal Registers Relating to Great Britain and Ireland vol. 1: 1198–1304* (London, 1893).

Bolton, Brenda, *Innocent III: Studies on Papal Authority and Pastoral Care* (Aldershot, 1995).

Clausen, Johannes, *Papst Honorius III (1216–1227)* (Bonn, 1895, reprinted Hildesheim, 2004).

Claussen, Peter, *Die Kirchen der Stadt Rom im Mittelalter 1050–1300*: vol. II: S. Giovanni in Laterano (Stuttgart, 2008).

Doran, John and Damian J. Smith, (ed.), *Pope Celestine III (1191–1198): Diplomat and Pastor* (Aldershot, 2008).

Franchi, A. *Il conclave di Viterbo (1268–1271) e le sue origini* (Assisi, 1993).

Laurent, M.-H., *Le bienheureux Innocent V et son temps* (Vatican City, 1947).

Linehan, Peter, *The Spanish Church and the Papacy in the Thirteenth Century* (Cambridge, 1971).

Moore, John C., *Pope Innocent III (1160/1–1216): to Root Up and to Plant* (Leiden and Boston, 2003).

Paravicini Bagliani, Agostino, *Il Trono di Pietro. L'universalità del papato da Alessandro III a Bonifacio VIII* (Rome, 1996).

Pennington, Kenneth, *Pope and Bishops: The Papal Monarchy in the Twelfth and Thirteenth Centuries* (Philadelphia, 1984).

Powell, James M. (trans.), *The Deeds of Pope Innocent III by an Anonymous Author* (Washington, D.C., 2004).

Sayers, Jane, *Innocent III: Leader of Europe 1198–1216* (London, 1994).

Sommerlechner, Andrea (ed.), *Innocenzo III. Urbs et Orbis: Atti del*

Congresso Internazionale Roma, 9–15 settembre 1998 (2 vols. Rome, 2003).

Tillmann, Helene, *Pope Innocent III* (English trans. Amsterdam, 1980).

CHAPTER 13

Baethgen, Friedrich, *Der Engelpapst* (Leipzig, 1943).

Barrell, A.D.M., *The Papacy, Scotland and Northern England, 1342–1378* (Cambridge, 1995).

Boase, T.S.R., *Boniface the Eighth 1294–1303* (London, 1933).

Burr, David, *The Spiritual Franciscans* (University Park, Pa., 2001).

Capezzali, Walter (ed.), *Celestino V Papa Angelico* (L'Aquila, 1991).

Favier, Jean, *Les Papes d'Avignon* (Paris, 2006).

Frugoni, Chiara, *Due Papi per un Giubileo* (Milan, 2000).

Gardner, Julian, *The Tomb and the Tiara: Curial Sculpture in Rome and Avignon in the Later Middle Ages* (Oxford, 1992).

Gatto, Ludovico, *Celestino V, pontefice e santo* (Rome, 2006).

Golinelli, Paolo, *Il Papa Contadino: Celestino V e il suo tempo* (Florence, 1996).

Guillemain, Bernard, *Les papes d'Avignon 1309–1376* (Paris, 1998).

Heft, James, *John XXII and Papal Teaching Authority* (Lewiston, N.Y., 1986).

Herde, Peter, *Coelestin V* (Stuttgart, 1981).

Housely, Norman, *The Avignon Papacy and the Crusades* (Oxford, 1986).

Jacopone da Todi e l'arte in Umbria nel suo tempo (Milan, 2006).

Larner, John, *The Lords of Romagna* (London, 1965).

Lunt, William, *Papal Revenues in the Middle Ages* (2 vols. New York, 1934).

Menache, Sophia, *Clement V* (Cambridge, 1998).

Mollat, Michel, *Les Papes d'Avignon 1307–78* (9th edn. Paris, 1949; 10th edn. 1965).

Morris, Bridget, *St. Birgitta of Sweden* (Woodbridge, 1999).

Musto, Ronald G., *Apocalypse in Rome: Cola di Rienzo and the Politics of the New Age* (Berkeley and London, 2003).

Nold, Patrick, *Pope John XXII and his Franciscan Cardinal* (Oxford, 2003).

Pauler, Roland, *Die deutschen Könige und Italien im 14 Jahrhundert* (Darmstadt, 1997).

Renouard, Yves, *The Avignon Papacy 1305–1403* (English trans. London, 1970).

Tosti-Croce, Marina Righetti, *Bonifacio VIII e il suo tempo* (Milan, 2000).

Vones, Ludwig, *Urban V. (1362–1370) Kirchenreform zwischen Kardinalkollegium, Kurie und Klientel* (Stuttgart, 1998).

Wood, Diana, *Clement VI* (Cambridge, 1989).

CHAPTER 14

Ady, Cecilia M., *The Bentivoglio of Bologna* (Oxford, 1937).

Blumenthal-Kosinski, Renate, *Poets, Saints, and Visionaries of the Great Schism: 1378–1417* (University Park, Pa., 2006).

Brandmüller, Walter, *Das Konzil von Kontanz 1414–1418* (2nd edn. 2 vols., Paderborn, 1997/9).

Chiabò, M. (ed.), *Alle origini della nuova Roma: Martino V (1417–1431)* (Rome, 1992).

Crowder, C.M.D., *Unity, Heresy and Reform 1378–1460* (London, 1977).

Delaruelle, Etienne, Edmond-René Labande, and Paul Ourliac (ed.), *L'Eglise au temps du Grand Schisme et de la crise conciliaire (1378–1449)* (2 vols. Paris, 1962).

Esch, Arnold, *Bonifatius IX und der Kirchenstaat* (Tübingen, 1969).

Genèse et débuts du Grand Schisme d'Occident. Colloque (Paris, 1980).

Gill, Joseph, *Eugenius IV, Pope of Christian Union* (London, 1961).

Glasfurd, Alec, *The Antipope. Peter de Luna 1342–1423* (London, 1965).

Harvey, Margaret, *The English in Rome, 1362–1420: Portrait of an Expatriate Community* (Cambridge, 2000).

Jacob, Ernest Fraser, *Essays in the Conciliar Epoch* (3rd edn. Manchester, 1963).

Kaminsky, Howard, 'The Great Schism', in Michael Jones (ed.), *New Cambridge Medieval History*, vol. 6 (Cambridge, 2000), 674–696.

Landi, Aldo, *Il papa deposto (Pisa 1409). L'idea conciliare nel Grande Scisma* (Turin, 1985).

Mongiano, Elisa, *La cancelleria di un Antipapa (Il bollario di Felice V)* (Turin, 1988).

Oakley, Francis, *The Conciliarist Tradition: Constitutionalism in the Catholic Church 1300–1870* (Oxford, 2003).

Partner, Peter, *The Papal State under Martin V* (London, 1958).

Perroy, Edouard, *L'Angleterre et le Grand Schisme d'Occident* (Paris, 1933).

Smith, J.H., *The Great Schism, 1378: The Disintegration of the Papacy* (London, 1970).

Suarez Fernández, Luis, *Castilla, el Cisma y la crisis conciliar (1378–1440)* (Madrid, 1960).

Suarez Fernández, Luis, *Benedicto XIII* (Barcelona, 2002).

Swanson, R.N., *Universities, Academics and the Great Schism* (Cambridge, 1979).

Trexler, Richard C., 'Rome on the Eve of the Great Schism', *Speculum* 42 (1967), 489–509.

Ullmann, Walter, *The Origins of the Great Schism* (London, 1948).

CHAPTER 15

Bonatti F. and A. Manfredi (ed.), *Niccolò V nel sesto centenario della nascita* (Vatican City, 2000).

Brezzi, P. (ed.), *Humanismo a Roma nel Quattrocento* (New York and Rome, 1984).

Carli, Enzo, *Pienza: la città di Pio II* (3rd edn. Rome, 1993).

Chambers, D.S., *Popes, Cardinals and War* (London, 2006).

Cloulas, Ivan, *Jules II* (Paris, 1990).

Corbo, Anna Maria, *Pio II Piccolomini, un Papa umanista* (Rome, 2002).

D'Amico, John F., *Renaissance Humanism in Papal Rome* (Baltimore and London, 1983).

Grafton, Anthony (ed.), *Rome Reborn. The Vatican Library and Renaissance Culture* (Washington D.C., 1993).

Howe, Eunice D., *Art and Culture at the Sistine Court* (Vatican City, 2005).

I Borgia (Milan, 2002).

Johnson, Marion, *The Borgias* (London, 1981).

Jones, Philip, *The Malatesta of Rimini and the Papal State* (Cambridge, 1974).

Lee, E., *Sixtus IV and Men of Letters* (Rome, 1978).

Mallett, Michael, *The Borgias* (London, 1969).

Martines, Lauro, *Scourge and Fire: Savonarola and Renaissance Italy* (London, 2006).

Miglio, Massimo, Francesca Niutta, Diego Quaglioni, and Concetta Ranieri (ed.), *Un pontificato ed una città. Sisto IV (1471–1484)* (Vatican City, 1986).

Mitchell, R.J., *The Laurels and the Tiara: Pope Pius II 1458–1464* (London, 1962).

Nucciarelli, Franco Ivan, *Pinturicchio: il bambin Gesù delle mani* (Perugia, 2007).

O'Malley, John W., *Praise and Blame in Renaissance Rome: Rhetoric, Doctrine and Reform in the Sacred Orators of the Papal Court, c. 1450–1521* (Durham, N.C., 1979).

Partner, Peter, *The Pope's Men: the Papal Civil Service in the Renaissance* (Oxford, 1990).

Partridge, Loren, *Art of the Renaissance in Rome 1400–1600* (Upper Saddle River, N.J., 1996).

Paschini, Pio, *Lodovico Cardinal Camerlengo (+1465)* (Rome, 1939).

Pastor, Ludwig, *History of the Popes*, vols. I–VI (London, 1908).

Reinhardt, Volker, *Der unheimliche Papst. Alexander VI Borgia 1431–1503* (Munich, 2005).

Secchi Tarugi, Luisa (ed.), *Pio II umanista Europeo* (Florence, 2007).

Shaw, Christine, *Julius II the Warrior Pope* (Oxford and Cambridge, Mass., 1993).

Sodi, Manlio and Arianna Antoniutti (ed.), *Enea Silvio Piccolomini, Pius Secundus Poeta Laureatus Pontifex Maximus* (Rome, 2007).

Stringer, Charles L., *The Renaissance in Rome* (rev. edn. Bloomington and Indianapolis, 1998).

Tafuri, Manfredo, 'Nicholas V and Leon Battista Alberti' in *idem, Interpreting the Renaissance: Princes, Cities, Architects* (English trans. New Haven and London, 2006), 23–58.

Terzoli, Maria Antonietta (ed.), *Enea Silvio Piccolomini: Uomo di lettere e mediatore di cultura* (Basel, 2006).

CHAPTER 16

Alexander, John, *From Renaissance to Counter-Reformation: The Architectural Patronage of Carlo Borromeo during the Reign of Pius IV* (Milan, 2007).

Aubert, A., *Paolo IV: Politica, inquisizione e storiografia* (2nd edn. Florence, 1999).

Borromeo, Agostino (ed.), *L'Inquisizione: Atti del Simposio internazionale* (Vatican City, 2003).

Chadwick, Owen, *The Reformation* (revised edn. London, 1972).

Fenlon, Dermot, *Heresy and Obedience in Tridentine Italy: Cardinal Pole and the Counter–Reformation* (Cambridge, 1973).

Firpo, Massimo, *Inquisizione Romana e Contrariforma: Studi sul Cardinal Giovanni Morone (1509–1580) e il suo processo d'eresia* (Brescia, 2005).

Fosi, Irene, *La società violenta. Il bandetismo nello Stato Pontificio nella seconda metà del Cinquecento* (Rome, 1985).

Gamrath, Helge, *Farnese: Pomp, Power and Politics in Renaissance Rome* (Rome, 2007).

Gattoni, Maurizio, *Leone X e la geopolitica dello Stato Pontificio (1513–1521)* (Vatican City, 2000).

Gouwens, Kenneth and Sheryl F. Reiss (ed.), *The Pontificate of Clement VII* (Aldershot and Burlington, Vt., 2005).

Hallman, Barbara McClung, *Italian Cardinals, Reform and the Church as Property* (Berkeley and London, 1985).

Hook, Judith, *The Sack of Rome 1527* (2nd edn. Basingstoke and New York, 2005).

Hyde, Helen, *Cardinal Bendinello Sauli and Church Patronage in Sixteenth-Century Rome* (London, 2008).

Jedin, Hubert, *A History of the Council of Trent* (English trans. 2 vols. London, 1957 and 1961).

MacCulloch, Diarmaid, *Reformation: Europe's House Divided 1490–1700* (London, 2003).

Mayer, Thomas F., *Reginald Pole, Prince and Prophet* (Cambridge, 2000).

Mullett, Michael A., *The Catholic Reformation* (London, 1999).

Oberman, Heiko A., *Luther: Man Between God and the Devil* (English trans. New Haven and London, 1989).

O'Malley, John W., *The First Jesuits* (Cambridge, Mass., and London, 1993).

O'Malley, John W., *Trent and All That* (Cambridge, Mass., and London, 2000).

Pastor, Ludwig, *History of the Popes,* vols. VII–XX (London, 1929–1930).

Prosperi, Adriano, *L'Inquisizione Romana. Letture e ricerche* (Rome, 2003).

Schenk, W., *Reginald Pole, Cardinal of England* (London, 1950).

Signorotto, Gianvittorio and Maria Antonietta Visceglia (ed.), *Court and Politics in Papal Rome, 1492–1700* (Cambridge, 2002).

Chapter 17

Bargrave, John, *Pope Alexander the Seventh and the College of Cardinals,* ed. James Craigie Robertson (London, 1867).

Barock im Vatikan. Kunst und Kultur im Rom der Päpste 1572–1676 (Leipzig, 2005).

Courtright, Nicola, *The Papacy and the Art of Reform in the Sixteenth Century* (Cambridge, 2003).

D'Addio, Mario, *The Galileo Case: Trial/Science/Truth* (English trans. Leominster and Rome, 2004).

Drake, Stillman, *Galileo* (Oxford, 1980).

Ehrlich, Tracey L., *Landscape and Identity in Early Modern Rome: Villa Culture at Frascati in the Borghese Era* (Cambridge, 2002).

Fehl, Philipp, *Monuments and the Art of Mourning: The Tombs of Popes and Princes in St. Peter's* (Rome, 2007).

Fosi, Irene, *La giustizia del papa* (Rome and Bari, 2007).

Gamrath, Helge, *Roma Sancta renovata: Studi sull'urbanistica di Roma nella Seconda metà del sec. XVI* (Rome, 1987).

Habel, Dorothy Metzger, *The Development of Rome in the Age of Alexander VII* (Cambridge, 2002).

Hammond, Frederick, *Music and Spectacle in Baroque Rome: Barberini Patronage under Urban VIII* (New Haven and London, 1994).

Hsia, R. Po-Chia, *The World of Catholic Renewal, 1540–1770* (2nd edn. Cambridge, 2005).

Karsten, Arne, *Kardinal Bernardino Spada. Eine Karriere im barocken Rom* (Göttingen, 2001).

Krautheimer, Richard, *The Rome of Alexander VII* (Princeton, 1985).

Madonna, M.L. (ed.), *Roma e Sisto V: Le arti e la cultura* (Rome, 1993).

Magnuson, Torgil, *Rome in the Age of Bernini* (2 vols. Rome, 1982 and 1987).

Mandel, Corinne, *Sixtus V and the Lateran Palace* (Rome, 1994).

McGinness, Frederick J., *Right Thinking and Sacred Oratory in Counter-Reformation Rome* (Princeton, 1995).

Miselli, Walter, *Il Papato del 1605 al 1669 attraverso le medaglie* (Pavia, 2004).

Negro, Angela, *La Collezione Rospigliosi: La quadreria e la committenza artistica di una famiglia patrizia a Roma nel Sei e Settecento* (Rome, 2007).

Nussdorfer, Laurie, *Civic Politics in the Rome of Urban VIII* (Princeton, 1992).

Pagano, Sergio M. (ed.), *I Documenti del processo di Galileo Galilei* (Vatican City, 1984).

Pastor, Ludwig, *History of the Popes*, vols. XXI–XXXI, ed. Ralph Francis Kerr (London, 1932–1940).

Reinhart, W., *Papstfinanz und Nepotismus unter Paul V. (1605–1621). Studien und Quellen zur Struktur und zu quantitativen Aspekten des päpstlichen Herrschaftssystems* (Stuttgart, 1974).

Rodén, Marie-Louise, *Church Politics in Seventeenth-Century Rome* (Stockholm, 2000).

Teodori, Marco, *I Parenti del Papa. Nepotismo pontificio e formazione del patrimonio Chigi nella Roma barocca* (Padua, 2001).

، Wright, A.D., *The Early Modern Papacy: From the Council of Trent to the French Revolution 1564–1789* (London, 2000).

Zirpolo, Lilian H., *'Ave Papa, Ave Papabile': The Sacchetti Family, the Art Patronage and Political Aspirations* (Toronto, 2005).

Zuccari, Alessandro and Stefania Macioce (ed.), *Innocenzo X Pamphili. Arte e Potere a Roma nell'Età Barocca* (Rome, 1990).

CHAPTER 18

Bowron, Edgar P. and James J. Rishel (ed.), *Art in Rome in the Eighteenth Century* (Philadelphia and London, 2000).

Callahan W.J. and D. Higgs (ed.), *Church and Society in Catholic Europe of the Eighteenth Century* (Cambridge, 1979).

Cecchelli, M. (ed.), *Benedetto XIV* (3 vols. Ferrara, 1981).

Chadwick, Owen, *The Popes and European Revolution* (Oxford, 1981).

Gisondi, F.A., *Innocenzo XII, Antonio Pignatelli* (Rome, 1994).

Gross, Hanns, *Rome in the Age of Enlightenment: the Post-Tridentine Syndrome and the Ancien Régime* (Cambridge, 1990).

Johns, C.M.S., *Papal Art and Cultural Politics: Rome in the Age of Clement XI* (Cambridge, 1993).

Lauro, A., *Il cardinale Giovan Battista de Luca: Diritto e riforme nello Stato della Chiesa 1657–1683* (Naples, 1991).

Papes et Papauté au XVIIIe siècle (Paris, 1999).

Raybaud, L.P., *Papauté et pouvoir temporel sous les pontificats de Clément XII et Benoit XIV* (Paris, 1963).

Theiner, A. *Histoire du pontificat de Clément XIV* (2 vols. Paris, 1852).

CHAPTER 19

Aubert, R., *Le pontificat de Pie IX* (Paris, 1952).

Bolton, C.A., *Church Reform in Eighteenth-Century Italy* (The Hague, 1969).

Chadwick, Owen, *A History of the Popes 1830–1914* (Oxford, 1998).

Collins, Jeffrey, *Papacy and Politics in Eighteenth-Century Rome: Pius VI and the Arts* (Cambridge, 2004).

Coppa, F.J., *The Modern Papacy since 1789* (London, 1998).

Dicey, Edward, *Rome in 1860* (London, 1861).

Hales, E.E.Y., *Pio Nono: a Study in European Politics and Religion in the Nineteenth Century* (London, 1954).

Hales E.E.Y., *Revolution and Papacy* (Notre Dame, 1966).

Hasler, A.B., *How the Pope Became Infallible: Pius IX and the Politics of Persuasion* (New York, 1981).

Leflon, J. *Pie VII* (Paris, 1958).

Manning, H.E., *The True Story of the Vatican Council* (London, 1877).

Mathieu, Le Cardinal (François-Désiré), *Le Concordat de 1801: ses origines - son histoire* (Paris, 1904).

Moore, John, *A View of Society and Manners in Italy with Anecdotes relating to some Eminent Characters* (2 vols. London, 1780).

Nicassio, Susan Vandiver, *Imperial City: Rome, Romans and Napoleon,* *1796–1815* (Welwyn Garden City, 2005).

Nodari, Antonio, *Vitae Pontificum Romanorum Pii VI, Pii VII, Leonis XII, Pii VIII addito commentariolo de Gregorio XVI feliciter regnante* (Pavia, 1840).

Reinerman, Alan J., *Austria and the Papacy in the Age of Metternich* (2 vols. Washington, D.C., 1979, 1989).

Vidler, Alec R., *The Church in an Age of Revolution* (Harmondsworth, 1961).

Wiseman, N., *Recollections of the Last Four Popes and of Rome in Their Times* (London, 1858).

CHAPTER 20

Besier, Gerhard, *The Holy See and Hitler's Germany* (English trans. Basingstoke and New York, 2007).

Cenci, Pio, *Il Cardinale Raffaele Merry Del Val* (Rome and Turin, 1933).

Chiron, Yves, *Pie XI: (1857–1939)* (Paris, 2004).

Conway, Martin, *Catholic Politics in Europe, 1918-1945* (London, 1997).

Ellis, J.T., *The Life and Times of James Cardinal Gibbons, Archbishop of Baltimore, 1834–1921* (2 vols. Milwaukee, 1952).

Falconi, Carlo, *The Popes in the Twentieth Century* (London, 1967).

Fogarty, Gerald P., *The Vatican and the American Hierarchy from 1870 to 1965* (Stuttgart and Collegeville, Minn., 1982).

Graham, Robert, *Vatican Diplomacy* (Princeton, 1959).

I Documenti Sociali della Chiesa da Leone XIII a Giovanni Paolo II (Vatican City, 1991).

Launay, Marcel, *La papauté à l'aube du xxe siècle* (Paris, 1997).

Moynihan, J.H., *The Life of Archbishop John Ireland* (New York, 1953).

Passelecq, Georges and Bernard Suchecky, *L'Encyclique cachée de Pie XI* (Paris, 1995).

Pollard, John F., *The Vatican and Italian Fascism, 1929–1932: a Study in Conflict* (Cambridge, 1985).

Pollard, John F., *The Unknown Pope: Benedict XV (1914–1922) and the Pursuit of Peace* (London and New York, 1999).

Pollard, John F., *Money and the Rise of the Modern Papacy* (Cambridge, 2005).

Semeraro, Cosimo (ed.), *Leone XIII e gli studi storici* (Vatican City, 2004).

Vidler, Alec R., *The Modernist Movement in the Roman Church* (Cambridge, 1934; reprinted New York, 1976).

CHAPTER 21

Alberigo, Giuseppe (ed.), *A History of Vatican II*, (English edn. 5 vols. Maryknoll, N.Y., and Leuven, 1995–2006).

Allen, John L., *All the Pope's Men* (New York and London, 2004).

Allen, John L., *Pope Benedict XVI* (London and New York, 2005).

Alvarez, David, *Spies in the Vatican: Espionage and Intrigue from Napoleon to the Holocaust* (Lawrence, Kans., 2002).

Bokun, Branko, *Spy in the Vatican, 1941–1945* (London, 1973).

Buonasorte, Nicolà, *Siri* (Bologna, 2006).

Cornwell, John, *A Thief in the Night: The Death of Pope John Paul I* (London, 1989).

Cornwell, John, *Hitler's Pope: the Secret History of Pius XII* (London, 1999).

Cornwell, John, *The Pope in Winter: the Dark Face of John Paul II's Papacy* (London, 2004).

Gibson, David, *The Rule of Benedict: Pope Benedict XVI and His Battle with the Modern World* (San Francisco, 2006).

Hebblethwaite, Peter, *John XXIII: Pope of the Council* (London, 1984).

Hebblethwaite, Peter, *Paul VI: the First Modern Pope* (London, 1993).

Stourton, Edward, *John Paul II: Man of History* (London, 2006).

INDEX

549